OF **1800**

Democracy, Race, and the New Republic

Edited by James Horn, Jan Ellen Lewis,
and Peter S. Onuf

University of Virginia Press
Charlottesville and London

University of Virginia Press
© 2002 by the Rector and Visitors of the University of Virginia
All rights reserved
Printed in the United States of America on acid-free paper
First published 2002

1 3 5 7 9 8 6 4 2

LIBRARY OF CONGRESS CATALOGING-IN-PUBLICATION DATA
The revolution of 1800 : democracy, race, and the new republic /
edited by James Horn, Jan Ellen Lewis, and Peter S. Onuf
p. cm. — (Jeffersonian America)
Includes bibliographical references and index.
ISBN 0-8139-2140-6 (cloth : alk. paper) — ISBN 0-8139-2141-4 (pbk. : alk. paper)
1. Presidents—United States—Election—1800 2. Jefferson, Thomas, 1743–1826.
3. United States—Politics and government—1797–1801. 4. United States—Race relations—
Political aspects. 5. Slavery—Political aspects—United States—History—19th century.
6. Political culture—United States—History—19th century. 7. World politics—
To 1900. I. Horn, James P. P. II. Lewis, Jan, 1949– III. Onuf, Peter S. IV. Series
E330 .R48 2002
324 .973 '044—dc21
002006429

Publication of this book was assisted by a gift from
the Martin S. and Luella Davis Publications Fund
of the Thomas Jefferson Foundation

Contents

The Revolution of 1800

Jeffersonian America

James Horn, Jan Ellen Lewis, Peter S. Onuf, Editors

THE **REVOLUTION**

Acknowledgments

As we gathered together at the beginning of December 2000 for a conference on "Thomas Jefferson and the Revolution of 1800," we could not have imagined finding ourselves discussing the bitterly contested presidential election of two hundred years ago in the midst of another hotly contested presidential election, the outcome of which was still in the balance, or, to be more precise, still in the courts. Between sessions we talked to eager journalists about the efficacy of the electoral college today, the role of the Supreme Court, and whether the Constitution needed to be amended. We watched TV and listened to the radio to catch the breaking news, followed the latest editorials, and from time to time, in strangely disoriented moments, caught ourselves repeating arguments in our own discussions that sounded all too familiar against the backdrop of the continuing political struggle being played out in Florida and Washington, D.C. Whatever unlikely combination of circumstances brought about the disputed election of 2000, we are grateful for one of those rare moments when historical and contemporary events converge, informing one another in a peculiarly dramatic way.

In bringing this book to completion we would like to thank a number of friends and colleagues who have made the task considerably easier and certainly more pleasant than it might otherwise have been. First and foremost, we are indebted to Daniel P. Jordan, president of the Thomas Jefferson Foundation, for making it possible to mount the conference at the International Center for Jefferson Studies (Monticello), and for his encouragement to publish the proceedings. Aurelia Brogan, then Jim Horn's assistant at the International Center, took care of all the conference arrangements with her usual efficiency and good humor, and other staff, notably Christine Coalwell, helped out in numerous ways during the meeting. At an early stage of planning, we benefited from the shrewd advice of Fredrika Teute and Ron Hoffman about possible participants and themes, and we were fortunate to be joined for discussion by several friends and colleagues: Matthew Holden, Lawrence Kaplan, Jeff Looney, Barbara Oberg, John Murrin, Fraser Neiman, Simon Newman, Jack Robertson, Leonard Sadosky, Cinder Stanton, Dianne Swann-Wright, David Waldstreicher, Gaye Wilson, Gordon Wood, and Rosemarie Zagarri. Their thoughtful comments enlivened proceedings and kept the paper givers on their toes.

We are most grateful to the two anonymous readers for their valuable critiques of the manuscript, pointing out errors of detail as well as providing substantive commentary, which saved us from many mistakes. Special thanks go to acquisitions editor Richard Holway, managing editor Ellen Satrom, and other staff of the University of Virginia Press for all their help, and to Laura Gross, of the International Center for Jefferson Studies, for the many hours spent working on the manuscript to get it into shape for submission to the Press. Finally, we wish to thank our authors for their remarkable patience and cooperation throughout the project, especially in meeting all our deadlines and demands in such a timely fashion and with such good grace.

James Horn, Jan Ellen Lewis, and Peter S. Onuf
December 2001

Abbreviations

AHP Harold C. Syrett and Jacob E. Cooke, eds. *The Papers of Alexander Hamilton.* New York, 1961–87. 27 vols.

AJL Lester J. Cappon, ed. *The Adams-Jefferson Letters: The Complete Correspondence between Thomas Jefferson and Abigail and John Adams.* Chapel Hill, N.C., 1959.

Ford Paul Leicester Ford, ed. *The Writings of Thomas Jefferson.* 10 vols. New York, 1892–99.

JAH *Journal of American History*

JER *Journal of the Early Republic*

JSH *Journal of Southern History*

JMP Robert Rutland et al., eds. *The Papers of James Madison.* 17 vols. Chicago and Charlottesville, Va., 1962–91.

L&B Andrew A. Lipscomb and Albert Ellery Bergh, eds. *The Writings of Thomas Jefferson.* 20 vols. Washington D.C., 1903–4.

Lib. Cong. Library of Congress, Washington, D.C.

Notes Thomas Jefferson, *Notes on the State of Virginia,* ed. William Peden. Chapel Hill, N.C., 1954.

Smith James Morton Smith, ed. *The Republic of Letters: The Correspondence between Thomas Jefferson and James Madison, 1776–1826.* 3 vols. New York, 1995.

TJ Thomas Jefferson

TJP   Julian Boyd et al., eds. *The Papers of Thomas Jefferson.* 29 vols. to date. Princeton, N.J., 1950 –.

TJW   Merrill D. Peterson, ed. *Jefferson's Writings.* New York, 1984.

WMQ   *William and Mary Quarterly*

Introduction

James Horn, Jan Ellen Lewis, and Peter S. Onuf

The election of 1800 was one of the most controversial and consequential in American history. A close look both at the 1800 campaign and at the electoral impasse in the House of Representatives in February 1801 reveals the wide range of possible outcomes. Focusing on these contingencies sets the agenda for this collection of essays. Knowing what might have happened in the election of 1800–1801 directs our attention outward, to seemingly far removed consequences and implications. Though we could not pretend to pursue all these implications in a single volume, it is nonetheless our intention to situate the American "revolution of 1800" in the broad context of geopolitical developments of the Atlantic world as a whole.

We begin by emphasizing the impact of international instability on "party" development in the United States. The "Quasi-War" with France (1798–1800) energized popular support for John Adams's administration, encouraging the Federalist Congress to clamp down on the Republican opposition in the controversial Alien and Sedition Acts. Adams's successful diplomacy defused the war crisis, but not soon enough to repair a deep rift within the ruling party or to influence wavering voters. To an extraordinary extent, developments in the French revolutionary and Napoleonic wars thus determined the course of American politics. The precise timing of the normalization of the Franco-American peace was crucial to Jefferson's election; so, too, the brief cessation of hostilities marked by the Peace of Amiens (1802) and continuing through Jefferson's first term allowed the Republicans to establish their dominance over the federal government.

International developments made Jefferson's "Revolution" possible, enabling Americans to preserve their fragile union and thus secure their independence in a dangerous world. Of course, Jefferson thought much more was at stake in his triumph—or, as he preferred to think, in the triumph of the

American *people,* as it shook off the incubus of reactionary, antirepublican Federalism. But how "revolutionary" was Jefferson's "revolution of 1800"? The question is an important one and is considered at length in several of the essays here. We would merely note at this point that the same international developments that made a peaceful transition of power possible in the United States had catastrophic consequences for Toussaint Louverture and the "Black Jacobins" of Saint Domingue. Napoleon's design for French empire in the Caribbean, with Louisiana serving as the source of food supplies for the sugar islands, reversed the French revolutionary commitment to emancipation and equal rights. Ironically, it was Napoleon's *failure* to crush the Haitian Revolution that made Louisiana worthless to the French and so prepared the way for the Louisiana Purchase of 1803. It is also ironic—or, if we may be permitted to moralize, tragic—that this vast addition to American territory, Jefferson's great diplomatic triumph, made possible the vast expansion and entrenchment of a brutal regime of plantation slavery.

A more capacious approach to the "revolution of 1800" enables us to provide a more complicated and nuanced answer to our question about its "revolutionary" credentials. It depended on who you were, and where you stood. For white "Americans," the new people whose triumph Jefferson celebrated in his first inaugural address, the Republican ascendancy marked an epochal shift in the fundamental character of the social and political relationships that defined their worlds. Jefferson defined this new nation in extraordinarily inclusive terms. Yet there were limits to Jefferson's definition, and they would become increasingly conspicuous in future years. In an unstable and dangerous world, Jefferson was hardly paranoid to fear foreign enemies. And there were enemies within as well as without: potentially hostile Indian nations in frontier regions that might ally with counterrevolutionary imperial powers; enslaved African Americans, a "captive nation" that might seek to overthrow and destroy the master class; and political opportunists and adventurers—like Aaron Burr, Jefferson's vice president and, unexpectedly, his rival for the presidency during the electoral crisis of 1801—who would recklessly jeopardize the Union. Jefferson's hostility to the Haitian Revolution reflected his deepest fears for the future of the American experiment, for the contagion of black republicanism threatened to spread north, challenging the racial hierarchy that secured peace and prosperity in Jefferson's Virginia and the other staple-producing slave states of the South.

These essays thus illuminate the boundaries of American nationhood, both in the conventional international context and by exploring hierarchies and distinctions *within* republican society and polity. The juxtaposition of "democracy" and "race" in our subtitle is not intended to discount, diminish, or deconstruct the former term by putting the latter into the foreground. Quite to the contrary, it is our intention to establish the broadest possible interpretative framework for Jefferson's election, one that situates the fragile American Union in a larger world. We would underscore the tenuousness of the republican experiment, emphasizing that developments in the European states' system over which Americans had little or no control determined in large measure the course of developments in the United States. Yet, as we do so, we will also show that American voters and politicians faced choices that would have momentous implications both for their own little worlds and the world at large.

Our approach to 1800 depends equally on a close examination of the particular circumstances of the election as well as a broader grasp of cultural and geopolitical implications. Collectively, the essays in part 1, "The Revolution of 1800," constitute the best new scholarship on the politics of 1800. James Lewis sets the tone with his careful study of the range of possible outcomes; his essay recaptures the sense of contingency that gripped the protagonists. Jack Rakove's penetrating analysis of the way the electoral college functioned demonstrates once again the profound disconnection between intentions and consequences in American constitutional history. There would have been no crisis if the presidency had not come to be so overwhelmingly important—and that would not have happened without the stimulus of deep disagreements over foreign policy.

Both of these first essays encourage us to think counterfactually about what might so easily have happened if, for instance, Burr had not so brilliantly managed the election of Republican legislators in New York City—or if Charles Pinckney had not been so effective in persuading his fellow South Carolina planters to support Jefferson. What would have happened if the election had turned out differently, or if the prize had finally been "stolen" from Jefferson in the House of Representatives? Michael Bellesiles's essay raises fascinating and important questions about the potential role of violence at a moment of crisis in the federal regime. Notwithstanding some blustering talk, Republicans probably would have submitted peacefully to the "stolen election," but they then would have been well situated to rise again in 1804. Bellesiles concludes that a brief postponement of Jefferson's "revolution" would have had little significant impact on long-term historical developments.

Bellesiles's conclusion is controversial, as subsequent essays will show, but he makes us confront the all-important question: what difference did Jefferson's election actually make? The next two essays suggest some answers. Joanne Freeman interprets the 1800 election as a great "honor event" in which anxious politicians sought to preserve the Union by pledges and commitments to each other as "gentlemen." They had to do so because partisan loyalties were so weak—and because parties in the institutional sense could hardly be said to exist at all. Yet if self-styled gentry politicians looked backward, invoking an apparently archaic conception of honor to avoid plunging into the abyss of anarchy and disunion, an emerging class of political operatives, Jeffrey Pasley's editors, were looking forward to new forms of popular political mobilization. Honorable gentleman politicians and partisan political editors (with their somewhat dubious social credentials) moved in to fill the vacuum that division and demoralization within Federalist ranks helped open, and their often uneasy collaboration would have a profound impact on the future development of American politics. Pasley makes the most forthright case for the democratizing effects of the 1800 election, suggesting that the relationship between leaders and followers, editors and their readers, constitutes the crucial site for revolutionary change.

The essays in part 2, "Jeffersonian America," assess the broader impact of the election on the history of the early Republic. Joyce Appleby asks us to reconsider the nature of the Republican appeal, suggesting that Jefferson himself was a kind of political "psychologist" who grasped the fundamental connections between democratization and broader transformations in postrevolutionary American culture. But Jefferson's psychological acuity had its limits, as Robert McDonald's essay on Jefferson and religion makes clear. Democratization was a two-way street, and an increasingly Christian electorate expected politicians to meet its pious standards. The Federalists may have lost the election, but they succeeded in focusing attention on the third president's religious life. As a result, the great foe of "priestcraft" and champion of Enlightenment rationality refashioned himself as a (very idiosyncratic sort of) "Christian."

Just as Freeman and Pasley offer complementary perspectives on the transformation of political culture in 1800, Appleby and McDonald give us two perspectives on a visionary Jefferson who sees far—but does not see everything. In subsequent essays we move away from this protean figure to a broader consideration of American society and culture in the era of the early Republic.

James Sidbury effects the transition from Jefferson to the world of "Gabriel's Virginia" by asking the simple question: what difference did Jefferson make for the slaves of Virginia, or for American slaves generally? In combination Jefferson's two major achievements, the Louisiana Purchase and the subsequent implementation of the ban on American participation in the transatlantic slave trade, had a horrific impact on the lives of Virginia slaves who were transported southward to develop the new cotton kingdom. Yet, as James Oakes shows, Jefferson's liberal-humanist commitment to the principle of human happiness presented a challenge to the institution of slavery, one that his fellow Virginians could meet only by insisting that their slaves were indeed happy. Happiness, Oakes argues, was one of the central terms in the debate over slavery.

Jefferson's democratic vision also had important implications for gender relations. Jeanne Boydston offers a perceptive account of Judith Sargent Murray's personal revolution. Murray and other privileged white women glimpsed new civic and social opportunities during the war and its immediate aftermath. Yet as Murray extrapolated a vision of the new Republic from her conception of "civic domesticity," she found herself increasingly marginalized and depoliticized by the rising tide of republicanism. The premises of the new gender regime were conspicuously articulated in the Jeffersonian program for the "civilization" of southeastern Indians, as Gregory Dowd shows in the final essay in this section. Dowd suggests that elite Indian slaveholders adapted to "American" culture—and were able to remove their women from field labor, as civilizers enjoined them to do—by embracing the "American" system of exploiting African American slave labor.

Dowd's essay takes us to the problematic limits—and literal boundaries—of American nationhood. In the volume's concluding section, "Revolutionary World," we explore the transatlantic and comparative dimensions of the "revolution of 1800." Our authors also offer some preliminary suggestions about the continuing contest for empire, both in North America and in the Caribbean. Laurent Dubois emphasizes how critical developments in European capitals, as well as in their provincial peripheries, would be for American history. Napoleon's western design converged with rising pressure from Creole elites in the sugar islands to reenslave the black working classes. Though Haiti remained nominally linked to metropolitan France, Toussaint Louverture explored the possibility of developing commercial and diplomatic ties with the United States to secure his revolution. Douglas Egerton shows how the Adams administration responded eagerly to this opening, authorizing a burgeoning trade with the island and taking preliminary steps toward recognition. But Jefferson's election changed the diplomatic situation in fundamental ways: Haiti would be isolated and "contained" and Napoleon would lose interest in Louisiana. The "revolution of 1800" thus made a critical difference in this part of the world. The United States might have become more secure as a result of the "normalization" of great power relations in the region. But security meant that plantation slavery would spread into the North American heartland, and that the black republic of Haiti would remain an unrecognized pariah state.

The sale of a Virginia slave to the Black Belt may epitomize what 1800 meant for African Americans. But the transatlantic movement of white radical refugees such as Joseph Gales reminds us that the liberatory promise of the American republican experiment was very real in Jefferson's day. Seth Cotlar complicates Gales's story, however, in interesting ways, for the expatriate newspaper editor settled down in—and adapted to—slave-holding North Carolina without any apparent sense of contradiction or inconsistency. Gales was not alone in making such a move—Jefferson's friend, the English radical Thomas Cooper, eventually moved to South Carolina, where he promoted the slaveholders' cause with ideological fervor—but the riddle remains. Perhaps, Cotlar suggests, the radicals' quarrel with the status-ridden social hierarchy of the Old World did not seem compelling in the "middle-class" Republic, where talented newcomers could pursue their happiness without hindrance—and even enjoy the benefits of slave ownership.

Bethel Saler's discussion of Federalist and Republican conceptions of continental empire emphasizes the geopolitical dimensions of American nation-making. Whatever their ideological predilections, Americans could not jettison a centralized, "imperial" government that could defend and promote the new nation's claims against hostile imperial policies and their Indian allies. In this respect, Saler shows, the continuities between Federalist and Republican administrations are striking. At the same time, however, ascendent Jeffersonians fostered a decentralized, homogenous national political community that disguised the continuing exercise of the central government's power on the imperial periphery. The genius of this new "republican empire" was to foster the rapid expansion of local political elites in the territories and new states, preempting the centralized, hierarchical authority that characterized European colonial regimes. Certainly, as Alan Taylor demonstrates in his fascinating history of a "revolution" in Upper Canada that never happened, British imperial authorities recognized the subversive potential of republican institutions and of emigrants from republican America. Taylor's essay thus ends our volume on an appropriately ambiguous note. The machinations of his would-be "rebels" reflected the pervasive democratization of values and attitudes among ordinary, enterprising Americans. Yet these rebels were cautious and calculating: they would not put their lives and property at risk by a frontal assault on British authority. And Jefferson himself was too absorbed with consolidating his authority at home and securing American interests abroad to risk rousing the British lion. Besides, it was Jefferson's nemesis Burr who had encouraged the quondam insurgents, and Burr had no influence on the new administration.

What does this all add up to? We do not suggest that all these essays elaborate a single, overarching thesis. Readers will discover that our authors differ on some questions—for instance, on the significance of Jefferson's election for the spread of plantation slavery. But we do believe that the various perspectives offered here—from the close examination of electoral mechanics to broader reflections on cultural change and finally to assessments of political and diplomatic developments in the Atlantic world—are reciprocally illuminating. Jefferson's election figures importantly in many stories, and not just in American political history narrowly defined. The authors in this volume have set the agenda for future scholarship. The challenge for their successors will be to develop these and other stories, and to show more clearly how they relate to one another.

Part 1

THE REVOLUTION OF 1800

CHAPTER 1

"What Is to Become of Our Government?"
The Revolutionary Potential of the Election of 1800

James E. Lewis Jr.

Writing to the Virginia jurist and essayist Spencer Roane in September 1819, Thomas Jefferson described his election to the presidency as "the revolution of 1800." It was, in Jefferson's view, "as real a revolution in the principles of our government as that of 1776 was in its form." He considered it revolutionary even though it had been effected not "by the sword, . . . but by the rational and peaceable instrument of reform, the suffrage of the people."[1] In juxtaposing these two "revolutions," Jefferson also united them; the "revolution of 1800," in his view, redeemed and extended the Revolution of 1776. Still, his dichotomies—1800 vs. 1776, principles vs. form, suffrage vs. sword—suggest the breadth of Jefferson's definition of "revolution." They also obscure the complexities and potentialities of the election of 1800, when a revolution in "form" effected by the "sword" seemed to many a real possibility.

Historians and political scientists have long accepted at least part of Jefferson's formulation. Even as they have debated whether the transfer of power from Federalists to Republicans actually involved a "revolution in principles," they have usually agreed that it occurred without anything even approaching a "revolution in form." In fact, it is frequently treated as the first instance—not just in American history but even in modern history—when control over a national government passed from the ruling party to the opposition party peacefully. One political scientist called it "the first . . . grand, democratic, peaceful transfer of power in modern politics." "*Violent resistance was never, at any time, discussed*," the historian Richard Hofstadter insisted; "neither was disunion

discussed as a serious immediate possibility." The "peaceful and orderly fashion" in which this transfer of power took place has often been treated as evidence of "the maturity of the nation's first system of political parties." [2]

Some contemporaries also remarked on the unrevolutionary nature of the
process by which power changed hands in 1801. "I have this morning witnessed
one of the most interesting scenes, a free people can ever witness," wrote Margaret Bayard Smith on the day of Jefferson's inauguration. "The changes in
administration, which in every government and in every age have most generally been epochs of confusion, villainy and bloodshed, in this our happy country take place without any species of distraction, or disorder." [3] Having lived in
the new national capital during the climactic stage of the recent election,
Smith — the daughter of a Federalist politician and wife of a Republican newspaper editor — certainly knew better. What the correspondence, newspapers,
and pamphlets of the time make clear, instead, is the great extent of "confusion," "distraction," and "disorder" generated by the election of 1800. While the
transfer of power may ultimately have come without "villainy and bloodshed,"
we need to recognize just how unlikely this result seemed in the months before
4 March 1801.

As they thought about the approaching election, Jefferson and his politically
active contemporaries predicted, imagined, feared, and in some cases advocated various outcomes that are probably best understood as revolutionary in
form. With the correct "form" for deciding the president and vice president
established by the Constitution, any extra-constitutional process in 1800 —
whether one as drastic as disunion or as mild as a new election — could be
viewed as revolutionary. Even if the election took place under the constitutional
rules, certain combinations of president and vice president might still have
brought forth revolutionary outcomes. Many commentators at the time recognized that given the intensity of the struggle between Federalists and Republicans and the instability of the new government and nation, the election of 1800
had the potential either to follow a truly revolutionary course or to produce a
truly revolutionary result. An examination of the concerns and intentions expressed at the time makes clear the alarming potential of the election of 1800, as
it was understood by contemporaries.

Before turning to the extra-constitutional potentialities, however, it seems
helpful to identify the possible constitutional outcomes. The election of 1800

occurred under a set of rules that were very different from the current ones. In fact, it was precisely in order to avoid a recurrence of the events of 1800 that Congress devised and the states ratified the Twelfth Amendment (1804), establishing much of the current system. We must understand, as well, that the organization of the candidates into competing political parties or factions had already created a situation by 1800 that differed significantly from what the framers of the Constitution had imagined in 1787.

The Constitution established a complex, multistage process for choosing the president. Article II, section 1 assigned the selection of the two highest executive officers to an electoral college composed of one member for each of a state's senators and representatives, to be chosen "in such Manner as the Legislature thereof may direct." On a day determined by Congress (later set as the first Wednesday in December), the electors would meet in their own states and cast their votes for two persons, at least one of whom could not be a resident of their state. The lists of votes in each state would be sent to the national capital, where the president of the Senate would count the votes in the presence of the Senate and House of Representatives. The person with the most votes would become president "if such Number be a Majority of the whole Number of Electors" (not of the total votes). If more than one person had such a majority, then the House would "immediately chuse by Ballot" between them. In doing so, the House would vote as states, rather than individuals, with a majority of the states needed to elect the president. The vice president would simply be whoever had the most electoral votes "after the Choice of the President."[4]

Assuming four candidates in the interest of clarity, this system would allow all of the potential outcomes diagrammed in figure 1.1. Four candidates produce twenty-four distinct results: twelve combinations of president and vice president, with each combination capable of resulting from the decision of either the electoral college or the House. The framers apparently viewed each of the twenty-four potential outcomes as equally acceptable and equally probable. They believed that the House rather than the electoral college would decide many elections. And they expected electors to cast both ballots for individuals whom they were willing to see become president. It is apparent from the Constitution and the convention debates, moreover, that the framers expected more than four individuals to receive electoral votes in most elections. As originally devised, the electoral system could accommodate neither political parties nor distinct presidential and vice presidential candidates.

In the three presidential elections before 1800, the impact of the deepening

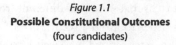

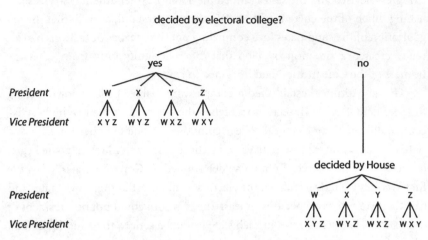

party divisions on the electoral process became increasingly obvious. Even with the unanimous support given to George Washington, the first election in 1789 proceeded much as the framers had expected. In addition to Washington, eleven men received electoral votes, ranging from just one for Georgia's Edward Telfair to thirty-four for John Adams, the eventual vice president. At the next election, in 1792, only five men received electoral votes. Among these five, moreover, it was relatively easy to distinguish between those who represented the current administration (Washington and Adams) and those who opposed it on key issues (George Clinton, Jefferson, and Aaron Burr). Party lines were even clearer in the election of 1796, even though thirteen men received electoral votes. While the presidential electors distributed their second ballots among a wide range of candidates, every one of them voted for one of the two party champions (Adams or Jefferson). The resulting election of Adams as president and Jefferson as vice president showed clearly how unsuited the constitutional system was to party competition.[5]

In 1800 the impact of party divisions and party loyalties became even more apparent. Each party had two candidates who were clearly distinguished by office between president and vice president. The Federalist caucus in Congress agreed to support Adams for president and Charles Cotesworth Pinckney for vice president. The Republicans in the nation's capital decided on Jefferson

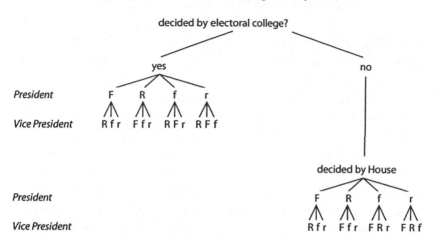

Figure 1.2
Possible Constitutional Outcomes
(two parties with candidates distinguished by office)

F = Federalist presidential preference
R = Republican presidential preference
f = Federalist vice presidential preference
r = Republican vice presidential preference

and Burr for their candidates. Since the rules fixed by the Constitution had not changed, the basic structure of choices remained the same (see figure 1.2). With four candidates, there were still twenty-four possible outcomes. But it is clear that these outcomes were no longer equally acceptable or equally probable. Any outcome with a president from one party and a vice president from a different party, as had happened in 1796, must be viewed as unintended and unexpected. The same could be said of any outcome in which a person intended for vice president was elected president. Only four of the twenty-four constitutional outcomes would have satisfied the avowed goals of the parties: Adams as president with Pinckney as vice president and Jefferson as president with Burr as vice president, whether elected by the electoral college or by the House.[6]

It is clear from contemporary correspondence, however, that many more than just these four outcomes were considered possible or even desirable at the time. Someone, at some time during the long election process, discussed almost every other combination of Adams, Jefferson, Pinckney, and Burr. Anti-Adams Federalists, including Alexander Hamilton, sought ways to reverse the order of their party's candidates, placing Pinckney above Adams either by manipulating electoral votes or by securing his election in the House. They also worried about what they saw as overtures from Adams to the Republicans. Some talked of another Adams-Jefferson administration; others, such as Massachusetts's George Cabot, believed that if Jefferson and Adams cooperated, the result might be "the elevation of the former to the President's chair, and [the] depressing [of] the latter to the Vice Presidency."[7] In the summer of 1800, the Massachusetts Federalist Fisher Ames could imagine Burr combining with any of the other candidates. "Col. B. of New York also is at market," he informed Rufus King, "and may give his influence to the highest bidder."[8] With South Carolina the last state to choose electors, a number of observers predicted that its votes would go to Pinckney (a favorite son) and Jefferson, though which candidate would become president and which vice president remained subject to dispute.

In the months before the eventual decision on 17 February 1801, however, observers projected many potential outcomes other than the twenty-four provided by the Constitution (see figure 1.3). Pointing to a number of dangers, some doubted that an election would even be held. Others feared that extra-constitutional maneuvering would destroy the integrity of the electoral college vote. The plotting and counterplotting only accelerated once it became clear that by giving Jefferson and Burr the same number of votes, the electoral college had failed to decide the contest. Throughout the tense electoral process, contemporaries worried about various extra-constitutional measures and outcomes, seeing in many of them grave consequences for the new nation. Having entered this process concerned that the election would produce a revolution, they increasingly realized that the election itself might be the revolution.

The election of 1800 capped a period of intense partisan rivalry in the United States. The Quasi-War with France, the Alien and Sedition Acts, the Virginia and Kentucky Resolutions, the expansion of the army, Fries' Rebellion, and countless other developments fueled a sense of crisis in the United States that lasted the entirety of Adams's presidency. The leaders of each party proposed dramatically different responses to each of these developments. Throughout this crisis, party conflict remained at a fever pitch, with effects that extended from Congress and the executive offices to the press, the dueling ground, the meeting hall, the tavern, and the street. Party rivalries did not just affect politics. They also strained and distorted business and social relationships.

Figure 1.3
All Possible Outcomes in 1800/1801

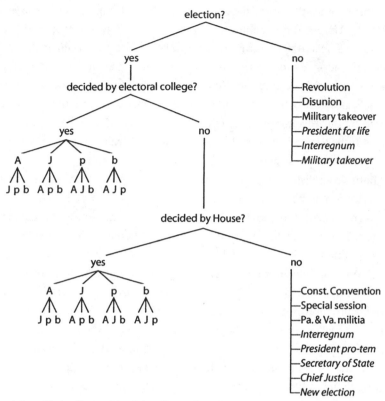

A = Adams (Federalist presidential preference)
J = Jefferson (Republican presidential preference)
p = Pinckney (Federalist vice presidential preference)
b = Burr (Republican vice presidential preference)
outcomes in *italics* were associated with the Federalists

In this superheated atmosphere, the election of 1800 assumed tremendous importance. Since each side believed that the other would destroy the nation if it controlled the executive branch, a revolutionary result seemed possible, even likely, even if the election itself proceeded in an unrevolutionary manner. Many Federalists worried that a victorious Jefferson would fritter away federal power, stir up class resentment, and bring about an alliance with France and a war against Great Britain. Robert Goodloe Harper warned that if the Federalists lost the election, they might "live to see our country mourn, in blood & ashes, over the consequences."[9] The rumors that reached Jefferson in early 1800 said that the Federalist "eastern states would . . . throw things into confusion, and break the Union" if a Republican won the election.[10] At the same time, many Republicans feared that four more years of Federalist rule would lead to a consolidated nation, a monarchical government, and a return—in form, if not in name—to British subjugation. Virginia governor James Monroe considered a Republican victory essential to "secure to us forever those liberties that were acquired by our revolution [and] which ought never to have been put in danger."[11] If the Republicans lost, Hamilton warned, Virginia would "resort to the employment of physical force" to gain power.[12]

Both Federalists and Republicans expressed doubts that there would even be an election in the two or three years before the electors finally cast their votes in December 1800. Outraged by the Republican response to the Quasi-War, the expanded army, and the Alien and Sedition Acts, Federalists calculated that their opponents might destroy the government before the election could take place. Writing from Europe in June 1798, for example, John Quincy Adams passed along a French report "that the *friends of liberty* in the United States . . . [would] probably not wait for the next election, but in the mean time [would] destroy the fatal influence of the President and Senate *by a Revolution*."[13] Both Theodore Sedgwick and Fisher Ames warned that the Republicans in the large mid-Atlantic states would attempt a military takeover once they finished "render[ing their] militia[s] as formidable as possible, and supply[ing their] arsenals & magazines."[14] "It is obvious to me," Ames explained in early 1800, "that all other modes of decision will be spurned as soon as the antis [the Republicans] think they have force on their side."[15] Another prospect that worried Federalists during the months before the election was Republican disunionism. Virginia Republicans, in particular, emerged as committed secessionists in Federalist correspondence. A rumor that William Branch Giles, a former Virginia congressman, had "expressly [stated] that he desired that the Union of the States might be severed" even crossed the Atlantic in both directions.[16] It traveled from Philadelphia to London in a private letter from the secretary of state to the minister to Great Britain and returned from Berlin to Philadelphia in a letter from John Quincy Adams to his mother.

Republicans similarly questioned whether the election would even occur. When the Federalists were at their strongest and the Republicans at their weakest, leading Republicans feared that their opponents would use their position to transform the government. In October 1798 Jefferson predicted a succession of steps by which the Federalists would establish a government that was both monarchical and aristocratic. If the public tolerated the Alien and Sedition Acts, he warned, "we shall immediately see attempted another act of Congress, declaring that the President shall continue in office during life." Additional acts would complete "the transfer of the succession to his heirs, and the establishment of the Senate for life." [17] Earlier that year, James Thomson Callender, a Republican essayist, suggested that President Adams might claim absolute power between the close of the Fifth Congress in March 1799 and the opening of the Sixth Congress in November. "Nine months of a royal *interregnum* might readily put an end to the government," he warned.[18] Once the tide began to turn against the Federalists and in favor of the Republicans, a different set of fears emerged. By early 1800 it seemed possible that the Federalists would try to seize power permanently before they lost it in the election. "The enemies of our Constitution [the Federalists] are preparing a fearful operation," Jefferson wrote his son-in-law in February. Chaotic conditions throughout the country, and especially in Pennsylvania, appeared "too likely to bring things to the situation they wish, when our Bonaparte [Alexander Hamilton], surrounded by his comrades in arms, may step in to give us political salvation in his way." [19]

During the last congressional session before the election, a new issue emerged that posed a direct threat to the integrity of the electoral college and the voting process. Federalists and Republicans viewed this threat very differently, of course. To many Federalists the danger came from Pennsylvania governor Thomas McKean, "who [was] certainly a mad man" in the view of Connecticut Federalist Roger Griswold. A stalemate between the Federalist-dominated upper house and Republican-dominated lower house of the Pennsylvania legislature had left the state with no law for choosing its presidential electors. Concerned that his state's fifteen electoral votes would go uncast, the Republican McKean hinted that if the legislature could not agree on an election law, he would "issue his own proclamation calling on the People to chuse electors." Federalists viewed it as indisputable that McKean's proposal was unconstitutional since the framers had entrusted the state legislatures with deciding the method for picking electors. "Whether Electors thus chosen can give any votes" Griswold considered "a question . . . of no difficulty." But he recognized that it would "occasion much clamour." [20]

In order to forestall this "clamour," Senate Federalists proposed a bill creating a new mechanism "for deciding disputed elections of President and Vice

President of the United States, and for determining the legality or illegality of the votes given for those officers in the different States."[21] First offered by Pennsylvania Federalist James Ross, this bill was understood, by both parties, to be directed largely at McKean and the situation in Pennsylvania. The bill that finally passed the Senate in late March 1800, essentially on a party vote, would have established a "grand committee" of thirteen members—six chosen by the Senate, six chosen by the House, and the chief justice. With a Federalist chief justice and a Federalist majority in each house, the composition of this committee was never in doubt. It would review each electoral vote "with ultimate powers of decision" about which should be counted and which should be rejected.[22] The bill was heavily amended in the House, however, as both Federalists and Republicans questioned the constitutionality of specific elements and the whole bill. In its amended form it passed the House in early May, but it no longer served the purposes of the majority in the Senate, who returned it with their own amendment. Even the Federalists in the House admitted that the Senate "amendment very materially changed the principle of the bill" by making it more likely that votes would be rejected.[23] Ultimately, enough Federalists joined Republicans in opposition to the bill in the House to defeat a measure that the Federalist Speaker of the House, Theodore Sedgwick, believed "wisely & effectually provid[ed] against the evil."[24]

Most Republicans viewed the problem very differently from most Federalists. For many Republicans, the Ross bill—rather than McKean's efforts to pressure the Pennsylvania legislature into passing an election law—posed the real danger. They certainly recognized that if it passed the bill would injure their cause in the upcoming election; John Beckley, for example, immediately described it as "a deadly blow . . . aimed at us."[25] But they also viewed it as a threat to the Constitution and to the very basis of a republican government, a meaningful popular suffrage. In private letters, congressional speeches, and newspaper editorials, Republicans attacked the Federalist effort to interpose an unconstitutional body between the people and the choice of the president and vice president. In a circular letter to his constituents, Kentucky congressman John Fowler depicted the bill as "creat[ing] a conservative senate" that would meet "in a secret conclave" to decide on the votes—a measure that he considered "repugnant to every principle of the constitution."[26] James Madison, one of the leading Republican strategists, shared these fears. "It is impossible to say," Madison noted when the bill was under debate, "how far the choice of the Ex[ecutive] may be drawn out of the Constitutional hands, and subjected to the management of the Legislature."[27]

The election of 1800 played out across a period of months, with the electors chosen through different means and at different times in the sixteen states. Some of these elections favored the Republicans; others favored the Federalists. Until the end, the final outcome remained in doubt. By late November both sides recognized that everything depended on the South Carolina legislature's choice of electors in early December, just one day before the electors were to cast their ballots in every state. Even those familiar with the state's politics, much less the many interested outsiders, found it difficult to predict how it would vote. As the Connecticut Federalist Oliver Wolcott recognized, South Carolina's votes were "claimed, and expected by both parties." [28] Insiders asserted confidently, and contradictorily, that its votes would be for Jefferson and Burr, for Adams and Pinckney, and even for Pinckney and Jefferson. The legislators believed that they would decide the election, but they could not have known just how close the votes would be in the other states (sixty-five each for Jefferson, Burr, and Adams and sixty-four for Pinckney). Ultimately the Republicans managed to fill all eight of the state's electoral college seats with men who were pledged to cast one ballot for Jefferson and one for Burr. "Our Country is yet safe," Peter Freneau, the Republican editor of the Charleston *City Gazette*, announced as soon as the electors were chosen. [29]

But Freneau began his celebration too soon. Even though the electoral votes would not be opened and counted until 11 February 1801, it became clear within a couple of weeks of the voting that both Jefferson and Burr would have seventy-three votes and that the House would have to choose between them. As late as 15 December, Jefferson still believed that one or more electors from Tennessee, South Carolina, or Georgia had withheld their second ballots from Burr in order to prevent a tie. Just a few days later, however, enough information had reached Washington to dispel this hope. By 19 December Jefferson saw no grounds for doubting "that there [would] be an absolute parity between the two republican candidates." This result, he informed Madison, had "produced great dismay & gloom on the republican gentlemen here, and equal exultation in the federalists." [30] The problem was that, while the Republicans dominated eight of the sixteen state delegations in the House, they needed a majority to decide the outcome. Of the remaining eight states, the Federalists held six and two were evenly divided. One of the Republicans who experienced "dismay & gloom" because of this unexpected result was Virginia congressman John Dawson. Writing to Madison, Dawson lamented the defect in the Constitution that had made possible this outcome. In despair, he wondered: "who is to be president? In short, what is to become of our government?"[31]

The final stage of the election of 1800 can be divided into two phases. The first began in mid-December 1800, when it became apparent that Jefferson and Burr had defeated Adams and Pinckney but had tied each other, and lasted until mid-February 1801. The second phase consisted of the actual balloting in the House from 11 February to 17 February. Different options and different dangers emerged in each phase. But, throughout, the election seemed likely to become a "revolution in form," as one side or the other or both considered extra-constitutional means to produce a desired outcome or prevent a dreaded result.

In the first phase, the Federalists enjoyed a wide range of options, since the election could not be decided without them. One obvious course was to acquiesce in the popular will by voting for Jefferson as president and Burr as vice president; there were Federalists, in and out of government, who supported this course. Another constitutional option was to vote for Burr as president, counting on some Republican congressmen to vote for their second choice. Finally, the Federalists might feign support for Burr in order to pressure Jefferson into pledges about principles, policies, and patronage. It was this approach that Hamilton, who considered "Burr the most unfit man in the U.S. for the office of President," urged in a series of letters to various Federalist congressmen.[32] Massachusetts's Fisher Ames also advocated the tactic of supporting Burr long enough to secure from Jefferson some sign that he would "not countenance democratic amendmts., dependence on France, a wrangle or war with G. Britain, plunder of the banks and [their] friends, or Madison's empiricism in regard to trade & navy."[33]

The Federalists did not limit themselves to constitutional measures, at least not indisputably constitutional measures, as they weighed their options during the first phase of the crisis, however. Some insisted that if no president was elected by the time that Adams's administration ended on 4 March 1801, the rules of succession would take effect, placing executive power in the hands of the president pro tempore of the Senate or, if none had been chosen, the Speaker of the House. Since the Federalists held a majority in both houses, either of these individuals would almost certainly have been members of their party. Some of the Federalists in Washington "propos'd to prevent any Election and thereby throw the Government into the Hands of a President of the Senate" as soon as it became clear that the electoral college had not decided the election. According to Gouverneur Morris, they "even went so far as to cast about for the Person."³⁴ Morris believed that this plan had immediately been abandoned, but the private letters of many Federalists show otherwise. Writing to a Federalist senator three weeks later, former secretary of state Timothy Pickering could ask: "Are we to have a President and Vice-President, or an interregnum" in which the president pro tempore served as president?³⁵ John Adams still treated such a temporary transfer of power as a legitimate option just days before the balloting in the House. It would involve "no more danger of a political convulsion," the president argued, "than if Mr. Jefferson or Mr. Burr [was] declared [president]."³⁶

Other Federalists advised preventing a decision in the House without offering any clear idea of what would follow. In late December Samuel Sewall suggested to one Federalist congressman that with "a steady and decided vote" for Burr, "it [was] possible that an election at this time and with the materials [the House was] confined to, [might] be wholly prevented."³⁷ For New Yorker William Cooper, "Burr or no President [was] the order of the day."³⁸ House Federalists apparently evaluated this tactic during a 9 January meeting to try to arrange a single approach to the crisis. As reported by a leading Republican newspaper, this "Federal Caucus was held . . . for the express object of organizing measures for defeating the election of Mr. Jefferson, or, to use the words of a member present, 'of any Election of a President.'" But, this account noted, "the *Caucus* broke up without concluding upon any decisive measures."³⁹

During this initial phase of the election crisis, between mid-December 1800 and mid-February 1801, the Republicans either learned of or surmised every tactic that was considered by the Federalists; they imagined many more. It occurred to them almost immediately that the Federalists might try to obstruct a decision in order to transfer executive power to someone of their own choosing. As early as 15 December Jefferson had already heard, and was already spreading, a rumor that the Federalists intended to "let the government devolve on a President of the Senate."⁴⁰ Over the next few weeks the Republican rumor mill added the chief justice, the secretary of state, and the Speaker of the House to the list of Federalists to whom power might be committed "by a legislative act."⁴¹ The very thought "of creating a president by Act of Congress," as Pennsylvania's John Beckley put it, struck most Republicans as unconstitutional and unrepublican.⁴² "Any Law empowering any Person to exercise the Presidency," Samuel Smith insisted, would be viewed "as an Usurpation."⁴³ That the Federalists might defeat an election without any definite sense of the consequences of their actions also terrified Republicans. To Jefferson, "prevent[ing] an election altogether" seemed certain to produce "a suspension of the federal government, for want of a head." This course, he informed one correspondent, would "[open] to us an abyss, at which every sincere patriot must shudder."[44]

Republican fears clearly exceeded Federalist plans. Many leading Republicans worried, for example, that the Federalists intended, by preventing a choice between Jefferson and Burr, to force an entirely new election. It seemed so obvious that such a course could only lead to a second Republican victory that Albert Gallatin wondered: "what interest can the Federalists have in defeating an election?" His answer—that "they mean to usurp government"—was far more revolutionary than anything Federalists in Washington ever discussed, as far as the existing evidence shows. Confident that they would not "run the immense risk" of usurpation merely to hold the presidency until a new election, moreover, Gallatin concluded that "they must mean something more than a temporary usurpation." "The intention of the desperate leaders," he informed his wife, "must be absolute usurpation and the overthrow of our Constitution."[45] Similarly, Virginia governor James Monroe calculated that Federalist plans to assign executive power by law to the president pro tempore or secretary of state only made sense if the Federalists actually intended "to disorganize" the United States. "If the union cod. be broken," he warned Jefferson, "that wod. do it."[46]

Republicans hoped that they could defeat Federalist plans—constitutional and unconstitutional—through constitutional means. Reasonably confident that eight state delegations would vote for Jefferson as president and Burr as vice president, they trusted that the moderate Federalists in the Maryland, Delaware, or Vermont delegations would provide the decisive ninth state. In order to sway these Federalists, the pro-Jefferson Republicans needed to demonstrate that their eight-state bloc would hold together. By mid-January they had taken a clear public stand, which they subsequently reaffirmed through pledges given in private caucuses such as that held by New York and New Jersey congressmen on 31 January. Republicans also counted on a simple constitutional measure to frustrate Federalist plans to transfer power to the president pro tempore. As the sitting vice president, Jefferson was the president of the Senate. The Senate could only elect a president pro tempore in his absence. But Jefferson, as Samuel Smith reported, decided not "to afford an oppy. to the Senate, to choose a President pro tem." Actually Smith claimed that Jefferson intended "to declare from the Chair [in the Senate] that he would not" make possible the selection of a president pro tempore.[47] There is no evidence that Jefferson made such a declaration, nor did he need to. All that he needed to do was make sure to be present to preside over the Senate whenever it was in session.

The correspondence of leading Republicans demonstrates that they were willing to take unconstitutional steps, if needed, to foil the unconstitutional designs of the Federalists. In early January Madison developed for Jefferson the possible Republican responses to Federalist efforts to produce "an interregnum in the Executive, or . . . a surreptitious intrusion into it." One option, according to Madison, was simply "to acquiesce in a suspension or usurpation of Executive authority till the meeting of Congs. in De[cember 1801]." But his preference was for Jefferson and Burr to summon a special session of Congress "by a joint proclamation," reasoning that "the prerogative of convening the Legislature must reside in one or other of them." He admitted that, "in reference to the Constn: [such a] proceeding [would not be] strictly regular," but he trusted that "the irregularity [would] be less in form than any other [solution] adequate to the emergency." And in this case the irregularity would be "in form only rather than substance." "The other remedies," he worried, "are substantial violations of the will of the people, of the scope of the Constitution, and of the public order & interest."[48] Jefferson, Burr, and other Republicans initially supported Madison's solution; Federalists viewed it with alarm. Georgia's Federalist senator, James Gunn, who had seen another letter of Madison's with the same proposal, described "the little Virginian" as "a little furious."[49]

Albert Gallatin, a leading House Republican, also questioned Madison's solution. He drafted his own "plan," which Jefferson apparently approved. In an undated memorandum of late January or early February, Gallatin examined the possible Federalist goals and weighed the various Republican options. He enumerated three Federalist "objects"—electing Burr, forcing a new election, and "assum[ing] *executive* power during *interregnum*." The first could "be defeated by our own firmness," the second by the Republican-dominated House that would meet in December and would have to certify the results of any election. What worried Gallatin most was an unconstitutional assumption of power by the Federalists. Such a course would place the party and the nation in a difficult position. Either of the extreme options—"total submission to usurpation on their part or . . . usurpation on our part"—could have alarming results. He preferred a middle course, treating the nine months until the next congressional session as an "interregnum" in which "the several Republican States [would] act either separately or jointly, according to circumstances." In this period the

Republican states would oppose new acts "flowing immediately from the person who shall have usurped," but accept and uphold those "which [were] not immediately connected with Presidential powers." This solution seemed safer than Madison's. To Gallatin, "the dangers of civil war, of the dissolution of the Union, [and] of the stab given to our republican institutions by any assumption of power on [the Republicans'] part not strictly justified by the forms of our Constitution, [were] the greatest" threats. A partial and temporary acquiescence involved less risk than assuming power "by a joint act of the two candidates."[50]

A crucial turning point in the election crisis occurred when the House established rules for the balloting. Adopted on 9 February, the rules had been drafted by a committee of sixteen—one from each state, but twelve Federalists to four Republicans. Three provisions were especially significant. First, the House agreed that there could be multiple ballots if necessary; some individuals in each party had earlier expressed doubts on this point. Second, the rules stated that once the voting began, "the House shall not adjourn until a choice be made." Finally, any question that arose during the balloting and was "incidental to the power of choosing the President" was to be voted on by states.[51] Even though the Federalists enjoyed a majority on the committee and in the House, they made most of the concessions. They agreed to allow multiple ballots, even though requiring a choice on the first ballot would have made it more likely either that some Republicans would vote for Burr or that someone other than Jefferson or Burr would receive interim power. And they adopted the principle of voting by states (where they did not have a majority) rather than as individuals (where they did) on any important matters that arose once the balloting began.

Most importantly, though, Federalists proposed and accepted the rule calling for the voting to continue without adjournment until a president was chosen. Congressmen on both sides griped that they might end up spending the final weeks of the session "sleep[ing] on blankets in the Capitol."[52] Delaware Federalist James A. Bayard even considered it necessary to reassure one correspondent that the representatives were "not to be without meat and drink[,] fire or candles."[53] But this rule would do much more than inconvenience the congressmen, as Gallatin and others immediately grasped. When the Federalist majority in the House adopted it, they sent a clear sign "that they mean[t] to choose" between Jefferson and Burr. "For if no choice was made," Gallatin explained, "they could neither pass a law for a new election or usurpation, nor indeed for any object whatever."[54] Monroe's observer in Washington concluded that the adoption of this rule showed that the Federalists' "object [was] apparently confined to electing Mr. Burr," whom they saw as "the instrument by which they [might] effect any worse purpose."[55]

Taken together, these rules significantly narrowed the range of options on the eve of the balloting. They seemed to eliminate solutions of questionable constitutionality, such as providing by law for a transfer of power to the president pro tempore or for a new election. What was left were the two clearly constitutional options—electing Jefferson and electing Burr—and many clearly unconstitutional options. The sense of crisis grew more intense the longer each side clung to its own preference—the eight Republican states for Jefferson and the six Federalist states for Burr, with the remaining two states evenly divided. On the first day of the balloting, the Federalist Roger Griswold wrote his wife that the House's decision was "big . . . not 'with the fate of Cato and of Rome' but with the destinies of America."[56] To Monroe, the "state of things [was] critical and alarming."[57] After two days of voting in the House and nineteen inconclusive ballots, one Virginia congressman warned Governor Monroe to take steps "to guard against a situation truly awful."[58]

In the view of some Federalists, the acceptable outcomes of the election had shrunk to electing Burr or going without a president. Writing to his wife after sixteen ballots, Griswold expressed this determination very simply: "I am willing to put the Constitution, Government, and everything which belongs to it upon the issue of this business, and if our opponents will not take Burr, they shall take nobody."[59] Many of the New England Federalists in Congress insisted to the very end of the crisis that they would "go without a Constitution and take the risk of a Civil War" rather than elect Jefferson.[60] Republicans actually worried less about the Federalists abandoning the Constitution and more about their effecting some form of usurpation. They saw indications that the Federalists intended to revive the scheme of transferring power to the president pro tempore of the Senate. This goal could no longer be accomplished through legislation. But the Federalists could block an election through the end of the session and then rely on the existing rules of succession. Republicans found confirmation for their fears when Adams called a special session of the Senate for 4 March. This session was ostensibly necessary to confirm the new president's cabinet appointments, but Republicans recognized that most of the senators would be Federalists and that, with Jefferson's term as vice president ended, they could not be prevented from choosing a Federalist president pro tempore to be an interim president.[61]

A commitment to thwarting unconstitutional usurpation by the Federalists led the Republicans to consider unconstitutional, or at least extra-constitutional, measures of their own. In Virginia and Pennsylvania the governors took preliminary steps toward readying their militias to descend on Washington. Precisely what they did, or were prepared to do, remains unclear, in part because key documents were deliberately destroyed. After the election, Pennsylvania governor McKean apprised Jefferson that he had prepared a public proclamation, arranged support in the state legislature, and secured cannons and arms for a militia of twenty thousand. While Jefferson had not yet learned "the particulars" from Monroe, he reported to McKean that he thought that "Virginia was bristling up" as well at the highpoint of the crisis.[62] The subject of anxious rumors in Washington, these preparations were apparently a matter of great concern to the Federalists. There are some signs that steps were taken by the administration or the army to take federal arms away from the militias in both states. After learning of rumors that the militia "had seized the public arms" in Pennsylvania, John Beckley sent word to Republicans in Washington that, in fact, "several hundred stand of Arms and 18 pieces of Cannon, heretofore in the hands of the Militia, [had] lately been taken by fœderalists and *removed* into the public arsenals of the U.S."[63] Jefferson viewed "the certainty that a legislative usurpation would be resisted by arms" as one of the principal factors that led the Federalists to relent.[64]

Jefferson also credited another extra-constitutional measure that was apparently discussed by the Republicans during the House vote—the idea of a constitutional "Convention to reorganise & amend the government."[65] Four days into the House balloting, Jefferson informed Monroe that the Republicans had "declare[d] openly and firmly, one and all," that any form of usurpation would lead to this recourse. "The very word convention gives [the Federalists] the horrors," Jefferson noted, "as in the present democratical spirit of America, they fear they should lose some of the favorite morsels of the Constitution."[66] Five decades later, after Jefferson's letters had been published, Gallatin insisted that "there was not the slightest intention or suggestion [of] call[ing] a convention to reorganize the government and to amend the Constitution." But he could only explain the letters by proposing that Jefferson might "have wished such a measure, or thought that the Federalists might be frightened by the threat." [67] In 1848, Gallatin clearly had good reasons to downplay the Republicans' willingness to consider such a revolutionary step. Still, his comment highlights a curious problem. Talk of a new convention could work as a "threat" only if the Federalists knew of it. But there is no indication that they did. Other than Jefferson's own statement about declaring it "openly and firmly," there is no evidence that the Republican solution of a new constitutional convention was made public at the time.

Although neither the preparations of the Pennsylvania and Virginia militias nor the prospect of a constitutional convention appear to have had the impact that Jefferson attributed to them, the possibility that the election of 1800 would devolve into a "revolution in form" certainly hastened the ultimate resolution of the crisis. After six days of voting and thirty-five ballots, Bayard—a Federalist and the only representative from Delaware—promised an end to the deadlock when he declared that he would abandon Burr and support Jefferson. Bayard broke with his party in part because he had concluded that Burr could not be elected and in part because he believed that Jefferson had pledged himself on a few key policies. But it is also clear that he feared what might happen if there was no election by the House. As he informed the governor of Delaware, he did not back down "till it was admitted on all hands that we must risk the Constitution and a civil war or take Mr. Jefferson." [68] Along with the Federalist congressmen from Vermont, Maryland, and South Carolina, Bayard devised a plan in which two states that had previously voted for Burr would cast blank ballots and two states that had previously been divided would vote for Jefferson. On 17 February, on the thirty-sixth ballot, they put this plan into action, with the result that ten states voted for Jefferson, four states continued to vote for Burr, and two states did not vote.

With all of this potential for the election of 1800 to take a revolutionary turn or produce a revolutionary outcome, we might ask: why did it not? And what does it mean that it did not? The answers to these questions reveal a good deal about the process of electing a president, the role of partisanship, the commitment to union, and the attachment to the Constitution. But what they reveal is generally ambiguous, even contradictory.

In 1800 the constitutional process for electing a president seemed at once a success and a failure. A widely shared belief that the electoral process could work and, more importantly, that it could be used to achieve desired results played a critical role in preventing extra-constitutional experiments. The letters of everyone, from Jefferson to Adams, Gallatin to Hamilton, and John Beckley to Theodore Sedgwick, show that men with varied goals calculated, throughout this process, that with just a little more effort—writing letters or circulating essays or persuading legislators or turning out voters—the results of this very close election would go their way. With reasonable hopes of effecting their goals through legitimate means, they eschewed illegitimate ones. As long as they expected to elect their candidates in the electoral college, they did not seriously consider preventing an election entirely. After it became clear that the choice would have to be made by the House, both sides recognized that it would only require a few men changing their votes to accomplish their goals. While the electoral process ultimately resulted in a constitutional outcome, however, it generated tremendous anxiety and appeared perilously close to producing anarchy and disunion. During the crisis, many people bemoaned the failure of the "Wise Men" who had framed the Constitution to foresee and prevent the potential problems in this system.[69] Within just a few years, Congress passed and the states ratified the Twelfth Amendment to address the problems that had appeared in 1800 (and 1796). In the next presidential election, in 1804, electors marked separate ballots for their presidential and vice presidential choices.

Parties and partisanship played an equally ambivalent role in the election of 1800. A sense of party loyalty, or at least a sense of personal loyalty among members of the same party, guided men's actions throughout the electoral process. It helped to get voters to the polls, organize the actions of legislators at the state and federal levels, decide the votes of electors, and determine the outcome in the House election. Men acted together in parties, but they did not accept the legitimacy of a party system. Each party believed that the other would destroy the government and the nation, not through mistaken policies but by conscious design. Accusations that the opposition was willing to sacrifice the Constitution and the Union rather than tolerate the loss of their candidate flew in both directions at the height of the crisis in the House. "The supporters of Mr. Jefferson had come to a determination, which was known to have been solemnly made, and was publicly avowed," South Carolina's Robert Goodloe Harper informed his constituents, "to risk the constitution and the union rather than give him up."[70] Bayard reported early on that the Republicans had "declare[d] that they [would] never concur in the vote for Burr, [and] that they would rather see the union dissolved for want of a head than give up Jefferson."[71] Jefferson said much the same thing about the Federalists, whose obstinacy created a "danger of the dissolution of our Union."[72] Each side viewed the loyalty of its own members as essential for resolving the crisis, while attacking the loyalty of the opposing party for creating the crisis in the first place.

The most significant factor in keeping the election of 1800 from taking a revolutionary turn or producing a revolutionary result was the commitment of enough men in each party to the Constitution and the Union. During the crisis over the Quasi-War and the Alien and Sedition Acts, this commitment led Republicans such as Jefferson and Madison to counter disunionist extremists in their own party, in part by pointing to the potential of the approaching election to dispel "the reign of witches."[73] The same commitment weighed heavily on Gallatin's mind as he drafted the blueprint for a restrained and cautious Republican response to the threat of Federalist usurpation in January 1801. And it produced the final resolution to the stalemate in the House. A number of Federalist congressmen began the balloting committed, as one explained, "to mak[ing] a choice, and to acced[ing] to the election of Mr. Jefferson, rather than expos[ing] the nation to the mischiefs which might result from leaving the government without a head."[74] Bayard, who ultimately broke the deadlock, stated flatly that he did so because he was "perfectly resolved not to risk the constitution or a civil war."[75] Men of both parties trusted, correctly as it happened, in what Gallatin described as a general "love of union and order" to preserve the Constitution.[76]

At the same time, it is clear that throughout the election process men on both sides seriously considered sacrificing the Union and the Constitution to state or local goals. Certainly Jefferson would not have had to assert his faith in the Union and the electoral process if other Virginians had not been actively suggesting disunion as the solution to the problem of Federalist dominance. Similarly, while the unionism of Bayard and the other Federalist defectors ended the crisis in the House, as many as two dozen Federalists from four New England states continued to support Burr even at "the risk of a Civil War."[77] Even Bayard's unionism arose as much from a commitment to his state's welfare as from one to the nation's. Justifying his actions to men from outside Delaware, Bayard repeatedly suggested that his greatest concern was his state. Representing "the smallest State in the Union," he informed President Adams, he had "to act so as not to hazard the constitution upon which the political existence of the State depend[ed]."[78] In the same way, Bayard explained to

Hamilton that since his state lacked "the means of self protection," he did "not dare to . . . jeopardize the constitution or the safety of the state."[79] Seen in this light, Bayard's unionism was no less calculated than that of the New England holdouts, even if his calculations ultimately differed from theirs.

The depth of the commitment to the Constitution apparent in the election of 1800 similarly requires reassessment. Jefferson in particular seemed to attach much greater importance to *a* constitution than to *the* Constitution. In a number of letters written during and shortly after the election crisis, Jefferson suggested that he viewed the prospect of a new constitutional convention, called by the people, with perfect equanimity. At the peak of the crisis, he argued coolly that if the House failed to choose a president before the end of the session "and the government should expire on the 3d of March by the loss of its head," the people could simply "authorize a convention to reorganize and even amend the machine."[80] For Jefferson the government could be understood as a machine that could "run down" and could be wound up again by a popular convention meeting to prepare a new or amended constitution. That he considered such conventions "a perpetual and peaceable resource . . . in whatever extremity may befall us" suggests the limits of his attachment to the Constitution of 1787.[81]

To understand what did not happen in 1800, we might invert the explanation of the "revolution of 1800" in Jefferson's 1819 letter to Spencer Roane. Jefferson clearly believed that the fact that the Republicans won in 1800 permitted a "revolution in principles." But we might argue, instead, that it was the fact that the Federalists lost that prevented a "revolution in form." To a much greater degree than most Republicans, most Federalists were willing to accept defeat in the election of 1800. Somewhat ungenerously, Jefferson ascribed the Federalists' devotion to the Constitution and the Union to "timidity of constitution"; the same fears that had originally led many Federalists to support "those who wished for a strong executive," he argued, later led them to accept his election "rather than risk anarchy."[82] Federalists often characterized themselves in the same way, if in different terms. Hamilton, for example, described Federalists as "men who have an interest in public Order."[83] Robert Goodloe Harper insisted that the Federalists had "justly obtained" their name through "their attachment to the union, and their support of the federal government."[84] With this self-identification, most Federalists were simply less likely than many Republicans to dissolve the Union or abandon the Constitution if the election went against them. Even the Federalists who voted for Burr to the very end could rely on their colleagues' defection to preserve the Constitution and the Union; according to Bayard, they even agreed that the defectors should "recede without loss of time."[85]

Writing to the English liberal Joseph Priestley just weeks after his election to the presidency, Jefferson downplayed the recent "storm." "I have been, above all things, solaced by the prospect which opened on us, in the event of a non-election of a President," Jefferson reflected. "In [that] case, the federal government would have been in the situation of a clock or watch run down." The solution was simple, in Jefferson's thinking. A convention "would have been on the ground in eight weeks, would have repaired the Constitution where it was defective, and wound it up again."[86] For Jefferson, it was the transfer of executive dominance from the Federalists to the Republicans that was truly revolutionary. But, for us, it is the things that might have happened but did not, and the solutions that might have been attempted but were not, that seem much more revolutionary. A "revolution in form"—whether disunion or a military takeover or usurpation or a new constitutional convention—appeared much more probable to Jefferson and his contemporaries than most accounts would suggest.

NOTES

1. TJ to Spencer Roane, 6 Sept. 1819, L&B, 15:212.

2. William Nisbet Chambers, *Political Parties in a New Nation: The American Experience, 1776–1809* (New York, 1963), 169; Richard Hofstadter, *The Idea of a Party System: The Rise of Legitimate Opposition in the United States, 1780–1840* (Berkeley, Calif., 1969), 131; Noble E. Cunningham Jr., "Election of 1800," in *History of American Presidential Elections, 1789–1968,* ed. Arthur M. Schlesinger Jr. and Fred L. Israel (New York, 1971), 1:101. For some important dissenting views, see Joanne B. Freeman, *Affairs of Honor: National Politics in the New Republic* (New Haven, Conn., 2001), 199–261; Joanne B. Freeman, "The Election of 1800: A Study in the Logic of Political Change," *Yale Law Journal* 108 (1999): 1959–94; James Roger Sharp, *American Politics in the Early Republic: The New Nation in Crisis* (New Haven, Conn., 1993); and Daniel Sisson, *The American Revolution of 1800* (New York, 1974).

3. Margaret Bayard Smith to Susan B. Smith, 4 March 1801, *The First Forty Years of Washington Society: Portrayed by the Family Letters of Mrs. Samuel Harrison Smith (Margaret Bayard),* ed. Gaillard Hunt (New York, 1906), 25.

4. For the emergence of the electoral college system at the Convention, see Jack N. Rakove, *Original Meanings: Politics and Ideas in the Making of the Constitution* (New York, 1997), and

Shlomo Slonim, "The Electoral College at Philadelphia: The Evolution of an Ad Hoc Congress for the Selection of a President," *JAH* 73 (1986): 35–58.

5. For concise accounts of the first three elections, see Marcus Cunliffe, "Elections of 1789 and 1792," in Schlesinger and Israel, *History of American Presidential Elections* 1:3–32; and Page Smith, "Election of 1796," ibid., 59–80.

6. In addition to the essay by Cunningham, the book and article by Freeman, and the books by Sharp and Sisson cited above, helpful accounts of the election of 1800 include Peter S. Onuf, *Jefferson's Empire: The Language of American Nationhood* (Charlottesville, Va., 2000), chap. 3; Bernard A. Weisberger, *America Afire: Jefferson, Adams, and the Revolutionary Election of 1800* (New York, 2000); Tadahisa Kuroda, *The Origins of the Twelfth Amendment: The Electoral College in the Early Republic, 1787–1804* (Westport, Conn., 1994); and Stanley Elkins and Eric McKitrick, *The Age of Federalism: The Early American Republic, 1788–1800* (New York, 1993), chap. 15. The biographies of most of the key figures involved in the election—Jefferson, Aaron Burr, Albert Gallatin, James Madison, Alexander Hamilton, James A. Bayard, and others—also provide useful insights and information.

7. George Cabot to Rufus King, 29 May 1800, *The Life and Correspondence of Rufus King: Comprising His Letters, Private and Official, His Public Documents and His Speeches*, ed. Henry Adams (New York, 1894–1900), 3:249 (hereafter *Life of King*).

8. Fisher Ames to Rufus King (to William Payne), 15 July 1800, *Works of Fisher Ames, as Published by Seth Ames*, ed. W. B. Allen (Indianapolis, 1983), 2:1365 (hereafter *Works of Ames*).

9. Robert Goodloe Harper to Harrison Gray Otis, 28 Aug. 1800, *The Life and Letters of Harrison Gray Otis, Federalist, 1765–1848*, ed. Samuel Eliot Morison (Boston, 1913), 1:196 (hereafter *Life of Otis*).

10. TJ, "Anas" entry of 19 Jan. 1800, L&B, 1:432.

11. James Monroe to Thomas McKean, 12 July 1800, *The Writings of James Monroe: Including a Collection of His Public and Private Papers and Correspondence Now for the First Time Printed*, 7 vols., ed. Stanislaus Murray Hamilton (New York, 1898–1903), 3:194 (hereafter *Writings of Monroe*).

12. Alexander Hamilton to Rufus King, 5 Jan. 1800, *AHP* 24:168.

13. John Quincy Adams to Abigail Adams, 27 June 1798, *Writings of John Quincy Adams*, 7 vols., ed. Worthington Chauncey Ford (New York, 1913–17), 2:323 (hereafter *Writings of Adams*).

14. Theodore Sedgwick to Rufus King, 15 Nov. 1799, *Life of King* 3:147.

15. Fisher Ames to Oliver Wolcott, 12 Jan. 1800, *Works of Ames* 2:1348.

16. Timothy Pickering to Rufus King, 4 May 1799, *Life of King* 3:13. See also John Quincy Adams to Abigail Adams, 3 July 1799, *Writings of Adams* 3:427.

17. TJ to Stephens Thompson [*sic*, Stevens Thomson] Mason, 11 Oct. 1798, L&B, 10:62.

18. James Thomson Callender, *Sketches of the History of America* (Philadelphia, 1798), 120.

19. TJ to Thomas Mann Randolph, 2 Feb. 1800, L&B, 10:151.

20. Roger Griswold to unknown correspondent, 9 Feb. 1800, Griswold, Wolcott, Williams, Woodbridge, and Rogers Family Papers (microfilm ed.), University of Virginia Library, Charlottesville (hereafter Griswold Papers).

21. James Ross, motion of 23 Jan. 1800, *The Debates and Proceedings in the Congress of the United States*, comp. Joseph Gales (Washington, D.C., 1834–56), 6th Cong., 1st sess., 29 (hereafter *Annals of Congress*).

22. Theodore Sedgwick to Rufus King, 11 May 1800, *Life of King* 3:237. No Senate Republicans voted in favor of the bill; only two Senate Federalists voted against it.

23. Robert Goodloe Harper and James A. Bayard, remarks of 9 May 1800, *Annals of Congress*, 6th Cong., 1st sess., 710.

24. Theodore Sedgwick to Rufus King, 11 May 1800, *Life of King* 3:237. A full discussion of the Ross bill can be found in Kuroda, *Origins of the Twelfth Amendment*, 78–82.

25. John Beckley to Tench Coxe, 24 Jan. 1800, *Justifying Jefferson: The Political Writings of John James Beckley,* ed. Gerard W. Gawalt (Washington, D.C., 1995), 164 (hereafter *Justifying Jefferson*).

26. John Fowler, circular letter to his constituents, 15 May 1800, *Circular Letters of Congressmen to Their Constituents, 1789–1829,* 3 vols., ed. Noble E. Cunningham Jr. (Chapel Hill, N.C., 1978), 1:209 (hereafter *Circular Letters*).

27. James Madison to TJ, 15 March 1800, *JMP* 17:372–73.

28. Oliver Wolcott to Jedidiah Morse, 28 Nov. 1800, *Memoirs of the Administrations of Washington and John Adams, Edited from the Papers of Oliver Wolcott, Secretary of the Treasury,* ed. George Gibbs (1846; rept. New York, 1971), 2:449.

29. Peter Freneau to Seth Paine, 2 Dec. 1800, quoted in Cunningham, "Election of 1800," 128.

30. TJ to James Madison, 19 Dec. 1800, *JMP* 17:444. For Jefferson's earlier hopes, see TJ to Aaron Burr, 15 Dec. 1800, *Political Correspondence and Public Papers of Aaron Burr,* 2 vols., ed. Mary-Jo Kline (Princeton, N.J., 1983), 1:469 (hereafter *Correspondence of Burr*).

31. John Dawson to James Madison, 18 Dec. 1800, *JMP* 17:443.

32. Alexander Hamilton to James A. Bayard, 27 Dec. 1800, *AHP* 25:277.

33. Fisher Ames to John Rutledge Jr., 26 Jan. 1801, *Works of Ames* 2:1405–6.

34. Gouverneur Morris to Alexander Hamilton, 19 Dec. 1800, *AHP* 25:267. Hamilton strongly opposed this approach; see Alexander Hamilton to Gouverneur Morris, 9 Jan. 1801, ibid., 304.

35. Timothy Pickering to Benjamin Goodhue, [ca. 5 Jan. 1801], *The Life of Timothy Pickering,* ed. Octavius Pickering and Charles Upham (Boston, 1867–73), 4:22 (hereafter *Life of Pickering*). See also Timothy Pickering to Rufus King, 5 Jan. 1801, *Life of King* 3:366.

36. John Adams to Elbridge Gerry, 7 Feb. 1801, *The Works of John Adams, Second President of the United States: With a Life of the Author, Notes and Illustrations,* ed. Charles Francis Adams (Boston, 1856), 9:98.

37. Samuel Sewall to Harrison Gray Otis, 29 Dec. 1800, *Life of Otis* 1:212.

38. William Cooper to John Jay, 19 Dec. 1800, quoted in Kuroda, *Origins of the Twelfth Amendment,* 104.

39. *Aurora General Advertiser* (Philadelphia), 16 Jan. 1801, quoted in *AHP* 17:302–3 n. 7.

40. TJ to Aaron Burr, 15 Dec. 1800, *Correspondence of Burr* 1:469.

41. James Monroe to TJ, 6 Jan. 1801, *Writings of Monroe* 3:254. See also TJ to James Madison, 26 Dec. 1800, *JMP* 17:448; and TJ to Tench Coxe, 31 Dec. 1800, L&B, 10:188.

42. John Beckley to Littleton W. Tazewell, 25 Jan. 1801, *Justifying Jefferson,* 228.

43. Samuel Smith to Aaron Burr, 11 Jan. [1801], *Correspondence of Burr* 2:488.

44. TJ to Judge John Breckenridge [*sic,* Breckinridge], 18 Dec. 1800, L&B, 10:183.

45. Albert Gallatin to Hannah Gallatin, 29 Jan. 1801, in Henry Adams, *The Life of Albert Gallatin* (1879; rept. New York, 1943), 257 (hereafter *Life of Gallatin*).

46. James Monroe to TJ, 6 Jan. 1801, *Writings of Monroe* 3:254.

47. Samuel Smith to Aaron Burr, 11 Jan. [1801], *Correspondence of Burr* 1:488. For the caucus of New York and New Jersey congressmen, see George Jackson to James Madison, 5 Feb. 1801, *JMP* 17:460–61.

48. James Madison to TJ, 10 Jan. 1801, *JMP* 17:454.

49. James Gunn to Alexander Hamilton, [9 Jan. 1801], *AHP* 25:303. For the support of Jefferson, Burr, and other Republicans for the idea of a special session of Congress called by joint proclamation, see Samuel Smith to Aaron Burr, 11 Jan. [1801], *Correspondence of Burr* 1:488.

50. Albert Gallatin, "Plan at Time of Balloting for Jefferson and Burr, Communicated to Nicholas and Mr. Jefferson," [late Jan.–early Feb. 1801], *The Writings of Albert Gallatin,* 3 vols., ed. Henry Adams (Philadelphia, 1879), 1:18–20 (hereafter *Writings of Gallatin*). Gallatin can be seen working his way through this problem in a pair of letters to his wife; see Albert Gallatin to Hannah

Gallatin, 22 and 29 Jan. 1801, *Life of Gallatin*, 255–58. The memorandum was certainly completed before the House decided on the rules for balloting on 9 February. For Gallatin's later recollections of Republican thinking, see Albert Gallatin to Henry A. Muhlenberg, 8 May 1848, in *Life of Gallatin*, 248–51.

51. Resolution of 9 Feb. 1801, *Annals of Congress*, 6th Cong., 2d sess., 1010, 1011. For the doubts about multiple ballots, see Timothy Pickering to Benjamin Goodhue, [ca. 5 Jan. 1801], *Life of Pickering* 4:22; and Gallatin, "Plan," *Writings of Gallatin* 1:21.

52. Albert Gallatin to Hannah Gallatin, 5 Feb. 1801, *Life of Gallatin* 260.

53. James A. Bayard to Richard Bassett, 10 Feb. 1801, "Papers of James A. Bayard, 1796–1815," *American Historical Association Annual Report for the Year 1913*, ed. Elizabeth Donnan (Washington, D.C., 1915), 124 (hereafter "Papers of Bayard").

54. Albert Gallatin to Hannah Gallatin, 5 Feb. 1801, *Life of Gallatin*, 260. See also John Beckley to Albert Gallatin, 15 Feb. 1801, *Justifying Jefferson*, 233.

55. Samuel Tyler to James Monroe, 9 Feb. 1801, "Original Letters," *WMQ* 1st ser., 1 (1892): 103 (hereafter "Original Letters"). The sources for a legislative history of these rules—whether in the *Annals of Congress* or in private letters—are not nearly as clear as one might wish. As a result, some seemingly important developments are difficult to explain. Why did almost every Republican vote to strike the rule that called for the balloting to continue without adjournment (see vote of 9 Feb. 1801, *Annals of Congress*, 1008)? Why did Bayard, who first proposed and later voted for this principle, inform the governor of Delaware that he disagreed with it (see James A. Bayard to Richard Bassett, 6 Feb. 1801, "Papers of Bayard," 123)? And why did leading Republicans vote against requiring voting by states, rather than individuals, on important issues once the balloting began (see Samuel Tyler to James Monroe, 9 Feb. 1801, "Original Letters," 102)?

56. Roger Griswold to Frances Griswold, 11 Feb. 1801 [morning], Griswold Papers.

57. James Monroe to John Hoomes, 14 Feb. 1801, *Writings of Monroe* 3:259.

58. John Dawson to James Monroe, 12 Feb. 1801, quoted in Harry Ammon, *James Monroe: The Quest for National Identity* (1971; rept. Charlottesville, Va., 1990), 192.

59. Roger Griswold to Frances Griswold, 11 Feb. 1801 [evening], Griswold Papers.

60. James A. Bayard to Allan McLane, 17 Feb. 1801, "Papers of Bayard," 127.

61. See, for example, Albert Gallatin to Hannah Gallatin, 5 Feb. 1801, *Life of Gallatin*, 260; and John Beckley to Albert Gallatin, 15 Feb. 1801, *Justifying Jefferson*, 233.

62. TJ to Thomas M'Kean [*sic*, McKean], 9 March 1801, L&B, 10:221. For the preparations in Pennsylvania and Virginia, see Sharp, *American Politics*, 268–71; Ammon, *James Monroe*, 192–93; Dumas Malone, *Jefferson the President: First Term, 1801–1805*, vol. 4 of *Jefferson and His Time* (Boston, 1970), 10–11; and Harry M. Tinkcom, *The Republicans and Federalists in Pennsylvania, 1790–1801: A Study in National Stimulus and Local Response* (Harrisburg, Pa., 1950), 255–56.

63. John Beckley to Albert Gallatin, 15 Feb. 1801, *Justifying Jefferson*, 232.

64. TJ to James Madison, 18 Feb. 1801, *JMP* 17:467.

65. Ibid.

66. TJ to James Monroe, 15 Feb. 1801, L&B, 10:201–2.

67. Albert Gallatin to Henry A. Muhlenberg, 8 May 1848, *Life of Gallatin*, 248.

68. James A. Bayard to Richard Bassett, 17 Feb. 1801, "Papers of Bayard," 127.

69. John Lawrence to Rufus King, 18 Feb. 1801, *Life of King* 3:393.

70. Robert Goodloe Harper, circular letter to his constituents, 24 Feb. 1801, *Circular Letters* 1:233–34. Whether this "determination" was, in fact, "publicly avowed" is unclear. But Republicans certainly thought that they would not have to relent. Vermont Federalist Lewis Morris and Maryland Federalists George Baer and William Craik, along with Bayard, were viewed as almost certain to accept Jefferson's victory rather than defeat an election entirely; see Samuel Tyler to James

Monroe, 9 Feb. 1801, "Original Letters," 103; and Albert Gallatin to Henry A. Muhlenberg, 8 May 1848, *Life of Gallatin,* 250.

71. James A. Bayard to [Richard Bassett], 3 Jan. 1801, "Papers of Bayard," 117.

72. TJ to Thomas Lomax, 25 Feb. 1801, L&B, 10:211.

73. TJ to John Taylor, 1 June 1798, ibid., 46.

74. Robert Goodloe Harper, circular letter to his constituents, 24 Feb. 1801, *Circular Letters* 1:232.

75. James A. Bayard to Richard Bassett, 16 Feb. 1801, "Papers of Bayard," 126.

76. Albert Gallatin to Hannah Gallatin, 22 Jan. 1801, *Life of Gallatin,* 256. See also George Cabot to Rufus King, 28 Dec. 1800, *Life of King* 3:354.

77. James A. Bayard to Allen McLane, 17 Feb. 1801, "Papers of Bayard," 128–29. According to Bayard, even these holdouts would have agreed to cast blank ballots "had it not been for a single gentleman from Connecticut"; when he refused, the other New England Federalists decided to vote for Burr to the end (James A. Bayard to Alexander Hamilton, 8 March 1801, *AHP* 25:345).

78. James A. Bayard to John Adams, 19 Feb. 1801, "Papers of Bayard," 129–30.

79. James A. Bayard to Alexander Hamilton, 8 March 1801, *AHP* 25:345.

80. TJ to B. S. Barton, 14 Feb. 1801, L&B, 10:200.

81. TJ to Nathaniel Niles, 22 March 1801, ibid., 233.

82. TJ to James Monroe, 7 March 1801, ibid., 219.

83. Alexander Hamilton to Gouverneur Morris, 9 Jan. 1801, *AHP* 25:305.

84. Robert Goodloe Harper, circular letter to his constituents, 5 March 1801, *Circular Letters* 1:248.

85. James A. Bayard to Allen McLane, 17 Feb. 1801, "Papers of Bayard," 127. It is rare to find a Federalist after the election echoing William Vans Murray's statement: "I deeply regret the election and wish there had been *none*" (William Vans Murray to John Quincy Adams, 30 March 1801, "Letters of William Vans Murray to John Quincy Adams, 1797–1803," ed. Worthington Chauncey Ford, in *American Historical Association Annual Report for the Year 1912* [Washington, D.C., 1914], 692).

86. TJ to Joseph Priestley, 21 March 1801, L&B, 10:229–30.

CHAPTER 2

The Political Presidency
Discovery and Invention

Jack N. Rakove

The providence that superintends the fortunes of the United States of America in mysterious ways planned a special bicentennial commemoration of the election of 1800–1801.[1] For the first time since 1888, it produced a presidential election in which the winner of the electoral vote did not secure a plurality of the popular vote, thereby reminding Americans of the curious mechanism for selecting a president that the framers of the Constitution had cobbled together in 1787. Yet during the five weeks of legal and political wrangling in the fall of 2000 over the recounting of the vote in Florida—a territory that President Thomas Jefferson once coveted—what was more striking was how few citizens appreciated the deeper irony revealed by the disputed results in that decisive state. If the returns demonstrated anything, it was that Florida's 6 million voters were divided into two perfectly equal blocs separated by a statistically insignificant margin of a few hundred (or perhaps a few thousand) votes. Yet under the winner-take-all rule that has prevailed in nearly every state since the early nineteenth century—and whose logic first became manifest in 1800—all of the state's twenty-five electors went to George W. Bush, who thereby became president of the United States by the grace and favor of the United States Supreme Court (not Jefferson's favorite institution of government) and the vagaries of the chad and the butterfly ballot.

The disparity between the popular and electoral votes in the 2000 presidential election fulfilled a scenario that had previously troubled only odd academics like Akhil Amar, whose thoughts on the subject, under the title "An

Accident Waiting to Happen," open a recent collection of half-whimsical, half-serious essays devoted to cataloguing *Constitutional Stupidities, Constitutional Tragedies.*[2] The volume's thirty-nine contributors[3] include thirty-two other professors of law, six political scientists, and no historians;[4] moreover, references to specific historical episodes are surprisingly few. Yet had the editors dedicated a category to "Stupidities: Historical Examples," an essay devoted to the election of 1800–1801, "An Accident That Did Happen," could have led the list. Indeed, such an essay would merit recognition on several counts. First, the election demonstrated how poorly the framers of the Constitution anticipated the dynamics of presidential politics. Had they imagined that a post–George Washington election could devolve into a clear contest between two nationally prominent candidates, they might have decided not to invent the electoral college in the first place. Second, the failure of the victorious Republicans to coordinate the votes of their electors—leaving Aaron Burr, the ostensible vice presidential candidate, tied with Thomas Jefferson, the ostensible head of the ticket—exposed the particular glitch in the original electoral formula that the Twelfth Amendment was subsequently adopted to rectify. Third, this tie in turn demonstrated the risks of allowing the final determination to be made by a lame-duck House of Representatives in which the defeated Federalists held the balance of power. Fourth, the Republican victory depended on the additional votes gained through the application of the three-fifths clause to the electoral college—but this factor arguably brings us within the realm of constitutional tragedy, rather than mere stupidity.

Historians should in any case feel more comfortable writing about tragedy than about stupidity. Tragedy can be an accurate characterization of the consequences of events, but stupidity does not provide a correspondingly useful explanation of their origins and causes. A historian who explained the outcome of an event in terms of the stupidity of the actors involved would rarely be taken seriously.[5] Even when we could plausibly assert that stupidity really was involved, as in the case of a dim-witted king or an obtuse general, we would still be obliged to explain events and outcomes in terms of the stupidity of the hereditary principle itself, or of the failures of staff and intelligence, traditions of deference to higher command, or simply the fog of battle.[6]

To treat the presidential election of 1800–1801 as a case study in constitutional stupidity would thus itself be stupid. To equate its constitutional importance with the adoption of the Twelfth Amendment to correct the framers' oversight would be more defensible, but unsurprising.[7] But to use the election to examine the processes of constitutional invention, implementation, and

innovation is another matter. The election was the culmination of three developments: the difficulty the framers faced in perceiving the political dimensions
of the presidency, which in turn meant that much would necessarily be left to
creative experimentation and discovery; the realization by the mid-1790s that
control of the government depended on control of the executive; and the recognition by 1798 that the brevity of the constitutional provisions governing the
electoral college created opportunities and therefore incentives to manipulate
the text in pursuit of political advantage. Taken together, these three developments led to what might be called the discovery and invention of the political
presidency: discovery, because it exposed inherent aspects of the office that its
designers had not perceived; and invention, because leaders of both parties actively innovated to manipulate the electoral system for their own ends.

THE VIEW FROM PHILADELPHIA

Discussions of the origins of the presidency often invoke the purported influence that the presence and image of George Washington exercised over the deliberations at Philadelphia. A contemporary letter from South Carolina framer
Pierce Butler corroborates this belief. Writing to an English relative in May 1788,
Butler observed that the powers of the presidency were "greater than I was disposed to make them," and then further wondered whether "they would have
been so great had not many of the members cast their eyes toward General
Washington as President; and shaped their Ideas of the Powers to be given to a
President, by their Opinions of his Virtue."[8]

This observation hardly accords with the record of the "tedious and reiterated discussions" from which the presidency emerged in the final fortnight of
debate in September 1787.[9] Even if Washington provided a stirring example of
the possibility of a trustworthy republican executive, the fact remains that the
presidency posed the single most perplexing problem of institutional design
that the Convention confronted. When the framers thought about the legislature, they could draw freely upon the rich history of Parliament and their own
assemblies. Similarly, while the concept of judicial review was certainly a great
innovation, the traditions of common law jurisprudence did offer shining illustrations of the merits of independent and learned judges. But in the case of
the executive, the examples and precedents to be evoked were either essentially
negative in character or at least had little bearing on the problems of constituting a national executive on republican principles.

To understand why this was the case, consider the differences between the still evolving form of ministerial government that existed in Georgian Britain, on the one hand, and its mature nineteenth-century state (as described by Walter Bagehot and admired by Woodrow Wilson). From the 1710s on, there were recognizable prime ministers in such eminent leaders as Sir Robert Walpole, the duke of Newcastle, William Pitt, and Lord North, and to stay in power these ministers had to command stable majorities in Parliament. But the choice of prime minister still depended significantly on the pleasure of the king, and in practice both houses of Parliament were highly susceptible to ministerial influence. Control of Parliament depended on negotiations among the aristocratic grandees who commanded their own factions in the Commons. Elections had little effect on the composition of the government, the electorate was small and easily influenced, and popular political parties simply did not exist. Eighteenth-century ministerial government still had a strongly monarchical cast.[10]

A second factor complicating American thinking about the political potentialities of the executive was the legacy of suspicion produced by decades of quarrels with colonial governors and reinforced by the fear of executive power fostered by radical Whig writers in England.[11] That bias was reflected in the evisceration of executive power that characterized the first state constitutions. These governors—Jefferson would have preferred the term "administrators"—were typically elected by the state legislatures for a single year and yoked to councils that were also meant to play a watchdog role. "Stripped of those badges of domination called prerogatives," as John Adams put it, these governors exercised powers that were conceived to be merely executive in nature: an agency power to implement the legislative will but not to influence it in a political capacity. True, the second-generation constitutions of New York (1777) and Massachusetts (1780) restored a modicum of authority and independence to the executive, most notably by providing for popular election of the governor. Not coincidentally, two of the most popular figures to emerge from the turmoil of state politics were the upstart George Clinton in New York and the aristocratic John Hancock in Massachusetts. But there is little evidence that their success encouraged observers to perceive the commanding political station that a popularly elected executive might occupy.[12]

Nor, finally, did the Continental Congress afford much in the way of positive experience on which to draw. For one thing, Congress itself was often regarded as an executive body because its essential responsibilities for war and foreign relations were traditionally associated with the prerogative powers of the monarchy. The presidency of Congress resembled a legislative speakership, while the heads of the executive departments that Congress established in 1781, though able men, occupied a distinctly subordinate position. Some historians have described Robert Morris, superintendent of finance from 1781 until 1784, as a virtual prime minister. Yet Morris's success in placing the war effort on a sound footing was not equaled by his ability to command a working majority in Congress. If anything, it was the frustration he felt when Congress balked at adopting his financial program that lured him into the dangerous expedient of fanning the fears of the public creditors and the officer corps of the continental army in a futile effort to pressure Congress. But this attempt to mobilize political assets "out-of-doors" had the opposite effect from what Morris intended, persuading James Madison, among others, to reject the superintendent's demands and fashion a compromise that disappointed Morris.[13]

Given these unpromising materials, it is not surprising that the task of establishing a national executive on republican principles puzzled the framers. Madison's uncertainty about the problem is suggestive. In 1785 he had wondered whether the executive deserved even the second place of importance behind the legislature, and on the eve of the Convention he told Washington that he had "scarcely ventured to form my own opinion either of the manner in which it ought to be constituted or of the authorities with which it ought to be cloathed."[14] Other delegates, such as Alexander Hamilton and James Wilson, came to Philadelphia with more advanced notions, but Madison's uncertainty better reflected the Convention's collective hesitancy.

Once the Convention got under way, discussion of the executive was subordinated to the more vexatious struggle over the reconstruction of Congress. In early June the delegates reached initial agreement on two important principles: to vest the executive power in a single person, and to arm him with a limited veto on legislation. The first measure was consistent with the idea of "responsibility," while the second is best explained as a weapon of self-defense against the threat of legislative encroachment. Both principles were concerned, in effect, with the administrative dimensions of the executive rather than its political puissance. Once the committee of the whole accepted these points, however, discussion of the executive flagged, to be resumed only after the key decision of 16 July resolved the protracted wrangle over the apportionment of representation in Congress.[15]

At this point the framers could finally give the executive sustained attention, and the immediate result was perhaps the single most perplexing passage in their entire deliberations. Over the next ten days (17–26 July), the Convention cycled through a variety of schemes for electing the executive while pondering such related issues as length of term, eligibility for re-election, and mode of removal. Three modes of election were possible: by the legislature, which presumably would possess the best knowledge of likely candidates; by the people at large, voting in one national electorate; and by a separate body of electors. As the debate unfolded, each of these schemes was subjected to sharp criticism, turning the debate into an exercise in comparing their relative disadvantages.

Election by the legislature, it was argued, would risk turning the executive into its toady, unless the incumbent was made ineligible for re-election. But that in turn would rob the president of the motive for excellent service that the incentive of re-election would create, while also lengthening the single term he would serve and encouraging presidents to profit as much as they could from the single opportunity they would enjoy. Popular election was vulnerable to other objections. In a national electorate, the disparity in the sizes of the free populations of the North and South might well prevent any southern candidate other than Washington from securing the office. More important, in a decentralized (and expanding) polity like the United States, it was difficult to imagine how any candidate other than the general would ever gain the national reputation required to enable a popular vote to make a decisive choice. What the framers feared was not that the people would fall prey to the first demagogue to canter along, but rather that lack of information would render a popular choice ineffective.

These objections briefly seemed strong enough to persuade the Convention to endorse a scheme of presidential electors. But this untried device had little inherent appeal; it was attractive primarily as an alternative to the other two modes, and when some delegates questioned whether the electors would have the requisite ability to make an informed choice, the delegates retreated to their original position, which was to have the legislature elect an executive for a single term of seven years. If this mode "was liable to objections," George Mason observed on 26 July, "it was liable to fewer than any others." [16]

There the question sat for another three weeks. In mid-August, however, a series of discrete discussions indicated that the framers' conceptions of the executive were evolving in ways favorable to its potential authority, and this had important implications for the question of election. Through the first fortnight of August, the framers evidently still thought of the executive primarily in agency terms, and not as an independent repository of political power. The best index of this lies in their inclination to vest powers over appointment and the conduct of foreign relations in the Senate. But by mid-August a reaction against the Senate had begun to set in, and the presidency emerged as its main bene-ficiary. When the mode of election was next considered on 24 August, the Con-vention, prodded by Gouverneur Morris, deadlocked on the "abstract ques-tion" of replacing legislative election with a system of electors. The matter then passed to the grand committee appointed to consider "such parts of the Con-stitution as have been postponed." Its report of 4 September proposed all but one of the critical changes that gave the presidency its final form. Now the ex-ecutive and Senate were joined in the exercise of the appointment and treaty powers. The president would be chosen by electors meeting separately in the states and balloting only once. Electors would be distributed among the states in numbers equal to their representation in Congress; each would cast two bal-lots, and the candidate receiving the second largest number of votes would be-come vice president. In the event that no candidate obtained a majority of all the electors, the choice would fall to the Senate. And the president would be el-igible for re-election.[17]

The political logic of this scheme tracked the compromise over representa-tion. Populous states would have the advantage in the first electoral round, but the small states would gain two important points: first, they would be overrep-resented in the initial vote because their senators would count in the allocation; second, should the electors not prove decisive, an eventual decision by the Sen-ate would give each state an equal vote. Southern states would also benefit from having the three-fifths clause augment their number of electors.

The ensuing debate offers a fascinating case study in the workings and lim-its of the political imagination. The report was immediately found objection-able on one critical ground. By joining the president and Senate in the exercise of specific powers while providing for the president to be elected (contingently) by the same body, the report would presumably make the executive politically dependent on the one institution with which it would be most closely linked. Had the framers believed that the electors would make a decisive choice, this objection might not have mattered. But many delegates sensibly assumed that the electors would act as the equivalent of a modern primary, making candi-dates but not producing a president. This prediction sustained the troubling conclusion that the Senate would become a nursery of aristocracy, dominating both the House and the presidency, and (*pace* "the celebrated Montesquieu") improperly combining all three forms of power (legislative, executive, and—through impeachment—judicial) in its avaricious paws.[18]

These telling criticisms stumped the delegates for three days. Transferring the contingent election to the House would give the large states the advantage at both stages, thereby vitiating the political compromise between large and small states. With some reluctance, the framers finally approved the committee's original proposal on 6 September. But then two members of the committee stumbled onto a solution. Hugh Williamson first moved to have the whole Congress, "voting *by states* and not *per capita,*" make the "eventual choice," and Roger Sherman then offered the winning amendment to have the House of Representatives, rather than Congress, make the decision using the same rule. This would preserve the political compromise while avoiding making the president politically dependent on the Senate.

The fact that this neat solution appeared almost as an afterthought is only one remarkable aspect of this curious debate. It is equally striking that so few delegates expressed any confidence that the electoral system would ever work in practice. Only Madison seemed to grasp, or even glimpse, the key point: that the goal should be "to render an eventual resort to any part of the Legislature improbable" by encouraging the large states "to make the appointment in the first instance conclusive." Rather than allow the eventual choice to be made among the top five electoral vote-getters, as proposed, Madison would limit the number of candidates passing to the second round to three, thereby encouraging the larger states to find ways to make an effective decision. The small states clung to an opposite view, holding the line at five nominees to preserve the influence they would enjoy during the second stage. Under either rule, however, many delegates assumed that electors would scatter their votes among favorite-son candidates, and that the difficulty of coordinating political activity in a decentralized polity would exceed the ingenuity of either state or national leaders.

Nor did the delegates have any better sense of the dynamics of presidential election should the choice fall to either the Senate, the House, or the whole Congress. The logic of balancing large and small states was more closely tied to the politics of the Convention than to any realistic assessment of the alignments that would emerge once the Constitution was adopted. For reasons Madison had explained during the debates over representation, the size of a state would not predict the behavior of either its citizens or their elected representatives. Size per se would matter only during the special circumstances of a constitutional convention, when each state's delegation could readily calculate which rule of apportionment would favor its constituents, and act accordingly. In a sense, size was a relevant factor in deliberations only when one was framing constitutional rules for voting. But once the system was running, electors, like members of Congress, would almost certainly act on other principles—not the size of their state but the real interests and preferences of its citizens.[19] In these terms, the real beneficiaries of the final decisions on presidential election were the slave states of the South, which had an enduring peculiar interest to protect. The dual compromise over the allocation of representatives and electors gave the South a measure of political leverage that it would exploit successfully over the coming decades.

The decisions on the electoral system followed those on representation in one other respect. Just as state legislatures were free to determine how members of the House were to be elected, the appointment of electors was left completely to their discretion as well. In both cases, the Constitution could in theory have stipulated essential rules of election, by mandating, for example, that electors and representatives be chosen statewide, or in districts (though the fact that electors would always outnumber representatives by two would prevent congressional and electoral districts from being coterminous), or even statewide by districts (that is, a statewide electorate could vote for an elector from each district). But any such decision would have required the framers to refine an already complicated system even further, perhaps more than they felt the Constitution could practically, or even rightfully, do. And the fact that these decisions were taken so late in the deliberations may also explain why further specifications were omitted. Or perhaps the framers simply did not perceive a problem in leaving the mode of appointing electors up to the states.

Whatever the explanation for this omission, its consequences were clear. Far from creating a neutral procedural rule, or one immune to manipulation, the Constitution created opportunities and therefore incentives to subordinate the procedures for the selection of electors to considerations of political advantage. In 1787, what form the calculation of such advantage would take lay among what John Adams once called "the arcana of futurity." The general expectation of Washington's election removed any urgency from the determination of the initial rules for appointing electors. As the states enacted enabling legislation for the first federal elections, they predictably adopted a variety of procedures for the electors, as they also did for the House of Representatives.[20] Moreover, no one in 1788 could predict whether, when, or how the election of a president would become a serious object of political contestation. The institution was so novel, its influence so hard to fathom, and the difficulty of coordinating efforts across state lines so daunting, that there simply was no basis upon which to offer any reliable opinion of its political potentialities. Moreover, by grounding their decision on the comparative disadvantages of different procedures, the framers never developed a positive theory of the political presidency—that is, one that grappled with the advantages it might acquire should the electors actually prove decisive. The presidency was the one office in the new government least amenable to prognostication, and its imminent occupation by the one living American whose unique political advantages history could never replicate meant that early precedents might not provide a reliable guide for the future.

DISCOVERING THE EXECUTIVE POWER

The presidency received far less attention during the ratification debates than might be expected. As Ralph Ketcham has noted, "There was surprisingly little concentration by the Anti-Federalists on executive powers as such." Anti-Federalists worried much more about the dangerous ties between the president and the Senate than they did about monarchical tendencies in the executive. Their perception of the Senate as the most sinister institution of the new government made it more difficult to consider the presidency in its own right.[21] The experience and vocabulary of republican politics simply proved inadequate for conceiving the political dimensions of the presidency, and as a result the ratification debates had strikingly little to say about this novel institution.

The most sustained and intriguing discussion of the potential character of presidential power appeared in Hamilton's essays on the subject in *The Federalist*. Modern readers, having the advantage of knowing what was to come, can detect insights and ambitions that presage the author's conduct as first secretary of the treasury. The image of executive power that emerges from these passages, however, is one that still emphasizes the importance of a vigorous administration of government and the value of enabling the executive to resist the "imperious control" and transient "humours" of the legislature.[22] The closest Hamilton came to a positive conception of the executive was when he reflected on "the love of fame, the ruling passion of the noblest minds."[23] Here he foreshadowed the active role that a minister of state—himself as secretary of the treasury, or Jefferson as secretary of state—might play in drafting state papers that would lay out ambitious enterprises of public policy, shaping the requisite congressional deliberations by the sheer depth and brilliance of his understanding.

Suggestive as such passages are of Hamilton's perception of the advantages of executive power, they fall short of envisioning the president as the focus of national political life; nor did Hamilton offer anything more than cursory remarks about the mechanism of the electoral college.[24] Not that he was oblivious to the problem. In his post-Convention "Conjectures about the new Constitution," he predicted that Washington's election as first president "will insure a wise choice of men to administer the government and a good administration," and this "will conciliate the confidence and affection of the people and perhaps enable the government to acquire more consistency than the proposed constitution seems to promise."[25] Washington's election, in this sense, was critical to the transition between the *ancien regime* of the Confederation and the *nouveau regime* of the Constitution. The initial political stability that the general would provide would enable the national government to consolidate political support by adopting exactly the kinds of policies that Hamilton, as his most influential adviser, would propose. But even these speculations are more concerned with bestowing advantages on the national government, in its anticipated zero-sum game competition with the states, than with projecting the ongoing locus of decision-making within the national government itself.

For what Hamilton undoubtedly knew was that there could be only one Washington. Just as the national government might benefit from the policies his administration promoted, so his successors in the presidency would presumably act upon, and perhaps be constrained by, the precedents his administration set. But no future president could expect to enjoy the unique political assets that would free Washington from having to nurture new political skills. As Ketcham observes, Washington "so completely embodied the patriot king model that had Lord Bolingbroke been able to observe his conduct as general and president he surely would have listed Washington along with Elizabeth and Henry of Navarre as an ideal leader"—that is, a leader who reigned above considerations of faction and party, seeking the true public good of the commonwealth.[26] Washington might set precedents for his successors to follow, and they in turn could attempt to emulate his example; but none would ever possess his unique stature and advantages.

Even so, politics never stands still, and Washington's two administrations marked the beginning of presidential politics in at least three respects. First,

Washington understood that the power of appointment should be wielded for political purposes, not to reward partisans in a narrow sense but to recruit national officials from the ranks of the Constitution's firm supporters. Second, as much as Washington, with his experience of military command, believed in delegating authority to his quite capable subordinates, their disagreements ineluctably reached his desk, compelling him to take decisions that reinforced the emerging political divisions within Congress. In this respect it is critical to note that during the dispute over the bank bill, Jefferson, Madison, and Attorney General Edmund Randolph advised the president to veto the measure on constitutional grounds, not because it would encroach on executive powers (which of course it would not), but rather because the bill relied on the broad Hamiltonian reading of the necessary and proper clause.[27] Regardless of whether the three Virginians would have endorsed that conception of the purposes of the veto in principle, political circumstances persuaded them to urge the president to apply it in this way. The constitutional opportunity to use the presidential veto for this end was a sufficient incentive in itself—the more so because the political arguments against it had registered so poorly both in Congress and out-of-doors.

This constitutional fissure over the bank, following the prior dispute over the assumption of state debts, is often seen as the point of departure for the emergence of the factions that soon evolved into the first political parties. But whether these issues were sufficient to sustain organized competition, much less encourage interstate mobilization to capture the presidency, is doubtful. Assumption, after all, did not operate to divide the polity into favored and disfavored blocs, nor did the primitive financial infrastructure of the United States in the 1790s provide the same basis for disagreement over federal policy that would shape the bank war of the 1830s. Looking backward from 1800, it is easy to understand how this initial falling-out within the national elite could be seen as the opening rupture from which all else followed. The fact that Madison's essays for the party press articulated the essential tenets of a platform also conveys a sense of inevitability about the descent into partisanship.[28] Yet we should be cautious about concluding that the domestic disputes of the early 1790s established an adequate basis for organizing partisan competition across state lines, much less for perceiving the presidency as the great prize of the competition. At some point the struggle between Hamilton and Jefferson over Washington's ear would have ended—perhaps simply through their shared desire to pursue their private cares—and it could then have been dismissed as the intensely personal quarrel that in many ways it was. Absent more salient issues, it is not difficult to imagine that national politics could have followed lines closer to the "pluralist" model of *Federalist* No. 10, in which a multiplicity of interests scattered through a decentralized polity would prevent the formation of durable blocs or coalitions. In this model, majorities would form and re-form around particular issues, but high rates of turnover in Congress and the difficulty of cordinating interstate political activity would produce a national politics without parties.

That American politics followed another course was the result of a third development that made control of the presidency the focus of political competition. This development coincided with the beginning of Washington's second administration, when events in Europe and the arrival of Citizen Genet made foreign relations the most urgent topic for government deliberation. The question of the posture the United States should adopt toward revolutionary France gave secretaries Hamilton and Jefferson another occasion to disagree over matters of policy, but that disagreement again quickly took constitutional form. In debating the appropriate response to Genet's activities, Hamilton argued that, with Congress in recess, the executive was fully competent to assert the neutrality of the United States in the war France had declared against Britain. By contrast, Jefferson argued that because the Constitution vested the power over war in the legislature, only Congress could conclusively decide whether neutrality was appropriate. In support of his position Hamilton began publishing his letters as Pacificus, the *locus classicus* in American constitutional theory of the broad statement of inherent executive power over foreign relations. In response Jefferson dragooned a reluctant Madison, then back home in Virginia, into entering the lists as Hamilton's opponent.

Like the earlier debate over the necessary and proper clause, the Pacificus-Helvidius exchange marked a further elaboration of the rival modes of constitutional interpretation that compounded the differences between the rival political coalitions. The articulation of these positions probably mattered less than the reaction to Genet's provocative activities, culminating in his efforts to appeal directly to the American people in order to muster support for France. Within the government, as among the population, the struggle was primarily about policy and politics, and only secondarily about the Constitution. Yet the primary emphasis on politics is less important than what this dispute reveals about the innate tendency of both parties to constitutionalize their disagreements. Nor can one readily distinguish the instrumental aspects of this tendency—the impulse to present differences over policy as matters of constitutional principle—from an authentic belief, on the part of Jefferson and

Madison, that Hamilton was indeed acting on proto-monarchical aspirations. That perception had already taken hold, and Hamilton's willingness to take his case to the public only confirmed views the two Virginia leaders already shared.

Hamilton's brief for executive discretion in foreign relations was noteworthy in two respects. First, it was consistent with his privately held views of how foreign policy ought to be made, representing, in a sense, a general application of a *raison d'état* mode of thinking about foreign relations to the peculiar character of the American constitutional system. A cynic might wonder whether Hamilton reached this position completely independently of the Constitution, but so long as he could make a constitutionally plausible case for his defense of prerogative, he was free to argue the point and leave it to his opponents to frame a suitable response. But the assertion of the executive's inherent power was significant for a more important reason: it identified an entire realm of governance in which the initiative and "energy" of the executive gave it decisive advantages over the legislature. In the realm of domestic policy, a different equation governed. There the balancing of a variety of local interests would inevitably have to occur within Congress before government could act, and there the most the executive could do would be to propose a course of action for the disposition (or the disposal) of Congress. But in matters of foreign relations, where external events could require action when Congress was not even in session, and where the conduct of diplomacy was not easily subjected to legislative scrutiny, other conditions governed. Whenever foreign relations took precedence over domestic affairs, the institutional advantages of the executive would leave Congress with the choice of acquiescence or reaction under circumstances in which its own field of action had been sharply constrained.[29]

The Pacificus-Helvidius exchange, however, was only a prelude to the more serious confrontation that developed from British seizures of American merchantmen in the West Indies in the spring of 1794. In their wake, Chief Justice John Jay was dispatched on his special mission to London, and the treaty he negotiated in turn became the source of a running controversy that preoccupied the country from Jay's return in March 1795 through the Republicans' effort a year later to make enforcement of the treaty dependent on the approval of the requisite appropriations by the House of Representatives. The thrust of the Republican argument was that, notwithstanding the plain language of the Constitution vesting the treaty power in the president and Senate, the House of Representatives retained residual authority to determine whether a treaty requiring public expenditures was to take effect; otherwise its independent power over appropriations, arguably its most important privilege, would be rendered null. In attempting to enforce this claim, the House called upon the president to present documents relating to the negotiation of the treaty, but Washington forthrightly refused, invoking the letter of the Constitution and the imperative of secrecy in diplomacy to explain why the House was not entitled to the papers. The Republicans opened this debate with a strong working majority in Congress, but by late April a swing of eleven votes enabled the Federalists to carry the appropriation measure.

It was during this debate that Madison made his most authoritative statement of the theory of constitutional interpretation we now call "originalism." That theory, too, was an invention: it had not been part of the original constitutional understanding of 1787–88 but instead evolved with—and obviously reflected—the politicization of constitutional interpretation in the years since.[30] But the deeper significance of this episode lay in the juxtaposition of the rival strategies pursued by the administration and its opposition in the House. Historically the power of the purse had been the most effective weapon that the House of Commons, and its colonial counterparts, had wielded in the ongoing struggles between legislative privilege and executive prerogative. In the abstract, the Republican majority in the House should have been able to deploy this weapon in the same way. But here it was prerogative that prevailed over privilege. And while some of that success doubtless reflected Washington's political potency, the outcome of the Jay Treaty controversy demonstrated that when matters of foreign relations were concerned, the executive enjoyed decisive advantages.

With Jefferson happily rusticated on his Virginia mountaintop, it was Madison who had to confront the implications of these developments. To the earlier concerns that he and Jefferson shared about the corrupt means Hamilton had purportedly used to influence Congress, Madison now increasingly reckoned with the institutional advantages of the presidency. This theme recurs in his correspondence from the spring of 1794 on. "The influence of the Ex. on events, the use made of them, and the public confidence in the P[resident] are an overmatch for all the efforts Republicanism can make," he wrote in May, when the rush of sentiment in favor of the Jay mission frustrated his efforts to impose an embargo on Britain.[31] After December 1794 the two Virginians began fencing over the question of which one should challenge for the first presidential succession. Jefferson first overcame "double delicacies" to express his hope of one day seeing his correspondent in "a more splendid and a more efficacious post"; Madison responded, several months later, with his own disclaimer against "any idea such as you seem to glance at," while pointedly informing Jefferson that "You ought to be preparing yourself however to hear truths, which no inflexibility will be able to withstand." But the truth Jefferson still preferred was that Madison was the person he wished to see "placed at the helm of our affairs," and "that the little spice of ambition, which I had in my younger days, has long since evaporated." [32] Madison did not take the hint. Though careful not to renew the discussion with Jefferson, by early 1796 he was actively engaged in promoting Jefferson's silent, ambivalent candidacy.

As much as this duet reveals about the mores of republican politics, it establishes one critical point. Both men now understood that the capture of the presidency was essential to the pursuit of their objectives and policies. It was an office that had to be actively contested, and that contest would take the form of sustained competition at both the state and national levels of politics. The real work of coordinating party strategy and activity fell not to Madison but to John Beckley and others like him—men at ease with the hurly-burly of popular politics in a way that the two eminences never pretended to be. That the electors would make an effective choice, and not leave the final decision to the House, also seems never to have been in doubt. However uncertain the intentions or expectations of 1787, the course of politics since 1789 had quickly conspired to make the presidency the focal point and prize of political competition, and to identify two preeminent candidates as potential successors to the nation's only indispensable leader.

It might of course be argued that the polity was still drawing on the talented pool of recognized and notable leaders that the Revolution had discovered. That characterization would certainly fit John Adams; whether it pertained equally well to Jefferson is another question. [33] His authorship of the Declaration of Independence was not yet a decisive factor in his reputation; his dismal record as governor of Virginia could have barred him from ever holding executive office again; and his service as minister to France, however much it helped to shape his political ideas, was not distinguished by great diplomatic achievements. Arguably it was only Jefferson's appointment as secretary of state, which in turn brought him to his leadership of the opposition, that rendered him eligible for national elective office. In this sense, Jefferson was as much a creature of the new national politics as one of its creators.

One crucial puzzle remains: would the disputes over domestic policy that dominated Washington's first administration have been sufficient to generate the same competition, and with it the corresponding impetus for interstate co-ordination that was already operating by 1796? Or did the foreign policy disputes of the second administration, culminating in the controversy over the Jay Treaty, provide the additional "inputs" required to convert an opposition faction operating primarily *within* the government into a political movement soliciting and securing significant public support? The counterfactual model of political development implicit in this formulation rests on two propositions: first, that the disputes over the Hamiltonian program lacked the impact and staying power to sustain competition among coherent political parties; and second, that domestic issues would not have provided either factions within the government or state-based interests with adequate incentives to collaborate to capture the presidency. In this scenario the political composition of any given session of Congress would have been more factious than partisan; that is, a variety of coalitions embracing diverse interests would have formed around particular issues, but without evolving into stable alliances. Further, and equally important, there would have been no great imperative to focus political activity on the presidency.

The corresponding positive hypothesis is that the foreign policy disputes that erupted in 1793 and dominated American politics for the next two decades altered the course of political development by making control of the presidency the decisive fact of American politics and governance. This departure was contingent upon events that no one in the 1780s anticipated. Then it might have been plausible to predict that occasional European wars would require presidents (and Congress) to maneuver skillfully amid the vicissitudes of Old World politics, with the opportunities and dangers such conflicts posed to a nation that always stood to profit from Europe's misery. But to imagine an event like the French Revolution, generating a quarter-century of conflict on a scale surpassing even the Thirty Years War, and resonant with ideological meanings that would reverberate in the streets and squares of countless American communities, was something else entirely. Not only did these events raise the most fundamental questions about the very definition of the national interest; they also acquired a popular appeal that merely domestic issues lacked and probably would not acquire until slavery became deeply controversial. And because in responding to these events the presidency enjoyed manifest advantages over

Congress, the Republicans had to contest the presidency in 1796 if they hoped to affect, much less control, foreign policy.

The originalist theory of constitutional interpretation that James Madison articulated during the House debate over the Jay Treaty can itself be interpreted in several ways. A narrowly political reading could suggest that Madison was driven, almost goaded, into delivering his key speech of 6 April 1796, recognizing that this mode of interpretation was fraught with difficulty but also feeling he had no alternative if the Republican case for the authority of the House over treaties was to be sustained.[34] Alternatively, it could be argued on normative grounds that Madison was in fact articulating the correct theory of constitutional interpretation. In this view, the Constitution became supreme law only because it was adopted through a direct expression of popular sovereignty, and the people's understanding of what they had adopted (as reflected in the debates of the state ratification conventions) was therefore a legitimate, indeed authoritative, guide to the meaning of constitutional language.[35]

Between these two polar interpretations, we can also discern a third possibility. The process of developing and deploying rival modes of constitutional interpretation—whether Madison's form of originalism or the loose canon of Hamiltonian construction—reveals a critical and inadequately conceptualized aspect of constitutional politics. Because the rival theories of constitutional interpretation associated with the different parties emerged and diverged so early, we tend to think of the values they represent as independent variables. That is, these differences in constitutional philosophy to some extent preceded, and therefore help to explain, the disagreements over policy in which they were expressed. This explanation may well be true in itself—especially as it pertains to Hamilton and Jefferson, though Madison makes a more complicated case. But it is inadequate or incomplete in several respects.

First, it ignores the incentive and impetus that the existence of a written constitution may provide to escalate disagreements over policy into disputes over constitutional principle. If any doubt about the allocation or extent of constitutional authority to undertake an action exists, the opponents of that action will have a natural incentive to convert such doubts into additional points of controversy. In pursuing this course, political actors will also have an incentive—both strategic and psychological—to assert the right of action by whichever institution (or institutions) they perceive to be most responsive to their interests or influence. In the case of the Jay Treaty, for example, a Republican opposition holding a majority in the House of Representatives, and with no immediate prospect of capturing either the Senate or the executive, will naturally incline to assert the constitutional privileges of the lower chamber, and to emphasize those provisions of the Constitution most conducive to supporting its authority. Moreover, when such questions arise in a rancorous atmosphere like that of the 1790s, one side's willingness to constitutionalize a political dispute, or to refuse to concede a constitutional point, will operate to compound and reinforce, not alleviate or defuse, initial sources of contention. Far from being a source of neutral rules conceived to contain disagreements without implicating the fundamental principles of the regime, a constitution may unavoidably operate to transform quarrels over policy into disputes over basic principles.

The dual American commitment to separation of powers and to federalism, by dividing power among several autonomous institutions at two levels of government, increases the likelihood that the contending political forces will each capture at least one institution with a plausible right of decision or action. In 1796 the Republicans believed they had an opportunity to use their apparent majority in the House to that effect, and their claims for its constitutional authority over treaties followed accordingly. In 1798, having lost control of any branch of the national government, their two principal leaders stated a new theory of the role that state governments might play in correcting constitutional deviations. Once the Republicans gained control of the political branches of the national government in 1801, the Federalists were similarly led to concentrate their constitutional assets in the judiciary. A decade later, reduced to their political toehold in the state governments of New England, Federalist opponents of the War of 1812 offered states' rights arguments little different from the heresies Jefferson and Madison had propounded in 1798.

To dismiss these transpositions as simple opportunism, or as evidence that all constitutional argument is merely instrumental, would overlook the encouragement that constitutionalism offers to political actors to pursue exactly this strategy. Such a situational approach to constitutional decision-making, moreover, would comport with the principles Madison laid down in the famous formulation of *Federalist* No. 51: that "ambition must be made to counteract ambition. The interest of the man must be connected with the constitutional rights of the place." That defense of separation of powers (and federalism) need not require individual political actors to hold the same constitutional philosophy or interpretation as they move from position to position. It presupposes, instead, that the equilibrium of the constitutional system depends on actors asking which action is appropriate to the institution to which each is attached. A constitutional system that establishes multiple repositories of authority and that cannot attain perfect accuracy in delineating and distinguishing the responsibilities of each—for reasons Madison explained in *Federalist* No. 37— thus gives political entrepreneurs strong incentives to innovate, either by making claims for the decision-making authority of the institutions where they enjoy the greatest influence, or by developing interpretative theories to support these claims, or by manipulating ambiguous provisions of the Constitution for partisan advantage.

Few provisions proved more open to manipulation than the rules for appointing electors. While carefully specifying some features of the electoral system, the framers left one critical aspect of the entire process—the mode by which each state would appoint electors—entirely to the discretion of the state legislatures. Members of Congress and other federal officials were ineligible for selection, but everything else was open to legislative decision: popular election by district or statewide; appointment by the legislature; even appointment from within the legislature. The resulting impossibility of specifying the constituency or constituencies the president would represent made it difficult to identify the political attributes of the chief executive. At Philadelphia the framers briefly considered allowing the executives of the states to appoint their national counterpart, but under the Constitution each legislature could have appointed an electoral committee from the ranks of its own members, thereby in theory making the presidency an institution representative of, or accountable to, the state assemblies.

Nor would an attempt to use the interpretative theory of originalism to fill in silences in the constitutional text have produced a more definitive result. Given that neither the framers nor the ratifiers had formed any coherent conception of the political dimensions of the presidency, there was no original understanding to recover and apply to the circumstances of 1796 or 1800. Nor was there any real occasion to look beyond the four corners of the document for clues to its meaning, for the Constitution unambiguously left the method of appointing electors to the state legislatures. In one important respect Article II was even more tolerant of state discretion in appointing electors than was the comparable provision of Article I, authorizing the state legislatures to regulate the election of congressional representatives. Exercise of the latter power was subject to congressional review under Article I, section 10, but no corresponding clause enabled Congress to override a state's decision about the appointment of electors. When it came to the appointment of electors, the Constitution was simply a license to innovate.

In preparing for 1800, leaders of both parties could already draw useful inferences from the first contested election of 1796.[36] Even though Washington's delay in announcing his retirement dampened preparations for the election, electoral scheming began quickly—principally among the Federalists. While the Republicans were united behind Jefferson, they were, as Richard McCormick has observed, "surprisingly indifferent on the matter of a vice-presidential candidate"; but Hamilton, the *eminence grise* of Federalist politics, hatched a complicated scheme to enable Thomas Pinckney, the apparent second man on the party ticket, to receive more electoral votes than its nominal head, John Adams. This scheme foundered on the suspicions of New England Federalists; eighteen of their electors voted for Adams but not Pinckney, thereby not only enabling Jefferson to take second place, three votes behind the victorious Adams, but preventing Pinckney's election *as president* outright.[37] The fact that the electors were constitutionally required to meet and cast their votes in the separate states on the same day had not prevented the evil the framers had dreaded: just the kind of manipulative maneuvers that they lumped together under the general heading of cabal.

One other aspect of the 1796 election pointed suggestively toward 1800: in each of three states (Pennsylvania, Virginia, and North Carolina) Adams had picked up a single elector against the Republican phalanx, and had two of these votes gone to Jefferson, the result of the election would have been reversed, making His Rotundity, John Adams, the nation's only three-term vice president. Not only did this result corroborate the obvious point that in a close election every electoral vote counted; it also demonstrated the advantage of adopting a winner-take-all rule in states where one party was confident of its superiority.[38] In September 1799 Charles Pinckney reminded Madison (who needed no reminding) "that Mr Adams carried his Election by One Vote from Virginia & North Carolina." The lesson was clear: Madison had "to Write to & speak to all your Friends in the *republican interest* in the state Legislature" to replace its existing mode of selecting electors by district with appointment by joint ballot of the assembly. "The Constitution of the United States fully warrants it," Pinckney observed, "& remember that Every thing Depends upon it."[39] In the absence of constitutional constraint, political necessity ("Every thing Depends upon it") was a sufficient justification.

Pinckney may have been thinking ahead, but his *aperçu* was hardly unique: any informed, calculating political actor would have been encouraged, indeed required, to reason in exactly the same way, and this is in fact what key leaders of both parties generally did. As Jefferson himself observed in the spring of 1800, "All agree that an election by districts would be best, if it could be general; but while 10 states chuse either by their legislatures or by a general ticket, it is folly & worse than folly for the other 6 not to do it."[40] Given the opportunity and the imperative to think strategically about manipulating electoral rules in the interest of securing maximum advantage, the parties responded exactly as one might predict, regardless of previously expressed commitments or anything resembling a normative or neutral conception of how the presidency should be selected. The evidence on this point is unambiguous, and though the prosaic details are familiar to students of the election of 1800, the implications for our understanding of constitutional politics deserve greater emphasis.

In Virginia the strong Federalist showing in the 1798 elections—including the election of John Marshall to Congress—provided additional support for the idea of replacing the existing rule of district election with a statewide, winner-take-all appointment. Rather than follow Pinckney's proposal for a legislative election, the assembly adopted a general ticket law, whereby a statewide electorate in effect voted for a party's entire slate of electors. Many legislators evidently felt qualms about this action, which passed the lower house by a mere five votes—but pass it did. The implications of this change in the state with the largest number of electors was not lost on Federalists, especially the Massachusetts congressional delegation. Fearful that Republicans might capture one or two electors should Massachusetts maintain its use of districts, the delegation urged the assembly to follow Virginia's example, which it did by reserving to itself the power of appointment.[41]

Arguably the most interesting—and consequential—developments unfolded in New York. In March 1800 a Federalist-dominated legislature, confident that its party would retain control of the assembly in the spring elections, rejected a Republican proposal to replace legislative election with a district scheme. But the skill with which that great political entrepreneur, Aaron Burr, organized New York City for the Republicans gave his party control of the legislature that would meet in the fall to cast the state's electoral votes. This dramatic reversal in political fortune inspired Hamilton to write his famous desperate letter urging Governor John Jay to reconvene the sitting legislature to adopt, in effect, the Republican proposal to choose electors by district. Like Pinckney, Hamilton argued from political necessity and constitutional permissibility. He did not mean to suggest "that any thing ought to be done which integrity will forbid—but merely that the scruples of delicacy and propriety, as relative to a common course of things, ought to yield to the extraordinary nature of the crisis. They ought not to hinder the taking of a *legal* and *constitutional* step, to prevent an *Atheist* in Religion and a *Fanatic* in politics from getting possession of the helm of the State."

And again: "As to its intrinsic nature it is justified by unequivocal reasons for *public safety*"; a measure "warranted," Hamilton continued, "by the particular nature of the Crisis and the great cause of social order." Given the willingness of the other party to summon "all the resources which *Vice* can give," the Federalist party could ill afford to "confin[e] itself within all the ordinary forms of delicacy and decorum." [42]

Jay seems not to have answered Hamilton in writing, but at the bottom of the letter he docketed his response: "Proposing a measure for party purposes wh. I think it wd. not become me to adopt." [43] Jay's refusal to further Hamilton's scheme demonstrates that honor and political propriety could sway individual actors to act on considerations other than the calculation of partisan advantage. The apologetic note struck by four Maryland Federalists in their campaign for the legislature reveals a similar discomfort with electoral manipulation. In Maryland Federalists favored replacing the existing district law with a legislative election, and the four candidates announced that they would "pursue every *proper* and *constitutional* measure to elect John Adams president"; but whatever decision the assembly took, they promised to "*consent to no law making a change in the election, unless it contain a clause expressly declaring that the present mode shall be revived after this election.*" [44] The district mode, in other words, appeared to be correct on its merits—except insofar as it augured the wrong results for the current election.

Still a different but equally revealing scenario unfolded in Pennsylvania. In 1796 the state's electors were selected by general ticket, but that law had lapsed, and the procedure to be used in 1800 had to be determined by an assembly in which Republicans controlled the lower house and Federalists the upper. If the general ticket law was revived, Republicans would carry the state, but a district system might allow Federalists to salvage some votes.[45] After the legislature adjourned without breaking the resulting impasse, Republican hopes fastened on the elections for the new assembly, which Governor Thomas McKean could call into special session in time to meet the statutory deadline for the appointment of electors. But in the October elections, Federalists narrowly retained control of the senate. The deadlock thus persisted at the special session that McKean promptly called, and it was widely speculated that Pennsylvania would simply sit the election out (as New York had done in 1789). In a last-moment compromise, William Findley, the old anti-Federalist, hatched a plan that led to the appointment of eight Republican and seven Federalist electors by joint ballot.

From a political perspective, there is nothing very surprising about the extent of these maneuvers or even the matter-of-fact candor with which political leaders discussed them. Even a second-level political actor like John Dawson, Republican congressman from Virginia, could draw the obvious strategic inferences from monitoring the other side's moves, or by anticipating worst-case contingencies requiring immediate counteraction. Should Federalists carry the Maryland legislative elections, Dawson wrote Madison in late July, "they will be immediately calld together, for the purpose of appointing electors of president themselves—this will give the whole vote to Adams & Pinckney & will endanger the prospect which otherwise we have before us. Under this view what ought N. Carolina to do? Ought she not to play the same game, & thereby [sic] place herself on an equal footing, & not loose the weight which she ought to have in the Election?"[46] In this context, to "play the same game" meant doing everything possible to maximize the harvesting of electoral votes, taking the structure of politics and decision-making in each state on its own terms. There was no principled basis from which to ask whether the proper theory of the Constitution might favor one mode of election over another—to ask, that is, whether some true conception of the presidency warranted the selection of electors by either district voters, a statewide electorate, or the legislature itself. The only logic that mattered was political.

It would be tempting to treat this instrumental attitude toward the appointment of electors as a function of the perceived urgency of the times— a mood partisans on both sides palpably shared. Their willingness to treat the possibilities created by the language of the Constitution so instrumentally, inconsistently, and even cynically could thus be explained by evoking the same appeals to necessity that were bandied about at the time. Political actors simply perceived the crisis in which they were immersed so gravely as to be unable to do otherwise.

Yet these maneuvers were arguably less a lapse from constitutional norms than their fulfillment. Without the sense of urgency and necessity fostered by the events of the late 1790s, the electoral provisions of the Constitution, by themselves, might not have been viewed as an open-ended invitation to political innovation. The state legislatures, in theory, would still have adopted a variety of procedures *ab initio,* but lacking the same stakes in the outcome of a particular election, inertia might have inclined them to leave their existing procedures intact. Or perhaps a principled conviction would gradually have taken hold that one procedure—say, popular election by districts—was the most attractive mode. But once a threshold level of political conflict had been reached, and the essential powers and influence of the presidency had been perceived, the license the Constitution gave to political innovation became an incentive as well as an invitation to the invention and manipulation of the electoral rules. Far from exemplifying a constitutional stupidity—or, more neutrally, a failure to anticipate—the provision for presidential election illustrated one of the central if latent tendencies of the Constitution. By making the attainment of national office dependent on the control of state political processes, the provision itself inspired the modes of political cooperation and integration that the first party system designed with such striking speed. In this respect the system of presidential electors resembled the analogous provisions for the election of the House. For there, too, the Constitution left critical details to the states (though subject to a rarely exercised congressional power of revision). It was the state legislatures that were free to draw congressional district lines how, where, and (occasionally) when they pleased; and, unsurprisingly, dominant political interests in the states have always exploited this license, too.

Seen from the vantage point of the late 1780s, the maneuvers over the appointment of electors a decade later offer a striking example of a phenomenon that might best be characterized as constitutional irony (another term with which historians are more comfortable than they are with stupidity). The best explanation of how the presidency and the electoral college finally did emerge from the "tedious and reiterated discussions" at Philadelphia would stress the framers' desire, first, to make the executive as politically independent of Congress as possible, and second, to avoid the danger of "cabal" in the election of a president. It was this specter of collusion that also explains why presidential electors could never meet at one central campus but instead had to convene as satellite faculties in the states; and equally important, why (unlike, say, the college of cardinals in Rome—not an institution that Americans were likely to emulate) electors were allowed to vote only once before dispatching their ballots to the central office of the capitol. Had the framers thought the problem through, or not been so fixated on the location of the contingent election, they might have perceived that allowing a state's electors to be appointed "in such Manner as the Legislature thereof may direct" could only displace the locus of collusion from one institution to another. Whether from fatigue, or lack of foresight, or even deference to federalism, the framers left the critical decision to the one institution that Madison, at least, regarded as the most worrisome source of factionalism in the Republic. Yet the Constitution could have specified the rule whereby *all* states would vote (by general ticket, district, or joint legislative ballot) and still have preserved at least the political compromise embodied in the allocation of electors and the contingent election by the House.

There is a further irony, too, in viewing the maneuvers leading up to 1800 from the perspective of the ratification debate of 1787–88. Federalists had repeatedly answered the charge that adoption of the Constitution would end in the consolidation of all real power in the Union and the corresponding withering away of the states by reminding their opponents that the state legislatures would have an active, necessary role to play in selecting both houses of Congress as well as the presidency. But this argument, conceived to reassure Anti-Federalists in benign and reasonable terms, turned out to prove far more than Federalists imagined or, arguably, desired. For the role that state legislatures could regularly play in setting the rules for election to the presidency and the House created a powerful incentive and opportunity for the integration of state and national politics.

As this process of integration unfolded—as the parties created the necessary mechanisms and linkages between state and national politics—it was the presidency that immediately emerged and repeatedly operated as the major stimulus for coordination. It is an open if necessarily speculative question whether this degree of innovation and coordination would have been required had the French Revolution not occurred, placing a great premium on the control of the presidency because its advantages in the conduct of foreign policy immediately became apparent. A domestic politics concerned with such exciting issues as banking, subsidies, post roads, and internal improvements might have left occupancy of the presidency a much less urgent matter, and might therefore have produced or required a lower level of political integration in the form of interstate parties. Once the foreign policy crises of the mid-1790s coincided with Washington's retirement, that course of development was foreclosed. Jefferson and Madison found themselves acting on a perception of the executive not so different from Hamilton's. And when it came to fashioning strategy for 1800, the two sides acted alike in at least one critical respect. Their approach to the gathering of electoral votes can be almost completely explained as a strategic response, independent of ideology, to the opportunity that the Constitution created simply because its framers, unable to conceptualize the political dimensions of the presidency, had left so much open to discovery and invention.

NOTES

1. This is, of course, a more accurate characterization of the election than the conventional phrase, "election of 1800." It also better conforms to the original expectations of 1787–88.

2. Akhil Reed Amar, "An Accident Waiting to Happen," in *Constitutional Stupidities, Constitutional Tragedies*, ed. William N. Eskridge Jr. and Sanford Levinson (New York, 1998), 15–17.

3. The number of contributors thus equals the number of signers of the Constitution.

4. Eskridge and Levinson, "Introduction: Constitutional Conversations," in *Constitutional Stupidities*, 1–2. I regret my omission from the contributors, not only because I would have loved to provide an essay on the stupidity of the non-amendable rule giving Wyoming the same number of senators as California, but also because (if memory serves) I was privy to the conversation from which the project was launched. Fortunately, the topic I would have discussed is treated in Suzanna Sherry, "Our Unconstitutional Senate," ibid., 95–97. For my own assessment of the stupidity of the current electoral college, see Jack N. Rakove, "The E-College in the E-Age," in *The Unfinished Election of 2000*, ed. Jack N. Rakove (New York, 2001), 221–34.

5. The same might be said of hypocrisy, a term that figures prominently in Jefferson scholarship but is devoid of analytical (as opposed to descriptive) power.

6. In this vein, see the observations about generalship in World War I, often taken as a low point in the annals of military folly, in John Keegan, *The First World War* (New York, 1999), 315–16.

7. For general discussion, see Tadahisa Kuroda, *The Origins of the Twelfth Amendment: The Electoral College in the Early Republic, 1787–1804* (Westport, Conn., 1994).

8. Pierce Butler to Weedon Butler, 5 May 1788, *The Records of the Federal Convention of 1787*, ed. Max Farrand (New Haven, Conn., 1966), 3:302.

9. James Madison to TJ, 24 Oct. 1787, *JMP* 10:208.

10. Betty Kemp, *King and Commons, 1660–1832* (London, 1959), 113–40.

11. The best short account of this is still Bernard Bailyn, *The Origins of American Politics* (New York, 1968), chap. 2.

12. For the standard account, see Gordon S. Wood, *The Creation of the American Republic, 1776–1787* (Chapel Hill, N.C., 1969), 132–50. For Jefferson's use of the term "administrator," see his draft constitution for Virginia, *TJP* 1:341–42, 349–50, 359–60; for the sharp quotation from Adams, see *Thoughts on Government* (Philadelphia, 1776), reprinted in *The Founders' Constitution*, ed. Philip Kurland and Ralph Lerner (Chicago, 1987), 1, 109.

13. Jack N. Rakove, *The Beginnings of National Politics: An Interpretive History of the Continental Congress* (New York, 1979), 297–329.

14. Madison to Caleb Wallace, 23 Aug. 1785, and to George Washington, 16 April 1787, *JMP* 8:350–52, 9:385.

15. For the conclusions presented in this and the following paragraphs, see Jack N. Rakove, *Original Meanings: Politics and Ideas in the Making of the Constitution* (New York, 1997), 256–62.

16. Farrand, *Records,* 2:118–21.

17. Ibid., 493–95.

18. The debate can be followed in Farrand, *Records,* 2:30.

19. To illustrate this point, imagine that the respective counties of Delaware, Maryland, and Virginia occupying the eastern shore of the Chesapeake (the Delmarva peninsula) were populous enough to constitute one congressional district for each state, and that these states could be labeled respectively as small, medium, and large. Would the representatives they elected vote differently on the basis of the size of their states, or similarly on the basis of the underlying identity among the socioeconomic characteristics of their common region?

20. The various acts can be found in Merrill Jensen, Robert Becker, and Gorden DenBoer, eds., *Documentary History of the First Federal Elections, 1788–1790,* 4 vols. (Madison, Wis., 1976–89).

21. Ralph Ketcham, *Presidents above Party: The First American Presidency, 1789–1829* (Chapel Hill, N.C., 1984), 82; Rakove, *Original Meanings,* 268–79.

22. *Federalist* No. 71.

23. *Federalist* No. 72.

24. In fact, Hamilton's account of the electoral college in *Federalist* No. 68 is noteworthy for presuming that electors would be chosen by the people. On the one hand, this is not what the Constitution requires; on the other, it does foresee the actual development of the election system. As we shall see, however, Hamilton's eventual support for popular election in 1800 owed nothing to democratic principle and everything to political opportunism.

25. Hamilton, "Conjectures about the new Constitution," [17–30 Sept. 1787], *AHP* 4:275–77.

26. Ketcham, *Presidents above Party,* 89.

27. On this debate, see Benjamin B. Klubes, "The First Federal Congress and the First National Bank: A Case Study in Constitutional Interpretation," *JER* 10 (1990): 19–42. The respective opinions are reprinted in M. St. Clair Clarke and D. A. Hall, eds., *Legislative and Documentary History of the Bank of the United States* (1832; rept. New York, 1967).

28. Reprinted in Jack N. Rakove, ed., *James Madison: Writings* (New York, 1999), 492–518, 530–34.

29. On this point, my conceptual debt to Harvey C. Mansfield Jr., *Taming the Prince: The Ambivalence of Modern Executive Power* (New York, 1989) is evident.

30. Rakove, *Original Meanings,* 339–65.

31. Madison to TJ, 25 May 1794, Smith, 2:845.

32. TJ to Madison, 28 Dec. 1794; Madison to TJ, 23 March 1795; TJ to Madison, 27 April 1795; ibid., 868, 875–76, 877–78.

33. For a particularly invidious comparison of the two men, which goes out of its way to disparage Jefferson, see John Ferling, *Setting the World Ablaze: Washington, Adams, and Jefferson and the American Revolution* (New York, 2000).

34. Rakove, *Original Meanings,* 361–65; for the speech itself, see *JMP* 16: 294–99.

35. Charles A. Lofgren, "The Original Understanding of Original Intent?" *Constitutional Commentary* 5 (1988): 77–113.

36. For general discussion, see Kuroda, *Origins of the Twelfth Amendment,* 107–14.

37. Richard P. McCormick, *The Presidential Game: The Origins of American Presidential Politics* (New York, 1982), 52–57; and see Joanne B. Freeman, *Affairs of Honor: National Politics in the New Republic* (New Haven, Conn., 2001), 219–23.

38. Kuroda suggests, however, that Democratic-Republicans may have been somewhat more inclined to prefer, in the abstract, a district system, as practiced in Virginia, because they were critical of the use of a unit system in the three small Federalist-leaning states of Delaware, New Jersey, and Connecticut. Kuroda, *Origins of the Twelfth Amendment*, 107–8.

39. Pinckney to Madison, 30 Sept. 1799, *JMP* 16:272, reiterating his earlier (and unanswered) request to the same effect in a letter of 16 May 16 1799, ibid., 250–51.

40. TJ to Monroe, 12 Jan. 1800, Ford, 7:401–2.

41. Noble E. Cunningham Jr., *The Jeffersonian Republicans: The Formation of Party Organization, 1789–1801* (Chapel Hill, N.C., 1957), 144–47.

42. Hamilton to Jay, 7 May 1800, *AHP* 24:464–66.

43. Ibid., 467 n. 4.

44. *Baltimore Federal Gazette*, 3 Oct. 1800, quoted in Cunningham, *Jeffersonian Republicans*, 189–90.

45. One scholar suggests that Federalists might have captured as many as nine electoral votes, and perhaps even more, under a district election scheme. G. S. Rowe, *Thomas McKean: The Shaping of an American Republicanism* (Boulder, Colo., 1978), 314. But that seems improbable, given that Republicans outnumbered Federalists eight to five in the state's House delegation in the Sixth Congress, and that they improved that margin to nine to four in the election for the Seventh Congress that coincided with the presidential election. A high concentration of the voters of one party in a handful of districts would of course make it possible for a party supported by a minority of voters statewide to capture a majority of a state's electoral districts.

46. Dawson to Madison, 28 July 1800, *JMP* 17:399.

CHAPTER 3

"The Soil Will Be Soaked with Blood"
Taking the Revolution of 1800 Seriously

Michael A. Bellesiles

The enduring achievement of historical study is the historical sense—
an intuitive understanding—of how things do not happen.
—Lewis Namier

They certainly sounded as though they meant to have a revolution. Alexander Hamilton cautioned that Republican victory in 1800 would lead to the "overthrow . . . [of] the Government." The result would be a "Revolution after the manner of Bonaparte."[1] Alternatively, one Connecticut Federalist wrote, "There is scarcely a possibility that we shall escape a *Civil War.*" His imagination ran away with him as he foresaw that "murder, robbery, rape, adultery, and incest will all be openly taught and practiced, the air will be rent with the cries of distress, the soil will be soaked with blood, and the nation black with crimes."[2] From the other side, John Preston, a Republican elector from Virginia, warned that if the Federalists won the election, "chains, dungeons, transportation and perhaps the gibbet" awaited the followers of Jefferson.[3] Other Jeffersonians threatened that "any man who should thus be appointed President by law and accept the office" other than Jefferson "would instantaneously be put to death."[4] Jefferson himself wrote that the Republican leadership had resolved "to declare openly and firmly, one and all, that the day such an act" to deny Jefferson the presidency "passed, the Middle States would arm, and that no such usurpation, even for a single day, should be submitted to."[5] It is important to note that these predictions were based just on electoral victory for their opponents; each expected violence and even civil war if the other side won. Yet Thomas Jefferson did win election as president, and Federalist fears went unrealized. The visions of social disruption remained self-generated terrors. When the Federalists lost the election to that evil man, Thomas Jefferson, they went home.

That is the most interesting aspect of the so-called "revolution of 1800": its tameness. For all their angry talk, prognostications of anarchy and tyranny, and threats of lethal action, Americans in 1800 were pussycats toward one another. Sure, they were violent people toward blacks and Indians. But when it came to their own political and social divisions, they were remarkably forgiving—or at least far busier with other matters. Federalists who really wanted to launch a coup, revolution, or punitive assault had ample opportunity in February 1801, when the House of Representatives could not choose a president until the thirty-sixth ballot. But they did not; they did not even make any plans to do so. Compared to Europeans, Americans at the beginning of the nineteenth century were remarkably passive when it came to politics. To call Jefferson's electoral victory a revolution is a misnomer, or at least a gross exaggeration. (And let's not forget that it was Jefferson who called his election a revolution.) This is not necessarily a trivial matter, as our choice of historical labels such as "the revolution of 1800" can often simplify or even obscure historical events.

It is therefore time to take the revolution of 1800 seriously.[6] It is appropriate to ask just how revolutionary it was. Was it revolutionary at all? One way of getting at such an essential question is to imagine what might have happened had the Federalists girded their loins and seized their chance to retain power. Since as great a scholar as E. P. Thompson dismissed counterfactual history as *Geschictswissenschlopff* (unhistorical crap),[7] it is appropriate to offer a brief justification of this exercise.[8] Counterfactual history allows us to explore the parameters under which historical figures acted. Too often the assumption is made that key historical actors had a limitless number of alternatives and selected the most rational.[9] R. G. Collinwood has pointed out that historians easily slip into this hyper-rational vision of the past—the perception that key figures, or at least the winners, knew exactly what they were doing—as a consequence of the teleological fallacy. It is convenient to believe that where we are today is the only possible end point of any historical narrative.[10] And yet historical analysis easily lends itself to the counterfactual. John Murrin has observed that historians do not realize the ways in which they regularly practice counterfactual thinking. "Every time a historian evaluates a particular decision or policy option in terms of contemporary alternatives, he is thinking counterfactually because he has to, unless he is prepared to assert that real choices did not exist in the past or that, if they did, historians should ignore them."[11] Or as Hugh Trevor-Roper put it, in what could serve as counterfactual history's motto, "History is not merely what happened: it is what happened in the context of what might have happened."[12]

This essay suggests that Republicans in 1800 faced severe limitations on their choice of action because they lacked the political will and practical means to employ violence, as well as an understanding that violence among whites might encourage a slave insurrection. The Federalists had access to better armaments, but they too demonstrated no real interest in a military confrontation. These perceptions circumscribed the extent of political change in the years after Jefferson's election.[13] If this was a revolution, it was a very mild one.

Far too often the revolution of 1800 is seen as part of a progressive plot line: the expansion of American democracy. This view is simplistic to the point of being ahistorical. Imagine, for instance, the position of slaves in American society. Did their situation improve in the early nineteenth century? I think not. In order to construct a progressive vision of America around the revolution of 1800 we need to reverse our chronology. To wit:

> In the years leading up to the revolution of 1800, the southern states slowly loosened their slave codes, removing some of their harshest controls. After the revolution of 1800, also known as Gabriel's Rebellion, the southern states allowed the manumission of slaves and even debated the justice of slavery. With the Constitution of 1788 the United States removed its hateful three-fifths and fugitive slave clauses. In the 1780s southern leaders like Thomas Jefferson publicly questioned the morality of slavery, a process that culminated in 1776 with his declaration that "All men are created equal." The struggle for equality took many decades, but with the imposition of British rule the slave codes slowly vanished and slaves enjoyed greater legal rights. Finally, in the years between 1700 and 1620, North American whites saw the error of their ways, freeing their slaves and sending them to freedom in Africa.[14]

This is of course a rather extreme version of counterfactual history, but it highlights, I think, the too-relaxed manner of many historians when it comes to sweeping generalizations about the past. Far too often these generalizations have a rather timeless quality, like the old assertions that America was the land of the free, always had been, always would be. History, if nothing else, is the story of change over time. Those changes are not—in the absence of evidence to the contrary—predetermined, but the product of human decisions. And those decisions are as often born of human passions—from love to hate, fear to self-righteous certainty—as of human reason. It seems almost too obvious, but it is worth reminding ourselves that the historical figures we study did not know what was going to happen next.[15]

There are, of course, some rules of the game. Most importantly, counterfactual history must be probable; it must not violate the laws of nature or of known human behavior. More than that, any guesswork must match the determinable pattern of the participants' lives and actions. Niall Ferguson set this as the single most important standard for counterfactual history: "We should consider as plausible or probable *only those alternatives which we can show on the basis of contemporary evidence that contemporaries actually considered.*"[16] In a way, these rules are no different from those set forth for history itself by Isaiah Berlin: "What is meant by historical sense is the knowledge not of what happened, but of what did not happen. When an historian, in attempting to decide what occurred and why, rejects all the infinity of logically open possibilities, the vast majority of which are obviously absurd, and, like a detective, investigates only those possibilities which have at least some initial plausibility, it is this sense of what is plausible . . . that constitutes the sense of coherence with the patterns of life."[17] Attaining this point of reference requires that we make the effort, as Hugh Trevor-Roper put it, to "place ourselves before the alternatives of the past."[18]

Counterfactual history sheds light on the reality beneath the legends. In this case it is hoped that an attempt to imagine a revolution in 1800 will focus historical attention on the political and military culture of the early Republic. The sober use of counterfactual history reminds us that the reality we think we know is not always quite what it seems.

So how might it have happened differently? Anyone who studies the election of 1800 in detail ends amazed at how close an affair it was and how easily it might have turned out differently. There are at least four moments when it could have gone the other way, especially as we must recall that the final electoral vote was seventy-three for Jefferson and Burr, sixty-five for Adams, sixty-four for Charles Cotesworth Pinckney, and one for John Jay.

In May 1800 New York's Republicans, guided by Aaron Burr, won a majority in the state legislature. The legislature selected the electoral voters, leaving little doubt that New York's twelve electoral votes belonged to Jefferson. But that election had been very close, a mere three hundred votes, the Republican victory highly dependent on the energy of Aaron Burr. Since the Federalists had won control of the legislature the previous year, it is easy to imagine their retaining that dominance had Aaron Burr been shot by an angry husband. But more to the point, Alexander Hamilton attempted to negate this loss by asking Governor John Jay to call an emergency session of the Federalist-dominated legislature to change the system of choosing presidential electors. Hamilton recommended that New York follow the example of Maryland, North Carolina, and Kentucky in having the electors chosen by districts, which, since the Republicans were concentrated in New York City, would give the Federalists a majority.[19] But Jay rejected this solution.[20] Had he listened to Hamilton and had the New York vote turned out the way Hamilton expected, Adams would have received eight electoral votes to Jefferson's four. That would have reversed the results exactly, giving Adams seventy-three votes to Jefferson's sixty-five.

Then there was Pennsylvania, with its fifteen electoral votes. Its legislature adjourned in the winter of 1800 hopelessly deadlocked over the method of selecting electors. With the Republicans controlling the House and the Federalists the Senate, there seemed no chance of any action and many observers, including Jefferson, predicted that Pennsylvania would just not participate in the election.[21] It was not until December, more than a month after they were supposed to have made the selection, that the two houses compromised by giving eight votes to Jefferson and seven to Adams. What would have happened had they not resolved that dispute or if the legislature had determined to put the matter before the voters in either a direct vote or by district? The first alternative would have left Jefferson the winner, but with a rather unimpressive sixty-five votes and a large hole on the electoral map that could have produced many challenges and cries of an illegitimate presidency. The second option, a winner-take-all vote, would have probably led to Jefferson getting all fifteen electoral votes. The third alternative, a district vote, would probably have ended with Adams getting ten of the electoral votes to Jefferson's five. In this case, Jefferson would have still won the election by seventy to sixty-eight. However, if both Pennsylvania and New York had used district votes, Adams would have won convincingly by a vote of seventy-six to sixty-two.

And then there was South Carolina. The Federalists had high hopes for South Carolina's eight votes; their vice presidential candidate was that state's immensely popular general Charles Cotesworth Pinckney.[22] Many southern Federalists even planned to promote Pinckney by awarding him all eight votes while withholding a few from Adams. Had they succeeded in this effort, the nation would have witnessed the inauguration of President Pinckney in March 1801. That this inaugural did not occur seems largely the result of the actions of Charles Pinckney, a second cousin of Charles Cotesworth Pinckney and a Republican. This Pinckney worked furiously in the legislature to prevent the election of his cousin, promising patronage to those who wavered, and successfully seeing that Jefferson and Burr received all eight votes. Though each of these electors won by a very small margin, their eight votes were exactly the Republican margin of victory.[23] What if the Republican Pinckney had put family values first and worked as hard for his cousin's victory? What if his patronage bribes had been exposed and the assembly had responded in disgust by turning to Adams and Pinckney? Obviously it did not happen, but it easily could have.

In addition to demonstrating that the electoral college is a stupid system (as if we needed further evidence), these scenarios give us a sense of how close a call was the 1800 election. But it is the fourth option that requires our attention, as I think it the only one that could have possibly produced an actual revolution of 1800.

The real problem with the election of 1800, as we all know, came in February 1801. With the electoral vote tied at seventy-three for Jefferson and Burr, the House of Representatives had to choose the president, with each state getting just one vote—another dumb system capable of creating real mischief. And this was the lame-duck Congress, with a Federalist majority. But the Federalists controlled only six of the sixteen state delegations, leaving the whole matter up in the air.

Adding to the emerging crisis was a sense of impending doom. Rumors of assassination, arson, military preparations, revolution, and civil war swirled around the new capital of Washington, D.C. Most fearful were the southern Republicans. They were certain that the Federalists had secretly sent arms to Toussaint Louverture for his slave rebellion in Saint Domingue. Many southern Republicans were convinced that two mysterious fires, one at the War Department in November, the other at the Treasury in January, were part of an effort to cover up this support for slave rebellions, perhaps even in the United States.[24]

Rumors flew that Republican militia and federal forces were marching on Washington to seize control. Each side seemed determined to terrify their own adherents. Thus Federalists spread rumors that the Republicans in Virginia's legislature were purchasing arms in France to launch an insurrection against the national government.[25] Meanwhile the Republican *General Advertiser* reported on several occasions that Adams had ordered troops into Washington to intimidate Congress.[26] Republican Henry Breckenridge warned Jefferson that federal forces were seizing all the armories so as to have a near monopoly on firearms for the coming civil war.[27] The Republican press warned that Federalists were threatening to destroy the Constitution "at the point of the bayonet" if the House selected Jefferson. If they did not assassinate Jefferson first, the Federalists would march on the capital with "70,000 Massachusetts militia . . . to support a usurper."[28] Jefferson thought the Federalist goal was no less than to "sap the republic by fraud, if they cannot destroy it by force, and to erect an English monarchy in its place."[29] Faced with such a threat, the Republicans had to fight to the end. Each side saw the other arming to take over the government; each swore to arm in protection of that government.[30]

The House of Representatives began its voting on 11 February 1801. The Constitution specified that the House was to choose from among the tied candidates, and the Federalists initially gave their votes to Aaron Burr in an effort to divide the Republicans.[31] With the congressional Federalists lacking clear leadership, they turned to the vague notion that they could work with Burr. There is much to suggest that if Burr had followed Gallatin's advice and gone to Washington, he might have succeeded in organizing a coalition of his Republican adherents and the Federalists to the detriment of Jefferson. But Burr hesitated at this key moment, and no one was left to orchestrate his possible election to the presidency.[32]

The House voted that no other business could be addressed until the president was selected. But after twenty-seven ballots the vote remained unchanged: Jefferson had eight states—New York, New Jersey, Pennsylvania, Virginia, North Carolina, Kentucky, Georgia, and Tennessee; Burr had six—New Hampshire, Massachusetts, Rhode Island, Connecticut, Delaware, and South Carolina; and Vermont and Maryland were equally divided and thus unable to vote. The government of the United States was paralyzed.[33]

At such an impasse, expectations of violence from members of both parties increased. At a time when "it is impossible to determine, which of the two candidates will be chosen President," Gouverneur Morris wrote, "rumors are various and intrigues great."[34] Representative Joseph Nicholson wrote that if anyone but Jefferson became president, "Virginia would instantly proclaim herself out of the Union."[35] The Philadelphia Federalist *Gazette of the United States* reported that "the bold and impetuous partisans of Mr. Jefferson" planned to march on Washington to remove with force anyone other than Jefferson selected for the presidency. "Are they then ripe for civil war, and ready to imbrue their hands in kindred blood?"[36] Republicans like Abraham Bishop of Connecticut warned that "A Monarchy is decidedly before us!"[37] John Quincy Adams thought that no matter what happened in terms of the election "the ultimate necessary consequence, if not the ultimate object of both the extreme parties which divide us, will be a dissolution of the Union and a civil war."[38]

It was in the midst of this uncertainty bordering on chaos that Alexander Hamilton stepped forth to play his pivotal role. Hamilton thought Jefferson "a contemptible hypocrite,"[39] but he hated Aaron Burr. When fellow Federalists approached him with the notion of cutting a deal with Burr, Hamilton worked to kill the idea, telling James Bayard that Burr was the "most unfit man in the U.S. for the office of President."[40] Initially he thrashed about seeking an alternative to Burr and Jefferson, without success. As we know, he eventually made clear his preference for Jefferson, firing off letters in every direction warning of the consequences of a Burr victory. Hamilton told Gouverneur Morris that the Federalists would be "mad" to vote for Burr, whose victory would "only promote the purposes of the desperate and proflicate [sic]."[41] To Oliver Wolcott he wrote that there "is nothing in his [Burr's] favor. . . . He is bankrupt beyond redemption except by the plunder of his country. His public principles have no other spring or aim than his own aggrandisement."[42] He warned John Rutledge that Burr was "the most unfit and most dangerous man" yet proposed for the presidency. "No mortal can tell what his political principles are. . . . The truth seems to be that he has no plan but that of *getting* power by *any* means and *keeping* it by *all* means."[43] James Bayard heard from Hamilton that Burr possessed "an ambition which will be content with nothing less than *permanent* power in his own hands. . . . Disgrace abroad ruin at home are the probable fruits of his elevation."[44] Hamilton must have regretted that he had once written, in *Federalist* No. 68, that the electoral college made it "a moral certainty that the office of President will seldom fall to the lot of any man who is not in an eminent degree endowed with the requisite qualifications." As he wrote in January 1801, when that very process seemed likely to disrupt the peace of the country, "Tis not to a Chapter of Accidents, that we ought to trust the Government peace and happiness of our Country."[45]

But other options were available to the Federalists. In December 1800 Gouverneur Morris hatched a wild scheme to prolong the electoral deadlock until

4 March 1801. At that time John Adams's presidency would end, and in the absence of a new president a 1792 federal statute declared that the president pro tempore of the Senate would become acting president of the United States. Jefferson most feared this plan of action, writing Madison that the Federalists "openly declare they will prevent an election, and will name a President of the Senate, *pro tem.* by what they say would only be a *stretch* of the constitution."[46] Jefferson was correct that many congressional Federalists supported this approach, one that could easily be attained simply by refusing to resolve the deadlock in the House. But Hamilton did his best to squash the project as "a most dangerous and unbecoming policy."[47]

A much more sensible plan, and one that Hamilton may have supported, was for the Federalists to invalidate some of the Republican electors on technical grounds, handing the election to Adams without need to resort to the House of Representatives. Had evidence from South Carolina of Charles Pinckney's manipulations—which could be interpreted as bribery—been more forthcoming, the Federalists would have had a sound case for rejecting those Jeffersonian electors. As it was, a serious challenge to Georgia's electors was launched in Congress, though narrowly defeated by the Republicans.[48]

Far too much seems to have depended on Hamilton's personality. He sat at a pivot of three possible presidents—Jefferson, Burr, and Adams—all of whom he hated. But he hated Burr most. Unfortunately he had already burned his bridges to Adams with the publication of his scurrilous *Letter Concerning the Public Conduct and Character of John Adams* attacking the president's character, a letter that may have cost Adams the election.[49] But he had once thought highly of Adams, often praising him for his "ardent love for the public good."[50] They had fallen out over Adams's willingness to compromise with the Republicans, which Hamilton saw as weakness. But now Hamilton feared that the Federalists were about to make Aaron Burr president. For two months he did his best to prevent this outcome, pleading with members of his party to "let not the Fœderal party be responsible for the elevation of this Man" to the presidency.[51] In late February 1801 it appeared to Hamilton that he was being ignored, and that the slightest twist could make the most dangerous man in America president. In such circumstances, Hamilton may have thought of reconciliation with Adams.

An effort to keep Adams on was perfectly reasonable and perhaps even legal. The Federalists were, after all, known for their loose construction of the Constitution. Article II, section 1 states that "if no person have a majority, then from the five highest on the list said House shall in like Manner choose the President."[52] Neither Burr nor Jefferson had a majority; that was exactly why there was a crisis. So the House could have felt justified in going further down the list, say to John Adams.[53] And such a possibility hinged on a few people in positions of responsibility.

A great deal hung on the health of Joseph H. Nicholson of Maryland. Only thirty years old, Nicholson was very ill and was carried through the snow every day to the Capitol so that he could write "Jefferson" on his ballot at each roll call. Had he taken a turn for the worse, or had the snow fallen too heavily to allow transportation, Maryland, which had four Republican and four Federalist representatives, would have gone Federalist. Such an event would have created a perfect tie between the Federalist and Republican states. However, the other divided state, Vermont, would have gone Federalist only if Republican Matthew Lyon, fresh from serving time in jail for violating the Sedition Act, had been murdered.

But there was another weak link on Jefferson's side in New York's Edward Livingston. A lame-duck member of the House, Livingston had wavered in the early ballots between Jefferson and Burr, and had apparently spoken with James Linn of New Jersey about breaking the deadlock by swinging their states to Burr.[54] Livingston was at the center of intrigues; he had studied law with Alexander Hamilton and James Kent, a rather conservative pair, was a friend of Burr's, and had already been offered the post of secretary of the navy by Jefferson.[55] Since he was leaving Congress, he was clearly angling for some position of even greater authority.[56] It is certainly conceivable that a man like Edward Livingston could have been bought off with a sufficiently attractive position from either of his fellow New Yorkers and personal friends, Hamilton or Burr. Such an arrangement, in conjunction with Nicholson taking a turn for the worse, would have swung the election to whomever the Federalists could agree upon. Just two votes stood between Jefferson's ascension to the presidency and a real "revolution of 1800."

Had the Federalists succeeded in preventing Jefferson's election in some fashion, the vast majority of Republicans would certainly have reacted with fury. There would have been loud proclamations that the election had been stolen, the Constitution violated, the public trust trampled. Throughout the nation bitter supporters of Thomas Jefferson might even have rushed to get their militia companies into shape. Had they done so, they very probably would have discovered that Washington, Knox, Hamilton, and the other Federalists had been right all along in their condemnation of the militia as a poorly armed and untrained fantasy.

For the previous ten years the Republicans had resisted every effort by the Federalists to modernize the militia of the United States. The Federalists had looked to Europe and seen that warfare was changing fast, with massive armies and well-trained corps of light infantry sweeping away the last remnants of medieval warfare. Harrison Gray Otis was not alone in thinking that in the United States the "art of war is least understood." He insisted that at least a few men must be trained in modern methods of warfare, if only to be on hand to advise the militia when war came. Otis and most Federalists pointed to the experience of the American Revolution and asked whether the United States was in a better condition for war now than in 1775. Their answer was a ringing negative. To prevent disaster the country needed a larger army staffed by professional soldiers and a centralized select militia subject to extended training. Federalist support for volunteer militia companies appeared to Republicans an obvious assault on the ideal of a universal militia. The fact that the universal militia had never existed and that the current militia showed no signs of life remained irrelevant to this ideological absolute.[57]

The Republican Party resembled its leader in generally refusing to back rhetoric up with action. Though giving consistent rhetorical support to the militia, Republicans refused actual financial or legal provision. They tended to oppose any legislative coercion of militia duty, placing their faith in the desire of farmers and artisans to spend a few months' wages acquiring a gun and then take several days off work to practice using it. Oddly, the Federalists, while supporters of a standing army and consistently contemptuous of the militia, worked hardest to arm and train the militia in the 1790s, seeking laws mandating militia service. To their eventual detriment, the Republicans kept winning these political battles, so that by 1800 militia companies throughout the country held few if any musters.[58]

The Republican position had one obvious effect: Federalist volunteer militia companies were far better armed. In early 1799 the Virginia government purchased several hundred guns from Europe, convincing many Federalists that the Republicans were planning an insurrection against the federal government.[59] Federalists in Richmond and Petersburg responded by organizing the first private militia companies.[60] Shortly thereafter, Republicans in Philadelphia organized the Republican Blues, a private militia company, "in order to defend the country against foreign and domestic enemies and [to] support the laws."[61] The private volunteer companies were generally better armed and far more enthusiastic than their state-sponsored counterparts, and mostly Federalist. Like the Washington Artillery of Washington, D.C., most volunteer militia maintained exclusivity through the required election of new members and supplied guns from the company's private armory.[62] In contrast, during the war scare in 1798, when the Quasi-War with France seemed likely to expand, the nearby Alexandria militia regiment, only 18 percent of whom bore arms, frantically turned to the Virginia government for an additional five hundred muskets. The governor offered 250, noting that requests for arms were coming in from militia companies all over Virginia. The Fairfax County militia was in slightly better shape, needing only 250 guns to finish arming their 563 militiamen.[63]

Republicans had further cause for hesitation if they bothered to study the militia returns for 1800. The most active state militia, and the one best prepared for war, was that of Massachusetts. Back in 1781 that state had created two kinds of militia: the Train Band and the Alarm List. The former, some five thousand volunteers, met and drilled regularly. The Alarm List was just that, a list of all fit males age sixteen to sixty-five, who were required to keep arms and equipment and appear with them once a year at muster. The state saw to the arming of the Train Band while the towns were responsible for the Alarm List. The result was predictable: the Alarm List met only as often as required by law, most without firearms, and quickly atrophied; the Train Band included a number of enthusiasts but generally took such poor care of equipment that the state employed gunsmiths to keep the guns in repair. But the Train Band did show some promise as a military force, and Massachusetts had more guns in both public and private hands than did any other state.[64]

Given the shortage of both trained militia and firearms in most of the states, any response to a "stolen election" in 1801 would have been fairly tepid. Those familiar with the nature of American crowds would have laughed at the very idea of a white revolution of 1800 based on a perceived usurpation of the presidency. One simply had to look back two years to Fries' Rebellion for sufficient indication of the relative passivity of the American people. Fries' Rebellion began in early 1799 in southeast Pennsylvania as a protest against the new direct federal taxes and the Alien and Sedition Acts. The rebels, most of whom belonged officially to the local militia, threatened tax assessors, forcing one to "dance around" a liberty pole, while another was "committed to an old stable and . . . fed rotten corn." Otherwise their only violence came with the beating of an assessor in a tavern. The rebels' greatest crime came when John Fries, a local militia commander, led more than one hundred men armed with swords, clubs, and muskets to free some prisoners. No shots were fired, the point being a traditional effort to protest corrupt authority by what Fries's attorney Alexander Dallas called a "system of intimidation." To President John Adams, this system was treasonous, and he ordered five hundred federal troops under General William MacPherson to put down the uprising. There was no resistance and no violence as this little army rounded up the leaders of the "rebellion." Fries and two others were arrested, tried, convicted, and pardoned, and that was the end of it.[65]

Alexander Hamilton understood well the danger of "magnifying a riot into an insurrection, by employing in the first instance an inadequate Force." He advised Secretary of War James McHenry that "Whenever the Government appears in arms it ought to appear a *Hercules,* and inspire respect by the display of strength." Apparently five hundred well-armed troops were enough to overawe the poorly armed rebels. The same might have been the case in 1801 had any rural Republicans actually risen in opposition to a Federalist victory.[66]

A more precise precursor of any "revolution of 1801" was the Whiskey Rebellion of 1794. The Federalists at least had learned from the Whiskey Rebellion that little or no reliance was to be placed on the militia. President Washington had called for thirteen thousand militia from Pennsylvania, Maryland, Virginia, and New Jersey. Many common members of the militia refused to turn out, while officers resigned their commissions. As in Shays' Rebellion, some militia companies were themselves the rebels. Those who did show up for service were mostly unarmed and untrained. Governor Henry Lee of Virginia called up 3,300 militia, 2,000 (61%) of whom were issued guns from the state arsenal; Lee called on the federal government to arm the rest. The officers of the Georgetown, Maryland, militia reported that they needed 370 muskets for their 390 men. Maryland's governor Thomas Lee wrote to Secretary of War Knox asking for guns, arguing that the federal government bore complete responsibility for the militia and that the states simply facilitated organization.[67]

Washington got his army by opening the federal armories. The president sent his army, larger than any force he had led in the Revolution, toward western Pennsylvania under the active command of Alexander Hamilton. The rebellion simply evaporated before such a show of force; the only deaths came from a pistol going off accidentally and a drunken brawl that ended with a fatal bayonet wound.[68] One can only speculate whether the Whiskey rebels would have behaved differently had they known just how ignorant of firearms were most of Washington's troops. Hardly a disciplined force, the government militia looted, drank heavily, and beat civilians randomly. It was neither well trained nor well armed. General Samuel Smith, commander of the Maryland militia, reported to the House of Representatives that the majority of the Virginia and Maryland troops were ignorant of the use of arms. Many did not know how to load a musket, and others had never carried one in their lives.[69]

It is little wonder that most Federalists appeared distinctively unconcerned with Republican threats of military action. Federalists repeatedly ridiculed the untrained and buffoonish militia in Republican-controlled states, which generally did not allow enough money to train and arm their companies. "What could Pennsylvania do aided by Virginia," a Federalist paper asked of two Republican states, "the militia of the latter untrained and farcically performing the manual exercise with cornstalks instead of muskets?" In contrast, the militia of the Federalist New England states were fairly well armed and had shown a willingness to march in defense of their government.[70]

The Republicans fantasized for years about tens of thousands of militia rushing forth to defend liberty. Thus at the height of the crisis of 1801, Representative Samuel Tyler wrote Governor Monroe that Pennsylvania had twenty-two thousand militia ready to march at a moment's notice on Washington. Tyler urged that Virginia mobilize its tens of thousands of militia to join them. Fortunately for Virginia, Monroe had more experience of the Virginia militia, which was good for terrorizing individual slaves but little else.[71] Those tens of thousands were rarely more than a few score members of the slave patrol. And yet Republicans clung to their militia myth despite a formidable amount of evidence to the contrary. When called to serve, most militia stayed home. Whether responding to Indian wars, threatened invasions, real and imagined slave insurrections, domestic uprisings, or regular musters, hundreds, not thousands, of militia would turn out. It was a sorry myth that prevented the country from creating a competent professional army.[72]

The U.S. Army had all the advantages when it came to armaments. Most importantly it had several hundred pieces of artillery, whereas each state's militia had only a few cannon. Additionally, there were tens of thousands of muskets left over from the Revolution, most rusting away in various federal repositories. Of greater value, the federal arsenal at Springfield, the first gun manufactory in North America, had reached production levels of three thousand guns per year, while Harpers Ferry was just coming on line in 1801. Though the army had been kept small by congressional Republicans, its few thousand men were basically well trained and actually had experience firing guns, unlike the majority of American men. And its officer corps was overwhelmingly Federalist.[73] Had the Federalists stolen the election in 1801, they would have held most of the cards militarily. But there is more to a revolution than guns.

The character of Thomas Jefferson was vitally important. Despite his rhetorical skill and style, Jefferson was not a charismatic leader who could mount the barricades in the vanguard of mass revolution. He also had a strange defeatist quality mixed with real political acumen. Initially he indicated a willingness to fight. As the crisis heated up in February, Jefferson wrote Governor Monroe that any effort by the Federalists to prevent his election would be resisted with force of arms. But he also suggested to Monroe that it might be better to call "a convention to re-organize the government, and to amend it"—a less threatening and more time-consuming prospect than armed resistance.[74] Jefferson wrote another supporter that "every sincere patriot must shudder" before this "abyss" of possible revolution.[75]

Jefferson had a cool head to match his temperament. He appreciated that the Federalists would commit political suicide by attempting to win the 1800 election through "legislative usurpation." He wrote Madison that the fear that such action might "be resisted by arms" was sufficient to bring "the whole body of the Federalists" to his support.[76] The Federalists valued order too much to risk its disruption. But then so did Jefferson.

Jefferson understood that the nonviolent approach was safer and more effective. As Gallatin advised him, the Republicans' best strategy in case of a Federalist coup was basically to do nothing, to use the state governments in order to negate the actions of the federal—in other words, to implement the Virginia and Kentucky Resolutions. In Republican states, Gallatin wrote, "supported by our State governments, we shall run no risk of civil war by refusing to obey only those acts which may flow from the usurper as President." After all, there was little that the federal government could have done in the face of widespread nullification of federal law. But it was vital that noncompliance not turn to violence. The Republican leadership must prevent "every partial insurrection, or even individual act of resistance, except when supported by the laws of the particular State." Nonviolent legal resistance would bring a Federalist government to its knees.[77]

Jefferson later reported that he "called on Mr. Adams" on 14 February 1801 in an effort to avoid bloodshed. He told Adams that he had heard of a "very dangerous" Federalist plan to string the election along until 5 March, when they would elect the Senate president pro tem. Jefferson asked Adams to announce that he would veto any such legislation, carefully implying that otherwise there would be "resistance by force, and incalculable consequences." More explicitly he threatened a new convention to rewrite the Constitution. Adams refused to commit himself and, more importantly, Jefferson did nothing.[78]

In early 1801 few Republican leaders could conceive of an alternative to simply waiting for revenge in 1804. In January 1801 James Madison considered two courses of action, should the Federalists attempt to prevent the election of Jefferson by the House. One, he told Jefferson, was to go along with a Federalist "usurpation of the Executive authority"; the other was to have Jefferson and Burr issue a joint call for the early meeting of the newly elected Congress to settle the issue. Neither alternative was particularly radical, and neither could be even loosely called revolutionary. Madison did not even consider the idea of violent resistance. In fact, he seems to have dismissed it with the slightly obscure statement that "the other remedies proposed are substantial violations of the will of the people, of the scope of the Constitution, and of the public order and interest." The idea of an armed insurrection against even an illegitimate American government made James Madison nervous.[79]

Most Republican leaders shared Madison's hesitation to act with force. A good indication of their caution can be found in what did not occur in Richmond the previous spring. Governor Monroe was on his way to plan election strategy at James Madison's home, Montpelier, when he heard that Republicans in the capital were planning protests to disrupt and perhaps even prevent the trial of John T. Callender. A journalist given to excessive language, Callender was being tried under the Sedition Act. Monroe rushed back to Richmond and persuaded his fellow Republicans that any sort of protest could be seen as setting federal authority at defiance and would therefore hurt their cause with the voting public. Monroe even rejected the suggestion that he should fund Callender's defense from state funds, following instead Jefferson's suggestion of establishing a private subscription for the journalist. These were hardly the actions of committed radicals willing to challenge established powers; they were the actions of clever politicians well aware of the difference between rhetoric and reality.[80]

As near as can be determined, only two Republican leaders actually made any plans for a possible armed conflict. Governor Thomas McKean of Pennsylvania informed Jefferson that "arms for upwards to twenty thousand were secured" by his government for the militia in case their service was required. Once armed, the militia would arrest "every member of Congress" guilty of "treason." McKean quickly discovered that he was overly optimistic, most state arms already being in the hands of the Federalists. Nothing came of his preparations other than rhetorical broadsides.[81]

More notable were the efforts of Governor James Monroe of Virginia. Monroe became suspicious when four hundred U.S. regulars camped not far from Richmond. He reasoned that they were there either to seize control of the capital or, more likely, to remove the federal arms stored in Virginia. Monroe planned to block this latter action by having his militia seize these guns for state use.[82] Monroe even sent a spy, Major Thomas M. Randolph of the state militia, to check out the quality of these arms. Randolph reported that these "4000 excellent muskets and bayonets" had been captured from the British at Yorktown and should be sufficient to arm the better trained members of the militia.[83] But Monroe knew well that his state's militia was in no position to launch a major military effort. After all, the real revolution of 1800 had already occurred in Virginia.

In 1797 Thomas Jefferson had looked at the slave rebellion in Saint Domingue and warned that "the revolutionary storm, now sweeping the globe, will be upon us." This was not the sort of revolutionary bloodshed that he felt should water the tree of liberty from time to time. He was terrified of it, as were most southern whites.[84] In August 1800 an African American named Gabriel rattled the South to its core with a vivid anticipation of the danger whites had created with their system of racial slavery. Gabriel's Rebellion also revealed a fundamental weakness in the South: the need of the state to hold guns that would be easily accessible to the militia but not to the slaves. These stored arms became the most tempting targets for any revolutionary force. Thus Gabriel's first goal was to capture the militia arms stored in the Capitol. Gabriel understood that his forces would initially be armed only with swords, knives, pikes, and what few muskets he could seize from the white planters.[85]

At the beginning of his rebellion, Gabriel had access to only six guns, but he reasoned that a sword was as good as a gun in a surprise attack. An ingenious blacksmith, Gabriel made a secret store of swords by splitting farm scythes in two. He planned to move quickly, using his homemade weapons to seize ever more guns for arming what he was sure would be increasing numbers of slaves. When he learned that a local tavern owner stored several firearms, he immediately made that tavern his first stop on the road to Richmond. He ordered a second group to the unfinished penitentiary, where powder was stored.[86]

When Monroe heard rumors of a slave uprising, he ordered all public arms moved from the Capitol to the penitentiary under a guard of thirteen armed militia. This may seem an amazingly small force for such a critical task, but it was all he had available at the time. The problem then became to issue some of these arms to the militia units called up by Monroe. One curious aspect of this revolution of 1800 was the governor's hesitance to call out the militia because of the expense involved. As Monroe discovered, militiamen, even in the face of a slave insurrection, extracted every possible penny from the state for their service. They did not rush to service when called, they had to be cajoled; and the prime incentive was pay. The cost of suppressing Gabriel's Rebellion ultimately absorbed a tenth of Virginia's annual budget.[87]

A general panic spread through much of Virginia at the start of Gabriel's uprising. Whites, even those who were officers in the militia, demanded immediate militia protection. The Suffolk militia found that they had too few guns to provide an effective defense and appealed to the governor for aid. Monroe promised to supply arms but then discovered that the state had insufficient guns even for the five hundred militia so far ordered into action. The militia officers appealed repeatedly for aid, without success, finally arming their troops with whatever they could lay their hands on, mostly bladed weapons.[88]

Many observers felt that only heavy rains and the early discovery of the uprising prevented a successful slave rebellion. As James Callender wrote Thomas Jefferson, the insurrection "could hardly have failed of success, . . . for after all, we could only muster four or five hundred men of whom no more than thirty had Muskets."[89] Norfolk mayor Thomas Newton was delighted to hear that the militia had been called out but complained that "they have not arms, and are on that account only equal to the slaves except in numbers." Newton insisted that it was the state's job to see that the militia was properly armed. Mayor John Bracken of Williamsburg felt the same, and frantically requested "the loan of 25 Stand of Arms & the necessary Accoutrements" from Monroe. Williamsburg received nothing from the state; its stores were already exhausted. Their opponents were not much better armed. The militia searched every slave quarter in the area for weapons. On the Prosser plantation, Gabriel's home, they found "a number of rude arms," and not much more.[90] And even so poorly armed, Gabriel and his followers had posed an enormous threat to the state. As James Monroe wrote Jefferson, "It is unquestionably the most serious and formidable conspiracy we have ever known of the kind: tho' indeed to call it so is to give no idea of the thing itself."[91]

In 1801 the South was paralyzed by fear of slave rebellion, yet the southern elite had no incentive to limit the number of slaves in their society. Slavery made their South, economically and politically. For instance, had there been no three-fifths clause in the Constitution, the southern states would have had fourteen fewer electoral votes. As William Freehling has calculated, Jefferson would have lost twelve of those votes, Adams two.[92] Absent the representation of slaves, the election of 1800 would have ended with an Adams victory by a vote of sixty-three to sixty-one.

The fear of slave insurrections precisely delimited Republican actions in the South. There was just no way Republicans were going to enter into a conflict with other whites, leaving themselves open to an assault from within their very homes. They were too poorly armed to fight either uprising anyway. France and the Netherlands had supplied 85 percent of America's guns in the Revolution; where would they now get their firearms if they launched some sort of mass resistance? After all, in 1797 Governor James Wood had informed the legislature that he could not locate a single person in Virginia able to make guns for the state, and even the federal government was having trouble buying guns from Europe, which was in the midst of the bloody Napoleonic wars.[93]

Many Federalists appreciated that this well-justified terror of slave uprisings made most threats from southern Republicans pure bluff. In December 1800 William Vans Murray wrote John Qunicy Adams that he had heard that Virginia was buying guns in Europe for a possible political confrontation. But Gabriel's Rebellion demonstrated that southern Republicans had much more to worry about than a Federalist president.[94] Many Federalists, and even some Republicans such as James Monroe, felt that the slaves could take the Republicans' revolutionary rhetoric too seriously and endanger white supremacy. This point became abundantly clear in the investigations of Gabriel's Rebellion after it was suppressed. It appeared that Gabriel knew of the political divisions among the whites and based his hope of ultimate freedom on manipulating this contest and negotiating with the Federalists. In such a context it was best to keep political passions cool.[95]

As a consequence of these key factors, fear of slave rebellion and poorly armed and unwilling militia, any uprisings in 1801 would probably have been a repeat of the Whiskey Rebellion, with local variations. Governor Monroe did more than any other Republican during the election crisis to prepare for an actual military confrontation. Making use of his informant's report that the federal government was about to move the "4000 excellent muskets and bayonets" from the arsenal at New London, Virginia, Monroe sent a militia company to guard these arms for the state. Major Randloph's cover story was that there was a plot by "a wicked negro or a madman [who] might blow them up," and the militia was "the surest control of the slaves." [96] But Monroe could do little more, as he feared the consequences of an actual civil war. He had little doubt that Virginia's slaves would seize upon the opportunity of whites fighting whites to strike for freedom.

It is telling that Republicans phrased calls for action in the passive voice; Albert Gallatin asserted that any Federalist denial of Jefferson's election "will most certainly be resisted." [97] He did not say by whom. Like most Republicans, Gallatin simply assumed that the people would act; he indicated no intention of either leading those people or organizing to ensure their success. If the Federalists retained executive power, Gallatin wrote, they would naturally be "resisted by freemen whenever they have the power of resisting." Failure to do so "would justify submission in every case, and encourage usurpation for ever hereafter." [98] And yet, when Gallatin heard a false rumor on 12 February that Philadelphia Republicans had "seized the public arms," he dashed off a hurried note to A. J. Dallas, calling on him to "By all means preserve the city quiet. Anything which could be construed into a commotion would be fatal to us." [99] Gallatin correctly identified the prime determinant of resistance as having "the power of resisting"; but he himself did nothing to facilitate that power.

Even though they tended to hyperventilate about an American reign of terror once Jefferson took office, most Federalists dismissed Republican threats of civil war should Jefferson be denied that office. The *Washington Federalist* wrote that "the tumultuous meetings of a set of factious foreigners in Pennsylvania, or a few fighting bacchanals of Virginia," hardly constituted a grave danger to national stability. [100] Just to make certain, though, the Federalists acted with greater foresight than did the Republicans. While Philadelphia's Republicans were issuing warnings that denying the election to Jefferson would be "the first day of revolution and Civil War," the Federalists were busily moving the artillery and firearms from the state arsenal in Philadelphia to the federal arsenal. Doing so deprived the local militia of all its cannon and most of its guns. [101]

There were many rumors of Republicans marching on Washington, but nothing of the kind happened. John Adams later wrote that he thought the two parties, "dizzy" with politics, did not realize "the precipice on which they stood" until the last minute, when "a civil war was expected." At the least hint of violence, both backed down.[102]

Just how revolutionary was the election of 1800? Most Americans were not eligible to vote; only voters in Rhode Island and Virginia could even elect their presidential electors directly. The president was chosen by the political classes, so how revolutionary is a contest among these groups? It is possible that the decision of the House of Representatives in February 1801 set the path that the nation would follow over the next half century; but such an assertion remains highly contested.

Why was the election revolutionary? Most books on the subject, and most U.S. history textbooks, find its revolutionary character in the peaceful change of government. For instance, Bernard A. Weisberger perceives the electoral turnabout in Congress as an "impressive" political revolution, with a Republican majority of five in the Senate and twenty-four in the House.[103] Daniel Sisson is even more enthusiastic, stating that the Jeffersonians "had achieved what no other group of revolutionaries had gained in the entire course of western political history: a change in the power of government, from one party to another, without a tremendous cost in violence and bloodshed."[104] As Page Smith has written, "it is a strange revolution indeed that is consummated by three hundred astutely managed votes in one state, for aside from New York Adams was stronger in 1800 than he had been in 1796."[105] Usually revolutions are about changing structures or systems. Jefferson did not institute any significant alterations in government; he was far too cautious a man for that.[106]

The Republican *Aurora* thought Jefferson's election marked the true "emancipation of the American states from British influence and tyranny."[107] Such imagined alternatives seem grotesquely exaggerated; a victory for the Federalists would certainly not have led to anything approximating a monarchy any more than Jefferson's instituted a reign of terror. But for some people the defeat of Thomas Jefferson would have been a far more revolutionary act. For most African Americans, Jefferson's election proved counterrevolutionary. Not only were the most prominent northern Federalists opposed to slavery, but so was Aaron Burr. In the 1790s Burr had worked with Hamilton and John Jay to pass a general manumission law in New York.[108] But once Burr had removed Hamilton from the political scene and then been banished himself, New York's Jeffersonians moved to limit the rights of free blacks. It was Jefferson's postmaster general, Gideon Granger, who reversed the policy of the Federalists and fired all free blacks working in the U.S. post office. The tone of these racist Republicans is revealed by the type of songs they favored for their political gatherings, for instance "Federalists with Blacks Unite." The Republicans did not mean that song as a compliment.[109]

Of course no counterfactual study can predict what might have happened had Jefferson not assumed the presidency in 1801. Counterfactual history only works in the short run, sifting a number of likely results from what we know were the choices of the participants. Every prediction beyond the first few years after an alleged turning point is unsustainable speculation, which does not mean that we should not try our hand at it. Had the election of 1800 ended differently, it is unlikely that the course of American development would have been much altered over the ensuing decade. But in the unpredictable long run, a few key aspects of American life might have changed had the Federalist Party held onto the presidency for another four years. Its domestic authority might have been nil, but a few often-ignored aspects of foreign affairs might have taken distinctive turns. Not that John Adams or whomever else the Federalists put in the presidency would have accomplished much with a hostile Republican Congress and several state governments ignoring every action of the executive branch. Thomas Jefferson would have orchestrated four years of resistance from Monticello, essentially operating a government in exile.

Congress probably would have blocked the Federalists' proposals for modernizing the army, navy, and militia, as they did in Jefferson's first term, and could have prevented any legislative initiative by the Federalists. Where a Federalist president would have made a difference is on the question of slavery in the United States. John Adams or Aaron Burr would have been unlikely to negotiate a Louisiana Purchase that recognized slavery in the new territory. One can only speculate as to the consequences of a free Louisiana territory. For instance, there would have been no need for the Missouri Compromise; the expansion of slavery would have ended at the Mississippi River; and very probably even Thomas Jefferson would have had no choice but to confront the reality of slavery in a free republic at a much earlier date.

Similarly, as the Republicans charged in 1800, the Federalists might have given generous encouragement to the new Republic of Saint Domingue. At the very least, a Federalist president would have extended diplomatic recognition, sending a powerful message that the United States would not act internationally in support of slavery, again forcing the Jeffersonians to come to terms with their position on that divisive issue.

Such actions would not have helped the Federalists, who would have been stigmatized for stealing the election of 1800. Jefferson would probably have won a sweeping victory in 1804, the Federalist Party would probably have died sooner than it did, and Jefferson might never have forgiven Adams and entered into that wonderful exchange of letters that historians so enjoy quoting. But it is all speculation based on the undeniable power of contingency in history. A consideration of these contingencies may lead to a questioning of the revolutionary nature of Jefferson's election in 1801.

NOTES

1. Hamilton to Jay, 7 May 1800, *AHP* 24:464–67. See also Hamilton to Sedgwick, 4 May 1800, ibid., 444–53.

2. *Connecticut Courant*, 20 Sept. 1800. See also William Linn, *Serious Considerations on the Election of a President: Addressed to the Citizens of the United States* (New York, 1800), 23–25; John Ward Fenno, *Desultory Reflections on the New Political Aspects of Public Affairs in the United States of America, since the Commencement of the Year 1799* (New York, 1800), 52–53; Oliver Wolcott Jr. to Alexander Hamilton, 2 Oct. 1800, *AHP* 25:145.

3. John Preston to John Breckinridge, 28 Dec. 1800, Breckinridge Papers, Lib. Cong.

4. Quoted in Raymond Walters Jr., *Albert Gallatin: Jeffersonian Financier and Diplomat* (New York, 1957), 129.

5. TJ to James Monroe, 15 Feb. 1801, L&B, 10:201. On the heated tone of the election of 1800, see Charles O. Lerche Jr., "Thomas Jefferson and the Election of 1800: A Case Study in the Political Smear," *WMQ* 3d ser., 5 (1948): 467–91.

6. As Bernard A. Weisberger has written, the electoral crisis of 1801 "was no laughing matter." Weisberger, *America Afire: Jefferson, Adams, and the Revolutionary Election of 1800* (New York, 2000), 257. Some historians have been rather dismissive about the revolution of 1800.

7. E. P. Thompson, *The Poverty of Theory* (London, 1978), 300.

8. The best justification I know can be found in *Virtual History: Alternatives and Counterfactuals*, ed. Niall Ferguson (London, 1997).

9. Two opponents of counterfactual history, Benedetto Croce and Michael Oakeshott, have acknowledged this one contribution of the form. See Croce's essay, " 'Necessity' in History," in *Philosophy, Poetry, History: An Anthology of Essays*, trans. Cecil Sprigge (London, 1966); Michael Oakeshott, *Experience and Its Modes* (Cambridge, Mass., 1933), 128–45.

10. R. G. Collingwood, *The Idea of History: With Lectures, 1926–1928*, ed. J. van der Dussen (Oxford, 1993), 390–410.

11. John M. Murrin, "The French and Indian War, the American Revolution, and the Counterfactual Hypothesis: Reflections on Lawrence Henry Gipson and John Shy," *Reviews in American History* 1 (1973): 307.

12. Hugh Trevor-Roper, "History and Imagination," in *History and Imagination: Essays in Honour of H. R. Trevor-Roper*, ed. Valerie Pearl et al. (London, 1981), 364.

13. See particularly Richard E. Ellis, *The Jeffersonian Crisis: Courts and Politics in the Young Republic* (New York, 1971).

14. I am borrowing this idea from something I heard R. F. Foster say about Ireland on Irish Radio in the early 1990s.

15. Interestingly enough, science (at least so far as I understand it) has also changed since the nineteenth century, basically becoming more historical, more contingent, more relativistic. See for instance Stephen Jay Gould, *Wonderful Life: The Burgess Shale and the Nature of History* (New York, 1989); Stephen W. Hawking, *A Brief History of Time: From the Big Bang to Black Holes* (New York, 1988).

16. Ferguson, *Virtual History,* 86 (italics in original).

17. Isaiah Berlin, "The Concept of Scientific History," in *The Proper Study of Mankind: An Anthology of Essays,* ed. Henry Hardy and Roger Hausheer (New York, 1998), 56.

18. Trevor-Roper, "History and Imagination," 363.

19. Hamilton to Jay, 7 May 1800, *AHP* 24:464–67.

20. James Roger Sharp, *American Politics in the Early Republic: The New Nation in Crisis* (New Haven, Conn., 1993), 234–35.

21. TJ to Madison, 4 March 1800, L&B, 10:154–59.

22. There is good evidence that the Federalists actually won in South Carolina. Few of the candidates who won election to the assembly identified themselves as Republicans, while the majority labeled themselves Federalist. Of Charleston's fifteen representatives, only John Drayton declared his support for Jefferson, eight ran on C. C. Pinckney's platform, and the remaining six were labeled Federalist but did not state a presidential preference. See Marvin R. Zahniser, *Charles Cotesworth Pinckney: Founding Father* (Chapel Hill, N.C., 1967), 224–25.

23. Ibid., 213–33; James H. Broussard, *The Southern Federalists, 1800–1816* (Baton Rouge, 1978), 30–31; Noble E. Cunningham Jr., *The Jeffersonian Republicans: The Formation of Party Organization, 1789–1801* (Chapel Hill, N.C., 1957), 231–36.

24. M. Clay to Monroe, 21 Jan. 1801, Monroe Papers, Lib. Cong.; *General Advertiser,* 26 and 27 Jan. 1801.

25. Harry Ammon, *James Monroe: The Quest for National Identity* (1971; rept. Charlottesville, Va., 1990), 192–93; quoting from the *Virginia Argus* (Richmond), 12 April 1799, 9 May 1800.

26. *General Advertiser,* 7 and 10 Jan., 3 Feb. 1801.

27. Breckinridge to TJ, 19 Jan. 1801, Thomas Jefferson Papers, Lib. Cong.

28. *General Advertiser,* 19 Feb. 1801. This charge seems to be based on an article in the *Washington Federalist* of 12 Feb. 1801, which boasted that the "70,000 (regulars let us call them)" of the Massachusetts militia would join with those of the other New England states and march on Washington "under the federal banner in support of the Constitution."

29. TJ to Levi Lincoln, 11 July 1801, L&B, 10:261. Jefferson made this feared monarchy the subject of several letters. See also letters to Samuel Adams, 26 Feb. 1800, Gideon Granger, 13 Aug. 1800, and Robert R. Livingston, 14 Dec. 1800, ibid., 153–54, 166–70, 176–80.

30. See for instance, William Cobbett, *Porcupine's Works,* 12 vols. (London, 1801), 12:175–78, 187–90; Alexander Hamilton to James A. Bayard, 6 April 1802, *AHP* 25:587–88; Ezra Witter, *Two Sermons on the Party Spirit and Divided State of the Country* (Springfield, Mass., 1801), 11–12.

31. For a series of Federalist articles in favor of Burr, see the essays of Epaminondas, *Washington Federalist,* 15, 16, 21, 23 Jan. 1801.

32. Roger G. Kennedy, *Burr, Hamilton, and Jefferson: A Study in Character* (New York, 2000), 167–68; Weisberger, *America Afire,* 269–70.

33. Samuel Tyler to James Monroe, 9 Feb. 1801, *WMQ* 1st ser., 1 (1892): 102–3; TJ to Madison, 18 Feb. 1801, Smith, 2:1161; Daniel Sisson, *The American Revolution of 1800* (New York, 1974), 422–34.

34. Morris to Nicholas Low, 8 Feb. 1801, Jared Sparks, *Life of Gouverneur Morris,* 3 vols. (Boston, 1832), 3:152.

35. Quoted in Sisson, *The American Revolution of 1800,* 420.

36. *Gazette of the United States,* 16 Feb. 1801, based on a report in the *Washington Federalist,* 12 Feb. 1801.

37. Abraham Bishop, *Connecticut Republicanism: An Oration, on the Extent & Power of Political Delusion* (New Haven, Conn., 1800), i. See also John Beckley, *Address to the People of the United States* (Philadelphia, 1800), 4–5; Marcus Brutus, *Serious Facts, Opposed to "Serious Considerations"* (New York, 1800), 2–5.

38. John Quincy Adams to Thomas B. Adams, 30 Dec. 1800, *Writings of John Quincy Adams,* 7 vols., ed. Worthington Chauncey Ford (New York, 1913–17), 2:491. See also Adams to William Van Murray, 17 and 27 Jan. 1801, ibid., 494–98.

39. Hamilton to James Bayard, 16 Jan. 1801, *AHP* 25:319–24.

40. Hamilton to James Bayard, 27 Dec. 1800, ibid., 275–77.

41. Hamilton to Gouverneur Morris, 26 Dec. 1800, ibid., 275.

42. Hamilton to Wolcott, 16 Dec. 1800, ibid., 257.

43. Hamilton to Rutledge, 4 Jan. 1801, ibid., 294, 297.

44. Hamilton to James Bayard, 27 Dec. 1800, ibid., 276–77.

45. Hamilton to Rutledge, 4 Jan. 1801, ibid., 294.

46. TJ to Madison, 19 Dec. 1800, Smith, 2:1154. See also TJ to Tench Coxe, 31 Dec. 1800, L&B, 10:187–88.

47. Morris to Hamilton, 1 Dec. 1800, Hamilton to Morris, 9 Jan. 1801, *AHP* 25:266–69, 304; TJ to Burr, 15 Dec. 1800, *Political Correspondence and Public Papers of Aaron Burr,* 2 vols., ed. Mary-Jo Kline (Princeton, N.J., 1983) 1:469–70; *General Advertiser,* 16 Jan. 1801.

48. Samuel Tyler to Monroe, 11 Feb. 1801, *WMQ* 1st ser., 1 (1892): 104.

49. For a full account of Hamilton's letter and its publication, see *AHP* 25:169–85, with the complete text of the letter ibid., 186–234. On the letter's effect on the election, see Page Smith, *John Adams,* 2 vols. (Garden City, N.Y., 1962) 2:1043–46.

50. Quoted in Smith, *John Adams,* 740. Other members of the revolutionary generation had their doubts about John Adams. It is well to recall Benjamin Franklin's astute evaluation of Adams from 1783: "He means well for his country, is always an honest man, often a wise one, but sometimes, and in some things, absolutely out of his senses." See L. H. Butterfield, *Diary and Autobiography of John Adams,* 4 vols., ed. L. H. Butterfield (Cambridge, Mass., 1961), 1:63.

51. Hamilton to Theodore Sedgwick, 22 Dec. 1800, *AHP* 25:270.

52. Article II, section 1 reads: "The person having the greatest number of votes shall be the President, if such number be a majority of the whole number of electors appointed; and if there be more than one who have such majority, and have an equal number of votes, then the House of Representatives shall immediately choose by ballot one of them for President; and if no person have a majority, then from the five highest on the list said House shall in like Manner choose the President. But in choosing the President, the votes shall be taken by States, the representation from each State having one vote; a quorum for this purpose shall consist of a member or members from two-thirds of the States, and a majority of all the States shall be necessary to a choice. In every case, after the choice of the President, the person having the greatest number of votes of the electors shall be the Vice President."

53. The other alternative was of course Charles Cotesworth Pinckney. But he was a man of surprising integrity, having already refused any deal that would have placed him in the presidency rather than John Adams. See Stanley Elkins and Eric McKitrick, *The Age of Federalism: The Early American Republic, 1788–1800* (New York, 1993), 735, 741–43; Zahniser, *Charles Cotesworth Pinckney,* 222–33.

54. According to Hamilton, Livingston initially "declared among his friends that his first ballot will be for Jefferson his second for Burr." Hamilton to Gouverneur Morris, 9 Jan. 1801, *AHP*

25:305. See also C. H. Hunt, *Life of Edward Livingston* (New York, 1864), 86; William B. Hatcher, *Edward Livingston: Jefferson Republican and Jacksonian Democrat* (Baton Rouge, 1940), 69.

55. Known as "Beau Ned" because of his preference for high fashion, Livingston had switched with most of his family to the Jeffersonians in hopes of gaining position and control of patronage in New York. See Hatcher, *Edward Livingston*, 18–25.

56. Ibid., 55–71. Jefferson appointed Livingston U.S. attorney for the district of New York, a position he held simultaneously with that of mayor of New York. However, Jefferson found Livingston corrupt and felt that his conduct as U.S. attorney brought the party into disrepute. Livingston resigned his offices and moved to New Orleans, where he would enter into further disagreements and court cases with Jefferson and his government.

57. Otis in the House of Representatives, *The Debates and Proceedings in the Congress of the United States*, 42 vols. (Washington, D.C., 1834–56) 10:304–6; United States Congress, *American State Papers: Documents, Legislative and Executive, of the Congress of the United States: Military Affairs*, class 5, 7 vols. (Washington, D.C., 1832–61) 1:133–35, 142–44; Lawrence Delbert Cress, *Citizens in Arms: The Army and the Militia in American Society to the War of 1812* (Chapel Hill, N.C., 1982), 136–49; Theodore J. Crackel, *Mr. Jefferson's Army: Political and Social Reform of the Military Establishment, 1801–1809* (New York, 1987), 17–35.

58. Michael A. Bellesiles, *Arming America: The Origins of a National Gun Culture* (New York, 2000), 219–53.

59. Sharp, *American Politics*, 203; Adrienne Koch and Henry Ammon, "The Virginia and Kentucky Resolutions," *WMQ* 5 (1948): 163–65; Richard R. Beeman, *The Old Dominion and the New Nation, 1788–1801* (Lexington, Ky., 1972), 202.

60. Sharp, *American Politics*, 222; Lisle A. Rose, *Prologue to Democracy: The Federalists in the South, 1789–1800* (Lexington, Ky., 1968), 219–23.

61. Sharp, *American Politics*, 252; quoting the *General Advertiser*, 11 Dec. 1800.

62. Martin K. Gordon, "The Militia of the District of Columbia, 1790–1815" (Ph.D. diss., George Washington University, 1975), 36–37.

63. Ibid., 58–59; *The Times and Alexandria Advertiser*, 18, 21, 31 May 1798; Roger West to James Wood, 6 June 1798, Statement of Public Arms, 22 June 1799, *Calendar of Virginia State Papers*, 11 vols., ed. William P. Palmer et al. (Richmond, Va., 1875–93), 8:487–88, 9:31–32.

64. Bellesiles, *Arming America*, 224–27.

65. Thomas Carpenter, comp., *The Two Trials of John Fries on an Indictment of Treason* (Philadelphia, 1800), 21, 75; Francis Wharton, ed., *State Trials of the United States* (Philadelphia, 1849), 545 (in general see 458–648); Sharp, *American Politics*, 209–10; Peter Levine, "The Fries Rebellion: Social Violence and the Politics of the New Nation," *Pennsylvania History* 40 (1973): 241–58.

66. Hamilton to McHenry, 18 March 1799, *AHP* 22:552–53; Levine, "Fries Rebellion," 249–50.

67. Lee to James Wood, 16 Sept. 1794, Edward Carrington to Wood, 16 Sept. 1794, Account against the U.S. for arms, 19 Sept. 1794, Thomas Mathews to Wood, 6, 12 Oct. 12, 1794, Palmer et al., *Calendar of Virginia State Papers* 7: 316–19, 341–43; Gordon, "The Militia of the District of Columbia," 29–30, 33, 53–54; Cress, *Citizens in Arms*, 121–27; Thomas P. Slaughter, *The Whiskey Rebellion: Frontier Epilogue to the American Revolution* (New York, 1986), 192–204.

68. Slaughter, *The Whiskey Rebellion*, 205–6.

69. Frank A. Cassell, "Samuel Smith: Merchant Politician, 1792–1812" (Ph.D. diss., Northwestern University, 1968), 44–45; *The Columbian Chronicle*, 23 Jan. 1795; Gordon, "The Militia of the District of Columbia," 32; Richard H. Kohn, "The Washington Administration's Decision to Crush the Whiskey Rebellion," *JAH* 59 (1972): 567–84; Russell F. Weigley, *History of the United States Army* (Bloomington, Ind., 1984), 100–103; Slaughter, *The Whiskey Rebellion*, 206–21; Saul Cornell, "Aristocracy Assailed: The Ideology of Backcountry Anti-Federalism," *JAH* 66 (1990): 1148–72.

70. Sharp, *American Politics*, 209–10; Levine, "Fries Rebellion," 267–68, quoting *Washington Federalist*, 12 Feb. 1801.

71. Tyler to Monroe, 11 Feb. 1801, *WMQ* 1st ser., 1 (1892): 104; Monroe to ?, 12 Feb. 1801, Monroe Papers, Lib. Cong.

72. See especially Cress, *Citizens in Arms,* and Mark Pitcavage, "An Equitable Burden: The Decline of the State Militias, 1783–1858" (Ph.D. diss., Ohio State University, 1995).

73. Weigley, *History of the United States Army,* 97–104.

74. TJ to Monroe, 15 Feb. 1801, L&B, 10:201.

75. TJ to John Breckinridge, 18 Dec. 1800, to Madison, 19 and 26 Dec. 1800, to Tench Coxe, 31 Dec. 1800, ibid., 182–88.

76. TJ to Madison, 18 Feb. 1801, Smith, 2:1161.

77. Albert Gallatin, "Plan at Time of Balloting for Jefferson and Burr, Communicated to Nicholas and Mr. Jefferson," [late Jan.–early Feb. 1801], *The Writings of Albert Gallatin,* 3 vols., ed. Henry Adams (Philadelphia, 1879), 1:18–23.

78. TJ, "Anas," L&B, 1:451–52; TJ to James Monroe, 15 Feb. 1801, ibid., 10:201. For Jefferson's account of these days, see "Anas," ibid., 1:439–53.

79. Madison to TJ, 10 Jan. 1801, *The Writings of James Madison,* 9 vols., ed. Gaillard Hunt (New York, 1900–1910), 6:410–16.

80. Ammon, *James Monroe,* 183–84.

81. Sharp, *American Politics,* 269; McKean to TJ, 19 March 1801 [a rewrite of a Feb. letter], Thomas McKean Papers, Historical Society of Pennsylvania (Philadelphia).

82. Monroe to Madison, 15 May 1800, Monroe Papers, New York Public Library; Sharp, *American Politics,* 269; Ammon, *James Monroe,* 193.

83. Ammon, *James Monroe,* 270; Randolph to Monroe, 14 Feb. 1801, Monroe Papers, Lib. Cong. In the same letter, Randolph warned Monroe that federal officials appeared to have removed some of the arms from the federal armory in Bedford County with the purpose of "disarming the state in order to secure an usurpation" of the presidency.

84. TJ to St. George Tucker, 28 Aug. 1797, quoted in Winthrop D. Jordan, *White over Black: American Attitudes toward the Negro, 1550–1812* (Chapel Hill, N.C., 1968), 386.

85. Douglas R. Egerton, *Gabriel's Rebellion: The Virginia Slave Conspiracies of 1800 and 1802* (Chapel Hill, N.C., 1993), 50–68. It is interesting how little attention Gabriel's Rebellion receives in standard studies of this period. For instance, neither Ralph Ketcham's biography of Madison nor Elkins and McKitrick's *Age of Federalism*—both massive books—mention this slave insurrection even in passing.

86. Egerton, *Gabriel's Rebellion,* 55–56, 64–65.

87. Ibid., 72, 75–79; Ammon, *James Monroe,* 185–87; see the payroll accounts for Gabriel's Insurrection, Military Papers, Library of Virginia, Richmond.

88. Egerton, *Gabriel's Rebellion,* 76; William Wilkinson to James Monroe, 1 Oct. 1800, Executive Papers, Negro Insurrection, Virginia State Library; *Norfolk Herald,* 2 Oct. 1800, *Virginia Argus* (Richmond), 10 Oct. 1800.

89. Egerton, *Gabriel's Rebellion,* 77; Callender to TJ, 13 or 18 Sept. 1800, Thomas Jefferson Papers, Lib. Cong.; John Randolph to Joseph Nicholson, 26 Sept. 1800, Nicholson Papers, Lib. Cong.; Ammon, *James Monroe,* 186.

90. Thomas Newton to Monroe, 29 Dec. 1800, John Bracken to Monroe, 20 Sept. 1800, Executive Papers, Negro Insurrection, Virginia State Library; Egerton, *Gabriel's Rebellion,* 75, 77.

91. Monroe to TJ, 15 Sept. 1800, *The Writings of James Monroe: Including a Collection of His Public and Private Papers and Correspondence Now for the First Time Printed,* 7 vols., ed. Stanislaus Murray Hamilton (New York, 1898–1903) 3:208.

92. William W. Freehling, *The Road to Disunion: Secessionists at Bay, 1776–1854* (New York, 1990), 147.

93. Giles Cromwell, *The Virginia Manufactory of Arms* (Charlottesville, Va., 1975), 2–28; Bellesiles, *Arming America,* 227–39.

94. William Vans Murray to John Q. Adams, 9 Dec. 1800, quoted in Herbert Aptheker, *American Negro Slave Revolts* (New York, 1963), 227.

95. Sharp, *American Politics,* 241–43; Egerton, *Gabriel's Rebellion,* 36–41.

96. Major Thomas M. Randolph to Monroe, 14 Feb. 1801, Monroe Papers, Lib. Cong.

97. Gallatin, 22 Jan. 1801, quoted in Henry Adams, *The Life of Albert Gallatin* (Philadelphia, 1879), 255; see also 248–54.

98. Gallatin, "Plan," in Adams, *Writings of Gallatin,* 1:18–23.

99. George Mifflin Dallas, *Life and Writings of Alexander James Dallas* (Philadelphia, 1871), 112–13. See also *General Advertiser,* 16 Feb. 1801.

100. *Washington Federalist,* 12 Feb. 1801 (quoted in *General Advertiser,* 17 Feb. 1801).

101. Beckley to Gallatin, 15 Feb. 1801, Gallatin Papers, New-York Historical Society.

102. John Adams to James Lloyd, 6 Feb. 1815, *The Works of John Adams, Second President of the United States,* 10 vols., ed. Charles Francis Adams (Boston, 1850–56), 10:115. Adams added that the Federalists "committed suicide; they killed themselves and the national President (not their President) at one shot, and then, as foolishly as maliciously, indicted me for the murder."

103. Weisberger, *America Afire,* 255.

104. Sisson, *The American Revolution of 1800,* 436.

105. Smith, *John Adams* 2:1058.

106. Ellis, *The Jeffersonian Crisis.*

107. The *Aurora,* 24 Dec. 1800, quoted in Richard N. Rosenfeld, *American Aurora: A Democratic-Republican Returns* (New York, 1997), 894.

108. Kennedy, *Burr, Hamilton, and Jefferson,* 89–110.

109. Ibid., 105; Anthony Gronowicz, *Race and Class Politics in New York City before the Civil War* (Boston, 1998), 21. As Gronowicz wrote, Jefferson's "party supplied the ideology—democratic republicanism—that rationalized inequality" (11).

CHAPTER 4

Corruption and Compromise in the Election of 1800
The Process of Politics on the National Stage

Joanne B. Freeman

Judging by the memoirs of those who lived through it, the presidential election of 1800 was a defining moment of epic proportions. A hotly contested campaign for the soul of the Republic, the contest had resulted in a tie vote between Republicans Aaron Burr and Thomas Jefferson; an extended standoff in the House, where the tie was to be broken; an outburst of intrigue, suspicion, and whispered fears of disunion and civil war; Jefferson's election to the presidency; and Burr's ultimate downfall.[1]

But it was not the high-stakes drama of the election alone that made it a magnet for controversy well into the nineteenth century. The tenor of mass politicking alone was remarkable. On a local level, the masses were mobilized as never before, and the burgeoning American press was beginning to reveal its full reach and power. Politicking on the national stage was no less dramatic in its implications. As explained by the national leaders at the center of this political maelstrom, this was a contest of corruption and deceit that put the very nature of the political process under debate. During the course of the campaign, rules were broken, standards shattered, loyalties tested, and ambitions exposed; put to the test, even the Constitution came up lacking. The crisis atmosphere of the six-day tie only made matters worse, forcing men to declare loyalties, and exposing distrust, regionalism, and personal ambitions in the process. In a political community grounded on political "friendship," highly attuned to subtleties of personal reputation, and still grappling with the logistics of federal politicking, such do-or-die line drawing was bound to have devastating consequences.[2]

The result was a stream of charges and countercharges that lingered until the deaths of the contest's principal players and well beyond. Although there were accusations of corruption and intrigue throughout the campaign, not surprisingly, it was the electoral tie and its resolution that attracted the most controversy. For six days of excruciating indecision in February 1801, the House voted again and again, unable to break the tie after thirty-five ballots, Federalists leaning toward Burr, Republicans standing behind Jefferson. Did Burr encourage the stalemate by covertly seeking Federalist support for the presidency? Such charges taint his reputation even today. Who were his agents of influence in this supposed plot? A host of friends were tarred by this brush.[3] And what resolved the tie? Federalists later claimed that they negotiated a deal with Jefferson through Delaware Federalist James Bayard—a charge that Jefferson vehemently denied in private memoranda.

It was these memoranda, published after Jefferson's death in the first edition of his works, that gave the 1801 controversy its remarkable staying power. Depicting Jefferson's personal perspective as objective history, they provoked a chain of responses for decades thereafter in a desperate appeal to posterity, each participant hoping to stamp the historical record in his favor. Burr undertook his memoirs explicitly to refute Jefferson's memoranda, as did many others.[4] James Bayard's descendants were particularly active in this debate, defending his claims about a deal with Jefferson—and thus Bayard's veracity and good name as well—in an ongoing string of newspaper defenses and pamphlets; as late as 1907, Bayard's great-grandson was defending his ancestor—and declaring Jefferson's guilt—in the public press.[5]

Modern studies of this pivotal contest offer little insight into such long-lived anxieties, generally viewing the election as a signpost of political development. Pointing to the Federalist and Republican "caucuses" to name candidates; the organization required to manage massive national publicity campaigns; the widespread popular mobilization; the party discipline that led to the tie between Jefferson and Burr (every Republican elector voted for both men); the first transfer of power from one party to the other; and the downfall of Federalism and its aristocratic Old World order, most scholars depict the election of 1800 as the first "modern" presidential election featuring distinct national political parties.[6] To the political elite, however, the contest was something far more complex, characterized by political corruption as well as advancement, fueled by an urgent sense of crisis as well as by forward-looking "modern" innovations, grounded on personal alliances more than group discipline, and steered by issues of character and reputation as well as by partisan ideals. This is a very different election of 1800, one of contingency, crisis, improvisation, and unexpected consequences—the very things most obscured by the conventional narrative that stresses modernity above all else. In essence, by imposing modern assumptions and inevitabilities on the distinctive politics of a time long past, we have obscured the reality of this pivotal contest to those who lived through it.

We have also masked the complexity of political change. Branding the 1800 contest "modern" suggests that participants of all ranks and stripes were united in a confidant partnership of political methods and styles, yet, as we shall see, elite national officeholders had serious reservations about their actions throughout the campaign. Even as politically minded citizens throughout the states aggressively organized themselves into partisan societies and committees, the political elite remained profoundly uncomfortable with such political methods, struggling to adapt their personal and political proprieties to the demands of the moment.[7] Their discomfort makes the 1800 campaign an ideal case study of their evolving political methods, for it raised a chorus of commentary about the prevailing rules of the political game from their perspective.[8] Persisting long after Jefferson ascended to the presidency, protests about the 1800 campaign were protests about the changing nature of politics itself.

THE CRISIS MENTALITY OF 1800

To national leaders, the significance of the presidential election of 1800 was clear. Long after the election, in his retirement years, John Adams had little trouble recalling its broader implications. Adams opened the topic for debate in the spring of 1813, in the midst of a conciliatory correspondence with his longtime political opponent, Thomas Jefferson. Reading the *Memoirs of the Late Reverend Theophilus Lindsey,* which included "Anecdotes and Letters of eminent Persons," Adams had noted a 21 March 1801 letter from Jefferson to renowned Unitarian thinker Joseph Priestley. "I wish to know, if you have seen this Book," Adams wrote to Jefferson. "I have much to say on the Subject."[9] Adams remained true to his word, two of his next three letters (written within five days of each other) opening with the phrase "In your Letter to Dr. Priestley." His biggest gripe, by far, concerned Jefferson's claims about the election of 1800. "The mighty wave of public opinion" that had "rolled over" the Republic and raised him to office was new, Jefferson had claimed. A "new chapter in the history of man" was opening on American shores. To Adams this was egocentric nonsense. "There is nothing new Under the Sun," he countered; great shifts in the tide of public opinion had been washing over peoples and civilizations throughout recorded time. Such was the nature of historical change.

Jefferson's election to the presidency was not revolutionary. Nor had he been swept into office on a wave of popularity. Speaking of the election's moment of crisis—the tie vote between Jefferson and Aaron Burr for the presidency—Jefferson had written that if the tie could not be broken, as seemed likely at the time,

> the federal government would have been in the situation of a clock or watch run down. There was no idea of force, nor of any occasion for it. A convention, invited by the Republican members of Congress . . . would have been on the ground in 8. weeks, would have repaired the Constitution where it was defective, & wound it up again. This peaceable & legitimate resource, to which we are in the habit of implicit obedience, superseding all appeal to force, and being always within our reach, shows a precious principle of self-preservation in our composition, till a change of circumstances shall take place, which is not within prospect at any definite period.[10]

To Jefferson, a constitutional convention and the spirit behind it—"a precious principle of self-preservation"—would have bridged this moment of crisis. Adams, however, was less optimistic. "I am not so sanguine, as you," he responded. "Had the voters for Burr, addressed the Nation, I am not sure that your Convention would have decided in your Favour."[11] In other words, Jefferson had no popular mandate. Burr easily could have won, his defeat resulting from one congressman's willingness to alter his vote and break the tie. Jefferson, infinitely more self-restrained than the impulsively confessional Adams, chose not to respond to this assertion, instead writing a long disquisition on political parties and their role in American politics.[12] Adams revisited the subject in his next few letters, but Jefferson's next letter, written more than a month later, spoke only of religion. For the present, at least, the two would agree to disagree.

They agreed, however, on one fundamental point: in 1801 the constitutional clock had almost run down. As suggested by Jefferson's letter to Priestley, the contest tested the Republic's durability, challenged political methods, revealed a constitutional defect, and raised important questions about legitimate modes of constitutional change. Contrary to Jefferson's rather rosy depiction of its resolution, there was talk of disunion and civil war, and, indeed, two states began to organize their militias to seize the government for Jefferson if Burr prevailed.

Clearly, this is political drama at its most dramatic. Surprisingly, however, the contest has received short shrift in the scholarly literature. In part this can be blamed on the advantages and disadvantages of hindsight. We know that a president was elected, the Republic survived, and future political contests continued to stretch and shape the political process for centuries to come. Set in this context, exclamations about the crisis of 1801 seem shrill indeed. Yet people living in the moment could have no such confidence. Not only did the contest seem Union-shaking in its significance, but also it was set in a larger context of political crises and anxieties that extended across the 1790s.

Foremost among them was a prevailing fear about the Union's very survival. National politicians were constructing a machine of governance that was already in motion—a machine for which there was no model of comparison in the modern world. A federal republic was supposedly superior to its Old World predecessors, but the validity of this assumption had yet to be determined. The stability and long-term practicability of such a polity was likewise a question, every political crisis raising fears of disunion and civil war. The founders had no great faith that the Union would survive, a prevailing anxiety that could not help but have an enormous impact on their politics. Alexander Hamilton and James Madison, the two driving forces behind the Constitution, went to their deaths with the Union's vulnerability on their minds. Both men wrote final pleas for its preservation on the eve of their demise, Madison composing a memorandum entitled "Advice to My Country," and Hamilton writing one last letter on the night before his duel with Aaron Burr, urging a friend to fight against the "Dismemberment [*sic*] of our Empire." Indeed, Hamilton dueled with Burr, in part, to preserve his reputation for that future time when the Republic would collapse, and his leadership would be in demand.[13] Virginian Henry Lee's offhand comment in a 1790 letter to Madison is a blunt reminder of the tenuous nature of the national Union. "If the government should continue to exist," he wrote in passing, evidence of a mindset that is difficult to recapture.[14]

In his 1813 exchange of letters with Jefferson, Adams gave ample testimony to this mindset. Speaking of acts of "terrorism" of the 1790s, Jefferson had written that "none can conceive who did not witness them, and they were felt by one party only."[15] Adams did not agree. "You never felt the Terrorism of Chaises [Shays'] Rebellion in Massachusetts," he began.

> I believe You never felt the Terrorism of Gallatins Insurrection in Pensilvania: You certainly never realized the Terrorism of Fries's, most outragious Riot and Rescue, as I call it, Treason. . . . You certainly never felt the Terrorism, excited by Genet in 1793, when ten thousand People in the Streets of Philadelphia, day after day, threatened to drag Washington out of his House, and effect a Revolution in the Government, or compell it to declare War in favour of the French Revolution, and against England. The coolest and the firmest Minds, even among the Quakers in Philadelphia, have given their Opinions to me, that nothing but the Yellow Fever . . . could have saved the United States from a total Revolution of Government. I have no doubt You was fast asleep in philosophical Tranquility, when ten thousand People, and perhaps many more, were parading the Streets of Philadelphia, on the Evening of my Fast Day; When even Governor Mifflin himself, thought it his Duty to order a Patrol of Horse And Foot to preserve the peace; when Markett Street was as full as Men could stand by one another, and even before my Door; when some of my Domesticks in Phrenzy, determined to sacrifice their Lives in my defence . . . when I myself judged it prudent and necessary to order Chests of Arms from the War Office to be brought through bye Lanes and back Doors: determined to defend my House at the Expence of my Life, and the Lives of the few, very few Domesticks and Friends within it.

"What think you of Terrorism, Mr. Jefferson?" he concluded. He himself thought that Federalists and Republicans were equally guilty: "Summoned as a Witness to say upon Oath, which Party had excited, Machiavillialy, the most terror, and which had really felt the most, I could not give a more sincere Answer, than in the vulgar Style 'Put Them in a bagg and shake them, and then see which comes out first.'"[16]

Adams's litany of horrors raises an important point about the crisis-ridden political climate of the 1790s. National crises occurred almost annually, and though not all of them percolated down to the realm of local politics with equal intensity, it took only the slightest spark to ignite an uproar of outraged entitlement and revolutionary fervor among populace and politicians alike. Witness the period's political chronology. In 1790 the intertwined controversies over the location of the national capital and Hamilton's financial plan convinced many that the Union was not long for this world. In 1792 partisan conflict exploded into the public papers, threatening, as George Washington put it, "to tare the [federal] Machine asunder." [17] In 1793 the inflammatory activities of "Citizen" Edmond Genet threatened to spread French revolutionary fervor to American shores, prompting even Francophile Republicans to abandon his cause. In 1794, when western Pennsylvania farmers refused to pay a national whiskey tax, President Washington called an armed force of fifteen thousand soldiers to the field—almost the size of the army that captured Cornwallis at Yorktown. In 1795 the lackluster Jay Treaty with Britain provoked angry public protests around the nation; thousands of people gathered in New York City alone (a handful of them reputedly throwing rocks at Hamilton's head). In 1796, with Washington's retirement, the nation had its first real presidential election, Washington's departure prompting many to fear the nation's imminent collapse. The 1797–98 XYZ Affair, the Quasi-War with France, the 1798 Alien and Sedition Acts, the Kentucky and Virginia Resolutions, Fries' Rebellion, and finally the presidential election of 1800—these are only the most prominent of the period's many crises, each one raising serious questions about the survival and character of the national government and its relationship with the body politic.

Indeed, among the political elite, the political process itself raised questions, fears, and insecurities. Increasingly throughout the 1790s politicians found themselves compelled to win power and prestige from ever more vociferous popular audiences with unpredictable demands and desires. Political methods were changing, as was the stance of political leadership—and the transition was a rocky one. Even for elite Republicans, who were friendlier to the idea of popular politicking, there was a vast difference between mingling with the masses in theory and actually doing so. Whether electioneering, running for office, or simply exercising the privileges of leadership, America's ruling elite was increasingly dependent on the whims of the democratic many, a state of affairs that contributed to the volatility of early national politics and the defensive spirit of political leadership. In essence, uncertainty ruled the day—uncertainty about the structure of the Constitution and the durability of the Union, the impact and implications of popular politics, the new Republic's place on an international stage, and the larger significance of a national partisan war.

Thus in many ways the 1800 contest was a capstone to ten years of ever-heightening partisan political tensions. Not only was there an ongoing partisan power struggle for control, but also this struggle itself seemed to put national constitutional governance into doubt. As New York Republican Matthew Davis

wrote in the spring of 1800, this election would "clearly evince, whether a Republican form of Government is worth contending for," deciding "in some
measure, our future destiny." Federalists were likewise uneasy as the contest approached, many convinced that this would be the last election.[18] Even President
Adams assumed that some of his colleagues desired the destruction of the Republic and, ultimately, a new constitution.[19] As early as May 1800, months before a vote was cast, there was anxious talk of civil war.[20]

The fuel for these fears was the seemingly implacable opposition of Federalists and Republicans, largely a battle between northerners and southerners.
With partisan animosity at an all-time high and no end in sight, many assumed
that they were engaged in a fight to the death that would destroy the Union. Of
course each side assumed that it alone represented the American people, its opponents a mere faction promoting self-interested desires. If the Union fell, it
would be the fault of the other side, a group of desperate men who had forsaken
the public good in the hope of winning power, fortune, and influence. Each side
was thus firmly convinced that its enemies had abandoned the rules of the
game, and that it must act accordingly. This mindset would have a profound
influence on the nature of politicking during the campaign, encouraging politicians to violate some of their most heartfelt political principles and ideals.

THE POLITICAL SINS OF 1800

The political sins of 1800 are well known today, though scholars often deem
them political virtues. Both Federalists and Republicans held congressional
caucuses to nominate candidates; there was the semblance of a national propaganda campaign; elite politicians electioneered among the common folk to an
unprecedented degree; and party discipline was strong enough to produce an
electoral tie—and almost to dissolve the Union. All of these practices seem like
harbingers of a modern politics-to-come. Yet, as demonstrated by the anxious
apologies, excuses, and justifications, to many participants these same practices
violated the ethics of national politics, grounding the national political process
on combat rather than compromise, moving the axis of politics away from the
accountability of the legislative floor, dividing the nation along a two-party axis,
and seemingly promoting factional ambitions over the general good. Scholars
who discuss this profound conflict between political ideals and realities rarely
do more than acknowledge it, noting that early national politicians formed parties despite themselves.[21] The precise way in which individuals reasoned their
way into such extreme practices remains unknown.

Certainly the cause of liberty had justified extreme measures before; with each side convinced that it was defending the promise of the Revolution, it was no great leap to conclude that the present combat demanded more of the same. As Hamilton wrote in the midst of the 1800 election, "in times like these in which we live, it will not do to be overscrupulous. It is easy to sacrifice the substantial interests of society by a strict adherence to ordinary rules." [22] Connecticut Republican Gideon Granger felt the personal impact of this mentality during a congressional debate in 1800. As he explained to Thomas Jefferson, a Federalist representative had been "insolent enough to dictate to me that tho' he esteemed me as a Man, yet we must all be crushed and that my life was of little Importance when compared to the peace of the State." [23] Extraordinary times demanded extraordinary actions. Such supposed moral lapses, in turn, fostered anxiety about the fate of the Republic. National politicians were caught in a vicious circle, torn between the demands and proprieties of national politics. By virtually demanding adaptation, this crisis mentality greased the wheels of political change.

The ever-impulsive Alexander Hamilton provides us with one such example. Many accounts of the election of 1800 mention disapprovingly his attempt to tamper with the electoral college.[24] Alarmed that the incoming New York state legislature was largely Republican and would thus select Republican presidential electors, Hamilton wrote to New York governor John Jay in May 1800, pleading for drastic measures: the old legislature should be called immediately and the mode of choosing electors changed to popular voting by districts. Hamilton was "aware that there are weighty objections to the measure," he confessed, but "scruples of delicacy and propriety . . . ought to yield to the extraordinary nature of the crisis. They ought not to hinder the taking of a *legal* and *constitutional* step, to prevent an Atheist in Religion and a Fanatic in politics from getting possession of the helm of the State." Jay did not know the Republicans as well as Hamilton did, Hamilton assured the governor; they were intent on either overthrowing the government "by stripping it of its due energies" or effecting a revolution. Given the threat to the Republic, the "*public safety,*" and the "great cause of social order," it was their "solemn obligation to employ" any means in their power to defeat these wrongdoers. Hamilton even told Jay how to inform the state legislature of this electoral maneuver. "If done the motive ought to be frankly avowed," he advised.

In your communication to the Legislature they ought to be told that Temporary circumstances had rendered it probable that without their interposition the executive authority of the General Government would be transfered to hands hostile to the system heretofore pursued with so much success and dangerous to the peace happiness and order of the Country—that under this impression from facts convincing to your own mind you had thought it your duty to give the existing Legislature an opportunity of deliberating whether it would not be proper to interpose and endeavour to prevent so great an evil.

There could be no hope for any popular government "if one party will call to its aid all the resources which *Vice* can give and if the other, however pressing the emergency, confines itself within all the ordinary forms of delicacy and decorum."[25]

Two things are worth noting about Hamilton's rather low moment. First, this was no simple grasp at power by a deceitful politician (deceitful as Hamilton might occasionally have been). There was method to Hamilton's seeming madness. With the Republic's survival at stake, rules and standards had to be bent and adapted, though not overthrown. "Call the legislature and change the electoral system," he suggested, not "Ignore the system and select electors of our own." And though Hamilton alone usually shoulders the blame for electoral sinning, in truth many others resorted to the same logic, manipulating the rules of the game at the last minute to ensure the public safety and the general good. Given the lessons of the presidential election of 1796—the first without George Washington and thus the first true presidential contest—such attempts seemed logical. The 1796 electors had proven entirely unpredictable, their loyalties ever shifting, the national election dissolving into a cluster of local debates and controversies.[26] In the crisis atmosphere of 1800, politicians thus did their best to secure reliable electors. Pleading for immediate electoral reform in Virginia, North Carolina, Kentucky, and Tennessee, South Carolina Republican Charles Pinckney explained, "I tell you I know nothing else will do and this is no time for qualms."[27] Maryland Federalist Charles Carroll likewise encouraged such reform, though he disapproved of "laws & changes of a moment."[28] The entire Massachusetts congressional delegation urged similar reform for its state; fearful that its allies back home might not realize the importance of Massachusetts's electoral votes from a national perspective, it made its request in a circular letter—an unusual act for New Englanders—apologizing for the demand even as it made it; "excuse us for suggesting these ideas," the delegation explained, "our anxiety for the event of the election must be our apology."[29] Other politicians waited until their states elected new legislatures; if their party had a clear majority, they lobbied to convene it immediately for the selection of electors, before their opponents could organize resistance.[30] These men justified their actions by declaring them public-minded during a time of crisis; rather than abandoning their ideals and morals, they were doing just the opposite, clinging to them as justification for their political sins. The Republic and the Constitution demanded such sacrifice.

This sense of crisis likewise inspired some electioneering innovations, compelling elite politicians to court the body politic to an unprecedented degree. The people needed to be aroused and enlightened to the danger at hand and induced to reveal their true sentiments—prompting many politicians to forge new and uncomfortable compromises. For example, the notoriously standoffish Jefferson, opposed in principle and personality to public ceremony and display, changed his tune in the spring of 1800. Writing to Virginia governor James Monroe, he expressed his willingness to arrange a "spontaneous" public demonstration of support for him on his way home from Washington. He hated ceremony, he acknowledged, and thought it better to avoid occasions "which might drag me into the newspapers." Yet "the federal party had made [powerful] use" of such demonstrations, and there was "a great deal of federalism and Marshalism" in Richmond. Was a reliance on "the slow but sure progress of good sense & attachment to republicanism . . . best for the public as well as [myself]?" In a contest between political proprieties and the demands of the moment, the latter prevailed. In the end, however, Monroe advised against such a display. Not only would it inspire "like attention by the tories," involving Jefferson "in a kind of competition," but the public might not readily rally to his cause. After inquiring "in a way wh[ich] compromitted no one," Monroe explained, "it was feared . . . that the zeal of some of our friends . . . had abated by yr. absence."—an interesting comment on the supposed wave of sentiment that swept Jefferson into office.[31]

Some of the most renowned electioneering innovations took place in New York City under the guidance of Aaron Burr.[32] The sense of crisis was certainly at an extreme in the spring of 1800, for New York City was the most crucial contest of the campaign. As Republican Matthew Davis explained, "it was universally conceded that on the state of New-York the presidential election would depend, and that the result of the city would decide the fate of the state."[33] Given Burr's perverse pleasure in violating prevailing standards and norms, it is difficult to ascribe his actions to a process of tortured compromise. But the challenge of the moment did spur him to institute a number of political innovations that proved highly effective. For example, he personalized his campaign to an extraordinary degree, purportedly compiling a roster with the name of every New York City voter, accompanied by a detailed description of his political leanings, temperament, and financial standing.[34] His plan was to portion the list out to his cadre of young supporters, who would literally electioneer door to door; in the process, he was helping to organize the citizenry politically— not his goal, but the logical outcome. Similarly, rather than selecting potential electors based on their rank and reputation, he selected the men "most likely to run well," canvassing voters to test the waters.[35]

Perhaps Burr's most striking innovations concerned his preparations for the city's three polling days. Creating a literal campaign headquarters, he "kept open house for nearly two months, and Committees were in session day and night during that whole time at his house. Refreshments were always on the table and mattresses for temporary repose in the rooms. Reports were hourly received from sub-committees, and in short, no means left unemployed."[36] As the polls opened, he dispatched German-speaking Republicans to the predominantly German seventh ward to "explain" the election in the voters' native tongue. When the polls had closed, guards were posted discreetly at each one to prevent inspectors from "inadvertently" making errors in their returns; guards likewise "narrowly and cautiously watched" the city's "leading Federal gentlemen."[37]

Though Burr was unequaled in his strategy and efforts, Hamilton matched his pace during the city's three days of balloting. Unequipped and unwilling to manage a large-scale democratic campaign, he could at least meet Burr's individual efforts during the ultimate moment of crisis. Both men rushed from ward to ward for twelve to fifteen hours a day, often neglecting to eat, their political aides hard put to keep up with them.[38] Both likewise took the unprecedented measure of speaking directly to the people. As Burr's political lieutenant Matthew Davis reported to Albert Gallatin, one of Jefferson's political intimates, Burr had "pledged himself to come forward, and address the people in firm & manly language on the importance of the election, and the momentous crisis at which we have arrived—This he has never done at any former election, and I anticipate Great advantages from the effect it will produce."[39] Significantly, Burr made this decision in response to the supposedly backward-looking high Federalist Hamilton, who had previously announced his intention to electioneer in the same manner.[40] Of course, their bold democratic gesture is unremarkable by our standards, the two men arguing "the debatable questions" before large assemblages at polling places, each politely stepping aside when it was the other's turn to speak.[41] But the partisan press recognized the novelty of such gestures. How could a "would be Vice President . . . stoop so low as to visit every corner in search of voters?" asked the Federalist *Daily Advertiser.* The *Commercial Advertiser* likewise commented on the "astonished" electorate that greeted Hamilton's efforts. "Every day he is seen in the street hurrying this way, and darting that; here he buttons a heavy hearted fed, and preaches up courage, there he meets a group, and he simpers in unanimity, again to the heavy headed and hearted, he talks of perseverance, and (God bless the mark) of virtue!"[42] Though as energetic as Burr, Hamilton electioneered with a decidedly Federalist flair. On at least one occasion, he offended the crowd at a polling place by appearing on horseback, prompting one disgruntled observer to literally force Hamilton off his high horse.[43]

Burr is often cited as one of the nation's first "modern" politicians, his efforts in 1800 a far cry from the genteel restraint displayed by most of his peers. But even Burr did not simply abandon past precedent in favor of a "more logical" mode of politicking. His genius was in his strategic deployment of his presence and reputation, enabling him to popular politick without dirtying his hands.[44] With the exception of his polling place orations, he himself did not mingle with the populace. Rather, he politicked through the agency of a league of energetic young lieutenants. As noted by Davis (himself one of Burr's lieutenants), this was his chief's most distinctive political skill: his ability to charm and persuade his supporters and the unconverted alike. "It was one of the most remarkable exhibitions of the force of his character," Davis wrote, "this bending every one who approached him to his use, and compelling their unremitted, though often unwilling, labours in his behalf."[45]

The power of such popular politicking was apparent—even to recalcitrant Federalists who disliked the disorder of an aroused democratic multitude.[46] The tone of politics was slowly shifting, as leaders and populace negotiated the best means of maintaining the constitutional order, as they envisioned it. Of course, Federalists and Republicans had very different visions of this sense of order. Yet their politicking in 1800 shared one fundamental assumption: popular political innovations were attempts to *preserve* their sense of the political system. Forged in a time of crisis, such compromises looked back to the past as well as forward to the future.

HONOR: THE BOND OF PARTY

Even the adventurer Burr did not repudiate the political system in the service of his goals. Rather, he adapted it to suit his purposes, stretching the bounds of propriety in the name of the Republicans, the people—and Aaron Burr, for his extreme measures won him the vice presidential nomination. Contemporaries deemed Burr's practices reprehensible but admirable, their conflicted emotions revealing the clash between political proprieties and demands. As New Yorker Robert R. Livingston noted, some men seemed to see in Burr "all the vices of a Cataline & yet assign those very vices as a reason for placing him at the head of the government."[47] They were equally conflicted about electoral caucuses— another feature of the 1800 election. To ensure an electoral victory, both Federalists and Republicans attempted to strengthen national partisan bonds by holding national congressional caucuses in May 1800, just before the adjournment of Congress. Close analysis of their logic and impact reveals the warping influence of modern assumptions. Led astray by the word "caucus," most scholarly accounts pinpoint these meetings as a "modern" innovation. But in truth they are something quite different—something not at all apparent unless we listen to the participants' precise words, reconstruct their precise logic, and look at these meetings through their eyes.

Context is vital to understanding these caucuses—political, intellectual, and cultural. Politically, they were a logical outgrowth of the confusion and unpredictability of the presidential election of four years past. This time, politicians thought, they would do better. They would have a plan. Intellectually, however, caucuses were problematic. Even as they acknowledged the need for organization, politicians were uncomfortable with these exclusive bodies, factional, seemingly secret, and extra-constitutional as they were. Federalist John Trumbull of Connecticut avoided them on principle: "I never attended a *Caucus*, & never intend to do it."[48] As the Philadelphia *Aurora* declared in a burst of self-righteous outrage, the Federalist congressional caucus was a "self appointed, self elected, self delegated club or caucus, or conspiracy, of about 24 persons, . . . unknown to the constitution or the law."[49]

There were several ways to grapple with this conflict between political proprieties and demands. You could "capture" a town meeting and commandeer it to serve partisan purposes; this was no secret caucus, but an open public discussion.[50] You could stage a separate public meeting, supposedly open to all but likewise partisan. The risk with such a ploy was that you could not exclude your political opponents without appearing partisan and exclusive—as in New Jersey, where Federalists insisted on attending a Republican meeting in the name of "free discussion."[51] You could openly declare that you were holding a caucus, your honesty intended to mitigate your sin—thereby opening yourself to attack by your opponents—as congressional Federalists did in May 1800.[52] You could stage a secret caucus, as congressional Republicans did, risking the penalties of exposure.[53] Or you could obscure the organizational nature of your meeting, presenting it as "a private meeting of our friends," as Matthew Davis did in 1800.[54] All such strategies were attempts to bend the rules without breaking them. Not surprisingly, within the next twenty years electoral politics would see a new adaptation—political conventions, seemingly popular organizations that, at least in their earliest incarnation, were often well-orchestrated public endorsements of privately selected candidates.[55] Again, rather than wholesale surrender to a properly democratic mode of politicking, we are seeing a gradual process of change.

Thinking back to the disorganization of 1796, when a total of thirteen candidates received presidential nominations, national politicians in 1800 saw congressional caucuses as both logical and necessary, justified by the crisis at hand. This time, with the fate of the Republic at stake, they would try to get national support for two "safe" candidates. It is here that close attention to cultural conventions—language, rituals, and customs—offers insight into the distinctive nature of the early national political process. The first hint at the purpose of these two congressional meetings of May 1800 can be found in the words that politicians used to describe them. Though they sometimes referred to them as caucuses, they also called them "the agreement," "the promise," "the compromise," and "the pledge," to which they would be "faithful" and "true."[56] Clearly these caucuses involved negotiation and compromise between men of differing views, rather than the simple confirmation of a presidential ticket. The result of these compromises—electoral tickets featuring a northerner and a southerner—was not a foregone conclusion, regardless of how obvious such a strategy seems to us. For national politicians a cross-regional ticket was risky, for it required a high degree of national partisan loyalty and mutual trust between North and South. Many politicians later regretted their faith in such a "scheme." For example, John Adams's son Thomas attributed his father's loss to the treachery of southern Federalist Pinckney supporters. As he explained, "It ought never to have been the plan of the federal party to support a Gentleman from the South, merely for the sake of securing the interest of [any] Southern

State in favor of the federal ticket. There was evidence enough on the former trial, what result might be calculated upon in making another." He now had no "confidence in the Southern people."[57] Although southern Republicans remained true to their promise, supporting both candidates equally, they regretted their actions once the tie was announced. To Maryland Republican John Francis Mercer, the lesson was obvious. As he wrote to Madison, "It all amounts to this[,] that we are *too honest.*"[58] They should have thought first of themselves.

The national caucuses of May 1800 were attempts to *create* national partisan unity, not expressions of it. Indeed, as suggested by words such as "pledge" and "promise," national partisan loyalty was so weak that it had to be supplemented by personal vows.[59] To compel politicians to stay the course, they had to commit themselves to it personally, pledging their word of honor and their reputations; the only way to unite northerners and southerners was to appeal to them as gentlemen rather than as political allies. These caucuses were thus not simple "modern" political innovations. Premised on bonds of honor and friendship as well as on partisanship, they were a political hybrid that enabled participants to envision themselves as one of a band of brothers rather than as members of a cold and calculating faction. Justified by the election's crisis mentality, national caucuses were adaptations of the prevailing political system, premised on the cultural importance of honor.

Personal honor was the ultimate bond of party when all else failed, the only way to overcome the many conflicting regional and personal claims that tore at a man's commitments of principle. In the absence of the firm partisan bonds that scholars often take for granted on the national stage, honor was a fundamental underpinning of national partisan combat—a heretofore neglected cultural influence that is crucial to understanding the nature of early national political change. Particularly during peak moments of crisis, such bonds of honor bolstered the national political system, using the power of a gentleman's personal reputation to overcome lapses in national coordination and vision.

Thus, in the crisis-ridden election of 1800, public figures clung to such pledges as the only hope for national political unity—the only way to save the Republic from what they perceived as the dire threat of their opposition. Panicky politicians who suggested last-minute changes were reminded that they could not do so without going back on their word. For example, when Hamilton began to urge Federalists to abandon Adams in favor of Pinckney, his friends brought him to account. "*We are pledged*" to give Adams "*the full chance of the united vote concerted at Philadelphia,*" urged Massachusetts Federalist

George Cabot. Cabot again reminded Hamilton of their pledge when the latter was contemplating his pamphlet attack on John Adams. "Good faith wou'd & ought to be observed as the only means of success," he insisted, for if Adams were dropped, his friends would drop Pinckney in return. Three months earlier it had been Hamilton himself who had propounded such "good faith." Fearful that the Federalists would fail to unite on a national level, he had pleaded with his friends at Washington to make a "distinct & solemn [con]cert" to support both candidates.[60] Such a personal vow seemed the only way to inspire mutual trust between North and South.

All over the nation Federalists were well aware that if they reneged on their half of the agreement—if they refused to support the candidate who was not from their region—the supporters of that man would do the same in return, and the Federalist cause would collapse. National unity depended on the personal honor of individual politicians; thus, throughout the election, they pledged their faith to men from other regions, in hopes of getting similar reassurances in return. South Carolinian John Rutledge Jr. described such an exchange in a letter to Hamilton. Shortly after arriving in Rhode Island, he received a "pressing invitation" for an immediate discussion of the election. When he explained that he could not journey into town, "the old Gentleman" who had requested the meeting traveled out to Rutledge for "an hour[']s conversation." The man asked Rutledge "to declare [for] the information of his friends . . . whether I really thought Mr A[dams] would have the votes of So[uth] Carolina. I told him I had on my return there fulfilled the promise I made at the Caucus held at Philada., & used every exertion within my power to induce the federalists to suport Mr A equally with Genl P. . . . He seemed pleased with this information—said we might rely upon P's getting all the votes in this State."[61] This "old Gentleman" of Rhode Island was desperate for personal reassurance of South Carolina's fidelity. Only then could he claim confidence in the national cause. Such personal pledges of honor were virtually the only thing holding North and South together.

Federalist worries centered around Massachusetts and South Carolina, the home states of the two candidates, for it was these states that were most likely to succumb to regional prejudice and abandon one candidate in favor of their regional favorite. As South Carolinian Robert Goodloe Harper wrote to Harrison Gray Otis of Massachusetts, "I fear you and your friends in Boston are ruining every thing. The federalists . . . in South Carolina, are making the fairest & the most zealous exertions in favour of Mr. Adams. . . . But can it be expected that they will continue the same efforts," if they know that Massachusetts has abandoned Pinckney?[62] Virginian Bushrod Washington—George Washington's nephew—likewise wrote a frantic letter to Oliver Wolcott in Connecticut, assuring him that South Carolina would support both Adams and Pinckney, for "they consider themselves imperiously urged to pursue this conduct by the soundest principles of good faith & of good policy." Even Pinckney was behaving "like a man of honor" by supporting Adams, Washington insisted. Should "distrust take place between the friends of the two federal candidates," he warned, "all must end in the election of Mr. J[efferson]—which God forbid."[63] So important was such personal reassurance that Wolcott commenced a letter campaign, quoting Washington's letter to friends throughout the North.[64] Pinckney himself wrote a similar letter to James McHenry in Maryland, assuring him that South Carolina would only abandon Adams if New England did so first—an interesting insight into Pinckney's ambitions.[65] All of these men recognized what Maryland Federalist James Bayard put into words: the Federalist Party's "efforts can not be united, but thro' mutual confidence," and the best way to ensure such regional trust was through pledges of personal honor.[66]

Republicans, too, clung to their caucus "pledge" as their only hope of surmounting regional differences. Like the Federalists, their concerns focused on the home states of the candidates, New York and Virginia, where regional biases would be strongest. Thus, throughout the election, a slew of anxious correspondence passed between New Yorkers and Virginians, each seeking constant reassurance from the other that their honor was pledged. Burr's friend David Gelston of New York—well aware of Virginia's disloyal abandonment of Burr four years before—was particularly nervous about that state's intentions, writing several anxious letters to Madison during the course of the election. "*Can we, may we* rely on the integrity of the southern States?" he wrote in October 1800. "We depend on the integrity of Virginia & the southern States as we shall be faithfull & honest in New York." Six weeks later, agitated by reports that Virginia was going to drop a few votes for Burr to ensure Jefferson's victory, he wrote again, reminding Madison that honor was at stake. "I am not willing to believe it possible that such measures can be contemplated," he wrote, suggesting just the opposite. "We know that the honour of the Gentlemen of Virginia. and N. Y. was pledged at the adjournment of Congress," and to violate such an agreement would be "a sacrilege."[67] A letter from Madison to Jefferson reveals that Gelston's fears were well founded. Gelston "expresses much anxiety & betrays some jealousy with respect to the *integrity* of the Southern States,"

Madison wrote. "I hope the event will skreen all the parties, particularly Virginia from any imputation on this subject; tho' I am not without fears, that the requisite concert may not sufficiently pervade the several States."[68] Such fears eventually compelled Jefferson himself, as he later explained, to take "some measures" to ensure Burr of Virginia's unanimous vote.[69]

In 1800 honor bound national politicians more than partisan loyalty did. Locally, politicians could agree on political priorities and principles far more readily than they could across regions. And indeed, local partisan organizations were more organized in 1800 than they had ever been before, creating statewide committees of correspondence and networks of influence. Because they posed little threat to the Union, local party organizations were far less threatening than their national equivalents, and far easier to institute among men who shared local interests. On a national level such organization proved more problematic; it seemed to threaten the existence of the Union itself. The national political arena had been designed to forge compromises among local interests in service of the public good; organized national parties seemed to declare such compromises impossible. In the face of such conflicts and fears, national politicians turned to what they knew best: they guided their actions according to the mandates of honor. Ironically, reliance on aristocratic tradition helped elite politicians adapt to the demands of a democratic politics.

The ultimate test of adaptive powers arose during the February 1801 electoral tie between Jefferson and Burr. Under the Constitution, the House of Representatives was responsible for resolving such an electoral deadlock, each state's delegation possessing one vote. However, to the horror of all involved, the House seemed unable to break the tie. For six days and thirty-five ballots, the contest dragged on, Federalists undecided on a course of action and Republicans insistent on Jefferson, to their minds the people's choice. With the constitutional process at a seeming standstill, many predicted its demise and, indeed, Representatives began to murmur about "usurpation" of the government or, worse, civil war. At this ultimate moment of crisis, national politicians revealed their commitment to the Constitution, but not without a price. For the nightmare of 1801 raised serious questions about the national political process.

The tie between Jefferson and Burr has long been attributed to intense party discipline: so loyal were Republicans to their party ticket that they unexpectedly caused a tie between the two candidates.[70] Yet there is another way of interpreting such unanimous support, as suggested by Connecticut Federalist Uriah Tracy. Writing from the capital to Maryland Federalist James McHenry, Tracy reported that the Republicans were in a rage "for having acted with good faith . . . each declaring, if they had not had full confidence in the treachery of the others, they would have been treacherous themselves; and not acted, as they promised, to act—at Philada. last winter."[71] In other words, no Republican dared drop a vote because each assumed that others would prove disloyal. To drop a vote would be to invite retributive vote dropping elsewhere, thereby destroying whatever national party unity existed, and probably throwing the election to the Federalists. It is true that given this scenario Republicans might have been surprised at the unanimous support of their caucus pledge; it is not true, however, that such behavior represented a great stride in national party spirit. Indeed, regional distrust and personal differences only worsened during the course of the election, as did party enmity, flaring into anxious talk of civil war. At this peak moment of crisis, it is highly significant that many politicians opted to support their region at the expense of their national party.

The detachment of hindsight makes it difficult for us to recapture the desperate anxiety that prevailed in the national capital during the duration of the tie. Given a choice between electing Burr or Jefferson to the presidency, many Federalists were willing to do anything rather than select the "fanatic" Virginian. Perhaps Burr would cooperate with them if they were responsible for his election. The idea received serious consideration. They also discussed simply refusing to break the tie, declaring the election inconclusive and naming a president pro tem until they could hold a second election.[72] Either one of these strategies blocked Republicans out of the political process, an extreme act with potentially severe consequences. Their political voices potentially cut off, Republicans gestured toward a violent extreme, the Republican governors of Pennsylvania and Virginia putting their state militias on alert should Jefferson not be chosen. As one New York Republican observed admiringly, Virginians had "pledged themselves to resist the authority" of any attempt to usurp the government, "decisively and effectively." To Jefferson it was this threat of armed resistance that ultimately forced the Federalists to fold. As we have seen, he later added that a "convention . . . would have been on the ground in 8. weeks" and "repaired the Constitution."[73]

Jefferson's mention of a "convention" reveals his underlying faith in the adaptive power of the Constitution. Others shared his conviction, holding on to the slim hope that the Federalists would ultimately bow to the public will and elect Jefferson. James Monroe felt sure that after an initial outburst of spleen, Federalists would assume "more correct views." The alternative was unthinkable: surely they would not usurp the election, for such a move "wod. require a degree of . . . wickedness in that party wh. I do not think it possessed of." Madison agreed: "certainly" the Federalists would put things right.[74] Many Federalists used this same logic when contemplating the possibility of having Jefferson or Burr as president: surely these men were not as bad as Federalists had been led to believe. Forced to define their terms by a national emergency, politicians revealed that underneath all of their partisan name-calling and threats, they believed that their opponents would act for the public good; by threatening to destroy the Union, the crisis of 1801 forced politicians to acknowledge their mutual commitment to it. In the same way that calls for national partisan unity revealed dangerous divisions, the threat of disunion revealed bonds of nationalism, tenuous as they were.[75]

This jumble of suspicions and expectations—some partisan, some regional, some personal, some ideological—was at the heart of the subsequent controversy over the tie between Jefferson and Burr. Forced to take a stand with their votes, national politicians found themselves torn between conflicting aspects of their public identity. Voting along partisan lines might do a disservice to one's region; voting along regional lines could endanger the Union; and either of these paths might damage one's public career. There was no single correct course of action, but a poor choice could bring dishonor, defeat, and disunion. In the end, most men remained true to partisan demands—Republicans voting for Jefferson, and Federalists withholding enough votes to allow Jefferson to win—but only after days of conflict, questions, persuasion, and suspicion.

Given the distrust between northern and southern Republicans, it should be no surprise that during the six days of balloting at least one New Yorker tried to entice New York and New Jersey Republicans to abandon Jefferson in favor of Burr. As Maryland Republican Samuel Smith told Burr, "A Mr. Ogden" had recently "Addressed the York Members on your Acct. directly & boldly," suggesting "how much New York would be benefited by having you for the President," and made similar suggestions to a New Jersey representative.[76] Already predisposed to distrust New Yorkers, many southern Republicans assumed that David Ogden had been sent by Burr to sway the election in his favor. The same was suggested of northern Republican Edward Livingston and Connecticut Republican Abraham Bishop. A New Yorker who was friendly with Burr, Livingston was assumed to be assisting Ogden as Burr's "confidential agent" in wooing Vermont and Tennessee delegates; Bishop was accused of traveling to

Pennsylvania with similar intentions.[77] Regardless of the truth of such claims, New York and New Jersey Republicans clearly feared the temptation of such a regional victory, for shortly after Ogden's departure they called a caucus "to pledge themselves to each other." In the face of such temptation, their loyalty to the national cause required the reinforcement of a personal pledge. Once again, honor was the ultimate bond of party. This type of ceremonial vow, entirely overlooked by modern accounts, meant enough to inspire at least one Virginia representative with hope.[78]

A group of six Federalists made a similar pledge, but for very different reasons; as representatives of small states, George Baer, William Craik, John Chew Thomas, and John Dennis of Maryland, James Bayard of Delaware, and Lewis Richard Morris of Vermont had an exorbitant amount of influence in breaking the electoral tie, for their individual votes could shift an entire state to one candidate or another and decide the election. Keenly aware that they would be held responsible for the outcome of the contest, unsure about Burr's viability, their votes courted on all sides, they made "a solemn and mutual pledge" to act together; aware that their seemingly disloyal actions could destroy their reputations and careers, they pledged themselves to a difficult course of action.[79] They would "defer to the opinions" of their "political friends" and support Burr as long as possible, but as soon as it was "fairly ascertained" that he could not be elected, they would surrender their votes to Jefferson; far better to have an unfit president than to be personally responsible for disunion and civil war.[80] Bayard had an additional reason for such a strategy: the best interests of his home state relied on the continuing existence of the Union. As he explained to John Adams after the election, "representing the smallest State in the Union, without resources which could furnish the means of self protection, I was compelled by the obligation of a sacred duty so to act as not to hazard the constitution upon which the political existence of the State depends."[81] Compelled to decide between loyalty to Federalism and to his home state, Bayard abandoned Federalism.

The lone representative from Delaware, Bayard felt particularly responsible for the election's outcome, for he had an entire state's vote in his power. The difficulty of his decision, joined with the controversy that surrounded it in later years, led him to document his reasoning in great detail, offering invaluable insight into the internal logic of one of the period's many personal compromises. A letter to Hamilton written shortly after the tie was announced suggests that Bayard viewed national politics through two lenses. He considered himself a

Federalist who would require "the most undoubting conviction" before he separated himself from his friends. He also considered himself a northerner whose intense dislike of Virginia seemed to make Burr the preferable choice.[82] Under normal circumstances these two perspectives were in accord, for the Federalists were largely a northern party with a particular hatred of Virginia, the heart of their Republican opposition. Bayard's problems arose when he perceived a conflict between national partisan considerations and the welfare of his state. New England Federalists seemed willing to sacrifice the Union rather than install Jefferson as president, a desperate act that compelled Bayard to redefine his priorities. Confronted with a regional faction that threatened the interests of his state, he first joined with Federalists from the middle states to protest such desperate measures. When the interests of Delaware seemed to stand alone, Bayard went one step further. As he explained when describing the violent Federalist reaction to his decision to support Jefferson, "I told them that if necessary I had determined to become the victim of the measure. They might attempt to direct the vengeance of the Party against me but the danger of being a sacrifice could not shake my resolution."[83] In the final moment of crisis, Bayard abandoned national Federalism.

A crisis justified desperate measures, freeing politicians to act as they saw fit; significantly, given the choice, most of them were willing to abandon national allies. Bayard and his five colleagues vowed to split with the Federalists at the final crisis. According to Bayard, New York, New Jersey, Vermont, and Tennessee made the same promise: they would "vote a decent length of time for Mr. Jefferson, and as soon as they could excuse themselves by the imperious situation of affairs, would give their votes for Mr. Burr, the man they really preferred."[84] As we shall see, at the peak moment of crisis, even Jefferson made a compromise. In the pressure-cooker atmosphere of the national capital, national bonds were dissolving into geographical and personal alliances.

THE BARGAIN OF 1801

The crucial moment of decision came after Federalists had surrendered their hopes for Burr, taking his continued silence as lack of interest. Rather than simply surrender the battle, some Federalists—most notably James Bayard—tried to strike a deal with Jefferson, to get his assurance on a few basic Federalist demands. Specifically, they wanted reassurance that he would support the navy, maintain public credit, and retain some Federalists in public office. Most

accounts of this key moment in the election crisis give short shrift to this negotiation. Historians recognize that Bayard decided the election but are unclear
about the precise chain of events that led to his decision, some suggesting that
he misunderstood Jefferson's response and surrendered the election under the
false assumption that they had come to an agreement.[85] The truth, however, is
far more complex—and it is Jefferson, not Bayard, who took the most decisive
course of action.

As Bayard himself later explained it, after countless ballots he made one last
attempt to "obtain terms of capitulation" from one of the candidates. Unable to
speak directly with them, Burr not on site and Jefferson maintaining a pose of
selfless detachment, he intimated his intentions to New York representative Edward Livingston—Burr's friend and supposed agent—and Virginian representative John Nicholas—Jefferson's "particular friend." Livingston denied having
any influence with Burr, leading Bayard to surrender his hopes for the New
Yorker. Nicholas, however, was willing to discuss Federalist terms and, having
heard them, declared them reasonable. Assuring Bayard that he was friendly
with Jefferson and the men who would be "about him" when president, he
stated that he could "solemnly declare it as his opinion" that Jefferson would
abide by Bayard's demands.[86] Bayard, however, refused to surrender the election without Jefferson's direct confirmation—which Nicholas refused to seek.
Before he conceded the election, Bayard wanted Jefferson's personal pledge;
once again, honor was the ultimate bond of political trust.

Unable to coax more out of Nicholas, Bayard repeated his terms to Samuel
Smith, who was likewise intimate with Jefferson. At the instigation of two different Federalists, Smith had already spoken to Jefferson twice about these same
terms, and he repeated Jefferson's comments to Bayard. Though the details of
the conversation between Jefferson and Smith have been left out of virtually all
contemporary analyses of the 1800 contest, it was the precise manner in which
Jefferson communicated his thoughts to Smith that ultimately determined the
election.[87] As Smith later recounted in a legal deposition, when he approached
Jefferson with the Federalist terms, the Virginian first declared that "any opinion that he should give at this time might be attributed to improper motives"—
in other words, he did not want to seem guilty of negotiating his way into the
presidency. Then—with a crucial twist of logic—he added that "he had no
hesitation" in discussing his sentiments privately with a friend. Engaged in mere
conversation, Jefferson then responded to each Federalist proposition in turn,
footnoting his assurances with citations to his writings that would prove his

views to the Federalists.[88] In essence, Jefferson took advantage of the blurred bounds between politicking and socializing to make an official statement by unofficial means.

The very ambiguity that enabled Jefferson to negotiate in this manner exploded into controversy when Bayard and Smith interpreted Jefferson's words in different ways. Bayard heard an official commitment to an agreement and thereby convinced Federalists to allow Jefferson to win. Smith insisted that he had simply relayed Jefferson's informal thoughts without any intention of making a deal. Of course, both men were right, as was Jefferson—in a formal sense—when he angrily declared that he had not bargained with Bayard (though he went too far when he asserted that the Federalist had invented the charge without "any other object than to calumniate me").[89] At fault were the ambiguities of a politics of friendship that blurred the public, the private, the political, and the personal. Depending on one's worldview, Jefferson's comments could be interpreted as anything one wanted them to be.

THE LEGACY OF 1800

Thus the ongoing debate over the election for decades thereafter. The very malleability that seemingly lifted a politics of friendship and personal loyalty above the political fray left a gaping hole of ambiguity at the center of the election's narrative that participants and their progeny tried to fill thereafter. This was a contest resolved by behind-the-scenes negotiations that were so removed from the public accountability of the political stage that even participants were not sure how they transpired. It was a contest that forced national politicians to declare their loyalties, rending friendships and political ties in the process. It was a contest that backed candidates against the wall, demanding that they acknowledge personal ambitions that were normally masked by a pose of detachment. It stretched the Constitution to the breaking point, hovering ever nearer to a worst-case scenario, challenging political conventions and violating political ideals and personal proprieties. And the causes of this mountain of sin and contention were personal ambition and factionalism, the ultimate bugbears of politicking among the elite.

It is no wonder that this election cast a long, dark shadow. It is likewise no wonder that this shadow had a profound personal impact on those who fell under it. For to the political elite, this was no abstract debate over the political process, no simple leap forward for the democratic process. It was an example of

everything gone wrong, a near disaster born of flawed characters, selfish interests, and shortsighted regionalism—or so it seemed to those who were there.
To national politicians, the crisis of 1801 was a direct reflection on the personal
reputations and public careers of its participants, and the image cast back was
none too flattering. And because of the linking of friend to friend in this contest of personal pledges and alliances, an attack on one man cast a wide net of
disgrace, tainting friends, allies, and even relatives by association. In essence,
the 1800 election threatened to undo a lifetime of careful attention to reputation, particularly when committed to paper as the historical record—a cruel
blow to a generation of men who were self-consciously declaring themselves
founders in the memoirs and reminiscences of their old age.

What appears to be a modern, structured party battle grounded on partisan
ideals and group discipline was thus something quite different. Forward-looking as the politicking seems—far-reaching as its impact on the political process
might have been—it was something far more anomalous to national leaders, a
highly personal struggle shaped by a series of individual compromises and innovations born of the demands of the moment. Claims about a "revolution of
sentiment"—a victory for republicanism—were more difficult to make on the
national stage, for regardless of the theoretical spin cast over the contest, a mo-
rass of accusations, ambiguities, and wounded reputations brewed underneath.

The implications of this insight are manifold. First, and most basic, it reveals the emotional reality of the event to the political elite, capturing something of the crisis mentality and sense of contingency that fueled the election. It
also reveals the cultural reality of elite politicking, highlighting its profoundly
personal nature and the ambiguities and repercussions of a politics of "particular friends"; similarly, it exposes a neglected dimension of this personal form
of politics—the culture of honor, a bundle of assumptions, standards, and rituals that shaped politicking on the unstructured national stage to an extraordinary degree. It likewise exposes the pros and cons of this personal form of politics, its malleability and ambiguity as potentially troublesome as they were
useful. Finally, and perhaps most important, it offers insight into a fundamental paradox of the period's politics, revealing how a political population backed
their way into political practices that violated some of their most heartfelt standards, principles, and ideals.

The precise means by which an anti-party population of elites moved toward party politicking is a question that hovers over the period's historical
narrative. Perhaps standards of virtue slipped a few notches—so suggests one

recent magisterial account, thereby dragging modern assumptions about political corruption into the narrative.[90] Perhaps the political elite saw the light and abandoned outmoded practices, a presentist claim that does a grave disservice to the distinctive integrity of the period's politics, dismissing prevailing anxieties about the political process as mere rhetoric deployed for political impact and little else.

In truth, the national elite did not assume that they were adopting "modern" political practices, nor did they simply toss old standards aside. They were responding to the demands of the moment one decision at a time, adapting their politics to an immediate crisis by compromising and bending—not abandoning—their political standards in the name of the public good as they understood it. To politicians firmly convinced of the righteousness of their convictions, and equally convinced of the corrupt intentions of their foes, this was a crisis that demanded such extreme action. Of course, public-minded Republican compromises seemed like self-interested factional sins to Federalists, and vice versa. Each side assumed that the other had abandoned all rules and standards, fueling a sense of crisis that stretched political and personal proprieties even more. It was their absolute conviction of the righteousness of their cause—a cause premised, in part, on the corruption of their adversaries—that enabled elite national politicians to justify their partisan politicking to themselves, and ultimately to posterity. Thus the series of accusatory memoirs and biographies that continued for years afterward, each writer justifying one man's extreme politicking, and thus his political career and reputation, by stressing the corruption of his foes.

This series of personal compromises helps explain the riddle of partisan politicking among the elite, a gradual, ground-level process of political change that has been obscured from view by presentist assumptions about the inevitability of a "modern" party politics as we understand it. To national leaders, adaptation—not abandonment—of long-held standards and practices would be the salvation of the Republic. To preserve the Republic, political proprieties would have to be stretched to the breaking point. Confronted with this dangerous logic, national politicians walked a thin line, struggling to balance their political ideals and assumptions with the demands of the moment. As the word "adaptation" suggests, they did not rush blindly into an inevitable two-party system. Rather, they forged an intricate series of compromises between their political and cultural imperatives as a ruling elite, and their desperate desire to steer an unwieldy democratic process. Imposing a modern structure on the

distinctive political dynamic of an earlier time has obscured this personal process of compromise. But examined closely, these compromises offer crucial insight into the complex dynamic of political change.

NOTES

1. This essay draws extensively on material included in my article, "The Election of 1800:
A Study of the Logic of Political Change," *Yale Law Journal* 108 (1999): 1959–94. Chapter 5 of my
recent book, *Affairs of Honor: National Politics in the New Republic* (New Haven, Conn., 2001),
develops this thesis in greater detail. On the election of 1800, see Noble E. Cunningham Jr., *The Jeffersonian Republicans: The Formation of Party Organization: 1789–1801* (Chapel Hill, N.C., 1957),
144–248; Stanley Elkins and Eric McKitrick, *The Age of Federalism: The Early American Republic,
1788–1800* (New York, 1993), 691–754; Daniel Sisson, *The American Revolution of 1800* (New York,
1974); Dumas Malone, *Jefferson and the Ordeal of Liberty* (Boston, 1962), 484–506; Dumas Malone,
Jefferson the President: First Term, 1801–1805, vol. 4 of *Jefferson and His Time* (Boston, 1970), 5–16,
487–93; Page Smith, *John Adams,* 2 vols. (Garden City, N.Y., 1962), 2:1052–62; Milton Lomask,
Aaron Burr: The Years from Princeton to Vice President, 1756–1805, 2 vols. (New York, 1979), 1:231–
95; Stephen G. Kurtz, *The Presidency of John Adams: The Collapse of Federalism, 1795–1800* (Philadelphia, 1957); and Manning J. Dauer, *The Adams Federalists* (Baltimore, 1953). For a more sectional reading of the election—though it remains focused on warring "proto-parties"—see James
Roger Sharp, *American Politics in the Early Republic: The New Nation in Crisis* (New Haven, Conn.,
1993), 226–75. Peter S. Onuf offers a provocative account of the election as a nationalizing—*and*
boundary-setting—event for the Republicans in *Jefferson's Empire: The Language of American Nationhood* (Charlottesville, Va., 2000), chap. 3.

2. On the political significance of "friendship," see Gordon S. Wood, *The Radicalism of the
American Revolution* (New York, 1992), 224, 178; Alan Taylor, "'The Art of Hook and Snivey': Political Culture in Upstate New York During the 1790s," *JAH* 79 (1993): 1382; Alan Taylor, *William
Cooper's Town: Power and Persuasion on the Frontier of the Early American Republic* (New York,
1995), 234–35; J. Mills Thornton III, *Politics and Power in a Slave Society: Alabama, 1800–1860* (Baton Rouge, 1978), 140–41. Interestingly, Thornton points out that by 1850 "friend" was a way of
masking personal "cliques," seemingly evil, oppressive, exclusive mechanisms (as opposed to regular, organized political parties, which were viewed as admirable aspects of the American democratic process).

3. Timothy Green, Abraham Bishop, John Swartwout, David A. Ogden, Edward Livingston,
Gideon Granger, and Pierpont Edwards (Burr's uncle) were all accused of assisting Burr in his intrigues for the presidency. See Matthew L. Davis, *Memoirs of Aaron Burr,* 2 vols. (New York, 1837),
2:91–98; John S. Pancake, *Samuel Smith and the Politics of Business, 1752–1839* (Tuscaloosa, Ala.,
1972), 55; Richard Bayard, "Documents Relating to the Presidential Election in the Year 1801: Containing a Refutation of Two Passages in the Writings of Thomas Jefferson, Aspersing the Character
of the Late James A. Bayard, of Delaware" (Philadelphia, 1831).

4. Davis, *Memoirs of Burr* 1:3. For other objections to Jefferson's memoranda, see Charles
Carter Lee, *Observations on the Writings of Thomas Jefferson* (1839); Theodore Dwight, *The Character of Thomas Jefferson as Exhibited in His Own Writings* (1839); George Gibbs, *Memoirs of the Administrations of Washington and John Adams, Edited from the Papers of Oliver Wolcott, Secretary of
the Treasury* (1846); John T. S. Sullivan, *The Public Men of the Revolution . . . in a Series of Letters by
the Late Hon. Wm. Sullivan* (1847). For a more detailed discussion of the response to Jefferson's
Memoirs, see Merrill D. Peterson, *The Jefferson Image in the American Mind* (New York, 1960), 32–
36, 130–35.

5. Merrill Peterson tracks the controversy until 1855, but Bayard's great-grandson republished the 1855 defense in 1907 when a Delaware newspaper published some of Jefferson's memoranda. See Thomas F. Bayard, "Remarks in the Senate of the United States, January 31, 1855, Vindicating the Late James A. Bayard, of Delaware, and Refuting the Groundless Charges Contained in the 'Anas.' of Thomas Jefferson, Aspersing His Character," (n.p., 1907). Peterson, *Jefferson Image*, 34. On Bayard, see Morton Borden, *The Federalism of James A. Bayard* (New York, 1954).

6. See, for example, Cunningham, *Jeffersonian Republicans*; Elkins and McKitrick, *Age of Federalism*, 691–754; Sisson, *The American Revolution of 1800*.

7. Studies of state-level political organization include Harry Ammon, "The Formation of the Republican Party in Virginia, 1789–1796," *JSH* 19 (1953): 283–310; Cunningham, *Jeffersonian Republicans*; Ronald P. Formisano, *The Transformation of Political Culture: Massachusetts Parties, 1790s-1840s* (New York, 1983); Delbert H. Gilpatrick, *Jeffersonian Democracy of North Carolina, 1789–1816* (New York, 1931); Rudolph J. Pasler and Margaret C. Pasler, *The New Jersey Federalists* (Rutherford, N.J., 1975); Carl E. Prince, *New Jersey's Jeffersonian Republicans: The Genesis of an Early Party Machine* (Chapel Hill, N.C., 1967); Marx L. Renzulli Jr., *Maryland: The Federalist Years* (Rutherford, N.J., 1972); Lisle A. Rose, *Prologue to Democracy: The Federalists in the South, 1789–1800* (Lexington, Ky., 1968); Arthur Scherr, "The 'Republican Experiment' and the Election of 1796 in Virginia," *West Virginia History* 37 (1976): 89–108; Harry M. Tinkcom, *The Republicans and Federalists in Pennsylvania, 1790–1801: A Study in National Stimulus and Local Response* (Harrisburg, Pa., 1950); Alfred F. Young, *The Democratic-Republicans of New York: The Origins, 1763–1797* (Chapel Hill, N.C., 1967); Norman L. Stamps, "Political Parties in Connecticut, 1789–1819" (Ph.D. diss., Yale University, 1950); Edmund B. Thomas Jr., "Politics in the Land of Steady Habits: Connecticut's First Political Party System, 1789–1820," (Ph.D. diss., Clark University, 1972).

8. Understanding this elite perspective is vital to understanding the larger democratic movement of the period's politics. As Norbert Elias points out, scholarship often concerns "itself only with the constraint to which less powerful groups are exposed. But in this way we gain only a one-sided picture. Just because in every society, in every interdependent network, there is a kind of circulation of constraints, exerted by groups on groups, individuals on individuals, the constraints to which lower strata are exposed cannot be understood without also investigating those affecting the upper strata." Elias, *The Court Society*, trans. Edmund Jephcott (Oxford, 1983), 266. See also 212, 271.

9. Adams to TJ, 29 May 1813, *AJL*, 325.

10. TJ to Dr. Joseph Priestley, 21 March 1801, *TJW*, 1085–87. On Jefferson's optimistic view of constitutional and human development, see Joyce Appleby, "What Is American in Jefferson's Political Philosophy?" in Joyce Appleby, *Liberalism and Republicanism in the Historical Imagination* (Cambridge, Mass., 1992), 291–319.

11. Adams to TJ, 14 June 1813, *AJL*, 329–30.

12. TJ to Adams, 27 June 1813, ibid., 335–38.

13. Madison, "Advice to My Country," 1834, in Irving Brant, *James Madison: Commander in Chief, 1812–1836* (New York, 1961), 6:530–31; Hamilton to Theodore Sedgwick, 10 July 1804, *AHP* 26:309–10; Hamilton, [Statement on Impending Duel with Aaron Burr], [28 June–10 July 1804], *AHP* 26:278–81. On leadership and dueling in general, and the Burr-Hamilton duel in particular, see Joanne B. Freeman, "Dueling as Politics: Reinterpreting the Burr-Hamilton Duel," *WMQ* 53 (1996): 289–318; Freeman, *Affairs of Honor*, chap. 4. Hamilton's 1804 duel with Burr, the culmination of a fifteen-year rivalry, resulted from Hamilton's criticism of Burr during New York's gubernatorial campaign that same year. Both men fought for essentially the same reason: to protect their claims to power and leadership in a political culture centered around reputation and the ethic of honor. Despite the pathos of Hamilton's deathbed plea, it was ineffective, failing to stem the secessionist impulse that resulted in the 1814 Hartford Convention. Written to a New Englander, his letter was probably aimed at the convention's first stirrings.

14. Lee to James Madison, 3 April 1790, *JMP* 13:136–37.

15. TJ to Adams, 15 June 1813, *AJL*, 331–33.

16. Adams to TJ, 30 June 1813, ibid., 346–48. "Gallatins Insurrection in Pensilvania" refers to the 1794 Whiskey Rebellion.

17. George Washington to Alexander Hamilton, 26 Aug. 1792, *AHP* 12:276–77. See also Washington to TJ, 23 Aug. 1792, *TJP* 24:317.

18. Matthew Davis to Albert Gallatin, 5 May 1800, Albert Gallatin Papers, New-York Historical Society. For other examples of pre-election jitters, see Abigail Adams to Thomas Adams, 12 Oct. 1800; William Tudor to John Adams, 5 Nov. 1800, Adams Family Papers (Massachusetts Historical Society, microfilm ed.); Gideon Granger to TJ, 18 Oct. 1800, Thomas Jefferson Papers, Lib. Cong.; *Aurora* (Philadelphia), 7 May 1800.

19. Adams to Abigail Adams, 15 Nov. 1800, Adams Family Papers.

20. See, for example, the *Aurora* (Philadelphia), 7 May 1800.

21. See, for example, Elkins and McKitrick, *Age of Federalism*, 24. Sharp offers a brief statement of each "proto" party's mind-set (*American Politics*, 8–13). Noble Cunningham's impressive study of party organization in the 1790s focuses on its mechanics rather than its logic, pointing out "in chronological sequence those political developments which suggest the germination of parties" and showing "the gradual progression of party growth." Cunningham, *Jeffersonian Republicans*, 7–8. Waldstreicher has a better discussion of the logic of "partisan antipartisanship," explaining how Republicans and Federalists identified themselves as the "real" nation and their opponents as a party. David Waldstreicher, *In the Midst of Perpetual Fetes: The Making of American Nationalism, 1776–1820* (Chapel Hill, N.C., 1997), 201–16.

22. Hamilton to John Jay, 7 May 1800, *AHP* 24:464–67.

23. Granger to TJ, 18 Oct. 1800, *Thomas Jefferson Papers*, Lib. Cong.

24. Designed as a nonpartisan system that would discourage regional prejudice in the selection of a president, the electoral college was composed of specially selected presidential electors. The precise method of their selection varied state by state; most states used their legislatures to nominate electors, while a few staged a popular vote. Each state's electors chose two men, at least one of whom could not be from their home state. A joint session of the House and Senate counted these electoral votes, naming the candidate with the most votes president and the runner-up vice president. On the electoral college, see Tadahisa Kuroda, *The Origins of the Twelfth Amendment: The Electoral College in the Early Republic, 1787–1804* (Westport, Conn., 1994); Peter H. Argersinger, "Electoral Processes," in *Encyclopedia of American Political History*, 3 vols., ed. Jack P. Greene (New York, 1984); Richard P. McCormick, *The Presidential Game: The Origins of American Presidential Politics* (New York, 1982); Shlomo Slonim, "The Electoral College at Philadelphia: The Evolution of an Ad Hoc Congress for the Selection of a President," *JAH* 73 (1986): 35–58; Richard B. Bernstein with Jerome Agel, *Amending America: If We Love the Constitution So Much, Why Do We Keep Trying to Change It?* (New York, 1993), 59–65, 150–54.

25. Hamilton to Jay, 7 May 1800, *AHP* 24:464–67. All emphases are Hamilton's. His closing— "Respectfully & Affect[ionatel]y"—reveals him appealing to Jay as both the governor and a friend. Jay was not persuaded, writing at the bottom of the letter: "Proposing a measure for party purposes wh. I think it wd. not become me to adopt."

26. On the lack of coordination in the presidential election of 1796, see Joanne B. Freeman, "The Election of 1796," in *John Adams and the Founding of the Republic*, ed. Richard A. Ryerson (Boston, 2001); and Freeman, *Affairs of Honor*, chap. 5. On the election of 1796 in general, see Cunningham, *Jeffersonian Republicans*, 89–115; Dauer, *Adams Federalists*, 92–119; Elkins and McKitrick, *Age of Federalism*, 518–28; Kuroda, *Origins of the Twelfth Amendment*, 63–72; Kurtz, *Presidency of John Adams*, 78–238; Malone, *Jefferson and the Ordeal of Liberty*, 273–94; Arthur Scherr, "The 'Republican Experiment' and the Election of 1796 in Virginia," *West Virginia History* 37 (1976): 89–108; Arthur M. Schlesinger Jr. and Fred L. Israel, eds., *History of American Presidential Elections, 1789–1968* (New York, 1971), 59–80; Smith, *John Adams* 2:878–917.

27. Charles Pinckney to James Madison, 30 Sept. 1799, *JMP* 17:272–74. See also Charles Pinckney to James Madison, 16 May 1799; John Dawson to James Madison, 28 Nov. 1799; Stevens Thomas Mason to James Madison, 16 Jan. 1800; Charles Peale Polk to James Madison, 20 June 1800, ibid., 17:250–51, 281–82, 357–58, 384–86. For a detailed discussion of electoral college reform in 1800, see Cunningham, *Jeffersonian Republicans,* 144–47.

28. Charles Carroll to Alexander Hamilton, 27 Aug. 1800, *AHP* 25:93–95.

29. Circular letter from Massachusetts Delegates in Congress, 31 Jan. 1800, in Cunningham, *Jeffersonian Republicans,* 146. Personal letters in printed form that were mailed to constituents, circular letters were largely a southern form of political communication, well adapted to a widely dispersed population. In densely populated, print-saturated New England townships, such personal appeals were unnecessary, and thus seemingly self-promoting. See Noble E. Cunningham Jr., ed., *Circular Letters of Congressmen to Their Constituents, 1789–1829,* 3 vols. (Chapel Hill, N.C., 1978).

30. See, for example, Gabriel Duvall to James Madison, 6 June 1800; Charles Peale Polk to James Madison, 20 June 1800; John Dawson to James Madison, 28 July 1800, *JMP* 17:392, 395, 399.

31. TJ to James Monroe, 26 March and 16 April 1800; James Monroe to TJ, [May 1800], *Thomas Jefferson Papers,* Lib. Cong.

32. The contest was for New York state legislators—the men who would select presidential electors and thereby determine the state's presidential preference. It is worth noting that Pennsylvania also saw dramatic electioneering innovations in 1796 and 1800, but their driving force—John Beckley—was not among the ruling elite; a man of more equivocal status, his activities were less shocking to contemporaries. On Beckley, see Edmund Berkeley and Dorothy Smith Berkeley, *John Beckley: Zealous Partisan in a Nation Divided* (Philadelphia, 1973); Jeffrey L. Pasley, "'A Journeyman, Either in Law or Politics': John Beckley and the Social Origins of Political Campaigning," *JER* 16 (1996): 531–69; Noble E. Cunningham Jr., "John Beckley: An Early American Party Manager," *WMQ* 3d ser., 13 (1956): 40–52.

33. Davis, *Memoirs of Burr* 2:54–55. As evidence, Davis cited a letter of 4 March 1800 from TJ to James Madison.

34. Lomask, *Aaron Burr* 1:239–40. Unfortunately, Lomask cites no source for this information, though it seems typical of Burr's political method as documented and described by his peers. He may be referring to Davis's account of Burr's checklist of the political elite. See Davis, *Memoirs of Burr* 2:434–35. Overall, however, Lomask offers a vivid description of Burr's politicking; many of the details in this paragraph can be found in Lomask, *Aaron Burr* 1:239–47.

35. Davis to Albert Gallatin, 29 March 1800, Albert Gallatin Papers (Philadelphia: Historical Publications, microfilm ed., 1969) (hereafter Gallatin Papers).

36. Diary of Benjamin Betterton Howell, 118–19, New-York Historical Society, in Lomask, *Aaron Burr* 1:244.

37. Davis, *Memoirs of Burr* 2:61.

38. Robert Troup to Peter Van Schaack, 2 May 1800, in Cunningham, *Jeffersonian Republicans,* 183; Davis to Albert Gallatin, 1 May 1800, Gallatin Papers.

39. Davis to Albert Gallatin, 29 March 1800, Gallatin Papers.

40. Davis, *Memoirs of Burr* 1:434–35.

41. Ibid., 1:434–35, 2:60.

42. *Daily Advertiser* (New York), 28 April 1800; *Commercial Advertiser* (New York), 3 April 1800, in Lomask, *Aaron Burr* 1:244.

43. John Church Hamilton, *History of the Republic of the United States of America, as Traced in the Writings of Alexander Hamilton and of his Contemporaries,* 8 vols. (New York, 1860), 7:375–76. The story may be apocryphal. John Church Hamilton reports that his father was on horseback because he was on his way to his country home and then offers a questionable anecdote about how his father swayed the "rabble." Hamilton's "history of the republic"—which is really a biography of

his father—is a prime example of the partisan, personal histories of the early and mid-nineteenth century.

44. On the difference between the "hands-off" politicking of the political elite and the popular politicking of lower level "professional" politicians, see Jeffrey L. Pasley, *"The Tyranny of Printers": Newspaper Politics in the Early Republic* (Charlottesville, Va., 2001).

45. Davis, *Memoirs of Burr* 2:15–17. I cannot resist including Davis's fascinating account of Burr's personnel management. Eager to gain as much financial and personal support as possible in 1800, Burr asked his assistants to draw up a list of the city's Republican elite. Proceeding down the list of names, he then calculated how much money or time to request of each man:

> An individual, an active partisan of wealth, but proverbially parsimonious, was assessed one hundred dollars. Burr directed that his name should be struck from the list; for, said he, you will not get the money, and from the moment the demand is made upon him, his exertions will cease, and you will not see him at the polls during the election. . . . The name of another wealthy individual was presented; he was liberal, but indolent; he also was assessed one hundred dollars. Burr requested that this sum should be *doubled,* and that he should be informed that no labour would be expected from him except an occasional attendance at the committee-rooms to assist in folding tickets. He will pay you the two hundred dollars, and thank you for letting him off so easy.

The moral of this political lesson, Burr noted, was *"that the knowledge and use of men consisted in placing each in his appropriate position."* Ibid., 2:16–17, emphasis in the original.

46. On Federalist attempts at democratic innovation, see David Hackett Fischer, *The Revolution of American Conservatism: The Federalist Party in the Era of Jeffersonian Republicanism* (New York, 1965).

47. Livingston to Gouverneur Morris, 2 Feb. 1801, Robert R. Livingston Papers, New-York Historical Society. Livingston was speaking of Federalist congressmen as they debated Jefferson's and Burr's qualifications for the presidency.

48. Trumbull to John Adams, 21 July 1801, Adams Family Papers.

49. *Aurora* (Philadelphia), 22 Sept. 1800, in Cunningham, *Jeffersonian Republicans,* 165. See also Old South [Benjamin Austin], *Constitutional Republicanism in Opposition to Fallacious Federalism; as published occasionally in the Independent Chronicle under the Signature of Old South* (Boston, 1803), ibid., 166 n. 84; Prince, *New Jersey's Jeffersonian Republicans,* 117–18, 155, 168; William Blount to John Sevier, 26 Sept. 1796, *Political Correspondence and Public Papers of Aaron Burr,* 2 vols., ed. Mary-Jo Kline (Princeton, N.J., 1983), 1:266–70.

50. Cunningham, *Jeffersonian Republicans,* 156–57.

51. Ibid.

52. Ibid., 163–65.

53. Ibid.

54. Davis to Albert Gallatin, 15 April 1800, Gallatin Papers. Cunningham describes this meeting as "presumably the general committee of the Republican party," thereby dismissing entirely the mindset of those involved. Cunningham, *Jeffersonian Republicans,* 180. See also Pasler and Pasler, *New Jersey Federalists,* 96–97, 107 n. 34; Fischer, *Revolution of American Conservatism,* 110–12.

55. Fischer, *Revolution of American Conservatism,* 73–74, 78; Prince, *New Jersey's Jeffersonian Republicans,* 64, 66–67, 72, 85. For an example of one of these well-choreographed "democratic" conventions, see Matthew L. Davis to Albert Gallatin, 15 April 1800, Gallatin Papers, where Davis explains how New York Republicans selected candidates in a private meeting and then held a public convention, during which a committee was "appointed," withdrew from the room, and returned with the preselected ballot in hand as though just created.

56. See, for example, James Monroe to James Madison, 21 Oct. 1800; George Jackson to James Madison, *JMP* 17:426, 460–61; Charles Cotesworth Pinckney to James McHenry, 10 June 1800, *The*

Life and Correspondence of James McHenry, ed. Bernard C. Steiner (Cleveland, 1907), 459–60; Robert Troup to Rufus King, 4 Dec. 1800; Fisher Ames to Rufus King, 26 Aug. 1800, *The Life and Correspondence of Rufus King,* 6 vols., ed. Charles R. King (New York, 1897), 3:295–97, 340–41; John Adams to Abigail Adams, 16 Dec. 1796, Adams Family Papers; John Rutledge Jr. to Alexander Hamilton, 17 July 1800, *AHP* 25:30–38; David Gelston to James Madison, 8 Oct. 1800 and 21 Nov. 1800, *JMP* 17:418–19, 438; George Cabot to Alexander Hamilton, 21 Aug. 1800, *AHP* 25:74–75.

57. Thomas Adams to John Adams, 22 Jan. 1801, Adams Family Papers.

58. John Francis Mercer to James Madison, 5 Jan. 1801, *JMP* 17:452–53.

59. For the similar use of oaths as a social glue, see Wood, *Radicalism,* 214–15.

60. Alexander Hamilton to Theodore Sedgwick, 4 May 1800, *AHP* 24:444–53; George Cabot to Alexander Hamilton, 21 Aug. 1800; ibid., 25:74–5. Emphasis theirs.

61. John Rutledge Jr. to Alexander Hamilton, 17 July 1800, ibid., 25:30–38. See also Alexander Hamilton to Theodore Sedgwick, 8 and 10 May 1800, ibid., 25:24; Robert Goodloe Harper to Harrison Gray Otis, 28 Aug. 1800, ibid., 25:59 n. 9; Theodore Sedgwick to Peter Van Schaack, 9 May 1800, Theodore Sedgwick III, Massachusetts Historical Society; Charles Cotesworth Pinckney to James McHenry, 10 and 19 June 1800, *Correspondence of McHenry,* 459–61; John Rutledge Jr. to Alexander Hamilton, 17 July 1800, *AHP* 25:30–38; Fisher Ames to Rufus King, 26 Aug. 1800, *Correspondence of Rufus King* 3:295–97.

62. Robert Goodloe Harper to Harrison Gray Otis, 28 Aug. 1800, *AHP* 25:59 n. 9.

63. Bushrod Washington to Oliver Wolcott Jr., 11 Nov. 1800, ibid., 25:249–50 n. 7.

64. George Cabot to Alexander Hamilton, 29 Nov. 1800, ibid., 25:247–49.

65. Charles Cotesworth Pinckney to James McHenry, 10 June 1800, *Correspondence of McHenry,* 459–60.

66. James A. Bayard to Alexander Hamilton, 18 Aug. 1800, *AHP* 25:68–71.

67. David Gelston to James Madison, 8 Oct. and 21 Nov. 1800, *JMP* 17:418–19, 438.

68. James Madison to TJ, 21 Oct. 1800, ibid., 17:425–26. See also James Madison to James Monroe, [ca. 21 Oct. 1800]; James Madison to David Gelston, 24 Oct. 1800, ibid., 17:426.

69. TJ, memorandum, 26 Jan. 1804, *The Complete Anas of Thomas Jefferson,* ed. Franklin B. Sawvel (New York, 1903), 224–28.

70. See, for example, Elkins and McKitrick, *Age of Federalism,* 744; Cunningham, *Jeffersonian Republicans,* 239, Sharp, *American Politics,* 249. Sharp discusses regional dissension between the largely northern Federalist party and the largely southern Republican party, but does not acknowledge such sectionalism within the parties themselves, still assuming that the nation was divided into two coherent parties—or "proto-parties."

71. Uriah Tracy to James McHenry, 30 Dec. 1800, *Correspondence of McHenry,* 483–84. See also John Francis Mercer to James Madison, 5 Jan. 1801, *JMP* 17:452–53.

72. See, for example, Albert Gallatin to Hannah Nicholson Gallatin, 5, 7, and 29 Jan. 1801; Aaron Burr to Albert Gallatin, 16 Jan. 1801; William Eustis to Albert Gallatin, 6 March 1801; John Beckley to Albert Gallatin, 15 Feb. 1801, Albert Gallatin Papers, New-York Historical Society; TJ to Andrew Ellicott, 18 Dec. 1800; Caesar Rodney to TJ, 28 Dec. 1800; TJ to Tench Coxe, 31 Dec. 1800; James Monroe to TJ, 6 Jan. 1801; Thomas McKean to TJ, 10 Jan. 1801; Horatio Gates to TJ, 9 Feb. 1801, *Thomas Jefferson Papers,* Lib. Cong.; TJ to James Madison, 19 and 26 Dec. 1800, *JMP* 17:444–46, 448; James Bayard to Alexander Hamilton, 8 March 1801; Gouverneur Morris to Alexander Hamilton, 19 Dec. 1800, *AHP* 25:266–69, 322–46. Hamilton declared usurpation of the government a "most dangerous and unbecoming policy." Alexander Hamilton to Gouverneur Morris, 9 Jan. 1801, ibid., 304–5.

73. Edward Livingston to Robert R. Livingston, 29 Jan. 1801, Robert R. Livingston Papers, New-York Historical Society; TJ to James Monroe, 15 Feb. 1801, in Cunningham, *Jeffersonian Republicans,* 246; TJ to James Madison, 18 Feb. 1801, *JMP* 17:467–68; TJ to Dr. Joseph Priestley, 21 March 1801, *TJW,* 1085–87.

74. James Monroe to TJ, 30 Dec. 1800 and 6 Jan. 1801, *Thomas Jefferson Papers,* Lib. Cong.; James Madison to James Monroe, [ca. 10 Nov. 1800], *JMP* 17:435. See also TJ to Thomas Mann Randolph, 9 Jan. 1801; Thomas McKean to TJ, 10 Jan. 1801; Horatio Gates to TJ, 9 Feb. 1801; Caesar Rodney to TJ, 28 Dec. 1800, *Thomas Jefferson Papers,* Lib. Cong.; James Madison to TJ, 20 Dec. 1800, *JMP* 17:446–48.

75. Peter S. Onuf, *Statehood and Union: A History of the Northwest Ordinance* (Bloomington, Ind., 1987), esp. chaps. 1 and 7; Peter S. Onuf, "Federalism, Republicanism, and the Origins of American Sectionalism," in *All Over the Map: Rethinking American Regions,* ed. Edward L. Ayers et al. (Baltimore, 1996), 11–37.

76. Samuel Smith to Aaron Burr, 11 Jan. 1801, Samuel Smith Papers, Alderman Library, University of Virginia.

77. All three men later denied the charges—Ogden at the urging of Burrite editor Peter Irving, Livingston at the request of Burr himself, and Bishop in response to the virulence of Republican editor James Cheetham. Though Ogden denied any connection with Burr, Livingston stated only that he had never heard Burr state anything to suggest that he would seek the presidency over Jefferson. Bishop dismissed the accusations against him as lies. On Ogden, see [Deposition of James Bayard], 1805; Peter Irving to David Ogden, 24 Nov. 1802; David Ogden to Peter Irving, 24 Nov. 1802; *Memoirs of Burr* 2:95–7, 124–26; Samuel Smith to Aaron Burr, 11 Jan. 1801, Samuel Smith Papers, Alderman Library, University of Virginia; Aaron Burr to Samuel Smith, 16 Jan. 1801, Kline, *Public Papers of Aaron Burr* 1:493, 489–90 n. 1. On Livingston, see [Statement regarding Aaron Burr], c. 1802; [Deposition of James Bayard], Davis, *Memoirs of Burr* 2:97, 125; Alexander Hamilton to Gouverneur Morris, 9 Jan. 1801, *AHP* 25:304–5; Aaron Burr to Albert Gallatin, 16 Jan. 1801, Kline, *Public Papers of Aaron Burr* 1:492–93 and n. 3. On Bishop, see Kline, *Public Papers of Aaron Burr,* 2:728–29 n. 2; Aaron Burr to Tench Coxe, 25 Oct. 1800 and Aaron Burr to Pierpont Edwards, 18 Nov. 1800, Kline, *Public Papers of Aaron Burr,* 1:452–53, 459. On intraparty distrust, see also Benjamin Hichborn to TJ, 5 Jan. 1801, *Thomas Jefferson Papers,* Lib. Cong.

78. George Jackson to James Madison, 5 Feb. 1801, *JMP* 17:460–61.

79. Davis, *Memoirs of Burr* 2:116, 130.

80. Ibid., 2:126, 115–16, 130.

81. James Bayard to John Adams, 19 Feb. 1801, "Papers of James A. Bayard, 1796–1815," *American Historical Association Annual Report for the Year 1913,* ed. Elizabeth Donnan (Washington, D.C., 1915), 129–30. See also [Deposition of Samuel Smith], 1802; [Deposition of James Bayard], 1805, Davis, *Memoirs of Burr* 2:108, 127; James Bayard to Alexander Hamilton, 8 March 1801, *AHP* 25:344–46; Borden, *Federalism of Bayard.*

82. James Bayard to Alexander Hamilton, 7 Jan. 1801, *AHP* 25:299–303.

83. James Bayard to Samuel Bayard, 22 Feb. 1801, *Annual Report of the AHA,* 131–32.

84. [Deposition of James Bayard], 1805, in Davis, *Memoirs of Burr* 2:122–28.

85. Sharp, *American Politics,* 27–33; Malone, *Jefferson and the Ordeal of Liberty;* Elkins and McKitrick, *Age of Federalism.* Malone wrestles with this in *Jefferson the President,* 12–15, 487–93.

86. [Deposition of James Bayard], 3 April 1806, in Davis, *Memoirs of Burr* 2:130–31.

87. See, for example, Malone, *Jefferson and the Ordeal of Liberty,* 505.

88. [Deposition of Samuel Smith], 15 April 1806, in Davis, *Memoirs of Burr* 2:133–37.

89. TJ, memorandum, 15 April 1806, Sawvel, *The Complete Anas,* 238.

90. Elkins and McKitrick, *Age of Federalism,* 740.

CHAPTER 5

1800 as a Revolution in Political Culture
Newspapers, Celebrations, Voting, and Democratization in the Early Republic

Jeffrey L. Pasley

The "revolution of 1800" appears to be one of the more heavily doubted historical labels in American historiography. Indeed, one might argue that the American historical profession was founded on the denial of this particular revolution. In his greatest work as a historian, Henry Adams patronized the idea of a revolutionary change as an old man's nostalgic yarn, a "claim which Jefferson . . . loved to put forward" in his dotage. Within a year of his election, Adams argued, Jefferson and his allies had reached "the limit of their supposed revolutionary projects," which in the domestic arena amounted only to budget and tax cuts. After that the Republicans rapidly moved back "toward Federalist practices," and once President Jefferson began using the powers of his office to conduct foreign policy, "it was hard to see how any President could be more Federalist than Jefferson himself."[1] Most later historians have reached similar conclusions. "There was no 'revolution of 1800' in any common use of the term," wrote Lance Banning in a typical statement. "The Jeffersonian ascendancy brought far too little change."[2]

This argument is difficult to dispute as it relates to national policy and congressional action. Any number of revolutionary steps that might have been taken were not. There was no declaratory act on the unconstitutionality of the Alien and Sedition Acts. The Bank of the United States was left in place. Tentative assaults on the independence of the federal judiciary were blunted or turned back partly with Republican votes. Radical supporters and sentiments from the 1790s were disavowed. Caution and sober second or third thoughts ruled the day.[3]

There is only one problem with this near historiographic consensus: accepting it requires throwing out much of the eyewitness testimony in the case. Though the precise term "revolution of 1800" was coined by Jefferson years later, there is abundant evidence that people who lived through the election of 1800 thought something momentous had just occurred. Writing two weeks after taking office, Jefferson explained to Joseph Priestley that they had just witnessed a literally epochal historical event: "We can no longer say there is nothing new under the sun."[4] Even contemporary commentators who were *not* the candidate waxed millennial about the meaning of his accession to the presidency. In a sermon delivered a few weeks after Jefferson took office, Baptist preacher John Leland of Cheshire, Massachusetts, saw the hand of God in the election results: "Heaven above looked down, and awakened the American genius, which has arisen, like a lion, from the swelling of Jordon [sic], and roared like thunder in the states, 'we will be free; we will rule ourselves.'" The next year Leland told a Fourth of July audience that the "late change has been as radical in its tendency, as that which took place in 1776," prefiguring Jefferson's phraseology so many years later.[5]

Others less religiously inclined nevertheless concurred with Leland as to the momentousness of Jefferson's election. The Baltimore *American* declared that no event "more completely evinces the progress of reason" than did the election. The people of the United States had faced a critical moment, and in their choice had recurred "to those first principles of social justice, which can alone sustain and perpetuate the blessings of national liberty."[6] In this view, 1800 amounted to nothing less than a second (or third) founding, a sentiment that was echoed in the lyrics of "The People's Friend," one of several popular songs that were written to celebrate Jefferson's victory: "Now ent'ring on th' auspicious morn / in which a people's hopes are born / what joy o'ersprads [sic] the land."[7]

Perceptions of revolution during and after 1800 were not limited to the victorious Republicans. Though John Adams ridiculed Jefferson's letter to Priestley when he read it in 1813, establishing a long family tradition of scoffing at Jefferson's claimed revolution, he and other Federalists back at the turn of the nineteenth century did not feel quite so relaxed about it.[8] Believing that the Republicans were Jacobin conspirators seeking a French-style revolution in the United States, President Adams and a Federalist-controlled Congress had promulgated the Alien and Sedition Acts in order to stop the conspiracy. When those efforts seemed to fail, Federalists took their rhetoric to even more apocalyptic levels, painting the consequences of a Jefferson victory as "the abasement of all that is venerable . . . the transmutation of all that is established."[9]

Such statements were no mere scare tactics arising from a bitter political campaign; similar talk continued and in some cases grew stronger after the 1800 elections. In New England, where Federalists were circling the wagons in the face of Republican efforts to win over the voters of their states, the hysteria grew almost comically intense. Attempting to rally Connecticut "to resist a foe, just entering the gates of your fortress," Theodore Dwight outlined "the consummation of Democratic blessedness" that awaited the Land of Steady Habits if it too succumbed to the revolutionary legions who had already overrun most of Europe and, in the 1800 election, achieved "dominion over a large portion of these United States." Unless Connecticut made a stand, her people faced the hellish prospect of "a country governed by blockheads, and knaves; the ties of marriage . . . destroyed; our wives, and our daughters . . . thrown into the stews; our children . . . forgotten . . . a world full of ignorance, impurity, and guilt; without justice, without science, without affection . . . without worship, without a prayer, without a God!"[10] Even after it had long been apparent that the God-fearing families of New England would survive Jeffersonian rule, conservative critics of American culture blamed Jefferson and 1800 for social and political changes that they perceived as a democratic revolution and heartily disliked. The German traveler Francis J. Grund's *Aristocracy in America,* published in 1839, includes a scene in the bar of an exclusive New York hotel in which a large company of gentlemen agree that the "god-less father of democracy . . . Jefferson has ruined the country!"[11]

How can we explain this striking contradiction between prevailing scholarly interpretations and contemporary beliefs regarding the election of 1800? That depends largely on where one looks for evidence of "revolution." Critics of the revolution of 1800 concept have always focused on Jefferson's administration, where few revolutionary developments are to be found. Proponents of the concept, including Jefferson himself, have looked elsewhere for their evidence. Rather than the putative content of the revolution, proponents have emphasized the changes that 1800 wrought on what later generations would call American political culture.

According to Merrill Peterson, Jacksonian-era conservatives who actually lived through the changes believed that Jefferson's election marked a decisive, transformative moment in the history of the Republic. As journalist and

clergyman Calvin Colton put it, the founders had created "a republican Constitution, imposing salutary checks on the popular will," which was to be filtered through multiple levels and branches of government and special democ-
racy-limiting institutions such as the electoral college. The framers of the
Constitution had no expectation that presidents would be chosen through national popular elections, believing not only that the electors appointed by the
states would make their own independent decisions, but also that Congress
would be the entity that usually chose the president, from a list set by the electors. Yet the competitive presidential elections of 1796 and 1800 created a system that, far from filtering the popular will or preventing national coalitions
and political competition, was structured by those forces. Numerous features
emerged that are now regarded as essential to free and democratic government:
political parties, competitive elections where more than personal rivalries were
at stake, peaceful transfers of power, even (in a broad sense) freedom of speech
and the press for partisan opponents of the government. From 1800 on, Colton
wrote, "The popular will in the shape of a dynasty of opinion, has habitually triumphed over" the antidemocratic provisions of the Constitution. "The government has been republican in form, but democratic in fact." [12]

We should not celebrate this development uncritically, but we should acknowledge it. While not fully democratic in the broader sense in which later
generations would use the term—most notably, only white men usually held
the franchise—American politics and government after 1800 were overwhelmingly and increasingly driven by popular voting, as even bastions of oligarchy
such as South Carolina and formerly independent institutions such as the judiciary and municipal government fell to the majority principle. This does not
mean that the real interests of most Americans, to say nothing of social justice,
were necessarily served by this system, but procedurally it was nothing if not
democratic, much more so than any other polity in the world at that time.

If we read Jefferson's infamous letter to Spencer Roane carefully, we can see
that he actually did not claim to have revolutionized American society or national policy. The events of 1800 and 1801 were "as real a revolution in the principles of our government as that of 1776 was in its form," he wrote, and in explaining this statement, Jefferson located much of his revolution's meaning in
the *means* by it was accomplished. It was "not effected indeed by the sword . . .
but by the rational and peaceable instrument of reform, the suffrage of the
people. The nation declared its will by dismissing functionaries of one principle, and electing those of another, in the two branches, executive and legislative, submitted to their election." This was perfectly consonant with his

statements to Joseph Priestley back in 1801, when he listed the "mighty wave of public opinion," which he believed had "rolled over" the country and deposed the Federalists, high among the new things under the sun that had launched a new chapter in the history of mankind.[13]

Jefferson was content to see mass public opinion applied to the selection of the president on this one occasion, but the intensity of effort and feeling that went into his election produced more general and durable changes. Foremost among these was the rejection of the principle of free choice at the higher levels of the electoral system that the founders had intended. John Adams believed that Americans would have accepted Aaron Burr as their legitimate president if Congress had selected him, but the contrary idea that Jefferson ought to be president because he was the people's choice was forcefully expressed in the popular political culture of 1800–1801. Reflecting the fearful atmosphere of the electoral college deadlock period, the Republican song "Jefferson and Liberty" promised dire retribution to anyone who tried to prevent the people from having their choice:

> Let foes to Freedom dread the name,
> But should they touch this sacred Tree,
> Twice fifty thousands swords shall flame,
> For *Jefferson* and *Liberty.*[14]

More typical than threats of violence in the popular cultural productions of the revolution of 1800 were expressions of the hope that one hundred thousand swords would not be necessary to wrest power from tyrants, that it could be managed instead through electoral politics. "Remember *election* is liberty's base, / By which noble *charter* our freedom we cherish," proclaimed another song, also entitled "Jefferson and Liberty."[15]

Though most Federalist and many Republican leaders feared overly direct democracy and deplored party spirit, they nonetheless made room for them after 1800 by framing and ratifying the Twelfth Amendment in time for the next presidential election. It required specific ballots for president and vice president. Through this constitutional change and the partisan national political culture that forced it, the electoral college was downgraded from a decision-making body and check on the popular will to merely a strange apportionment device. The ultimate role of Congress in selecting a president was left intact, but it would be rarely invoked in after years. Indeed, those who used this procedure to deviate from rather than ratify the popular vote did so at their peril, as John Quincy Adams and Henry Clay discovered after the election of 1824.

At least as important as these formal and informal changes in political structure were the changes that the revolution of 1800 wrought in the areas of voting, campaigning, and other forms of political behavior and culture. The election of the man perceived as "The People's Friend" gave a strong dose of legitimacy to democratic values and procedures, and by some measures brought more democracy in its wake than was actually practiced in 1800. Though Jefferson preferred to call his followers "Republicans," many of them were already adding the adjective democratic and moving toward the later appellation Democrats. In a recent but already classic article and book, Alan Taylor has described a dramatic shift that occurred in the "political personae" that successful leaders projected, portraying the shift as both a cause and a result of the Republican victory. Federalist politicians tended to be men who posed as "'Fathers of the People'—well-meaning superiors ready to assist their lessers" but not take their bearings from them. This could only work as long as voters were willing to accept the traditional view, prevalent in Great Britain and in colonial British America, that "social, political, and cultural authority should be united in an order of gentlemen" who "combined superior wealth with genteel manners, classical learning, and a reputation for integrity" and thus really deserved to hold power over the rest of the community. In the period around 1800, Taylor shows, such would-be paternalists were successfully challenged by followers of Jefferson, who posed, like their leader, as "'Friends of the People'—equals rather than superiors." Though often themselves beneficiaries of the new opportunities for wealth, leadership, and social mobility opened up by the American Revolution, the Federalists fell from public grace when they tried to "bring the Revolution to a premature end" in the 1790s, too openly expressing elitist values and too often looking to government power rather than popular electoral politics in resisting challenges to their leadership.[16]

The change in the way political leaders presented themselves was part of a larger shift in the practical and rhetorical conduct of politics. Campaigning grew more intense in many localities after 1800 than it had been before, and voting became a much more salient activity for politicians and citizens alike. One telling indicator of this is that post-1800 newspapers were much more likely than their predecessors to publish detailed election returns. Before 1800 newspapers rarely published full election returns, often reporting only the names of the winners and perhaps their margin of victory or some gross vote totals. After 1800, in most localities, it became common for the newspapers to print detailed tables of election results, carefully broken down by candidate, county, and township.[17]

Along with the more intense focus on voting went significant changes in the availability of voting rights and the scope and importance of the offices voters were allowed to fill. The conventional discussion of democratization in American history syntheses and textbooks locates the trend in the Jacksonian era, thirty years or so after Jefferson's election. Yet a closer look at the key changes—the rise of universal white male suffrage and the shift to choosing presidential electors by popular vote—shows that they actually occurred in the immediate aftermath of 1800, leaving only a mop-up operation for the supposed Age of the Common Man.

The typical property requirement for voting became a controversial issue in many states during the first years of the nineteenth century, and while some strongly Jeffersonian states (such as Virginia) lagged behind the trend, a burst of suffrage reform activity began that soon made economic restrictions on voting relatively rare.[18] In 1800 a majority of states (nine of sixteen) still had property qualifications, and four of the states without property qualifications limited voting to taxpayers. By 1830 only one-third of the states still had property qualifications on the books, and many of them significantly diluted the restriction by providing alternative means of qualifying to vote, such as paying taxes or serving in the militia. The vast majority of these changes were made before 1821.[19]

The switch to popular voting in presidential elections is even more closely and directly associated with the legacy of Jefferson's election. In 1800 state legislatures chose presidential electors in twelve of the sixteen states. By the very next presidential election, in 1804, four other states had switched to popular voting, and though there were many changes from election to election after that, legislative appointment of electors was never again the predominant method. By 1824 the ratio was down to six of twenty-four states.[20]

Of course, none of this matters much unless we can see that there was some discernable effect on the voters who were gaining all this new attention and power, and no such effect jumps out from the standard accounts of the era. Yet if one goes back far enough in the literature, evidence of a dramatic effect can be found. Statistics gathered by J. R. Pole and Richard P. McCormick in the 1950s and 1960s indicate that voter participation approached 70 percent of adult white males during the campaigns of 1799 and 1800 in heavily politicized states such as Pennsylvania and New Jersey, and trended up elsewhere in an "extraordinary surge" over the period 1800–1816. According to the numbers generated by McCormick and Pole, it was not until 1840 or so that the more elaborately organized parties of the Jacksonian era managed to match that record.[21]

Unfortunately, the Pole-McCormick data has been largely ignored by historians for decades. Because no states other than Massachusetts systematically collected electoral statistics before 1824, the data was declared fragmentary and shunted aside by scholars who were eager in any case to emphasize the sharpness of the break between the supposedly deferential, somnolent, top-down political culture of the founders' era and the rise of highly democratic and wildly popular "mass parties" in the 1830s or so.[22]

Future historians and political scientists should find the early nineteenth century much more difficult to ignore thanks to the First Democracy Project, a long-term effort to fill the gaps in the early electoral data that is now nearing completion. Conducted primarily by Philip Lampi of the American Antiquarian Society, the project has painstakingly compiled early election statistics town by town, state by state, year by year out of whatever sources are available: newspaper reports, legislative committee records, county courthouse archives, and even private manuscript collections.[23]

The data thus amassed place the surge of voting discovered by McCormick and Pole, and thus the revolution of 1800 itself, on much firmer and more thoroughly mapped ground (see figures 5.1–5.3 at end of this essay for examples).[24] In places as diverse as Massachusetts, Pennsylvania, and Delaware, there were similarly high and increasing levels of voter participation in an atmosphere of strenuous competition, bitter ideological division, and high turnover in officeholders. Competition seems to have been the key to increased turnout, a principle familiar to students of modern politics.

To see these changes in action, we can take the arbitrarily selected example of Lancaster County, Pennsylvania (see table 5.1), a case study that will be returned to later in this essay. Pennsylvania's governor for most of the 1790s was General Thomas Mifflin, a popular though allegedly bibulous Revolutionary War hero who tried to stay above the political fray. He was unopposed in 1796, and turnout was quite low, less than 30 percent statewide and a little under 20 percent in heavily Federalist and German Lancaster County. In 1799 Mifflin retired, and there was a bitter partisan contest between Republican candidate Thomas McKean and Federalist candidate James Ross. Turnout more than doubled statewide and tripled in Lancaster. Pennsylvania Federalists were so frightened that they used the state senate to block any popular voting for presidential electors at all in 1800, robbing Thomas Jefferson of what would have been his strongest and largest state outside of the South. Subsequent gubernatorial elections would push Lancaster's turnout even higher, peaking at over 70 percent in 1808.[25]

Table 5.1

Lancaster County, Pennsylvania, Voting 1796–1808

(Extra space demarcates founding of Lancaster *Intelligencer*, July 1799)

Year	Federalist candidate	Votes	%	Republican candidate	Votes	%	Total vote	Est. turnout
Congress								
1796	Kittera	1679	95.62	Webb	77	4.38	1756	19.52
1798	Kittera	1403	77.51	Barton	407	22.49	1810	19.49
1800	Boude	2274	54.13	Whitehill	1927	45.87	4201	43.87
1802	three-candidate avg.	2222	43.32	three-candidate avg.	2907	56.68	5129	53.06
1804	two-candidate avg.	1079	35.22	three-candidate avg.	1985	64.78	3064	30.05
1806	three-candidate avg.*	2666	59.35	three-candidate avg.	1826	40.65	4493	42.77
1808	three-candidate avg.*	4147	53.64	three-candidate avg.	3584	46.36	7731	71.50
State Senate								
1796	Burton	953	51.51	Scott (F?)	897	48.49	1850	20.57
1798	Boude	877	47.95	Carpenter (F)	952	52.05	1829	19.70
1800	Burton	2286	54.65	Schaffner	1897	45.35	4183	43.68
1802	Carpenter	2223	43.50	Steele	2887	56.50	5110	51.69
1804	Burton	1096	40.16	Mayer	1633	59.84	2729	26.77
1806	Slaymaker	2706	60.08	Steele	1798	39.92	4504	42.88
1808	Mayer*	4138	53.61	Messencope	3581	46.39	7719	72.43
Governor								
1796	Mifflin (unopposed)	1758					1758	19.54
1799	Ross	3285	59.26	McKean	2258	40.74	5543	58.77
1802	Ross	2183	42.85	McKean	2911	57.15	5094	54.01
1805	McKean*	3978	63.29	Snyder	2307	36.71	6285	60.73
1808	Ross	4089	53.19	Snyder	3598	46.81	7687	71.10

*Running as "Constitutional Republicans"
Source: First Democracy Project data

Nationwide, the trends show that the revolution in voting was as much a legacy of Jefferson's election (and its attendant state-level conflicts) as a cause of it. Voter participation rose during the 1790s in some places, but the more widespread surge occurs just after 1799–1800. In the long run, the forces that actually elected Jefferson are less important than what politicians at the time thought elected him and how they reacted to his election. In Delaware, for instance, newly confident Republicans nominated former Revolutionary War officer David Hall for governor in 1801, and even mobilized the Society of the Cincinnati (usually a Federalist stronghold) in his favor, sending the Federalists into a panicked frenzy of activity. "Let No Man Stay at home thats able to ride or Walk to the Election," wrote one Delaware Federalist. "They have got a

Jacobin President & if they git a Jacobin governor all is lost, there will be no more security for person Liberty or property in this State, Nothing but Tyrany [*sic*] Anarchy & confusion & distress." Turnout shot up above 79 percent in two of the three counties, and Hall won. But all was not lost. The Federalists took the governorship back in 1804, driving turnout even higher, up to nearly 90 percent in Sussex County.[26]

Federalists responded to 1800 and other local Republican victories by trying to adapt themselves to the perceived new political culture. Theodore Dwight's hysterical 1801 oration, already quoted above, included a stern call for Federalists to recognize how they had been defeated and to learn to imitate the methods of their foes. In particular, Dwight argued, Federalists needed to learn not to think of themselves simply as the nation's constituted authorities or as the society's wisest and best people. Instead, they needed to conduct themselves like a political party that must compete for power by gaining the people's support:

> Let us profit by the lessons which the Jacobins have taught us. We have learned
> from experience, what great things may be accomplished by a spirit of union, vigi-
> lance, and activity. We have seen a vicious combination, composed of the most
> discordant materials, agreeing to bury their individual, and separate interests, and
> passions, and uniting, with one heart, and hand, to forward by every mean, and at
> all hazards, the general plans of the party. We have also seen them succeed. That
> government, which the collected wisdom, virtue and patriotism of the United
> States originally planned . . . is the now the sport of popular commotion—is
> adrift, without helm or compass, in a turbid and boisterous ocean. To be prepared
> against the hour of its shipwreck, or to bring it back in safety to its wonted haven,
> the Federal party must also unite, be watchful, and active. . . . They must move in
> a firm, compact, and formidable phalanx, which no common force can resist, &
> no ordinary danger intimidate.[27]

One of many such calls made by Federalists in the first years of the nineteenth century, Dwight's remarks helped launch a process in which the Federalists tried to democratize their political style, if not their basic beliefs. Party organizations were created (often more systematic and hierarchical than what the Republicans had), newspapers were set up, and appeals to the voters became more common. The elitist rhetoric was toned down, and more libertarian doctrines of press freedom were espoused, at least in cases where Federalist editors faced Republican-controlled governments. The scramble for every available voter even led the antidemocratic Federalists to support expansion of the suffrage at times.[28]

Political renovations following the Republican blueprints allowed the Federalists to hold Theodore Dwight's fortress of Connecticut and, eventually, when the issue environment allowed, to regain competitiveness throughout New England and even in parts of the middle states. While never close to gaining a majority of the House of Representatives after 1800, the Federalists held well over a third of the seats during the two Congresses of the War of 1812, and as late as 1820, New York and Pennsylvania together sent seventeen Federalists to Congress. Vigorous competition drove participation levels up sharply and the erstwhile victims of the revolution of 1800 thus made a major contribution to it.[29]

What happened to the Federalists is an example of perhaps the most important and revolutionary legacy of 1800, an imitative process of partisanization and democratization that, while by no means constant or irreversible after 1800, would not be altered in its general direction until the Progressive voting reforms were imposed at the turn of the twentieth century.[30]

The party politics that emerged from the revolution of 1800 was, to be sure, a strange animal by modern standards. There were as yet no formal platforms, nominating conventions, party chairmen, paid operatives, or national committees—few permanent institutional structures of any kind—and there would not be for years. The nature of the party organizations and even their names would remain tenuous, unstable, and regionally varied for many decades. Campaigning and voting were often more intense at the state and local levels than in presidential elections. As Ronald Formisano has argued, there was no centralized national party "system" of the type that existed in 1900 or 2000.[31] This lack of the familiar characteristics of modern politics was one of the most important reasons that political historians largely abandoned the study of early partisan politics (apart from ruminating on the founders), brushing off the Pole-McCormick numbers and missing the real revolution of 1800. Failing to fit the existing models and apparently data-impaired, the Federalist-Republican era became the unwanted "stepchild of party history."[32]

With the First Democracy Project statistics on the table, however, the challenge becomes not explaining away the perceptions of democratic revolution and indications of high participation, but understanding the realities that underlay them. The first step in reaching that understanding is to abandon the idea that modern American party forms are normative or teleological.

A successful and popular party politics was created *without* all the modern trappings and institutional structures, and the question is, how was this accomplished?

The answer seems to be that political activists simply improvised, appealing for popular support with whatever means came to hand. They first politicized and then partisanized a number of traditions, institutions, and practices that were already part of Anglo-American popular culture. These included holiday celebrations, parades, taverns, town meetings, petitions, militia company training days, orations, sermons, and various products of local printing presses, including songs, broadsides, handbills, almanacs, pamphlets, and, especially, the small-circulation local and regional newspapers that sprang up everywhere after the first American Revolution.

Each region had some unique local practices that were drawn into partisan politics. In the South, the famous court-day barbecues were transformed in some locations from rituals of noblesse oblige into competitive partisan debates; in New England, the election sermon and the jeremiad were updated into orations and sermons (often delivered in church) that added partisan political instruction to the usual religious kind. One-time incidents like the "mammoth cheese" of Cheshire, Massachusetts, and the "mammoth veal" produced by two Philadelphia butchers, were very much in keeping with the general spirit of politically exploiting whatever local materials happened to be available. Also politicized were the fraternal orders and voluntary associations that were so popular in the early Republic. Nationalists trying to build patriotic support for the new nation during and after the Revolutionary War were the first to mobilize some of these practices, but it was the Jeffersonian Republicans of the 1790s who took the lead in turning them into partisan vehicles and knitted them loosely together into the decentralized but intensely committed network that became the Republican Party.

While a bit ridiculous to modern eyes, and greatly lacking in the kind of uniformity and consistency that some social scientific scholars would like to see in a party "system," this political culture was successful precisely because it was *not* a standardized national system. Instead, it was thoroughly embedded in, and built out of, the culture of everyday life. Sermons, newspapers, barbecues, and cheese had all long existed in these local cultures. What early American party politicians did was adapt these local customs into something that was politically usable. David Waldstreicher has applied the general rubric "celebratory politics" to this political culture. Though carrying forward some aspects of colonial and revolutionary politics and presaging the bloated campaign extravaganzas of the mid-nineteenth century, it was in many ways unique to the period from the late 1790s through the 1820s, and quite successful on its own terms.[33]

The various elements of the early Republic's political culture all came together in the holiday celebrations that dotted the civic calendar. By far the most important of these celebrations (out of many) was the Fourth of July, a holiday that the Republicans both popularized and made their own politically. Promoting the Fourth of July, a commemoration of Jefferson and his egalitarian Declaration of Independence, as the nation's primary patriotic holiday over Washington's birthday or some other date did a good deal of political work on its own, but holiday celebrations had many other political functions as well, some quite practical in nature. Typically included were a parade or procession; a program including music, a reading of a sacred document (especially the Declaration of Independence), and an oration or sermon or both; and then banquets that culminated in a carefully crafted and dangerously lengthy set of toasts. The celebrations energized and rewarded activists by honoring them as officials of the celebration or orator of the day; attracted votes by providing entertainment to the populace; and sent political messages through the medium of the speeches, songs, and toasts, all designed for publication.

The toasts were in many ways the most important business of any partisan celebration, and probably the most widely published genre of popular political culture. Appearing in local newspapers and often in other regions of the country, toasts served as informal platforms for whatever local community, party, or faction had organized the gathering, and they were carefully parsed for the subtle and not-so-subtle indications they gave as to the balance of political forces and the state of public opinion in a given area.

As the emphasis on publishing toasts and other political ephemera suggests, the most important and ubiquitous form that the early Republic's popular political culture took was the partisan press. As David Waldstreicher argues in his seminal description of celebratory politics, it was print, and especially newspapers, that made celebrations work as politics. Since public events like a Fourth of July celebration could be attended only by a minority of the population of one small region at any given time, even an extremely well-attended event could not engender wide concert of opinion or action unless an account of it was printed in a newspaper. Given the vast extent of the nation and even some individual states and congressional districts, we can see that party activists and

voters needed (as Alexis de Tocqueville, who was fascinated by American partisan newspapers, pointed out), "some means of talking every day without seeing one another and of acting together without meeting."[34] Publication in the
newspapers transformed toasts, holiday celebrations, and parades from quaint
local customs into vital forms of political communication.

At the same time, newspapers played the even more fundamental role of
embodying the early parties. To understand this, we must recall that American
political parties developed very unevenly. A functioning party politics came
into being long before the parties themselves became fully institutionalized.[35]
Newspapers filled many of the gaps left by the party system's uneven development, providing a fabric that held the parties together between elections
and conventions, connected voters and activists to the larger party, and linked
the different political levels and geographic regions of the country. Newspaper
offices were unofficial clubhouses and reading rooms of local parties, and newspaper columns were the major source of party doctrine and strategy for activists
and voters alike. In most communities, the local party newspapers were the
only corporeal or ongoing form that party institutions had. A subscription to
a newspaper, or regular readership of one in a tavern or reading room, was
the only real form of party "membership" that existed in this age before voter
registration.

This was as true for candidates as it was for voters. Since few authoritative
or officially sanctioned party organizations (and no official ballots) existed before the dawn of national conventions, a candidate's partisan identity was defined entirely by privately printed matter such as newspapers and tickets printed
in newspaper offices. Among the local party newspaper's most important jobs
were clarifying party labels and their meanings and authenticating candidates
on that basis. This was especially true before the late 1830s, when party organizations became more elaborate. Until then labels could be fluid and nominations of uncertain provenance. In many cases, being the candidate of a particular party consisted only in making a convincing *claim* to being the candidate,
and members of new or dying parties, or apostate factions, often had incentives
to misrepresent themselves.

Party newspapers thus contributed in fundamental ways to the very existence of the parties and to the creation of a sense of membership, identity, and
common cause among political officeholders, candidates, activists, and voters. Newspapers performed much the same function for parties that Benedict

Anderson has assigned them in the formation of national identities: the establishment of a set of common reference points—names and images of social events, public figures, or places—allowing a group of unrelated people to imagine themselves as a community. Partisan newspapers went further than merely providing reference points for an imagined partisan community. Readers got not only a common set of candidates but also a common rhetoric, a common set of political ideas, and a common interpretation of current affairs. In other words, partisan newspaper readers got the content of their imagined community life, rather than just the fact of it.[36]

Tocqueville noticed the imagined community building that newspapers performed, for parties and many other voluntary associations, even without the fashionable academic terminology. He argued that because large numbers of private, working citizens could never meet together, broad, democratic associations could be formed *only* in newspapers: "Newspapers make associations, and associations make newspapers."[37]

The role of early American newspapers in the building of political movements and associations shows in the patterns of newspaper expansion. Political crises and transformations coincided frequently with the establishment of large numbers of new newspapers, with the pace of newspaper creation spiking in such periods as the Revolution, the War of 1812, and, of course, the revolution of 1800 (see figure 5.4 at end of this essay). Taking all this together, I would argue that we should think of the early political parties and the political press not just as intimately associated but as fused, as constituent elements of the same system. This convergence of parties and the press, which I have called "newspaper politics," was most evident between the turn of the nineteenth century and the Civil War, but it remained strong in many places until the twentieth century.

One index of the importance of newspapers to early American politics was the ubiquity of newspaper editors in public life during the nineteenth century. Newspaper politics naturally placed editors in a crucial position. While newspapers themselves provided the medium for the linkages described above, it was the editors who controlled them, using their newspapers to direct the affairs of the party and coordinate its message. Each editor was his party's principal spokesman, supplier of ideology, and enforcer of party discipline in the area and political level he served. Often he was chief strategist and manager as well. He and his newspaper defined the party line on issues as they arose and maintained it between party conventions and caucuses. He defended his party's candidates and officeholders and attacked its opponents. Newspaper editors were the most professional politicians in the political system. They actually ran businesses devoted to politics, making their living from politics and devoting their time to it in a way that lawyers serving in Congress a few months out of the year did not.

Exploiting their position in the party system, large numbers of editors found their way into office, in everything from low-level patronage jobs to seats in Congress and high posts in the federal government. While a full-scale study of the question has not been attempted, it is likely that thousands of editors held office over the course of the nineteenth century, and hundreds in any given decade after the 1820s. A few examples should make the point: Andrew Jackson appointed more than seventy newspaper editors to posts in his administration. Five of the seven men that the Hamilton, Ohio, area elected to Congress between 1825 and the Civil War were local editors. There were six former editors in the Senate at one time during the late 1830s, and three in Abraham Lincoln's cabinet. As late as 1920 the influence of newspaper politics could still be seen, when the presidential election of that year pitted two Ohio newspaper editors, Republican Warren G. Harding and Democrat James M. Cox, against each other.[38]

Commenting on the mistaken network calls of the 2000 presidential election, "presidential historian" Allen Lichtman lamented that the news media had "inserted itself as part of the political process rather than as observers or analysts of it."[39] In the nineteenth century, the press did not have to insert itself: it was already there, not just influencing the political system though its mistakes and enthusiasms but acting as a basic working component whose members were fully engaged in and partly responsible for the system's political outcomes.

The clear point of origin for this system of newspaper politics was Thomas Jefferson's victory in the election of 1800, and indeed, besides democracy itself, newspaper politics may have been the revolution of 1800's most enduring legacy. One of the very few points of agreement between Federalists and Republicans concerning the politics of the 1790s was the decisive role of newspapers in determining the outcome of their struggle. In the aftermath of the 1800 election, Federalists and Republicans alike blamed or credited the nationwide network of Republican newspapers for Jefferson's triumph. A Delaware Republican attributed the "great political change in the Union" largely to the "unremitting vigilance of Republican Printers," and Massachusetts Federalist Fisher Ames agreed that "the Jacobins owe their triumph to the unceasing use of this engine." Jefferson subscribed to similar views, and to dozens of newspapers to prove it.[40]

The use of newspapers to accomplish political ends had roots in America that went back as far as the 1730s, but the press first gained its tremendous reputation for political efficacy during the American Revolution. Many of the founders believed that newspapers had been a crucial tool in their efforts to build opposition to the British in the 1760s and 1770s, and then again in selling the Constitution to the new nation in 1787 and 1788.[41] The early Congresses wrote the founders' reliance on newspapers into national policy when they created favorable postage rates for newspapers, arranged to pay certain newspapers to reprint the laws of the United States, and codified the longstanding custom of allowing newspaper printers to exchange newspapers with each other through the mail without charge. This latter practice allowed a host of small weekly newspapers, each with a circulation of only a few hundred to a few thousand, to form a kind of national network. Each printer needed to supply relatively little original material himself, but anything he did originate had a potentially large audience extending far beyond his local area. When newspapers began to identify with the Republicans or Federalists, what was in essence a subsidized national system of political communication sprang into being. The partisan bonds were cemented further by the fact that most of these newspapers were sold chiefly by subscription, with further funding coming, in time, from printing contracts directed by officeholders to printers of their own political persuasion.[42]

Newspaper politics as described above began to take shape in the early 1790s, when Jefferson and Madison recruited Philip Freneau to start a Philadelphia newspaper that would be their surrogate in the battle against Alexander Hamilton for public opinion and the soul of the new government. Though battle lines had appeared in congressional voting and cabinet infighting over a number of issues by 1791, the dissidents had no common basis for identifying themselves and communicating their ideas to the voters. The emerging party battle took concrete, public, and self-identified form only with the establishment of Freneau's *National Gazette*. A string of items in the *National Gazette*, some written by James Madison himself, boiled down the welter of arguments, preferences, and fears that government opponents had expressed to a few crisp points and gave a collective name, "Republican," to the politicians and citizens who held them. Though electoral organizing was at a very nascent stage of development, Freneau's newspaper provided the critical service of creating at least an imaginary body for readers to identify with and "join." At the same time, the furious reactions of John Fenno's pro-administration *Gazette of the United States* set up the prototype partisan newspaper dyad that in time would be replicated in every significant town and become the basic unit of early American party politics.[43]

When Freneau's journal folded in 1793, the burden of promoting what Madison had named the Republican cause shifted away from high-level statesmen and their handpicked spokesmen to newspapers of more conventional origins such as the Philadelphia *General Advertiser* (later renamed the *Aurora*) and the Boston *Independent Chronicle*. These journals went beyond constituting a mere arena for public debate and even beyond the *National Gazette*'s imaginative construction of party. They not only promoted particular sets of beliefs but, in time, particular sets of candidates associated with those beliefs, forging a critical link between the battle for public opinion and the battle for actual political power. Political candidates had been promoted in newspapers before, but never on such a sustained and ideological basis.[44]

Increasingly, partisan newspapers allowed new voices into American politics as well. Where in the past newspapers had been mostly conduits for the political writings of educated gentlemen, the partisan editors of the 1790s (especially on the Republican side) were much more likely to control the political direction of their journals themselves, publishing their own writings and often becoming committed political activists and leaders in their own right. Most of these editors were printers by training, artisans or "mechanics" who generally lacked the education, breeding, family connections, and other marks of gentility that would have allowed them to be part of the traditional "speaking" leadership class. Also writing for the Republican press and becoming political figures were a number of radical journalists who had been exiled from England, Scotland, and Ireland.[45]

Following in the footsteps of Thomas Paine, partisan printers and the immigrant radicals brought a blunt emotional style and strongly democratic beliefs into American political debate. In particular, they bitterly resented and skewered the pretensions to social and moral superiority that were increasingly expressed by Federalist speakers and writers, and they feared to attack no public figure, not even George Washington, who proved himself in their eyes an impediment to democracy and republicanism. Where colonial printers had usually at least paid lip service to the ideal of giving all viewpoints equal access, the new journals tended to be or quickly become committed, admitted partisans.

The Republicans had a small network of such newspapers in place by the time John Adams took office, with outlets in many of the principal towns. Congressional Federalists felt threatened enough by this network to try to stamp out or intimidate it with the Alien and Sedition Acts of 1798. The framers of the Sedition Act believed that Republican printers and writers were mere mercenaries, hired help controlled by ambitious Republican gentlemen. Government pressure, they believed, would quickly rearrange printers' calculations of self-interest and disperse the Republican press. This analysis of the common political activists' motives was consonant with the Federalists' street-level strategy of dealing with Republican journalists, which was to shame or threaten them into silence. This was done by publicizing their relatively low social status in the press, or demonstrating it in the streets with beating or whippings. Dueling was the honorable means of redressing a wrong from an equal, but corporal punishment was the appropriate remedy for insults that came from a presumptuous inferior or anyone else deemed not worthy of respect.[46]

This approach usually did not work, as shown by the extensive accounts of attacks on Republican editors that appeared in the Republican newspapers. Most editors regarded Federalist shaming as a badge of honor, and rejected the common Federalist view that social respectability and political leadership should be reserved for those well born, well educated, or wealthy enough not to have to work with their hands. When Wilmington printer James J. Wilson was taunted as a "damn'd upstart" and cowhided by Federalist lawyer Richard Stockton, he responded with a lengthy narrative that embraced the insult, "if he meant by it, as he apparently did, that I depended on my own industry for support, that I wished no surreptitious merit, and that I would rise, if I rose at all, by personal exertion, in an honest occupation."[47] Shaming and other persecutions only confirmed Republican printers and immigrant radicals in their commitment to the cause, because the Republican Party not only had a place for men like them but allowed them to become major spokesmen and leaders.[48]

Based as it was on a gross underestimate of the Republican editors' level of political commitment and self-respect, the Federalist campaign of repression backfired badly. Though almost all the major pre-1798 Republican journals were hit, and several crippled, by sedition prosecutions, the overall number of Republican journals and the geographic area they covered increased greatly. Moreover, the new journals were much more intensely political than their predecessors had been, and they found a tremendous source of political hay in the very "reign of terror" (as they called it) that was supposed to be shutting the press network down.[49] One of their most productive methods of defiance was simply to reprint stories of other editors' persecutions under the Alien and Sedition Acts and other forms of Federalist harassment. So former printer and current congressman Matthew Lyon, who had once brawled with a Federalist on the House floor, became a national figure through the extensive and histrionic coverage of his sedition trial and imprisonment.[50]

Exchange papers and mutual adversity also brought the Republican newspapers into closer coordination with each other. Since most newspapers had small and relatively localized circulations, editors regularly carried announcements of new journals in other towns and reprints of their "proposals" and introductory "addresses" to readers, and often took subscriptions for each other's newspapers. There were proposals, and one serious effort by Matthew Lyon's printer-son James, to create an out-and-out chain of Republican newspapers. This effort failed, and in truth it was probably not necessary. Even in its relatively informal and decentralized state, the network was already identifiable and cohesive enough that it was possible to toast and write about it as a collective entity, as the Trenton *True American* did in July 1801. Most of the journal's first page was taken up one week by a kind of review essay listing all the active "*RE-PUBLICAN NEWS-PAPERS*" across the country, naming their proprietors and assessing the "laurels won" by each of "our Editorial Brethren, in the late Republican victory." According to the *True American*'s census, there were active outlets in Portsmouth, New Hampshire; Bennington, Vermont; Salem, Pittsfield, and Boston (2), Massachusetts; Hartford and New London, Connecticut; New York and Albany, New York; Newark, Elizabethtown, and Trenton, New Jersey; Philadelphia, Lancaster, and Pittsburgh, Pennsylvania; Wilmington, Delaware; Baltimore, Maryland; Washington, D.C.; Richmond (2), Petersburg, and other locations in Virginia; Charleston, South Carolina; and Raleigh, North Carolina, in addition to other newspapers in the South and West that were "principally Republican" in their politics but "confin[ed] themselves mostly to detailing news or selecting from other papers."[51] One of the more graphic representations of the network, showing the level of cooperation, was an advertisement listing some sixty-one "agents," Republican printers and postmasters from the District of Maine to the Mississippi Territory, who would receive subscription orders for the Walpole, New Hampshire, *Political Observatory,* one of the many new Republican journals started after 1800 to help bring New England into the Republican fold.[52]

Federalists and other observers were amazed at how quickly and effectively themes, arguments, information, and particular articles moved back and forth across the Republican press network. The Irish radical refugee William Duane's Philadelphia *Aurora* was the clear ideological leader and chief source of information for the others on politics at the seat of government. It seems to have taken from two to four weeks for *Aurora* material to get over the mountains to the network's extremities in Kentucky and western Pennsylvania, but only a few days to get as far away from Philadelphia as Pittsfield, Massachusetts, and Raleigh, North Carolina.[53] This was blinding speed by eighteenth-century standards. Duane's newspaper was "the heart, the seat of life" of the Republican Party, argued the Federalist *Connecticut Courant*. "From thence the blood has flowed to the extremities by a sure and rapid circulation, and the life, and strength of the party have thus been supported and nourished. It is astonishing to remark, with how much punctuality and rapidity, *the same opinion* has been circulated and repeated by these people from the highest to the lowest." [54]

The *Courant* exaggerated, but the thematic unity shown in the various far-flung journals was striking. In early 1801, for instance, with suspicions roiling about Federalist intentions in the coming congressional voting for the presidency, one of the *Aurora*'s chief themes concerned the "Federal Firework." This was a fire at the new Treasury Department building in Washington that Duane suspected was an act of arson aimed at destroying records that would prove the accusations of financial malfeasance that Republican newspapers had been making for months. A random sampling of other newspapers shows the "Treasury Bonfire" popping up frequently in various forms, from relatively neutral reports in the *Kentucky Gazette* to dark rumors in more radical journals, which alleged that wagon loads of Treasury Secretary Oliver Wolcott's personal property were carried off just before the fire began, and that mysterious men were found working feverishly in the building, at night, as citizens arrived to put out the blaze.[55]

Yet just as striking as the *Aurora*'s influence is the evident decentralization of the Republican newspaper network. An effective theme or strong essay or telling bit of information could originate in any local Republican newspaper, no matter how obscure, and fan out from there in any direction. The saga of Matthew Lyon's time in a "loathesome" Federalist "dungeon" emanated from the Vermont press, and, while promoted by the *Aurora,* the Treasury fire story actually originated in the Georgetown *Cabinet,* a publication that was in existence for only six months. Duane also found space to reprint from many other small local newspapers over the same period, including the Salem *Register,* the New London *Bee,* the Boston *Constitutional Telegraphe,* and the Pittsburgh *Tree of*

Liberty, among others.[56] Lateral exchanges across the newspaper network were just as common as vertical ones between Philadelphia and the hinterlands. During its first year, the Lancaster *Intelligencer* repeatedly ran material from newspapers in New London, Albany, Newark, Poughkeepsie, Wilmington, Richmond, Norfolk, Fredericksburg, "Niagara," Easton (Md.), and Washington (Pa.), in addition to multiple journals in Philadelphia, New York, Boston, and Baltimore.[57]

The same principles applied to newspapers of the opposing political persuasion. Most newspapers were Federalist-leaning in the 1790s, but most older printers were commercial in orientation and much preferred to publish shipping notices, price lists, and advertisements over political essays. There were a number of virulently Federalist or anti-Republican journals, however, and these gradually developed into more of a network, especially after 1800. The creation of a rival network was critical to both the continued health of the Republican one and to the promotion of party competition. Printers seem to have exchanged newspapers across political lines, allowing them to carry on battles with enemy editors in distant towns. William Duane found Federalist partisan newspapers "very unfortunate" in their views, but opined that "these papers have, however, their *use*. They promote discussion, and by putting their rivals on the defensive, sometimes promote new facts."[58]

While centralized command and control might seem to be indicators of a strong political organization, partisan newspaper networks thrived and drew some of their effectiveness from their very decentralization. The party's general message could be filtered or adjusted to suit local predilections. Southern Republican newspapers tried to justify and refine the extreme states'-rights principles of the Virginia and Kentucky Resolutions, for instance, while northern Republican journals largely avoided the topic after 1798.[59] Perhaps responding to Federalist rhetoric about being ruled by Virginia slave lords, northern Republican editors openly expressed their antipathy to slavery, despite their leader's undeniable status as a Virginia slave lord.[60]

Reports and extracts from one section or state could sometimes be usefully imported to another region for political impact. The *Aurora* did this with its constant stream of material on the depredations of the Federalist-Congregational "Standing Order" in Connecticut, whose stalwarts—such as "Pope" Timothy Dwight—were relentlessly compared to a certain Enlightenment caricature of the Catholic Church; they became the "fiery bigots" mentioned in the song "Jefferson and Liberty," ready to "Lay waste our fields and streets in blood."[61] A final benefit of newspaper networks was their modularity. Any individual unit could be marginalized or dispensed with, as even the *Aurora* eventually was, without affecting the health of the larger network much at all.

Contemporaries were deeply impressed with what the Republican press network was able to accomplish, often flatly attributing not only Jefferson's victory to the newspapers, but also some kind of deeper democratic awakening of the people to the defense and exercise of their rights. "Had it not been for the patriotic exertions . . . of Republican Papers," declared the Trenton *True American,* "the People would have indulged their love of peace and quiet, until the yoke of tyranny would have been insidiously fixed on their necks."[62] The Reverend Samuel Miller wrote shortly after the election of 1800 that newspapers had become "immense moral and political engines," presenting a "spectacle never before displayed among men . . . not of the learned and the wealthy only, but of the great body of the people; even a large portion of that class of the community . . . destined to daily labour, having free and constant access to public prints, receiving regular information of every occurrence, attending to the course of political affairs, discussing public measures." And unlike the *True American*'s editor, Miller was no cheerleader for the Republican press. He feared that society would pay a terrible price for the influence of the new political journals, run as they were by artisan printers or bottom-feeding lawyers, "persons of less character, and of humbler qualifications" than ought "to undertake the high task of enlightening the public mind."[63]

While most Federalist and many elite Republican politicians shared the Reverend Mr. Miller's fears, political leaders and activists of all stripes learned a practical political lesson during the revolution of 1800. This was simply that newspapers were in many ways the one essential tool necessary to gain support and votes for any party or cause. Anyone who wanted to get anywhere politically knew they had to have newspapers in their arsenal, and preferably a network of them. So Jefferson's attorney general, Levi Lincoln, was quite certain in July 1801 that his home state of Massachusetts could be brought around immediately with an infusion of Republican journalism: "A few more republican newspapers and the thing is accomplished. Exertions are making to obtain them." Lincoln's exertions were part of a journalistic arms race that broke out between Federalists and Republicans after 1800, focusing on New England through Jefferson's 1804 landslide but then spreading out across the rest of the country, with town after town acquiring at least one paired set of Republican and Federalist newspapers. In the same period, numerous intra-Republican factional battles led to the creation in many towns of a second or third Republican newspaper to represent the breakaway factions. The arms race peaked just before the War of 1812, appropriately enough, as the Federalists made their electoral comeback. This basic strategy was employed hundreds of times throughout the nineteenth century, and its entry into conventional wisdom just after 1800 marks the moment when newspaper politics came into its own.[64]

Of course, as historians, we must not accept these high estimates of the democratic powers of the press uncritically. Certainly modern students of political communication would regard such views as naive in assuming a direct and unproblematic relationship between media messages and political support. Were the lessons of 1800 correct? Certainly not in their most extreme forms. But was there any truth to them? Did partisan newspapers really translate into political participation, and votes?

The First Democracy Project data allow us to test this proposition, at least circumstantially, by examining local voting patterns in areas where partisan journalism was first introduced. While more systematic research needs to be done, early indications are that the political leaders of 1800 were not wrong to perceive that partisan newspapers made a strong electoral impact. In several locations Republican voting and voting in general seem to have increased sharply after an outlet of the Republican newspaper network was established.

One such location was our chosen case study of Lancaster County, Pennsylvania, a strongly Federalist area where Republican candidates either did not run or were overwhelmingly defeated as late as 1796. When Lancaster got its first Republican newspapers, the German-language *Correspondent* in May 1799 and the English-language *Intelligencer* in July 1799, everything seemed to change.

The Lancaster *Intelligencer* was a particularly tough-minded and effective example of the breed. While not as free of advertising as some Republican papers, it was wall-to-wall politics, presenting its material with striking attention to maintaining ideological clarity, defending the party's candidates, and getting out the vote. Gubernatorial candidate Thomas McKean's circuitous ideological path to Democratic Republicanism was straightened, charges that he was an Irish Catholic were refuted, and the past anti-federalism of many Pennsylvania Republicans was leavened with their vociferous defense of the Constitution and union in the present. Republican activists believed that wealthy Federalists were trying to suppress the Republican vote by withdrawing their business from Republican artisans and shopkeepers and falsely telling poor men and immigrants that Pennsylvania's electoral laws did not allow them to vote. So Republicans used the *Intelligencer* to encourage their humbler supporters. A detailed primer on the state election law was printed repeatedly, including the qualifications for citizenship and voting, with instructions on how to prove citizenship and where and how to vote. One of the paper's many reports of Republican meetings promised an investigation of the Federalist pressure and urged "the Tradesmen of this Borough to come forward boldly, and give in their Votes with the Dignity of Freemen."[65]

The *Intelligencer*'s printer, William Dickson, was even more deeply and directly involved in campaigning than most Republican printers were. A few weeks after the *Intelligencer* first appeared, Lancaster Republicans held a public meeting to organize themselves for the campaign, and Dickson's name appeared on the committee of correspondence. A political disciple of William Duane, Dickson reserved particular disgust for printers who could not take the political heat. The *Intelligencer* ridiculed the *Lancaster Journal*'s William Hamilton, a Republican and onetime *Aurora* apprentice, for having "completely veered about" after Federalists squeezed him financially and attacked him in print. Dickson remained a Democratic Republican activist in Lancaster for years, an important enough figure that when he was imprisoned for libel in 1802, the local party held a banquet for him at the jail and timed a county meeting and celebration to coincide with his release. Dickson served as county treasurer and borough councilman during the War of 1812 era and on the town's first elected city council in 1818. Later Andrew Jackson recognized the *Intelligencer*'s long service when he appointed Mary Dickson, William's widow and successor as publisher, as postmaster of Lancaster in 1829.[66]

Voting patterns in Lancaster changed rapidly after the *Intelligencer*'s 1799 debut. Republican gubernatorial candidate Thomas McKean and the rest of the ticket did not carry Lancaster County in that year's elections, but Republicans were competitive there for the first time, and voter participation exploded, as mentioned above. In 1800 Republican congressional candidate John Whitehall actually won a majority in Lancaster itself while losing the election district-wide by the relatively small margin of 347 votes. More significantly, more than twice as many votes were cast in 1800 as in the 1798 congressional race, even though Pennsylvanians were prevented from voting in the presidential election that year. By 1802 then-incumbent governor McKean won the county handily, while the Republican congressional candidates—it was now a three-man district— averaged over 56 percent of the vote.

Although Republican schisms greatly confused the political lines in Pennsylvania during the remaining Jefferson years, the once monolithic county became permanently competitive. It sustained not only two vigorous Republican factions but also one of the longer-lasting local Federalist parties, of which future president James Buchanan was a product. Local turnout peaked at over 70 percent during the election year of 1808, when the legislative, congressional, and presidential elections coincided with one of Pennsylvania's bitter triennial governor's races (see table 5.1, p. 129). The Lancaster *Intelligencer* probably did not cause all of this, but its publication undoubtedly coincided with a remarkable outbreak of democratic partisan politics in a place where that article had previously been little known.

Some even more striking instances of apparent newspaper influence on political participation occurred as the lessons of 1800 were implemented, with both the general results and the local statistics seeming to bear out Levi Lincoln's expectations to an almost shocking degree. Some eighteen new Republican newspapers appeared in New England between 1801 and 1804, and Jefferson carried every state there but Connecticut. To name only one example, the printer Nathaniel Willis, a former apprentice at the Boston *Independent Chronicle,* came to Portland in mid-1803 to establish the District of Maine's first Republican newspaper, the *Eastern Argus.* Only two years later, he reflected that "his efforts [had] not been ineffectual." After the spring state elections of 1805, Willis printed a table showing the Republicans' changing fortunes over the not quite two years that he had been in business:

Federal Majority in 1803	4,881
Republican Majority in 1804	64
Republican Majority in 1805	1,905

Such was the "powerful effect of *correct politics*" and political newspapers, Willis believed.[67]

Though Jefferson's Republicans created the model and always maintained an advantage, the voting statistics show that both parties could play successfully at newspaper politics, and that if voter participation was the goal, it was better if they both played. This principle acted powerfully in Columbia County, New York, for instance, where the lessons of 1800 were applied with particular effectiveness. Between 1800 and 1804, first the Federalists, then the Republicans, and then the Federalists gained an allied newspaper in the county and stormed to victory in the subsequent election. The total vote in the county increased with every election, and by more than 23 percent overall, between 1801 and 1804, a period when the county's population was actually declining.[68]

These statistics should be taken as suggestive only. There were some clear extrinsic reasons for greater turnout and increased Republican voting around

1800, such as the existence of a hotly contested presidential race with a certain popular hero at the head of the Republican ticket. In Pennsylvania the heavy-handed suppression of the so-called Fries Rebellion in 1800 is said to have soured German voters on the Federalists. On the other hand, few extrinsic causes, other than the Republicans' increasing popularity and strenuous, newspaper-based campaigning, can be named for the voting changes observed in the elections immediately following 1800. In any case, no certain or one-way link can or should be made between newspapers and voting. Newspapers were only one part of the popular political culture that coalesced in 1800, with celebrations and partisanship itself—the mere fact of organized, ideological political competition—all working with newspapers to politicize and energize the nation's expanding electorate.

At the very least, the statistics are one more piece of evidence that the widespread perceptions of political change during and after the revolution of 1800 really did have some basis in reality. We do not have to give Jefferson much personal credit for this, though his ringing language and carefully shaped image as "The People's Friend" surely played an important role. Nor should resurrecting the idea of a democratic revolution of 1800 lead us to overlook or downplay the many negative consequences of the Republican victory for Native and African Americans. Indeed, the massive territorial expansion and westward population movement that followed Jefferson's victory might be seen as part of a white democratic revolution prepared to mow down everything in its path. Nevertheless, it is surely wrongheaded to follow the Adamses in pretending that nothing much happened when John lost that election back in 1800.

Figure 5.1

**Estimated Percentage of Adult White Males Voting
in Pennsylvania Gubernatorial Elections, 1790–1823**

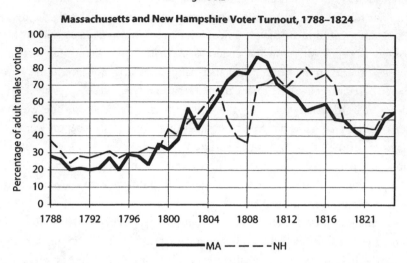

Figure 5.2

Massachusetts and New Hampshire Voter Turnout, 1788–1824

MA — — — NH

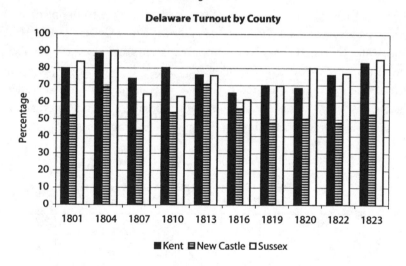

Figure 5.3

Delaware Turnout by County

■ Kent ▤ New Castle ▢ Sussex

Voting statistics courtesy of First Democracy Project

Figure 5.4

The Pace of Newspaper Creation, 1780–1820

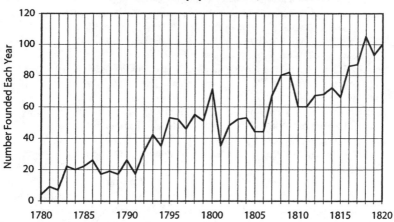

Source: Pasley, *"Tyranny of Printers,"* 404.

NOTES

1. Henry Adams, *History of the United States of America during the Administrations of Thomas Jefferson* (1903; rept. New York, 1986), 145–47, 164, 190, 226, 354. For a more extended treatment of this and most other points in this chapter, see the much longer original paper from the Revolution of 1800 conference, "A Revolution of 1800 after All: The Political Culture of the Earlier Early Republic and the Origins of American Democracy," posted on the Internet at http://jeff.pasleybrothers.com/writings/Pasley1800.htm.

2. Lance Banning, review of *The American Revolution of 1800* by Daniel Sisson, *WMQ* 3d ser., 32 (1975): 539; Dumas Malone, *Jefferson the President: First Term, 1801–1805* (Boston, 1970), 27. Noble Cunningham and Jacob Cooke also used reviews of the Sisson book to denounce not only the book but the "revolution of 1800" concept more generally. See *JAH* 62 (1975): 383–85; and *American Historical Review* 81 (1976): 964–65.

3. For instance, see Richard E. Ellis, *The Jeffersonian Crisis: Courts and Politics in the Young Republic* (New York, 1971).

4. TJ to Spencer Roane, 6 Sept. 1819, TJ to Joseph Priestley, 21 March 1801, *TJW*, 1425, 1086.

5. L. F. Greene, ed., *The Writings of the Late Elder John Leland* (New York, 1845), 255, 263.

6. "On the Election of Thomas Jefferson to the Presidential Chair of the United States," *American* (Baltimore), 31 Jan. 1801.

7. The sheet music for "The People's Friend" is reproduced in Vera Brodsky Lawrence, *Music for Patriots, Politicians, and Presidents: Harmonies and Discords of the First Hundred Years* (New York, 1975), 169.

8. John Adams to TJ, 14 June 1813, *AJL*, 330.

9. Fisher Ames, "Laocoon II," *Works of Fisher Ames, as Published by Seth Ames*, ed. W. B. Allen (Indianapolis, 1983), 207. This is a random example from among hundreds of similar statements.

10. Theodore Dwight, *An Oration Delivered at New-Haven on the 7th of July, A.D. 1801 before the Society of the Cincinnati for the State of Connecticut for the State of Connecticut, Assembled to Celebrate the Anniversary of American Independence* (Hartford, Conn., 1801), 6–7, 27–28, 29–30.

11. Merrill D. Peterson, *The Jefferson Image in the American Mind* (New York, 1960), 87–99; Francis J. Grund, *Aristocracy in America* (1839; New York, 1959), 15, 16.

12. Peterson, *Jefferson Image,* 89. On the framers' expectations, see Jack N. Rakove, *Original Meanings: Politics and Ideas in the Making of the Constitution* (New York, 1997), 89–90, 266.

13. TJ to Spencer Roane, 6 Sept. 1819, TJ to Joseph Priestley, 21 March 1801, *TJW,* 1425, 1086.

14. *Aurora General Advertiser* (Philadelphia) (hereafter *Aurora*), 24 Jan. 1801.

15. Lyrics reprinted in Lawrence, *Music for Patriots,* 163, 165.

16. Alan Taylor, "From Fathers to Friends of the People: Political Personae in the Early Republic," in *Federalists Reconsidered,* ed. Doron Ben-Atar and Barbara B. Oberg (Charlottesville, Va., 1998), 225–45.

17. Philip Lampi and Andrew Robertson, "The First Democracy Project: Politics, Participation, the Press, and the First Party System" (presentation at the annual meeting of the Social Science History Association, Pittsburgh, 28 Oct. 2000).

18. Chilton Williamson, *American Suffrage: From Property to Democracy, 1760–1860* (Princeton, N.J., 1960), 138–222.

19. Charles O. Paullin, *Atlas of the Historical Geography of the United States* (Washington and New York, 1932), 126–27, and plates 124c, 125a; Alexander Keyssar, *The Right to Vote: The Contested History of Democracy in the United States* (New York, 2000), 29–30 and tables A.2 and A.3. Keyssar's appendix on state suffrage laws is now the most convenient and comprehensive source on the expansion of voting rights in various localities.

20. U.S. Bureau of the Census, *Historical Statistics of the United States, Colonial Times to 1970* (Washington, 1975), 1071.

21. Richard P. McCormick, "New Perspectives on Jacksonian Politics," *American Historical Review* 65 (1960): 288–301; J. R. Pole, *Political Representation in England and the Origins of the American Republic* (Berkeley, Calif., 1971), 543–64; David Hackett Fischer, *The Revolution of American Conservatism: The Federalist Party in the Era of Jeffersonian Democracy* (New York, 1965), xiv–xv. The Pole data was originally published in a series of articles in the late 1950s and early 1960s.

22. Ronald P. Formisano, "Deferential-Participant Politics: The Early Republic's Political Culture, 1789–1840," *American Political Science Review* 68 (1974): 473–87; Ronald P. Formisano, *The Birth of Mass Political Parties: Michigan, 1827–1861* (Princeton, N.J., 1971); Ronald P. Formisano, *The Transformation of Political Culture: Massachusetts Parties, 1790s–1840s* (New York, 1983); Paul Kleppner et al., *The Evolution of American Electoral Systems* (Westport, Conn., 1981); Joel H. Silbey, *The American Political Nation, 1838–1893* (Stanford, Calif., 1991), 5–32; Paul Goodman, "The First American Party System," in *The American Party Systems: Stages of Political Development,* ed. William Nisbet Chambers and Walter Dean Burnham (New York, 1967), 56–89.

23. Overviews of the project were provided in Lampi and Robertson, "The First Democracy Project." The information amassed thus far can already be accessed, in raw form, at the American Antiquarian Society (AAS) in what that institution calls the Lampi Collection of Early American Electoral Data.

24. The voting information throughout this essay and in the appended charts and tables comes from the Lampi Collection, AAS. The Delaware and Pennsylvania statewide data were compiled by, and are provided here courtesy of, Andrew W. Robertson and the First Democracy Project.

25. On Pennsylvania politics during the 1790s, see Harry M. Tinkcom, *The Republicans and Federalists in Pennsylvania, 1790–1801: A Study in National Stimulus and Local Response* (Harrisburg, Pa., 1950).

26. Quotation and background information from John A. Munroe, *Federalist Delaware, 1775–1815* (New Brunswick, N.J., 1954), 208–12, 231–38. See figure 5.3 for turnout data.

27. Dwight, *Oration Delivered at New-Haven,* 5.

28. This is all detailed in Fischer, *Revolution of American Conservatism,* which sometimes exaggerates the genuineness and effectiveness of the changes.

29. On Federalist strength in Congress, see Kenneth C. Martis, *The Historical Atlas of Political Parties in the United States Congress, 1789–1989* (New York, 1989), 76–86.

30. Keyssar, *Right to Vote*, 81–171.

31. Ronald P. Formisano, "Federalists and Republicans: Parties, Yes—System, No," in Kleppner et al., *Evolution of American Electoral Systems*, 33–76.

32. Formisano, "Deferential-Participant Politics," 481. The works of Alan Taylor, Joyce Appleby, and James Roger Sharp have been lonely exceptions to the general trend.

33. This discussion draws heavily on David Waldstreicher, *In the Midst of Perpetual Fetes: The Making of American Nationalism, 1776–1820* (Chapel Hill, N.C., 1997); and Jeffrey L. Pasley, "The Cheese and the Words: Popular Political Culture and Participatory Democracy in the Early American Republic" (paper presented at the seventh annual conference of the Omohundro Institute of Early American History and Culture, Glasgow, Scotland, 12 July 2001). For other works covering aspects of this festive political culture, see Peter Thompson, *Rum Punch and Revolution: Taverngoing and Public Life in Eighteenth-Century Philadelphia* (Philadelphia, 1999); Simon P. Newman, *Parades and the Politics of the Street: Festive Culture in the Early American Republic* (Philadelphia, 1997); Len Travers, *Celebrating the Fourth: Independence Day and the Rites of Nationalism in the Early Republic* (Amherst, Mass., 1997).

34. Alexis de Tocqueville, *Democracy in America*, ed. J. P. Mayer, trans. George Lawrence (New York, 1969), 518.

35. The arguments in the next few paragraphs are made and documented more fully in Jeffrey L. Pasley, *"The Tyranny of Printers": Newspaper Politics in the Early Republic* (Charlottesville, Va., 2001) chap. 1; and Jeffrey L. Pasley, "The Two National Gazettes: Newspapers and the Embodiment of American Political Parties," *Early American Literature* 35 (2000): 51–86.

36. Benedict Anderson, *Imagined Communities*, rev. ed. (London, 1991), 62.

37. Tocqueville, *Democracy in America*, 518.

38. Based primarily on information gathered from Kathryn Allamong Jacob and Bruce A. Ragsdale, eds., *Biographical Directory of the United States Congress, 1774–1989*, bicentennial ed. (Washington, D.C., 1989). All of the data I have gathered on officeholding by nineteenth-century editors is available on the Internet at http://pasleybrothers.com/newspols/officeholding.htm. The three former editors in the Lincoln cabinet were Simon Cameron, secretary of war; Gideon Welles, secretary of the navy; and Caleb Blood Smith, secretary of the interior. In addition, Vice President Hannibal Hamlin had once worked as a compositor.

39. Jotted down by author from election night 2000 coverage on the cable television network MSNBC.

40. Donald H. Stewart, *The Opposition Press of the Federalist Period* (Albany, N.Y., 1969), 3; TJ to James Monroe, 19 Oct. 1823, Ford, 10:275; "On the Utility of Education," *Wilmington Mirror of the Times,* 4 March 1801; Fisher Ames to Theodore Dwight, 19 March 1801, Allen, *Works of Ames,* 2:1410–11; Pasley, *"Tyranny of Printers,"* 105.

41. Pasley, *"Tyranny of Printers,"* chap. 2.

42. On the various government policies benefitting newspapers, see Richard R. John, *Spreading the News: The American Postal System from Franklin to Morse* (Cambridge, Mass., 1995); Culver H. Smith, *The Press, Politics, and Patronage: The American Government's Use of Newspapers, 1789–1875* (Athens, Ga., 1977).

43. Pasley, "Two National Gazettes."

44. The basic narrative of the development of newspaper politics in the next few pages summarizes material presented in Pasley, *"Tyranny of Printers,"* chaps. 5–8. Many of the specific points and examples, however, are unique to this essay.

45. Michael Durey, *Transatlantic Radicals and the Early American Republic* (Lawrence, Kans., 1997); Michael Durey, "Thomas Paine's Apostles: Radical Émigrés and the Triumph of Jeffersonian Republicanism," *WMQ* 3d ser., 44 (1987): 661–88.

46. For a detailed account of honor culture and the *code duello* as practiced in the founding era, see Joanne B. Freeman, *Affairs of Honor: National Politics in the New Republic* (New Haven, Conn., 2001).

47. *Mirror of the Times* (Wilmington), 8 Nov. 1800.

48. For example, see William Duane's eloquent embrace of the intended insult "journeyman printer" in the *Aurora* (Philadelphia), 1 Sept. 1802.

49. Pasley, *"Tyranny of Printers,"* chap. 6.

50. On Lyon's ascent to stardom, see Aleine Austin, *Matthew Lyon: "New Man" of the Democratic Revolution, 1749–1822* (University Park, Pa., 1981), 90–130.

51. *True American* (Trenton), 21 July 1801.

52. *Political Observatory* (Walpole), 25 Feb. 1804. One version of the ad can be viewed on the author's website at http://pasleybrothers.com/newspols/images.htm.

53. Examples of how quickly *Aurora* articles traveled: "The Two Reigns," *Aurora,* 27 Jan. 1801; *Raleigh Register,* 2 Feb. 1800; *Sun* (Pittsfield), 10 Feb. 1801; *Herald of Liberty* (Washington, Pa.), 16 Feb. 1801. "Of Parties in the U.S.": *Aurora,* 17 Feb. 1801; *American* (Baltimore), 20 Feb. 1801; *City Gazette and Daily Advertiser* (Charleston), 8 March 1800. Reports of Senate contempt proceedings against William Duane: *Aurora,* 1 March 1800, and following issues; *Herald of Liberty* (Washington, Pa.), 17 March 1800; *Kentucky Gazette* (Lexington), 27 March 1800; *Raleigh Register,* 1 April 1800.

54. *Connecticut Courant* (Hartford), 18 Aug. 1800.

55. *Aurora* (Philadelphia), 23, 24, 26, 27 Jan., 3, 6 Feb. 1801; *American* (Baltimore), 26, 31 Jan. 1801; *Herald of Liberty* (Washington, Pa.), 2 Feb. 1801; *Kentucky Gazette* (Lexington), 9, 16 Feb. 1801.

56. Austin, *Matthew Lyon,* 118–30; *Aurora* (Philadelphia), 2, 5, 22, 29 Jan., 9 Feb 1801.

57. *Intelligencer* (Lancaster), 31 July 1799–6 Aug. 1800.

58. *Aurora,* 21 Jan. 1801.

59. For examples of the former, see *Raleigh Register,* 4, 18, 25 Feb., 3, 10, 17, 24 March, 1 April, 23 Sept. 1800, 3 Feb. 1801.

60. For examples, see *Intelligencer & Weekly Advertiser* (Lancaster), 19, 26 Feb., 5 March, 13 Aug. 1800; *Sun* (Pittsfield), 20 Oct. 1801; *True American* (Trenton), 15, 22, 29 Dec. 1801, 2 March, 1 Nov. 1802, 9 April, 9 July 1804; *Norristown Register,* 14 Feb. 1804.

61. On Duane's demonization of New England, see Alan V. Briceland, "The Philadelphia Aurora, the New England Illuminati, and the Election of 1800," *Pennsylvania Magazine of History and Biography* 50 (1976): 3–36; quotation from *Aurora,* 24 Jan. 1801.

62. *True American* (Trenton), 21 July 1801.

63. Samuel Miller, *A Brief Retrospect of the Eighteenth Century* (New York, 1803), 2:247–51, 252–53, 254–55.

64. Levi Lincoln to TJ, 28 July 1801, Thomas Jefferson Papers, Lib. Cong.; Pasley, *"Tyranny of Printers,"* chaps. 9–10.

65. *Intelligencer* (Lancaster), 7, 14, 21, 28 Aug., 4, 11, 18, 25 Sept., 2, 5 (pre-election extra), 9 (quoted), 16 Oct. 1799.

66. Ibid., 21 Aug. 1799, 12 Feb. 1800 (quoted); Sanford W. Higginbotham, *The Keystone in the Democratic Arch: Pennsylvania Politics 1800–1816* (Harrisburg, Pa., 1952), 110, 231, 353; Franklin Ellis and Samuel Evans, *History of Lancaster County, Pennsylvania* (Philadelphia, 1883), 216, 374, 402, 499; William Riddle, *The Story of Lancaster: Old and New* (Lancaster, Pa., 1917), 115–16.

67. *Eastern Argus* (Portland), 6 Jan., 30 Aug., 16 Nov. 1804, 4 Jan., 30 Aug. 1805. See also Frederick Gardiner Fassett Jr., *A History of Newspapers in the District of Maine, 1785–1820* (Orono, Maine, 1932), 118–19, 195–201.

68. On the newspaper situation in Columbia County, see Pasley, *"Tyranny of Printers,"* chaps. 6 and 10. For more on newspapers and voting in the county, see Pasley, "A Revolution of 1800 after All."

Part 2

JEFFERSONIAN AMERICA

CHAPTER 6

Thomas Jefferson and the Psychology of Democracy

Joyce Appleby

To speak of "the psychology of democracy" may startle readers. It may even strike some as an incongruous phrase, like the politics of the stomach or the economics of pride. I acknowledge the cognitive dissonance the concept creates; we are not used to linking a form of government with human consciousness. Still, talking about the psychology of democracy enables me to get at an elusive feature in the transformation of the United States from a postcolonial society to a democratic nation. It came to me after years of trying—often under the pressure of criticism—to express what I considered Thomas Jefferson's most distinctive contribution to the political mores of his country.

The thesis that I shall put forward is that his election to the presidency in 1800 enabled Jefferson to embark on a campaign to expunge the colonial residues that cluttered Americans' path—at least the white, male portion of them—to a democracy that was social as well as political. A student of both politics and people, Jefferson had a keen sense of the psychological component in the change from a monarchy to a democracy. He knew that it would take more than well-meaning prescriptions to change the political consciousness of his countrymen. While the colonists had never acquired the aristocratic manners or royal ceremonies of Great Britain, the ideals associated with them had exerted a strong influence on them, particularly among the upper class.

As president, Jefferson steered the country toward a fresh, indeterminate, emotional space where citizens, not subjects, might experiment with new ways of being free. Jefferson's success in promoting democracy and freedom produced a blend of egalitarianism and individualism that has characterized American culture ever since. What was truly remarkable was that Jefferson was astute enough to see that to liberate and democratize Americans would entail changes in attitudes, behavior, affect, and desire, not just opinion. Our own familiarity with democratic mores has obscured the fact that, like any set of cultural preferences, democratic ones had to be carefully learned, and then only after the habits and sensibilities of American adults—once monarchical subjects—had been eradicated.

Democracy, Jefferson realized, was as much about social interactions as political beliefs, demanding behavioral changes as urgently as new convictions. This was not an obvious conclusion, especially at a time when the most enlightened thinkers tended to talk about transforming society in strictly cerebral terms. Nor was the insight typical of reformers who are usually animated by the didactic impulse to tell people what is good for them. Long before behavioral responses became the domain of social psychologists and reality television, Jefferson analyzed the effects of the decorum of everyday life. He perceptively gauged the insufficiency of lecturing his people into progressive practices. Instead he set in motion a variety of convention-shattering initiatives, based on the assumption that the body had to move out of the box before the brain could imagine different ways of behaving.

The past for Jefferson contained frozen privileges and moribund arrangements. People lived, as it were, in a mask cut off from their real selves as they performed the parts imposed by the hierarchical institutions of church and state. He understood that formality was the handmaiden of hierarchy, heightening the consciousness of rank and promoting lower-class deference. The presumption of social superiority, conveyed in dress, carriage, voice, and gesture worked through a sociology of forms that, once internalized, served as a pervasive check to democratic action. Entirely congruent with Adam Smith's *Theory of Moral Sentiments,* Jefferson's campaign to rouse his fellow countrymen from the habits of monarchy sought to awaken the self to its routinized responses.

Richard Sennett titled his influential study on contemporary society *The Hidden Injuries of Class;* Jefferson might have written a book on the conspicuous slights of rank. His actions demonstrate his awareness that equality of esteem could flourish only after the psychological underpinnings of a hierarchical society had been deconstructed.[1] Jefferson opened his contemporaries to the sensations and feelings of an egalitarian world through action, as demonstrated in the notorious and exemplary Merry affair.

In 1803 Great Britain sent Anthony Merry as its first minister to the United States. He came with his wife. A wealthy and sociable couple, the Merrys entered Washington while it still retained its bucolic features amid the various building sites scattered across the rural landscape, to which they contributed their own construction plans by devising a residence remodeled from two existing houses. Accompanied by a parade of white servants carrying an endless succession of crates, boxes, and trunks, the Merrys made a grand entrance. Their arrival alerted the denizens of the capital city that their social betters had arrived.[2]

On 28 November, Secretary of State James Madison brought the new ambassador to the White House for his formal presentation to the president. Merry, in full diplomatic regalia, wore a coat trimmed in black velvet and gold braid, a plumed hat, handsomely buckled shoes, and that European mark of high status, a sword. The president, disconcertingly, was nowhere to be found when they arrived. Minutes elapsed while Madison looked for him among the downstairs rooms of the White House. When Jefferson finally emerged from his study through a side door, he horrified Merry, who later reported that the president was not merely in a state of undress, but *"actually standing in slippers down at the heels,"* his *"*pantaloons, coat, and under-clothes indicative of utter slovenliness and indifference to appearances and in a state of negligence actually studied."* We have to give Merry credit for that last observation—"in a state of negligence actually studied"—for he discerned that the president's attire had been well thought out.[3] He protested vigorously about this and further breaches of etiquette, but Madison, speaking for the new administration, pointedly told Merry that he could no more demand social distinctions in the United States than an American emissary could ask for equality at the Court of St. James's.[4]

While some at the time attributed Jefferson's dismissive reception of Merry to his well-known Anglophobia, it bore a striking resemblance to the behavior he had cultivated from the outset of his administration. At his inauguration he had failed to wear even the ceremonial sword that John Adams had sported four years earlier.[5] Disdaining the company of dignitaries, marching band, or honor guard, Jefferson had walked to the Capitol accompanied by friends and supporters. When he concluded his inaugural address and the crowd dispersed, he returned to his lodgings, where he took a place among his fellow boarders at the noon dinner table.

Once ensconced in the White House, Jefferson banished protocol— that system of formalities carefully calibrated to reflect publicly the relative importance of dignitaries at official gatherings. He even chose a round table for his dinners to avoid arraying his guests in any semblance of a hierarchical order. At Jefferson's parties, he who was standing nearest to the dining room door when the meal was announced went in first. On other occasions, the president was quite capable of answering the front door of the White House if he happened to be walking by, even if dressed in his lounging robe. He also abandoned the levees and receptions of the Washington and Adams eras, leaving only the Fourth of July and New Year's Day for "open houses" when all in the capital were invited to drop in.[6]

Far from indicating thoughtlessness or negligence on the president's part, these measures had been carefully considered. They provided the contrast with the Federalists that Jefferson wished to sharpen; they embodied the republican simplicity that he had extolled in his presidential campaign. More to the point of my thesis, they nurtured a psychology of democracy.

Jefferson's preference for *pêle-mêle* over protocol pulled forms out from under men and women, placing them in situations that might be characterized as coerced spontaneity. These gestures startled, provoked, pleased, and irritated, depending on one's attachment to formality. By removing the venerable props to a society of ranks and degrees, Jefferson weakened the entire edifice, for the essence of formal behavior is its routinization, its unquestioned channeling of movements into the mannerisms that choreograph status. Making men and women aware of their actions broke through the sense of naturalness that always gives force to habit. They also flushed out the political messages inherent in etiquette.

Under the veil of anonymity Jefferson called attention to the implications of his confrontations with the arbiters of polite society. In a piece in the Philadelphia *Aurora* he proclaimed dramatically that since 4 March 1801 there had been a repudiation of a "Court of the United States." "That day," he wrote, "buried levees, birthdays, royal parades, processions with white wands, and the arrogance of precedence in society, by certain self-styled friends of order, but truly styled friends of privileged orders."[7] Further to advertise these convictions, Jefferson took daily horseback rides about Washington, unaccompanied by a servant. Such indifference to etiquette disgusted Federalists like New Hampshire senator William Plumer, who confided in his diary that the president's appearance was so at variance with the practices of gentlemen that it "ill accords with the dignity of the Chief of a great nation."[8]

Clearly Jefferson had precipitated a clash of sensibilities, but he understood the political overtones better than those he offended did. Recognizing that a social system operates through habit, he exposed the routinized shame, embarrassment, envy, gratification, confidence, and fear that invisibly policed the interactions among men and women, children and adults, and social inferiors and their presumed superiors. In the economy of forms, emotions act as the switching boxes triggering movement in the service of a reigning set of precepts, just as clothes, speech, and body language provide the cues. Strengthened by daily exercise, established ways are usually strong enough to repel intellectual challenges to their legitimacy. Jefferson took advantage of a citizenry critical of elite rule to challenge the old forms and steered his countrymen toward democratic ways.

It was the genius of Jefferson to give substance to the bombast of revolutionary rhetoric by clarifying and politicizing the latent democratic tendencies of ordinary American men. As Jeffrey Pasley and Seth Cotlar have demonstrated, Jefferson's party pioneered the techniques of political mobilization.[9]

What made the Jeffersonian campaign necessary were the differing lessons America's leaders took away from their experience with resistance and revolution. Even though the violent assertions of American rights had shaken adults from their colonial cocoon, the American Revolution could still be interpreted atavistically as a recapturing of a more perfect past, leaving novelties suspect. Ancestor worship might be turned to the advantage of the revolutionary leaders themselves, as the Federalists began doing with their adulation of Washington. Like their parents, they had long lived under the shadow of seventeenth-century founders, whether the founders were the romanticized cavaliers of the South or New England's intrepid Puritans.

Once the war for independence had been won, the majority of Federalists were ready to settle down and enjoy self-government much on the social terms that existed in their youth. Those drawn to the Constitution's construction of central power hoped that the country might grow more like Great Britain as it acquired stability, wisdom, and refinement. They wanted to seal off the revolutionary era and teach a new generation of young Americans the truths of good government. Alexander Hamilton's reaction to Adam Smith's idea of self-regulating trade without "a common directing power," is illustrative. He called it "one of those wild speculative paradoxes, which have grown into credit among us, contrary to the uniform practice and sense of the most enlightened nations."[10]

For the Federalists the story of the American Revolution followed the sons of liberty from their spirited rebellion against a tyrannical mother country to their maturation through trials of fire into founding fathers. Because so much of the account was rendered through the individual biographies of patriots and leaders, it became a collective record of virtuous lads breathing the free air of a simple land—a virginal England—and growing straight enough as men to stand up for their rights. Local heroes fought a corrupt, autocratic, distant parent in King George. Opportunity was wrested from oppression, sacrifice and courage rewarded with independence. The countries in that candid world that Jefferson evoked in his famous declaration had acted as witnesses to these acts of vigorous manhood.

Not surprisingly, this version of the nation's beginnings attracted the Federalists because it was assimilable to older heroic sagas in which leaders and people were divided like actors and chorus. The past contains all the story lines for the future. Deeds of collective violence and law breaking were redeemed by demonstrations of civic responsibility. Institutions were not overthrown so much as improved, only the unworthy British custodians of those institutions being personally repudiated. Chastened by their own experience with tyrants, Americans were expected to show due respect for legitimate authority and eschew dissent, having won the prize of self-government. Above all, those who enjoyed the vote should appreciate the inherent dangers to a well-ordered state from enthusiastic excesses and unchecked impulses.

In the Federalists' drama of nationhood, Americans had fought a war for independence, a remarkable event but no more so than those contained in the ancient histories that the classically educated American gentry knew by heart. Young men became their own masters as in classical tales. Indeed, those stories provided a treasury of allusions for the leaders who presided over America's destiny in war and peace, rebellion and constitution making, supplying as well the pseudonyms of Publius, Agrippa, Cincinnatus, Cato, and Brutus. America's birth might represent a *novus ordo seclorum,* as the dollar bill proclaims, but the gentry origins of the founders guaranteed that they would be looking to the Old World for both precepts and approval. It is a perspective that Hamilton again inadvertently gave away when he wrote in a letter, "with Virginia on my right and New England on my left." Facing toward Europe could be assumed.[11]

The specialness of the United States for most Federalists lay not in signaling a new dispensation for the human race but in offering enlightened statesmen an opportunity to apply the lessons of the past. According to these national leaders, when the American colonies separated from Great Britain, they freed themselves from the mother country's corruptions, but not from the pure model itself. Their history taught that order preceded liberty and that gentlemen filtered from the mass of the voters could best preserve that order. These Federalists, true sons of Englishmen, extolled personal freedom, but it tended to be the freedom of independent gentlemen.

The first elections under the newly constituted United States gave responsibility to men who were socially conservative and intellectually unadventurous. Many, including Vice President John Adams, drew their truths from a kind of secular Calvinism, an amalgam of wisdom drawn from the classics and the Bible: men are prone to sin, and society is subject to degenerative diseases. While in Europe as the French and English emissaries from the United States, Adams had confided to Jefferson his fears that elections would open the nation to the dangers of foreign influence. "Elections to offices which are great objects of Ambition," he wrote Jefferson, "I look at with terror." [12]

The Jeffersonian idea of freedom did not accord with the public philosophy of the Federalist leaders, who viewed through classical and Christian glasses the state of nature in the unkind light that Thomas Hobbes made famous. Government offered a haven from the heartless war of all against all. When men sought to throw off authority, it was Old Nick speaking through them. Where the Federalists connected man's fallen nature to the civic duty to follow righteous leaders, Jefferson indicted just this disempowering belief, isolating it as the obstacle to fulfilling America's revolutionary potential. He blamed elitist political practices, not the fallen state of man, for the misrule history recorded.

James Duane described Jefferson as the best rubber-off of dust that he had ever met.[13] The metaphor is apt because it was Jefferson's peculiar relation to the settled and stationary—those things that collect dust—that separated him from almost all of his peers in the revolutionary elite. His campaign to reorient American voters involved cultivating an appreciation of novelty, undermining deference, and enhancing the self-confidence of ordinary white men. The natural rights philosophy did not represent for Jefferson, as it did for others, an intellectual discourse going back to the Stoics. Rather it announced a new liberation from the old social order that men, so long alienated from their true natures, might recover. For Jefferson as for Thomas Paine, the implementation of natural rights required radical surgery on the traditional body politic. More urgently, the dead hand of the past had to be lifted from the shoulders of the living. Liberation had to be actual, psychological, to become politically effective. But unlike Paine, Jefferson was no deracinated intellectual. His abhorrence of privilege and prerogative swelled within the bosom of Virginia's haughty, slaveholding elite. Anomalous as his views were, considering his birth, this at least gave him the advantage of knowing his opponents as an inside observer.

The elements in Jefferson's psychology of democracy were intertwined and overlapping, as the Merry incident illustrates. He initiated new forms for White House etiquette that treated ambassadors with the same respect as average visitors. By raising typical Americans to the same plane as foreign dignitaries, these new manners instilled self-respect and obliterated deference in the same stroke.

Like any dabbler in human nature, Jefferson understood others to the extent that he understood himself. Indeed, one gets the strong impression from Jefferson's writings that he sought to release the Thomas Jefferson in every man. Bristling with more curiosity than time to satiate it, Jefferson directed his social engineering to liberation. While virtue and responsibility were the esteemed civic ideals of the Federalists, he responded more rapturously to the freedom to explore, to express, to think, to travel, and to form opinions. Far more comfortable with fellow intellectuals, Jefferson gave no evidence of having learned firsthand what ordinary men wanted. Rather he knew better what they ought to desire, politically and socially, and was fortunate that they responded to his didactic program.

During his years as American minister in Paris, Jefferson became fascinated with the idea of replacing the tacit consent of the governed with a genuine, explicit endorsement of current laws. "The earth belongs in usufruct to the living," he wrote Madison. Then, taking the proposition quite literally, he set about calculating the optimal space of years between appeals to the electorate if each generation were to hold its own referendum on the body of legislation regulating their lives. His absorption with this idea exposed his penchant for acting on a philosophical proposition. In many ways a truism, this assertion about the proprietorship of the living prompted Jefferson to nudge his correspondents with provocative proposals about regular plebiscites to ensure the living generation's active consent to laws.[14] Viewed as capricious even by his close associates, the notion makes sense within the concept of a psychology of democracy. In going to the polls to register approval of past legislation, American citizens would be actively reclaiming authority over all of the institutions that made a claim to their loyalty. As in the philosophical treatises of Hobbes and Locke, all obligations would be voluntarily assumed.

Working compatibly with the proprietorship of the living, the expectation of inexorable improvement undercut the importance of past knowledge, an attitude Jefferson nicely epitomized when he hailed the principle of representative government as a stunning, modern reworking of republican institutions.

"The introduction of this new principle of representative democracy," he said, "has rendered useless almost everything written before on the structure of government." And then, delivering the coup de grace to classical learning, he added that this fact "in a great measure relieves our regret if the political writings of Aristotle, or of any other ancient, have been lost." [15] Obeisance to the past was exactly the kind of disempowering emotion that Jefferson isolated and attacked. In language, too, he saw the past's restrictive force. If existing laws constrained each cohort of the living, how much more profoundly inhibiting was the conceptual vocabulary that each child inherited through language?

Jefferson targeted the purist as the enemy of linguistic freedom. Dilating on two words he had just learned, purism and neologism, he announced, "I am no friend, therefore, to what is called Purism, but a zealous one to the Neology which has introduced these two new words without any authority of any dictionary." "I consider purism," he went on to say, "as destroying the verve and beauty of the language," while neology "improves both and adds to its copiousness." [16] In the purist Jefferson espied the snob and the expert, two social arbiters that created distance among men—and we must acknowledge that only men rose to the level of political concern for him. Here the aesthete and the scholar worked at odds with Jefferson, the political leader. He unambiguously strove to reduce those gulfs between men that slowed the progress of democratic practices, not to mention attitudes. Language, that most human of all endowments, carried with it the power to humble those who used it poorly. Inadequate schooling, always productive of humility, stood in the way of that confidence in one's innate abilities that he associated with democracy. Despite his own mastery as a stylist, he reacted viscerally to the conservatism of grammarians, recognizing in "purism" an authority arrogated by those who knew how to speak correctly, even as they actually thought within a tiresomely conventional social idiom.

Even the lexicon of diplomatic negotiations carried subtle messages for Jefferson. Working over a draft treaty sent to him by John Adams in 1785, he replaced the word "necessities" with "comforts." The new American nation would establish commercial treaties on the basis of exchanging comforts, not necessities or luxuries, categories appropriate for the poor and wealthy but not the average American he addressed. [17] Charles Ingersoll, an ardent Jeffersonian, gives us an idea of just how closely the concept of comfort became associated with the United States. Addressing the American Philosophical Society in 1823, Ingersoll announced, "Where American ingenuity has been put to trial it has never failed. In all the useful arts, and in the philosophy of comfort—that word which cannot be translated into any other language, and which . . . was reserved for maturity in America, we have no superiors." [18] Like Jefferson, Ingersoll read the future through the preferences and accomplishments of ordinary men.

Imagining free conversation as the source of innovations in language, Jefferson called society the workshop for words while dictionaries were but the repositories of those terms already legitimated by usage.[19] In his own day the principal neologisms came from variations on the suffix "ism." Proliferating much as "wise" flourished among us two decades ago (as in language-wise or relationship-wise), the new conceptual universe of "isms" suited Jefferson to a T. In a democratic society he saw that shared conviction—the "isms"—could create political affinities as easily as economic interests or inherited allegiances could.

Sensing on another occasion that his Federalist contemporaries were trying to elevate the new U.S. Constitution into a national shrine, Jefferson ridiculed those who looked on constitutions with "sanctimonious reverence and deemed them like the Ark of the Covenant too sacred to be touched." He touted his party as following "the guidance of . . . theory." [20] In countries "left free," the forms of social existence would be emergent and fluid. Without set practices, enduring laws, revered constitutions, and confining vocabularies, experience itself would furnish the mind with the material for making decisions. One can see in all these assertions the source of Jefferson's enduring appeal, for he articulated the values that continue to resonate today, with the less happy corollary that his success has encouraged an uncritical acceptance of their underlying assumptions.

The democratic sentiments that Jefferson expressed hardly compute with the prudish attitudes he inculcated in his daughters or the strict control he maintained over all the animate subjects and inanimate objects that filled Monticello. Did chucking out social protocols offer release from the tensions of his own legendary discipline? Or were relaxed manners and what today we would call self-actualization the logical extensions for him of his liberal commitments? An avid consumer and inveterate plantation improver, Jefferson may have detected in the tempo of the market a dynamic compatible with democratic practices. Neither slaves nor the members of the female sex could quite march to the beat of this drum, a fact he failed to discern as social when he called on nature to do the necessary discriminating. At a distance of two centuries, we can see that a distaste for racial mixing and emancipated women marked the limits of his social imagination.

Jefferson's championing of innovation cast him onto an uncharted road, totally off the map of the Federalists' path to stability. Thrusting himself against the common conviction that the state of human knowledge was optimal, that what was known was the sum total of what could be known, he conjured up a social world as yet unexplored and unexperienced. The French Revolution played an important part in this story. Its opening events in the spring and summer of 1789 sent Jefferson back to the United States thrilled with the swift translation of Enlightenment thought into revolutionary action. His timing could not have been worse, for in the temporary American capital of New York he discovered in George Washington's official family only elitists busy congratulating themselves on having put the lid on the same democratic impulses that had recharged Jefferson's commitment to change. At dinner parties he remembered that he found himself the only advocate of popular government.[21]

What the French Revolution offered Jefferson and those who rallied to his cause was the inspiration for a different understanding of the American Revolution, one that turned it into a rejection of the past, a rebellion of the spirit, a revolt against traditional sensibilities. The execution of Louis XVI energized a new generation of political aspirants already predisposed to attack Washington's pro-British policies. With act two running in France, the American Revolution could be reinterpreted as the opening of a drama about human liberation. The intoxicating cry of "liberty, equality, and fraternity" drowned out the sober invocation of "a more perfect union." Unbounded approval and dumbstruck horror emerged swiftly once word reached the United States that the French had killed a king and formed a republic. The equally astounding news that the French armies had defeated the Prussians at Valmy thrilled Jefferson supporters, with its proof that soldiers led by lawyers, saddlers, and stonecutters could defeat one headed by noblemen.

Writing to Adams when they resumed their friendship after 1813, Jefferson unequivocally described their respective parties as "the enemies of reform" and its champions, the two sides splitting on the question of "the improvability of the human mind, in science, in ethics, in government." "Those who advocated reformation of institutions, pari passu, with the progress of science," he lectured Adams, "maintained that no definite limits could be assigned to that progress."[22] Extolling the present while predicting an utterly new future,

Jefferson dispensed confidence to those who lacked both a knowledge of history and a vivid connection to the past through a distinguished family line. As strictly as any French *philosophe,* Jefferson marked his own age as a great divide. Writing to James Madison, he banished the legitimacy of force in international relations to "the dark ages which intervened between ancient and modern civilization."[23]

Having laid out my claim that Jefferson launched a campaign to detach American mores from their aristocratic British moorings with his psychology of democracy, I would like to speculate about the source of his animus to ceremonial formality. It is rather perplexing since he loved so dearly the embellishments of European culture—its music, architecture, literature, decorative arts, and salon sociability. Yet he evidently walled these tastes off from his political goals. Perhaps ordinary American householders—disciplined, unassuming, responsible—became Jefferson's ideal of democratic citizenship. Certainly common white men and women astounded foreign visitors with their intelligence, their self-assertiveness, and their disinclination to be taken for servants.[24] Rather than chafe at the brashness of average Americans, like many of his gentry associates, Jefferson politicized these qualities. It would be hard to find in his voluminous correspondence any dismissive statement about those of middling and lower rank. He saved his barbs for the grandees of Tidewater Virginia, who were capable of showing cold contempt to those beneath them.

Most probably Jefferson's impressions of lower-class behavior came to him circuitously, through the Scottish Common Sense thinkers who had incorporated the rationality displayed by untutored market participants into their new concept of commercial society. Another source for his iconoclastic views might have been the contrast that his much admired father offered to the haughty ways of his mother's Randolph relatives. From his father's successful exertions on the Virginia frontier, perhaps a young Jefferson crafted a model for all bootstrapping white men. While he discussed the fate of the African Americans in his midst with perceptive detachment, ordinary white men aroused his reformist passions. Without being able to identify with them, Jefferson abstracted their virtues into a vision of a liberal, progressive democracy.

Three aspects of Jefferson's own psychology figure in his engagement with a psychology for a democratic people. They all deal with absences: his inattentiveness to the problem of order; his lack of concern about measuring up to

European standards; and his apparent indifference to sneers about the femininity of his political style. Working together, these negative qualities sealed him off from worries and insults that might have inhibited other men. To start with the issue of order, most of America's revolutionary leaders became apprehensive at any sign of instability, as witness their reactions to Shays' Rebellion. When in 1786 an armed band of indebted farmers in western Massachusetts closed the county courts to prevent foreclosure proceedings, they frightened no less a cool head than George Washington. Jefferson, who heard the news in Paris, responded differently. He interpreted the little rebellion as a healthy outburst, penning his famous lines: "The tree of liberty must be refreshed from time to time with the blood of patriots and tyrants. It is it's natural manure." [25]

Achieving order had no salience for Jefferson, either as a goal or a problem. He believed in the self-regulating capacities of ordinary men, subscribing to the distinction Paine made in the opening of *Common Sense,* where he wrote, "society is produced by our wants, and government by our wickedness; the former promotes our happiness *positively* by uniting our affections, the latter *negatively* by restraining our vices." [26] Beneath government and holding it up was a natural social harmony, a conviction totally different from the view that it took government to enable people to cooperate. This indifference to ordering people, so strange in a slaveholder, left Jefferson unsympathetic to the anxieties, not to mention the accomplishments, of the Federalists, or even to the concerns of his great friend and collaborator, James Madison. Much like Jean Jacques Rousseau, Jefferson blamed the artificial inventions of rank and the overweening arrogance of authority for interfering with men's natural goodness. Nature, on the other hand, had barred women and blacks from the freemasonry of equals that he esteemed. In raising nature to this pitch of social authenticity, Jefferson was closing the doors to critical thinking about race and gender.

Jefferson was unfazed by fears of being provincial. Much of the presidential formality of Washington and Adams can be attributed to their longing to appear correct in the eyes of Europeans. Jefferson flouted the rules of etiquette and abandoned protocol when he assumed office. He threw open the White House to the general public long before Andrew Jackson did. His lack of formality—what some called his negligence about forms and dress—outraged the Federalists. It violated their sense of propriety and affronted their sensibilities. (Those who are "proper" tend to invest the quality with great importance.) One senses the parochial desire to avoid criticism—or worse, ridicule—from their unacknowledged cosmopolitan mentors in Washington's elaborate receptions and John Adams's fretting over the proper way to address officials. Jefferson, by contrast, gloried in his rejection of ostentation, as his Philadelphia *Aurora* article indicated, laying it at the feet of "certain self-styled friends of order, but truly styled friends of privileged orders."[27]

From the point of view of Jefferson's "self-styled friends of order," widespread white male suffrage was laudatory as long as the common people deferred to the political wisdom of their superiors. It was exactly the removal of crucial areas of national governance from vulgar majorities in the individual states that had recommended the new Constitution. An elite leadership, filtered for talent, probity, and virtue, would reclaim a reputation that had been sullied by the excessive democratic outbursts of the revolutionary period. The decorum, formality, even the secrecy, of Washington's two administrations embodied the political mores of an American gentry eager to stabilize the structure of government with time-honored hierarchies of authority. These leaders deliberately distanced themselves from those who simply voted. To inspire awe was to elicit compliance with measures deemed beyond the ken of plain voters. Without the Federalists' goals and devoid of their provincial social attitudes, Jefferson could chart a fresh course for the nation.

One more feature of Jefferson's character compels our attention: his indifference to proving his manhood. Defenders of the status quo invariably equate change with challenges to gender roles. The concept of democracy drew many egregious characterizations from Federalists, and a lack of virility was one of them. Despite Jefferson's hostility to the civic participation of women, his psychology of democracy had a feminine undercurrent, with its egalitarian spirit and evocation of man's peaceful, benign qualities. Hamilton referred to Jefferson's "womanish" attachment to the French Revolution. The flamboyant general James Wilkinson said "that the very existence of an army and democracy was incompatible; that republics were ungrateful; jealous of . . . military merit," and stingy. At a time when political duels proliferated, as partisans proved their manhood along with their political probity, Jefferson counseled his grandson to avoid duels and certainly not to fight to defend his grandfather's name, because, as he explained, it lies "in the hands of my fellow citizens at large, and will be consigned to honor or infamy be the verdict of the republican mass of our country, according to what themselves will have seen, not what their enemies and mine shall have said."[28]

The peculiar fusion of egalitarianism and individualism that has long typified American political values grew directly out of Jefferson's understanding of the psychology of democracy. Unlike classical political philosophy, which linked democracy to the collective will of the people, Jefferson disaggregated the people into a majority of individuals, each seeking to pursue happiness in his own way. Emphasizing liberation over collective power, he idealized democracy as a system for nourishing curiosity, talent, and personal responsibility. While the French revolutionaries across the Atlantic focused on the general will and strove to create the corporate entity of the nation, Americans created a version of republicanism that was highly individualistic. Their ideal was man the doer, the inventor, the adapter, the improver—*homo faber*—the universal man hidden from himself by tyrants, priests, and overlords. The conflict between the good of the whole and the interests of individuals was washed away by the facile assumption that all individuals had the same interests—that of making free choices. With perfect equanimity Jefferson could write, "so invariable do the laws of nature create our duties and interest, that when they seem to be at variance, we might suspect some fallacy in our reasoning."[29]

The enemies of Jefferson's program were hostile to parity, unwilling to think and feel as equals with their fellow men. The way their snobbery was transformed into political wisdom through the imaginative devices of culture outraged the new president. Helpless to change the elitism of the elite, Jefferson sought instead to limit their scope of power. Once in office, he dismantled as much of the Federalist armature for a vigorous central government as was practical. He cut taxes, reduced the size of the civil service, and let centralizing laws lapse.

Jefferson's efforts to contract the size of government and the revenues that supported it shrank the overall importance of government, redistributing attention away from the polity toward the economy, where everyone—women, adolescents, the propertyless, and the enslaved—had a place. While Jefferson certainly never sought an enlarged public role for either women or African Americans, his campaign to level hierarchies worked in diverse ways to hasten their day of civic recognition. Like the ordinary men whose emancipation from the serried ranks of traditional society preceded theirs, they found in the expanded commerce of the early Republic openings to a larger world. For women in particular the print revolution and religious reform movement brought an unprecedented scope for action, despite a popular rhetoric that idealized their domestic immurement. In a thousand new ways they were able to give the lie to assertions about their incapacity to participate in the public realm.

America offered Jefferson fertile soil for planting the seeds of free expression, political participation, and limited government. Like many a political theorist, he examined his own heart to find a formula for the right kind of government and discovered how much he hated the politics of deference. From this he concluded that his countrymen would not be ready for democratic action before they had dropped all habits of servility. Or more precisely, he saw in the typical American assertiveness the human material crying out for political validation. He never sought the interdependency of fraternity, nor did he fret about order, worry about European ridicule, or fear for his masculine reputation. Had he done these things, he might not have been able to think his way to a democratic psychology. Sometimes superficial, often optimistic without sufficient warrant, Jefferson established a powerful tie between ordinary citizens and American possibilities with an easiness captured in a line he wrote a friend in 1817: "My theory has always been, that if we are to dream, the flatteries of hope are as cheap, and pleasanter than the gloom of despair." [30]

Tocqueville got American democracy only half right. He correctly registered the power of majority will in the United States that he visited in 1833. With every office in its gift and without competition from nobles or kings, the majority ruled. He also saw how the spirit of equality threatened liberty: the joys of equality were experienced daily, while liberty needed defending infrequently and then at the risk of enraging the dominant majority. He even seemed to enjoy the irony of the tyrant-slaying Americans raising a new tyrant in themselves. What Tocqueville missed was the aspiration, even hubris, built into American individualism. He construed individualism as a form of self-indulgence that led self-satisfied Americans to withdraw from the public realm, the better to enjoy friends and family around their own hearth. What he failed to perceive was that the democratic psychology Jefferson had promoted liberated Americans from unwarranted authority and unacceptable gestures of superiority. In their fantasies, ordinary Americans imagined themselves as extraordinary. Social leveling had the inverse effect of infusing common men with a pride in their humanity that brooked no interference, not even from the tyrannical majority.

Jefferson's most enduring contribution to American politics came from his awareness of the debilitating effect of a ranked society's deferential manners. The latent possibility for politicizing these ways opened up when the French Revolution turned violent with the execution of the king and the declaration of the French Republic. The two presidential campaigns that followed gave him and his supporters occasions for arguing against hierarchical, authoritarian central government. After victory in 1800 Jefferson consciously set out to involve Americans in social situations primed to promote egalitarian practices.

The policies of limiting government, undertaken during his presidency, linked individualism to antistatism.

By the end of Jefferson's presidency, the once tight braid of social, economic, and political authority came untwisted, leaving the separate strands exposed and weakened. Those with social preeminence had to contend for political power; those with political power were not necessarily accorded social prestige. Those with wealth often failed to command social respect. Those newly admitted to citizenship challenged the authority of those who considered themselves born to govern. The vitality of America's democratic individualism tempts us to minimize the effort it took to eradicate Old World notions. Was Jefferson pushing on an open door? Have I been talking about a paper tiger?

In the contemporary intellectual milieu, indignation at the hypocrisy of a slaveholder's championing of natural rights, not to mention his patronizing attitudes toward women, has once again exposed Jefferson to angry criticism. A century ago he suffered similar abuse, but then it was for the democratic enthusiasm that I have been discussing. As Paul Leicester Ford, the New England editor of his collected writings wrote disparagingly, "Unlike the Federalists, Jefferson was willing to discard the tradition of ages—that the people must be protected against themselves by the brains, money and better 'elements' of the country."[31]

Jefferson deserves the scrutiny of every generation of Americans, but we will lose our grasp of historical reality if we underestimate the power of the aristocratic values that flourished in 1800. He imagined a different kind of social world, and the peculiarities of time and place gave him a historic opportunity to act on that vision. Even with new and important questions to address to the past, we should not forget that Thomas Jefferson jump-started democracy in the United States and, by extension, the world.

NOTES

1. Richard Sennett, *The Hidden Injuries of Class* (New York, 1993); the phrase "equality of esteem" comes from J. R. Pole, *The Pursuit of Equality* (Berkeley, Calif., 1978).

2. Catherine Allgor, *Parlor Politics: In Which the Ladies of Washington Help Build a City and a Government* (Charlottesville, Va., 2000), 35.

3. Ibid., 36.

4. Malcolm Lester, *Anthony Merry Redivivus: A Reappraisal of the British Minister to the United States, 1803–06* (Charlottesville, Va., 1978), 33.

5. Bernard A. Weisberger, *America Afire: Jefferson, Adams, and the Revolutionary Election of 1800* (New York, 2000), 1.

6. Allgor, *Parlor Politics*, 22, 24. See also Robert R. Davis Jr., "Pell-Mell: Jeffersonian Etiquette and Protocol," *Historian* 43 (1981): 509–29.

7. Lester, *Anthony Merry*, 41.

8. William Plumer, *Memorandum of Proceedings in the United States Senate, 1803–1807*, ed. Everett Somerville Brown (New York, 1923), 550.

9. See chaps. 5 and 14 in this volume.

10. *Continentalist* No. 5 (April 1782), *AHP* 3:76.

11. Gerald Stourzh, *Alexander Hamilton and the Idea of Republican Government*, (Stanford, Calif., 1970).

12. Adams to Jefferson, 10 Nov. 1787, *AJL*, 210–12.

13. Entry for 25 Oct. 1775, *Diary and Autobiography of John Adams*, 4 vols., ed. L. H. Butterfield (Cambridge, Mass., 1961), 2:218.

14. TJ to Madison, 6 Sept. 1789, *TJP* 15:392–97.

15. As quoted in John Dewey, ed., *Living Thoughts of Jefferson* (London, 1941), 59–60.

16. TJ to John Waldo, 16 Aug. 1813, L&B, 13:13; Dewey, *Living Thoughts*, 9.

17. TJ to John Adams, 27 Nov. 1785, *AJL*, 103.

18. Charles Ingersoll, *A Discourse Concerning the Influence of America* (Philadelphia, 1823), 24.

19. Dewey, *Living Thoughts*, 9. The *Oxford English Dictionary* has credited Jefferson with coining the word "Americanism"; he actually borrowed it from a Scottish clergyman, John Witherspoon.

20. TJ to Samuel Kercheval, 12 July 1816, Ford, 10:42; TJ to William Short, 3 Jan. 1793, *The Life and Selected Writings of Thomas Jefferson*, ed. Adrienne Koch and William Peden (New York, 1944), 321–22.

21. TJ, "Anas," Ford, 1:160.

22. *AJL*, 500–50l.

23. TJ to James Madison, 28 Aug. 1789, *TJP* 2:308.

24. Charles William Janson, *The Stranger in America* (London, 1807), 19, 197.

25. TJ to William Stephens Smith, 13 Nov. 1787, *TJP* 12:355–56.

26. Thomas Paine, *Common Sense* (Philadelphia, 1776), 1.

27. Lester, *Anthony Merry*, 41.

28. 24 Nov. 1808, *The Portable Thomas Jefferson*, ed. Merrill D. Peterson (New York, 1975), 510. For political dueling see Joyce Appleby, *Inheriting the Revolution: The First Generation of Americans* (Cambridge, Mass., 2000), 41–45.

29. TJ to J. B. Say, 1 Feb. 1804, L&B, 11:2–3.

30. TJ to Monsieur Barre de Marbois, Monticello, 14 June 1817, L&B, 15:130–31.

31. Ford, 1:12–15.

CHAPTER 7

Was There a Religious Revolution of 1800?

Robert M. S. McDonald

So virulent was the rhetoric and so desperate were the measures of Thomas Jefferson's religious opponents in 1800 that accounts of their excesses strain credulity. Pious New Englanders, warned by Congregational clergymen of Jefferson's hostility to all things Christian, on hearing news of his election reportedly buried their Bibles in kitchen gardens and hung them down wells for fear that federal troops would soon come to seize them. Then there is the tale of one Connecticut woman who, not satisfied with conventional strategies of concealment, took her Bible to the only Republican in town. "My good woman," he supposedly said, "if all the Bibles are to be destroyed, what is the use of bringing yours to me?" Keep it, she insisted. "They'll never think of looking in the house of a Democrat for a Bible."[1] These stories, while probably apocryphal, hardly exaggerate the mixed emotions of fear and hostility with which numerous sectarians regarded Jefferson. For much of the previous decade, Federalist divines had told churchgoers that Jeffersonian Republicans aimed to mold the United States into a nation of atheists. In 1798, for example, Yale president Timothy Dwight prophesied that, should Republicans gain power, "we may behold a strumpet personating a Goddess on the altars of JEHOVAH." The Bible would be "cast into a bonfire, the vessels of the sacramental supper borne by an ass in public procession, and our children, either wheedled or terrified, uniting in chanting mockeries against God." To the list of travesties he added "that we may see our wives and daughters the victims of legal prostitution."[2]

The crucial role of religion in the election of 1800 has not been ignored by scholars, many of whom have ably surveyed the sometimes hysterical jeremiads of Dwight and other leaders of established churches, as well as the numerous pamphlets and newspaper essays of Federalist laymen bent on exposing Jefferson as an enemy of God. Similarly, the responses of Republican partisans, many of whom maintained that matters of personal faith had no place in public debate, have been amassed, dissected, and analyzed.[3] But previous work leaves largely unanswered important but all-too-often implicit questions: What were the origins of Jefferson's image as an enemy to Christianity? To what extent were his attackers—and defenders—sincere? Did citizens really believe that on the outcome of the election of 1800 hinged the future of faith in America? To what extent did the "revolution of 1800," as Jefferson in 1819 described his elevation to the presidency, have revolutionary implications for the role of religion in public life?[4]

The answers can be found only by situating the religious rhetoric surrounding the election of 1800 within a period of profound uncertainty for the nation's faithful. Jeffersonian calls for the separation of church and state promised great opportunities for proponents of upstart, minority faiths but portended great pitfalls for advocates of establishment religions. In the 1790s this latter group grew increasingly hostile to Jefferson and made common cause with Federalists, his political enemies, who claimed that he supported the measures of French revolutionaries to purge their nation of Christianity. Frightened by the growing popularity in America of French philosophy and fearful that Jefferson might institute his own reign of terror, the coalition of Federalist clergy and newspapermen tainted Jefferson's reputation with charges of hostility to religion during the presidential campaign of 1796 and then amplified their aspersions four years later. These harangues damaged not only Jefferson's image but also, perhaps, his hope that the nation would set aside sectarian squabbling and unite around a more rational, more secular morality. From 1801 onward Jefferson worked to contradict charges of his hostility to religion and rescue his vision of interfaith harmony by fashioning himself into a role model of toleration. He led toward the center, where he would meet his opponents halfway, for his tenure in office coincided with a careful, systematic, and largely private effort to reassure himself—as he did others—that he was as true as anyone to the authentic principles of Christianity. But these efforts met with only partial success. Jefferson was never able to scrub completely from his reputation the stain of atheism—nor did he live to see Americans coalesce around the rationalistic creed that he considered self-evident. In the end, the revolution of 1800 resulted in changes less revolutionary than Jefferson's enemies feared and his allies hoped.

The presidential election of 1796, which pitted Jefferson against John Adams, set the stage for 1800 by bringing religion to the fore as a political issue. Jefferson's Federalist detractors, aware of his calls for disestablishment in Virginia as well as his early affinity for the French Revolution and his friendships with radicals such as Thomas Paine, took notice of attacks on religion in revolutionary France and used them to cultivate fear for the safety of Christianity in America. Republicans responded by affirming their support for the separation of church and state. Jefferson would and should do nothing, they contended, to prevent Americans from worshiping as they chose, nor should Americans do anything to disqualify from office men such as Jefferson whose private religious sentiments remained unknown to the public.

Jefferson's connection with the French Revolution turned Federalist stomachs. While their opponents painted Adams as a British supplicant, they could scarcely resist coming to the opposite conclusion about Jefferson. Rather than elevate him to the presidency, one writer suggested, "we might as well . . . become a Colony of France at once." The former secretary of state fully embraced the Gallic rebellion, his opponents charged, and this alone made him unfit to lead America. "The revolution of France has been distinguished by many scenes of cruelty that shock humanity," noted one pro-Adams newspaperman, a fact that Federalists understood but some Republicans seemed to overlook. He reminded readers of the "sacrilegious attacks on popular religion" in France, of the revolutionaries' violations of church property and religious rights.[5]

Such characterizations hardly exaggerated the harm done to the French church. Nearly as corrupt and corpulent as the monarchy, to which it was financially connected, the French religious establishment provided an inviting target for the ire of revolutionaries, many of whom attacked not only religious institutions but also religion itself. As one member of the French National Assembly informed his countrymen, "Kings and priests are leagued in *one cursed* design—and the cursed instrument of the latter is *eternal fire.* Let others tremble at this terrific bugbear . . . as for myself, I here honestly confess to this Assembly I am an atheist." Following the fall of the Bastille in July 1789, the Assembly confiscated church property, abolished tithes, outlawed clerical oaths, and suppressed monastic orders. A succession of revolutionary regimes then further undermined Christianity and Christian institutions, co-opting the remaining clergy and declaring its independence from Rome, allowing the massacre of hundreds of priests, forcing at least thirty thousand into exile, and pressuring clerics to renounce celibacy by entering into marriage. By 1794 the last vestiges of the old establishment stood almost completely dismantled. Church buildings not sold off or torn down had been reconsecrated as "Temples of Reason," where actresses impersonating philosophy were seated on thrones and serenaded by choirs of children.[6] Given this context, Dwight's 1798 prediction of religious ruin does not seem so delusional.

Compounding the fears of Dwight and other influential clergymen was the conviction that rationalist deism was on the rise in America and that outright atheism was sure to follow. So popular was the first installment of Paine's *Age of Reason,* which appeared in seventeen American editions between 1794 and 1796, that attacks on it emanated from pulpits from Maine to Georgia and thirty-five clerics published rejoinders to the work. The "infidel and irreligious spirit" of deism, which William E. Channing said at least one fellow Harvard student attributed to the *"French mania,"* had thoroughly infected the future stewards of the Republic. Lyman Beecher, Channing's contemporary, found Yale in "a most ungodly state," for "infidelity of the Tom Paine School" was much in fashion. Not usually prone to political risk taking, the growth of skepticism galvanized mainstream religious leaders. As Gary Nash has noted, French revolutionary attacks on the Roman Catholic Church failed to elicit an outcry from America's clergy until after 1794, when deism supplanted Catholicism in France and seemed to threaten Protestantism in America.[7]

Thus much of the American clergy joined with lay Federalists in viewing Jefferson's candidacy as evidence of a transatlantic conspiracy to supplant constitutional order and Christianity with anarchy and atheism. France was cast as an evil empire; its supporters, in turn, plotted to wage on American soil a culture war. The soul of the nation hung in the balance. John Fenno's Federalist *Gazette of the United States* observed that "the 'excessive patriots' of Paris . . . appear to be with the same cast with the enemies of the constitution of this country." Another penman asserted that "the democratic faction is wholly *foreign.* Not a drop of American blood" pulsed in its leaders' veins, and "not a drop that is not degenerate." Even after citizens and legislators had cast their votes, but before the electoral college outcome became certain, a Federalist warned that the "shoutings of *'liberty and equality'* [and] the mercenary cries of no 'king,' which disgraced" the election, were "so closely copied from the proceedings in

France, which first prepared and afterwards established the arbitrary power of Robespierre, that there is no little reason to apprehend a similar tyranny in this country."[8]

Republicans, however, insisted that while Jefferson supported France's experiment with popular government, he did not condone the Jacobins' Reign of Terror. Tench Coxe, for example, assumed the unlikely pen name "Federalist" and contended in a November pamphlet that Jefferson's opponents wrongly accused him of being "so much disposed to justify the French Revolution, as to overlook all the excesses which that nation has committed." On the contrary, he stood alongside George Washington, admiring the principles and promises of 1789 but "lamenting . . . aberrations from moderation and humanity" and the recent "stupendous despotism." Still, given the open warfare between France and Britain and the uneasy state of Franco-American relations, Jefferson's election could work to the advantage of the United States. As one writer observed, "it will conciliate the people of France who have the idea that he has been leaning in their favor."[9]

With all of its heady implications, the election of 1796 appeared to offer irreconcilable choices. How, with their diametrically divergent outlooks, could Americans navigate the treacherous channel between a French Scylla and a British Charybdis? For Republicans and Federalists alike, the contest between Jefferson and Adams loomed as a defining moment for a nascent nation still struggling to determine its role in world affairs. Unmistakably, however, the election also exposed bitter feuds on the domestic front. It called on citizens to confront cardinal questions about the nature of their polity, issues inflamed by international concerns but deeply rooted in their history. For the most part, Federalists raised these points of contention as they attacked Jefferson's character, deriding his religious beliefs and asking voters if a man of such doubtful faith should lead their Christian nation.

At least two factors had combined to create an image of Jefferson as irreligious. The first linked him with his old friend Paine, whose *Age of Reason,* according to one pamphleteer, constituted a collection of *"impious doctrines."* Written, significantly, in France, Paine's pronouncements came on the heels of the Jacobins' secularization and de-Christianization campaigns. He espoused the ideals of Enlightenment deism, attacked Christian dogma, and held that "I do not believe in the creed professed by . . . any church that I know of. My own mind is my own church." Jefferson, in the eyes of Federalists, stood allied with Paine's heretical clique of radical revolutionaries.[10] His connection to the controversial writer had been well known since 1791, when his public endorsement of the first volume of Paine's *Rights of Man,* a barbed rejoinder to Edmund Burke's condemnation of the French Revolution, not only praised Paine but also took a not so subtle swipe at Adams, setting off a political maelstrom. Meanwhile, Paine's involvement in French affairs resulted in treason charges against him in his native Britain and, shortly thereafter, imprisonment in France. Successful efforts by Jefferson confidant James Monroe to win his release reminded the public of the Jefferson-Paine connection; so did Benjamin Franklin Bache, the staunchly Jeffersonian editor of the Philadelphia's *Aurora,* who imported from Paris fifteen thousand copies of the *Age of Reason* for sale in America.[11]

As additional proof of Jefferson's un-Christian principles, his opponents pointed to his 1786 bill to disestablish the Anglican Church in Virginia. They ridiculed the "frivolous and impious passage" justifying the proposal in his *Notes on the State of Virginia,* where he contended that "it does me no injury for my neighbor to say there are twenty gods, or no god. It neither picks my pocket nor breaks my leg." "Good God!" exclaimed one indignant writer, "is this the man the *patriots* have cast their eyes on as successor to the *virtuous Washington,* who, in his farewell address, so warmly . . . recommends to his fellow citizens, the *cultivators of religion*"? America's status as a predominantly Christian nation was one of the most important factors distinguishing it from the French Republic. "We are not Frenchmen," a Connecticut penman asserted, "and until the Atheistical Philosophy of a certain great Virginian shall become the fashion (which God of his mercy forbid) we shall never be."[12]

"An American" astutely exposed the sources and contours of Federalists' ruminations regarding Jefferson's religion. Britain, Spain, and other enemies of France assiduously worked to spread the belief "that the French are intent on destroying all religious impressions," he explained, and "the writings of Thomas Paine have greatly contributed" to this fear. "Having appeared as a conspicuous political writer, the moment he undertook to doubt" sectarian teachings, "his opinions as to religion were supposed to be adopted by those who thought like him in politics." As a result, "to be a republican, or an admirer of the French revolution, was supposed to be synonymous" with being "an infidel, anxious to overthrow every vestige of the Christian system." Readers of this essay learned one thing more: not all Federalists condoned portrayals of Jefferson as an atheist. "An American"'s defense of the Republican candidate was implicit but clear, and it appeared, remarkably, in the New York *Minerva,* Noah Webster's Federalist sheet.[13]

Other essayists issued principled defenses of religious freedom, a right they traced to the foundation of American government. The *Aurora*, for example, quoted William Penn's writings on toleration to answer "an abuser of Thomas Jefferson." It also printed an amicable "Dialogue between an Aristocrat and a Republican." The aristocrat maintained that Jefferson "is not a friend to the old established religion of this country" and "does not hold that religious faith in which we have been brought up as a nation." The republican did not disagree, but he reminded his companion that "the religious sentiments of a man" remained a private matter. Individuals, he said, possessed "a right" to their beliefs in accordance with "the light of understanding which God has given to him." After all, he added, the Constitution "held sacred" the "freedom of conscience and religious sentiment." In matters of faith, "the ideas of a statesman, a Philosopher, or a gentlemen" could only be "determined to be of little consequence in public life."[14]

The Republicans' strategy did little to persuade strict sectarians to ignore Federalist charges. But it allowed them to avoid issuing a religious avowal in Jefferson's behalf, which, given his steady reticence regarding his faith, remained a problematical undertaking.[15] In an important way, however, their defense of Jefferson's right to religious freedom worked to their advantage. It gave them an opportunity to demonstrate the nature of their commitment to the Constitution, a document to which—Federalists frequently contended—they had little commitment at all.[16] Unlike proponents of Adams, who saw it as an instrument of order, for Republicans America's political charter stood as a guarantor of liberty. Jefferson, by implication, agreed.

The religious debate of 1796 can thus be cast as a contest between those fearful of the French Revolution's excesses and those dissatisfied with the American Revolution's limitations. While Federalists labored to reverse the secularization of public life, Republicans struggled for its advancement. While establishmentarians worked to retain religion as the foundation of political virtue, disestablishmentarians—the deists among them, especially—carried forward an Enlightenment faith in rational individual choice and common moral sense.[17]

Despite the divisiveness of the election of 1796, its polarizing effects did not influence all. Political centrists cheered the narrowness of Adams's victory over Jefferson, who finished second in the electoral college and would therefore serve as vice president in the new administration. Congressman William Barry Grove and his friend James Hogg, for example, were North Carolinians who did not fit neatly into either of the two developing factions. As Grove informed Hogg, "Mr. Adams is Elected President & Mr. Jefferson Vice—this is as we both wished." He welcomed Jefferson's acquiescence to the second post, as well as his magnanimous "satisfaction at the Election of Mr. A[dams], whose Character & Patriotism it seems he does and [has] respected." In Chester County, Pennsylvania, celebrants at a banquet honoring Washington toasted "Moderation" and raised their glasses to both Adams and Jefferson in hopes that "they, when at the head of the family of the United States, go hand in hand" in their duties. "There is no doubt they will act harmoniously together," wrote Unitarian theologian Joseph Priestley, "which shall greatly abate the animosity of both the parties."[18] Even strident partisans expressed hope that they could praise the outcome of the Adams-Jefferson partnership.[19] The four years to follow, however, only increased political factionalism, and the religious strife evident in 1796 intensified to the point that, in the election of 1800, it reappeared as the most defining issue.

The second contest between Jefferson and Adams struck supporters of both as an extended moment of true crisis. Republicans believed that another Adams victory would lead to the suppression of civil liberty. Federalists feared that the election of Jefferson would result in the final disruption of America's shaky constitutional experiment. Each side considered itself the permanent representative of the people's best interests and viewed the other as a sinister, illegitimate faction.[20] Republicans hoped that the record of the Adams administration, which approved, among other measures, the unpopular 1798 Alien and Sedition Acts, would tilt the election in their favor. Federalists chose to focus on Jefferson's character. "The question is not what he will *do*" as president, one of his opponents claimed, "but what he *is.*"[21]

For several reasons the decision by Federalists to politicize Jefferson's private life made strategic sense. First, it drew attention away from Adams, who, as the British ambassador complained, stood out as "the most passionate, intemperate man he ever had anything to do with." A Treasury Department official from North Carolina described him as "a man of jealous temper" who "has lately acted so strange . . . that many do not hesitate to assert that he is deranged in his intellect." Other Federalists also questioned his mental health.[22] A good many more complained about his effort to improve relations with France, which minimized an issue that had boosted his popularity. As a result Adams "lost many friends," according to Priestley, because to them the French Republic loomed as an evil "with which they wish to be at war." John Marshall gossiped that the decision caused people in the Northeast to feel "very much dissatisfied with the President" and left some "strongly disposed to desert him & to push for some other candidate." That other candidate was South Carolina's Charles Cotesworth Pinckney, who, although officially the Federalist vice presidential contender, would win the top office if a few electors dropped support for Adams. Hamilton exposed the rift in Federalist circles by calling Adams to task in a published pamphlet, and some in 1800 so much doubted the president's scruples that they wondered aloud if he and Jefferson had "made a coalition." A sizeable part of Adams's own faction doubted his fitness to lead and had scant enthusiasm for reelecting him.[23]

Federalists found themselves with neither an attractive leader nor a compelling agenda. For more than a decade they had controlled the government; they had united around Washington and a vague constitutional vision as well as an opposition to Jefferson and the changes for which they believed he stood. But for what did *they* stand? A New Jersey Federalist tried to lure voters with lukewarm assurances of "firm government" and "temperate liberty," promises that countless Americans viewed as threats. As New Yorker Robert Troup told diplomat Rufus King, "we have no rallying point."[24]

While targeting Jefferson diverted attention from Adams and their own malaise, the Federalists' campaign represented more than mere opportunism. As William C. Dowling writes, they viewed Jefferson "as the visible embodiment of invisible forces of social disintegration or decline." Conversely, they viewed themselves as virtuous and enlightened men, unselfish, disinterested, independent—unlike the mobs of common folk who, some of them thought, answered Jefferson's siren song. Dwight, for example, looked down on the "class of men" who lived along Vermont's frontier—the same sort who supported Jefferson—as individuals "who cannot live in regular society. They are too idle, too talkative, too passionate, too prodigal, & too shiftless to acquire property of character." Impatient with "restraints of Law, Religion, Morality & Public opinion," they grumbled "about the taxes by which rulers, ministers & school masters are supported." Even though they managed "their own concerns worse than any other men [they] feel perfectly satisfied that they could manage those of the nation far better than the persons to whom they are committed by the public." Dwight resented their "contentions for power & wealth." Others shared his disdain. Fenno proposed dissolving the states, establishing ten to twenty districts commanded by presidential appointees, cutting off the franchise "from all paupers, vagabonds and outlaws," and placing all legislation "in those hands to which it belongs, the proprietors of the country." Only "the best men"—"men of property, and of landed property, who must stand or fall with their country"—should rise to elective posts, a Rhode Islander claimed. "The intelligent and virtuous," wrote another Federalist, "have, at all times, been on the side of government." But Jefferson, like the people who supported him, apparently had neither quality, for he wanted to "crush the systems of *Washington* and *Adams*" and overturn the established orer. Federalist skepticism about the common people's capacity for self-rule helped to spur their insistence on the importance of religion as an issue in 1800. While the well educated might let reason guide them, the less fortunate needed faith's moral compass.[25]

Jefferson, Federalists warned the public, wanted to take that compass away. A South Carolina pamphleteer claimed that Jefferson "abhors the Christian system." The Reverend John Mason called him "a confirmed infidel" known for "vilifying the divine word, and preaching insurrection against God." Thomas Robbins, a young Connecticut parson, described him as a "howling atheist." In the *Connecticut Courant*, a "Humble Citizen" proclaimed that Jefferson and his band "oppose every thing sacred" and that if he and his "democrats could acquire control of our religious establishments . . . they would destroy them." The *Gazette of the United States* maintained that a voter need ask himself one easy question: "Shall I continue in allegiance to God—and a Religious President; Or impiously declare for Jefferson—and No God!!!"[26]

How did Federalists substantiate this view? New Yorker William Linn, whose anonymous pamphlet constituted one of the most thorough attempts to prove the vice president's "disbelief in the Holy Scriptures," culled his evidence "principally from Mr. Jefferson's own writings." As Mason boasted in his own tract, "the charge, unsupported by other proof, could hardly be pursued to conviction. Happily for truth and for us, Mr. Jefferson has *written;* he has *printed.*" While his religious freedom bill first alerted the pious to his damnable intentions, his enemies claimed, his *Notes on the State of Virginia* removed all doubts about Jefferson and his "fraternity of infidels."[27]

His heresies included doubting that fossilized shells found near mountaintops proved a universal deluge; he calculated that even if all the atmosphere turned to water and fell for forty days and nights, sea levels would rise less than fifty-three feet. His speculations about the world's languages and the time necessary for them to have become distinct—more "than many people give the age of the earth"—demonstrated that he rejected the Bible's chronology of the history of mankind. By wondering if Africans constituted a distinct race, he degraded them, according to Linn, "from the rank which God hath given them" as descendants of Adam and Eve. Worse yet, he proposed that instead of "putting the Bible and Testament in the hands of the children" of Virginia's schools "at an age when their judgments are not sufficiently matured for religious enquiries," they should read histories of Greece, Rome, Europe, and America. His remark that "it does me no injury for my neighbour to say there are twenty gods, or no god" because it "neither picks my pocket nor breaks my leg" revealed not tolerance but flagrant disregard for the souls of fellow citizens. "Ten thousand impieties and mischiefs" lurked within this sentiment, Mason warned. If all these blasphemies did not convince voters of his apostasy, they should consider his statement that farmers "are the chosen people of God, if ever he had a chosen people." This dumbfounded his critics: *if ever*?[28]

Jefferson proved his irreligion through deeds as well as words. He worked on Sundays, they contended, and did not attend church. He neglected to demonstrate "so much as a decent external respect for the faith." The public also learned of a story, related by Linn and confirmed by Mason, that Jefferson's loose-lipped confidant Philip Mazzei supposedly told a respected Virginia divine. "Your great philosopher and statesman, Mr. Jefferson, is rather farther gone in infidelity than I am," Mazzei was said to have bragged to the clergyman. Once, as he and Jefferson rode through the countryside, he pointed to a decrepit church, shocked that parishioners would allow it to fall into such a condition. "*It is good enough,*" Jefferson supposedly said, "*for him that was borne in a manger!*" That the vice president had made this "contemptuous fling at the blessed Jesus" Linn did not doubt, nor did he consider that Jefferson might have meant to praise Jesus' humility.[29]

The Federalists who cast these aspersions, of course, had earlier labored to link Jefferson with the excesses of revolutionary France, and in doing so had formulated their faction's enduring view of the man. During America's "Quasi-War" with France charges of Jacobinism had been especially damning, but now—thanks largely to the willingness of Adams to push for a peaceable settlement of the two nations' troubles—they had lost some of their force. A 1799 assessment that New Englanders generally held "*friends of France . . . in the greatest abhorrence*" still retained its accuracy, but elsewhere Americans began to manifest a "general, conclusive and . . . fixed dislike of the English nation," which stood as France's archenemy. Thus Federalist contentions of Jefferson's Francophilia were more oblique in the election of 1800 than they had been in 1796, but they still existed. "Burleigh," a frequent contributor to the *Connecticut*

Courant, urged people to view "every leading Jacobin as a ravening wolf, prepared to enter your peaceful fold, and glut his deadly appetite on the vitals of your country." "It was in France," South Carolina's Henry DeSaussure maintained, "that his disposition to theory, and his skepticism in religion, morals, and government, acquired full strength and vigor." He was a *"philosophe* in the modern French sense of the word." Because he stood as *"the favorer, and the favorite of a nation, which has heaped injuries on the head of his country, he is the last man to whom his fellow-citizens should entrust the government."* He was a Jacobin, and "Jacobins in all countries are destitute of morality and religion" for they craved "an opportunity to be as cruel and abandoned as those of France." More French than American, he would make a good Bonaparte, perhaps, but a terrible president of the United States.[30]

The vice president's un-American character and opinions made him entirely unsuitable for high office. As DeSaussure asserted, the election of Jefferson would place the nation "nearly in a revolutionary state." If "unprincipled and abandoned Democrats" came to power, Noah Webster observed, "Deists, Atheists, Adulterers and profligate men" would take charge of the country. For many, a Jefferson victory meant domestic disorder or, as Fenno wrote, "a warfare of confusion against order." At least one writer believed that a Republican victory might bring a *"Civil War,"* during which "murder, robbery, rape, adultery, and incest will all be openly taught and practiced." In nearly all Federalist polemics, whether in newspapers or pamphlets, the message was clear: Jefferson was evil, and he must be stopped.[31]

One Federalist could not fathom that even Republicans could regard "the measures he is expected to pursue [as] so essential to the welfare of our country" that they could possibly "outweigh every moral consideration flowing from his *unbelief."* Another scorned the people who said that *"religion has nothing to do with politics!"* The Bible, he contended, "is full of directions for your behavior as *citizens"* and the president is *"God's officer."* Dwight had proclaimed in 1798 that "individuals are often apt to consider their own private conduct as of small importance to the public welfare. This opinion is wholly erroneous and highly mischievous."[32]

But the Federalists had cried wolf. As a North Carolina congressman later commented, the "sound of alarm" passed "with little more effect, than sound itself." A Rhode Islander, comparing the merits of Jefferson and Adams, took care to "preserve a distinction between the moral qualities which make a man amiable in private life, and those strong virtues which alone fit him for elevated public station. A very good man may indeed make a very bad President." Adams, for example, possessed an exemplary "private character" as father, husband, and friend, but his personal goodness would never compensate for his "political crimes" and "official deformities." On the other hand, the Devil himself could serve the public with distinction, "provided that he disturbs not the public tranquility, nor abuses the high influence of his office, for the establishment of his favorite system." The very fact that the presidential election had aroused so much passion, another Republican said, exposed the extent to which Adams had placed power and glory in the hands of the executive, and not the more representative Congress, where it belonged. The *National Intelligencer* implied that Federalists' emphasis on character reflected their "servile spirit of adulation" for supposedly great men. "It becomes the enlightened friends of republicanism to cling *exclusively to principle,* and to commend, not men but measures." [33]

Perhaps Federalist attacks provoked such assertions. Webster, for instance, had avowed that "no men fawn, cringe, and flatter, so much as democrats" who "extol Jefferson to the skies." But no one should doubt the power of denial to shape one's view of oneself. The fact that the vice president's opponents sensed that adoration of him eclipsed support for his ideas does not diminish the conviction with which Republicans regarded their stated agenda. Quite possibly Jeffersonians' desire to prove critics wrong caused them to convince themselves of what they told others: some people were "too apt to confound principles with men." [34]

Even so, Jefferson had defenders who answered the attacks on his character. More than a few Republicans refused to sit silent while Federalists slung mud at the individual who, as Priestley reported, they considered "the first man in this country." A writer calling himself "Marcus Brutus" described Jefferson's religious beliefs as "wholly unexceptional." He believed in a "superintending providence" and "is at least as good a christian as Mr. Adams, and in all probability a much better one." Another penman asserted that Jefferson was no deist; even if he were, however, he would make a better president than "secret friends to aristocracy or monarchy" like Adams and Pinckney. In addition, he was "superior" to all other contenders as a writer, negotiator, thinker, scholar, statesman, and scientist, an "invincible patriot" who embraced law, liberty, and "the original principles of our revolution." Despite assertions to the contrary, the vice president, "not the man of France," was "the man of public liberty—the man of the people—the man of the constitution." Another writer lauded "Mr. Jefferson's good sense and moderation."[35]

Perhaps no one did as much to bolster the vice president's personal credibility as Congressman John Beckley, the Pennsylvania partisan stalwart whose *Address to the People of the United States* described Jefferson as "a man of pure, ardent and unaffected piety; of sincere and genuine virtue; of an enlightened mind and superior wisdom; the adorer of our God; the patriot of his country; and the friend and benefactor of the whole human race." Beckley appended to the pamphlet a biographical "Epitome" of Jefferson's "public life and services." His work reached a wide audience; in 1800 no fewer than five printers in five cities issued five thousand copies.[36]

Oftentimes, however, defenders skipped over his goodness to censure those who made "the incomparable JEFFERSON . . . the theme of incessant slander and abuse. The man who could pen the Declaration of Independence," had "no Sedition Law to protect him" against vicious calumniators—scandalmongers Beckley derided as "fanatics, bigots, and religious hypocrites." A Delaware Republican also attacked the attackers when he contended that, compared to aspersions against Jefferson's morality and religion, "there is nothing so lame and base . . . except the moral and religious principles of his revilers." Connecticut's Abraham Bishop noted that the Federalists' "great art . . . has been to paint up a certain character in every deformity of vice" while they styled themselves as "men famous for piety, goodness and science." They even went so far as to claim "all holy men of every age as federalists."[37]

The attacks on Jefferson's private faith, some suggested, also aimed to divert attention from the administration's record. It was a shoddy tactic, contended a *National Intelligencer* editorialist. Federalists should not confuse personal and public concerns, and "religion ought to be kept distinct from politics." Shoemakers and tailors did not quarrel because they had made different choices, reasoned another writer, and neither should "men who entertain different moral principles." Bishop, moreover, asked how much religion had been advanced by the clerics who claimed that "Satan and Cain were jacobins?" Would the bishop of Ephesus leave "the care of soul to ascertain the number of votes . . . his favorites could get for a seat in Congress? Would Paul of Tarsus have preached to an anxious listening audience on the propriety of sending envoys?" Jefferson, conversely, had written Virginia's religious freedom law. It proved that he was a "truly religious man," for it assumed "no dominion over the faith of others" and returned "the rites of religion" to the realm of individual choice. According to "Timoleon," the vice president's tolerance for different sects flowed from an understanding that coercion "never has been, and never will be of service to christianity." Persecution, he maintained, "may generate and multiply hypocrites, but will never produce a single convert." [38]

Not surprisingly, Catholics, Baptists, Unitarians, Jews, and members of other minority faiths generally concurred, and together they stood as an important source of support for Jefferson. Perhaps they suspected that Federalists wanted to establish a national church, or maybe they empathized with Benjamin Noves, a veteran of the Revolution who wrote that "I am a *Jew* and . . . for that reason I am a *republican.*" In monarchies Jews were "hunted from society," but in "Republics we have *rights.*" [39]

Jefferson's eventual success in the contest, his electoral tie with Aaron Burr and the ensuing Federalist maneuvering for the promotion of Burr to the presidency notwithstanding, gave Noves and other Republicans cause for celebration. But those with a dimmer view of Jefferson cringed, foreseeing dark days for the Republic. As Cato West reported from the Mississippi frontier, "those who were friends to the late Administration are quite long fac'd." Parson Robbins confided that "I have never heard bad tidings on anything which gave me such a shock." A man in Deerfield, Massachusetts, who had started building a house during Adams's presidency, vowed not to complete it until true Christians returned to power. Although these Federalists probably disagreed with nearly everything else in the *National Intelligencer,* they must have concurred with its assertion that people viewed the election's "importance as little short of infinite." [40]

Jefferson's presidency did not usher in the apocalypse that some of his detractors predicted. Strumpets did not parade across church altars, Bibles remained unburned, children went unmolested by the forces of atheism, and the virtue of wives and daughters endured no unusual challenges. The commander-in-chief worked hard, in fact, to prove wrong the Federalist jeremiads through public displays of moderation and tolerance as well as more private efforts to redefine himself as a Christian. His labors, however, resulted in only limited success.

Jefferson's inaugural address aimed to reassure enemies and allies that he was neither radical nor ready to relax his drive to advance the cause of liberty. He said that he stood not for anarchy but for "harmony and affection without which liberty and even life itself are but dreary things." But he opposed "that religious intolerance under which mankind so long bled and suffered." Americans possessed "the strongest Government on earth" because "every man, at the call of the law, would fly to the standard of the law, and would meet invasions of the public order as his own personal concern. Sometimes it is said that man cannot be trusted with the government of himself. Can he, then, be trusted with the government of others?" The United States was a big country with a diverse population; it was removed from the influence and troubles of Europe, and it acknowledged and adored "an overruling Providence."[41]

Jefferson joined deeds to words in his efforts to reassure sectarians. In the aftermath of his inauguration, he aimed not only to reward and embolden the Republican faithful but also to bring into his circle everyday pious critics, the common men and women who wished him no harm but who prayed that he would do no harm to goodness, good order, decency, and God. On 1 January 1802, the same day that he accepted from the Baptists of Cheshire, Massachusetts, a 1,235-pound "mammoth cheese" tendered as a "freewill offering" in anticipation of his zealous support for religious freedom, he wrote a letter to the Baptists of Danbury, Connecticut, that expressed his moderation. In this epistle, which he knew would send a message to the faithful throughout America, he laid out a careful and temperate course on matters of belief.

He welcomed the opportunity to set matters straight. Like Washington, who through a 1797 note to Timothy Pickering (which Pickering immediately published) put to rest as forgeries letters circulated twenty years earlier that purported to reveal his doubts about the Revolution, Jefferson wished to deny the charges against him. Like Washington, he realized that a direct response would appear unseemly and self-interested, and would therefore lack credibility. Unlike Washington, however, whose mediated rebuttal appeared after his retirement from public office, Jefferson was forced to compete in a combative political arena where he would not pull his punches—at least not after his elevation to the presidency, which provided him with the pretense of speaking for the nation rather than for himself. As he told Levi Lincoln, his attorney general, the "Baptist address" created "an occasion . . . which I have long wished to find."[42] The Danbury Baptists, who had complained about their state's Congregational establishment and affirmed that acts of toleration of their faith existed "as favors granted, and not as inalienable rights," gave Jefferson an excuse to tell them—and America—"that religion is a matter which lies solely between man and his God, that he owes account to none other for his faith or his worship," and "that the legislative powers of government reach actions only, and not opinions."[43]

Despite this restatement of his disestablishmentarianism, Jefferson also took care to pay homage to "the common Father and Creator of man." Notwithstanding his dictums about walls of separation between religion and public policy, he deleted from his letter a disparaging comparison between Britain's religious establishment and Federalists' proclamations of days of prayer and thanksgiving—"practised indeed by the Executive of another nation as the legal head of his church"—which remained popular in northern states. The result was a written commitment to toleration calculated to offend neither his Baptist supporters nor the many others who remained wary of his stance on religion. Here emerged most manifest his desire to unite all Americans, flappable Federalists included, around the banner of common people's faith. He made additional gestures that signified his approbation of public worship. He regularly appeared at Sunday services held in the chamber of the House of Representatives, for example, where ministers of various denominations preached to officeholders and members of the public. He also attended—and financially supported—the Reverend Andrew McCormick's Christ Church in Washington, and he allowed Presbyterians to hold communion services in the building occupied by the Department of the Treasury.[44]

The fact that Jefferson could not have helped but to understand the reassuring message conveyed by his patronage of religion need not be taken as evidence of insincerity, especially in light of his concurrent, mostly private, and almost obsessive pursuit of the authentic teachings of Jesus. Jefferson worked to establish his Christian credentials not only for the public but also in his own mind. His careful reexamination of Jesus' precepts began after his retirement as secretary of state, when he read Priestley's two-volume *History of the Corruptions of Christianity.* The work rejected the Trinity and asserted that early clerical accommodations to pagan practices, together with later attempts by priests to increase their importance by mystifying followers, muddled the more enlightened teachings of Jesus, a prophet who never claimed his own divinity. Priestley's arguments appealed to Jefferson, who had earlier rejected Christian dogma as irrational but now sought to reconcile his beliefs with those of the historical Jesus. Prodded by Priestley and Benjamin Rush, another proponent of rational Christianity, by the time of his inauguration he predicted that the "good sense" of New Englanders would free them from "the domination of the clergy" and help them to realize, as he did, "that the Christian religion when divested of the rags in which [ministers] have inveloped it, and brought to the original purity and simplicity of it's benevolent institutor, is a religion of all others most friendly to liberty, science, and the freest expansions of the human mind." These remarks, which he conveyed to former Vermont senator Moses Robinson, can be taken as yet another indirect answer to those who cast him as an enemy of religion; so can his 1803 "Syllabus," a document that favorably compared the beliefs of Jesus with those of classical philosophers and Jews, which he shared not only with Rush and Priestley but also with members of his cabinet and Virginia Governor John Page. But only twice did he invite others to peruse his 1804 scissor-edit of the gospel verses that he believed reflected Christianity's seminal teachings, a forty-six-page collection of biblical extracts entitled "The Philosophy of Jesus"—at the time the single most laborious expression of his faith—and not once did Jefferson authorize anyone to publish any of these texts with his name attached.[45]

This understood, his religious pilgrimage seems mainly personal in nature. Although happy to refute the charge that he was hostile to Christian worship, he understood that a public avowal of his private beliefs would expose him to further criticism and undermine his conviction, shared by many of his followers, that even officeholders' religion remained "a concern purely between our god and our consciences." Yet the fact remains that his most intense period of religious reflection coincided with Federalists' long and intense campaign to portray him as irreligious. His correspondence with Rush and Priestley commenced after the earliest assertions of his support for French infidelity; his private missive to Robinson followed the scrutiny of his faith in 1800; he authored the "Syllabus" after renewed charges of atheism followed his controversial sponsorship of Paine's 1802 return to America; and he compiled "The Philosophy of Jesus" at the same time that he prepared for another round of religious attacks in the 1804 presidential election. Ever eager to prove critics wrong, if only in his own mind, Jefferson's studious reconsideration of Christian principles may have been an attempt less to reassure others than to reassure himself.[46]

Jefferson's effort to reconstruct his religious reputation and remove himself from the center of America's religious debate was only partly successful. Because his first term as president did not bear out the dire predictions of his detractors, the question of his faith received much less attention in the months preceding his landslide re-election.[47] But despite his attempts to dodge the bullets of sectarian controversy—so nicely exemplified by his claim in his second inaugural address that it was the Constitution that made "matters of religion . . . independent of the powers of the general government" and prevented him from authorizing days of national prayer—the perception that he stood opposed to Christianity lingered in some circles, and his defense of the virtues of rational religion inspired few followers.[48]

Consider the controversy over religion at his University of Virginia, the institution that he envisioned as the "bulwark of the human mind" in the Western Hemisphere. Incorporated by the state in 1819, it could have no religious affiliation, but Jefferson proscribed the teaching of theology altogether. "Here we are not afraid to follow truth wherever it may lead," he boasted, "nor to tolerate any error so long as reason is left free to combat it"; but he planned not to tolerate as part of the curriculum the teaching of sectarian dogma. As a result, the university emerged from often ugly and complicated legislative proceedings. This "strenuous labor," which Jefferson described as "the greatest" of all his services, made him feel like "a physician pouring medicine down the throat of a patient insensible of needing it." [49]

The proposed institution drew fire from religious leaders who opposed its alleged anticlericalism. The tirades of John Rice, a Presbyterian clergyman, for example, threatened to quash the proposal altogether. In 1820, when Rice got wind of the theological skepticism of Thomas Cooper, whom Jefferson had selected as professor of chemistry, mineralogy, and natural philosophy, he lashed out in his *Virginia Evangelical and Literary Magazine.* He portrayed Cooper as either a Unitarian or an atheist (there was little difference, he thought), and hinted that such heresies corrupted the entire enterprise. He forced on Jefferson the old dilemma of either professing his own religious beliefs or silently enduring a timeworn charge that had always endangered his reputation but now also injured his plans for higher education. Even before the Rice episode, Jefferson understood that smoldering suspicions about his views on God and man could ignite criticism of his university. "There are fanatics in both religion and politics," he wrote two years earlier, "who, without knowing me personally, have long been taught to consider me as a raw head and bloody bones." This time, he decided on a middle course and accepted Cooper's resignation. In private correspondence he scorned "the priests of the different religious sects," particularly Presbyterians, in this case the "loudest" and "most intolerant," whose "spells on the human mind" cast doubt on "its improvement." Even so, he said, rather than fight back, "it might be better to relieve Dr. Cooper, ourselves and the institution from this crusade." [50]

Although Jefferson refused to concede it, Rice had a point. After Cooper's withdrawal the university looked to two other Unitarians to replace him. Rice and his allies assumed what Jefferson's own letters seem to suggest: that the former president did not intend the University of Virginia to remain neutral on religion but meant it to promote, at least through its selection of faculty, religious rationalism. The conundrum, of course, was that any composition of the faculty or organization of the curriculum could affect morality. Even an institution that ignored religion might have a religious impact, secularizing its students at the public expense. And even an institution based on a nonsectarian philosophy would, at its core, rely on fundamental principles, seminal beliefs that could not be proven and must be considered matters of faith. Jefferson and other members of the university's board of visitors eventually agreed to settle the dispute by inviting sectarians to set up seminaries at the institution, where in public buildings they could educate students with private funds.[51]

Such acts of penance, however, would not erase lingering notions of Jefferson's irreligiosity. Even before the Cooper controversy, the publication in 1819 of *Bawlfredonia,* a political parable by Baltimore minister Jonas Clopper, underscored the resilience of decades-old criticisms of the former president's religious views. Clopper's satirical account of American history, which cast Jefferson as "Thomas Tammany Bawlfredonius," portrayed the former president in the same terms as had his earlier detractors: he led a faction that "rejected the Christian religion," which he badmouthed with friends "Pigman Puff" (Madison) and "Thomas Anguish" (Paine); he asserted that mankind had evolved from tadpoles, believed that winds and tides rather than God created the continents, and embraced the notion "that a man might have as many wives as he could keep, provided the majority of them were black."

Unlike his predecessors, however, Clopper was no Federalist. He was merely a Christian, a fact that he thought put him at odds with nearly all the leading figures of the founding generation, who were, he claimed, not Christians but deists. John Adams, for example, appeared in the parody as "Lord John of Onionville," who, "having been elevated by the votes of the Christians, and believing that in certain districts, it was necessary to keep up appearances, affected to treat the name of the Redeemer with holy veneration, notwithstanding his secret denial of his divinity." Adams was not the only hypocrite, Clopper charged, for there existed a secret fraternity of skeptical statesmen who, although they begrudgingly affected displays of respect for Christianity, resolved to undermine it by magnifying the sins of wayward ministers, corrupting the morals of the young, circulating irreligious tracts, and suggesting "doubts which may perplex and stagger the faith of the illiterate."[52]

In the decades to follow, others also moved beyond the factional loyalties of Jefferson's era but, like Clopper, not the memories. Whigs of the 1830s pinned charges of Jeffersonian skepticism on Jacksonian Democrats who refused to support public days of prayer. Some of the South's proslavery thinkers derided not only Jefferson's natural rights theories but also Jefferson, who was "not a Christian, but a disciple of the French philosophy." Connecticut theologian Horace Bushnell blamed the Civil War on southern impiety, a blot on the nation that he said Jefferson exemplified. At the turn of the twentieth century, the Methodist president of North Carolina's Trinity College, later renamed in honor of its benefactors in the Duke family, urged parents not to send their sons to state universities, where, he claimed, students imbibed the secularism of Jefferson—"a deist, an infidel, agnostic and materialist." In the face of this lingering odium, some of Jefferson's biographers and descendants worked to Christianize his image, a project aided by the reemergence a century ago of his "Philosophy of Jesus" and his later and larger compilation of gospel extracts, "The Life and Morals of Jesus." The success of their efforts can be gleaned from the fact that William Jennings Bryan, the fundamentalist who drafted and defended legislation forbidding the teaching of evolution in Tennessee schools, hung a portrait of Jefferson in his office and kept close at hand an edition of the third president's works—after the Bible, his favorite reading.[53]

Attempts by Jefferson's posthumous supporters to defend him by revising his faith speak volumes about the limitations of the election of 1800's religious legacy. Their strategy represents a clear retreat from the battles of 1796 and 1800, when Republicans answered charges of infidelity with principled defenses of free thought. Was the religious impact of the "revolution of 1800" revolutionary at all? Was Jefferson's victory merely a successful skirmish against a political-clerical alliance that won a war for American piety—a virtual counterrevolution that reversed the tide of deism and skepticism?

Certainly Jefferson was wrong to assume that the separation of church and state, a campaign that his Virginia religious freedom bill helped to spur and Massachusetts's 1833 disestablishment concluded, would cause Americans to coalesce around a creed of rational morality. Ignoring all evidence to the contrary, in 1822 he was still predicting "that there is not a *young man* now living . . .

who will not die an Unitarian." Even his own grandchildren, brought up as deists, entered their dotage as evangelical Christians.[54]

Disestablishment and deism actually aided the growth and proliferation of Christian faiths by destabilizing the religious marketplace, encouraging competition between churches, and contributing to what historian Nathan Hatch describes as "a period of religious ferment, chaos, and originality unmatched in American history." By 1845 Congregationalists, who in 1775 possessed twice the clergy of any other church, had preachers amounting to only one-tenth of the number of Methodist ministers. As Baptist, Methodist, and other evangelical faiths swelled in size, churches once at the center of American society became increasingly peripheral. But so did rational Christianity and deism, which, despite Jefferson's predictions, lost momentum in the new era of emotional revivals and camp meetings.[55]

The prominence of the religion issue in the election of 1800 was less a cause than an effect of these larger developments. Even so, the election's legacies should not be minimized. The successful campaign to elevate Jefferson to the presidency emboldened religious minorities and underscored the importance of people of all faiths in the American political process. At the same time, however, the vociferous opposition of his sectarian enemies had a chilling effect on the most radical forms of religious experimentation. Even Jefferson, ever sensitive to the barbs against him, redefined himself as a Christian, but only after first redefining Christianity. To Benjamin Rush he pledged his allegiance to the "genuine precepts" of Jesus: "I am a Christian, in the only sense in which he wished any one to be; sincerely attached to his doctrines, in preference to all others; ascribing to himself every human excellence, and believing he never claimed any other."[56]

NOTES

1. Frank L. Mott, *Jefferson and the Press* (Baton Rouge, 1943), 39; Paul F. Boller Jr., *Presidential Campaigns* (New York, 1984), 17–18.

2. Timothy Dwight, *Duty of Americans, at the Present Crisis, Illustrated in a Discourse, Preached on the Fourth of July, 1798 . . . at the Request of the Citizens of New-Haven* (New Haven, Conn., 1798), 20.

3. See Edwin S. Gaustad, *Sworn on the Altar of God: A Religious Biography of Thomas Jefferson* (Grand Rapids, Mich., 1996), 90–96; Frank Lambert, " 'God—And a Religious President . . . [or] Thomas Jefferson and No God': Campaigning for a Voter-Imposed Religious Test in 1800," *Journal of Church and State* 39 (1997): 769–89; Charles O. Lerche Jr., "Thomas Jefferson and the Election of 1800: A Case Study in the Political Smear," *WMQ* 3d ser., 5 (1948): 468, 470, 472–75; Charles F. O'Brien, "The Religious Issue in the Presidential Campaign of 1800," *Essex Institute Historical*

Collections 107 (1971): 82–93; Constance B. Schultz, "'Of Bigotry in Politics and Religion': Thomas Jefferson's Religion, the Federalist Press, and the Syllabus," *Virginia Magazine of History and Biography* 91 (1983): 73–91.

4. TJ to Judge Spencer Roane, 6 Sept. 1819, *TJW*, 1425.

5. "Extract of a letter . . . dated Sept. 30," *New York Minerva, & Mercantile Evening Advertiser,* 18 Oct. 1796; 25 Oct. 1796.

6. Charles Downer Hazen, *Contemporary American Opinion of the French Revolution* (Baltimore, 1897), 268; Adrien Dansette, *Religious History of Modern France,* trans. John Dingle (New York, 1961), 1:12–97; Florin Aftalion, *The French Revolution: An Economic Interpretation,* trans. Martin Thom (New York, 1990), 119ff; Christopher Hibbert, *The French Revolution* (London, 1980), 181–289; George Rudé, *The French Revolution* (New York, 1988), 82–122.

7. Gary B. Nash, "The American Clergy and the French Revolution," *WMQ* 3d ser., 22 (1965): 392–412, 402, 403.

8. *Gazette of the United States, & Philadelphia Daily Advertiser,* 1 Sept. 1796; A Correspondent in Connecticut, "Remarks on the *Aurora,* No. I," *Minerva, & Mercantile Evening Advertiser,* 3 Sept. 1796; [John Fenno], *Aurora & General Advetiser* (Philadelphia), 11 Nov. 1796, reprinted from the *Gazette of the United States.* Alexander Hamilton, about a year before the election, claimed to suspect Jefferson's hand in preparing "an intimate & close alliance with france subject[ing] us to the vortex [of] European politics." See Hamilton to Oliver Wolcott, 30 Oct. [to 12 Nov.] 1795, *AHP* 24:376.

9. [Coxe], *The Federalist: Containing Some Strictures upon a Pamphlet, Entitled, "The Pretensions of Thomas Jefferson to the Presidency. . ."; Part the Second* (Philadelphia, 1796), 14–15; "Elector of Electors," *Aurora & General Advertiser* (Philadelphia), 5 Nov. 1796.

10. [Smith], *The Pretensions of Thomas Jefferson to the Presidency . . . ,* 4; Thomas Paine, *The Age of Reason, First Part* (1794), in *Thomas Paine: Political Writings,* ed. Bruce Kuklick (New York, 1989), 208; Aftalion, *The French Revolution,* 61–67; Hibbert, *The French Revolution,* 230–33.

11. Robert M. S. McDonald, "Jefferson and America: Episodes in Image Formation" (Ph.D. diss., University of North Carolina at Chapel Hill, N.C., 1998), 61–67; Nash, "The American Clergy and the French Revolution," 402–3.

12. [Smith], *The Pretensions of Thomas Jefferson to the Presidency . . . ,* 37; *Notes,* 159; "From a Correspondent in Connecticut," "Remarks on the *Aurora,* No. I," *Minerva, & Mercantile Evening Advertiser,* 3 Sept. 1796.

13. "An American," "Of Religion," *Minerva,* 26 Sept. 1796, reprinted from the *Philadelphia New World.* On Webster's advocacy of toleration and his moderation as a Federalist, see Alan K. Snyder, *Defining Noah Webster: Mind and Morals in the Early Republic* (Lanham, Md., 1990), 148, 153, 162–63, 164, 173, 174–75.

14. "Extract," *Aurora* (Philadelphia), 4 Nov. 1796; "Dialogue between an Aristocrat and a Republican," ibid., 12 Nov. 1796.

15. On Jefferson's maintenance of religious privacy, see TJ to Adams, 11 Jan. 1817, *AJL,* 506; Paul K. Conkin, "The Religious Pilgrimage of Thomas Jefferson," in *Jeffersonian Legacies,* ed. Peter S. Onuf (Charlottesville, Va., 1993), 35–36. For cogent analyses of Jefferson's evolving faith, see Conkin, "Religious Pilgrimage," 19–49, and the introduction by Eugene R. Sheridan in *Jefferson's Extracts from the Gospels: "The Philosophy of Jesus" and "The Life and Morals of Jesus,"* ed. Dickinson W. Adams (Princeton, N.J., 1983), 3–42.

16. See McDonald, "Jefferson and America," 63–64, 71, 72, 76–77, 91, 114–16, 146–48.

17. For a thoughtful analysis of Jefferson that argues persuasively for his inclusion in the latter group, see Jean M. Yarbrough, *American Virtues: Thomas Jefferson on the Character of a Free People* (Lawrence, Kans., 1998), esp. chap. 2.

18. William Barry Grove to James Hogg, 4 Jan. 1797, William Barry Grove Papers, Southern Historical Collection, University of North Carolina Library; *Gazette of the United States,* 4 March

1797; Priestley to Lindsey, 13 Jan. 1797, Original Letters from Dr. Joseph Priestley, Dr. Williams's Library, London.

19. See, for example, "An American," *Aurora* (Philadelphia), 9 Jan. 1797; Robert Goodloe Harper, Circular Letter to Constituents, 13 March 1797, *Circular Letters of Congressmen to Their Constituents, 1789–1829,* ed. Noble E. Cunningham, (Chapel Hill, N.C., 1978), 78–79.

20. See Joanne B. Freeman, "The Election of 1800: A Study in the Logic of Political Change," *Yale Law Journal* 108 (1999), 1959–94; James Roger Sharp, *American Politics in the Early Republic: The New Nation in Crisis* (New Haven, Conn., 1993).

21. William Linn, *Serious Considerations on the Election of a President: Addressed to the Citizens of the United States* (New York, 1800), 32.

22. Gouverneur Morris, [diary entry for 13 May 1800], *The Diary and Letters of Gouverneur Morris, Minister of the United States to France; Member of the Constitutional Convention, etc.,* 2 vols., ed. Anne Cary Morris (New York, 1888), 2:387; John W. Steele to John Haywood, 11 March 1801, Earnest Haywood Collection, Southern Historical Collection, University of North Carolina Library; J. W. Steele to Anne Steele [1800], Steele Papers, Southern Historical Collection, University of North Carolina Library; Stanley Elkins and Eric McKitrick, *The Age of Federalism: The Early American Republic, 1788–1800* (New York, 1993), 736.

23. Joseph Priestley to Theopolis Lindsey, 21 March 1799, Manuscripts Department, Dr. Williams's Library, London; John Marshall to James Markham Marshall, 16 Dec. 1799, *The Papers of John Marshall,* 8 vols. to date, ed. Charles T. Cullen (Chapel Hill, N.C., 1974–), 4:44–45; Alexander Hamilton, *Letter from Alexander Hamilton, Concerning the Public Conduct and Character of John Adams, Esq., President of the United States* (New York, 1800), reprinted in *AHP* 25:186–234; Morris, [diary entry for 13 May 1800], *Diary and Letters of Gouverneur Morris,* 2:387. See also Priestley to Lindsey, 29 May 1800, Manuscripts Department, Dr. Williams's Library, London. On the plot to elect Pinckney, see Elkins and McKitrick, *Age of Federalism,* 734–36. On rumors of an Adams-Jefferson alliance, see the account in *AHP* 24:483–86 n. 3.

24. David Hackett Fischer, *The Revolution of American Conservatism: The Federalist Party in the Era of Jeffersonian Democracy* (New York, 1965), 52–54, 150–52; *Address to the Federal Republicans of the State of New-Jersey* (Trenton, N.J., 1800), 6; Robert Troup to Rufus King, 1 Oct. 1800, *Life and Correspondence of Rufus King,* 6 vols., ed. Charles R. King (New York, 1896–97), 3:315.

25. William C. Dowling, *Literary Federalism in the Age of Jefferson: Joseph Dennie and The Port Folio, 1801–1812* (Columbia, S.C., 1999), 4–12, 6; Timothy Dwight, *Vermont Travel Journal,* n.d., Dwight Family Papers, Manuscripts and Archives, Yale University Library; John Ward Fenno, *Desultory Reflections on the New Political Aspects of Public Affairs in the United States of America, since the Commencement of the Year 1799* (New York, 1800), 52–53; *A Candid Address, to the Freemen of Rhode-Island, on the Subject of the Approaching Election* (Providence, 1800), 1; *Address to the Federal Republicans of the State of New-Jersey* (Trenton, N.J., 1800), 8.

26. "A Federal Republican" [Henry William DeSaussure], *Address to the Citizens of South-Carolina on the Approaching Election of a President and Vice-President of the United States* (Charleston, 1800), 17 n; [John Mason], *The Voice of Warning, to Christians, on the Ensuing Election of a President of the United States* (New York, 1800), 8, 27; Thomas Robbins [diary entry for 8 May 1800], *Diary of Thomas Robbins,* 2 vols., ed. Increase N. Tarbox (Boston, 1886–87), 1:114; "A Humble Citizen," *Connecticut Courant,* 17 March 1800; *Gazette of the United States,* 10 Sept. 1800.

27. Linn, *Serious Considerations,* 4, 5; [Mason], *The Voice of Warning,* 8, 35.

28. [Mason], *The Voice of Warning,* 9–18; Linn, *Serious Considerations,* 6–8, 13–19. See the relevant passages in *Notes,* 31, 102, 138–39, 147, 159, 164–65.

29. Linn, *Serious Considerations,* 20–21, 25, 16–17; [Mason], *The Voice of Warning,* 21–23.

30. Priestley to Lindsey, 21 March 1799, Manuscripts Department, Dr. Williams's Library, London; Hugh Williamson to TJ, 6 July 1801, Thomas Jefferson Papers, Lib. Cong.; Burleigh, *Connecti-*

cut Courant, 15 Sept. 1800; "A Federal Republican" [DeSaussure], 10, 15, 14; Lerche, "Jefferson and the Election of 1800," 480–81. On America's rapprochement with France, see Elkins and McKitrick, *Age of Federalism,* 618–23, 635–90.

31. A South-Carolina Federalist [DeSaussure], *Answer to a Dialogue between a Federalist and a Republican,* (Charleston, S.C., 1800), 21; [Noah Webster], *A Rod for the Fool's Back* (New Haven, Conn., 1800), 7; Fenno, *Desultory Reflections,* 9. See also Lewis R. Morris to Jacob Morris, 28 Oct. 1800, Morris Papers, Manuscripts Department, New-York Historical Society; Burleigh, *Connecticut Courant,* 20 Sept. 1800.

32. "A Layman," *The Claims of Thomas Jefferson to the Presidency,* 52; [Mason], *The Voice of Warning,* 26, 30; Dwight, *Duty of Americans,* 16.

33. Richard Stanford to James Patterson, 28 Feb. 1803, Miscellaneous Manuscripts, North Carolina State Archives, Raleigh; "A Republican" [Jonathan Russell], *To the Freemen of Rhode-Island, &c.* ([Providence?], 1800), 2; "A Republican," *National Intelligencer,* 31 Oct. 1800, 2 March 1801.

34. [Webster], *A Rod for the Fool's Back,* 7–8; "Grotius" [DeWitt Clinton], *A Vindication of Thomas Jefferson, against the Charges Contained in a Pamphlet Entitled, "Serious Considerations," &c.* (New York, 1800), 11.

35. Priestley to Lindsey, 19 May 1800, Manuscripts Department, Dr. Williams's Library, London; "Marcus Brutus" [Benjamin Pollard?], *Serious Facts, Opposed to "Serious Considerations": Or, The Voice of Warning to Religious Republicans* (n.p., 1800), 11, 12, 2; "Timoleon" [Tunis Wortman], *A Solemn Address, to Christians and Patriots, upon the Approaching Election of a President of the United States: in answer to a pamphlet, entitled "Serious Considerations," &c.* (New York, 1800), 13, 15, 34; "Civis," *National Intelligencer,* 11 Nov. 1800.

36. Americanus [John Beckley], *Address to the People of the United States: With an Epitome and Vindication of the Public Life and Character of Thomas Jefferson* (Philadelphia, 1800), 32. On the circulation of Beckley's pamphlet, see Noble E. Cunningham Jr., *The Jeffersonian Republicans: The Formation of a Party Organization, 1789–1801* (Chapel Hill, N.C., 1957), 198.

37. *Address to the Citizens of Kent, on the Approaching Election* (Wilmington, Del., [1800]), 4; [Beckley], *Address to the People of the United States,* 7; "A Voter," *To the Voters of Cecil: No. I* (Wilmington, Del., [1800]), 4; Abraham Bishop, *Connecticut Republicanism: An Oration, on the Extent & Power of Political Delusion* ([New Haven, Conn.], 1800), 44.

38. "Timoleon," *National Intelligencer,* 10 Nov. 1800, 31 Oct. 1800; Bishop, *Connecticut Republicanism,* 20; Anonymous, *A Test of the Religious Principles of Mr. Jefferson* (Philadelphia, 1800), ii; "Timoleon" [Wortman], *A Solemn Address,* 9.

39. Fischer, *Revolution of American Conservatism,* 224–25; Letter of Benjamin Noves, *Aurora* (Philadelphia), 13 Aug. 1800.

40. Cato West to Andrew Jackson, 26 June 1801, *The Papers of Andrew Jackson,* 5 vols., ed. Sam E. Smith et al. (Knoxville, Tenn., 1980–96), 1:246; Robbins, [diary entry for 21 Dec. 1800], *Diary of Thomas Robbins* 1:127; Fischer, *Revolution of American Conservatism,* 185; *National Intelligencer,* 3 Nov. 1800.

41. TJ, First Inaugural Address, 4 March 1801, *TJW,* 492–96.

42. L. H. Butterfield, "Elder John Leland, Jeffersonian Itinerant," *Proceedings of the American Antiquarian Society* 62 (1952): 219–29; McDonald, "Jefferson and America," 156–57; TJ to Levi Lincoln, 1 Jan. 1802, Ford, 9:346–47.

43. Danbury Baptist Association to TJ, 7 Oct. 1801, Thomas Jefferson Papers, Lib. Cong.; TJ to Messrs. Nehemiah Dodge and Others, a Committee of the Danbury Baptist Association, in the State of Connecticut, 1 Jan. 1802, *TJW,* 510.

44. TJ to Messrs. Nehemiah Dodge and Others, a Committee of the Danbury Baptist Association, in the State of Connecticut, 1 Jan. 1802; James H. Hutson, "Thomas Jefferson's Letter to the Danbury Baptists: A Controversy Rejoined," *WMQ* 3d ser., 56 (1999): 775–90, and James H. Hutson, "James H. Hutson Responds," *WMQ* 3d ser., 56 (1999): 823–24.

45. Sheridan, introduction to Adams, *Jefferson's Extracts from the Gospels*, 14–30, 35; TJ to Moses Robinson, 23 March 1801, ibid., 324–25.

46. TJ to Margaret Bayard Smith, 6 Aug. 1816, ibid., 376. On attacks on Jefferson occasioned by Paine's return, see Jerry Wayne Knudson, "The Jefferson Years: Response by the Press, 1801–1809" (Ph.D. diss., University of Virginia, 1962), 162–96.

47. Gaustad, *Sworn on the Altar of God*, 105. Although diminished in quantity, attacks on Jefferson's religious views in 1804 differed little substantively from those of 1800; see, for example, Clement C. Moore, *Observations upon Certain Passages in Mr. Jefferson's Notes on Virginia, which Appear to Have a Tendency to Subvert Religion, and Establish a False Philosophy* (New York, 1804).

48. TJ, Second Inaugural Address, 4 March 1805, *TJW*, 519–20.

49. TJ, "A Bill for the Establishment of an University," [1818], Thomas Jefferson Papers, University of Virginia Library; TJ to Thomas Cooper, 14 Aug. 1820, L&B, 25:269; TJ to Augustus B. Woodward, 3 April 1825, Ford, 12:408; TJ to William Roscoe, 27 Dec. 1820, L&B, 15:303; TJ to Joseph C. Cabell, 7 Feb. 1826, Thomas Jefferson Papers, University of Virginia Library.

50. Dumas Malone, *The Public Life of Thomas Cooper* (New Haven, Conn., 1926), 239–45; TJ to Cabell, 26 Feb. 1818, Thomas Jefferson Papers, University of Virginia Library; TJ to William Short, 13 April 1820, L&B, 15:246; TJ to Robert B. Taylor, 16 May 1820, Thomas Jefferson Papers, Lib. Cong.

51. James G. West Jr., *The Politics of Reason and Revelation: Religion and Civic Life in the New Nation* (Lawrence, Kans., 1996), 61–67.

52. Jonas Clopper, *Bawlfredonia* (1819; Upper Saddle River, N.J., 1969), esp. 73–74, 103, 126–27, 147.

53. Merrill D. Peterson, *The Jefferson Image in the American Mind* (New York, 1960), 92–94, 165, 219, 243, 158–59, 300–304, 259.

54. TJ to Benjamin Waterhouse, 26 June 1822, *TJW*, 1459. On the religious pilgrimage of Jefferson's grandchildren and their generation of Virginians, see Jan Lewis, *The Pursuit of Happiness: Family and Values in Jefferson's Virginia* (New York, 1983), 40–68.

55. Nathan O. Hatch, *The Democratization of American Christianity* (New Haven, Conn., 1989), 4, 64; Joyce Appleby, *Inheriting the Revolution: The First Generation of Americans* (Cambridge, Mass., 2000), 182–89, 191–93; Gordon S. Wood, *The Radicalism of the American Revolution* (New York, 1992), 329–33.

56. TJ to Benjamin Rush, 21 April 1803, Adams, *Jefferson's Extracts from the Gospels*, 331.

CHAPTER 8

Thomas Jefferson in Gabriel's Virginia

James Sidbury

From the publication of Robert McColley's *Slavery and Jeffersonian Virginia* more than three decades ago through the very recent appearance of *Sally Hemings and Thomas Jefferson,* many fine historians have struggled to make sense of the seemingly anomalous title of McColley's book.[1] If the term "Jeffersonian Virginia" is meant as shorthand for the society that produced so many of our "founding fathers," then how do we reconcile the picture of many of these icons of "American liberty" and the equality of "all men" with their reliance on a brutal and coercive labor regime that turned humans into chattels? Because this question speaks to fundamental issues about the nature of the nation that these fathers founded, and because it has uncertain but undeniable relevance for those who seek to make sense of the meaning of race in modern America, it is not surprising that work addressing it has garnered so much public attention. Of course the story's "ratings" have also been helped by the degree to which it is entangled in serious questions about an ex-president's sex life. No matter how legitimate and important these questions may be from a scholarly perspective, they have contributed to the soap-opera atmosphere surrounding contemporary discussion of race, slavery, and the founders, especially in light of the ardent efforts of some to "defend" Jefferson from the "charge" of having fathered "black" children.

Much has come from this work. Most importantly, historians have come to a consensus on the general claim that the simultaneous growth of black slavery and white freedom was no anomaly and that the egalitarian rhetoric of the

American Revolution rested in important ways on the exclusion of black people from its seemingly inclusive terms.[2] Arguments about the psychological roots of the founding fathers' behavior may not have produced the same level of agreement, but they have deepened our understanding of the meanings of race and servitude in the lives and thought of the first generation of national states-men. And recent work on the relationship between Sally Hemings and Thomas Jefferson has offered a stark warning about the role that racial assumptions con-tinue to play in shaping historians' decisions about the "reliability" of the evi-dence they use to reconstruct the past.[3] In short, analyses of the place of slavery in Jeffersonian Virginia have greatly enriched our understanding of American history and culture.

That said, it is also true that this scholarship has often remained within pa-rameters that mirror the exclusions for which Jefferson is often held account-able. It has done so by focusing primarily on the place of slavery and race in white Virginians' (or Americans') minds, rather than on the lives and percep-tions of the enslaved. Scholars have explored Jefferson's antislavery pronounce-ments and his racist statements about black people with great subtlety. They have pointed out the importance of the three-fifths clause to his victory in the presidential election of 1800—the "revolution of 1800"—and they have often excoriated him for condemning efforts to keep slavery out of Missouri in 1820. They have sought to understand the complexities of his support of African col-onization and "diffusion." They have juxtaposed the evidence that he was, by the standards of his class, a benign slavedriver with his callous assertion that slave women were more valuable than slave men because they produced human capital rather than merely perishable commodities.[4] It often seems as if we know as much as can be known about Jefferson the master, Jefferson the racial theorist, and Jefferson the moralist.[5] Neither he himself nor his fellow Virginia founders have come out of this extended reexamination with intact reputations as lovers of liberty and equality.

Of course the stakes of this examination have always been higher than just the reputations of a group of dead statesmen. These stakes have been deter-mined by an assumption that is best summed up in the frequently quoted as-sertion of a nineteenth-century historian that "if Jefferson was wrong," then "America is wrong."[6] Pointing out just how wrong Jefferson and his white con-temporaries were on questions of race and slavery has been a way of showing the degree to which racism and slavery lay near the center of American history and culture. Understanding the ways that they were wrong has been part of a project to confront those wrongs in order to begin to make them right.

The obvious attractions of this project, however, may have obscured the degree to which the black people living in Virginia around the time of the "revolution of 1800" are rendered objects by this analysis. A very few black people—especially the Hemingses, but other residents of Monticello as well (and by extension their counterparts at, for instance, Mount Vernon or Montpelier)—could influence and were influenced by Jefferson's racial theories and sexual practices. But nearly half of Virginia's population in 1800 was black, and precious few black Virginians would have known or cared what the sage of Monticello thought about the respective shares of beauty given by the divine creator to black and white people, nor would they have known or cared about Jefferson's critique of Phillis Wheatley's poetry. Nor can one assume that they would have much cared whom he was sleeping with. I would like to redirect attention, at least temporarily, from the place of slavery in Jeffersonian Virginia to the very different question of the place of Thomas Jefferson in the lives of enslaved Virginians.

This project should remind us of some of the obvious limitations of the "revolution of 1800." However fundamental Jefferson may have believed the changes in government caused by his election to have been, the Democratic-Republican platform was nowhere near the most radical alteration in government envisioned in Virginia that year. An enslaved blacksmith named Gabriel and his fellow Richmond-area conspirators attempted to foment a much more revolutionary movement during the summer of 1800, a movement built on a conception of Virginia's history that differed radically from the one held by whites. At the very time when Jeffersonian Republicans were organizing to "save" the new Republic from monarchical Federalism, Gabriel organized his followers to rise up and abolish slavery within the Commonwealth. While Jefferson and his followers worried about a foreign policy that favored Britain and a centralizing government that reflected British principles, Richmond slaves came together in churches and at social gatherings to express their faith that God would favor their struggle for liberty. They planned to sneak into Virginia's capital on the evening of 30 August, set fire to warehouses in order to draw townsmen away from their homes, and then seize Governor James Monroe and hold him hostage for black liberty. Theirs would have been a true "revolution of 1800."

Historians differ over the specific goals of Gabriel's conspirators, but they clearly sought far more than Jefferson's revolution offered. If the ideology behind the conspiracy was inspired by the most egalitarian strains of Jeffersonian thought, then the conspirators sought to build a society without slavery or racial discrimination, one in which artisans' property rights in their skills were as worthy of legal protection as planters' property rights in the soil. If, on the other hand, the conspiracy was motivated by a millennialist vision of God's justice on earth, then the conspirators envisioned armies protected by divine favor punishing slaveholders and elevating the chosen people to rule over their oppressors. In either case, black Virginians attempted to come together behind a vision of the Commonwealth that was rooted in their history in America, a history of forced labor in Virginia's fields and workshops, of family life in the state's plantation communities, of cooperative resistance to masters, and of religious conversion in Virginia's remarkably egalitarian evangelical churches.[7] It is not surprising that the political program that inspired black Virginians differed from, and sought more fundamental change than, that pursued by their masters. It is also unsurprising, if perhaps less obvious, that Thomas Jefferson, their masters' chosen political leader, had a relatively small place in their world.

Scholars examining Jefferson's stances on slavery and race have certainly uncovered some aspects of his life that influenced enslaved Virginians. He most affected the small fraction of enslaved Virginians whom he owned—roughly between one and two hundred people at any given time. The conventional view during Jefferson's life was that he was a benign master who was relatively solicitous of his bondsmen's welfare.[8] Given the hagiographic tone of so much that has been written about him, one might be forgiven for being skeptical of these claims, but it is worth noting that two black men who grew up on Monticello—Madison Hemings and Israel Jefferson—provided limited confirmation of the claim when they were interviewed following the Civil War.[9] And there is other contemporary evidence as well, from his injunctions to supervisors to avoid the whip, to descriptions of his slaves' housing as "much better than . . . on any other [Virginia] plantation," to reports that he preferred to stimulate productivity through positive incentives rather than through punishment. A former overseer who was interviewed years after Jefferson's death remembered his former employer as "always very kind and indulgent to his servants." Jefferson also delegated substantial supervisory responsibilities to elite slaves on his plantations, a management decision that may have been more humane toward the enslaved than hiring more white overseers.[10]

There is, however, countervailing evidence that suggests that Jefferson may have been a tougher master than convention suggests. In part, this was all but inevitable given his extensive career in public service. Jefferson spent most of the period from 1770 to 1810 away from Monticello, and during these forty years he neither could nor did closely monitor the treatment that his slaves received at the hands of his overseers. Moreover, as the historian Joseph Ellis has pointed out, even while resident at Monticello, Jefferson arranged his life in such a way as to shield himself from much of the brutality of slavery. Though he rode among the fields surrounding the big house each day, many of his slaves lived on outlying quarters that he rarely visited. Despite his famous claims for the nobility of agricultural labor, he directed his primary attention when at Monticello not to the fields but to his various workshops, so it seems clear that even when resident he left most decisions about most of his slaves' daily welfare to overseers and drivers.[11] Another way he sought to shield himself from slavery's brutality was by avoiding the whip, but he could not escape the need to punish slaves who refused to respond to "incentives," acknowledging that the whip must be "resorted to . . . in extremities."[12] He preferred to deal with "recalcitrant" bondspeople by selling them away from their friends and family, a punishment at least as brutal as flogging.[13]

Jefferson's relationship with Sally Hemings, like his actions as a master, profoundly affected a small circle of enslaved people, in this case one that radiated outward with decreasing influence from Hemings herself to her enslaved kin and thence to other black residents of Monticello and the neighborhood. It is perhaps inevitable that much speculation about this relationship has centered on the question of the two principals' feelings toward each other. Should they be considered lovers? A rapist and his victim? An affectionate if exploitive master and a more or less calculating concubine? But if curiosity about this question is unavoidable, it should not obscure the small number of questions whose answers would be changed if the truth could be known. Divining an answer is certainly important for those who seek to pass moral judgment on Jefferson, and the nature of the relationship must have been of enormous importance to Hemings herself. To the extent that the emotional nature of his relationship with Hemings contributed to Jefferson's decision to free her children, it had a deep influence on them (beyond that rooted in their love and concern for their mother).[14] And if the answer was known to neighbors living near Monticello, it may have had very limited influence on informal norms governing local sexual relationships between masters and slaves.[15] Nonetheless, neither Jefferson's behavior as a plantation owner nor his relationship with Sally Hemings would have loomed very large in the lives of most enslaved residents of Virginia. Historians' intense interest in these questions has usually grown out of their conviction that Jefferson is a figure upon whom it is important to pass moral

judgment—if Jefferson is wrong, then America is wrong—rather than on a belief that the experiences of enslaved Virginians are worthy of sustained inquiry.

If Jefferson's relationship with Sally Hemings has led many to cast aspersions on his private morality, his efforts to explain racial difference have left the
darkest stain on his public record. Beginning with an extended passage in *Notes
on Virginia* and continuing through shorter comments in various letters, Jefferson expressed something considerably stronger than a suspicion (though
sometimes it appears weaker than an absolute conviction) that black people
were inherently inferior to white people. In the most famous of these expressions, he speculated on the scientific explanation for differences in skin color
and then insisted that such differences laid the foundation for "a greater or
lesser share of beauty in the two races." Blacks, he suggested, were almost as far
below whites in natural endowment as they were above "oran-utan[s]." He also
found them smellier, less farsighted, more libidinous, and "in reason much inferior" to their distant white cousins.[16] As many scholars have pointed out, this
language anticipated the turn toward scientific explanations of racial difference
that came to dominate nineteenth- and early-twentieth-century racist thought
with such poisonous consequences. The importance of this strain of Jefferson's
thought for moral judgments about his statesmanship is obvious, and Winthrop Jordan has led the way in using this aspect of Jefferson's thought to provide a window on the pathology of racist thought that emerged out of the revolutionary era.

The immediate importance of these pronouncements for black Virginians,
however, remains murky. There is no reason to believe that other Virginia masters looked to Jefferson for guidance in their racial thought, nor is it clear that
slaves would have received worse treatment from masters who shared Jefferson's
racial theories than from those who did not. Had there been any realistic chance
for a voluntary general emancipation in Virginia during or after the revolutionary period, then Jefferson's pronouncements might have lessened them, but
no such chance existed.[17] Jefferson's prominence did, of course, mean that his
views were widely read, and his became an important voice affecting the hard-
ening of racist thought throughout the West during the early nineteenth century. Northern black intellectuals recognized his influence and sought to refute
his racist language. The New Yorker William Hamilton, for example, derided
Jefferson for "blasphemously" suggesting that "Negroes have no soul, they are
not men, they are a species of the ourang outang," and asked how a man could
continue to own slaves after admitting in writing that God could not "favour

the cause of the master in case of an insurrection."[18] David Walker extended the attack, asking incredulously how "Mr. Jefferson" could possibly think blacks "unfortunate" for having been given the color that "pleased our Creator." Walker warned, in fact, that Jefferson was too important among whites for his racist "assertions" to "pass away into oblivion," and thus that blacks had to answer them.[19] The poisonous effects of Jefferson's racist pronouncements were real, but the poison worked slowly. Its influence was obvious to black Americans like David Walker by 1829. By then, however, Gabriel's Virginia had been transformed—virtually destroyed—by more prosaic forces like changing commodity prices, alterations in planters' crop mixes, and, of course, the invention of the cotton gin.[20] Jefferson's statecraft did in fact contribute to this process, but through the unintended consequences of actions that were, at least to Jefferson's mind, relatively unrelated to slavery, rather than through those acts for which he has so often been blamed.

Two of the major events of Jefferson's presidency—the Louisiana Purchase and the closing of the African slave trade—had devastating effects on enslaved Virginians, though in neither case does Jefferson appear to have thought much about the consequences of his actions for black Virginians. One can, of course, question the degree to which Jefferson should be individually credited or blamed for either event. While he seized the opportunity afforded by Napoleon's willingness to sell the Louisiana Territory, he himself had previously maintained that much of that land was destined by nature to enter into the friendly orbit, if not the possession, of the United States. Nonetheless, his ardent efforts to acquire New Orleans, and his willingness to stretch his own constitutional principles to annex the huge territory that France sold to the United States, rightly convinced his contemporaries, as they have subsequent historians, that he should be considered the architect of the Louisiana Purchase.[21]

Jefferson has generally not been credited with as decisive a role in the closing of the Atlantic slave trade. This is partially because one can too easily assume that the constitutional provision preventing congressional action to close the slave trade prior to 1808 did in fact mandate that it close at that point. This was not, of course, the case: Congress had to pass a law to close the trade, and did so. The near unanimity of the Congress in support of closing the trade also contributes to the superficial treatment the passage of the act has often received, treatment summarized by the historian William Freehling's complaint that it too often appears to be a "non-event worthy of no more than a sentence."[22] But Jefferson did take the lead in asking Congress to close the trade at the earliest

possible moment, and he did so with a characteristically stirring appeal to natural rights: he called for an end to American "participation in those violations
of human rights which have been so long continued on the unoffending inhabitants of Africa, and which the morality, the reputation, and the best interests of
our country, have long been eager to proscribe."[23] After penning this stirring
call to immediate action, Jefferson largely avoided the contentious congressional debates that arose over what penalties should be invoked against those
who carried on the international slave trade in violation of the new law and what
should be done with, to, or for the people saved from illegal slavers. The law as
passed certainly left large loopholes, which slavers could and did exploit to
carry on an illicit international trade.[24] Nonetheless, Jefferson's leadership contributed to the rapid passage of the law, and the law did in fact end the large-
scale importation of enslaved Africans into the United States.[25]

These two acts—the closing of the Atlantic slave trade and the acquisition
of Louisiana—helped set in motion a series of events that proved disastrous for
residents of Gabriel's Virginia. By themselves they greatly increased the demand
for slaves living in longer-settled regions of the South by incorporating lightly
settled French territory into the Union. They also greatly accelerated the rate
at which southerners were expropriating Indian land and expanding into western land already claimed by the United States. Once Louisiana was part of the
United States, West Florida—the gulf coast of present-day Mississippi and Alabama—became more likely to pass from Spanish to American hands. In reasonably short order following the War of 1812 the United States had gained
the Floridas and had largely broken the Creek Confederacy. This opened the
rich river bottomland between Georgia and the Mississippi River for settlement, while simultaneously providing aspiring cotton planters an outlet to the
Atlantic market through Mobile Bay. Cotton planters flooded into the newly
opened territory.[26] This produced an unmitigated disaster for the residents of
Gabriel's Virginia because, without access to African slaves, would-be planters
who moved to the territories then in the process of becoming Louisiana, Mississippi, and Alabama were destined to look primarily to the southeast—especially the Chesapeake—for sources of slave labor.[27]

The effect of this confluence of forces on the enslaved residents of the
Chesapeake was immediate and enormous. Historian Allan Kulikoff has shown
that between 1810 and 1820 approximately 124,000 slaves were exported from
Maryland and Virginia, this from a total enslaved population of roughly half a
million, according to the 1810 Census. Of those, well over half (approximately

77,000) were forced to move to land opened up as a partial result of these Jeffersonian policies. The process only accelerated in the succeeding years: "During the 1820s and 1830s, from 350,000 to 450,000 slaves were forced . . . from the upper to the lower South."[28] Clearly the interstate slave trade grew in the wake of expansionist Jeffersonian policies, and those policies, along with the closing of the Atlantic slave trade, constituted Jefferson's most important legacy for Gabriel's Virginia.

To some degree the contours of that legacy are obvious. Historians have disagreed over the extent to which marriages were broken and parents separated from their children; they have also argued over the number of slaves sold to slave traders as opposed to being moved with masters who were themselves striking out for the southwest. Regardless of the answers to these technical questions, the emotional toll of the trade on black families and individuals seems incontrovertible.[29] Relatively few of those who suffered through these disruptions left written evidence of their distress, but the emotions involved are straightforward enough that a single surviving example should suffice. In 1835, when the Brownrigg family moved from North Carolina to Mississippi, they forced their nearly one hundred slaves to leave their homes for the southwest. Among the involuntary migrants was an enslaved woman named Phebe Brownrigg who was forcibly separated from a daughter living on a neighboring plantation. When Phebe Brownrigg realized that she would not get to say goodbye, she wrote to say that she "expect[ed] to start" the following month for "the Mississippi river." Though she feared that she would "never [again] meet" her daughter "in this world," she looked forward to the time they would "meet in heaven where . . . [they would] part no more."[30] Jeffersonian policies were not alone responsible for the innumerable mothers separated from daughters, husbands separated from wives, or friends separated from friends by the interstate trade, but they contributed to these repeated personal tragedies that devastated the residents of Gabriel's Virginia.

The costs of the interstate trade to black Virginians were not limited to heartbreakingly brutal disruptions of family and communal ties. Enslaved people had been planting roots in Virginia and Maryland for better than a century prior to the advent of the interstate slave trade. During that time they had forged plantation communities with a distinctive culture. They had battled their masters over the terms under which they were forced to work, over their customary rights to food and leisure, and over numerous other issues. None of this had been done in the absence of physical mobility: in addition to steady arrivals of people torn from their African homes during the first half of the eighteenth century, many black Virginians had undergone forced migration into the Virginia Piedmont and beyond during the second half of the century. As runaway advertisements, planter papers, church records, and evidence produced by Gabriel's Conspiracy make clear, however, migration within the state led to the extension of the scope of plantation communities and the forging of a sense of history among black Virginians as a people.[31] The experience of being ripped out of a deeply rooted community and culture to be forcibly transported and sold into a frontier setting peopled not only by unknown white people but by blacks from Africa and the Gullah coast of South Carolina must have been a disruptive experience analogous, though not equal, to that of Africans sold into the Atlantic trade.[32]

Friends and relatives of Gabriel suffered through a painful move of just this sort. The state of Virginia hanged Gabriel in the winter of 1800, but the enslaved people with whom he lived, presumably including his wife Nanny and any children they might have had, continued to live on Thomas Henry Prosser's plantation outside Richmond after the rebel leader's death. That an attempted revolution had been conceived on his land may have troubled Prosser, but it did not stop him from marrying a member of the locally prominent Hylton family in 1801. Presumably Lucy Hylton followed local convention by bringing a number of enslaved people from her father's household into that of her new husband, perhaps helping to replace the six conspirators whose labor Prosser had lost to the hangman's noose and the seventh who had been deported by the state. Gabriel's spirit seems to have remained within the Prosser plantation's community after his death, for there was a second, smaller insurrection scare on the plantation in 1806 that led to the trial and acquittal of three men who belonged to Prosser. At about the same time, however, Prosser began to fall into financial difficulty—he executed a deed offering nine slaves as security for debt that same year—and by 1819 he decided to pull up stakes, sell his Henrico County plantation, and move to the fertile cotton fields of the Deep South. In 1820 he was living with his family and twenty-seven slaves in Mississippi's Black Belt on land that Jeffersonian statecraft had helped bring into the plantation complex.[33]

It is difficult to know how many of those twenty-seven people had grown up on Prosser's plantation on the outskirts of Richmond, or what percentage of Prosser's Virginia slaves moved with the household. Even if Prosser took all the slaves he owned and only those he owned—the model of westward migration that least disrupted upper southern slave communities—the effects of this migration on Gabriel's former kin and friends would have been enormous. Those who had married off the plantation or had children living on neighboring plantations were permanently separated from their families. Even those whose families were not broken lost friends. And all were involuntarily ripped from what was, by southern standards, a cosmopolitan neighborhood that afforded them easy access to urban life in Richmond, and deposited in one of the most rural and isolated places in the United States.[34]

The slaves Prosser transported to Mississippi, like other residents of Gabriel's Virginia who, partly because of Jeffersonian policy, were sold into the Deep South, had to revisit battles over customary rights, labor regimes, and subsistence that had largely been settled in Virginia. And they had to do so in the face of cultural and material hurdles that complicated their struggles. Some of these complications were rooted in material conditions of life: cotton was much better suited to closely monitored gang labor than was tobacco, so masters and their overseers began the struggles to increase slave productivity with an advantage they had lacked in the Chesapeake.[35] Slaves' disadvantages on this material plane were intensified by the cultural heterogeneity that must have characterized many, perhaps most, Deep South cotton plantations. These plantations were larger in scale than Chesapeake tobacco quarters, and their slave communities would have included people from different traditions. Both of these factors must have made forging cooperative communal resistance more complicated. Though it is difficult to prove, it seems certain that long-settled, stable plantation communities must have found it easier to work together to subvert masters and overseers. Black Virginians who were sold into the Deep South traveled from a plantation world largely characterized by such communities to one in which they were exceedingly rare.

Nor was grief for lost kin and friends the only effect on those left behind in Virginia. Escaping sale to the South once did not, after all, exempt anyone from the threat of future sale, as Charles Ball, Frederick Douglass, and other authors of slave narratives made clear.[36] Masters certainly used the threat of sale (and the example of the sale of others) to weaken black Virginians' ability to resist. Historian Walter Johnson notes that several slave narratives reported masters threatening their slaves with sale to the South—with "put[ting] us in his pocket quick"—if they proved uncooperative.[37] Thus it is not simply that black Virginians sold into the interstate trade lost their positions in stable communities that had fought for and often won contingent recognition of customary rights—the only form of recognition that the enslaved could win. The trade also tipped the balance in those ongoing battles further in the favor of masters and overseers. And while Thomas Jefferson probably did not think through the connection between his policies and these effects on black Virginians, he was well aware of the extra power that blacks' fear of being sold south put into his own hands as a master. In 1803, the very year of the Louisiana Purchase, he instructed Thomas Mann Randolph, his son-in-law, to "make an example" of Cary, an enslaved man who had injured another in a fight. Jefferson asked Randolph to find one of the "negro purchasers from Georgia." If a Georgia trader could not be found, Randolph was to sell Cary to another buyer who would remove him to a "quarter so distant as never more to be heard of among us." In this way Jefferson hoped to create the impression among members of his slave community that Cary was as far removed from them as if "he were put out of the way by death." [38] Such an example, he realized, would be long remembered by those who knew and worked with Cary. That the combination of the cotton gin, the Louisiana Purchase, and the closing of the Atlantic slave trade came together during a period in which agricultural innovators were seeking to increase production on Virginia plantations must have given planters an important extra weapon in their struggles to convert more of their slaves' labor time into salable commodities. [39] To the extent that masters were strengthened by Jeffersonian policies, residents of Gabriel's Virginia were weakened.

These same policies also lessened the chances for large-scale slave rebellion in Virginia—for a revolution that would have put that of 1800 to shame—but only to a very marginal degree. Gabriel and Nat Turner, the leaders of the two biggest insurrectionary movements in nineteenth-century Virginia, were native-born residents of the communities they galvanized into conspiracy or rebellion. Their well-established local reputations—Gabriel's as someone willing to stand up to whites, Turner's as a religious visionary—helped them win followers. [40] Gabriel's Conspiracy was organized by slaves visiting neighboring plantations after dark or on Sundays, attending church on Sunday and then gathering to socialize afterward, and attending communal barbecues and fish fries. The majority of those tried for participating in the conspiracy were accused with at least one other resident of their home plantations, another indication of the degree to which the movement grew out of the communal world created by collective day-to-day slave resistance. In short, Gabriel's Conspiracy was organized by slaves enjoying customary rights that their communities had won in battles with local slave owners. [41] Far more went into decisions by enslaved Virginians to risk large-scale rebellion than membership in a vibrant local slave community, but such a community was central to Gabriel's Conspiracy in 1800. The disruptions caused by the interstate slave trade and the increased incentives that fear of being sold South must have created for potential informers can only have increased the already exceedingly long odds against a successful rebellion.[42]

Perhaps extending this analysis to the question of slave rebellion—to the question of the degree to which the revolution of 1800 helped forestall a more radical revolution—risks pushing too far into the realm of speculation. There are, however, several non-speculative points that can be made. First, historians who have examined Jefferson's attitudes toward slavery and the place of slavery in Jeffersonian Virginia have greatly enriched our understanding of American history, but they have concentrated on issues that were of marginal importance in the lives of Virginia's slaves. Second, the two specific results of the "revolution of 1800" that most affected black Virginians were the Louisiana Purchase (and the generally expansionist Jeffersonian policies for which it stands) and the closing of the Atlantic slave trade. Third, the two together contributed to a disaster for the relatively stable world that black Virginians had developed over the course of the second half of the eighteenth century.

Those contributions, however, were modest. One need not raise tired questions about the influence of great men on history to believe that U.S. participation in the Atlantic slave trade would have come to an end in 1808 if John Adams had won the presidential election of 1800. Nor was Jefferson's undeniable support for expansion and for the extension of plantation agriculture into the southern Mississippi Valley responsible in any important sense for the emergence of the Deep South. Adams might have been less enthusiastic about such expansion, but it is hard to imagine that he could have stopped it. The place of Jefferson and the revolution of 1800 in Gabriel's Virginia was not one of honor, but even in those realms in which Jefferson was most influential and malignant, his importance was negligible compared to the invention of the cotton gin, the emergence of the British textile industry, and the lust for land exhibited by run-of-the-mill white southerners. And to some degree the damage that was done to black Virginians by Jeffersonian policies falls into the category of unintended consequences, given the lack of evidence that Jefferson or any other contemporary statesman gave much thought to the way these policies would affect black Virginians.

Jefferson did, however, leave evidence that had he been aware of the effects on Virginia's blacks of his support for expansion, he would only have regretted that those effects were not greater. In 1820 Congress and the political nation were split into anxiously sectional camps over Missouri's attempt to enter the union. Missouri petitioned to enter as a slave state; James Talmadge, a congressman from New York, offered an amendment to Missouri's proffered constitution designed to ease white Missourians away from slavery and create a state free of the peculiar institution. The furor that arose is well known, as is Jefferson's response to it. He called the Missouri controversy a "fire-bell in the night," and predicted that the disputes settled by the Missouri Compromise heralded the end of the Union. This he considered "treason against the hopes of the world." Perhaps most interestingly, he argued that keeping slavery out of Missouri weakened the battle against the institution because it slowed the process through which slavery could "diffuse" across the continent. Only as a result of such "diffusion," of the spreading of the black population of the South across a growing geographical expanse (and thus a lessening of the density of the black population in the South), could voluntary emancipation coupled with African colonization proceed. And only that path offered what Jefferson considered an acceptable or achievable solution to American slavery.[43]

As countless critics have pointed out, Jefferson's reasoning does not stand up to scrutiny. By 1820 slavery had become firmly established in Kentucky, Tennessee, Louisiana, and in significant parts of Alabama and Mississippi; it had spread rapidly through the upcountry cotton regions of South Carolina and Georgia. Many of the slaves living in these new plantation regions had been born in Virginia, but their "diffusion" across the continent had been accompanied by a decision within Virginia to limit severely the right of an owner to manumit his or her slaves. And as a master who resorted to selling slaves into the interstate market in order to make ends meet, Thomas Jefferson surely recognized why the growing market for slaves strengthened the commitment of white Virginians to the protection of their property in humans. But Jefferson's more fundamental level of self-deception came when he sought to explain that "diffusion" would benefit blacks. Despite knowing well enough how enslaved Virginians felt about "Georgia traders" to use them as a threat against "recalcitrant" slaves, Jefferson maintained that "their diffusion . . . would make them individually happier." Having discounted the possibility that limiting slavery might benefit the enslaved, he had cleared the ground to maintain that advocates of a free Missouri pursued a purely "abstract principle," and that they did so to the detriment of the true happiness of their country.

Peter Onuf's recent exploration of the way Jefferson conceived of his country suggests a way to understand the benefit Jefferson hoped to gain through diffusion, and thus the degree to which he was, in his heart, an inveterate enemy of Gabriel's Virginia. As Onuf points out, Jefferson "casually and reflexively" spoke of Virginia rather than the United States as his "country," and in doing so he excluded from the "people" who were Virginians any "slaves forcibly removed from their homeland to work for others." Through diffusion, Onuf suggests, Jefferson hoped to make "slavery a national problem," and thus relieve Virginia and the other southern states of sole responsibility for "solving" it.[44]

But Jefferson may have counted on diffusion to solve the "national" problem of slavery in a different way. To the degree to which he conceived of Virginia as his "country," the diffusion of slavery into the "empire" of the west offered a way for white Virginians as a nation to free themselves from the stain of slavery without creating in free black people a new "nation" of enemies within. As slavery spread across the continent, slave-owning Virginians could cash out their investment in human capital. The closure of the Atlantic slave trade ensured that they would receive increasingly high prices for doing so. While the number of enslaved people in the United States would continue to grow, and while new plantation regions to the south and west might acquire growing concentrations of enslaved black people, the concentration of blacks within Jefferson's "country" might conceivably decline. Perhaps Virginia could be "relieved" of enough of its black population to render colonization a reasonable solution to its national "problem." Then Virginia could finally become a truly free, truly white Commonwealth. Gabriel's Virginia had to be eradicated to fulfill the sage of Monticello's vision for Jeffersonian Virginia.

This never came close to happening. Forty years after southern victory in the congressional battle over Missouri had permitted virtually unlimited "diffusion," Virginia's black population totaled almost two hundred thousand more people than it had in Gabriel's day.[45] The failure of Jefferson's advocacy and statecraft to make significant progress toward this goal serves as a reminder of the limits to Jefferson's influence on the lives of those who lived in Gabriel's Virginia. A small incident that took place on Richmond's waterfront several months after Jefferson retired from the presidency brought the celebrity-statesman into direct contact with Gabriel's world and showed how Jefferson's and Gabriel's Virginia lived in constant contact with each other without ever quite joining as one.

On 14 July 1809—only one date could have been more ironic—a "Negro-man Slave the property of the Estate of Jas. B. Couch dec'd." was arrested in Lynchburg, Virginia, and charged with having taken a "certain trunk the property of Thomas Jefferson Esquire" off a boat that had been docked in the basin of the James River Canal in Richmond.[46] Apparently Jefferson had shipped various papers, as well as "a pocket Tellescope with a brass case," and other things from Washington back to Monticello through Richmond. The trunk entered a world of goods carried along Virginia's rivers and roads by mostly enslaved black watermen, dockworkers, and draymen. One of the costs of a transportation system run on uncompensated labor was a vigorous market in stolen goods.[47] Ned's motives in the robbery went unreported, but there is little chance that he targeted the former president. It is far more likely—virtually certain—that while working on the docks, as did many slaves hired into the city by deceased master's estates, Ned spied an unattended trunk and made off with it. He appears to have turned to black friends and associates when trying to fence the goods he had taken.[48] No doubt he and his accomplices believed themselves to be home free when the trunk made it into Lynchburg. Had it belonged to anyone else, they would have been.[49]

The trunk did not, however, belong to anyone else, and though evidence has not survived of the hue and cry that inspired a multi-town search for Jefferson's goods, there can be little doubt that it went out. Ned had not, after all, merely liberated some of the goods traveling through Richmond. White townspeople disapproved of such slave "larceny" and periodically they sought to repress and prosecute it, but more often they treated it almost like a business expense. Jefferson's trunk could not, however, be written off as the cost of doing business in a slave society. Its disappearance would embarrass the town, and so it was tracked down within the day. The man responsible for taking it was hauled before a court, branded on the thumb, and subjected to thirty-nine lashes with the whip. When the meaning of the trunk for Jefferson and his followers conflicted with its meaning in Gabriel's Virginia, there was little doubt which meaning would get trumped. That important fact should be neither forgotten nor allowed to overshadow the persistence of the two different systems of meaning within the state. Thomas Jefferson was central to one of those systems, but remarkably peripheral to the other.

NOTES

1. Robert McColley, *Slavery and Jeffersonian Virginia*, 2d. ed. (Urbana, Ill., 1973); Jan Ellen Lewis and Peter S. Onuf, eds., *Sally Hemings and Thomas Jefferson: History, Memory, and Civic Culture* (Charlottesville, Va., 1999).

2. Edmund S. Morgan, *American Slavery, American Freedom: The Ordeal of Colonial Virginia* (New York, 1974), and Winthrop D. Jordan, *White over Black: American Attitudes toward the Negro,*

1550–1812 (Chapel Hill, N.C., 1968) are the two most significant works that have helped create this consensus.

3. I refer to Annette Gordon-Reed's discussions of the ways in which racial assumptions influenced historians' judgments about the reliability of different kinds of evidence regarding Hemings and Jefferson. See Gordon-Reed, *Thomas Jefferson and Sally Hemings: An American Controversy* (Charlottesville, Va., 1997). The recent DNA test results have virtually clinched the case that Gordon-Reed made so convincingly through traditional historical analysis.

4. In addition to chap. 12 of Jordan's *White over Black,* see Fawn M. Brodie, *Thomas Jefferson: An Intimate Biography* (New York, 1974); John Chester Miller, *The Wolf by the Ears: Thomas Jefferson and Slavery* (New York, 1977); Paul Finkelman, "Jefferson and Slavery: 'Treason against the Hopes of the World,'" in *Jeffersonian Legacies,* ed. Peter S. Onuf (Charlottesville, Va., 1993), 181–221; Paul Finkelman, "Thomas Jefferson and Slavery II: Historians and Myths," in *Slavery and the Founders: Race and Liberty in the Age of Jefferson,* ed. Paul Finkelman (Armonk, N.Y., 1996), 138–67.

5. Given the remarkably fresh interpretations of the languages of racial difference, nation, and empire that Peter Onuf has recently offered, however, as well as the work of Gordon-Reed, I am not suggesting that such work should stop.

6. Quoted in the introduction to Lewis and Onuf, *Sally Hemings and Thomas Jefferson,* 3.

7. Douglas R. Egerton, *Gabriel's Rebellion: The Virginia Slave Conspiracies of 1800 and 1802* (Chapel Hill, N.C., 1993), part 1 (artisanal republicanism reading); James Sidbury, *Ploughshares into Swords: Race, Rebellion, and Identity in Gabriel's Virginia, 1730–1810* (Cambridge, England, 1997), esp. chaps. 1–3 (black Virginians' historical consciousness and my reading of the conspiracy as rooted in a religious worldview).

8. Joseph J. Ellis, *American Sphinx: The Character of Thomas Jefferson* (New York, 1998), 149. Ellis provides a gloss on Jefferson as a *relatively* benign master, although he complicates this portrayal in the following pages. Also see the sometimes contradictory treatment of the subject in Jack McLaughlin, *Jefferson and Monticello: The Biography of a Builder* (New York, 1988), chap. 4. A sense of the contradictions is embodied in the following sentence: "On the other hand, although he was consistently humane and compassionate in his treatment of his slaves, he was also capable of acting like a hardened slave breaker by having a runaway slave 'severely flogged in the presence of his old companions'" (96). Lucia C. Stanton, "'Those Who Labor for My Happiness': Thomas Jefferson and His Slaves," in *Jeffersonian Legacies,* ed. Peter S. Onuf (Charlottesville, Va., 1993), 147–80. Stanton provides the best general interpretation of Jefferson's interaction with slaves at Monticello.

9. Madison Hemings, a son of Jefferson and Sally Hemings, described Jefferson as "uniformly kind to all about him," and Israel Jefferson reported that his former master was "esteemed by both whites and blacks as a very great man." "The Memoirs of Madison Hemings" and "The Memoirs of Israel Jefferson" are reproduced as Appendix B and Appendix C of Gordon-Reed, *Thomas Jefferson and Sally Hemings,* 245–53. Isaac Jefferson, another enslaved man who lived at Monticello, also described Thomas Jefferson as "very kind to servants" in a dictated narrative published in 1847 (see James A. Bear Jr., ed., *Jefferson at Monticello* [Charlottesville, Va., 1967], 13).

10. Edwin Morris Betts, ed., *Thomas Jefferson's Farm Book, with Commentary and Relevant Extracts from Other Writings* (Princeton, N.J., 1953), 442; Merrill D. Peterson, ed., *Visitors to Monticello* (Charlottesville, Va., 1989), 47, 28; McLaughlin, *Jefferson and Monticello,* 104; Bear, *Jefferson at Monticello,* 97.

11. Ellis, *American Sphinx,* 150; Peterson, *Visitors to Monticello,* 39; Gordon-Reed, *Thomas Jefferson and Sally Hemings,* 247 (Madison Hemings reports that Jefferson, "unlike Washington . . . had but little taste or care for agricultural pursuits" and left the plantations to "his stewards and overseers," preferring instead to engage with the work of his "mechanics").

12. Betts, *Jefferson's Farm Book,* 442. For two reports that Jefferson was less hesitant to use the whip than other observers claimed, see McLaughlin, *Jefferson and Monticello,* 97, and Anthony

F. C. Wallace, *Jefferson and the Indians: The Tragic Fate of the First Americans* (Cambridge, Mass., 1999), 115.

13. Betts, *Jefferson's Farm Book,* 10, 12, 13, 14, 19, 21, 35, 45, 47 (for orders to sell slaves, often as punishment, sometimes to pay debts, and sometimes for a combination of the two; he also sometimes sold or bought slaves to unite families, so not all sales count as evidence of brutality).

14. Madison Hemings's claim that Sally had returned to Virginia from France in response to Jefferson's promise to free her children supports the view that their relationship involved a strong emotional tie, at least on his part (see Gordon-Reed, *Thomas Jefferson and Sally Hemings,* 246).

15. Joshua D. Rothman, "James Callender and Social Knowledge of Interracial Sex in Antebellum Virginia," in Lewis and Onuf, *Sally Hemings and Thomas Jefferson,* 87–113, shows that many in the area knew of the relationship. Whether they "knew" how the two principals felt about each other remains unclear. Of course local rumors regarding Jefferson's feelings toward Hemings might have had the same limited influence on local norms regardless of their accuracy.

16. Jordan, *White over Black,* chap. 12, remains the best analysis. Also see Miller, *Wolf by the Ears,* esp. chaps. 6–9; and the works cited in note 4 above. Quotes are from Adrienne Koch and William Peden, eds., *The Life and Selected Writings of Thomas Jefferson* (New York, 1944), 256–57, and are drawn from Jefferson's answer to Query 14 in the *Notes.*

17. Peter S. Onuf, *Jefferson's Empire: The Language of American Nationhood* (Charlottesville, Va., 2000), chap. 5 points out, in fact, that most of these offensive statements were made as part of Jefferson's explicit condemnation of slavery and generally in support of emancipation through colonization. The spectacular failure of colonization despite the ardent support of Jefferson and many other prominent statesmen casts a substantial cloud over the claims of historians like Paul Finkelman that general emancipation could have been measurably advanced had Jefferson's racism not undercut his antislavery stances.

18. See William Hamilton, *An Address to the New York African Society, for Mutual Relief, Delivered in the Universalist Church, January 2, 1809,* in *Early Negro Writing, 1760–1837,* ed. Dorothy Porter (Boston, 1971), 36 (in which Hamilton takes on Jeffersonian language without mentioning Jefferson); and William Hamilton, *An Oration Delivered in the African Zion Church, on the Fourth of July, 1827, in Commemoration of the Abolition of Domestic Slavery in This State,* ibid., 98–101.

19. Peter P. Hinks, ed., *David Walker's Appeal to the Coloured Citizens of the World* (University Park, Pa., 2000 [1829]), 14, 17.

20. Lois Green Carr and Lorena S. Walsh, "Economic Diversification and Labor Organization in the Chesapeake, 1650–1820" in *Work and Labor in Early America,* ed. Stephen Innes (Chapel Hill, N.C., 1988), 144–88; and Philip D. Morgan, "Task and Gang Systems: The Organization of Labor on New World Plantations," ibid., 189–220 (esp. 212–13), for the ways these broader issues affected black life.

21. Dumas Malone, *Jefferson the President: First Term, 1801–1805* (Boston, 1970), chaps. 14–19 discuss the events surrounding the Louisiana Purchase with characteristic thoroughness. See Onuf, *Jefferson's Empire,* esp. introduction and chap. 2, for an important discussion of Jefferson's conception of empire.

22. William W. Freehling, *The Reintegration of American History: Slavery and the Civil War* (New York, 1994), 26–29. In these few pages Freehling explains why historians' inattention to this act is ill advised.

23. H. A. Washington, ed., *The Writings of Thomas Jefferson* (Washington, D.C., 1854), 8:67. This passage came in his sixth annual message to Congress, dated 2 Dec. 1806.

24. Donald L. Robinson, *Slavery in the Structure of American Politics, 1765–1820* (New York, 1971), chap. 8 (esp. 324–38); W. E. Burghardt Du Bois, *The Suppression of the African Slave-Trade to the United States of America, 1638–1870* (New York, 1954), chap. 8 (esp. 94–108); Dumas Malone, *Jefferson the President: Second Term, 1805–1809* (Boston, 1974), 546.

25. David Eltis, *Economic Growth and the Ending of the Atlantic Slave Trade* (New York, 1987), chap. 3 (esp. 43–46).

26. Jefferson and his followers had sought to convince the Spanish that West Florida (the Gulf Coast to the Perdido River on the east) was included in the Louisiana Purchase. Ulrich B. Phillips pointed out long ago the importance of this acquisition: "Alabama in particular, which comprises for the most part the basin draining into Mobile Bay, could have no safe market for its produce until Spain was dispossessed of the outlet. The taking of Mobile by the United States as an episode of the war of 1812, and the simultaneous breaking of the Indian strength, removed the obstacles. The influx then rose to immense proportions" (Phillips, *American Negro Slavery: A Survey of the Supply, Employment and Control of Negro Labor as Determined by the Plantation Regime* [1918; Baton Rouge, 1966], 171).

27. That those discussing the closing of the slave trade realized that this would be an effect is underscored by southern congressmen's insistence on language that would protect the coastal interstate slave trade. See Robinson, *Slavery*, 335–37; Du Bois, *Suppression*, 104–8.

28. Allan Kulikoff, *The Agrarian Origins of American Capitalism* (Charlottesville, Va., 1992), chap. 8. Michael Tadman uses different techniques to estimate the numbers of slaves sold in the interstate trade and comes up with different figures, but those differences are not significant for this argument. See Tadman, *Speculators and Slaves: Masters, Traders, and Slaves in the Old South* (Madison, Wis., 1989), esp. chaps. 2 and 3 and appendix 1.

29. Robert William Fogel and Stanley L. Engerman, *Time on the Cross: The Economics of American Negro Slavery* (Boston, 1974), 44–53 provides the most famous argument for the relative unimportance of the interstate trade. Paul A. David et al., *Reckoning with Slavery: A Critical Study in the Quantitative History of American Negro Slavery* (New York, 1976), chap. 3, offered the first refutation of their claims. The absence of a prolonged discussion of these issues in Robert W. Fogel, *Without Consent or Contract: The Rise and Fall of American Slavery* (New York, 1989) reveals the success of that particular critique. Kulikoff's *Agrarian Origins* analyzes the interstate slave trade to understand the influence of capitalism on migration in antebellum America, while Tadman's *Speculators and Slaves* seeks to refute Eugene Genovese's work on paternalism. Their differences notwithstanding, both agree on the significance and brutality of the trade. More recently, see Walter Johnson, *Soul by Soul: Life Inside the Antebellum Slave Market* (Cambridge, Mass., 2000).

30. Quoted in Tadman, *Speculators and Slaves*, 156. As Tadman points out, the Brownrigg move involved not sale to a trader but a whole plantation's moving, and thus this heartrending letter was produced by exactly the sort of move that some have seen as relatively benign.

31. I make this case in Sidbury, *Ploughshares into Swords*, chap. 1 (esp. 29–49). My claims are heavily indebted to Allan Kulikoff, *Tobacco and Slaves: The Development of Southern Cultures in the Chesapeake, 1680–1800* (Chapel Hill, N.C., 1986); Rhys Isaac, *The Transformation of Virginia, 1740–1790* (Chapel Hill, N.C., 1982), esp. his "Discourse on Method"; Mechal Sobel, *The World They Made Together: Black and White Values in Eighteenth-Century Virginia* (Princeton, N.J., 1987); Philip D. Morgan and Michael Lee Nichols, "Slaves in Piedmont Virginia, 1720–1790," *WMQ* 3d ser., 46 (1989): 212–51. Also see Philip D. Morgan, *Slave Counterpoint: Black Culture in the Eighteenth-Century Chesapeake and Lowcountry* (Chapel Hill, N.C., 1998), part 3, which was not then available.

32. This point (without the analogy to the Atlantic trade) is made powerfully by Kulikoff, *Agrarian Origins*, chap. 8 (esp. 255–63).

33. I am grateful to Philip J. Schwarz, who generously gave me this material on Thomas Henry Prosser. His sources include the *Richmond Argus*, 30 June 1801 (marriage); Henrico County Deed Book 7 (1803–6), 409–10, Library of Virginia, Richmond, Virginia (debt); *Mississippi Genealogical Exchange* 7 (1961): 37 (27 slaves). Wilkinson County, where Prosser settled, had a black and enslaved majority in 1820 (4,028 free whites, 5,761 enslaved blacks; see http://fisher.lib.virginia

.edu/cgi-local/censusbin/census/cen.pl?year=820). For the fates of accused conspirators, see Philip J. Schwarz, *Twice Condemned: Slaves and the Criminal Laws of Virginia, 1705–1865* (Baton Rouge, 1988), 324, 328.

34. See Winthrop D. Jordan, *Tumult and Silence at Second Creek: An Inquiry into a Civil War Slave Conspiracy* (Baton Rouge, 1993) for a portrayal of life in Wilkinson and neighboring Adams counties forty years after Prosser's move. See Sidbury, *Ploughshares into Swords,* part 2, for urban life in Richmond.

35. Fogel, *Without Consent or Contract,* chap. 1 (esp. 26–36).

36. Charles Ball, *Fifty Years in Chains* (New York, 1970 [1837]), 18–21; Frederick Douglass, *Narrative of the Life of Frederick Douglass, An American Slave,* ed. David W. Blight (Boston, 1993 [1845]), 89–90; Charles L. Perdue Jr., Thomas Barden, and Robert K. Phillips, eds., *Weevils in the Wheat: Interviews with Virginia Ex-Slaves* (Charlottesville, Va., 1976), 153 (for an elderly ex-slave's memory of slave traders). Solomon Northup, *Twelve Years a Slave,* ed. Sue Eakin and Joseph Logsdon (1853; Baton Rouge, 1968) shows that even northern free blacks had to live in fear of slave traders.

37. Johnson, *Soul By Soul,* chap. 1. As Johnson eloquently points out, a sale that would be recorded by a master as a single discrete event might be better comprehended as "a slave's lifelong fear" (14).

38. Betts, *Jefferson's Farm Book,* 19. Jefferson was so intent on making an example of Cary through this sale that he instructed Randolph to "regard price but little in comparison with so distant an exile of him as to cut him off compleatly from ever again being heard of" (19).

39. For the intensification of labor in the Chesapeake during the period of the early Republic, see Carr and Walsh, "Economic Diversification"; and Lorena S. Walsh, "Work and Resistance in the New Republic: The Case of the Chesapeake, 1770–1820" in *From Chattel Slaves to Wage Slaves: The Dynamics of Labour Bargaining in the Americas,* ed. Mary Turner (Kingston, Jamaica, 1995), 97–122. This process, of course, involved Jefferson, who experimented with naileries and other innovations (most involving manufacturing rather than agriculture) in his attempts to turn larger profits on the labor of his slaves.

40. Philip J. Schwarz, "Gabriel's Challenge: Slaves and Crime in Late Eighteenth-Century Virginia," *The Virginia Magazine of History and Biography* 90 (1982): 283–307 (for Gabriel's earlier run-in with the law); for the basic outlines of Turner's Rebellion, see Stephen B. Oates, *The Fires of Jubilee: Nat Turner's Fierce Rebellion* (New York, 1975); for my take on Turner, see Sidbury, "Reading, Revelation, and Rebellion: The Textual Communities of Gabriel, Denmark Vesey, and Nat Turner," in *Judgment Day: Nat Turner,* ed. Kenneth S. Greenberg (New York, forthcoming).

41. Sidbury, *Ploughshares into Swords,* part 1 (esp. chap. 2). The figures are as follows: 37 of the 66 black people tried for participating in the conspiracy were tried with at least one other person owned by the same master. Of these, 8 were tried with one other member of their home community; 12 with 2 other members; 8 with 3 other members; 5 with 4 other members; and 7, including Gabriel, were owned by Thomas Henry Prosser. These figures are compiled from the list in Schwarz, *Twice Condemned,* 324–27.

42. It may be true that Turner's decision to limit severely the number of his followers who knew of the planned rebellion in advance was tied to these issues. But given the degree to which Turner believed himself to be directed by God, there are other equally or more plausible explanations for differences in the way he and Gabriel organized their movements.

43. William W. Freehling, *The Road to Disunion: Secessionists at Bay, 1776–1854* (New York, 1990); chap. 8 is the best treatment of the national politics of the compromise. For a recent discussion of Jefferson's response to the compromise that supplants earlier work, see Onuf, *Jefferson's Empire,* chap. 4. Chaps. 24–26 of Miller's *Wolf by the Ears* also remain useful. The source for the famous quotes regarding Missouri is TJ to John Holmes, 22 April 1820, in Koch and Peden, *The Life and Selected Writings,* 698–99.

44. Onuf, *Jefferson's Empire*, 121, 167, 186. This paragraph is indebted to all of chaps. 4 and 5 rather than simply to the quoted pages.

45. According to the 1800 Census, 367,164 black people (346,671 of them enslaved) lived in Virginia; according to the 1860 Census, 548,907 black people (490,865 slaves) lived in the state. Despite the massive exportation of Virginia slaves that resulted from high cotton prices during the 1850s, the percentage of Virginia's population that was black had only fallen from 41 percent in 1800 to 33 percent in 1860. See http://fisher.lib.virginia.edu/cgi-local/censusbin/census/cen.pl?year=860.

46. Trial of Ned, Richmond Court Order Book 8, 326 (25 July 1809); John Lynch Jr., Mayor of Lynchburg, to the Serjeant of the Corporation, 14 July 1809, Richmond Suit Papers, Box 52, folder July, Sept., Oct., Dec. 1809, part 1, Library of Virginia, Richmond, Virginia; and Appearance Bond for Michael Smythers, Daniel Couch, John Y. Johnson, and Daniel Ellis, ibid., contain the surviving records of the case. All quotations are from those documents.

47. Sidbury, *Ploughshares into Swords,* chap. 5, for contemporary life on Richmond's waterfront.

48. In the appearance bond signed in Lynchburg, Daniel Couch pledged to deliver "his Negro men slaves Peter and Billy" to testify against Ned, and John Y. Johnson pledged for the appearance of "his Negromen slaves Jack Toast and George Pryor." Daniel Ellis, who also pledged to appear, was "a free Negro of Campbell county." See n. 46 for location of the appearance bond. Sidbury, *Ploughshares into Swords,* chaps. 5–6; Alex Lichtenstein, "'That Disposition to Theft, with Which They Have Been Branded': Moral Economy, Slave Management, and the Law," *Journal of Social History* 21 (1988): 413–40.

49. In reading through all of the Richmond and Henrico County Court Order Books between 1782 and 1810, and all of the Richmond Suit Papers for the same period, I do not recall a single other case of a slave being arrested outside the immediate Richmond area for a property crime committed within the city.

CHAPTER 9

"Whom Have I Oppressed?"
The Pursuit of Happiness and the Happy Slave

James Oakes

Can a slave be happy? Frederick Douglass was sure the answer was no. "The re-mark is not unfrequently made, that the slaves are the most contented and happy laborers in the world. They dance and sing, and make all manner of joy-ful noises," he wrote, "—so they do; but it is a great mistake to suppose them happy because they sing. The songs of the slave represent the sorrows, rather than the joys of the heart; and he is relieved by them, only as an aching heart is relieved by its tears."[1] Douglass was replying to the southern slaveholders who argued with increasing unanimity that their slaves were not merely happy but were among the happiest people on earth. In retrospect the debate seems alien and not a little absurd. But it was a serious issue at the time, and it exposed a way of thinking that was central to the political culture of early America. On one side were those who accepted the liberal-humanist idea that happiness de-pended on the quality of one's social life; on the other was nineteenth-century Romanticism, with its conviction that humans had an innate capacity for hap-piness that society could only encourage or thwart. Thomas Jefferson straddled these competing conceptions of human happiness and his ascendancy in 1801 helped establish the terms of the debate over whether a slave could be happy. The revolution of 1800 was, at least in part, an intellectual revolution.

In his first inaugural address Jefferson expressed humility about the re-sponsibilities he was about to assume, responsibilities that included securing "the happiness . . . of this beloved country." Fortunately he could recite a litany of "felicities" with which the American people were already blessed. After acknowledging "an overruling Providence, which . . . delights in the happiness of man here and his greater happiness hereafter," Jefferson wondered "what more is necessary to make us a happy and prosperous people." His answer—"a wise and frugal government"—is well known, but the fact that Jefferson repeatedly used "happiness" as a benchmark for evaluating the success of the American experiment as well as of his own administration is worth considering.

Jefferson referred at least four times to happiness and felicity in the space of a fairly brief inaugural address. This was not unusual for him. An online search of the Jefferson papers at the Library of Congress turned up 274 references to happiness. The University of Virginia's online version of Merrill Peterson's Library of America edition of the Jefferson papers turned up 196 references to "happiness" in Jefferson's writings. The most famous examples, of course, are the two uses of happiness in the Declaration of Independence. The first posited "the pursuit of happiness" as one of those inalienable rights—along with life and liberty—belonging to every individual. The second referred to the right of the people to replace tyrannical government with a regime that would better secure an entire society's safety and happiness.[2] From his earliest public documents to his last private letters, happiness appears as a central value in Jefferson's vision of the world. If his election to the presidency was a vindication of that vision, perhaps the "revolution of 1800" should be understood—at least in part—as having inaugurated the reign of happiness here on earth.

Fortunately, Jefferson's relatively unoriginal mind spares us from having to make such a case. For one thing, James Wilson probably inspired Jefferson to include the "pursuit of happiness" in his Declaration of Independence. But Wilson was no more original than Jefferson. The papers of the founders are littered with references to happiness as a standard by which to evaluate the worth of any given society or polity, and those references were the common coin of the liberal Enlightenment. It was John Locke, in his *Essay Concerning Human Understanding,* who, in Garry Wills's word's, "launched 'the pursuit of happiness' as the supreme determiner of man's action." Locke introduced the formula that defined happiness and misery in relation to each other, the greatest happiness being the least misery and vice versa. His followers would transform Locke's simple arithmetic into an elaborate calculus of pleasure and pain, but the basic formula remained unchanged.[3]

The universal search for happiness was a bit frightening to Locke, since no one seemed to agree on a socially benign standard for what happiness actually was. Some took pleasure in the satisfaction of purely sensual desires, others in the acquisition of knowledge.[4] Hoping to moderate Locke's ambivalence, his Scottish followers—beginning with Francis Hutcheson—argued that human beings found happiness in benevolence, what Adam Smith called "moral senti-ments." The Scots also coined the phrase—the greatest happiness for the great-est number—that would endure for centuries as the standard for evaluating the worth of any given society. From Scotland the happiness standard was picked up by the French—Helvetius, Burlamaqui, and Voltaire especially. And from France it spread to Italy, where Cesare Beccaria invoked it in his classic Enlight-enment study of crime and punishment.[5] Happiness, then, was one of the most powerful elements of eighteenth-century political thought. Its popularity in America places the colonists within a transatlantic culture that was heir to the humanist traditions of Montaigne and, more directly, the Enlightenment ideals of Great Britain and the continent.

The founders argued repeatedly that happiness was a political as well as a personal goal. John Dickinson opened his "Letters from a Farmer in Pennsyl-vania" with a blissful commendation of his private contentment. I "am now convinced," he wrote, "that a man may be as happy without bustle as with it." But happiness was as much an attribute of societies as of individuals. "Benevo-lence toward mankind, excites wishes for their welfare," Dickinson explained, "and such wishes endear the means of fulfilling them. *These* can be found in lib-erty only, and therefore her sacred cause ought to be espoused by every man on every occasion."[6] In John Adams's words, "the science of politics is the science of social happiness." Indeed, "the happiness of society is the end of govern-ment."[7] So Jefferson's inaugural preoccupation with happiness reveals him, once again, as a useful barometer of his own era. But the ordinariness of Jeffer-son's commitment to happiness does nothing to diminish the extraordinariness of the idea itself. The elevation of human happiness—happiness understood as domestic bliss and material comfort—was one of the most astonishing intel-lectual developments of early modern Europe. None of the great classical polit-ical theorists upheld that kind of happiness as a standard of judgment for any social and political order. Nor was earthly happiness part of the cosmology of medieval Christendom.

There has always been something utopian about this elevation of human happiness, and it flies in the face of the charge that liberalism lacks any vision of the larger good or the "ends" of government. In the years after World War II it was fashionable for scholars to point to the absence of utopianism in Ameri-can political culture. With the horrors of Nazism and Stalinism fresh in their minds, men like Daniel Boorstin and Louis Hartz noted the lack of comparable ideological extremes on this side of the Atlantic. For Boorstin Americans were the consummate pragmatists and had been since the earliest settlements. Colonial America, he said, was a "disproving ground for utopias," and Richard Hofstadter later quipped that "the same could be said about most of human history."[8] But wasn't universal happiness a utopian standard? The idea that every human being is endowed with the right to pursue his or her happiness and that a good society is a "happy" society was a revolutionary development in the history of Western political thought. Yet the standard, once developed, has remained with us, if only in the degraded form of the therapeutic culture. From Montaigne to Montel, ordinary human happiness has been central to the culture of the Western world.

What made the utopian idea of human happiness so potent was that—unlike the thousand-year Reich or the universal brotherhood of man—it seemed within reach. Here was a "pursuit" that was not obviously doomed to failure. For the happiness envisioned by the founders, while irreducibly utopian, was not simply a metaphysical abstraction. At its core, happiness had two very distinct but closely related meanings, one psychological and one social.[9] Personal or psychological happiness depended on concrete material and political conditions, particularly political freedom and a decent standard of living. In Adams's words, "the form of government which communicates ease, comfort, security, or, in one word, happiness to the greatest number of persons and in the greatest degree is best."[10]

Ease, comfort, and security, at home and at work: these were ordinary things. They represent what the philosopher Charles Taylor calls "the affirmation of ordinary life."[11] Work should be rewarding and family life fulfilling. And because they were things that ordinary men and women could aspire to, they were the egalitarian core of the liberal Enlightenment's vision of society. Aristotle would have been shocked. For him work and family were elements of "mere life." The good life, by contrast, could only be pursued in the polis. Work and family existed within the realm of necessity, driven by the fact that humans—like animals—must produce and reproduce simply to survive. For the ancients, humans were political beings, and this elevated them above mere animal existence. For enlightened liberals humans were social beings, and they put the social aspects of life on a par with the political.

Hannah Arendt pronounced the triumph of "the social" a disastrous turn in modern political life. With other neo-Aristotelians she was appalled by what she saw as the blurring of the lines between the public and the private.[12] But for

Jefferson and his contemporaries the fact that public and private life were related to each other did not mean that the lines between them were blurred. To be sure, the relationship between public and private was brokered by the liberal state.

Thus for Jefferson those governments that allowed men to claim the largest portion of the fruits of their labor were most conducive to human happiness. His awareness of the role of government in the establishment of human happiness was evident in a letter he wrote to Thomas Shippen in 1788. Shippen was visiting Europe, and Jefferson urged him to observe the effects of politics "on the happiness of the people: take every possible occasion of entering into the hovels of the labourers," Jefferson wrote. "See what they eat, how they are cloathed, whether they are obliged to labour too hard, whether the government or their landlord takes from them an unjust proportion of their labour; on what footing stands the property they call their own, their personal liberty, &c." [13] Jefferson apparently believed that in the United States the government was so organized as to promote the utopian standard of the greatest happiness for the greatest number. In his inaugural address of 1801 he ran through the elements that made America such a happy place, notably abundant land and the equal right to "the acquisitions of our industry." His "wise and frugal government" would, he promised, leave Americans "free to regulate their own pursuits of industry and improvement, and shall not take from the mouth of labor the bread it has earned."

Jefferson's commitment to happiness, and to the dignity of labor that was part of it, place at least one of his feet firmly within the eighteenth-century Enlightenment. But to appreciate what happened to the debate over happiness and slavery in the antebellum South, it is important to recognize that Jefferson's other foot was rooted in nineteenth-century Romanticism. If Enlightenment thinkers believed that humans could flourish only in society, for Romantics society threatened to suppress the innate essence that made humans what they were. In Ralph Waldo Emerson's words, "Society everywhere is in conspiracy against the manhood of every one of its members." [14] Society was the enemy because it interfered with the *natural* desire for freedom. And freedom, in the Romantic understanding, was the unfettered expression of one's innate, natural self. It was foolish to look for happiness in the trivial comforts of ordinary life, in the association of friends and family. Nature, not society, was the ultimate source of human happiness.

By 1825 the Romantic fetishization of nature had taken hold of American culture. It could be seen in frontier mythology and in the Hudson River school of painting, in Thoreau's retreat to Walden Pond, Andrew Jackson's rejection of social niceties, and Daniel Boone's escape to the West. From high culture to mass politics, the idea spread that nature was the realm of freedom, whereas society and its institutions were obstacles to the natural expression of freedom. In America as in Europe, Romanticism was the intellectual and cultural reaction against the Enlightenment and its emphasis on the social.

Jefferson lived in both these worlds; his public life from 1775 to 1825 straddled the intellectual transition from reason to Romanticism. When he spoke of letting bad ideas float freely to be corrected by the light of reason, he was the consummate Enlightenment liberal, as he was in his fascination with technology, progress, and, of course, the pursuit of happiness. But when he said that those who labor of the earth were the chosen people of God, Jefferson was starting to romanticize nature and the earth in ways that would become familiar in the nineteenth century. And when he suggested that Africans were naturally inferior to whites, he was stimulating the shift from the social categories of the eighteenth-century Enlightenment to the natural categories of nineteenth-century Romanticism. The next essay in this volume, by Jean Boydston, traces a similar shift by Judith Sargent Murray in the 1790s—from "rank" to race and gender as the determinant of political participation, or, to put it in more general terms, from social to natural categories.

The political implications of this shift were dramatic. If "white" and "male" became the criteria for membership in the electorate, "rank" was thereby eviscerated, with genuinely democratic consequences. But the same "natural" standard that extended the franchise to propertyless white men simultaneously and by definition closed it off to women and blacks. Thus did a single shift—a shift that Thomas Jefferson epitomized—from the social to the natural self, inject into the political culture a set of categories that help explain why the Jeffersonian ascendancy of 1800 could be both revolutionary and reactionary at the same time.

Jefferson himself never actually shifted. From the beginning of his career to the end of his life his writings reflected the sensibilities of both the Enlightenment and Romanticism. To the extent that Jefferson's election in 1800 brought this tension into the center of American political culture, he helped establish the terms of the debate over whether slaves could be happy. On the one hand, that Americans even asked the question revealed how influential Enlightenment standards remained in the nineteenth century. On the other hand, by positing an innate desire for freedom and, against that, the innate suitability of Africans for enslavement, Romanticism dramatically altered the terms of the debate over the happy slave. This was the intellectual revolution of 1800, and it began to play itself out in the antebellum South within a few years of Jefferson's death in 1826.

Having made ordinary life—a decent standard of living, a loving family, economic security—the basis of human happiness, was it possible to create material conditions for slaves that would render them happy? Liberal theory was ambiguous on this issue. On one reading, individual freedom, or at least a free government, was an essential component of human happiness. Certainly Jefferson believed that personal freedom was a prerequisite to personal happiness, and he considered the relation of master and slave to be grounded in abominable tyranny. But on another reading, the point of personal freedom and the value of free government was that they were most conducive to the ease and comfort, the material well-being, that made for human happiness. If that well-being could be secured under slavery, the question remained: could a slave be happy?[15] Historians have been too apt to pass over this debate without appreciating the fundamental issues at stake. Antebellum Americans were not simply tossing off banalities when they fought over whether or not slaves were happy. Jefferson had helped establish happiness as one of the highest standards to which any society could be held. It was inevitable that when his fellow southerners were forced to engage the great question of slavery and freedom, happiness would become one of the central terms of their debate.

Nowhere did southerners explore the issue with greater depth and passion than in the famous dispute over slavery in the Virginia legislature in 1832. The discussion had been provoked by Nat Turner's brutal but failed slave insurrection in Southampton. And although the legislators took up many other themes, the question of the slaves' happiness emerged as a kind of debate within the debate. It had a logic and a trajectory all its own, even though it was fully embedded in other problems, such as the practicality of colonization or the profitability of a slave economy.

Samuel Moore opened the debate by raising the question of the slaves' happiness immediately but indirectly. Arguing from Enlightenment premises, Moore deduced the demoralization of the slaves from the fact that they were, by necessity, imprisoned in ignorance. "I think I may safely assert, that ignorance is the inseparable companion of slavery, and that the desire of freedom is the inevitable consequence of implanting in the human mind any useful degree of intelligence," Moore argued. "It is therefore the policy of the master, that the ignorance of his slaves shall be as profound as possible." Thus steeped in ignorance, the slaves were incapable of distinguishing right from wrong, virtue from vice. Moore never actually said that the slaves were "unhappy," but his portrayal of slaves left little room for doubt. The Scots had argued that benevolence and morality were the most perfect source of human happiness, and Moore made moral sentiment, and therefore happiness, incompatible with slavery.[16]

James Gholson snapped at Moore's bait and spit back an argument that was rapidly becoming an orthodoxy among slaveholders: "I will say that the slaves of Va. are as happy a laboring class as exists upon the habitable globe," Gholson declared. They were well fed, well clothed, and well treated. Only "reasonable" labor was expected of healthy slaves; the sick were cared for properly. Slaves lived "in waste" during good times; in bad times their needs were met. They lived carefree lives, contented today and with no anxieties for the future. Cruelty was "discountenanced by society," while the slaves' "priveleges" were extended over the years. "Among what labouring class will you find more happiness and less misery?" Moore asked. "Not among the serfs and labouring poor of Europe!" With that the pattern was established. The material conditions Gholson described were precisely those held out by Jefferson and others as most conducive to human happiness. Indeed, there are echoes in Gholson of Locke's formula that weighed happiness and misery in the balance. By that standard, he concluded, "our slave population is not only a happy one, but it is a contented, peaceful and harmless one."[17]

William Brodnax emphatically seconded Gholson. Judged by "the ordinary comforts of life," Broadnax argued, the slaves' condition "is superior to that of the peasantry of any other country." Jefferson had used the misery of the European peasantry as the standard by which he had calculated the human price of political tyranny. Within a generation other Virginia slaveholders were using the same standard to extol the virtues of southern slavery. In Broadnax's words, Virginia's slaves were "exempt from many of the evils incident to laboring classes in other countries." Cruel and improper treatment was condemned by public sentiment. Well fed and clothed, the slaves were untouched by the famines that afflicted laboring classes elsewhere. Freed from the need to provide their own subsistence, the slaves "are, when they have good masters, I believe in a happy condition."[18]

The condition of the European peasantry and urban working class quickly emerged as the standard by which to measure the happiness of southern slaves. William Daniel Jr. offered a characteristically forthright comparison.

Compared to "the poorer classes" elsewhere, Daniel claimed, Virginia's slaves "are happy, and feelings of gratitude have, in most instances, attached them to us." Indeed, if it were not for the attempts by abolitionists ("philanthropists" was the epithet of choice) to persuade the slaves that they were miserable, "they would continue to be happy and to love us." In his closing peroration Daniel waxed positively ecstatic. "Show me, Sir, a happier man than one of those domestics in the possession of a kind and indulgent owner. Proud of his master, he assumes his name, apes his manners, puts on his air of dignity, and is, as has been said by a most observant writer, 'one of the veriest aristocrats of the world.'" [19]

At this point the debate took a curious turn. Thomas Marshall, one of the most vocal critics of slavery in the Virginia legislature, endorsed the claim that the slaves were well off and then promptly pronounced it irrelevant. "The ordinary condition of the slave is not such as to make humanity weep for his lot," Marshall announced. "Compare his condition with that of the laborer in any part of Europe, and you will find him blessed with a measure of happiness, nearly, if not altogether equal." To be sure, this was a much more tepid endorsement than those of Gholson, Broadnax, and Daniel. Marshall was stating simply that the slaves of Virginia were "nearly" as happy as the oppressed laborers of Europe. Still, in the part of Virginia where he lived, Marshall was prepared to make even stronger claims. "The negro there is happy—he is treated with the most indulgent kindness—he is required to do the same work, and no more, than is performed by the white man—he is clothed with the best fabrics of the factores, and he is fed literally with the fat of the land." [20] The crucial difference for Marshall was that this did not constitute a justification of slavery. If anything, the indulgence of the slaves contributed to the economic calamity that the slave economy was wreaking on his state. Thus the claim that slaves were happy was not, at least in the Virginia legislature, evidence of proslavery convictions. Nevertheless, in vouching for the well-being of the slaves Marshall was making a concession that slavery's remaining critics would have to confront.

The first to do so was William B. Preston. Speaking directly to the claim that the situation of the Virginia slave was "preferable to that of the labouring classes in Europe," Preston was perfectly incredulous. "Mr. Speaker, this is impossible: happiness, is incompatible with slavery." Why? Because, the "love of liberty is the ruling passion of man; it has been implanted in his bosom by the voice of God, and he cannot be happy if deprived of it." [21] This was an entirely new way of framing the issue, but Preston made the point only to drop it without elaboration. It was left to others to carry the argument forward.

Before that happened, slavery's defenders took up the challenge. Alexander G. Knox entered the fray with a refutation of Samuel Moore's opening claim that because slaves were ignorant they were incapable of distinguishing morality from immorality. On the contrary, Knox claimed, "the slave in Virginia, reared as he is to the knowledge of moral principle, is in a more happy condition than the African, wandering as he does in ignorance and wretchedness, over the sun-scorched deserts of his native land, a stranger to the lights of moral or revealed religion."[22] This was a curious argument. Knox did not respond to Moore's claims by defending the necessity of keeping the slaves in ignorance, as some other proslavery writers did. On the contrary, Knox claimed that because Virginia slaves were exposed to the Bible, they were actually rescued from the ignorance that allegedly enveloped blacks in Africa. As a result the slaves were morally sentient beings and therefore able to meet one of the basic liberal-humanist standards for human happiness.

But Knox turned out to be the last legislator to make an unambiguous case for the slaves' happiness. The tide of the debate turned with George W. Summers. He acknowledged that the material conditions of slave life were perfectly decent but was careful to separate those conditions from the question of whether the slaves were happy. At the present day, he argued, the "mere animal" comforts available to slaves compared favorably with those available to "the labouring classes in other countries, particularly in the severer governments of Europe." He was willing to admit that "many" of the slaves "are content with their destiny" and that others displayed "undying friendship" toward their owners.[23] But none of this was enough to persuade Summers that the slaves were actually happy. Indeed, he viewed the slaves as a threatening presence in Virginia. "There is a continual and abiding danger of insubordination," he insisted, and it stemmed inevitably "from the natural love of liberty, which the great Author of our being has imparted to all his creatures." Summers then fleshed out a line of reasoning advanced earlier by William Preston. The love of liberty was an innate trait common to all human beings, he argued. "It belongs to every thing which breathes the breath of life. . . . It is a portion of the divine essence, which can never be wholly destroyed. Oppression cannot eradicate it. Amid the profoundest mental darkness, its feeble ray will sometimes light up the gloom within. It is a scintillation struck from the eternal rock of being, which can only be extinguished in the tomb."[24]

Call this the Romantic trump. For Enlightenment liberals freedom was an inalienable right that could only be enjoyed in society and under the proper forms of government. For nineteenth-century Romantics liberty was an innate, almost biological desire that could be thwarted by society and repressed by governments. But the desire itself could never be eradicated. By naturalizing— as we say these days, "essentializing"—liberty in this way, Romanticism re- jected the eighteenth century's conviction that happiness depended on free governments that allowed human beings to claim the full fruits of their labor and thus live in ease and comfort. For Romantics happiness depended on the individual's ability to express him- or herself freely, without the interference of government or the restraints of "society." This reasoning had tremendous consequences for the debate over the happiness of the slaves. In the context of the Virginia debate, Romanticism allowed slavery's opponents to bypass the claims that the slaves were happy because their social and material lives were comfortable.

Ironically, it was the defenders of slavery who held most fiercely to the older, Enlightenment standard of human happiness. John T. Brown contended "that the happiness of the slave does not call for his emancipation." He then moved the discussion back into familiar territory. The slave, Brown insisted, "enjoys far more of the comforts of life, than the peasantry of many of the na- tions in Europe." In good times and bad, the slave "is sure of a subsistence." Brown even defended the internal slave trade, arguing that if a master becomes impoverished, "he is sure to sell" his slave "to someone who is able" to main- tain him. Secure in old age and protected by both law and public opinion from "cruel and abusive" treatment, the slave could only be worse off if free. Having gone this far, there was no holding Brown back from a generic assault on free- dom. "Man must be civilized, his mind enlightened, and his feelings refined for the enjoyment of liberty. . . . The greater part of mankind must, in the nature of things, be poor and ignorant, toiling anxiously for their daily bread. All cannot be raised to the top of the scale," Brown concluded, "and the negro, of all oth- ers, is the least susceptible of elevation." [25]

Call this the racial trump. Romantics, naturalizing the desire for freedom, all but declared the slaves intrinsically unhappy. Their opponents responded by naturalizing the concept of race, all but declaring blacks inherently unsuited for freedom. The debate over the slave's happiness was devolving into a battle of dueling essences.

For sheer rhetorical bravado, however, the Romantics had the upper hand, at least in the Virginia legislature. George I. Williams, for example, heaped rid- icule on Brown. He has "endeavored to maintain that our slaves do not wish to be liberated—that servitude is sweet; and that the yoke and the fetter sit as lightly on their limbs, as garlands of flowers and wreaths of palm. The gentleman was led away by his exuberant imagination into a picture of patriarchal simplicity and passionless content, which exists only in the dreams of fancy." Maybe so, but in this case it was Williams whose Romantic effusions were about to take wing.

> The poorest tattered negro, who tills the planter's field, under his task-master, and labors to produce those fruits which he may never call his own, feels within him that spark which emanates from the deity—the innate longing for liberty—and hears in the inmost recesses of his soul, the secret whispering of nature, that tell him he should be free. The love of freedom is a universal animal principle—it is concomitant with vitality. No human being was ever born without the wish for liberty implanted in his breast. God never made a slave—for slavery is the work of man alone." [26]

The seductive appeal of Williams's glorious phrasing was characteristically Romantic, as were the assumptions underlying his sweeping claims: social institutions, indeed society itself, invariably acts as a restraint on the inherent impulses that make human beings human. In this case the institution was slavery and the impulse was freedom, but it was stock Romanticism all the same.

Nor was Williams alone in his use of it. If anything, James McDowell outdid him. He, too, readily conceded that there was "no laboring peasantry in any other part of the world, who, in all external respects, are better situated than our slave—who suffer less from want—who suffer less from hardship—who struggle less under the toils of life or who have a fuller supply of the comforts which mere physical nature demands." Here again was the implicit denigration of "mere physical" needs and "external" comforts. Here again was the claim that the slaves were not the victims of cruelty and "rarely, if ever, of oppression." Quite the opposite: "year after year," McDowell affirmed, the "harshness" of slavery was "abating" while the slave "is admitted to every privilege which the deprivation of his liberty can allow." But of course this was just the setup for the Romantic trump. For it was precisely the improvement in the slaves' condition that gave McDowell "cause of apprehension."

> You raise his intelligence with his condition, and as he better understands his position in the world, he were not man if it did not the more inflame his discontent. That it has this effect we all know; for the truth is proverbial, that a slave is the more unhappy as he is the more indulged. He could not be otherwise; he follows

but the impulse of human nature in being so. . . . Sir, you may place the slave
where you please—you may dry up, to your uttermost, the fountains of his feeling, the springs of his thought—you may close upon his mind every avenue of
knowledge and cloud it over with artificial night—you may yoke him to your
labors as the ox which liveth only to work and worketh only to live—you may put
him under any process which, without destroying his value as a slave, will debase
and crush him as a rational being—you may do this and the idea that he was born
to be free will survive it all. It is allied to his hope of immortality—it is the ethe-
real part of his nature which oppression cannot reach; it is a torch lit up in his
soul by the hand of the Deity and never meant to be extinguished by the hand
of man.[27]

With that the debate over the slaves' happiness pretty much ended in the
Virginia legislature, the Romantic trump having silenced all claims that the
slaves were "happy." But the Romantic turn created more problems than it resolved, in part because its high quotient of rhetorical overkill effectively masked
some deeply troubling assumptions. In the wake of the Virginia debate, as the
southern critique of slavery withered and all but died, the proponents of the
happy slave exploited two critical weaknesses in the Romantic assault. First,
they eagerly capitalized on the Romantics' concession that by strictly material
measures the southern slaves were well treated, especially by comparison with
the miserable masses of Europe and the degraded savages of Africa. For those
who invoked liberal-humanist standards, this made the slaves "happy." Second,
proslavery writers took up the Romantics' naturalistic rhetoric and ran with it,
arguing that nature itself had so constituted the African race that it could be
happy when subjected to a form of slavery that white people would find intol-
erable. Having shifted the terms of debate from natural rights to innate traits,
Romantics could not easily answer the claim that blacks were innately suited to
slavery. In the aftermath of the Virginia slavery debate, proslavery writers who
argued that slaves were happy did so on the two grounds left open to them by
the weaknesses of the Romantic trump.

Both of these arguments were hinted at during the Virginia debate itself.
John Brown had opened the racial argument when he claimed that happiness
depended on a level of civilization that blacks could never reach. And at the
very end of the debate William O. Goode made chastened claims for the happiness of the slave by exploiting the concessions of his opponents. They "have
admitted," Goode pointed out, that "the slave is humanely treated. He has an

unrestrained abundance of good, substantial, wholesome food—as well for his family, as for himself. He and his family have an ample allowance of comfortable clothing. He is, for the most part well housed. He enjoys many reasonable indulgences." He has access to "some of the luxuries of life," is cared for in sickness, and is allowed a "fair, public trial" when charged with a crime." [28] The only thing Goode refrained from saying, perhaps because he didn't have to, is that the ease and comfort of their lives made the slaves happy. But the door had been left open for others to say just that and Thomas Roderick Dew marched right through it.

In his famous commentary on the Virginia slavery debate, a commentary widely seen as the beginning of the mature southern defense of slavery, Dew pointed explicitly to the crucial concession made by every legislator who had spoken in opposition to slavery. "In the debate in the Virginia legislature," Dew wrote, "no speaker *insinuated even*, we believe that the slaves in Virginia were not treated kindly; and all too agreed that they were most abundantly fed." For Dew that was more than enough to revive the claim that the slaves were happy. In fact, he argued, the slaves were happier even than their masters. We have "no doubt," Dew solemnly declared, "but that they form the happiest portion of our society." But why stop there? "A merrier being does not exist on the face of the globe," Dew announced, "than the negro slave of the United States." [29]

To reach this astonishing conclusion all Dew and subsequent proslavery writers had to do was jettison the dubious Romantic conceit that the longing for freedom stirs irrepressibly in the breast of every living human. Instead they simply returned to the standards of happiness that Americans carried out of the eighteenth century. William Harper appropriated those standards in his "Memoir on Slavery." Happiness, he wrote, "is the great end of existence, the sole object of all animated and sentient beings. This is the only *natural* right of man." The natural right to happiness came straight out of Burlamaqui, and it is what distinguished the eighteenth-century Enlightenment from nineteenth-century utilitarianism. For the latter, "the greatest good for the greatest number" was a purely pragmatic proposition and had no grounding in a concept of natural right. This made Harper uncomfortable, though in the end he acknowledged that the greatest good for the greatest number "is the best [standard] we have." And by that standard, Harper argued, civilization was happier with slavery than without. [30]

James Henry Hammond reverted to the Lockean calculus in his claim that the slaves were happy. "If pleasure is correctly defined to be the absence of pain—which, so far as the great body of mankind is concerned, is undoubtedly its true definition—I believe our slaves are the happiest three millions of human beings on whom the sun shines."[31] In retrospect, the claim that the slaves were at least as happy as the European peasants was downright modest. In the face of rising abolitionist criticism, proslavery writers increasingly claimed that the southern slaves were the happiest human beings on the entire planet.

Dew, Harper, and Hammond rested their case on elements of the liberal-humanist definition of human happiness. But as the decades passed proslavery writers supplemented their arguments with novel theories of African racial distinctiveness, claiming that blacks could be happy in conditions of enslavement that white people could never tolerate. Samuel Cartwright, one of the South's leading practitioners of the new science of "ethnology," presented the argument as clearly as anyone else. Scientific experiments satisfied Cartwright that blacks inhaled less oxygen than whites, rendering blacks both physically and mentally slower. Incapable of motivating themselves, blacks were appropriately stimulated to productive labor only by the institution of slavery. Furthermore, in the sugar, cotton, and rice fields of the slave South, Cartwright explained in 1852, "the white man, from the physiological laws governing his economy, *can not labor and live*." But in those same fields, "the negro thrives, luxuriates and enjoys existence more than any laboring peasantry to be found on the continent of Europe." Thus did nature predispose whites to be happy in freedom and blacks to be happy in slavery.[32]

By the 1850s racial ideology had been absorbed into most defenses of slavery. For example, after a lengthy historical introduction, Thomas R. R. Cobb opened his 1858 *Inquiry into the Law of Negro Slavery* with an elaborate summation of the findings of racial theorists, all of which led Cobb to the conclusion that Negroes were most happy when they were slaves. Such was their "moral character," Cobb explained, that blacks were "happy, peaceful, contented, and cheerful in a status that would break the spirit and destroy the energies of the Caucasian or the native American." Cobb then borrowed the classic language of eighteenth-century liberals and nineteenth-century utilitarians, fusing it with racial theory, to explain the happiness of slaves. In the state of bondage, Cobb wrote, the slave "enjoys the greatest amount of happiness, and arrives at the greatest degree of perfection of which his nature is capable."[33]

In fact, racial ideology added little to the argument that the slaves were happy. Cartwright's claim that southern slaves were happier than European peasants did not require the pseudo-science of "ethnology" to back it up. By the

1850s such rhetoric was a commonplace among proslavery writers. Indeed, they were not that far from Jefferson's conviction that American workers were happier than their miserable European counterparts. Similarly, Cobb's claim that slavery offered Africans "the greatest amount of happiness" possible was not much more than a utilitarian reworking of the eighteenth-century claim that humans had a natural right to happiness. Racial ideology added a new element to Enlightenment theory, but it did not alter the terms of the debate.

The real significance of racial ideology to the discussion of the slave's happiness lay in its trumping of the Romantic trump. In the Virginia slavery debate, the Romantic claim that humans were innately disposed to freedom effectively silenced the claims that the slaves were happy in their condition. But racial ideology posited the Africans' innate suitability to slavery, a claim that almost no one in the Old South bothered to dispute. As a result, the discussion of slaves' happiness returned to the question of their material well-being.

The clearest evidence of this tendency was the vast literature on the management of plantations that accumulated in the various agricultural periodicals published in the antebellum South. One of the staples of that literature was the claim that a well-managed plantation would ensure the happiness of both master and slave. "When the negro is treated with humanity and subjected to constant employment without the labor of thought and the cares incident to the necessity of providing for his own support," a Mississippi planter wrote in 1851, "he is by far happier than he would be if emancipated and left to think and act and provide for himself." [34]

In all of this literature the question of human happiness was framed in the terms established during the eighteenth century. The duties of the master with regard to the slave were widely acknowledged. He must provide the slaves with comfortable houses, sufficient wholesome food, decent clothing, proper medical care, clear rules that, when violated, would result in moderate but predictable punishments. "Negroes thus treated and managed are prolific, cheerful, industrious and happy," one planter wrote. After considering the material conditions of slave life—the size and location of their cabins, the quality of their clothing and blankets, the way their food was prepared, the quality of their medical care, the restraint on physical cruelty—another slaveholder argued that a plantation that so insured the material and physical well-being of the slaves would "promote the greatest good to the greatest number of all concerned." Under the system of management he had outlined, "the slaves are generally a happy, contented people." [35]

Over and over the slaveholders claimed that the happiness of the slaves was essential to a profitable and harmonious plantation. A "proper system of discipline" would make the slaves "much more contented and happy." It was the master's "duty" to "treat and govern" his slaves "with a view to their comfort and happiness." When properly treated, the slaves "are the happiest laboring class in the world." The slave's family should be left undisturbed; he is thereby "made happier and safer, put beyond discontent." [36]

But if the slaveholders invoked Enlightenment standards of human happiness, they did so selectively. Their arguments for the happiness of the slave were as interesting for what they left out as for what they included. They emphasized the purely material and physical elements of human happiness, repeatedly claiming that the slaves were well provided with good food, adequate clothing, and decent housing. They claimed that their slaves were not physically brutalized. The truth of these claims is not the issue. For our purposes, it is important only that the masters insisted that they had provided for the "mere animal" comforts of the slaves, who were therefore "happy."

But eighteenth-century liberals, while they had certainly elevated the material conditions of daily life to an unprecedented place in the configuration of human happiness, had never claimed that material life *alone* was enough to insure human happiness. In several crucial areas the argument for the slaves' happiness carefully sidestepped the legacy of the eighteenth century. The first was the sanctity of the family. It was a given among Enlightenment liberals that a private life grounded in affection and secure against the competitive pressures of the outside world was one of the basic sources of emotional satisfaction and, as such, of human happiness. The intrinsic insecurity of the slave family, along with the paternalistic intrusion of the master in the daily lives of the slaves, precluded the kind of private "happiness" that was so important to the Enlightenment vision.

Similarly, the satisfaction that came from self-directed and self-disciplined labor was denied to the slaves. When Jefferson claimed in his inaugural address that a wise and frugal government would never "take from the mouth of labor the bread it has earned," he was speaking of something more than labor's right to the material rewards of hard work. The dignity of labor was prized for its own sake, and for men like Jefferson labor could not be dignified if it was not free. The right to the fruits of one's labor thus presupposed *political* as well as personal freedom, and it was here that the argument for the slave's happiness collapsed. For in reducing human happiness to its material components, slavery's defenders ripped happiness from its broader emotional and political contexts. For Locke and his followers, the distinction between public and private was basic to human freedom, and freedom was essential to human happiness. But no slaveholder could guarantee the sanctity of the slave's private life; no slaveholder could sanction the slave's participation in the public sphere. By these standards—the standards of early modern humanism and the liberal Enlightenment that Jefferson had so effectively articulated—the inalienable right to the pursuit of happiness was denied to the slaves, by definition.

From this perspective, Jefferson's inaugural litany of the specific "felicities" with which the American people were blessed raised questions about the happiness of the slaves. He was not thinking of the Atlantic slave trade when he pointed to the "wide ocean" that "kindly separated" Americans from "the exterminating havoc of one quarter of the globe." Nor was he referring to the expansion of slavery when he cited his "chosen country, with room enough for our descendants to the thousandth and thousandth generation." He could not have meant slavery when he declared that America was further blessed by a citizenry that entertained "a due sense of our equal right to the use of our own faculties, to the acquisitions of our own industry." And if the happiness of Americans stemmed also from the "honor and confidence" they extended to each other "not from birth, but from our actions," Jefferson could not have believed that the national happiness extended as well to the slaves. These—along with the right to the fruits of our labor—were the standards for happiness that Jefferson laid down at the outset of his presidency in 1801. He knew, he had to know, that slavery did not meet those standards.

When he retired to Albemarle County eight years later, Jefferson was still concerned with the question of happiness. But perhaps chastened by his experience of the presidency, he spoke more modestly. In his inaugural address he had laid down the conditions for public happiness. In his address "To the Inhabitants of Albemarle County" of April 1809, Jefferson related those conditions to his own circumstances. "The anxieties you express to administer to my happiness," he wrote, "do, of themselves, confer that happiness." He then submitted his own record of public service to the judgment of his neighbors, asking them "in the face of the world, 'whose ox have I taken, or whom have I defrauded? Whom have I oppressed . . . ?'" Thus did Jefferson once again set the standard by which he himself is found wanting.

NOTES

1. Frederick Douglass, *My Bondage and My Freedom* (New York, 1855), 99.

2. Morton White, *The Philosophy of the American Revolution* (New York, 1978), 232–33.

3. Garry Wills, *Inventing America: Jefferson's Declaration of Independence* (New York, 1978), 250, 149–64, 248–55.

4. John Locke, *An Essay Concerning Human Understanding* (Oxford, 1975), bk. 2:42–43.

5. Wills, *Inventing America.* Morton White argued that Americans took the idea of happiness from Burlamaqui, but Wills shows that Burlamaqui and other French writers were influenced by the Scots.

6. John Dickinson, *Letters from a Farmer in Pennsylvania* (1767), reprinted in Forrest McDonald, ed., *Empire and Nation,* 2d ed. (Indianapolis, 1999), 3.

7. Adams, "Thoughts on Government," *The Political Writings of John Adams,* ed. George A. Peek Jr. (Indianapolis, 1954), 84–85.

8. Daniel J. Boorstin, *The Americans: The Colonial Experience* (New York, 1958), 1; Richard Hofstadter, *The Progressive Historians: Turner, Beard, Parrington* (New York, 1968), 450 n.

9. White, *Philosophy of the American Revolution,* 233, argues that in the Declaration Jefferson used "happiness" in two distinct senses. Along with life and liberty, the "pursuit of happiness" was a right vested in every individual. But he also speaks of happiness as a characteristic of entire societies, as in: "that whenever any form of government becomes destructive of these ends, it is the right of the people to alter or to abolish it, and to institute new government, laying its foundation on such principles and organizing its powers in such form, as to them shall seem most likely to effect their safety and happiness."

10. Adams, "Thoughts on Government," 84–85. Jack P. Greene, *Pursuits of Happiness: The Social Development of Early Modern British Colonies and the Formation of American Culture* (Chapel Hill, N.C., 1988), 196–98, specifies the demographic, material, and political components of happiness as understood by American colonists.

11. Charles Taylor, *Sources of the Self: The Making of Modern Identity* (Cambridge, Mass., 1989), 210–302. Taylor sees this affirmation as something other than liberalism.

12. Hannah Arendt, *The Human Condition* (Chicago, 1958), 38–49.

13. Quoted in Wills, *Inventing America:* 158–59.

14. Ralph Waldo Emerson, "Self Reliance," in *Selected Essays,* Penguin ed. (New York, 1982), 178.

15. The analytical problem arising within liberalism is brilliantly dissected in Don Herzog, *Happy Slaves: A Critique of Consent Theory* (Chicago, 1989).

16. Joseph Clarke Robert, ed., *The Road From Monticello: A Study of the Virginia Slaver Debate of 1832* (Durham, N.C., 1941), 62.

17. Ibid., 67.

18. Ibid., 71.

19. Ibid., 74.

20. Ibid., 78.

21. Ibid., 83.

22. Ibid., 84.

23. Ibid., 85.

24. Ibid., 85.

25. Ibid., 90–91.

26. Ibid., 93–94.

27. Ibid., 103.

28. Ibid., 106.

29. Drew Gilpin Faust, ed., *The Ideology of Slavery: Proslavery Thought in the Antebellum South: 1830–1860* (Baton Rouge, 1981), 66.

30. Ibid., 88–91.

31. Ibid., 192.

32. S. A. Cartwright, "Slavery in the Light of Ethnology," in *Cotton is King, and Proslavery Arguments,* ed. E. N. Elliot (Augusta, Ga., 1860), 691–728.

33. Thomas R. R. Cobb, *An Inquiry into the Law of Negro Slavery in the United States of America,* ed. Paul Finkelman (1858; Athens, Ga., 1999), 46–47, 51.

34. Quoted in James O. Breeden, ed., *Advice among Masters: The Ideal in Slave Management in the Old South* (Westport, Conn., 1980), 18.

35. Ibid., 15, 24, 25.

36. Ibid., 32, 33, 35, 58.

CHAPTER 10

Making Gender in the Early Republic
Judith Sargent Murray and the Revolution of 1800

Jeanne Boydston

In the early 1790s Judith Sargent Murray was one of the most influential writers in New England and arguably in the United States. The author of a children's religious catechism and numerous poems, Murray was best known for her social and political commentary, which appeared in essays published regularly from 1790 to 1794 in New England's most prestigious journals. Murray's interests ranged widely, but the subject on which she wrote most often and with the greatest authority was the civic and political culture of the new nation. Commenting on topics ranging from the character of representation, the rights of women, and the origin of legitimacy in a republic to specific government policies, by the mid-1790s she counted among her readers President George Washington, Vice President John Adams, Abigail Adams, and Mercy Otis Warren.

By the late 1790s, however, Murray's reputation was in decline. Two of her plays, performed in 1795 and 1796, brought an indifferent response. A 1798 collection of her essays, poems, and plays entitled *The Gleaner: A Miscellaneous Production in Three Volumes* failed to sell as well as she hoped. By 1806 at least one reviewer denounced *The Gleaner* as "stiff, forced, inelegant, coarse, affected, and feeble," and, perhaps more to the point, "oftentimes, incorrect."[1]

Murray blamed party politics for her troubles. An outspoken Federalist, she believed that the Republicans deliberately undermined sales of the 1798 *Gleaner*. By 1806 she was convinced that political opponents had "long since" put in operation "a systematic plan" to destroy her reputation.[2]

Although the demise of Murray's career obviously derived from many factors (some readers disliked her Universalist religious views and even her printer was chagrined at her syntax),[3] she was probably not altogether misguided in her analysis. Years later Thomas Jefferson would famously muse that the Republican victory in 1800 "was as real a revolution in the principles of our government as that of 1776 was in its form."[4] The principles that underpinned that victory were not purely or exclusively *governmental*, however. Jefferson's rise to the presidency was enabled by the diffusion of "principles" of a social and cultural kind—changes in the everyday assumptions of many Americans about the character of republican society and about who could enter with authority into public discussions of life and politics in a republic. As these "principles" of inclusion shifted, individuals and even variants of republican thought that had earlier commanded attention (if not necessarily assent) within the public debate lost stature and eventually relevance. Viewed in this way, the revolution of 1800 signaled a transformation not only of the early American party system but also of the early American public itself, and it speaks to larger questions of the historical processes through which publics gain and lose legitimacy and through which other publics are constituted.[5]

Murray's career as an author, both her public reputation and her sense of her own claims as a public actor, illuminate this shift in the authorizing discourse of American republicanism, particularly as it affected women. Murray entered the debates over the character of the new Republic confident that she, and other women like her, belonged there. Even in the 1790s, as she chronicled what were to her disturbing developments in the character of the American public sphere, Murray considered herself a member of that public, qualified to assume the position of the critical spectator.[6] By the turn of the century, however, not only Murray's reputation but also her confidence had begun to waver. Her published and private writings revealed a growing alienation from the public sphere as she perceived it to be forming and an uncertainty about how and whether women like her could claim a legitimate identity as public actors within its new vocabulary.

Murray's career also sheds light on the ways in which individuals displaced in transformations of the public sphere respond to and participate in those changes. When Murray was rediscovered by women's historians in the 1980s, she was noted as a symbol of women's postrevolutionary powerlessness. As Linda Kerber argued, "the political community that was fashioned by the American war was a deeply gendered community" in which the best that women could do was to fashion an indirect political status through their roles as mothers of future citizens, the relation identified by Kerber as "republican motherhood." According to Kerber and others, Judith Sargent Murray was "perhaps the most vigorous single voice" for that compromise position.[7] Yet this historical verdict seems at odds with Murray's early work, which asserts a far more direct relation to the new American public. It was only in the late 1790s, I will suggest, that Murray's writings betrayed acquiescence to a discourse of public authority in which gender designated a distinct relation to the public for women. With that acquiescence appeared a newly explicit willingness to repudiate other groups as the condition of her own qualified inclusion as a female. Ultimately women like Murray, white women struggling for new grounds upon which to legitimate their identities as members of the respectable classes, would actively police those boundaries of qualification.

Judith Sargent Murray was a member of New England's colonial elite, a background that deeply shaped her expectations of a public identity and her work. She was born in 1751 into a prosperous Massachusetts ship-building and merchant family, old and influential on both her father's and mother's sides. Judith's paternal grandfather was educated at Harvard and served as justice of the peace and a deputy to the Massachusetts General Court. Her father and uncles were the wealthiest merchants in Gloucester.[8] As she later acknowledged, Judith learned early to expect "*ease* and *affluence.*"[9] She also learned to assume that with rank and property came not only economic but also social and political power. In 1769 Judith Sargent married John Stevens, also from a prominent Gloucester family, moved into an elegant and imposing house overlooking Gloucester harbor, and prepared to begin her life as an adult member of Gloucester's merchant class.

This identity of rank—this confidence of membership in the ruling class of colonial society—was the constituting condition of Murray's sense of her public identity in American society, the conviction through which other elements of her experience found particular meaning and achieved coherence over time. It was an identity that assumed whiteness (throughout most of her publishing career, Murray simply did not bother to take much note of the presence of African Americans or Native Americans in the Republic), and it steadily shaped her understanding of what it meant to be female. Within her family, men ran the merchant enterprises, held public office, and enjoyed superior access to education. Her own later economic troubles would lead Murray to argue that women should have the capacity to be self-supporting, but the great sense of inequality she carried from her own childhood was in terms of education. She was tutored at home with her brothers but unlike them did not attend college— a point of contention that would recur as a central theme throughout her writings. Nevertheless, she was clearly raised to be confident in her own judgments and comfortable with authority, not unlike her less well educated mother, whose "very deportment commanded respect." Murray herself was polite but adamant about her independence of judgment. Using a trope that would later figure at the center of her republican political theory, in 1769 she wrote to her uncle that although she appreciated his expression of "paternal regard," she preferred to consider his friendship "fraternal" in character: "a brother is my equal, and I can communicate my ideas freely as they arise—but my Father is my sup[erior] and this idea contracts the freedom of my expressions." [10]

Although Murray was only eighteen when she wrote those lines, her assertion and expectation of a certain autonomy of identity was not atypical among women of her class. As a number of recent studies have suggested, in colonial America the achievement of social, economic, and political power required family-based strategies in which women played active roles. There is evidence that women in the colonial elites asserted a considerable authority over both their own choice of husbands and the marital alliances of other men and women. Throughout their adult lives, as representatives of prominent families, wives (and daughters) often helped to establish and maintain trade connections and entered into the management of estates, keeping accounts, managing correspondence, and making a variety of daily operational decisions. As embodiments of family power, they dispensed patronage, nurtured social and economic partnerships, and choreographed the public rituals of the ruling classes, enjoying an influence over their social, economic, and even political communities that was no less real for being claimed through their membership in leading families. [11]

By the time Murray married John Stevens, the world of colonial America was caught up in the revolutionary crisis. The war itself soon followed. Although the war brought devastation and danger to women across class lines, politicizing the poor and the privileged alike, women in prominent families appear to have expressed their political identities in distinct, class-identified ways. They seem to have avoided participating in patriotic crowds and other activities that required them to mingle with women of lower ranks. Mary Beth Norton has observed that the highly celebrated "spinning bees" of the late 1760s were the particular province of "eminently respectable young ladies." Other women used their station to draw public attention to the signing of patriotic pledges. Still others published poems and plays and sponsored and participated in salons, displays of political sentiment not readily available to women of lower rank or lesser education. More discreetly, women in socially prominent families took advantage of their connections "to collect some political intelligence," as Murray put it in 1778.[12]

Murray's wartime correspondence reflected both her optimism that elite women would enjoy a continuing, and perhaps expanded, political agency in the new Republic and the terms within which she framed that agency. She acknowledged that not everyone liked the idea of a "female politician." In a 1778 letter to her brother, she referred to "the tide of vulgar prejudice" that "a female is out of her sphere" to express political views. Yet clearly she did not expect the "vulgar" tide to affect her. Her letters showed a lively and informed interest in politics, political theory, and women's participation in the affairs of state. She claimed "the sacred rights of mankind" and "the welfare of my Country" as "subjects very near my heart" and appropriate for her consideration. Murray did ground her understanding of female patriotism in the relations of the household, in women's positions "as wives, as mothers and as friends." But she conceived the household so expansively, as a trope for all desirable civic identities, that its relevance to their identities did not *necessarily* attenuate women's relation to the state. She often represented men's political loyalties in familial tropes and did not hesitate to claim for herself the status of "Citizen."[13]

Murray's 1779 essay "On the Equality of the Sexes" also suggested the importance she attached to the household as the model of civic life. The explicit object of the essay was to argue for improved education for women. Murray's analysis was one that would later be associated with Mary Wollstonecraft: that to the extent that women behaved in less rational ways than men, their conduct was the result of inadequate education, not natural incapacity. Murray listed larger social costs of women's inferior training, but she conceived the problem figuratively as one of the household, and she dramatized it through a fictive chronology of a woman's life as a family member: a baby as bright as her brother, a sister less well educated, an unfulfilled and frustrated young woman, and a mortified wife. Poorly educated, the woman was unable to fulfill the highest callings of family membership.[14]

Those callings were not of a peculiarly female, or domestic, character. Murray made no mention of mothering and was openly contemptuous of the idea that women should be "wholly domesticated" or that the activities of "the needle and kitchen" were sufficient occupation. "Will it be urged that those [educational] acquirements would supercede our domestick duties," she wrote, "I answer that every requisite in female economy is easily attained; and, with truth I can add, that when once attained they require no further *mental attention.*" Instead, the essay evoked the family as a small civic society, a republican salon in miniature, whose excellence was burnished by the strengthened ability of each member to engage in informed discussion, reflection, and judgment. Nothing about women's equality in this republican society was inflected through motherhood.[15]

The household was a time-honored trope in New England, and Murray's conception of it as a civic location reflected well the world of postrevolutionary America, where paid and unpaid labor often occupied the same spaces and where households were often the locations of town meetings, political rallies, and prayer circles. The status of the household as a social and political institution had only been heightened by the revolutionary crisis. As Murray's own letters revealed, the war recognized no boundaries between private and public, domestic and civic life. Troops drilled menacingly in the streets of residential neighbors, sequestered houses, and sent Bostonians fleeing to the countryside with only the clothes on their backs. As Jan Lewis has observed, women's association with the household as "wives" did not necessarily disqualify them from political identities, since "the conjugal unit served as the ideal for political as well as familial relationships" in postrevolutionary American culture.[16]

Clearly, however, the 1779 essay did not refer to a generic revolutionary-era household. Her model was transparently the household of her own class experience. The women in the essay had access to fashionable dress, books, and telescopes, were above the "sewing of the seams of a garment," and enjoyed sufficient free time to engage in rational discussion and perhaps even literary production. Only from such a household, Murray implied, could spring the habits of mind necessary for personal and public cultivation.[17] Although her rendering of the households of leading families was surely romanticized, the choice was telling. Not only did it implicitly define and limit the universe of women who might be capable of "great activity of mind," but it also revealed Murray's own standpoint: she offered her criticisms of the education of women from within the community of public actors, as one who already enjoyed membership and argued for reform, not as an outsider.[18]

Murray may have been encouraged to speak out by the general mood of political experimentation in postrevolutionary America and by the persistence, as a part of that ferment, of aspects of the political practice that had supported elite women's power in the colonial era. First, to the extent that the franchise was the marker, the state was not clearly gendered. Although all but one of the original state constitutions failed to include women in the franchise, New Jersey's 1776 constitution was silent on the matter, allowing all adults possessing fifty pounds who had resided in the state for at least one year to claim the franchise.[19] Moreover, where free women lacked the franchise, they were not the only free adults barred. Virtually all of the state constitutions also excluded at least some free men. Rather than "gender," the single most consistent criterion for voting was economic rank (as attested to by property, either real estate or tax payment), which restricted suffrage in the original constitution of every state.

Equally important, as Gordon Wood has observed, the place of formal suffrage, understood either as the essential act of individual political agency or as the necessary vehicle for effective representation, was itself far from settled. Although the demand for actual representation that would eventually identify the right to vote "with the very essence of American democracy" was clearly present in the postrevolutionary era, at the founding many Americans believed that protecting discrete interests depended on suppressing their direct impact on policymaking. What was wanted from legislators was not the capacity to represent individual voters but rather the ability to discover the common interests of their constituents comprehended as a whole, a quality of stewardship women in prominent households had long been deemed capable of embodying.[20]

Their behavior indicates that many women from leading families asserted strong public, and even partisan, identities at the founding of the Republic. In the early 1790s elite women of various sympathies donned political badges, delivered political speeches to militias, offered political toasts in public settings, and, as Jan Lewis has suggested, made their presence felt as a critical public even when they remained silent. In these acts they were approximating in the new political regime the sorts of public performances long expected of them as members of prominent households. In her salutatory oration at the 1793 commencement of the Young Ladies' Academy of Philadelphia, Pricilla Mason reminded her listeners that the founding of the Republic offered an opportunity to reinvent government and society. She claimed for women the right to leadership positions in religion, at the bar, and in public office, going so far as to suggest that Congress create a separate all-female Senate "composed of women most noted for wisdom, learning and taste, delegated from every part of the

Union." In New Jersey, where propertied single females were (for the moment) securely enfranchised, the debate moved to the next level: whether women should be allowed to stand for office.[21] For these women the early years of the Republic were years of enormous potential in terms of women's relation to the state.

By the early 1790s, nevertheless, the fluidity of the postwar years was giving way to party formation, a process that served to organize the multiple differing views of public authority into two opposing discourses. In Philadelphia Jefferson and Hamilton were squaring off in Washington's cabinet, and Hamilton and Madison's differences in Congress spilled over into a venomous newspaper war. By 1792 two more or less distinct political philosophies began to dominate the American political life: the Federalists favored the leadership of the prosperous and educated, while the Republicans feared that the merchants and speculators were trying to steal their revolution. Throughout the states, the throes of early party formation resulted in a more contentious public. By 1793 political passions ran so high that, as one observer remarked, "Whenever two or three people are gather'd together it is expected there is a Quarrel and they crowd around, hence other squabbles arise." Increasingly, what they were squabbling about was the value of social hierarchy, the structure on which Murray rested her own public identity and her hopes for an orderly society. Especially in the cities, Republican societies announced their determination to remain vigilant against the designs of the wealthy and Republican newspaper editors condemned and ridiculed the pretensions of "the 'wellborn' among us." Common craftsmen processed through the city streets in pointed reminders that they did not intend to be led by their "betters."[22] The emerging public culture seemed increasingly unable to contain what Murray recognized as orderly dispassionate debate.

Murray's Gleaner essays (published between February 1792 and December 1794 in the *Massachusetts Magazine*) reflected these, to her, troubling developments in American public life and asserted an alternative vision of the public. To frame her views Murray drew on the English periodical essay, a genre defined less by its form than by its subject (the daily life of the new bourgeoisie) and by its didactic purpose: the discovery of a system of informed civic morality. Sometimes epistolary, the periodic essay drew upon a range of other literary forms—drama, poetry, biography, fiction, and dialogue—to evoke an imagined community where a rich cast of archetypal characters paraded their vanities and virtues before the gaze of a benevolent narrator. The narrator functioned as the all-knowing critical observer of this community and the embodiment of the virtues toward which it strove.

Murray made several revealing modifications to the genre. Generally the periodical essay focused on, and ultimately celebrated, urban life, its cosmopolitan characters, and institutions of the critical public presumed endemic to urban life, especially coffeehouses and newspapers. Murray shifted the focus of her essays away from the "metropolis" (Boston) to one of its nearby suburbs (her native town of Gloucester). More telling, as in her essay on the equality of the sexes, she located the model of social relations not in the coffeehouse but in the household and chose as her cast of characters not city sophisticates but a suburban family (Mr. Vigillius, his wife Mary, and their adopted daughter Margaretta). She used a doubled narrative voice: Mr. Vigillius served as the narrator within the action of the essays; Murray herself (signing as "Constantia") was the ultimate critical spectator.

From the very first essay forward, Murray made clear her contempt for the public culture of the city, which she viewed as impulse-driven and superficial. Newspaper essays were little more than vehicles of personal vanity, she suggested. Tongue in cheek, she avowed that even her own narrator was drawn to essay writing, and to the use of the *nom de plum* "The Gleaner," not by high principle or serious purpose but by an "inordinate ambition" and a passion for pseudonyms. The effect of such productions was not to create an educated and disciplined public but to stir up passions and encourage gossip: "Who is he? Where does he live? What is his *real name,* and occupation? And to the importance of these questions, considerations of real weight give place; as if the being able to ascertain a name was replete with information of the most salutary kind."[23]

In fact, Vigillius was not like other narrators in the genre. As Murray immediately made clear, whatever foibles of vanity led him to writing, he was distinctive for his very *lack* of cosmopolitan identity. "Neither in my person, or habilments," he confessed, was there "any distinguishing mark" to draw anyone's attention. Vigillius was one of "the strangers in the metropolis" and always eager to withdraw.[24] His qualities were unrepresented, perhaps unrepresentable, in *that* public.

Vigillius existed and was recognizable within his family, and it was that family that Murray held up as the ideal model of public life. In contrast to the vapid and irrational public of the city, the Vigillius household was characterized by a devotion to order and to the well-being of the whole. As early as the third essay, Vigillius offered an abstract rumination on the well-run household as the exemplum of the "well ordered community," unified in purpose and fully civic in its values. In subsequent essays Murray represented the virtues of the "well regulated family" as precisely those of the well-regulated state, arguing that in the "well regulated family" (unlike the political society she saw taking shape around her) "the domestic departments [are] filled in an allotted and regular manner" with "individuals . . . reciprocally assist[ing] one another." "In the varied and interesting offices of social life" household members "cheerfully engage . . . apprized of what their characters demand of them." Murray asserted as the fundamental and distinguishing quality of the well-regulated family not sentimental domesticity but "rational elevation"—the rational elevation necessary to preserve the republic from "destruction," "discord and malice."[25]

The history of the Vigillius family paralleled the trials of the Republic. Like the new nation, the Vigillius family was self-chosen "at the close of the late war," when husband and wife traveled to South Carolina to acquaint themselves with the state of affairs in a region where they were "entire strangers." There they met the child Margaretta, on the verge of being orphaned, and agreed to adopt her. Having thus eliminated any "natural" bonds of affection or interest, Murray was free to portray Margaretta's development from child to adult as an extended meditation on the challenges of nation building, where the historical bonds of peoplehood had been severed by revolution and had to be deliberately constructed. The values that informed Margaretta's education (reason and moderation) were the values Murray espoused for the new nation. The specific trials through which Margaretta was required to pass (for example, learning to behave rationally, to ward off self-interested impostors, and to conduct an economy successfully) were ordeals facing the Republic.[26]

Murray's optimism about the place of upper-rank women in the new public sphere persisted in the early Gleaner essays. The Vigillius household was strikingly ungendered. Although she represented Mary Vigillius and, later, Margaretta, as caring mothers and expert household managers, Murray did not assign to the female characters a special association with home, family, or parenting. Neither did Murray assign to the father a special association with a detached public sphere. Vigillius was a man happiest in his household, every bit as interested in and involved in the education of Margaretta as was his wife. The quality of that involvement was not discernibly different for father and mother. Both parents fretted. Both patiently modeled habits of reason and altruism, attributes that did not assume gendered forms.[27] Indeed, Murray chose a female, Margaretta, as the representative republican citizen. Although the essays clearly continued to make older arguments about the need to provide elite women with better education, the education of Margaretta was first and foremost a national narrative of the education of the American citizen.

Murray explicitly rejected patriarchal household structures. As in her 1769 letter to her uncle, in the Gleaner essays she identified the relationship of siblings as the ideal republican relationship, and the brother as the ideal male citizen. "Genuine and sincere," "disinterested," and "generous," the bond of brother and sister seemed to Murray to embody the highest aspirations of virtue.[28] The choice was no doubt a reflection of Murray's own particularly close attachment to her brother Winthrop Sargent, and it may have been a reaction against the patriarchalism that characterized wealthy families, including her own. But Murray's celebration of the sibling relationship also reflected the tendency of the revolutionary generation to conceive the act of revolution as an overthrowing of the father. Murray was suggesting that if this was the case, daughters (sisters) as well as sons (brothers) were included in the founding act of the Republic and that the social contract underpinning the Republic was not fraternal but among siblings.

If political authority was not distinguished by gender in the Gleaner essays, it *was* distributed by rank. The essays were a paean to the importance of social hierarchy in republican society—a point Murray made comically explicit in Essay 27. Emphasizing that "there is no calculating the disorders which may result from relaxing the series of subordination," the narrator offered the example of a meal prepared by assorted individuals without any abiding plan or oversight: "one bears a cup, another a saucer; a table is dragged from that apartment, and a tea-kettle from this." "Ignorant of each other's plans, and having no one to direct," he continued, "the process is impeded and confused" and the meal spoiled. "But if the theory of equality is not practicable in the contracted circle of domestic life," Murray concluded, "much less will that experiment succeed which would realize it, in regard to the heterogeneous collection of beings who constitute a nation." In such a case, she wrote, "anarchy reigneth supreme, and desolation administereth her commands."[29]

Although Murray opened the essays with an attack on party spirit, in its celebration of hierarchy and its endorsement of the stewardship of the leading classes, the Gleaner was transparently Federalist in philosophy. As early as the fourth essay of the series, Murray temporarily set aside her fictive persona to praise the new nation's "symmetry and its concomitant harmony" with "feder-alism . . . the talisman of their importance," and to defend fellow Massachusetts native John Adams against criticism. By the final essays of the original group, Murray's alarm over the growth of what she saw as a dangerous public culture assumed the form of a more overt oppositional stance. She closed the twenty-seventh essay with a discussion of parties that suggested that she had at least come to accept them as necessary evils—and perhaps even as necessary goods. "Parties, in a state of civil and political liberty, have been compared to the pas-sions of an individual," she wrote. "As the passions are said to be the elements of life, so the animated and resuscitating spirit of party is observed to be essen-tial to the existence of genuine freedom. Be it so; and may the public weal, the public tranquility, be, by every means, promoted."[30]

By that time Murray had grown more concerned about the growth of the Republican Party and what she viewed as its unruly impact on the civil and political life of the nation. In an essay written in April 1794 (but later inserted immediately before Vigillius's lecture on insubordination), she rose again to Adams's defense. This time, however, Murray anticipated the need to defend herself against criticism that she was "ambitious of forming an *aristocracy* in the midst of your brethren." By 21 July 1795 she would write to Mary Sargent Allen and Sarah Sargent Ellery that even the Fourth of July orations had become "tinctured with the acrimonious spirit of party" that evinced "antifederal sen-timents." Soon Republican objections to the Jay Treaty were depressing her. "If my letter assumes the melancholy complexion of the times, its hue will be sufficiently gloomy," she wrote in April 1796. "A portentous kind of despon-dency seems to pervade every description of people among us! . . . Peace, spreading her downy wings, appears on the eve of departing from our bor-ders. . . . We are threatened not only with the horrors of a foreign, but a civil war." Later that year, she returned to her defense of Adams, once again lament-ing the rise of private ambition and the loss of rectitude and propriety in the public arena. "It is true," she confessed, "I cannot regard a *pure unmixed de-mocracy* as that precise form of government, which is, in all its parts, the most friendly to the best interests of mankind."[31]

The democracy Murray feared and dreaded was the democracy embodied in the Republican Party, whose ascendancy had consequences for women like Murray beyond the general question of class leadership. Republicans sought to reform the public sphere by enlarging white male suffrage. This goal forced the issue of suffrage to the center of the political debate, identifying voting as the defining political act. Lori D. Ginzberg and others have noted the galvanizing effect of a similar set of circumstances fifty years later: it was, Ginzberg argues, when male reformers began to abandon moral suasion and take recourse to electoral strategies to achieve their ends that female reformers experienced their own deep political marginalization. As Zagarri and others have noted, that consequence was not accidental. The expansion of white male suffrage "rested on—in a sense depended on—the subordination of women, as well as blacks and Indians." Preserving an older belief that participation must be restricted on some grounds, Republicans sought to substitute categories of gender and race for earlier categories of economic and social rank.[32]

By the end of the 1790s the question of suffrage had become central to discussions of women's political status, a point made by Charles Brockden Brown in *Alcuin,* published in 1798, the same year in which Murray published her full Gleaner compendium. Brown wrote the book as a dialogue between a rather callow young man and an older woman (a property owner and a Federalist). In Part II, the female imagined herself watching as a succession of men were denied the right to vote, one because he was too young, one because he was too new to the state, one because he was not a taxpayer, and one because he was black. Being of age, a native to the state, a taxpayer, and a white person, she approached the poll confidently, only to be turned away because she was a woman. She dismissed utterly an argument that she might be indirectly represented by the men who admired her (a plea for "republican motherhood"). "I shall ever consider it as a gross abuse that we [women] are hindered from sharing with you in the power of chusing our rulers," she declared, "and of making those laws to which we equally with yourselves are subject."[33] In the world of *Alcuin,* the vote was the single instrumentality of citizenship.

In addition to watching as the growth of the Republican Party altered the landscape upon which the early Gleaner had been constructed, Murray weathered a number of personal difficulties in the mid-1790s. Between 1794 and 1798 she sustained assaults on virtually every aspect of the identity that girded her claims to public authority: her rank, her attempts to exercise of public influence, and the broad Federalist philosophy that integrated her views into the political discourse of the nation. Murray had experienced hard economic times before the 1790s. Her first husband, John Stevens, eventually went bankrupt as a result of the revolutionary-era disruptions to commerce, leaving Judith to meet her expenses by selling personal possessions and doing some needlework. By the mid-1790s her financial security was once again in doubt. Her second husband, John Murray, was a minister with low pay and no sense of money. Proud of her ancestry and position in the community, Judith may have been the guiding spirit behind the couple's decision to rent a "spacious, lofty, commodious, and elegant" house at Number 5 Franklin Place when John took a position at Boston's Universalist Church. Throughout the 1790s the Murrays felt the pinch of their personal finances. By 1795 Murray was writing not simply for pleasure but for "pecuniary reasons."[34]

Although the Gleaner essays were popular, by 1794 Murray's efforts to assert a public influence had become a source of frustration, even humiliation. First, in 1794, the Gleaner fell victim to sharp criticism, probably for expressing too fervently Murray's Universalist religious convictions. In March of the following year Murray's first play, *The Medium,* appeared at the Federal Street Theater. *The Medium* continued some of Murray's earlier themes, depicting the household as deeply immersed in the civic and political life of its world and representing the relation between husband and wife as one of rational equals. Not only was the production badly under-rehearsed but (perhaps more mortifying for the woman who proudly signed the piece "written by a citizen of the United States"), at least one critic denied it could have been the work of a woman alone and accused Murray's husband of being co-author. John Murray was forced to disavow the work, declaring in a published letter "that I never saw a single sentence, line, or even word of the comedy . . . until I saw it . . . presented to the public." The conflict took its toll on Judith Murray. Two days after John Murray's letter was published, Judith confided to a friend, "to confess a truth, I grow weary of the pen."[35]

But she did not stop writing. Later that year she completed a second play, *The Traveller Returned,* which bore some interesting resemblances to the story of Margaretta in the early Gleaner. It can be read as the tale of the education of a female character, set against the celebration of national independence. Yet *The Traveller Returned* was a confused text that lacked the authorial confidence of the early essays, reflected an uncertainty about the position of women in public, and ultimately located reason and judgment in men. Two of the three main female characters, Mrs. Montague and her daughter Harriot, were defined by their dangerous lack of self-discipline. It was Mrs. Montague's near "fatal indiscretion" with another man that drove away her husband, who took their son with him. Her daughter Harriot had grown into a good-hearted but dangerously undisciplined young woman, who risked her reputation by consenting to a secret rendezvous with her beau. The single rational female character, Emily

Lovegrove, was notable chiefly for the decorousness and discretion of her conduct. Together the three characters suggested not only a new preoccupation
with female respectability but also a new defensiveness on the subject. Various
scholars have noticed the growing sexualization of women at the end of the
eighteenth century and the increasing tendency to depict females in public
spaces—for example, on the streets unescorted—as morally suspect. Murray's
faltering construction of female characters may have been a response to this
growing association of women in public with sexual libertinism.[36]

The lack of confidence that characterized the play itself was also evident in
Murray's handling of the business end of the production. When Murray offered
The Traveller Returned to the Federal Theater, she was at great pains to suppress
her identity as author. Her letter to Charles Powell, manager of the theater,
seems worth quoting at length:

> Sir, . . . No person in existence, not even Mr M—— has ever had the smallest
> idea of my designing or writing this play—I have been willing to spare Mr M——
> that anxiety which he experienced relative to the Medium—If the Traveller re-
> turned meets with your approbation, I make the following proposals relative
> thereto. The piece shall be taken to Newport, and some person employed to copy
> it, who never heard of me—the several parts for each Player, shall be transcribed
> from that copy, while the original shall be laid by again to be placed in my hands,
> on your return to Boston. . . . It shall be the first play presented on opening the
> Boston Theater the third season . . . [because] the immediate advertisement of the
> piece, will be most likely to preclude every idea of its being mine. . . . I think every
> suspicion of its being mine will be thus prevented . . . not even hinting at it being
> an American production.

The depth of Murray's caution may be measured from her closing remarks. "I
request," she wrote, "that your rejection, or approbation, may be signified to me
in a way which will not excite the suspicion either of Mr Murray or any other
individual of my family." She arranged to receive news of Powell's decision from
his wife "in a private apartment." *The Traveller Returned* was produced twelve
months later (in March 1796) to insipid praise that turned to hostile criticism
when Murray protested privately.[37]

These experiences appear to have registered in Murray's 1798 *Gleaner* compendium, in which the author began to step back from her earlier insistence
that women could participate in the Republic as nongendered citizens. Much of
the 1798 publication was not devoted to new essays, strictly speaking, but to

Murray's two ill-fated dramas, *The Medium* (now renamed *Virtue Triumphant*) and *The Traveller Returned,* broken into essay-length segments. Among the new essays, however, was a quartet of pieces in which Murray returned to the theme of women's education, or "female capability," long central to her vision of the ideal republican society. Murray explicitly requested the reader "to consider the four succeeding numbers as supplementary" to the essay "On the Equality of the Sexes."[38]

Although the four new essays continued the argument for women's education and were often triumphal in tone, they were not simple supplements to the earlier piece.[39] In important ways they revised it, shifting the ground upon which Murray both argued for and celebrated the progress of women in the new Republic. Betraying some of the confusion of position evident in *The Traveller Returned,* the essays revealed Murray's ongoing retreat from her earlier vision of the ungendered republic and her growing willingness to entertain a theory of female authority based on women's special attributes and social position as mothers. The almost glib dismissal of the relevance of women's domestic responsibilities to their civic identities in the 1779 essay was gone, replaced by an elaborate assurance that although "it is true, that every faculty of their minds will be occasionally engrossed by the momentous concerns," nevertheless "as often as *necessity* or *propriety* shall render it incumbent upon them, [women] will *cheerfully* accommodate themselves to the more *humble duties* which their situation imposes."[40]

The first three of the four new essays were catalogues of the qualities of female intellect that proved women the equals of men, and of women who illustrated those qualities (selected from Roman and modern European history). Murray's choice of exemplars again suggested a certain defensive attentiveness to the salience of women's household identities. Her models of female capability now fell into two quite polarized categories: women of intelligence, talent, or heroism whose accomplishments were achieved entirely outside their household relations (for example, Issotta Nogarolla, Modesto Pozzo, and Anna Maria Schurman, all of whom Murray cited for their distinction as scholars), and women of patriotism and fortitude, whose public identities were manifested indirectly in self-sacrificial motherhood. Prominent in the latter group were the women of Sparta. Although Murray emphasized that "the name of Citizen possessed, for them, greater charms than that of Mother," she was clear that the fullest expression of that citizenship resided in the perfection of their sons' republican virtues: "so highly did they prize the warrior's meed, that they are said to have shed tears of joy over the bleeding bodies of their wounded sons!" Apparently no longer confident that women could enter the republic purely on the terms of their class membership and rational abilities, in these three essays Murray began to develop a second line of argument, in which women's domestic identities justified but also delimited their claims to public authority. Indeed, the essays hinted at a particular, essentializing association of women with sentiment. In Essay 90, Murray praised Venturia and Volumnia, "the wife and mother of Coriolanus," as exemplars of patriotism. In both cases, their patriotic influence was effectuated not through rational argument but through their special capacities of emotion: the "mother's tenderness," the women's "torrents of tears," through which "the hero is disarmed—his heart melted . . . and Rome is saved."[41]

In many respects, the fourth essay in the series, in which Murray attempted to situate her argument for female intellectual equality in her own times, approached most closely the character and tenor of her earlier argument for a "civic household." Most of the essay was devoted to a description of a single woman who ran her own farm, although Murray also included a second brief vignette of a widow, Mrs. Birmingham, who raised her daughters to be successful independent merchants. The values of both stories were the abiding values of Federalism: industry, order, and judgment. The essential argument of the essay, that women should be brought up to be independent, was one that Murray had been making at least as long as she had been writing.[42]

Yet this essay was different from its early 1790s variants in a number of ways. Perhaps most noticeably, unlike Mary or Margaretta Vigillius, and in spite of Murray's emphasis on the importance of the "united efforts of male and female" in supporting a family, the autonomous women so fully realized in Essay 90 lived in households without men. Although Mrs. Birmingham was a mother and had been a wife, her husband was dead and her sons were eliminated from the story by her decision to place them in the military. The main character of the essay (an unnamed resident of Massachusetts) was not married and evidently had no living parents or siblings. "Although far advanced in years," Murray observed, "without a matrimonial connexion . . . she realizes all that independence which is proper to humanity; and she knows how to set a just value on the blessings of humanity."[43] Paralleling their seclusion from men, these women seemed remote from civic life, watching over their gardens and their countinghouse, undoubtedly embodying republican virtue yet doing so indirectly and in some sense unmindfully. Unlike females in Murray's earlier essays, they did not actively contemplate or comment on the character of the civic fabric, and their interaction with their communities was largely as passive examples of virtue rather than as energetic advocates. In the world of turn-of-the-century America, the essay seemed to suggest, female autonomy had become circumscribed to the question of economic independence, was difficult to conceive within the marital relation, and required a withdrawal from the state.

The final paragraphs of the essay underscored the ways in which Murray was now at war with herself and with her earlier certainty about women's place in the Republic. From the beginning Murray had published the Gleaner essays under a pseudonym, "Constantia," and had moved back and forth between the voice of Vigillius and the voice of Constantia. Although the two voices were distinct (Constantia spoke as a serious intellectual, Vigillius as a good and caring clown), their values were identical. Essays 88, 89, and 90 were written entirely in the voice of Constantia. Only at the end of Essay 91 did Murray return to the conceit of Vigillius. But this was a vastly altered male narrative voice and one from which Murray as "Constantia" seemed jarringly alienated. Asked by a female reader whether he meant to suggest that all women should be consigned to the countinghouse, Vigillius demured, and then took quick and defensive refuge in essentialism. Assuring the reader that he intended only to defend "the *capability* of your Sex," he denied any "wish to *unsex* you." There followed a catalogue of "those amiable traits that are considered as characteristic" of females: modesty, gentleness, faithfulness, affection, and most especially "superiority in the feelings of the heart." Vigillius concluded the essay by approvingly quoting a passage which fully identified women with *motherhood* rather than directly with citizenship or stewardship (or, indeed, even with the family generally):

> What are the powerful emotions of nature? Where is that sentiment, at once sublime and pathetic, that carries every feeling to excess? Is it to be found in the frosty indifference, and the sour severity of some fathers? No—but in the warm and affectionate bosom of a *mother*. It is she who, by an impulse as quick as involuntary, rushes into the flood to preserve a boy, whose imprudence had betrayed him into the waves—It is she who, in the midst of a conflagration, throws herself across the flames to save a sleeping infant.

"These great expressions of nature—these heart-rending emotions, which fill us at once with wonder, compassion and terror," Vigillius quoted, "have always belonged, and always will belong, only to Women."[44] The passage constituted a sharp retreat from Murray's earlier portrayal of Vigillius, the household, and ultimately the Republic as nongendered. This Vigillius headed a household to which Constantia, the female who claimed her citizenship through her powers of reason and her membership in a class rather than through her gender, was an outsider.

Her correspondence indicates that in the years after the publication of the three-volume *Gleaner,* Murray became ever more defensive of women's public and political authority. In a letter written in November 1800, as the nation voted for its first Republican president, Murray upbraided a friend for writing "that you have *ever* hated female politicians!" "Surely you will, upon reflection, confess that you have expressed yourself rather too strongly," she urged. "May not a female be so circumstanced, as to render a correct, and even profound knowledge of politicks, the pride and glory of her character? How egregiously deficient would that woman appear, who, succeeding, by the constituted authority of her country, to sovereign power, should be unable to investigate, to direct, and to balance the various views, and interests of her subjects." She closed grimly, "Yes indeed, all the relative duties, every philanthropic, every patriotic virtue, are proper to women—if we concede one point, we throw down the barriers, and it will not be easy to determine where they may again be erected."[45]

Yet in her own world the barriers protecting women's claims to full citizenship seemed to be collapsing. The social and political conditions that supported Murray's early arguments had been gradually disappearing, replaced by a political system that equated political agency with the franchise and by a society that distinguished the household from the community and a feminine private morality from a masculine civic virtue. The 1807 disfranchisement of propertied New Jersey women officially rendered the "female politician" a national oxymoron. By that time the arguments of Murray's early essays may have seemed impossibly far-fetched to many Americans—as, indeed, they have to many historians since.

When she was not blaming the Republicans for her declining popularity, Judith Sargent Murray blamed a fickle public taste. In 1808 she declared that she would never again "venture upon so fluctuating an ocean as public opinion, except my invitation to embark should be both public and unequivocal."[46] It is hard to imagine that the young Judith Sargent, who in 1769 confidently instructed her uncle on the terms of their relationship, would have required an invitation to speak in a public voice, or that she would have conceived the "public" as an arena separate from "private" life. But forty years had passed. Not only had Murray been buffeted by the experiences of adulthood, but the larger social and cultural context within which her experiences occurred, and from which they derived meaning, had also changed.

The decline of Murray's reputation as an author paralleled and reflected shifts in the broad political culture of the new nation. Not only had Americans begun to repudiate the Federalist principles that helped give Murray's early views plausibility and resonance in the postrevolutionary world, but Federalism as a civil and social discourse was being supplanted by an alternate discourse of authority, present but not fully realized during the revolutionary struggle. Among the most apparent and substantive elements of the new discourse were a distrust of established and inherited hierarchies, a growing conviction that the energies of common Americans could ensure social stability, and a predisposition to locate republican virtue in the community of white males. These were the principles of American "democracy." Over the 1780s and 1790s these principles gained more currency in the cultural and social practices of the new nation. As they did, they not only laid the foundation for the electoral revolution of 1800 but also subtly altered the grounds upon which various Americans could make claims to political authority and public influence. For many Americans, particularly for free white men, the union of political thought and cultural practice signified in the revolution of 1800 promised greater liberty of action and expression. For other Americans, the gathering force of these ideas as social prohibition had very different meanings.

Within its more democratic rhetoric, Republicanism (in its party manifestation) shared with Federalism an anxiety about social dissolution, an anxiety that intensified over the decade of the 1790s, as the French Revolution disintegrated into the Terror. Also like Federalism, Republicanism imagined a hierarchical social order in which groups better fitted to public engagement would moderate the excesses of those less well fitted. Unlike Federalist discourse, which represented unequal access to the public sphere in external terms of property ownership, Republicanism located the source of inequality in a Romantic concept of nature. It was, Republicans divined, the nature of white manhood to combine the liberty and restraint necessary to achieve and maintain political freedom; it was the nature of women, African Americans, and Native Americans *not* to be capable of achieving and maintaining that combination. As the community of free white males came increasingly to constitute the legitimate public, female voices like Murray's seemed out of place, unrecogniz-able, and, as the 1806 reviewer put it, "incorrect."

Murray's later essays suggest an attempt, confused and incomplete, to come to terms with this new discourse by discovering ways to assert her claims to public authority within it, a strategy that required compromise. Most striking, the essays accepted (at least in a troubled way) the explicit Republican deploy-ment of gender as a system of markers delineating the contours of the public sphere. Conceding that females as a category had claims to political identity only indirectly, in her later essays Murray represented women as either deriving public identities from their relation to men as mothers or wives or retreating from the public sphere altogether. Indeed, it was this long negotiation with Re-publicanism that produced the discourse of "republican motherhood" in Mur-ray's work.

But the new woman Murray offered as a concession was not altogether a capitulation. The public mother of her later essays did preserve certain aspects of her earlier argument for social authority, most notably the explicit impor-tance of class (and the implicit salience of race). Whether Roman or American, whether self-sacrificing mothers or isolated *femmes sole* traders, the model fe-males of Murray's later writings remained women of class privilege patterned after the white women among whom Murray had grown up. They were wives and daughters and sisters of noble and aristocratic men. For Murray, "female" thus denoted an identity that existed and was recognizable only in combination with the social symbols of elite rank. In the idiom of the later essays, those sym-bols—leisure and refinement, for example—became not the prerogative of class but the expression of female nature itself. By implication, women not as-sociated with prosperous families, women unable to avail themselves of the privilege or reputation of rank (understood also as race), women who labored visibly or were uneducated were only marginally recognizable as women at all. In the context of the religious revivals of the early nineteenth century, this de-pendency of womanhood on class markers was increasingly represented in terms of private morality, a phenomenon noted by many women's historians.[47]

The discursive privileging of elite women was not new, of course, and it was not unique to Murray. What may be most notable about it in terms of the his-tory of gender is that it does not appear to have accompanied a parallel process for men. That is, for men the old language of rank was not so determinatively inflected into the new discourse of democracy. Men constituted a collectivity based first and foremost on their gender (and almost always their race). Few

Americans attached a class (or religious) marker to manliness analogous to the one associated with womanhood, leaving women who aspired to public identity as both the discursive symbols and the daily sentinels of class (and race) boundaries.

It is harder to detect the specific ways in which Murray embraced a distinctively Republican emphasis on "race" as a qualifier for public recognizability, in part because she had always assumed a hierarchy of race. She carried that assumption silently into her reconfigurations of womanhood—silently, at least, until the sixty-fifth essay of the 1798 *Gleaner* compendium, where she introduced a character she called Plato. Described as "a black man, born in Africa," Plato was the only character in all of Murray's essays explicitly named as black.[48]

The essay in which Plato appeared described the narrator's journey into the Massachusetts countryside in celebration of American progress. Apparently unrelated to this theme is the the narrator's encounter with Plato, who was making his way south to avoid the harsh northern winter. The narrator hailed Plato as a friend and identified him as a former slave, now free and living with his wife in Massachusetts, and passed on.

Yet anxiety permeated the telling of this simple episode. At the moment of Plato's appearance, the narrative voice of the essay abruptly and confusingly shifted from the first to the third person. Although the narrator described Plato as an independent farmer, his character was vouchsafed through reference to his former master, "who evinced his high sense of the merit of Plato, by bestowing on him his liberty." Plato's speech was rendered exotic by a heavy artificial dialect, and the suitability of his presence in the North was destabilized by his hatred of the northern climate. Indeed, he was so chilled by "*e cold weder* and *e torms* [that] come one after *anoder*" that every spring he journeyed back to his former master's residence. Perhaps most tellingly, although he was married Plato was utterly isolated socially: not only had he never made friends as a free man but even when he went south it was not to see his relatives or friends but to "see maser's friends." Murray seemed unable to conceive familial and community bonds among African Americans (beyond simple marriage).

The ultimate effect of Plato's appearance in this essay, then, was not to dissolve the racial collectivity of New England but to state and reinforce it—as white. Plato lived in the North, but the winds and landscape of Massachusetts were alien to him, or he to them. Much less was he a part of the collective public sphere of Massachusetts's free society. Indeed, Murray seemed unable to identify African Americans apart from the physical and political landscape of

slavery and unable to conceive familial and community bonds among them beyond simple marriage. Although the narrator of the essay greeted Plato as a
friend, he seemed to value the black man's presence primarily as a sign of spring.

In 1804 Murray wrote a third play, which she entitled *The African*. Given her
prior obliviousness to the presence of African Americans in the Republic, the
title itself would seem to reveal a newly explicit racial consciousness. Unfortunately no copy of the play has survived, and Murray's correspondence on the
matter discloses nothing about its content. We are left to speculate on the extent to which these references expressed a new willingness to *specify* Africans as
a distinct "other" in Murray's efforts to reconstruct and identify her own position as a female in the new public culture.[49]

Over time women like Murray would help to embed these idioms as the
conventions of Victorian female domesticity, a discourse of class and of race
that relied on a naturalized concept of womanhood as its key marker. Nothing
in the discourse of Republicanism rendered such a representation implausible.
Indeed, much in Republican discourse invited this strategy of reconstituting
elite white women's claims to public authority through a domestic discourse. In
this sense the term "republican motherhood" is perhaps mostly appropriately
capitalized, as "Republican motherhood," to locate it both chronologically in
the late 1790s (rather than in the postrevolutionary years) and discursively
within the rhetoric of Jefferson's particular brand of republican thought.

Educated white women from prosperous families were not the only casualties in the rise of Jeffersonian Republicanism, and they were not the only Americans to seize on the hidden hierarchies of the Republican Party as a means of
preserving former privileges and constituting new ones. In its long career,
American republicanism, in some senses certified as the national idiom in the
revolution of 1800, would demonstrate again and again its paradoxical capacity
to absorb old hierarchies and construct new ones within a radical language of
"democracy."

NOTES

I would like to thank the editors of this volume, fellow participants in the International Center for Jefferson Studies Conference on "Thomas Jefferson and the Revolution of 1800," and Joy P.
Newmann, Susan Zaeske, Nan Enstad, and Suzanne Desan for their comments on earlier drafts of
this essay.

1. "American Literature Reviewed," *The Monthly Register, Magazine and Review of the United
States* (Dec. 1806): 27.

2. Judith Sargent Murray to Colonel H——— 8 June 1798, Letterbook 10, Correspondence of Judith Sargent Murray, Mississippi Archives, Jackson, Miss. (Unless otherwise noted, all subsequent quotations from Murray's correspondence are from this collection.) Judith Sargent Murray to Sir [Mr. Carpenter] 4 Oct. 1806, Letterbook 14.

3. See, for example, Judith Sargent Murray to Epes Sargent, 6 Nov. 1797, Letterbook 10:173.

4. TJ to Spenser Roane, 6 Sept. 1819, Ford, 10:140.

5. I am indebted to the considerable recent literature on the formation of "publics" and on the many, often accidental ways in which individuals use their discursive environments to recognize, articulate, and enter collective identities that interact with institutions of the state. The relevant literature is now too voluminous to cite in full. Especially important in my thinking are Jürgen Habermas, *The Structural Transformation of the Public Sphere,* trans. T. Burger and F. Lawrence (Cambridge, Mass., 1989); Michel de Certeau, *The Practices of Everyday Life,* trans. Steven F. Rendell (Berkeley, Calif., 1984); Nancy Fraser, "Rethinking the Public Sphere: A Contribution to the Critique of Actually Existing Democracy" in *Habermas and the Public Sphere,* ed. Craig Calhoun (Cambridge, Mass., 1992); and Nan Enstad, "Fashioning Political Identities: Cultural Studies and the Historical Construction of Political Subjects," *American Quarterly* 50 (1998): 745–82. I use the concept of recognizability in the sense in which Judith Butler used that of "acknowledgment": "The domains of political and linguistic 'representation' set out in advance the criterion by which subjects themselves are formed, with the result that representation is extended only to what can be acknowledged as a subject" (Judith Butler, *Gender Trouble: Feminism and the Subversion of Identity* [New York, 1990], 1).

6. I am indebted to Susan Zaeske for this observation.

7. Linda K. Kerber, "'I Have Don . . . much to Carrey on the Warr': Women and the Shaping of Republican Ideology after the American Revolution," in *Women and Politics in the Age of the Democratic Revolution,* ed. Harriet B. Applewhite and Darline G. Levy (Ann Arbor, 1993), 228. Kerber first used the term "republican motherhood" in "The Republican Mother: Women and the Enlightenment—An American Perspective," *American Quarterly* 28/2 (Summer, 1976): 187–205, and developed it in her study of women in the American Revolution, *Women of the Republic: Intellect and Ideology in Revolutionary America* (New York, 1980), 269–88. Although she did not use the term "republican womanhood," Mary Beth Norton came to a similar argument at virtually the same moment. As Norton put it, the American Revolution produced no "androgynous" theory of political authority in which women and men might be identically comprehended. If women were to claim a public role, according to Norton, it would have to be "complementary, not identical" to men's and based in women's "domestic responsibilities." See Mary Beth Norton, *Liberty's Daughters: The Revolutionary Experience of American Women: 1750–1800* (Boston, 1980), 297. On Murray as the chief spokesperson for "republican motherhood," see Kerber, *Women of the Republic,* 204, 229, and Nina Baym's introduction to Judith Sargent Murray, *The Gleaner* (Schenectady, N.Y., 1992), 14. See also Nina Baym, *American Women Writers and the Work of History: 1790–1860* (New Brunswick, N.J., 1995), 36; and Rosemarie Zagarri, *A Woman's Dilemma: Mercy Otis Warren and the American Revolution* (Wheeling, Ill., 1995), 71. Historians of women in the nineteenth-century United States take this gendered state as a given. See, for example, Christine Stansell, *City of Women: Sex and Class in New York: 1789–1860* (New York, 1986), 20; and Mary P. Ryan, "Gender and Public Access: Women's Politics in Nineteenth-Century America" in Calhoun, *Habermas and the Public Sphere,* 259–88.

8. See Sheila L. Skemp, *Judith Sargent Murray: A Brief Biography with Documents* (Boston, 1998), 9.

9. Skemp, *Murray,* 53.

10. Judith's mother is described in the diary of Susan Lear, quoted in Vena Bernadette Field, *Constantia: A Study of the Life and Works of Judith Sargent Murray: 1751–1820* (Orono, Maine, 1931),

13; Judith Sargent Murray, "To a Widowed and Unfortunate Uncle," Gloucester, Oct. 1769, Letterbook 1.

11. Cynthia A. Kierner, *Beyond the Household: Women's Place in the Early South: 1700–1835* (Ithaca, N.Y., 1998), 1–2; Sarah Fatherly, "Gentlewomen and Learned Ladies: Gender and the Creation of an Urban Elite in Colonial Philadelphia" (Ph.D. diss., University of Wisconsin, 2000), esp. chap. 5. See also David S. Shields, *Civil Tongues and Polite Letters in British America* (Chapel Hill, N.C., 1997). Some historians interpret the presence of women as spectators to political rituals as evidence of their marginalization. See, for example, Simon P. Newman, *Parades and the Politics of the Streets: Festive Culture in the Early American Republic* (Philadelphia, 1997), 19. As the title of Addison and Steele's *Spectator Papers* reminds us, however, the position of "spectator" was, in many respects, the characterizing and constituting position of the seventeenth- and eighteenth-century critical public.

12. Norton, *Liberty's Daughters*, 167. Other examples are drawn from Zagarri, *A Woman's Dilemma*, 43–44. On women signing the Solemn League and Covenant, see 85. On Warren's poem on the Boston Tea Party, see 88. Judith Sargent Murray, "To my Aunt C. S.," Boston, 10 April 1778, Letterbook 1.

13. Judith Sargent Murray to Mr. Murray Gloucester, 31 Aug. 1778, Letterbook 1; Judith Sargent Murray "To my brother," Gloucester, 25 Feb. 1778, Letterbook 1. For examples of Murray's avid interest in wartime politics, see her running correspondence with her future husband, John Murray. Judith Sargent Murray to Mr. Murray, 3 April 1778, 11 Aug. 1778, and 31 Aug. 1778. See also Murray Winthrop Sargent, Gloucester, 15 May 1789, Letterbook 1 (the letter is probably misdated and should be 1781). This reading of Murray is supported by a growing literature that argues implicitly that women's exclusion from the Republic may not have been so absolute immediately after the Revolution as we have previously assumed. See, for example, Jan Lewis, "The Republican Wife: Virtue and Seduction in the Early Republic," *WMQ* 3d ser., 44 (1987): 689–712; Judith Apter Klinghoffer and Lois Elkis, "'The Petticoat Electors': Women's Suffrage in New Jersey, 1776–1807," *JER* 12 (1992): 159–93; Jan Lewis, "'Of Every Age Sex & Condition': The Representation of Women in the Constitution" *JER* 15 (1995): 359–87; Rosemarie Zagarri, "The Rights of Man and Woman," *WMQ* 3d ser., 55 (1998): 203–30; Rosemarie Zagarri, "Gender in the First American Party System" in *Federalists Reconsidered*, ed. Doron Ben-Atar and Barbara B. Oberg (Charlottesville, Va., 1998), 118–34; and Linda K. Kerber, "The Paradox of Women's Citizenship in the Early Republic: The Case of Martin vs. Massachusetts: 1805" in *Toward an Intellectual History of Women: Essays by Linda K. Kerber* (Chapel Hill, N.C., 1997), 261–302, esp. 282–88 (orig. pub. *The American Historical Review* 97/2 [April 1992]: 349–78).

14. Although the essay was written in 1779, it was not published until 1790. Judith Sargent Murray, "On the Equality of the Sexes," *Massachusetts Magazine*, March 1790: 132–35, and April 1790, 223–26. I am quoting from the reprinted version; see Murray, "On the Equality of the Sexes" in Skemp, *Murray*, 178.

15. Murray, "On the Equality of the Sexes," in Skemp, *Murray*, 177–79.

16. See, for example, Judith Sargent Murray, "To My Father and Mother," Boston, 15 Aug. 1769, Letterbook 1. See also Kerber, *Women of the Republic*, esp. 35–67; Norton, *Liberty's Daughters*, esp. 155–228; and Lewis, "The Republican Wife," 690.

17. Murray, "On the Equality of the Sexes" in Skemp, *Murray*, 179. It was an assumption shared by other women of her class, even women like Mercy Otis Warren, whose specific political party views were quite different from Murray's. Perhaps it was in this spirit that Abigail put her famous request to John to "remember the ladies," asking less about the fortunes of females as a group than about the future of "ladies" of the first rank. See Zagarri, *A Woman's Dilemma*, 100–103, and L. H. Butterfield, ed., *The Book of Abigail and John: Selected Letters of the Adams Family, 1762–1784* (Cambridge, Mass., 1975), 121–23.

18. Much of the recent literature on the public sphere examines ways in which individuals not included in the Habermasian "bourgeois public sphere" form alternate "counterpublics" to command interactions with the dominant discourse of legitimacy. My interest here is in the process by which a collective identity that is initially recognizable in the dominant discourse becomes unrecognizable, and in the ways in which at least one woman, Murray, responded to that shift. For an excellent overview of recent work on "counterpublics," see Robert Asen and Daniel C. Brouwer, "Introduction: Reconfigurations of the Public Sphere" in *Counterpublics and the State,* ed. Robert Asen and Daniel C. Brouwer (Albany, N.Y., 2001), 1–32.

19. On women's suffrage in New Jersey's 1776 constitution, see Klinghoffer and Elkis, "'The Petticoat Electors,'" 159–93.

20. For a discussion of theories of representation in the postrevolutionary era, see Gordon S. Wood, *The Creation of the American Republic, 1776–1787* (New York, 1969), 162–96.

21. Lewis, "'Of Every Age Sex & Condition,'" 371. See also "The Salutatory Oration, Delivered by Miss Mason" in *The Rise and Progress of the Young-Ladies' Academy of Philadelphia: Containing an Account of a Number of Public Examinations and Commencements; The Charter and Bye-laws; Likewise, a Number of Orations Delivered by the Young Ladies, and Several by the Trustees of Said Institution* (Philadelphia, 1794), 990–95; Klinghoffer and Elkis, "'The Petticoat Electors,'" 173.

22. On the newspaper war see Stanley Elkins and Eric McKitrick, *The Age of Federalism: The Early American Republic, 1788–1800* (New York, 1993), 282–93. The comment on public fighting is from Alexander Anderson, "Diarium," 1793–1795, as quoted in Paul A. Gilje, *The Road to Mobocracy: Popular Disorder in New York City: 1763–1834* (Chapel Hill, N.C., 1987), 102. The newspaper quotation is from the *Boston Gazette and the Voluntary Journal,* as quoted in James Roger Sharp, *American Politics in the Early Republic: The New Nation in Crisis* (New Haven, Conn., 1993), 73.

23. Murray, *The Gleaner* 12:105.

24. Ibid., 1:15–18; 12:105; 23:178.

25. Ibid., 19:154; 3:27; 19:154, 26:207.

26. For the history of the making of the Vigillius family, see ibid., essay 2. The themes of reason and moderation run throughout the essays. Here see 7:63–4.

27. Ibid., 1:15.

28. Ibid., 30:248. On the fraternal contract, see Carole Pateman, *The Disorder of Women* (Stanford, Calif., 1989), esp. chap. 2, "The Fraternal Social Contract," 33–57. Pateman argues that the fraternal paradigm necessarily excluded women. Murray's emphasis on the sibling (rather than fraternal) character of the relation suggests that the exclusion of women was not so conceptually fixed as Pateman concludes. The distinction is particularly interesting in light of Joseph Ellis's recent work on the importance of the fraternal bond among members of the founding generation. See Ellis, *Founding Brothers: The Revolutionary Generation* (New York, 2000).

29. Murray, *The Gleaner* 27:216–17, 218.

30. Ibid., 4:35–6; 27:222.

31. Ibid., 26:211. It is interesting here that Murray did not yet anticipate criticism based on her gender. See also Judith Sargent Murray to the Two Girls Mary Sargent Allen and Sarah Sargent Ellery, Boston, 21 July 1795, Letterbook 9; Judith Sargent Murray to [?], Boston, 23 April 1796, Letterbook 9; Murray, *The Gleaner* 87:695.

32. Lori D. Ginzberg, *Women and the Work of Benevolence: Morality, Class, and Politics in the Nineteenth-Century United States* (New Haven, Conn., 1990); Zagarri, "Gender and the First Party System," 119.

33. Charles Brockden Brown, *Alcuin: A Dialogue* (New York, 1970), 31–33, 37.

34. Skemp, *Murray,* 44–51. John Stevens died in the West Indies on 8 March 1787. On the Franklin Place house, see Skemp, *Murray,* 52–53. Judith Sargent Murray to Miss [Mary] A—— Boston, 26 April 1795, Letterbook 8.

35. See Field, *Constantia*, 32; *Federal Orrery*, 5 March 1795, as quoted in Field, *Constantia*, 34; Judith Sargent Murray to Miss Saltonstall, Boston, 7 March 1795. For a brief discussion of Murray's career as a playwright, see Skemp, *Murray*, 102–3.

36. See, for example, Ruth H. Bloch, "The Gendered Meanings of Virtue in Revolutionary America," *Signs* 13 (1987): 37–59; Christine Heyrman, *Southern Cross: The Beginnings of the Bible Belt* (New York, 1997); Jeanne Boydston, "The Woman Who Wasn't There" in *The Wages of Independence: Capitalism in the Early American Republic*, ed. Paul Gilje (Madison, Wis., 1997).

37. Judith Sargent Murray to Mr. Powell, Manager of the Boston Theater, Boston, 16 May 1795, Letterbook 8. On the response to the play, see Field, *Constantia*, 38–39.

38. Murray, *The Gleaner* 89:702.

39. For example, Murray exulted that "in this younger world, 'the Rights of Women' begin to be understood" and even predicted "a new era in female history." Ibid., 703.

40. Ibid., 704.

41. Ibid., 706, 90:717–18.

42. It is interesting to note, however, that Essay 91 was virtually the only essay in the entire Gleaner series that described an economically autonomous female with any degree of plausibility. Most of Murray's homilies on female economic independence were actually celebrations of orderliness in the running of a prosperous household in which the mistress apparently did not herself perform the labor. The woman described in Essay 91 was, once again, from a privileged background, having inherited a farm. As in other essays, one suspects the presence of unseen workers just offstage. But Murray did note that her character learned how to farm, making herself into "a complete *husbandwoman*." Ibid., 91:729.

43. Ibid., 728–30.

44. Ibid., 731. Italics in the original.

45. Judith Sargent Murray to Mrs. K—— 25 Nov. 1800, Letterbook 11.

46. Judith Sargent Murray to [?], 6 Oct. 1808, Letterbook 15.

47. The scholarship here is far too voluminous to cite in full. The classic work is Bloch, "The Gendered Meanings of Virtue."

48. Murray's 1796 drama *The Traveller Returned* included a character, Obadiah, who may have been conceived as African or African American. Murray wrote Obadiah's lines in a heavy, artificial dialect identical to the dialect she created for the later "Plato." I am indebted to Lisa Kelber for observing the close resemblance of the two dialects based on the version of the play included in the 1798 collection. See *The Gleaner* 80–84:637–82.

49. Ibid., 65:513. For discussions of race in the early-nineteenth-century United States, see Dana D. Nelson, *National Manhood: Capitalist Citizenship and the Imagined Fraternity of White Men* (Durham, N.C., 1998), esp. chaps. 1 and 2, and Margaret M. R. Kellow, "The Divided Mind of Antislavery Feminism: Lydia Maria Child and the Construction of African American Womanhood," in *Discovering the Women in Slavery: Emancipating Perspectives on the American Past*, ed. in Patricia Morton (Athens, Ga., 1996), 107–26.

CHAPTER 11

Spinning Wheel Revolution

Gregory Evans Dowd

Thomas Jefferson saw sexual tyranny in America: men, "natural aristocrats of the most brutal sort," lording it over degraded women, exercising "unnatural prerogatives, not natural rights." This "barbarous perversion of the natural destination of the two sexes," he meant to set aright with a peaceful revolution. And he was not alone. Federalist Benjamin Hawkins, a former North Carolinian senator, hoped that women in parts of what are now Georgia and Alabama would "break the chains which degrade them." When these two southern slaveholders advocated a federally sponsored gender revolution, they thought not of their fellow citizens, nor certainly of their slaves, but of their neighboring Indian nations. The revolution they intended was part of a larger civilizing plan.[1]

In his first address to Congress, Jefferson praised Federalist efforts to introduce agriculture and the "household arts" to Indians; later that month he recommended to the legislators a report by Hawkins, whom George Washington had appointed to serve as chief Indian agent for the South and who had begun to advocate the liberation of Indian women. Nowhere, however, did Jefferson advocate that the Indians follow the white example in adopting African American slavery, though slavery had been embraced by a narrow elite of leading Indians.[2] So what was the relationship of Jefferson's Indian policy to that of his Federalist predecessors? And what was the relationship between slavery and gender, as his administration determined to foment a revolution for Indian women in the Indian southeast?

Southeastern Native Americans had little reason to notice the "revolution of 1800." The Federalist-appointed Indian agents in the southeast, including most prominently Hawkins, kept their jobs. The Republican administration embraced and "re-animated" the policy of "civilization" that had been drawn by Federalist Henry Knox, implemented by George Washington, and continued half-heartedly by John Adams. Though Jefferson had once opposed the centralizing tendencies of the key bills relating to Indian affairs—the temporary Trade and Intercourse Acts of 1790, 1793, and 1796—he more durably embedded their provisions in the Trade and Intercourse Act of 1802, the ruling statute for more than thirty years.[3] Federalists and Republicans may have differed over such issues, critical to Native Americans, as territorial expansion, federal regulation of the economy, and the size of the standing army, but those differences were insignificant when viewed from Indian country.

If southeastern Indians had little immediate reason to notice the election of Thomas Jefferson, Indian historians are another matter: Jefferson's name is attached to an important cluster of works in the area of Native American studies. It is hard to imagine a book or even an article on the Indian policy of his predecessor, John Adams, whose vast curiosity was more transatlantic than transcontinental. Unlike Adams, Jefferson left a long paper trail—despite the loss of a chest of his most cherished Indian drafts in the James River in 1809—along which to explore his philosophical interest in Native Americans. Tragedy and paradox, both attractive to writers and scholars, surround Jefferson's Indian work, for Jefferson, far more than his peers, defended the natural equality of Indians and unequivocally asserted their prospective citizenship, even while he laid the foundations for Indian removal.[4]

Unlike Adams, Jefferson cared passionately about Indians. Above all he sought to avoid costly wars with them, and his two terms in office saw far fewer armed, federal invasions of Indian lands than had occurred in the preceding eight years. For all the Jeffersonians' celebration of an expansive Republic, they proved as willing as Federalists to employ federal forces against squatters on Indian lands, which is faint praise. As Jefferson put it as early as 1792, "Indian war [is] too serious a thing, to risk incurring one merely to gratify a few intruders" on Indian lands at the cost of "a thousand times their value in taxes for carrying on the war they produce." He preferred instead to remove squatters, to "send armed force and make war against the intruders as being more just and less expensive." His conviction was that the states could gain Indian land more cheaply and justly by peace than by war. Jefferson loathed war; he knew it produced the massive fiscal-military states of Europe. Even an Indian war would cost far more, not merely in dollars, but in overall political effect, than it was worth. His determination to lower taxes, erase the debt, and shrink the army made peaceful expansion essential and the civilizing mission imperative.[5]

Jefferson and his agents would not invade but would negotiate, cajole, promise, purchase, and bribe America's way westward. In 1802 Jefferson persuaded Georgia to relinquish its remaining western claims to the Union in exchange for a promise, known as the Compact of 1802, that the government in Washington would soon purchase Cherokee and Creek title within the state's boundaries. Federal agents persuaded the Creeks to surrender most of their claims by 1806, but Cherokees tenaciously held on to their Georgian lands until the state, citing the Compact of 1802, forced the issue of Cherokee removal under President Andrew Jackson.[6]

If the Compact of 1802 helped lay the groundwork for Creek and Cherokee removal, more distant events of 1800–1803 portended even more revolutionary changes for the entire Indian southeast, greatly restricting Indian access to potential European allies and providing boundless spaces for the Jeffersonian imagination. For almost a decade after the Revolution had ended, southeastern Indians, and particularly the numerous Creeks, had been able to leverage Spanish power against the United States. Spain's influence slipped decisively in the 1790s, a process marked by the Treaty of San Lorenzo (1795), in which Spain surrendered almost two-thirds of its claims to what are now Alabama and Mississippi, retaining, east of the Mississippi River, only Florida and the Gulf Coast to thirty-one degrees north. But when Americans learned that Spain, in the secret Treaty of San Ildefonso (1800), had signed away the Louisiana Territory to an increasingly powerful France, they could imagine both the reversal of this process of Europe's withdrawal from North America and the revival of Indian confidence. Jefferson feared that the French occupation of New Orleans would be felt "like a light breeze by the indians," whose general affection for the French was, among Anglo-Americans, legendary.[7]

The Louisiana Purchase (1803) had effects as far-reaching among Indians as any event in mainstream American diplomatic history since the Treaty of Paris (1783). Not only did it deny southeastern Indians a potentially powerful ally against American expansion, it made westward removal imaginable. Having acquired the Louisiana Territory and made difficult promises to Georgia, Jefferson schemed to persuade Indians to cross the Mississippi and American citizens already living in the West to "depopulate" their territories and remove eastward. Protected from intrusion by the wide river, and by federal forts and federal diplomacy from Plains Indians, the emigrant Indians would gain education and security at the high price of ceding their eastern lands. Jefferson promoted a constitutional amendment to provide for removal and appealed personally to Indians to embrace it. Both efforts largely failed, but not before generating a Cherokee political crisis in 1807–9, when a faction headed by Doublehead ceded lands to the federal government. Even after Doublehead's assassination in 1807, his followers traveled to Washington to discuss removal, and within a few years almost one out of twelve Cherokees was living west of the Mississippi. Removal had Jeffersonian roots.[8]

The effort to persuade Indians to cede their lands east of the Mississippi was closely related to the civilizing mission, which had sought, since its early implementation under Henry Knox, honorable American expansion. When Indian men farmed rather than hunted, when they wore clothes spun by their women rather than purchased from the unscrupulous trader, they would live well on less land, leaving a surplus they could sell to the United States. Historians have long noted that under Jefferson the process became inverted. He urged Indian agents not to wait for the fabled surpluses of lands to emerge but to purchase lands whether Indian men were farming or not. Cessions of Indian land would restrict Indian hunting and compel the men to work the fields. To obtain cessions Jefferson applied the pressure not of war but of debt. Henry Adams keenly observed that the third president "deliberately ordered his Indian agents to tempt the tribal chiefs into debt in order to oblige them to sell the tribal lands, which did not belong to them, but to their tribes."[9]

Benjamin Hawkins worked hard at both the acquisition of Indian land and the plan of civilization. He credited Jefferson with redoubling the federal civilizing mission after it had languished under John Adams. By the end of Jefferson's second term, Indians in the southeast and the Cherokees in particular had acquired a reputation for "civilization." Yet as southeastern Indians embraced the federal plan they did so on their own terms, often demonstrating a stout commitment to their own cultures, frustrating the Jeffersonian hope for the rapid assimilation of Indians as fee-simple landholders, farming country yeomen, and spinning domestic wives. Equally frustrating was the fact that the southeastern Indian reputation for civility rested in no small part on slavery.[10]

The gender revolution that Jefferson advocated would render Indian men less warlike, less dangerous, and less corruptible by European enemies, while it freed women from drudgery. Jefferson's own dependence on the field labor of enslaved women bred tyrannies he knew all too well, but he did not openly reflect on them when advocating the civilizing mission in the southeast. Here, to borrow a phrase, was gendered "confusion" at the heart of one of the federal government's earliest and most perplexing social experiments.[11]

The Indians whom Jefferson sought to transform understood gender and slavery in ways no less complicated than his own, and they included their own confusion, some of it the result of colonialism, some indigenous. Much as Jefferson differentiated between the Indian women he thought should withdraw from their fields and the slave women who were forced to labor in his own, and much as he differentiated between the free ladies and slave women of Virginia, Indians also differentiated between male slaves and Indian men. Gender, the cultural understandings and conventions surrounding sexual difference, powerfully shaped both the rise of black slavery and the history of the federal government's "plan of civilization" in the Indian southeast.

Theda Perdue's forceful study of Cherokee chattel slavery argues that it had been made possible by a thorough transformation in the Cherokee's division of labor and conventions of kinship. More recently, however, Perdue has discovered that Cherokees tenaciously maintained their understandings and conventions of gender at least until removal, by which time slavery had become firmly established. We may now ask the questions that Jefferson and Hawkins could not ask as they sought to liberate southeastern women: how did it become as proper for black men to work the fields in Cherokee Echota as it was for black women to work the fields in the shadow of Monticello? How did Indians (and perhaps by reflection southern whites) form "race-specific" concepts of gender?[12]

Among all corn-fed Indian peoples east of the Mississippi River, women directed and performed most agricultural labor. Southeastern Indian men generally helped with the clearing, planting, and harvest, but the women did the rest. Jefferson, like most writers from the colonial through the early republican periods, saw in women's labor evidence of idle male domination. Not all American citizens agreed. American Board missionary Daniel S. Butrick observed that Cherokee women took on "the heaviest part of the labor, . . . yet they were cheerful and voluntary in performing it." He saw no "slavish, servile fear on the part of women."[13]

Europeans had tried to grasp southeastern women's authority in politics as early as 1540, when Hernando de Soto famously encountered the ruling woman of Cofitachequi in South Carolina's interior. In 1564 Jacques Le Moyne painted a Timucuan queen, whose image, born aloft by porters, circulated widely as an engraving by Theodore de Bry. In 1775 James Adair accused—that is the only way to put it—the Cherokees of being under "petticoat government." Scholars today focus less attention on such claims to female authoritarianism than on the more routine authority of women in the household, in the village, and in the production and distribution of food, authority that regularly reached into the political realm.[14]

However that may be, Indian women surely did not see their authority in such early modern European terms as monarchy or in such postmodern Western terms as household government. Rather, Indian women and men conceived of their own powers as proper manifestations of creative and sustaining spiritual forces. To take the most relevant example, because Indians understood the power of women and the power of corn to be compatible, the field during the growing season suited women but did not suit most men. Jefferson and Hawkins, attempting to turn Indian men into farmers and Indian women into spinners and weavers, threatened to turn the world on its side, to derange the powers that governed fertility of all kinds, even to end life's renewal.[15]

In a keen manifestation of the separate natures of women and men, menstruating women avoided hunters and warriors. Colonists and American citizens who encountered the Indian approaches to menstruation tended to associate the practices either with biblical Judaism (as evidence that Native Americans indeed descended from Israel's lost tribes) or, more narrowly, with degrading filth and pollution. But anthropologists since at least Mary Douglas have revealed that menstrual proscriptions in some societies encode special powers; such strictures do not necessarily degrade women.[16] Southeastern Indian men, after all, also had to keep their sexual fluids in the proper place. John Howard Payne, a vigorous collector of Cherokee information in the early nineteenth century, noted that semen became dangerous when out of place, so "every garment and every skin whereon is the seed of copulation, must be washed with water."[17]

Menstrual blood, a dangerous power, was also a vital, life-giving power. In a sacred Creek story, an old woman (probably the important spirit Corn Woman) stepped over a log and "saw a drop of blood in her track. Stooping down, she carefully scraped up the dirt around the blood and carried it home." She hid the blood in an earthen jar. Soon, the old, probably postmenopausal woman "discovered that the blood clot was growing. . . . In ten months it was developed into a little boy."[18]

Vital enough to make life, menstrual blood could also kill, as it did in the Cherokee story of Stoneclad, a "wicked," stone-skinned, man-eating giant, who was defeated by seven menstruating women. They had blocked the monster's path as he advanced hungrily on a village. "He came along the trail to where the first woman was standing, and as soon as he saw her he started and cried out: '*Yu!* my grandchild; you are in a very bad state!' He hurried past her, but in a moment he met the next woman, and cried out again: '*Yu!* my child: you are in a terrible way,' and hurried past her, but now he was vomiting blood." Stoneclad weakened with each woman he passed. At the sight of the seventh, whose period "had just begun, the blood poured from his mouth and he fell down on the trail." Anthropologist Raymond D. Fogelson suggests that, for the Cherokees, Stoneclad embodied the masculine realm of nature as opposed to the feminine realm of culture. Perhaps women, as keepers of the village, as cultivators, stood in greater opposition to the monster than did men, who operated as hunters in "nature." [19]

The association of cultivation, fertility, and menstrual blood appears most widely in myths about the Corn Mother. In one common tale in the greater southeast, a boy (or pair of boys) discovered his mother as she secretively prepared his food. He saw her "place a riddle [i.e., a sieve] on the floor, stand with one foot on each side of it and scratch the front of one of her thighs, whereupon corn poured down the riddle. When she scratched the other thigh beans poured into the riddle." With vaginal symbolism, the story associates procreation and cultivation as feminine.[20] When the woman later noticed that the boy would no longer eat her food, she gave him detailed instructions that included her own death at his hands, a journey, a marriage, and a return. After carrying out all the instructions, the boy, now a young man, returned with his spouse to the spot where he had slain his mother. He saw that "all sorts of corn and beans had grown up in it." This Creek version of the myth ends with the admonition that corn had to be "treated well" or "it would become angry."[21]

To treat the corn well, southeastern Indians held Green Corn Ceremonies. Payne got it right when he noted of the Cherokee pantheon that "A female . . . is held in special honor, and identified with Indian Corn, or Maize. Most of the All Night Dances refer in some way to her, as did some of the Ceremonies in the Green Corn Festivals." He recorded the Cherokee name of the Green Corn Ceremony as "Sah, looh, stuknee, heeh, steh, steeh," the first two syllables of which appear to identify the feast with "Selu," the Cherokee Corn Mother.[22] James Adair noticed another of the Cherokees' associations of corn with female fertility. They called the corn crib "*Watóhre* and the penis of any creature, by the same name, intimating, that as the sun and moon influence and ripen the fruits that are stored in it, so by the help of Ceres and Bacchus, Venus lies warm, whereas on the contrary, *sine Cerere et Bacchus, friget Venus.*" [23]

Theda Perdue observes that changes in the Cherokee settlement pattern over the course of the late eighteenth and early nineteenth centuries both compressed the Cherokee ceremonial calendar and diminished the importance of the village—in which women had before had great say—in Cherokee politics. The adoption of pastoral agriculture, the cultivation of cotton, and the assaults of imperial and republican armies from 1759 through 1794 had encouraged the Cherokees and Creeks to shift from a settlement pattern dominated by towns, villages, and hamlets to one dominated by farmsteads and ranches. Choctaw and Chickasaw settlements changed similarly, if less dramatically, for before their wider dispersal away from the great rivers they had rambled broadly along riverbanks.[24] In the isolated farmsteads spreading out away from the rivers, in cabins rather than the larger households that characterized a denser village life before the onslaughts of disease and warfare, it may well be that menstruation became a more isolating experience, that the menstrual synchrony and suppression evident among large congregations of cohabiting women would have been disrupted, and that more women would go to the menstrual dwelling alone. This may have had implications for female power in the southeast.[25]

In addition to the basic distinctions between Indian men and women, it is conceivable that the concepts of woman and man did not alone account for the Indian construction of gender. Sometimes there was another category, composed of males who have most commonly been called by a French term of Persian derivation: *berdache*. This, in its original meaning, implies passive, male concubines, kept for an elite's homosexual pleasure, which is so far from the Indian practice that other terms have recently been coined, though many choose to stick with *berdache* despite its etymological disadvantages. Perdue calls them "men who became women," but most anthropologists disagree that gender crossing is what this cultural form accomplished. Others call them "two-spirit people," or "men-women." The implication of these terms is that, at least in some North American Indian communities, these males stood as an alternative gender, males who could work the fields alongside women without upsetting order. There are no definite references to Cherokee or Creek menwomen from the eighteenth or early nineteenth centuries, though there are such references from the sixteenth through the eighteenth centuries for other southeastern coastal and lower Mississippi Valley peoples (some of whom the Creeks assimilated).[26]

Men-women, as an alternative gender, suggest the rigidity, not the flexibility, of Indian understandings of sexual difference. Men-women stood on the potent boundary between masculine and feminine things. Believed to be extraordinary, they were not treated casually. Endowed with sacred powers because of their position on the border, the men-women, or two-spirit people, far from crossing or blurring the divide between male and female, cast it into bold relief.[27]

Jefferson's civilizing mission was not the first to confront southeastern Indian understandings of gender. Indian men in the seventeenth-century Franciscan mission system labored on Spanish ranches and farms, while in their own "native community" women remained the chief agriculturalists.[28] Long after that mission system collapsed under English, Creek, and other Indian attacks, southeastern women remained reluctant to see their countrymen in the fields, a cultural attitude that persisted for centuries. In their early-nineteenth-century efforts to convert Indian men into yeomen, federal agents asked Indian women to give up their communal labors, to surrender what may have been an economic base for female influence in Indian politics, and to interfere with the fundamentals of life itself. To ask women to leave the fields to their men was to invite disruption of sacred forces that kept fields and wombs fertile. After a long period of demographic crisis, this was to ask a great deal.[29]

The religious and cultural missionaries of the young Republic had set for themselves a difficult task, and in the years before the forced removal of the southeastern Indians, the missionaries' failures were more complete than they led their supporting societies to believe. Even the minority of Cherokees and Creeks who embraced the plan of civilization, like the Apalachee males who had labored on Spanish farms but not in Apalachee fields, did not consistently challenge the old way. Cherokee and Creek men continued to avoid their people's fields during the growing season. A small but powerful planter elite emerged, especially among the Cherokees. The new leaders subjected the ways of their neighboring Anglo-American southerners to the patterns of southeastern Indian culture. Husbands in many cases took to plowing, extending their traditional roles as clearers of the fields and working, as was also traditional, in association with animals. But they rarely took up the hoe. Regular care of growing crops remained the work of women and slaves.[30]

Men had predominantly composed the slave labor force among both

Cherokees and Creeks in the eighteenth century. These men entered the fields through traditional paths. Enslaved, non-adopted captives had always been permitted, indeed had regularly been forced, to handle the hoe. Slaves had long been aliens among the people. Because slaves lived outside clans, they had no claim to full humanity.[31] Male slaves were not, it appeared to their captors, true or real men. Like the men-women discussed above, they occupied an order apart from that of the male hunters and warriors; unlike the men-women, they had no relatives, they were not viewed as real people, they cast no bright light on the gender divide, and they faced the degradation of bondage. They were also far more common than men-women.

Traders and official British Indian commissaries and agents established slavery in southeastern Indian villages by the eve of the Revolution. Many of these colonial men married Indian women, and their children, who became full Indians by southeastern matrilineal reckoning, inherited their slaves, giving rise to the small but influential planter elite. Slavery became bound up with traditional forms of warfare, especially during the American Revolution, as young Cherokee and Muskogean men raided colonial farms and seized black people for ransom, resale, or slavery itself. Southeastern Indian slavery took many forms: African-Seminole slaves tended to live as tributaries in semi-autonomous communities; African-Cherokee or Chickasaw slaves often became chattels; Creek slaves ran the full spectrum in between. Everywhere, slaves might gain full incorporation into society by purchase, by manumission, or by marriage; such incorporation was most common among the Seminoles, least common among the Cherokees, and increasingly uncommon among all the tribes in the late eighteenth and early nineteenth centuries.[32]

The Revolutionary War decisively established slavery in the Indian southeast. The chaos of southern warfare rapidly depleted slaves from the plantations of South Carolina and Georgia even as it rapidly expanded slaveholding among the southeastern Indians, who not only took slaves during their scattered raids on American settlements but received them as presents from British officials impressed with their services. An estimated three hundred to four hundred loyalists also fled to Indian country from Georgia and South Carolina, bringing their slaves with them. Alexander McGillivray, the self-consciously Creek son of a loyalist father and Creek mother, maintained a large plantation of some sixty slaves by 1793; in 1798 one of his sisters owned some eighty.[33] Among the Creeks, Choctaws, and Chickasaws alone, who numbered perhaps thirty thousand, there were roughly thirty-five hundred black slaves and two hundred African

American free people in 1795. Hawkins, among the Creeks in 1801, noted that slaves bitterly called themselves "King's Gifts."[34]

By the turn of the nineteenth century slaveholding Indians, intermarried Indians, and Indians of mixed European and Indian descent had come to dominate the centralizing Creek and Cherokee governments—the very bodies with the authority to approve both the new "plan of civilization" and any further land cessions. Some among the new elites, committed to slavery, also turned to the cultivation of cotton.[35]

Even before he had established his own plantation nearby, Hawkins noted of the black slaves among the Creeks that "where they are there is more industry and better farms."[36] Settling himself on the Flint River, he provided a model for the developing Creek elite. By the time of his death in 1816 his holdings included seventy-two slaves worth $28,800, almost half the value of all his personal property.[37] And there were Indians to rival him. Benjamin Gold, visiting the prominent Cherokee families in New Echota in 1829, noted in a letter to his brother in Connecticut that the Ross family had "negroes enough to wait on us," and that the Vann household had "six or seven hundred acres of the best land you ever saw, and negroes enough to manage it." Evaluating Joseph Vann's status, Gould told his brother that it would "make you feel small to see his situation."[38]

Blacks came to Indian agriculture without the local knowledge of the Indian women but with considerable background in farming and with far more knowledge of commercial crops. Some had other skills—making barrels, shoeing horses, raising cattle, proficiency in English—that might be useful in the growing and even marketing of crops or livestock for the few Indians who would enter the wider agricultural market.[39] Black slaves of both sexes joined Indian women in the fields, and slaves belonging to the elite families eventually took over the work. Slaves both male and female worked the crops of a tiny but influential planter class, adding a new dimension to the southeastern Indian division of gender and labor.

The adoption of slavery carried implications for gender that stretched into the elite's understanding of kinship and the laws of property inheritance. By 1808 the Cherokee elite adopted written laws that opened the way for the patrilineal descent of personal property, including slaves, despite the matrilineal traditions of the Cherokees.[40] As it refined the laws in the years before removal, the Cherokee elite recoiled from the Anglo-American practice of coverture; an 1817 law made it clear that all transactions involving a married woman's property required "her will and consent."[41] The pattern remained operative throughout the antebellum period, as Cherokee freedman Morris Sheppard recalled for a WPA writer as late as the 1930s. "Old Mistress" he said, inherited "about half a dozen slaves," and she insisted they were "her own and old Master can't sell one unless she given him leave to do it."[42] Retaining rights to property was an important achievement, but slavery and intermarriage with white Americans did have a corrosive effect on the standing of women, as the Cherokee elite excluded women from politics and provided for citizenship's bilateral, as opposed to matrilineal, descent when it adopted a constitution, based in part on the American Constitution, in 1827. Though fewer than one-tenth of Cherokee households included slaves, eleven of the twelve known signers of the constitution were slave owners.[43]

The new understanding of gender, codified in the laws adopted by the slaveholding elite in these years, took greater hold among that elite (perhaps only among the elite) than among the great mass of non-slaveholders. Federal agent Return Jonathan Meigs estimated that some two hundred to three hundred families had potential as "useful citizens" of the United States, which probably establishes the rough size of the elite in 1808. Most litigants who appeared before Cherokee courts belonged to the slaveholding class, which suggests that ordinary folk had little use for the laws. A decade after 1808 most Cherokees still ignored that year's law providing for the patrilineal descent of property.[44]

Slavery and intermarriage profoundly shaped the lives of people in the narrow upper crust that had formed on southeastern Indian society. But Jefferson's hoped-for revolution in gender, which did not even completely reshape the elite, made little headway among most Indian people. Struggling to lead that revolution, Hawkins had chosen to work through women, whom he saw as "capable of and willing to become instrumental in civilizing the men." In 1797 the Creek wife of a British trader had warned Hawkins that though hard work was not foreign to Creek women, they would not attend to his scheme. In another instance that year, Hawkins had hired an English-speaking Creek woman and her two daughters to take up the spinning wheel as a model for others. Eight years later he noted that the three had disappointed him.[45] Because he paid so little attention to the religious dimensions of women's fieldwork, Hawkins grossly overestimated women's desire to "liberate" themselves from the fields.

Nor were Creek women alone in resisting the American plan. In an event that blends our investigation of myth with the historical record, Cherokees preached a religious revival in 1811–12. Two women and a man received eschatological warnings from a spiritual messenger who demanded that the

Cherokees both abandon the cultivation of nonnative grains and pound, not grind, the native corn. Recalling southeastern Indian myths concerning the origin of corn in the person of the Selu, the spirit warned that "The Mother of the Nation has forsaken you because all her bones are being broken through the grinding of the mills." [46] When federal agent Meigs reported on the Cherokee revival in March 1812, he implied that women were more active than men in attacking imported styles: "Some of the females are mutilating the fine muslins that are very common among the young people being told by the fanatics that these are amongst the causes of the displeasure of the Great Spirit." [47] The religious revival did not succeed in arresting the conscious adoption of Anglo-American ways by the Cherokee elite, but it may have given force to the resistance to acculturation that characterized many lesser-known Cherokees for the next half century.

Among non-slaveholding Indians field labor remained traditionally female, although because it was performed on smaller, poorer plots of land it probably became less cooperative. In 1808 a third of the Cherokees lived in the rugged "valley towns" amid the Great Smoky Mountains. Only five black slaves lived among these 3,500 people, who had a strong reputation for traditionalism. [48] Likewise among the Creeks, at the town of Cosito (Cussetah) in 1820, the British traveler Adam Hodgson noted that traditional patterns prevailed, as women weeded small fields, pounded corn, and carried water. Elsewhere among the Creeks Hodgson saw more "flourishing little farms," adding that "the labour generally devolved either on the African Negro, or the Indian wife." Hodgson associated the larger and more productive farms with slavery. He pointed out, however, that few Creeks owned slaves; most women engaged in agriculture.

Hodgson later passed into the Cherokee nation and visited the Presbyterian Brainerd Mission, where some fifty boys, sons for the most part of elite Cherokees, worked crops. Even their fathers, men who clearly embraced a degree of missionary instruction, could be anxious about violating the fields with a male Cherokee presence. One, reluctant to have his son weed fields, unsuccessfully offered to provide the school with a slave as a substitute. Plowing fields was another matter, a part of the preparation of the fields that had always been men's work. In June 1822 a busy captain of the Cherokee Light Horse Patrol kept his son away from the mission—not to avoid field work but to have the boy "plow out his corn." [49]

As the threat of removal intensified, slaveholders remained a small minority, and non-slaveholding women continued to work most fields. Only about 8 percent of Cherokee households owned slaves in the 1830s, and only a handful of these possessed more than twenty.[50] Based on the number of plows in the nation, Albert Gallatin guessed that a third of the men were farming among the Cherokees on the eve of removal, but plows do not point to male fieldwork between plowing and harvest.[51] Missionaries, who were usually from the northern states or Great Britain, generally stood against removal, and to advance their opposition they put the best face on the "civilization" of the Cherokees, publishing reports that Cherokee women spun most of the nation's cotton cloth and that the plow was in widespread use. There is no reason to dismiss either claim as rhetorical spin. But while these reports emphasize Cherokee strides toward an Anglo-American model, they avoid any discussion of slavery—increasingly controversial among their readers. And even these reports do not place adult Indian men in the fields between plowing and harvest. The reports, in other words, are remarkable for what they do not say; considering the importance of the division of labor to these proponents of the "civilizing mission," their failure to discuss it suggests that they failed measurably to revise it. The Indians took slavery, plows, and spinning wheels and adapted them to their own preferred patterns of culture.[52]

Nor did removal completely tear apart the old cultural fabric. In the 1840s, among southeasterners who had removed west of the Mississippi, Josiah Gregg found that the ordinary poor women commonly cultivated the soil. Although they had also taken up the spinning and weaving of cloth, they spun only "occasionally, during recess from the labors of the field."[53] By the 1860s only 2 to 3 percent of Indian citizens of the five western nations soon to be known as the civilized tribes owned slaves; almost two-thirds of these owned fewer than five, and perhaps 7 percent of the slaveholders owned more than twenty.[54] Among the vast non-slaveholding majority, women continued to tend the crops after the clearing (and increasingly after the plowing) of the fields. A Choctaw freedman whose master had been white recalled of his non-slaveholding neighbors that "the average Choctaw didn't do much farming . . . the women did what little farming that was done" until well after the Civil War. "I have seen," Jefferson L. Cole reported, "an Indian woman make her complete crop with nothing but a grubbing hoe; break the ground, lay off rows, and till the plants."[55] Black Cherokee and Creek freed people, remembering in the 1930s their own antebellum labors, rarely mention the labor of their male Indian owners; when they do they describe, for the most part, herding, hunting, and fighting.[56] Ed Butler, recalling his life among the Choctaws, succinctly describes the roles of slaves and of male Indian slaveholders: "The slaves did all the work, and the Indians hunted, and fished, attended councils and guided the work done by the slaves." [57] When Cherokee Lucy Keys, or Wahnenauhi, recalled in 1889 certain improvements made on the Cherokee George Lowrey's farm in the first half of the century, she emphasized Lowrey's tension with his slave, Billy, and said that Lowrey "had" the work done: he "had a large piece of ground cleared . . . and planted with watermelons, he had it fenced with pickets, a strong gate made, fastened with a lock and two keys, one of which he gave to Billy." [58] The Indian slaveholders did not themselves tend crops; they preferred to send in field hands, who like non-adopted captives were not considered full persons and accordingly, even if male, could threaten neither the crops nor the people's good relations with the sacred forces that produced them.

There would be no Jeffersonian revolution in gender in most Creek or Cherokee households. But there would be, as Hawkins had long hoped, men working in the Creek and Cherokee fields. Many, it turned out, would be African American. The American missionaries and those Indians who were most attentive to them found in the development of an Indian system of black slavery a partial—and racist—solution to the gender dilemma. What success was achieved in "civilizing" the southeast rested in part on a circumvention of the gender barrier accomplished by slavery.

If slaveholders were few and if their way of life differed from that of the great majority of their peoples, they were nonetheless powerful. Their slaves gave them wealth and visibility, the latter both at home and among their Anglo-American neighbors. In the 1860s slaves themselves amounted to almost 14 percent of the people living in the western lands of these nations and the Seminoles. As early as 1825 the fifteen thousand eastern Cherokees owned some thirteen hundred slaves.[59] The rising wealth of the planter class in slaves gave it increased influence, and it did more than that.

The emerging wealth of the slave-owning classes gave the southeasterners the quality of Anglo-American culture that led observers like Jefferson to set these nations apart in the nineteenth century.[60] Slavery, however uneven its form and depth among the peoples of the southeast before and after removal, partially resolved the dilemma of gender faced by the agents of the "plan of civilization" because it both allowed male slaveholders to retain their traditional distance from the crops and permitted elite Indian women to withdraw from the fields. Indian women who owned slaves accepted the increasing role of their men in agriculture because that role was indirect.

Gallatin, formerly Jefferson's secretary of the treasury and in many ways Jefferson's protégé, was one of the few to recognize the pattern, and it concerned him. He speculated that as slavery had given rise to the great Native American civilizations of Mexico and Peru, it had likewise introduced "cultivation" to the Cherokees, whom he deemed the only "agricultural nation" among all the Indians of the United States. He defined "agricultural nation" as "that state of society, in which the men themselves actually perform agricultural labor." Though Gallatin believed slavery had improved the Cherokees, he did not want it to "enable them to live without labor." Supporting Indian removal in 1836, he hoped that in "a permanent place of refuge" Indians would come to obey "that first decree which, allotting to each sex its proper share, declared labor to be the condition, on which man was permitted to exist." [61]

Euro-Americans had long bound notions of savagery to the labors of Indian women. Anglo-American missionaries—religious and secular—had long attempted, with little success, to convert Indian men into yeomen. Thomas Jefferson and Benjamin Hawkins had made a revolution in gender the centerpiece of their "civilizing mission." Things did not turn out as they had hoped. Southeastern Indian men took to the raising of livestock and even to the plowing of fields, but not to the regular crop work. Some elite Indian women released their hoes into the hands not of their husbands but of their slaves, both male and female. We might conceive of slavery as adding new forms of gender to Indian societies, or we might conceive of it as adding greater gendered complexity and confusion. In either case the Indian adoption of slavery transferred, from the point of view of many Anglo-American observers, the exploitation of Indian women to what the Hawkinses and Jeffersons saw as the more acceptable exploitation of black slaves of both sexes.

Among the rising southeastern Indian elite, slavery masked widespread cultural resistance to the central feature of the federal "civilizing mission," the redefining of Indian manhood and womanhood. Although the Indian elite did not conform fully to Anglo-American patterns, and although the mass of southeastern Indians continued to develop independently of the missionaries' conscious designs, the adoption of slavery by an Indian elite that was highly visible to American citizens disguised the surprising fixity of fundamental Native American notions of gender. Accomplishing this trick, black slavery became one of the developments among the Cherokees, Creeks, Chickasaws, and Choctaws that encouraged Anglo-Americans to coin these peoples "civilized tribes."

The contest over southeastern Indian civilization involved not only the social organization of men and women but also the meaning of manhood, womanhood, and field labor. When Jefferson and Hawkins degraded Indian women's field labor, most southeastern Indians ignored them, but southeastern

Indian leaders could not. These men, in their own ways, accepted the view of fieldwork as demeaning. Elevating themselves above women and slaves, they negotiated with a new Republic that, in return, congratulated them for their civility, degraded their people, and took their lands.

NOTES

The middle third of this essay revises my paper, "North American Indian Slaveholding and the Colonization of Gender: The Southeast before Removal," *Critical Matrix: Princeton Working Papers in Women's Studies* 3 (1987): 1–30; thanks to Ada Verloren, Suellen Hoy, and Gail Bederman for examining more recent versions.

1. Jefferson is quoted in Peter S. Onuf, *Jefferson's Empire: The Language of American Nationhood* (Charlottesville, Va., 2000), 25, 26, 32; Benjamin Hawkins to secretary of war, Coweta, 6 Jan. 1797, in Benjamin Hawkins, *Letters of Benjamin Hawkins, Collections of the Georgia Historical Society* 9 (Savannah, Ga., 1916), 57.

2. Anthony F. C. Wallace, *Jefferson and the Indians: The Tragic Fate of the First Americans* (Cambridge, Mass., 1999), 278; TJ, First Annual Message, 8 Dec. 1801; TJ to Senate, 22 Dec. 1801, *Messages and Papers of the Presidents,* ed. James D. Richardson (Washington, D.C., 1899) 1:326, 333; "Journal of the Commissioners of the United States," 8 May–29 June 1802, *American State Papers, Class II, Indian Affairs,* ed. Walter Lowrie and Matthew St. Clair Clarke (Washington, D.C., 1832), 4:670, 674, 676.

3. "Journal of the Commissioners" 4:677; Francis Paul Prucha, *American Indian Policy in the Formative Years: The Indian Trade and Intercourse Acts, 1790–1834* (1962; Lincoln, Neb., 1971), 50, 141; Wallace, *Jefferson and the Indians,* 166–69, 171, 278, 189, 207, 209, 220, 279.

4. Onuf, *Jefferson's Empire,* 18–52; Wallace, *Jefferson and the Indians,* 152; Bernard Sheehan, *Seeds of Extinction: Jeffersonian Philanthropy and the American Indian* (Chapel Hill, N.C., 1973); William G. McLoughlin, "Thomas Jefferson and the Beginnings of Cherokee Nationalism, 1806– 1809," in *Cherokee Ghost Dance,* ed. William G. McLoughlin (Macon, Ga., 1984), 73–110.

5. Prucha, *American Indian Policy,* 138, 144–55, 159; Robert W. Tucker and David C. Hendrickson, *Empire of Liberty: The Statecraft of Thomas Jefferson* (New York, 1990), 41, 87–88, 132.

6. Clarence Edwin Carter, *Territorial Papers of the United States, The Territory of Mississippi, 1798–1817* (Washington, D.C., 1939) 5:143–44; Reginald Horsman, *Expansion and American Indian Policy, 1783–1812* (Norman, Okla., 1967), 66–83, 115–41; Sheehan, *Seeds of Extinction,* 10, 122, 123, 137, 140, 172–73, 180, 212.

7. Tucker and Hendrickson, *Empire of Liberty,* 132; Gregory Evans Dowd, "The French King Wakes Up in Detroit: 'Pontiac's War' in Rumor and History," *Ethnohistory* 30 (1990): 254–78.

8. Onuf, *Jefferson's Empire,* 19; Wallace, *Jefferson and the Indians,* 274–75, 224–25, 254–60; McLoughlin, "Thomas Jefferson," 73–110.

9. Horsman, *Expansion,* 110; Henry Adams, *History of the United States during the Administration of Thomas Jefferson and James Madison* (1889–90; New York, 1986), 2:343–44.

10. "Journal of the Commissioners," 4:677. Jefferson praises the southeastern Indians in his Seventh (27 Oct. 1807) and Eighth (8 Nov. 1808) Annual Messages to Congress, in Richardson, *Messages* 1:428, 454.

11. Laura Edwards, *Gendered Strife and Confusion: The Political Culture of Reconstruction* (Champaign, Ill., 1997); Onuf, *Jefferson's Empire,* 31–32.

12. Contrast Theda Perdue's *Slavery and the Evolution of Cherokee Society, 1540–1866,* (Knoxville, Tenn., 1979), 50, 53, with her *Cherokee Women: Gender and Culture Change, 1700–1835*

(Lincoln, Neb., 1998), 69, 126. For the Anglo-American racialization of gender, see Kathleen Brown, *Good Wives, Nasty Wenches and Anxious Patriarchs: Gender, Race, and Power in Colonial Virginia* (Chapel Hill, N.C., 1996), esp. 107–36.

13. Daniel Butrick to John Howard Payne, Carmel, 15 Dec. 1835, in John Howard Payne, "Indian Antiquities," Typescript, 14 vols.; "Letters to Payne from John Ross, Daniel Butrick, and Others," 4:28, Newberry Library, Chicago. Also quoted in Theda Perdue, "Southern Indians and the Cult of True Womanhood," in *The Webb of Southern Relations: Women, Family, and Education,* ed. Walter J. Fraser, R. Frank Saunders Jr., and Jon L. Wakelyn (Athens, Ga., 1984), 36; Kathryn E. Holland Braund, "Guardians of Tradition and Handmaidens to Change: Women's Roles in Creek Economic and Social Life during the Eighteenth Century," *American Indian Quarterly* 14 (1990): 240–44.

14. Europeans, of course, also had female rulers. See Jerald T. Milanich, "The Timucua Indians of North Florida and South Georgia," in *Indians of the Greater Southeast,* ed. Bonnie G. McEwan (Gainesville, Fla., 2000), 6; Raymond Fogelson, "On the Petticoat Government of the Eighteenth-Century Cherokees," in *Personality and the Cultural Construction of Society,* ed. D. Jordan and M. Swartz (Tuscaloosa, Ala., 1990), 161–81; Perdue, *Cherokee Women,* 10, 13, 25; Anthony F. C. Wallace, *The Death and Rebirth of the Seneca* (New York, 1969); Judith K. Brown, "Economic Organization and the Position of Women among the Iroquois," *Ethnohistory* 17 (1970): 155–56; Theda Perdue, "Cherokee Women and the Trail of Tears," *Journal of Women's History* 1 (1989): 14–30.

15. Braund, "Guardians of Tradition", 244.

16. James Adair, *Adair's History of the American Indians, 1775,* ed. Samuel Cole Williams (1776; New York, 1966), 129–30; Perdue, *Cherokee Women,* 29–30, says that menstrual blood was "polluting" but not "unclean." In other words, menstruation was polluting when out of its proper context. Mary Douglas, *Purity and Danger: an Analysis of Concepts of Pollution and Taboo* (London, 1966), 35; Thomas Buckley and Alma Gottlieb, introduction; Alma Gottlieb, "Menstrual Cosmology among the Beng of the Ivory Coast"; and Thomas Buckley, "Menstruation and the Power of Yurok Women," all in *Blood Magic: the Anthropology of Menstruation,* ed. Thomas Buckley and Alma Gottlieb (Berkeley, Calif., 1988).

17. Payne, "Indian Antiquities" 3:76.

18. John R. Swanton, *Myths and Tales of the Southeastern Indians, Bureau of American Ethnology Bulletin* 88 (Washington, D.C., 1929), 15–16.

19. James Mooney, "Myths of the Cherokee," *Annual Report of the Bureau of American Ethnology* 19 (1900), 319–320. Raymond Fogelson analyzes this myth in "Windigo Goes South: Stoneclad among the Cherokees," in *Manlike Monsters on Trial: Early Records and Modern Evidence,* ed. Marjorie M. Halpin and Michael M. Ames (Vancouver, 1980), 133–35; for a similar analysis of a Shawnee analogue see Gregory Evans Dowd, *A Spirited Resistance: The North American Indian Struggle for Unity, 1745–1815* (Baltimore, 1992), 7.

20. Åke Hultkrantz, *The Religions of the American Indians,* trans. Monica Setterwall (Berkeley, Calif., 1979), 53; Bruno Bettelheim, *Symbolic Wounds: Puberty Rites and the Envious Male* (Glencoe, Ill., 1962), 22, 44, 112–15.

21. Swanton, *Myths,* 10–13. For a Cherokee version see Mooney, "Myths of the Cherokee," 242–49; Jack Frederick Kilpatrick, "The Wahnenauhi Manuscript: Historical Sketches of the Cherokees, Together with Some of Their Customs, Traditions, and Superstitions," *Bureau of American Ethnology Bulletin* 196, *Anthropological Papers* No. 77 (Washington, D.C., 1966), 189.

22. Payne, "Indian Antiquities" 1:24, 46–53.

23. Adair, *Adair's History,* 78.

24. Perdue, *Cherokee Women,* 65–158; Kathryn E. Holland Braund, *Deerskins and Duffels: The Creek Indian Trade with Anglo-America, 1685–1815* (Lincoln, Neb., 1993), 185; Claudio Saunt, *A New Order of Things: Property, Power and the Transformation of the Creek Indians, 1733–1816*

(Cambridge, Mass., 1999), 156–63; James T. Carson, "Native Americans, the Market Revolution, and Culture Change: The Choctaw Cattle Economy, 1690–1830," *Agricultural History* 71 (1997): 1–18; Gregory A. Waselkov and Marvin T. Smith, "Upper Creek Archaeology," in McEwan, *Indians of the Greater Southeast,* 252; Gerald Schroedi, "Cherokee Ethnohistory and Archaeology from 1540–1838," in McEwan, *Indians of the Greater Southeast,* 207; Clara Sue Kidwell, *Choctaws and Missionaries in Mississippi, 1818–1918* (Norman, Okla., 1995), 63.

25. Buckley, "Menstruation," 199.

26. Charles Callender and Lee M. Kochems, "The North American Berdache," *Current Anthropology* 24 (1983): 443–70, remains the best introduction to the distribution of the form in North America. See also Jonathan Katz, *Gay American History: Lesbians and Gay Men in the U.S.A.* (New York, 1973), 285, 288–89, 291; Perdue, *Cherokee Women,* 37; Adair, *Adair's History,* 109; Raymond E. Hauser, "The *Berdache* and the Illinois Tribe during the Last Half of the Seventeenth Century," *Ethnohistory* 37 (1990): 55–63; Walter L. Williams, *The Spirit and the Flesh: Sexual Diversity in American Indian Culture* (Boston, 1986); Robert Fulton and Steven W. Anderson, "The Amerindian 'Man-Woman': Gender, Liminality, and Cultural Continuity," *Current Anthropology* 33 (1992): 603–10; Wesley Thomas and Sue-Ellen Jacobs, "'. . . And We Are Still Here': From *Berdache* to Two-Spirit People," *American Indian Culture and Research Journal* 23 (1999): 95.

27. Hauser, "The *Berdache*," 55–63.

28. Bonnie G. McEwan, "The Apalachee Indians of Northwest Florida," in McEwan, *Indians of the Greater Southeast,* 66.

29. Peter Wood, "The Changing Population of the Colonial South: An Overview by Race and Region, 1685–1790," in *Powhatan's Mantel: Indians in the Colonial Southeast,* ed. Peter H. Wood, Gregory A. Waselkov, and M. Thomas Hatley (Lincoln, Neb., 1989), 38; Russell Thornton, *The Cherokees: A Population History* (Lincoln, Neb., 1990) 37–54.

30. Kathryn E. Holland Braund, "The Creek Indians, Blacks, and Slavery," *JSH* 57 (1991) states that among the Creeks, "black men, at least early on, were not required to participate in . . . horticulture" (623). Her evidence shows only that Benjamin Hawkins felt that the slaves were not put to full commercial use. Elsewhere she notes that slaves, the majority of whom were men, sometimes paid tribute in crops to their Creek masters, and sometimes grew rice. They labored in the fields.

31. Perdue, *Slavery and the Evolution of Cherokee Society,* 12–16; see also John Lawson, *A New Voyage to Carolina, 1709,* ed. Hugh Talmage Lefler (Chapel Hill, N.C., 1967), 210.

32. Verner Crane, *The Southern Colonial Frontier, 1670–1732* (Ann Arbor, 1956), 139–40, 152; Perdue, *Slavery and the Evolution of Cherokee Society,* 12–16; Michael F. Doran, "Negro Slaves of the Five Civilized Tribes," *Annals of the Association of American Geographers* 68 (1978): 337; Peter Wood, "Indian Servitude in the Southeast," in *History of Indian-White Relations,* ed. Wilcomb E. Washburn, vol. 4 of *Handbook of North American Indians,* William C. Sturtevant, gen. ed. (Washington, D.C., 1988), 407–10; Daniel F. Littlefield Jr., *Africans and Creeks: From the Colonial Period to the Civil War* (Westport, Conn., 1979), 6–56; Jay K. Johnson, "The Chickasaws," and George Sabo III, "The Quapaw Indians of Arkansas," both in McEwan, *Indians of the Greater Southeast,* 85, 91–92, 185.

33. William Panton to John Leslie, Pensacola, 28 Aug. 1793, and Panton to Lachlan McGillivray, Pensacola, 10 April 1794, *McGillivray of the Creeks,* ed. John W. Caughey (Norman, Okla., 1938), 359–60, 363, but see also 171–72, 212–13; Merritt B. Pound, *Benjamin Hawkins—Indian Agent,* (Athens, Ga., 1951), 111.

34. Benjamin Hawkins, "A Sketch of the Creek Country in the Years 1798 and 1799," *Collections of the Georgia Historical Society* 3 (1848): 66; Martha Condray Searcy, "The Introduction of African Slavery into the Creek Indian Nation," *Georgia Historical Quarterly* 1 (1982): 28–30; Edward Cashin, *Lachlan McGillivray, Indian Trader: The Shaping of the Southern Frontier* (Athens, Ga., 1992), 313; Daniel H. Usner Jr., "Changing Economic Relations with Citizens and Slaves in the Mississippi Territory," *JAH* 72 (1985): 297–317.

35. Usner, "Changing Economic Relations," 306.

36. Hawkins, "A Sketch of the Creek Country," 66.

37. Pound, *Benjamin Hawkins,* 247.

38. Benjamin Gold, letter to his brother, Cornwall, Conn., New Echota, Cherokee Nation, 8 Dec. 1829, copied from Theodore S. Gold, ed., *Historical Records of the Town of Cornwall* (1904), 37–39, National Anthropological Archives, no. 4747, Smithsonian Institution.

39. Littlefield, *Africans and Creeks,* 38, 40–41, 44.

40. Mary E. Young, "Women, Civilization, and the Indian Question," in *Clio was a Woman: Studies in the History of American Women,* ed. Mabel E. Deutrich and Virginia C. Purdy (Washington, D.C., 1980), 106; Rennard Strickland, *Fire and Spirits: Cherokee Law from Clan to Court* (Norman, Okla., 1975), 93–102; and William G. McLoughlin, *Cherokee Renascence and the New Republic* (Princeton, N.J., 1987), 140–41. Choctaws enacted similar laws beginning in the 1820s; see Clara Sue Kidwell, "Choctaw Women and Cultural Persistence," in *Negotiators of Change: Historical Perspectives on Native American Women,* ed. Nancy Shoemaker (New York, 1995), 123–29.

41. Strickland, *Fire and Spirits,* 100; Perdue, *Slavery and the Evolution of Cherokee Society,* 51; McLoughlin, *Cherokee Renascence,* 225.

42. Morris Sheppard's account is in *The American Slave: A Composite Autobiography,* ed. George P. Rawick, (Westport, Conn., 1972), 7:285.

43. Perdue, *Slavery and the Evolution of Cherokee Society,* 57; McLoughlin, *Cherokee Renascence,* 396–98; Strickland, *Fire and Spirits,* 66; Perdue, "Cherokee Women and the Trail of Tears," 14–30.

44. Strickland, *Fire and Spirits,* 73–84, 96; Return Jonathan Meigs to secretary of war, Highwassie Garrison, 11 July 1808, National Archives, microfilm, M208-4.

45. Hawkins, "Journal," *Letters of Hawkins,* 40, 48, 65.

46. [Anna Gambolt and John Gambolt], "Springplace Diary, 1811–1812," trans. Elizabeth Marx, ed. William G. McLoughlin; McLoughlin, *Cherokee Ghost Dance,* 143–44.

47. Return Jonathan Meigs, "Some reflections on Cherokee concerns, manners, state &c., not a letter," in Meigs to Eustice, 19 March 1812, National Archives, microfilm, M208-5.

48. George B. Davis to Return Jonathan Meigs, Lovies, 17 Oct. 1808, National Archives, microfilm, M208-4; McLoughlin, *Cherokee Renascence,* 171.

49. Adam Hodgson, *Remarks during a Journey through North America in the Years 1819, 1820, and 1821,* ed. Samuel Whiting, (New York, 1823), 265, 268–69, 287; Joyce B. Philips and Paul Gary Philips, eds., *The Brainerd Journal: A Mission to the Cherokees, 1817–1823* (Lincoln, Neb., 1998), 279. For boys and work at the mission see 126, 268, 275.

50. Perdue, *Slavery and the Evolution of Cherokee Society,* 57; McLoughlin, *Cherokee Renascence,* 328.

51. Albert Gallatin, *A Synopsis of Indian Tribes within the United States East of the Rocky Mountains, and in the British and Russian Possessions in North America,* (1836; New York, 1973), 157–158; Perdue, *Cherokee Women,* 128.

52. See, for example, the notice by Samuel A. Worcester, New Echota, Cherokee Nation, 1830, and the "Resolution by American Board of Commissioners, United Brethren, and Baptist Missionaries," in *Cherokee Phoenix,* 1 Jan. 1831, *New Echota Letters: Contributors of Samuel A. Worcester to the Cherokee Phoenix,* ed. Jack Frederick Kilpatrick and Anna Gritts Kilpatrick (Dallas, 1968), 71–92; "The Brainerd Journal" pays little attention to Cherokee farming outside the mission.

53. Josiah Gregg, *The Commerce of the Prairies,* 4th ed. (Philadelphia, 1849), 259.

54. Doran, "Negro Slaves of the Five Civilized Tribes," 347–48.

55. Jefferson Cole, 17 March 1938, (James Russell Gray, interviewer), *The American Slave: A Composite Autobiography, Supplement,* ser. 1, 12, ed. George P. Rawick (Westport, Conn., 1977), 121–22.

56. For labor see Rawick, *The American Slave* 7:238, 258; for violence see ibid., 7:59, 117, 257, 259, 260, 289, 290.

57. Ed Butler, 17 July 1937 (Etta D. Mason, interviewer), Rawick, *The American Slave, Supplement* 12:87.

58. Kilpatrick, "The Wahnenauhi Manuscript," 201.

59. Doran, "Negro Slaves of the Five Civilized Tribes," 346–47.

60. See his Seventh (27 Oct. 1807) and Eighth (8 Nov. 1808) Annual Messages, in Richardson, *Messages* 1:428, 454.

61. Gallatin, *Synopsis,* 157–58.

Part 3

REVOLUTIONARY WORLD

CHAPTER 12

"Troubled Water"

Rebellion and Republicanism in the Revolutionary French Caribbean

Laurent Dubois

In 1802 a group of exiled French administrators seeking to isolate the insurgents who had expelled them from the island of Guadeloupe complained about the actions of North American merchants. Ignoring the blockade of the renegade regime in Guadeloupe, which was in the hands of men of African descent, such merchants readily sold goods to the island. One such merchant had been so bold, the administrators reported, as to say that "it didn't matter to him whether he was trading with blacks, yellows, or whites, as long as they had business, and that it was in troubled water that one caught the best fish." [1]

Perhaps this merchant saw a connection between the actions of the insurgents of Guadeloupe, who were rebelling against oppressive metropolitan administrators, and the revolution that had created his own country a few decades before; or perhaps he was just eager to take advantage of a complicated political situation to turn a profit. But the angry reaction of the French administrators to his actions and his statement spoke volumes about the situation of the French Caribbean at the time. Only eight years earlier, slavery had been abolished in Guadeloupe by a mission sent by the French Republic. Emancipation was the centerpiece of France's colonial policy, which tightened the legal and political bonds between the metropolis and the colony, establishing an order in which the same set of revolutionary laws were to be applied on both sides of France's Atlantic empire. This new policy, based on the elimination of distinctions between regions within the Republic, was also predicated on the elimination of racial distinctions between citizens. It was a symptom of how rapidly things were changing in 1802 that it was precisely the *lack* of respect for racial hierarchies on the part of one North American merchant that enraged French administrators. Indeed, these same administrators had written in late 1801 that the insurgents of Guadeloupe had given "new proof" of their hatred of France's consular government by "proclaiming, publishing and posting the decree of 16 Pluviôse and the Rights of Man, which they carry to all the plantations."[2]

The decree of emancipation whose distribution these administrators saw as proof of subversion was still officially the law in France, although Bonaparte's consular government was rapidly moving toward eliminating it. That it was through this decree—and the Declaration of the Rights of Man that was drawn up in 1789 as the foundation for all of the nation's future laws—that the insurgents of Guadeloupe expressed their political agenda, and that French administrators admonished them for this, illustrates the tensions and contradictions that characterized the period from 1798 to 1802 in the French Caribbean. During this period a profound shift occurred in the region, one that grew out of but ultimately destroyed a radical project of political and social transformation. Even as groups on both sides of the Atlantic rallied to defend the idea of racial equality and emancipation, powerful forces were at work pushing for the reversal of the existing colonial policies.

This essay describes the shifting policies and political choices enacted in the French Caribbean during this period by first briefly exploring the foundations and impact of the French colonial policy put into place in 1794, and then outlining how this policy was both attacked and defended at the turn of the nineteenth century. It provides a general description of the events in the French Caribbean, notably the transformations that led to the creation of the new nation of Haiti on the ashes of colonial Saint Domingue. It then concludes with some broader reflections—which I hope will complement the detailed exploration of U.S. policy toward Saint Domingue in the essay by Douglas Egerton that follows this one—about the possibilities of making connections between the French Caribbean and the United States during this period of transformation. The Jeffersonian "revolution of 1800," I hope to suggest, can be better understood when situated in relation to the major transformations that took place in the Caribbean during this period. Through the successful action of slave insurgents, the radical political project that emerged there in the early 1790s destroyed slavery and granted citizenship to all men, regardless of race. Universalist and egalitarian principles were applied in the French Caribbean to an extent that far surpassed what had taken place—perhaps even what was imaginable—in the United States. As Jefferson came to power, however, these transformations were coming under sharp attack from a variety of groups in the French Atlantic. The expansion of rights, the counterattack against this expansion, and the vigorous defense of freedom on the part of individuals of African descent in the Caribbean all had a profound defining impact on the meaning of democracy in the Atlantic world at the dawn of the nineteenth century.[3]

How did such an extreme change occur in the French Caribbean? The decree of emancipation of 1794 was the result of the transformation of slave insurgents into defenders of the French Republic. Through a process I have explored in detail elsewhere, slave insurgents and *gens de couleur* (free coloreds) in both Guadeloupe and Saint Domingue during the early 1790s began fighting—uninvited—for a besieged Republic. They did so in part by calling on and actively aiding Republican officials from the metropolis who found themselves attacked by royalist, proslavery whites anxious about the implications of the increasingly radical policies of the Revolution. In a particularly illustrative incident in Guadeloupe in 1793, rebellious slaves, after killing most of the whites in the town of Trois-Rivières, actually presented themselves to local officials and boldly claimed that they had done what they had to save the white patriots of the island and serve the Republic.

What drove the major transformations of the period, however, were the massive uprisings that took place in parallel in Saint Domingue during the same period.[4] An early insurrection took place there in October 1790, when a group of *gens de couleur*—free coloreds—under the leadership of Vincent Ogé took up arms demanding political equality and an end to the forms of racial exclusion that had been built into the legal order of the colony. The brutal repression of their revolt in October 1790, after which Ogé and other leaders were tortured and killed, helped propel the first set of concessions to the *gens de couleur* by the metropolitan government—a May 1791 decree granted political equality to those *gens de couleur* men born of two free parents. This new law still excluded the majority of *gens de couleur*—it in fact applied to only about five hundred individuals in Saint Domingue—but it nevertheless enraged many white planters in the colony. It was all the French revolutionary government had managed to do, however, in addressing the major political contradictions represented by the colonial order, by late 1791.

Everything changed in August of that year, when the slaves of the northern province of Saint Domingue began what became the largest and most successful slave revolt in history. Burning the rich cane fields of one of the most profitable plantation regions in the Americas, they killed many whites, forced many others to flee to the capital of Le Cap, and constituted themselves into a formidable rebel force. They were aided by the Spanish, who, from across the border in Santo Domingo, supplied weapons, and eventually military commissions, to groups of insurgents. The revolt completely changed the terms of political debate in the metropolis. As Robin Blackburn has noted, "Like the first tremors of an earthquake the slave revolt had shaken every colonial institution, leveling a few structures but also weakening those which remained standing. The argument about mulattoes' rights had been transformed by the sight of the smoke rising from burnt-out plantation buildings and cane fields." Some *gens de couleur* representatives, drawing on their long history of service in the island's militia, argued that they were the only bulwark against the slave insurrection; in the new situation, many in the metropolis were receptive to the argument. In April 1792 the National Assembly granted full political rights to all *gens de couleur*.[5]

It was not to be the last time citizenship was extended to a previously excluded group in an attempt to save the colony for the Republic. The metropolitan commissioner Légér Félicité Sonthonax, sent to Saint Domingue to institute the April decree, increasingly alienated planters there as he recruited large numbers of *gens de couleur*—now called "new citizens"—into his regime. With war exploding between Britain and France, planters made increasingly open overtures to the British in the hope that an occupation by this power could preserve the rapidly crumbling slave system. Slave insurgents, many of them fighting as "auxiliaries" for Spain, survived the French missions sent against them. In May 1793 an uprising in Le Cap threatened Sonthonax, and he invited a group of slave insurgents camped outside the city to come to his assistance in return for freedom and citizenship. They responded, falling on Sonthonax's enemies and quickly overcoming them. A seemingly unstoppable process had been set in motion, and Sonthonax expanded his offer to larger and larger groups of insurgents and their families as a way of securing Republican control on the island. Soon he decreed an outright abolition of slavery in the north province, and his colleague did the same in the rest of Saint Domingue. The heroism of the republican ex-slaves of Saint Domingue, presented to the National Convention in February 1794, propelled the declaration of France's emancipation decree. It was the culmination of what we might call the first phase of the Haitian Revolution, one in which—in a curious reversal of what would happen a decade later—planters had sought autonomy and even independence for the colony, while slave insurgents had formed an alliance with the metropolis that saved the colony for France.[6]

Within the French Caribbean the advent of emancipation and the particular process through which it occurred ushered in a profound shift in the terms of political and social power. The majority of the planters, once the forceful lords of the plantations and the entire society, had been politically discredited by their anti-Republican and anti-metropolitan activity (inspired in part by the example of their neighbors to the north, who had escaped from colonial control and maintained slavery). And large numbers of them had been either massacred or forced into exile. The slaves, once nothing more than legal objects and sources of labor, now served as citizen-soldiers, having already proved the central importance as guarantors of the Republic. They had made the republicanism of the age their own, and in so doing propelled it in new directions.

The mobilization of ex-slave troops was in fact a powerful weapon for France throughout the Caribbean region. A small mission of French Republicans managed to take back Guadeloupe from the British, who had occupied it a few months before, by spreading the news of emancipation and recruiting slaves into their ranks. Soon Guadeloupe became a base for attacks against Saint Lucia, Grenada, and Saint Vincent. In these campaigns, French troops comprised of whites, *gens de couleur,* and ex-slaves allied themselves with slaves on the islands, as well as with groups such as the Black Caribs of Saint Vincent. In both Saint Domingue and Guadeloupe (which were the centers of the revolutionary French Caribbean, since Martinique was occupied by the British during the entire period), the army became a central site for the social rise and political mobilization of both *gens de couleur* and ex-slaves. Thousands of ex-slaves acquired new identities through their military careers. In addition to the economic support they gained from their service—which could be significant especially for those who served on the Republican corsairs and were paid with a portion of the loot from the ships they captured—they gained the dignity of being soldiers and defenders of the Republic. The more visible officers, such as Toussaint Louverture and Jean-Jacques Dessalines in Saint Domingue and Louis Delgrès and Magloire Pélage in the Eastern Caribbean, also became political leaders who played central roles in the struggles of the late 1790s and early 1800s. In a context in which the freedom of the ex-slaves on the plantations was often limited in a variety of ways, officers of African descent were the most visible examples of the success of the policies of republican emancipation and assimilation. The fact that they were loyal servants of the Republic, however, also enabled them to issue and defend claims to power and equality that were received with increasing hostility by metropolitan administratos and politicians as the French Revolution grew more reactionary.

At the same time, in Paris itself, several individuals of African descent served in the various Parliaments that succeeded one another during these years. Perhaps the best known of these, because of the famous portrait of him by Anne-Louis Girodet, was the African-born Jean-Baptiste Belley. He was elected in 1793 in Saint Domingue, was one of those who propelled the abolition of slavery in 1794 in Paris, and continued to serve until 1798. But there were others as well, notably the free coloreds Etienne Mentor and Pierre Thomany, who served in the *Conseil des 500* after 1798. Mentor was allied with a number of metropolitan Republicans, most notably Etienne Laveaux, who as an officer in Saint Domingue in the mid-1790s had been an important ally to Toussaint Louverture, and had been instrumental in his rise to power on the island.[7]

The period from 1794 to 1798 can be seen as the second phase of the Haitian Revolution, a time in which the principles of racial equality and emancipation were implemented and drove powerful social and political transformations in Saint Domingue. But by the end of the 1790s, in the midst of increasingly conservative political context in the metropolis, exiled planters and other proslavery advocates who saw the policies of slave emancipation as a disaster started to find a receptive audience in certain sectors of the metropolitan government. As the metropolitan regimes of the late 1790s and early 1800s began to dismantle the republican project of emancipation, Antillean officers and political figures on both sides of the Atlantic rallied to defend it, at first within the structures of republican empire but ultimately by declaring war against the French metropolis. It was the slow dismantling of the French republican regime of emancipation, and the various attempts on the part of the people of the French Caribbean to guarantee the freedom they had gained, that began the last phase of the Haitian Revolution, which ultimately led to brutal wars in the French Caribbean and the birth of a new nation.

We can get a good picture of the beginnings of this process from events that took place in 1798 and 1799, when two very different visions of the colonies collided. In February 1799 the decree of abolition of slavery was five years old, and its defenders united to commemorate what had been done in 1794. In a speech at an anniversary celebration, Etienne Laveaux proclaimed, "On the 16 Pluviôse, the Republic achieved a conquest of a kind that until then was unknown. She conquered, or rather created, for the *human race,* through a single powerful idea, a million new beings, and so expanded the family of man." "In our colonies, *everything is French. This system of absolute unity* makes our disconcerted enemies go pale with rage," he continued, "and from it the signal for colonial prosperity will be sent." The British had lost thousands of soldiers trying to take over Saint Domingue; "but all paled in front of the loyalty of those men that the 16 Pluviôse made French citizens." The chief architect of the preservation of the colonies was, Laveaux claimed, Toussaint Louverture, who was "intimately linked to the Republic" and "penetrated" with the principle that the colonies were an integral part of that Republic. The people of Saint Domingue "never have, and never will, lose sight of the glorious title of the French citizens," and they had proven that through their liberty the colonies could be preserved and commerce could prosper. The deputy Thomany similarly argued that the history of the Caribbean had shown that "the French have no friends more impassioned, the Republic has no citizen more zealous, than he who has become free." [8]

There were others, however, who had a very different vision of the place Antilleans were to have in the French imperial order. In May 1798 the minister of the colonies, a planter from Saint Domingue named Baron de Bruix had sent out a call for the creation of a segregated military unit that would regroup all of the "black or colored" soldiers in metropolitan France. This included all soldiers of African descent serving in the French armies in Europe, not only those from the French colonies—one such soldier, named Henry Fruchon, had in fact been born in Philadelphia. The soldiers who reported for duty for this new unit were subjected to various indignities, including several demotions, and there were many illnesses and a few deaths among the troops. Many of them wrote to deputy Mentor asking him to intervene on their behalf. Mentor took up their case in Parliament, sharply attacking the formation of the battalion, arguing that it set up a situation in which these soldiers were "isolated from their European comrades, so that it seems that they are being punished for having supported, in the New World, the principles of the Republic." How could governors dare "to re-establish such insulting distinctions"? Mentor's intervention was convincing to the other representatives; his proposition to retract the order was "unanimously adopted." Soon afterward, Bruix was relieved of his functions. [9]

Etienne Laveaux and the others who defended republican emancipation also won other victories. In 1797 Laveaux drew up a law on the colonies, which was passed in January 1798. This law affirmed the juridical assimilation between metropolis and colony, and gave those ex-slaves who had fought in the Republican armies a dispensation from the poll tax that would have prevented most of them from voting. Indeed, Laveaux had even argued that all those who worked on the plantations should also be given such a dispensation, since they were just as central to the defense of the colonies as soldiers were. The law as it ultimately passed did not include this latter provision, however. Although quite radical in its intent, the law as it was eventually applied in the colonies was weakened by one crucial loophole that undermined the principle of unity between metropolitan and colonial juridical structures. While it was declared that all laws decreed for the "continental departments" were in principle applicable to the colonies, it was added that the government and their representatives could selectively apply them. As a result, the majority of the ex-slaves of the Caribbean essentially experienced only the more oppressive aspects of the law, which tied their citizenship to their continuing labor on the plantations. The law also facilitated the return of certain émigrés, and so accelerated the return of ex-masters to their plantations. Ironically, the application of a law originally meant to tighten the bonds of the metropolis and colony into a "system of absolute unity" ultimately did the opposite, propelling the centrifugal forces that ultimately brought the ex-slaves of the Caribbean into a violent conflict with metropolitan forces.[10]

The agent who left France to apply the new law in Saint Domingue, General Hédouville, was given explicit orders to limit the power of Toussaint Louverture, which was causing growing anxiety in the metropolis, especially among planters and their allies. Indeed, after having expelled Sonthonax from the island, and with Julien Raimond, the last of the commissioners, deferring to his authority, Louverture had become the de facto ruler of the colony. On his arrival Hédouville pushed Louverture to resign and gave his support to his main rival, André Rigaud. He also replaced black troops with white ones in strategic locations, antagonized *cultivateurs* by issuing a decree that required them to sign contracts on their plantations, and ordered the punishment of all "vagabonds." These measures incited revolt, particularly in the south province, where Hédouville put them down with the help of Rigaud. In the north province Hédouville arrested Moïse, a commander who was popular among *cultivateurs*. Moïse escaped and mobilized an army of *cultivateurs* to attack Hédouville, and Louverture gave orders to arrest and expel the French agent. Hédouville's mission deepened the conflict between Rigaud and Louverture, which exploded in the next years into a bloody civil war.[11]

In struggling against Rigaud, Louverture turned to Britain and the United States for supplies and weapons, boldly going against the current of metropolitan policy and developing an autonomous foreign policy. The U.S. Navy helped Louverture and his General Jean-Jacques Dessalines by blockading the port of Jacmel in order to isolate Rigaud in the south. Dessalines, however, made clear that he considered himself and his army equals to the United States. When a U.S. ship mistakenly captured and detained a white officer who was fighting with him, Dessalines wrote angrily to the captain of the ship that he should remember that he had made a "treaty with an open and frank nation." Louverture, in the conciliatory letters he soon wrote apologizing for Dessalines's angry words, noted that he wished to avoid anything that would "tend to disturb the good understanding between our two Nations." Although he expressed no intention of separating from the Republic, the fact that Louverture was dealing directly with foreign representatives alarmed French metropolitan authorities. During this period, Louverture also struggled to rebuild the plantation economy of Saint Domingue and instituted labor laws that, like those instituted by Sonthonax in 1793 and administrators in Guadeloupe after 1794, required ex-slaves to keep working on their former plantations in return for a portion of the plantation production. Louverture granted plantations to officers in the army and enforced his labor regime with military courts and strict punishment. He was, in fact, successful at rebuilding the economy of Saint Domingue, which allowed him to continue purchasing weapons and ammunition from U.S. merchants.[12]

Into this already tense situation stepped Napoleon Bonaparte, whose rise to power after the coup d'état of 1799 profoundly shifted the terms of metropolitan colonial policy. Bonaparte staffed the ministry of the colonies with a number of figures who had defended slavery in the early 1790s. They included Barbé-Marbois, who had been an *intendant* in Saint Domingue in 1789 and retained royalist sympathies throughout the Revolution, and Pierre Malouet, a property owner from Saint Domingue who was a member of the proslavery Club Massiac in 1791 and in 1793 led the negotiations through which the planters of Saint Domingue offered to hand the colony over to the British. Also part of the new ministry was Moreau de Saint-Méry, who, in exile in Philadelphia in 1797, had published his magisterial *Description* of colonial Saint Domingue, lamenting that the prosperous colony he described had been destroyed since 1789. Perhaps, he noted then, the details he provided might help in making the colony back into what it once had been. In December 1799 Bonaparte issued a proclamation to the "Brave Blacks of St. Domingue," assuring them that the de-cree of 1794 would be maintained. His proclamation also, however, announced the promulgation of the year 8 constitution, which explicitly abandoned the policy of integrating metropolis and colony and announced that a particular set of laws would be created for each colony. This signaled a profound transforma-tion in the political situation of the Caribbean: the inhabitants of the colonies would no longer have the same rights as those of the metropolis, and the colo-nies would no longer have representatives in the French Parliament.[13]

Three agents were dispatched by Bonaparte to Saint Domingue to apply his new constitution there. Since there was no mention of emancipation in the constitution, Bonaparte gave his envoys a statement making assurances that the freedom of the ex-slaves would not be taken away. Louverture responded to the new constitution's policy of juridical separation by producing his own con-stitution for Saint Domingue, which defined the "territory" of Saint Domingue a colony "which is part of the French empire but is governed by a particular set of laws." The constitution guaranteed "the individual property of people and the liberty of the negroes, the *gens de couleur* and all people" and declared that "slaves are not permitted in this territory" and that "slavery is forever abol-ished." "All men born in this land live and die free, French men."[14]

Although it was in many ways simply what C.L.R. James called the "formal embodiment" of the regime of autonomy he had been building since at least 1798, Louverture's constitution enraged Bonaparte. In making Louverture the "governor for life" of the island, it made him, and the colony of Saint Domin-gue, equal to Bonaparte and France. In declaring that all its citizens would be both "free" and "French," it also posed a challenge to Bonaparte's ultimate wish to return the colonial system to what it once had been. Within Saint Domingue *cultivateurs* revolted against the constitution's labor policies, but Louverture steadfastly crushed the revolt and executed its leader, Moïse. These internal conflicts presaged those that would explode during the war against the French that would soon begin. For having learned of Louverture's new constitution, Bonaparte sent a massive expedition to Saint Domingue under the command of General Leclerc with the mission to crush his power.[15]

By then the international situation had changed in ways that were to have a profound impact on the Caribbean. In the fall of 1801 Henry Addington and Charles Talleyrand-Périgord began the negotiations that would lead to the Treaty of Amiens, which in 1802 would officially end the war between France and Britain. Addington raised the issue of Saint Domingue, noting that he expected that France would send troops to "reestablish completely the authority of the metropolis." He added that the British might also have to send reinforcements to the Caribbean, and that since the object of the two nations was to maintain order in their "respective possessions," the governments should keep one another informed of their missions. A few weeks later, Addington said, "The interests of the two governments is absolutely the same: the destruction of Jacobinism, and above all that of the Blacks." As news of Louverture's constitution and the insurrections in Guadeloupe arrived in Europe, the mission of the projected expedition to the Antilles increasingly was cast in terms of the reestablishment of metropolitan power over rebellious black leaders. Talleyrand wrote that "the interest of civilization in general is to destroy the new Alger that is organizing itself in the center of America."[16]

After the preliminaries of the Treaty of Amiens were signed in October 1801, Bonaparte announced that the whites in the French possessions where slavery had not been abolished—both those in the Indian Ocean who had refused emancipation and those in the Caribbean who had been in the hands of the British—"did not need to fear the liberation of the slaves."[17] No public decision was made at the time regarding the future of those colonies where slavery had been abolished. But when Leclerc left for Saint Domingue in November 1801, he was carrying special orders from Bonaparte instructing him to disarm the black armies and prepare the return of slavery. As Carolyn Fick writes, on his arrival in Saint Domingue, Leclerc was to "win over the black generals with assurances of his peaceful intentions and good will," telling them that his massive expedition had come only to "protect the colony" and "preserve its peace and tranquillity." Once they had gained control of the port cities and landed their forces, the French troops were to "wage an unremitting war against the black army generals" such as Louverture and Dessalines. Finally, once the morale of the army was broken, the "entire black population was to be disarmed, forced back onto the plantations, and the groundwork laid for the restoration of slavery." Bonaparte famously commanded, "Do not allow any blacks having held a rank above that of captain to remain on the island." The "secret instructions" given to Leclerc had their parallel in orders given to the General Richepanse, who was sent to Guadeloupe during the same period.[18]

The metropolitan government had made a clear choice to retreat from the republican polices of emancipation that had been the hallmark of French colonial policy for the preceding years. But how would the republicans of the Antilles react? They were faced with a profoundly difficult choice. The French

Republic had, since 1794, rallied to the struggle for emancipation, and had provided the context for the promotion and rise to positions of leadership of ex-slaves and free coloreds of the colonies. Once France began retreating from these policies, the potent combination embodied in France's emancipatory colonial policies was fractured. To defend the republican policies of the previous years meant to struggle against France. If the choice was not difficult in enough in principle, the situation on the ground made choosing even more difficult. For Leclerc's instructions were indeed intentionally kept secret, as were Richepanse's. The French commanders deliberately hid their intentions, and the citizens of the colonies were not always able to see the real goals of the French administration. Many expressed and demonstrated a profound loyalty to France, blaming local administrators for errors they assumed would be corrected by the benevolent leaders in Paris. Ultimately, many in both Saint Domingue and Guadeloupe took up arms against the French. In Guadeloupe they were defeated in May 1802, but in Saint Domingue, after two years of struggle, they defeated the French and created the new nation of Haiti, founded on the policy of emancipation that had been produced there in 1793 and became the law of the French empire in 1794.

After defeating the insurgents in Guadeloupe, General Richepanse was convinced that the preservation of the colony depended on the elimination of all former slaves or *gens de couleur* who had served the army. Accordingly, he had over a thousand *hommes de couleur* and *noirs* who had been "part of the armed forces" and were "recognized in the colony as dangerous men" arrested and placed on a convoy of ships that was ordered to drop them off in New York. Some of these ships seem to have stopped off Le Cap, where prisoners who escaped from the ships spread the news of the brutality of the French in Guadeloupe and the reestablishment of slavery there. This helped spur leaders such as Jean-Jacques Dessalines and Henri Christophe to turn against the French in Saint Domingue, and was therefore a turning point in the long struggle for independence that created Haiti. The rest of the imprisoned insurgents from Guadeloupe, however, spent months on ships as their captains searched for a good place to get rid of their unruly cargo. In fact, several months after the deportation an administrator from Guadeloupe sent orders to the commander of the prison convoy ordering him, if the previous plan had failed, "to use all means possible to get rid of the deportees," including leaving them on unpopulated beaches along the U.S. coast. It was probably these French ships that appeared in the "waters of the Gulf" in an attempt to "sell renegade negroes," and

that helped troubled James Monroe in his attempt to deport some of those convicted of participating in Gabriel's Rebellion.[19]

This story suggests some of the ways in which events in the French Caribbean ended up affecting events in the United States. It can therefore serve to
open up some broader questions with which I wish to conclude this essay. How
did the United States react to events in the French Caribbean during the 1790s
and early 1800s? In what ways was the French experiment in slave emancipation
during the 1790s, and its ultimate disintegration in the early 1800s, connected to
and refracted in debates in the United States? Certain aspects of these questions
have been answered by scholars. The insurrection of 1791 that shattered the colonial economy in Saint Domingue had a profound impact in North America,
frightening slave owners and inspiring slaves, and sending some of both groups
fleeing into towns like Philadelphia and Charleston. This migration had multiple effects in the United States—humanitarian efforts on the part of white
refugees, fears of contagion in Philadelphia in 1793, mobilization on the part
of abolitionists for the rights to freedom of those slaves who were part of the
emigration, laws regulating the movement of people of African descent, even
temporary cessation of the slave trade in certain places. At the other end of
the epoch, the ultimately independence of Haiti also had well-known consequences, most notably the setting of a policy of isolation of the new black republic—which lasted until Charles Sumner led its destruction in 1862—a policy put in place by the collaboration of the United States with Britain and, of
course, France, all of which sought to contain the ramifications of this new nation's threatening arrival. In both these periods, events in the French Caribbean
and particularly in Saint Domingue sent shockwaves through the plantation societies of the U.S. South and served as an example for slaves such as Gabriel, because they represented a threat to the slave system of a degree and extent that
had never been seen before.[20]

Reactions to the revolutions in the French Caribbean varied between different social groups in the United States. Northern merchants who wished
to trade in the French Caribbean had very different interests from southern
planters, whose chief concern was avoiding the contagion of rebellion among
their own slaves. Thomas Jefferson had to confront and deal with these various
northern interests. His policies toward the French Caribbean were also profoundly influenced by his desire to acquire Louisiana. From month to month
and year to year, the changing situation in the French Caribbean elicited varied
and complex responses in the United States. Jefferson ultimately contributed to

aiding the rebellion against France in Saint Domingue, and then pioneered the policies of isolation that would profoundly affect Haiti during the first half of the nineteenth century.[21]

In both the French Caribbean and the United States the 1790s were a decade of profound transformation of political identities and institutions, and in both contexts the question of slavery was crucial in defining the possibilities and limits of democracy and the idea of rights. Both regions faced parallel problems, and yet the approaches of political leaders to these problems were ultimately quite different. To understand this difference and its significance requires moving beyond a focus on the fears incited by slave insurrection in the Caribbean and toward a deeper analysis of the new political visions that emerged from such insurrection. To put it another way, the existence of the slave revolt in 1791, and the circulation of news about it in slave communities, posed an obvious threat to slaveholders everywhere. What happened in 1793 and 1794, when the French Republic essentially ratified the actions of these insurgents by proclaiming emancipation throughout its empire, was in a sense even more threatening. What was unique in the French Caribbean was the rise of a class of ex-slave and *gens de couleur* political leaders who not only took leading roles in military, economic, and diplomatic choices in the Caribbean, but also were important participants in the formation of metropolitan policy in France itself. These figures, first as insurgents and then as representatives of the "new citizens" of the colonies, helped created a particular political formation with far-reaching implications.

The 1794 decree of emancipation instituted a completely new relationship between metropolis and colony, one that was strikingly different from the compromise reached in the United States after independence. In the French case the emancipation decree was the victory of an argument that basic rights had to be applied universally and without distinction in all territorial regions of France. This argument was articulated in the early 1790s by members of the *Société des Amis des Noirs* and *gens de couleur* activists in Paris, who argued that all *free* people, regardless of race, should have the same rights in the Caribbean as in metropolitan France. This shift in policy had a profound meaning in the reigning context of the late-eighteenth-century Atlantic world. Imperial relations in North America had, obviously, been predicated on legal distinctions between colonies and the metropolis; the same was true in the Spanish case. Furthermore, in North America various regimes of slavery coexisted within one nation. The French revolutionary policy was very different, declaring that "universal" laws necessitated the interlinked ending of slavery and juridical differentiation.

The changes that took place in the French Caribbean during this period, then, represented a fundamental break with, and a challenge to, what had come before, because it represented a radical new approach to the problem of governance, the application of rights, and the issue of slavery that was so central in both the Caribbean and the United States.

The particular way in which this new policy came into being was also remarkable, since it involved alliances between metropolitan officials and slave insurgents. When Gabriel sought to organize his 1800 revolt with the idea that slave insurgents would find allies with republican whites, he was perhaps drawing not only on the inspiration provided by the success of insurgents in the Caribbean but more particularly on the exact form through which this success had taken place. Often we cannot know the exact information that traveled along the routes of communication that tied slave communities of the Atlantic world, having only imperfect echoes of them in the written record (notably in newspapers), but there is a good chance that the particular mechanics of the slave victory in the French Caribbean would have been known in at least some of its details. In May 1793, for instance, a ship bound from Guadeloupe for Portland stopped in Baltimore and reported that "the negroes had killed a number of whites of that island a few days before the brig leaving that place." This report was then published in the *Philadelphia General Advertiser*. The event being described was almost certainly the revolt at Trois-Rivières. If the newspaper published a much reduced narrative of the events (and did not mention the fact that republican whites had actually lauded the actions of the slaves), the conversations between various members of the ship's crew and others in Baltimore could well have been more developed and included more details about the alliances between slaves and republicans in this particular case. With artisans in places like Richmond inspired by the example of the French Revolution, the specific examples of the alliances that had had such a profound impact in the French Caribbean could have been an inspiration for the kinds of plans made by Gabriel in 1800.[22]

During the 1790s and early 1800s the French Caribbean was the site of an enormously radical experiment in emancipation, followed by a brutal, and at least in Haiti ultimately failed, attempt to reverse this history. What would have happened if Bonaparte had not embarked on his plan to reestablish slavery in Saint Domingue? Would the history of the United States have been different? In answering this question we can follow the diplomat Talleyrand into a brief foray into counterfactual history. In 1801, in the midst of his negotiations with Britain, Talleyrand briefly imagined what might happen if Bonaparte opted to ally himself with Toussaint Louverture instead of attacking him. If he were to "recognize Toussaint," and "constitute French blacks," in Saint Domingue, Talleyrand mused, commerce would certainly suffer, but the "military force" of France would gain a great advantage. "The government of the Blacks recognized in St. Domingue and legitimated by the French would be in all times an incredible point for action in the New World." One can imagine that Bonaparte and Louverture together would have been fearsome allies, endangering the British colonies of the Caribbean as they mobilized armies of black citizen-soldiers to expand the French holdings in the region. Perhaps Louisiana, which had remained chronically unsettled under its earlier French rule and had recently been ceded back to France, could have been settled and developed with ex-slaves who would have been eager for land, just as one writer who had advocated bringing Africans to the colony and transforming them into "true citizens of Louisiana" had imagined in the 1760s. Of course it may be true that in the long term little would have changed, for the presence of a region populated by free ex-slaves on the border of the United States would probably have incited invasion in the long run.[23]

But remembering that there could have been other outcomes—that there were other political possibilities available to the leaders of the time—can help us better perceive the profound nature of the choices made during this period to close down the radical possibilities for freedom and racial equality that had briefly opened up during the 1790s. During this period republicans—some of them owners of slaves, and others slaves themselves—struggled over the meaning of citizenship, over their future and the future of their communities. Ultimately the sweeping vision of racial equality that briefly took hold in the French Caribbean of the 1790s was contained, and then pushed back. It was maintained in some ways in the war-scarred world of post-independence Haiti, and in the minds of slaves throughout the Americas. But it would take many years—and many dead—to bring the remaining colonies of the Caribbean and the United States to the point at which the colonies of the French Caribbean stood briefly in the middle of the 1790s—to a world in which the promise of full citizenship was held out to all people, of all races.

NOTES

1. Lacrosse and Lescallier to Minister, 7 Floréal An 10 (27 April 1802), Archives Nationales—Section Outre-Mer (hereafter ANSOM) C[7A] 56, 5–7.

2. Lacrosse to Minister, 26 Frimaire An 10 (17 Dec. 1801) in ANSOM C[7A] 55, 102–5.

3. I draw in this essay on my broader work on the Revolutionary French Caribbean: *A Colony of Citizens: Revolution and Slave Emancipation in the French Caribbean, 1787–1804* (Chapel Hill, N.C., forthcoming); *Les Esclaves de la République: l'histoire oubliée de la première émancipation, 1789–1794* (Paris, 1998); "'The Price of Liberty': Victor Hugues and the Administration of Freedom in Guadeloupe, 1794–1798," *WMQ* 3d ser., 56 (1999): 363–92.

4. The literature on the Haitian Revolution is extensive; for the following discussion I draw on Carolyn Fick, *The Making of Haiti: The Saint-Domingue Revolution from Below* (Knoxville, Tenn., 1990); C.L.R. James, *The Black Jacobins: Toussaint L'Ouverture and the San Domingo Revolution,* 2d ed. (New York, 1963); David P. Geggus, *Slavery, War, and Revolution, The British Occupation of Saint Domingue, 1793–1798* (New York, 1982); and Robin Blackburn, *The Overthrow of Colonial Slavery* (London, 1989). For the best brief overview of the Haitian Revolution see David P. Geggus, "The Haitian Revolution," in *The Modern Caribbean,* ed. Franklin Knight and Colin Palmer (Chapel Hill, N.C., 1989), 111–28.

5. See Blackburn, *Overthrow of Colonial Slavery,* 206. On the *gens de couleur* and the tradition of militia service, see John Garrigus, "Redrawing the Colour Line: Gender and the Social Construction of Race in Pre-Revolutionary Haiti," *Journal of Caribbean History* 30 (1996): 28–50.

6. This process is described in detail in Fick, *The Making of Haiti,* esp. 161–63, as well as in Robert Louis Stein, *Légér Félicité Sonthonax: The Lost Sentinel of the Republic* (London, 1985).

7. On Belley's portrait see Helen Weston, "Representing the Right to Represent: The Portrait of Citizen Belley, Ex-Representative of the Colonies by A. L. Girodet," *Res* 26 (1994): 83–109; on Mentor and his allies, see Marcel Dorigny and Bernard Gainot, *La Société des Amis des Noirs, 1788–1799: Contribution à l'histoire de l'abolition de l'esclavage* (Paris, 1998). The relationship between Laveaux and Louverture is documented in a series of letters written between them which are in the Bibliothèque Nationale (BN), Manuscrits Occidentaux, France, Nouvelles Acquisitions, 6894, and 12101 T. 1–3.

8. "Discours prononcé par Laveaux, sur l'anniversaire du 16 Pluviôse An 2," Corps Législatif, Conseil des Anciens; "Motion d'ordre, faite par P. Thomany, Député du Département du Nord, sur l'anniversaire de la liberté des noirs dans les colonies Françaises," Corps Législatif, Conseil des Cinq Cents, both from 16 Pluviôse An 7 (4 Feb. 1799), located in the Bibliothèque Nationale, Paris.

9. "Motion d'ordre faite par Mentor," AN AD^{VII} 21A, #52; on the company see the law from 3 Prairial An 6 (22 May 1798), AN AD^{VII} 20B; see also documents in Archives Historiques de l'Armée de Terre, Vincennes (AHAT) X^i, Carton 80; on the letters sent by the soldiers, see Mentor's angry letter to the Baron de Bruix, from 21 Ventôse An 7 (10 March 1799), reprinted in Dorigny and Gainot, *La Société,* 385–92.

10. See Bernard Gainot, "La constitutionalisation de la liberté générale sous le Directoire," *Les Abolitions de l'esclavage de L. F. Sonthonax à V. Schoelcher, 1793, 1794, 1848,* ed. Marcel Dorigny (Paris, 1995), 213–29. For the law see "Loi concernant l'organisation constitutionelle des colonies," 12 Nivôse An 6 (1 Jan. 1798), AN AD VII 20A.

11. On this period in Saint-Domingue, see Fick, *The Making of Haiti,* 196–203; James, *Black Jacobins,* 188–208.

12. The correspondence between Dessalines, Toussaint Louverture, and Captain Perry is in the Clements Library, Perry Papers, vol. 1; in addition to the sources noted above, see also Mats Lundahl, "Toussaint L'Ouverture and the War Economy of Saint-Domingue, 1796–1802," *Slavery and Abolition* 6 (Sept. 1985): 122–38.

13. Yves Benot, "Bonaparte et la démence coloniale (1799–1804)," in *Mourir pour les Antilles: Indépendance nègre ou esclavage, 1802–1804,* ed. Michel Martin and Alain Yacou (Paris, 1991), and *La démence coloniale sous Napoléon* (Paris, 1991); Louis Médéric Moreau de St.-Mery, *Description topographique, physique, civile, politique et historique de la partie française de Saint-Domingue* (1797; rept. Paris, 1959) 1:5–7; Fick, *The Making of Haiti,* 204–5.

14. See the "Constitution Française des Colonies de Saint-Domingue," Cap-Français, 13 Messidor An 9 (2 July 1801), BN; see also Fick, *The Making of Haiti,* 204–6.

15. See James, *The Black Jacobins,* 263–66, 275–78; Fick, *The Making of Haiti,* 206–8; the best history of the expedition is Claude B. Auguste and Marcel B. Auguste, *L'expedition Leclerc, 1801–1803* (Port-au-Prince, 1985).

16. Benot, "La démence coloniale," 20–22.

17. Germain Saint-Ruf, *L'Epopée Delgrès: La Guadeloupe sous la Révolution française (1789–1802)* (Paris, 1977), 88; see also the correspondence relating to this in Minister to Lacrosse, 25 Vendémiaire An 10 (17 Oct. 1801), and Lacrosse to Minister, 26 Frimaire An 10 (17 Dec. 1801) in ANSOM C^{7A} 55, 267, 102–5.

18. Fick, *The Making of Haiti,* 210; for the instructions see *Lettres du général Leclerc, commandant en chef de l'armée de Saint-Domingue en 1802* (Paris, 1937), 264–75; see also Auguste and Auguste, *L'expédition Leclerc.*

19. Richepanse to Minister, 11 Prairial An 10 (31 May 1802), ANSOM C^{7A} 57, 1; Lacrosse to Minister, 1 Vendémiaire An 11 (23 Sept. 1802), ANSOM C^{7A} 56, 157–158; Douglas R. Egerton, *Gabriel's Rebellion: The Virginia Slave Conspiracies of 1800 and 1802* (Chapel Hill, N.C., 1993), 158.

20. The best study of the impact of the news of events in Saint Domingue is Julius Scott's "The Common Wind: Currents of Afro-American Communication in the Era of the Haitian Revolution" (Ph.D. diss., Duke University, 1986); on Haitians in Philadelphia see Gary B. Nash, *Forging Freedom: The Formation of Philadelphia's Black Community* (Cambridge, Mass., 1988), 140–42, 174–76; on the general reaction in the U.S. South see Alfred N. Hunt, *Haiti's Influence on Antebellum America: Slumbering Volcano in the Caribbean* (Baton Rouge, 1988); on Gabriel's rebellion see Egerton, *Gabriel's Rebellion,* and James Sidbury, *Ploughshares into Swords: Race, Rebellion and Identity in Gabriel's Virginia, 1730–1810* (Cambridge, Mass., 1998), as well as his "Saint Domingue in Virginia: Ideology, Local Meanings, and Resistance to Slavery, 1790–1800" *JSH* 63 (1997): 531–552.

21. See Tim Matthewson, "Jefferson and Haiti," *JSH* 61 (1995): 209–47.

22. *Philadelphia General Advertiser* 835, 31 May 1793; see Egerton, *Gabriel's Rebellion,* Sidbury, *Ploughshares,* and Scott, "The Common Wind," as well as "Afro-American Sailors and the International Communication Network: The Case of Newport Bowers," in *Jack Tar in History: Essays in the History of Maritime Life and Labour,* ed. Colin Howell and Richard Twomey (Fredericton, New Brunswick, N.J., 1991), 37–52; Julius Scott, "Crisscrossing Empires: Ships, Sailors and Resistance in the Lesser Antilles in the Eighteenth Century," in *The Lesser Antilles in the Age of European Expansion,* ed. Robert Paquette and Stanley Engerman (Gainesville, Fla., 1996), 128–46.

23. Benot, "La démence coloniale," 23, 35; on the idea of colonizing Louisiana with Africans see Edward Seeber, *Anti-slavery Opinion in France during the Second Half of the Eighteenth Century* (Baltimore, 1937), 99. My thanks to the participants in the "Revolution of 1800" conference, particularly Jim Sidbury and Douglas Egerton, who helped me walk through this counterfactual exercise.

CHAPTER 13

The Empire of Liberty Reconsidered

Douglas R. Egerton

One month after retiring from the presidency, Thomas Jefferson gazed back with satisfaction on his tenure in the executive mansion. The Republican victory of 1800 began a peaceful march westward, he mused, that established "such an empire for liberty as [the world] has never surveyed since the creation." The Virginian was so enamored of this oft-repeated phrase that it came to define his foreign policy and gave title to influential modern studies of his diplomacy.[1]

This essay suggests, however, that a North American, perhaps even a hemispheric, empire of liberty, would have been better served by the re-election of John Adams. Expansion into the American Midwest was sure to have continued regardless of what party controlled Washington. But with Adams in power the Louisiana Territory might have arrived on very different terms, due to Federalist detente with Toussaint Louverture. President Jefferson's willingness to support Napoleon Bonaparte's 1802 invasion of Saint Domingue has been well documented. Yet historians rarely pause to consider how a Federalist victory could have altered that unhappy scenario. Haitian independence in, say, 1801 under a President Louverture, protected by an Anglo-American naval agreement, might have prevented the final implementation of the treaty of San Ildefonso, in which Spain transferred control of Louisiana to France. Indeed, given Madrid's escalating disenchantment with its Corsican ally, a second Adams term might have resulted not merely in a greater Spanish-American understanding but even in a possible Federalist acquisition of the Louisiana Territory from Spain under free-soil conditions.[2]

For many scholars, the very idea that the decidedly inegalitarian Adams forged a more enlightened foreign policy than the urbane Jefferson appears self-evidently absurd. Biographers of the Virginian uniformly depict their subject as a rational philosopher in pursuit of reason, whereas Adams's biographers can scarcely muster a kind word in his behalf. "Vain, irritable, irascible, supercilious, and even tactless" are just some of the unhappy character traits chronicled by the leading authority on Adams's life, while an equally distinguished diplomatic historian describes Secretary of State Timothy Pickering—fellow architect of the president's Haitian policy—as "stern and overbearing, stubborn and inflexible, volatile and combative." No less than the author of the standard account of the Adams administration refers to "the more democratic years of Jefferson." [3]

All of these uncharitable pronouncements are unfortunately true. The president was too often pompous and stubborn and proud, and like many a man raised in Calvinist New England he nursed an abiding suspicion of his fellow man; Secretary Pickering, who was equally wary of the common sort, stood very high in Secretary Pickering's opinion. Yet abrasive and arrogant as they appeared to white southern agriculturalists, Adams and Pickering were also anti-slavery politicians who—unlike their southern successors—saw little reason to craft their foreign policy to fit the peculiar labor demands of their region. When it came to issues of race and slavery, particularly in the Caribbean, the conservative Adams and his cabinet pursued a more liberal diplomacy than that of any administration prior to 1861. [4]

Many early national statesmen, of course, including more than a few Virginians, professed to oppose slavery. But Adams was granted the occasion to translate word into deed, when on 2 March 1797—two days before he assumed the presidency—the French Directory annulled the Franco-American commercial treaty of 1778 and allowed French warships to drag neutral prizes into home or colonial ports. Congress retaliated on 13 June 1798 by imposing an embargo on all shipping between the United States and France or its colonies. But because many American vessels sailed not for the war-torn continent but for the Caribbean, where they were easy prey for French privateers, insurance underwriters demanded special "war premiums" for those ships trading with British merchants in Jamaica or Barbados. Consequently, the emerging Quasi-War between France and the United States was largely waged in the Caribbean, and not in the North Atlantic. [5]

At the same time that American seamen began to prepare for a fight in the Caribbean, one potential confederate, Great Britain, made ready to retreat from a losing battle in the same region. Shortly after the bloody 1791 slave uprising in the French colony of Saint Domingue, War Minister Henry Dundas proposed a preemptive invasion to restore order—and reenslave black labor. The chaos wrought by the slave revolt had not only destroyed the re-export trade in Africans throughout the Caribbean, it also presented Britain with the opportunity to seize what had been the most lucrative of all Caribbean sugar islands. Dundas advocated invading with seventeen thousand men by the end of 1793, to be followed by naval attacks on French arsenals at Toulon and Brest in 1794. The latter actions were to destroy French naval power, while the loss of riches derived from Saint Domingue would deny Paris the resources required to rebuild its fleet.[6]

The British invasion proved a spectacular failure. Prime Minister William Pitt foolishly divided his forces in an effort to capture Guadeloupe, Martinique, and Saint Lucia as well as Saint Domingue. British efforts were further weakened by the need to crush slave revolts in their own colonies of Jamaica and Grenada. As 1796 drew to a close, Dundas calculated that his government had spent £4,400,000 in its unsuccessful attempt to wrest the French Caribbean from the mercantilist grip of the Directory, and Saint Domingue from of the hands of former Dominguan slaves. Total casualties approached eighty thousand, of which forty thousand lay dead, a ghastly figure that exceeded the total losses of the Duke of Wellington's army from the start to finish of the Peninsular War. It only remained for the English commander in Saint Domingue, General Thomas Maitland, to salvage what he could from such an utter defeat and abandon the island.[7]

Heading the negotiations with Maitland was the victorious Dominguan general, ex-slave Toussaint Louverture. Despite their previous enmity, the two soldiers shared surprisingly similar goals. Although he obviously preferred to add the Dominguan jewel to the British crown, Maitland's ancillary position was the protection of Jamaican slavery from any future Franco-Dominguan intrusion. For his part, Louverture had no interest in Jamaica, having been warned by Julien Raimond, a Paris member of the *Amis des Noirs,* that the Directory regarded a suicidal attack on British holdings as a fine opportunity "to get rid of T[oussain]t, his principal Officers and his Army." Both generals also hoped to establish a profitable commercial arrangement. Maitland wished to puncture French mercantilism in the Caribbean, while Louverture hoped to rebuild his island's shattered economy and lure back as many white colonists as possible. To that end the two officers signed a convention on 31 August 1798. In a document consisting of five articles, Britain promised not to again invade

Saint Domingue for "the entire duration of the present [European] war," so long as Louverture refused to allow his "colonial troops" to attack Jamaica during the same period. Maitland also vowed to hasten "a quantity of provisions" to the colony in exchange for "colonial products" of sugar and coffee. In early October British forces sailed from their northern stronghold of Mole Saint Nicholas.[8]

Despite the fact that Secretary Pickering regarded Pitt as a potential confederate in the looming conflict with France, even to the extent of considering a formal military alliance, rumors of the Maitland agreement "excited serious apprehensions in the minds of [American] West-India merchants." New England traders in particular had expected "the new independence of the Blacks" to result in the cessation of a "European yoke," but now it appeared that Saint Domingue had merely exchanged one mother country for another. In London the worried American minister, Rufus King, promptly called on Pitt, who referred him to Henry Dundas. King warned that continuing "amity and good understanding" between their two nations could exist only so long as no "American Prize shall be received or sold in any" port under Louverture's control. Philadelphia newspapers hinted that Maitland had "recognized the independence" of Saint Domingue, and if that was the case, King insisted, "*we* as well as *you* may *trade* there."[9]

Equally skeptical of English motives was General Louverture. Having waged a bloody three-year campaign against a British army that wished to reenslave his soldiers, the shrewd Louverture recognized that British goodwill would last not a moment longer than the French threat in Europe. Yet neither could he turn to Paris for support. The French Convention had abolished slavery in France's Caribbean holdings in 1794, and the current government, the Directory, had no intention of going back on that decree. But as the composition of the Directory changed each year, when a new member replaced a departing constituent, Paris rarely maintained a steady policy on any crucial matter. "The negroes & people of colour of St. Doming[ue]," Pickering advised King, "believe with reason that France [intends] to bring them back again to Slavery." In short, Louverture needed an ally, and preferably one with provisions and warships. On 6 November 1798 Louverture took up his quill pen and began an extraordinary letter to President Adams. The old general expressed the "greatest surprise" that American traders had "abandoned the ports of St. Domingue." Affecting to understand nothing about the Quasi-War between the United States and the country to which he allegedly remained loyal, Louverture did "not pretend to know" why American bottoms no longer filled his harbors. But he "assured [Adams] that Americans will find protection and security in the ports of St. Domingue." As to French cruisers operating out of his waters, "appropriate orders will be issued in this matter." [10]

The president had numerous reasons to be interested, not the least of which was foreign trade and protection for American shipping. Even before the Franco-American commercial accord of 1778, American merchants in search of sugar, molasses, and coffee quietly slipped into Dominguan ports. Shortly after the trade became legal, Saint Domingue became the young Republic's second-most-valuable trading partner. This traffic was especially important to New England; Saint Domingue purchased 63 percent of the dried fish and fully 80 percent of the pickled fish exported from the United States. By the eve of the Quasi-War, more than six hundred American vessels ran direct routes to Saint Domingue, all of them dangerously vulnerable to privateers operating out of the French Caribbean. [11]

Given the growing estrangement of Philadelphia and Paris, military considerations also made it imperative to seduce Saint Domingue out of the French orbit. Not only had the Directory turned its Caribbean colonies into bases from which to attack American shipping, the French government even seriously considered sending an African army under General Theodore Hédouville, the infamous "Pacifier of the Vendee," to "invade both the Southern States of America and the Island of Jamaica" to "excite an insurrection among the negroes." Among those concerned about the very real possibility of a Franco-Dominguan invasion force was George Washington, who had been called back into service to organize the recently enlarged army. "*If* the French should be so *mad* as" to invade the United States, he warned Secretary Pickering, "their operations will commence in the Southern quarter [as] there can be no doubt of their arming our own Negroes against us." [12]

Modern scholars tend to dismiss the rumors regarding Hedouville as the groundless fears of a paranoid American planter class, but Pickering and Washington may be forgiven if they did not fancy themselves foolish or irrational men. During the American Revolution, the British had made every effort to disrupt the patriot war effort through the liberation of American bondpeople, and the Directory would be astonishingly imprudent if it failed to pursue a similarly shrewd policy in 1798. Secretary Pickering cautioned both John Adams in Braintree and Rufus King in London of the dangers posed by a Louverture loyal to Paris: "France with an army of those black troops might conquer all the

British Isles and put in jeopardy our Southern States." Pickering had no worries about the former slaves "if left to themselves," but as "subjects of France" Louverture's legions might become a "military corps of such strength in a future war, as no European or other white force could resist." [13]

Yet it is also clear that for Adams and Pickering this was no trifling matter of trade or privateers. Their hemispheric vision was far grander than that. Four months before Louverture contacted the president, John Quincy Adams, writing from his post in Berlin, urged the administration to "do something" for the "West India Islands." Louverture and most of the "generals of color are decidedly with us," he suspected. "Those islands will not be English if they can help it," but neither should they become American colonies. The relationship he advocated was "a more natural connection than that of metropolis and colony, or in other words, master and servant." John Quincy Adams was no more in favor of African American social equality than was his father, yet his diplomacy knew neither color nor servitude; he regarded Louverture as an African Burke, the sort of man who could restore order to the region, and so he wished to see Saint Domingue "free and independent." [14]

Whatever his motivation, the elder Adams soon had the opportunity to demonstrate the utter lack of racial animosity in his statecraft. Not trusting his correspondence to British ships, Louverture chose to send his missive to Philadelphia with Joseph Bunel, a trusted advisor. Bunel arrived in the capital in early December 1798, where he was greeted by Secretary Pickering. Bunel reiterated Louverture's guarantee that "American commerce should be protected in all the ports under his jurisdiction" and requested an audience with the president. Several nights later Bunel dined with Adams, the first-ever breaking of bread between an American president and a man of color. Bunel pressed for an immediate renewal of trade and hinted that any hope of an understanding with his general required the utmost haste. Louverture's ragged army was hungry and unpaid, Bunel explained, and "the distress was so great as to endanger his authority." [15]

Bunel's assurances were all that New England Federalists required. When Congress reconvened in January, Harrison Gray Otis, chairman of the Committee of Defense and leader of the six-member Massachusetts delegation, called upon the House to amend the June 1798 embargo with France to allow a resumption of trade with Saint Domingue. "If St. Doming[ue] becomes independent," Otis argued, "we shall have the right to treat with" its new government. Conversely, since Congress had stopped short of formally declaring war on France, the 1778 trade agreement with Paris ostensibly remained in effect, and so if the colony did *not* break free, "no objection can be made even by France, to our furnishing it with supplies." Otis slyly observed that Jefferson once urged the recognition of Minister Edmond Genet on the grounds that he represented the *de facto* government of France. "Shall we now begin to examine into the legality of the powers of persons in authority" simply because of race, Otis wondered. The "Black General" Louverture "is a very able and influential character [who] justly appreciates the advantages of a free trade with the United States." [16]

The thought that the Adams administration was prepared to recognize a government led by men of African ancestry infuriated even northern Republicans. Swiss-born Albert Gallatin rose in rebuttal. Louverture's army had only recently "been initiated to Liberty" through "rapine, pillage, and massacre." To trade with or diplomatically recognize the rebellious colony might spread the contagion of freedom "to the Southern States" and "excite dangerous insurrections" among "the negro people there." It was even folly, Gallatin fumed, for Adams to dine with the light-skinned Bunel, a mulatto "married to a black woman." Watching from his post as vice president was Thomas Jefferson. Otis's bill, commonly called "Toussaint's clause," was openly designed "to facilitate the separation of the island from France," he sighed. Yet he had little doubt that the "clause will pass." [17]

The vice president proved correct. On 28 January, after only seven days of deliberation, the Federalist majority approved the bill by a party-line vote of fifty-five to thirty-seven; of the Massachusetts delegation, only Joseph B. Varnum, a Republican, cast a negative vote. Adams now enjoyed the authority to reopen trade with any port in Saint Domingue he deemed safe for American vessels. "We may expect therefore black crews, & supercargoes & missionaries" to pour "into the Southern States," Jefferson worried.[18]

To investigate the situation in the colony and to represent American commercial interests, Adams appointed Dr. Edward Stevens consul general to Saint Domingue. The Federalist majority in the Senate overrode Republican objections once more and confirmed Stevens on 21 February. Two weeks later Adams commandeered a private vessel, the *Kingston,* to ferry Stevens to Cap François, as well as to "conciliate the good opinion of [Louverture] and his people." Stevens was a curious if logical choice. Although born and bred in Nevis and knowledgeable about the Caribbean people, Stevens evidently owed his appointment at least in part to Adams's hopes of placating the high Federalist wing of his party. Pickering often commented on the "extraordinary similitude" between Stevens and Alexander Hamilton, and Adams had little doubt that the two men were biological brothers.[19]

Although American negotiators in Paris two years before had angrily rebuffed French demands for tribute, Pickering now deemed it wise to sweeten their Dominguan overture with "fifty thousand dollars" worth of specie, clothing, and luxury items. Part of this valuable cargo was entrusted to Bunel to carry back to Louverture, but most of it sailed with Stevens on the *Kingston*. Of the cabinet members, only Attorney General Charles Lee, a Virginia slaveholder, denounced the bribe as "neither *lawful* nor *expedient*." Pickering had little use for such technicalities. The "*supplies* or *presents*" constituted "a *political measure*," he lectured Adams, "necessary to improve an important commercial intercourse" and "put down privateering."[20]

On 18 April Stevens arrived in Cap François. The consul was greeted by Philippe Roume, the agent of the Directory in Saint Domingue. But Pickering had made it clear to the envoy that the "Negro general Toussaint now commands" the government in Saint Domingue, and Stevens requested an audience with the old soldier. Louverture arrived early the next morning and "received [Stevens] very favorably." The general was delighted by the supplies for his men but even more so by "the attention which had been paid to his letter by" President Adams. Stevens also presented a missive from Pickering, which laid out the conditions for a restoration of trade established by the law of 28 January (a copy of which was also enclosed). Nothing less than an immediate end "to these depredations" by French privateers would "permit a renewal of commercial intercourse." As he handed the documents over, Stevens noticed that Louverture's army had "not a single Pound of Flour or Salt Provisions." Like Bunel he feared that if trade was "delayed much longer, all [Louverture's] Plans will be deranged."[21]

During the course of the following day, 20 April, Stevens "received a copy of [Louverture's] intended Proclamation" regarding the United States. The American consul, already impressed with the "penetration and good sense" of the general, was gratified to discover that Louverture completely accepted "the Justice and Propriety of the President's Demands." Although Louverture's power was nominally confined to the colony's military administration, on 25 April he and Stevens signed an agreement consisting of nine articles. The accord banned French privateers from the ports under his control yet opened the docks to "the Merchant Vessels and Ships of War of the United States." So complete was Louverture's pretended capitulation that even the staunchly Republican *Aurora,* which had of late castigated both Adams and Louverture as English dupes, praised the "renewal of our former Commercial relations" with Saint Domingue.[22]

General Louverture, of course, well knew what he was about, and his slow but perceptible movements away from the French empire meant that he had to isolate Roume and those yet loyal to the Directory. Chief among them was Andre Rigaud, the mulatto general who controlled most of the southern portion of the colony. Foolishly loyal to Paris and its assurances of Dominguan freedom, Rigaud regarded the Stevens agreement as treason, and the long simmering animosity between the two general erupted into civil war. In an effort to ensure that the conflict "terminate in Favour of Toussaint," Stevens urged Pickering to reopen trade only with those northern ports under Louverture's jurisdiction, "provided the President sees no Objection to it." Adams did not object. "I will not disappoint those islanders if I can help it," he promised Navy Secretary Benjamin Stoddert.[23]

Because of strategic considerations born of the Quasi-War, Adams wished to work closely with the British—and their formidable navy—in the Caribbean, where French privateers were increasingly outgunned. "Harmony with the English in all this business of St. Doming[ue]," he lectured Pickering, "is the thing I have most at heart." The Haitians, however, did not share that view. Following Maitland's withdrawal from the colony, Louverture initially allowed British warships to enter his waters, but he was far less interested in a permanent alliance with London than in one with Philadelphia. This presented a problem for Adams, who recognized the need to conciliate England. "If an agent from the British government is not admitted [into Cap François], while one from the United States is," he worried, "this will render it more necessary for us to be particularly delicate and compliant towards the English," at least as long as the fighting continued in Europe.[24]

As a former slave who owed his advancement in life to armed revolution, Louverture had no fondness for Pitt or his reactionary government. Secretary Stoddert correctly regarded the convention between Louverture and Maitland as "no more than a Truce for the [duration of the] War," and even that modest withdrawal agreement handed those loyal to France "a powerful Weapon" to use against Louverture. As the summer of 1799 wore on, Adams still hoped to work "in concert with Maitland." But the administration increasingly understood Louverture's hostility to Britain. "The British will never encourage a

[Haitian] declaration of independence" for fear of its impact on Jamaica, the attorney general warned Adams, and the president himself conceded that the English invasion "made much mischief for themselves [on] that island." Word soon arrived from Stevens that any trade agreement "embracing equally the British and American commerce, may not be adopted" by Louverture.[25]

Maitland was many things, but never a fool. Still hoping to forge a good commercial relationship with Louverture, he determined to sail for Philadelphia. On Tuesday, 2 April, the warship *Camilla* arrived at the docks. Maitland was displeased to hear that Bunel had departed for Cap François "a few days" before, but what he really desired was the administration's intercession on Britain's behalf. Pickering was more than affable. Yet the secretary of state, who today is commonly depicted as blindly Anglophilic, perceived that Adams held the whip hand. At a meeting with Maitland and Robert Liston, the British minister in Philadelphia, Pickering coolly suggested that his majesty's government "state in writing the precise plan which they wished to have adopted in respect to the intercourse of both nations with St. Doming[ue]." [26]

Maitland especially hoped that Britain might obtain the same rights that Louverture granted to American warships and privateers in his 25 April accord with Stevens. Pickering raised no objections but doubted there was anything the administration could do to sway the suspicious Louverture on this subject. At length Maitland reluctantly agreed to accept a position subordinate to the United States in hopes that a lucrative trading agreement, at the very least, might follow. Writing from Braintree, Adams was pleased to hear that Maitland had given way on "this point without any difficulty to us." If Louverture, who had only recently driven the British army into the sea, "will not admit British ships of war or commerce into their ports," he counseled Pickering, "the British government ought to be contented with sufficient assurances of the neutrality of that island" and "not insist on defeating the connection between the United States & St. Doming[ue]." [27]

With that Maitland sailed again for Cap François, which he reached on 15 May. As Stevens had predicted, the black general refused to yield on the issue of the British navy, but trade was quite a different proposition. With his colony devastated by a bloody slave revolt, the British invasion, and now a civil war with Rigaud, Louverture needed considerable economic aid, and commercial relations with Jamaica and Barbados, not to mention London and Liverpool, could supply his tattered army and feed his starving people. On 13 June 1799 Maitland, Stevens, and Louverture signed a tripartite treaty—both the American consul and the black general described it as a "Convention secrette"—in which the latter again guaranteed "that no [French] Privateers should in future be commissioned from this Island" in exchange for Anglo-American trade. He promised also to actively protect Jamaica and the southern United States from any attacks by blacks serving under French colors, in exchange for further British assurances of armed neutrality. Secret or not, in putting his name to a treaty with the enemies of France, Louverture had all but declared independence.[28]

Even before word of the treaty reached Pickering's desk, Adams moved to formally normalize relations with Saint Domingue. In keeping with the law of 28 January the president announced on 26 June the resumption of trade with all ports under Louverture's control as of 1 August. Ships heavily laden with supplies promptly weighed anchor; within months commerce between the American mainland and Saint Domingue was roughly seven times that between the colony and its mother country. General Louverture lost no time in thanking Adams for the proclamation, but he also used the opportunity to request that the United States do more than simply refuse provision to ports held by troops loyal to Rigaud—and France. An embargo against the southern parts of the colony "will remain ineffective," Louverture warned, so long as it was not backed up by "a plainly coercive force [such as] warships." If Rigaud's "rebellion" succeeded, he hinted, the Quasi-War might yet be lost in the Caribbean.[29]

The imaginative mind of John Adams had no intention of allowing that to happen. In late October Stevens wrote from Cap François with word that Louverture would soon purge Roume, the Directory's agent, and replace him with lieutenants more sympathetic to his increasingly autonomous course. Although his sources of information were far less reliable, Minister Liston expressed few doubts that the administration hoped to see "a separation of the island of St. Doming[ue] from the mother country." Indeed, as early as the previous spring Adams advised Pickering "that we should accede" to "the independence of the island," provided "the senate advise & consent." Treasury secretary Oliver Wolcott also refused to "conceal an opinion" that Louverture would shortly "assert and maintain [his] independence" to prevent the Directory from ever returning "the negroes to slavery." Easily the most sanguine was the secretary of state, who "confidently" informed Rufus King in London that Louverture's appetite for American commerce was but a prelude to "the Independence of St. Doming[ue]."[30]

With this the Quasi-War, always centered in the Caribbean, now moved onto the island itself. As Stevens predicted, the escalating conflict between Paris and Philadelphia meant the time had arrived for Louverture to rid himself of both Roume and Rigaud. Four years prior, in the Treaty of Basle—22 July

1795—Spain had promised to surrender Santo Domingo to its French allies. To protect his back from the French invasion he knew would one day come, Louverture instructed Roume to take possession of "the whole Spanish Part of the Island." The Directory's agent refused and was imprisoned. But Roume's recalcitrance, together with orders from Paris to move on Jamaica, emboldened Rigaud. As the black general explained it to Adams, his lieutenant "raised the standard of revolt" and would soon return to privateering in the south. Unless the United States threw "several armed vessels of war" into the conflict, Saint Domingue could yet become a staging ground for a French invasion of the American mainland. Louverture also confided in Stevens and repeated "in very Strong Terms his ardent Desire to do every Thing which can preserve the existing Harmony between this Colony and the U[nited] States."[31]

It is John Adams's fate, and perhaps his deserts, to be remembered as the president who signed the Sedition Act into law; yet it was this same commander-in-chief who dispatched American ships to crush both French power and the conservative *gens de couleur* under Rigaud. Stevens begged the administration to impose a naval blockade "on the south Side of the Island" so as to cut off "all Supplies of Provision and Ammunition" to those ports. By the spring of 1800 the frigates *Boston, Connecticut,* and *General Greene* cooperated with the royal navy along the southern coast, while the *Constitution* and the *Norfolk* attacked and captured "a small french Luggar" carrying instructions from Roume. "As soon as Rigaud falls, Roume will be sent off," Stevens crowed to Pickering, "and from that Moment the Power of the Directory will cease in this Colony."[32]

With American and British frigates acting the part of Louverture's military allies by guarding his southern coast, the general made short work of Rigaud's mutiny. His campaign against his rebellious lieutenant ended successfully by August. Rigaud fled the colony and was captured at sea by the American schooner *Experiment.* Roume, weary of imprisonment, agreed to follow Rigaud into exile on the continent. The "black Chiefs," as Stevens dubbed officers Jean Jacques Dessalines and Paul Louverture, "now talk loudly and openly" in favor of autonomy. For his part, Louverture wished to move "slowly but *securely*" and "make no open Declaration of Independence" until compelled to by Napoleon Bonaparte, who had recently deposed the Directory. But his victory over Rigaud and Roume left Louverture with both military and civil authority on the entire island. "*All connection with France* will *soon* be *broken off,*" Stevens informed Philadelphia by cipher.[33]

On 2 August 1800 the American consul apprised his superiors of the end to "the destructive Civil War which has so long raged in this Colony." One month later Adams amended his previous proclamation by opening "every part of the said island" to American shipping. At almost the same moment, however, the president urged his disloyal cabinet to support yet another peace delegation to Paris. At least one contemporary critic—and numerous modern scholars—suspected that Adams's friendship toward Louverture would last only as long as the Quasi-War. How could Adams reconcile his hopes for Haitian independence, Alexander Hamilton fumed, with sending "a Minister to France to negotiate an accommodation"? But the president saw no paradox. American political and economic stability required both peace with Europe and black liberty in the Caribbean. The administration's support for Louverture, Adams assured Pickering, would continue "as if no negotiation was going on."[34]

So deeply invested was the administration in Haitian liberty that the secretary of state even thought it worthwhile to advise Louverture on the shape of his emerging government. Having little experience in constitution building, Pickering naturally turned to one who did. Hamilton's response indicated that Federalist confidence in the black general did not extend to his populace; but then the New Yorker was never one to exhibit much faith in popular democracy. "The Government if independent must be military," he advised Pickering, "partaking of the feudal system." Echoing, ironically, Albert Gallatin's doubts about the ability of former slaves to govern themselves, Hamilton preferred a monarchy for the island but recognized that such an idea was "impracticable." Instead, in words reminiscent of the position he had adopted in Philadelphia twelve years before, he recommended a "single Executive to hold his place for life." Land was to be divided among young men following obligatory military service. No extant evidence proves that Hamilton's missive reached Louverture's hands but, in a coincidence worthy of Dickens, in July 1801 the general announced the first-ever constitution for Haiti (which technically remained a colony). According to the American consul, it "declare[d] Genl. Toussaint Louverture Governor for life, with the power of naming his successor."[35]

American amity with Saint Domingue even survived the acrimonious departure of Pickering from the State Department on 12 May 1800. His replacement, John Marshall of Richmond, was a slaveholder but not a planter; he maintained no estate outside the city and his few slaves performed household chores and cared for his habitually distracted wife. Marshall's correspondence with the president reveals that he differed not at all with the other "heads of departments" on relations with the island. Upon taking office he hastened to assure Louverture of his "most sincere desire to preserve the most perfect harmony and the most friendly intercourse with St. Doming[ue]."[36]

What altered the course of American relations with the island, and ultimately the nature of westward expansion as well, was the election of 1800. Ironically, those issues that most damaged Adams, particularly in the critical state of New York, were those he was most dispassionate about. Increased taxes, party intrigue, and the infamous Sedition Act trials all contributed to what Abigail Adams later characterized as a "jungle-growth" of unpopular, repressive measures. Yet given the close election, there can be little doubt that had the nation learned earlier of the Peace of Mortefontaine, which was signed on 30 September, several crucial states would have cast their electoral ballots for Adams. In fact, had depoliticized slaves in the American South not been counted for purposes of representation, Adams would have been reelected handily, and his support for politicized former slaves in the Caribbean would have continued.[37]

It requires no counterfactual flight of fancy to perceive how a Federalist victory, together with continuing support for Louverture's cause, could have allowed for a very different kind of westward movement. Although something of a historiographical cottage industry has sprung up around Jefferson's admittedly keen fascination with the West, the fact remains that Adams and Pickering had long demonstrated a similar interest in the gulf South. When it became clear that Madrid hoped to abrogate several provisions in the 1795 Pinckney Treaty, Pickering adopted an inflexible position toward Minister Marqués de Casa Yrujo and forced Spain to dismantle its forts along the Mississippi (thereby weakening its ability to resist further territorial demands). When rumors began to reach Philadelphia that France wished to retake control of New Orleans from its Spanish ally, Adams seriously considered the advice of secretary of war James McHenry, who recommended seizing the city "until a treaty could be entered into with Spain for the greater security of our frontiers." The president himself well understood that "the free navigation of the Mississippi was essential to [the Union's] preservation"; as a politician who looked south when replacing Pickering, he was hardly opposed to the prospect of gaining Federalist converts among southern and western voters.[38]

Secretary Pickering is commonly depicted as a man who gazed only toward the east and Britain, yet the same Francophobic strategic considerations that motivated him to befriend Louverture aroused his interest in Louisiana. Fully three years before the Treaty of San Ildefonso restored New Orleans to France, the secretary of state worried about a possible transfer. The "Spaniards will certainly be more safe and quiet neighbors," he warned Rufus King in words curiously similar to those his enemy Jefferson adopted in later years. Pickering even envisioned a scenario in which a resurgent France might recapture Canada and fulfill "the ancient plan of her Monarch, of *circumscribing* and encircling what now constitutes the Atlantic states." Unlike Jefferson, Secretary Pickering never spoke of western lands in terms of the American yeomen, yet he was every bit as adamant about keeping New Orleans out of the clutches of a major European power.[39]

Equally plausible is that Pickering's departure from the State Department might have led to a closer relationship with Madrid. The New Englander's adroit diplomacy with Yrujo—whom he publicly branded as a "Spanish puppy"—was as damaging to long-term Spanish-American relations as it was effective in the short term. With Pickering and McHenry banished from the cabinet, there was no voice supporting Alexander Hamilton's ambitious plan of joining forces with Franciso de Miranda, the Venezuelan soldier of fortune. All of Europe knew of Hamilton's dream of seizing "the Floridas and Louisiana" before ultimately "detach[ing] South American from Spain." Adams had no interest in Miranda's scheme, and when the adventurer approached the president in 1798, Adams publicly refused to answer his missive. Instead, Adams and Marshall, given their growing cooperation with the British navy in the Caribbean, were in a position to apply subtle pressure on France's wavering Iberian ally to cede more western lands. Indeed, the tension between Paris and Madrid had become so pronounced that as late as December 1801 Spain still refused to hand over the documents necessary for the formal transfer of New Orleans.[40]

Even less conjectural is the fact that Adams's re-election would have left European diplomacy in the staunchly anticolonial hands of John Quincy Adams and William Vans Murray, both of whom were deeply sympathetic to General Louverture. The younger Adams hoped to "protect [Haitian] independence" with the American navy, while "leaving them as to their government totally to themselves." Instead, the Republican triumph placed James Monroe again in Europe, and the Virginian was far less enamored of black liberty in the Caribbean. Writing in the wake of Gabriel's slave conspiracy (which coincided with the election of 1800), Monroe worried that the "occurrences in St. Doming[ue] for some years past were calculated and doubtless did excite some sensation among our Slaves."[41]

Monroe's fears of black rebellion, both at home and abroad, were shared by President Jefferson.[42] Despite scholarly efforts to suggest that the Louisiana Purchase of 1803 "was another vast extension of the Empire of Liberty,"[43] it is hard not to conclude that for Americans of African descent, Jefferson's election meant a diminution of liberty both in the Caribbean *and* on the western frontier. Indeed, although Adams and Pickering had long expressed concern about French designs on New Orleans, Jefferson was surprisingly slow to grasp Bonaparte's spectacular ambitions in the Americas. In July 1801, after only four months in office, Jefferson was approached by Louis Andre Pichon, the French *charge d' affaires,* who wished to know the president's opinion on a possible invasion of Saint Domingue. According to Pichon's report to his superiors, Jefferson assured the charge that "nothing would be more simple than to furnish your army and your fleet with everything and to starve out Toussaint." [44]

Jefferson's failure to appreciate the connection between the island and his western frontier has been shared by more than a few historians. But on this point hindsight is the enemy of understanding; because today the American heartland serves as breadbasket to much of the world, while Haiti has collapsed into abject poverty, it is easy to assume that Louisiana was more important in Bonaparte's mind. Yet prior to 1791 Saint Domingue accounted for roughly 40 percent of France's external trade. That level of prosperity, Bonaparte concluded, could only be reestablished under slavery. The land west of the Mississippi River was intended to supply the island with foodstuffs and beef, while the reenslaved Haitian people furnished the continent with sugar and prosperity enough to challenge Britain's commercial hegemony. Had he succeeded in recapturing the island's African population, the *premier consul* would surely have refused to sell Louisiana. Notwithstanding his public promises to wed his republic to the British fleet upon the French acquisition of New Orleans, Jefferson and Monroe would have been forced to bargain with a powerful foe deeply entrenched in the gulf coast.[45]

John Adams forged a pragmatic diplomacy in both the Caribbean and the Spanish west out of economic considerations, geopolitical realities, but also, it should be noted, a sense of justice that defied racial considerations. Conversely, Jefferson's precarious overtures toward France were based fully as much on fear of slave resistance as they were on a desire to acquire the West. John Quincy Adams hoped to see Saint Domingue as an equal partner in the expanding republican sphere, but the author of the Declaration of Independence informed Pichon that he "had no reason to be favorable" to revolutionaries like Toussaint Louverture. Color meant little enough to Adams, but it was everything for Jefferson. When Tobias Lear, the new American consul, arrived in Cap François without so much as a perfunctory letter from the Virginian, Louverture "express[ed] his disappointment and disgust." His "Colour was the cause of his being neglected," he fumed, "and not thought worthy of the Usual attentions" paid by Adams and Pickering.[46]

And so it happened that with the "revolution of 1800," the empire of liberty vanished from the Caribbean. Upon leaving the executive mansion Pichon hurried the president's response to Charles Maurice de Talleyrand, where it played no small part in Bonaparte's decision to proceed with his invasion of Saint Domingue. Instructions handed to General Victor Leclerc spoke of American collaboration in the destruction of Louverture's regime, and even the death of Leclerc failed to nudge Jefferson into recognizing the independence of the colony. Nor did he ever concede that the Haitian people saved Louisiana for the United States. Only when the French dream of a reenslaved island lay in ashes did Bonaparte determine that he no longer required mainland foodstuffs. As Alexander Hamilton archly observed, Jefferson's greatest achievement came not through adroit diplomacy or skillful negotiation but because of "the courage and obstinate resistance made by [the] black inhabitants" of Saint Domingue.[47]

If the acquisition of the vast Louisiana territory was made possible by Haitian intransigence, it nonetheless arrived on Jeffersonian terms. To appease French and Spanish nationals along the Mississippi, American negotiators in Paris agreed to the protection of slave property in the region. Given Bonaparte's desire to obtain ready capital to use in his renewed war against Britain, one suspects that Monroe and Robert Livingston could have forced Paris to give way on this issue—had they wanted to. Certainly it is hard to imagine John Quincy Adams or William Vans Murray conceding this point. In short, even as the American empire of liberty faded from the Caribbean, it arrived on the frontier, but only for white settlers, many of whom journeyed west with their human chattel. Nor was the third clause in the treaty soon forgotten. Two decades later, as politicians in Washington wrestled with the question of slavery's expansion into Missouri, western settlers loudly embraced it as their Magna Carta, their organic right to hold other people as property under the French Treaty of 1803.[48]

Each year brings the publication of several new biographies or specialized studies about Thomas Jefferson, and perhaps with good reason. Upon capturing the executive mansion, Jefferson promptly pardoned the editors convicted under the Sedition Act and remitted their fines with interest. The required period for naturalization was returned to five years, and the Republican majority in Congress reduced the enlarged army, thereby eliminating the need for higher taxes. Yet it should also be remembered that for many in the Western Hemisphere, there was no "revolution of 1800," but rather a reactionary, even a counterrevolutionary backlash to black liberty. Toussaint Louverture froze to death in a French dungeon, and his already devastated nation was further impoverished by the American-supported invasion of General Leclerc. For countless thousands of black Americans, the acquisition of what would become Louisiana, Arkansas, and Missouri under slave state auspices meant forced separation and sale away from enslaved families in the border South. Louverture's soldiers had once dubbed Adams and Stevens "the good whites," but that sentiment vanished soon after 4 March 1801.

NOTES

1. TJ to James Madison, 27 April 1809, Smith, 3:1586. See, for example, Julian P. Boyd, "Thomas Jefferson's 'Empire of Liberty,'" *Virginia Quarterly Review* 24 (1948): 549–50, who believed Jefferson first used the phrase in 1779, and Robert W. Tucker and David C. Hendrickson, *Empire of Liberty: The Statecraft of Thomas Jefferson* (New York, 1990), who, curiously, never cite any of the letters in which Jefferson used the phrase.

The author thanks John M. Belohlavek, Ronald Hatzenbuehler, James Horn, Roger Kennedy, Peter Onuf, and Rosemarie Zagarri for their kind advice and suggestions.

2. Adams's diplomacy toward Saint Domingue—or the anger it generated among Republicans—has not received the attention it deserves. The standard account of the election of 1800, Daniel Sisson, *The American Revolution of 1800* (New York, 1974), mentions neither Saint Domingue nor Louverture. Neither does Stephen G. Kurtz, *The Presidency of John Adams: The Collapse of Federalism, 1795–1800* (Philadelphia, 1957), Manning J. Dauer, *The Adams Federalists* (Baltimore, 1953), or John Ferling's masterful *John Adams: A Life* (Knoxville, Tenn., 1992). Thomas O. Ott, *The Haitian Revolution, 1789–1804* (Knoxville, Tenn., 1973), 108, 123, mentions Timothy Pickering but not Adams. Page Smith, *John Adams*, 2 vols., (Garden City, N.Y., 1962), 2:1008, reduces Adams's Haitian policy to a single paragraph, relevant to nothing else in the chapter. David McCullough, *John Adams* (New York, 2001), 519, covers the affair in a single page and sets it in the nonexistent colony of "San Domingo." Conor Cruise O'Brien, *The Long Affair: Thomas Jefferson and the French Revolution, 1785–1800* (Chicago, 1996), 289, is typical of recent literature in that it castigates Jefferson for his diplomacy toward Saint Domingue but relegates Adams to a single sentence.

3. Ferling, *Adams*, 170–71; Donald R. Hickey, "Timothy Pickering and the Haitian Slave Revolt: A Letter to Thomas Jefferson in 1806," *Essex Institute Historical Collections* 120 (1984): 151; Ralph Adams Brown, *The Presidency of John Adams* (Lawrence, Kans., 1975), 6. This is not to suggest, of course, that Adams was a social liberal who crusaded for black equality in Massachusetts; my argument is that he was antislavery, not pro-black.

4. Adams even scolded Jefferson over Virginia's refusal to eliminate unfree labor, which he called "a black cloud" that debased the entire nation. See John Adams to TJ, 3 Feb. 1821, *AJL*, 571. Pickering, who later became an avid supporter of the American Colonization Society, denounced slavery as a "portentous evil . . . surpassing any other that can be conceived." See Gerald A. Clarfield, *Timothy Pickering and the American Republic* (Pittsburgh, 1980), 264, and P. J. Staudenraus, *The African Colonization Movement, 1816–1865* (New York, 1961), 10, 72.

5. Alexander DeConde, *The Quasi-War: The Politics and Diplomacy of the Undeclared War with France, 1797–1801* (New York, 1966), 17–20; Rayford W. Logan, *The Diplomatic Relations of the United States with Haiti, 1776–1891* (Chapel Hill, N.C., 1941), 65–66.

6. David P. Geggus, "Jamaica and the Saint Domingue Slave Revolt, 1791–1793," *The Americas* 38 (Oct. 1981): 230–31; Michael Duffy, "The French Revolution and British Attitudes to the West Indian Colonies," in *A Turbulent Time: The French Revolution and the Greater Caribbean,* ed. David Barry Gaspar and David P. Geggus (Bloomington, Ind., 1997), 83.

7. C. L. R. James, *The Black Jacobins: Toussaint L'Ouverture and the San Domingo Revolution,* 2d ed. (New York, 1963), 200; Charles C. Tansill, *The United States and Santo Domingo, 1798–1873* (Baltimore, 1938), 19–22.

8. David P. Geggus, *Slavery, War, and Revolution: The British Occupation of Saint Domingue, 1793–1798* (New York, 1982), 381; Edward Stevens to Timothy Pickering, 30 Sept. 1799, "Letters of Toussaint Louverture and of Edward Stevens, 1798–1800," *American Historical Review* (hereafter AHR), 16 (Oct. 1910): 83–84; Thomas Maitland, "Previous to entering on the exact restrictions," n.d., Public Record Office, War Office, 1/71 (hereafter PRO, WO). There is as yet no first-rate biography of Louverture; scholars await the publication of David P. Geggus, *The Saint Domingue Slave Revolt and the Rise of Toussaint Louverture.*

9. *Aurora* (Philadelphia), 4 Feb., 28 March 1799; Rufus King to Timothy Pickering, 7 Dec. 1798, *The Life and Correspondence of Rufus King,* 6 vols., ed. Charles R. King (New York, 1896–97), 2:476; Rufus King to Henry Dundas, 8 Dec. 1798, in King, *Life and Correspondence,* 2:484.

10. Timothy Pickering to John Adams, 7 June 1799, Adams Papers, Massachusetts Historical Society (hereafter MHS), Reel 395; Timothy Pickering to Rufus King, 22 April 1799, MHS, Reel 10; Toussaint Louverture to John Adams, 6 Nov. 1798, "Letters of Louverture," *AHR* 16 (1910): 66–67. (Translations of Louverture's letters kindly provided by John W. Langdon.)

11. Donald R. Hickey, "America's Response to the Slave Revolt in Haiti, 1791–1806," *JER* 2 (1982): 362–63; John H. Coatsworth, "American Trade with European Colonies in the Caribbean and South America, 1790–1812," *WMQ* 3d ser., 24 (1967): 245–46; DeConde, *Quasi-War,* 124.

12. Rufus King to Henry Dundas, 8 Dec. 1798, in King, *Life and Correspondence* 2:483–84; Edward Stevens to Thomas Maitland, 23 May 1799, "Letters of Louverture," *AHR* 16 (1910): 73; Robert Goodloe Harper to Constituents, 20 March 1799, "Papers of James A. Bayard, 1796–1815," *American Historical Association Annual Report for the Year 1913,* ed. Elizabeth Donnan (Washington, D.C., 1915), 2:90; George Washington to Timothy Pickering, 11 July 1798, in Dorothy Twohig, ed., *The Papers of George Washington: Retirement Series* (Charlottesville, Va., 1998), 2:397.

13. Timothy Pickering to John Adams, 7 June 1799, Adams Papers, MHS, Reel 395; Timothy Pickering to Rufus King, 12 March 1799, in King, *Life and Correspondence* 2:557.

14. John Quincy Adams to William Vans Murray, 14 July 1798, Adams Papers, MHS, Reel 133. The interpretation presented here differs from that presented by DeConde, who argued that Adams only decided to cooperate with Louverture "because the Negro general was an enemy of France" (*Quasi-War,* 208–9), and also from Logan, who suggested that Adams's diplomacy toward Saint Domingue had no basis in "idealism" (*Diplomatic Relations,* 89). Considerations of trade and military power need not, of course, exclude idealism, and in this case the three objectives dovetailed perfectly.

15. Timothy Pickering to Regis Leblanc, 20 Feb. 1799, *Naval Documents Related to the Quasi-War between the United States and France,* ed. Dudley W. Knox (Washington, D.C., 1935), 2:242; Oliver Wolcott to John Adams, 20 Feb. 1799, *Memoirs of the Administrations of Washington and John Adams, Edited from the Papers of Oliver Wolcott, Secretary of the Treasury,* ed. George Gibbs (1846; rept. New York, 1971), 2:300–301.

16. *Aurora* (Philadelphia), 28 Jan. 1799; *Abridgement of the Debates in Congress* (New York, 1851), 2:335–36.

17. *Abridgement of Debates* 2:339; TJ to James Madison, 5 Feb. 1799, *JMP* 17:225–27.

18. *Abridgement of the Debates* 2:347; Timothy Pickering to Alexander Hamilton, 9 Feb. 1799, *AHP* 22:473–74; TJ to James Madison, 12 Feb. 1799, *JMP* 17:230–31.

19. Timothy Pickering to Alexander Hamilton, 20 Feb. 1799, *AHP* 22:491; Robert Liston to Lord Grenville, 30 March 1799, PRO, Foreign Office, 5/25A; *Aurora* (Philadelphia), 20 Feb. 1799; Benjamin Stoddert to Thomas Tingey, 16 March 1799, in Knox, *Naval Documents* 2:479; Pickering quoted in James T. Flexner, *The Young Hamilton: A Biography* (Boston, 1978), 18–19 (who found no evidence to substantiate rumors that Thomas Stevens was Hamilton's father); John Adams to William Tudor, 14 Nov. 1800, Adams Papers, MHS, Reel 399.

20. Timothy Pickering to Edward Stevens, 26 Feb. 1799, Timothy Pickering Papers, MHS, Reel 10; Oliver Wolcott to Samuel Smith, 20 March 1799, in Gibbs, *Memoirs of the Administrations,* 228; Charles Lee to John Adams, 20 Feb. 1799, Adams Papers, MHS, Reel 393; Timothy Pickering to John Adams, 20 Feb. 1799, Adams Papers, MHS, Reel 393 (second letter of that date).

21. Timothy Pickering to Edward Stevens, 7 March 1799, Pickering Papers, MHS, Reel 10; Edward Stevens to Timothy Pickering, 3 May 1799, "Letters of Louverture," *AHR* 16 (1910): 67; Timothy Pickering to Toussaint Louverture, 4 March 1799, Pickering Papers, MHS, Reel 10; Edward Stevens to Timothy Pickering, 23 June 1799, "Letters of Louverture," *AHR* 16 (1910): 75–76.

22. Timothy Pickering to Edward Stevens, 7 March 1799, Pickering Papers, MHS, Reel 10; Edward Stevens to Timothy Pickering, 3 May 1799, "Letters of Louverture," *AHR* 16 (1910): 67–69; *Aurora* (Philadelphia), 28 May 1799.

23. Edward Stevens to Timothy Pickering, 3 Dec. 1799, "Letters of Louverture," *AHR* 16 (1910): 87; John Adams to Benjamin Stoddert, 8 June 1799, Adams Papers, MHS, Reel 119.

24. John Adams to Benjamin Stoddert, 27 April 1799, Adams Papers, MHS, Reel 119; John Adams to Timothy Pickering, 2 July 1799, Adams Papers, MHS, Reel 119; John Adams to Timothy Pickering, Adams Papers, MHS, Reel 119.

25. Benjamin Stoddert to Samuel Smith, 16 March 1799, in Knox, *Naval Documents* 2:480; Edward Stevens to Timothy Pickering, 23 June 1799, "Letters of Louverture," *AHR* 16 (1910): 74–75; Charles Lee to John Adams, 20 Feb. 1799, Adams Papers, MHS, Reel 393; John Adams to Benjamin Stoddert, 7 June 1799, Adams Papers, MHS, Reel 119; Timothy Pickering to John Adams, 7 June 1799, Adams Papers, MHS, Reel 395. Martin Ros, *Night of Fire: The Black Napoleon and the Battle for Haiti* (New York, 1994), 98, which mentions neither Adams nor Pickering, curiously suggests that Louverture "refrain[ed] from undertaking anything in foreign politics without consulting the British."

26. *Aurora* (Philadelphia), 4, 30 April 1799; Thomas Maitland, "Previous to entering on the exact restrictions," n.d., PRO, WO, 1/71; Timothy Pickering to Rufus King, 23 April 1799, Pickering Papers, MHS, Reel 10.

27. John Adams to Timothy Pickering, 1 May 1799, Adams Papers, MHS, Reel 119; John Adams to Timothy Pickering, 15 June 1799, Adams Papers, MHS, Reel 119. Bradford Perkins, *The First Rapprochement: England and the United States, 1795–1805* (Berkeley, Calif., 1967), 109, suggests that "Liston and Maitland felt the Americans had driven a hard bargain." Perhaps so, but Adams's letters indicate an honest desire to cooperate with the British in the Caribbean. The administration simply recognized that given Louverture's animosity toward the British military, better terms were unattainable.

28. Suite de L' Article cinquieme de la Convention secrette, 13 June 1799, PRO, WO, 1/71; Edward Stevens to Timothy Pickering, 23 June 1799, "Letters of Louverture," *AHR* 16 (1910): 74. C. L. R. James's classic study of the revolt, *The Black Jacobins,* 229, is flawed by its determination to depict Louverture as a loyal subject of France: "Toussaint attempted no secrecy" with Maitland and engaged in "no treason to France."

29. John Adams, "A Proclamation: Renewal of Commerce with St. Domingo," 26 June 1799, *State Papers and Publick Documents of the United States* (Boston, 1819), 4; Roger G. Kennedy, *Orders from France: The Americans and the French in a Revolutionary World, 1780–1820* (New York, 1989),

151; Toussaint Louverture to John Adams, 14 Aug. 1799, "Letters of Louverture," *AHR* 16 (1910): 82. Joseph Charles, *The Origins of the American Party System* (Williamsburg, Va., 1956), 134 n. 105, contends that Pickering's diplomacy was "carried out behind Adams's back" and hoped "to put Toussaint in the power of our merchants and politicians." The Adams Papers demonstrate, however, that Adams was not only fully apprised of events in Philadelphia and Cap François but that, as he told Pickering on 1 May 1799, the negotiations with Maitland and Louverture enjoyed his "fullest approbation." See Reel 119.

30. Edward Stevens to Timothy Pickering, 26 Oct. 1799, "Letters of Louverture," *AHR* 16 (1910): 86; Robert Liston to Governor Russel, 6 May 1799, *The Suppressed History of the Administration of John Adams,* ed. John Wood (New York, 1846), 230; John Adams to Timothy Pickering, 17 April 1799, Adams Papers, MHS, Reel 119; Oliver Wolcott to Samuel Smith, 20 March 1799, in Gibbs, *Memoirs of the Administrations,* 228–29; Timothy Pickering to Rufus King, 12 March 1799, in King, *Life and Correspondence* 2:557.

31. Edward Stevens to Timothy Pickering, 27 April 1800, "Letters of Louverture," *AHR* 16 (1910): 97–98; Edward Stevens to Thomas Maitland, 23 May 1799, ibid., 73; Toussaint Louverture to John Adams, 14 Aug. 1799, ibid., 82; Edward Stevens to Timothy Pickering, 24 April 1800, ibid., 97.

32. Larry E. Tise, *The American Counterrevolution: A Retreat From Liberty, 1783–1800* (Mechanicsburg, Pa., 1998), 485; Ott, *Haitian Revolution,* 114; Edward Stevens to Timothy Pickering, 24 June 1799, "Letters of Louverture," *AHR* 16 (1910): 80; Edward Stevens to Timothy Pickering, 16 Jan. 1800, *AHR* 16 (1910): 90.

33. Stanley Elkins and Eric McKitrick, *The Age of Federalism: The Early American Republic, 1788–1800* (New York, 1993), 659; Edward Stevens to Timothy Pickering, 24 May 1800, "Letters of Louverture," *AHR* 16 (1910): 98–99; Edward Stevens to Timothy Pickering, 19 April 1800, *AHR* 16 (1910): 94–96; Edward Stevens to John Marshall, 10 Sept. 1800, *AHR* 16 (1910): 101; Edward Stevens to Timothy Pickering, 13 Feb. 1800, *AHR* 16 (1910): 93. Paul Louverture was Toussaint's brother; it is unclear at what date he assumed Toussaint's adopted surname, which many historians, such as McCullough, *Adams,* 519, incorrectly spell as L'Ouverture.

34. Edward Stevens to John Marshall, 2 Aug. 1800, "Letters of Louverture," *AHR* 16 (1910): 100–101; John Adams, "A Proclamation," 6 Sept. 1800, *National State Papers of the United States, 1789–1817,* ed. Martin P. Claussen (Wilmington, Del., 1980), 240; Alexander Hamilton to Timothy Pickering, 21 Feb. 1799, *AHP* 22:493; John Adams to Timothy Pickering, 6 Aug. 1799, Adams Papers, MHS, Reel 120.

35. Alexander Hamilton to Timothy Pickering, 21 Feb. 1799, *AHP* 22:492–93; Tobias Lear to James Madison, 17 July 1801, *JMP: Secretary of State Series* 1:427–29.

36. Jean Smith, *John Marshall: Definer of a Nation* (New York, 1996), 162; John Marshall to John Adams, 6 Sept. 1800, Adams Papers, MHS, Reel 398; John Marshall to Toussaint Louverture, 26 Nov. 1800, *The Papers of John Marshall,* 8 vols. to date, ed. Charles T. Cullen (Chapel Hill, N.C., 1974–), 6:22.

37. Ferling, *Adams,* 405; Brown, *Presidency of Adams,* 190; Paul Finkelman, "The Problem of Slavery in the Age of Federalism," in *Federalists Reconsidered,* ed. Doren Ben-Atar and Barbara B. Oberg (Charlottesville, Va., 1998), 138.

38. Brown, *Presidency of Adams,* 139–40; James McHenry to John Adams, 25 Nov. 1798, Adams Papers, MHS, Reel 392; Smith, *John Adams* 2:1094.

39. Clarfield, *Pickering,* 198; Timothy Pickering to Rufus King, 15 Feb. 1797, Timothy Pickering to Rufus King, 20 June 1797, both in King Papers, Huntington Library.

40. Henry J. Ford, "Timothy Pickering," in *The American Secretaries of State and Their Diplomacy,* ed. Samuel Flagg Bemis (New York, 1928), 2:224–25; Richard Brookhiser, *Alexander Hamilton, American* (New York, 1999), 140–41; Alexander Hamilton to Harrison Gray Otis, 26 Jan. 1799, *AHP* 22:440–41; Perkins, *First Rapprochement,* 112.

41. John Quincy Adams to William Vans Murray, 14 July 1798, Adams Papers, MHS, Reel 133; James Monroe to Thomas Mathews, 17 March 1802, Executive Letterbook, Library of Virginia.

42. Clifford Egan, *Neither War Nor Peace: Franco-American Relations, 1803–1812* (Baton Rouge, 1983), 51.

43. Boyd, "Thomas Jefferson's 'Empire of Liberty,'" 552.

44. Tucker and Hendrickson, *Empire of Liberty,* 126.

45. Alan Schom, *Napoleon Bonaparte* (New York, 1997), 225, 321, 389; and Henry Adams, *History of the United States of America during the Administrations of Thomas Jefferson* (1903; rept. New York, 1986), 256, both suggest Louisiana was more important in Bonaparte's mind. Tucker and Hendrickson, *Empire of Liberty,* 299, 301 n. 83, and esp. Robert L. Paquette, "Revolutionary Saint Domingue in the Making of Territorial Louisiana," in Gaspar and Geggus, *Turbulent Time,* 206–7, 210–11, rightly, in my view, emphasize that France was far more interested in the island than in the American mainland.

46. Michael Zuckerman, *Almost Chosen People: Oblique Biographies in the American Grain* (Berkeley, 1993), 204–5; Tobias Lear to James Madison, 17 July 1801, *JMP: Secretary of State Series* 1:427–29. Tim Matthewson, "Jefferson and Haiti," *JSH* 61 (1995): 224, argues that in his conversation with Pichon, Jefferson "had called for neither the restoration of slavery nor for the French to make an example of the blacks." That theory, however, begs the question of what the president thought Bonaparte planned to do after "starving" out the rebels. To defend Jefferson on this point is to make him a fool, blind to French objectives regarding the island.

47. Alexander DeConde, *This Affair of Louisiana* (New York, 1976), 100; John Chester Miller, *The Wolf by the Ears: Thomas Jefferson and Slavery* (New York, 1977), 139–40; Alexander Hamilton, "Purchase of Louisiana," *New-York Evening Post,* 5 July 1803, *AHP* 26:130. Dumas Malone, *Jefferson the President: First Term, 1801–1805* (Boston, 1970), 253, theorized that Jefferson's response to Pichon was designed to demonstrate "his excellent disposition toward the French," and Lawrence S. Kaplan, *Jefferson and France: An Essay on Politics and Political Ideas* (New Haven, Conn., 1967), 118, suggests that Jefferson "was giving France an earnest of American good will," which assumes that Bonaparte could be persuaded to base his Caribbean diplomacy on morality and gratitude toward the United States.

48. Glover Moore, *The Missouri Controversy, 1819–1821* (Lexington, Ky., 1953), 47–48. Admittedly, even had the Louisiana region arrived without slavery, white settlers might have tried to overturn that restriction at a later date. Yet as Robert McColley rightly suggested in *Slavery and Jeffersonian Virginia* (Urbana, Ill., 1964), 125, Jefferson "has been recognized universally as the father of exclusion in the Old Northwest, but has never been labeled as the father of slavery in Louisiana."

CHAPTER 14

Joseph Gales and the Making of the Jeffersonian Middle Class

Seth Cotlar

A rough historiographical consensus seems to have emerged that the Jefferson-ian principles of 1800 flowed unproblematically from the radical Enlighten-ment doctrines that legitimated the Atlantic world's popular political activism of the 1790s. Like Paine, the United Irishmen, the members of the London Cor-responding Society, and most of the French revolutionaries, this account goes, the Jeffersonians were bourgeois radicals who believed that the establishment of a progressive, just society required little more than expunging the world of the vestiges of aristocratic privilege, instituting representative governments, and letting the free market run its course. If several recent studies of the Atlan-tic radicalism of the early 1790s are correct, however, American historians may have to reconsider this narrative of congruity.[1] Indeed, when compared to the more radically democratic and egalitarian elements of Painite radicalism that European historians have recently uncovered, the dominant political vision be-hind the "revolution of 1800" appears profoundly limited in scope. The mod-est nature of the principles of 1800 is particularly glaring considering that many rank-and-file Jeffersonians had previously participated in Irish, British, and French movements that had endorsed a far more sweeping, socially transfor-mative politics. This essay uses the career of one of these transatlantic radicals, Joseph Gales—the editor of North Carolina's leading Jeffersonian newspaper during the election of 1800—to argue that the Jeffersonian persuasion of 1800 rested on a rejection and a willful forgetting of many of the key elements of the radical, transatlantic, Painite political ideology that emerged in the early 1790s.

Joseph Gales makes his first appearance as a figure of historical note in E. P. Thompson's classic *The Making of the English Working Class*.[2] He shows up there as the quintessential radical in the provinces, the editor of the *Sheffield Weekly Register* (1787–94), which was probably the most widely circulated opposition paper produced outside of London. In Thompson's book, Gales plays the role of the lower-middling printer who used his literacy and access to print to galvanize those below and slightly above him on the socioeconomic ladder into a powerful, potentially revolutionary political movement on behalf of the rights of man. Gales's paper was the voice of Sheffield's notoriously radical cutlers, and he corresponded with some of Britain's most vehemently Francophilic democrats during his stint as the secretary of the Sheffield Society for Constitutional Information. Gales used his newspaper to advocate not only the end of the slave trade but also the complete abolition of slavery in England's colonial possessions—a position he defended by noting that the idea of "the blacks being inferior to the whites in their capacities, is a vulgar prejudice, founded only in pride and ignorance."[3] Gales also reprinted cheap editions of Paine's works, as well as a weekly periodical entitled *The Patriot,* designed to supply laborers with political theory, opinion, and information in an affordable and easily readable form. After being accused in 1794 of hoarding pikes for an eventual overthrow of the British government, Gales and his family fled the country.

After a year in Germany and France Gales emigrated to America, where he largely disappears from the historiography. He surfaces briefly in William Ames's book-length study of his son, Joseph Gales Jr., who edited the national mouthpiece of the Jeffersonian party, the *National Intelligencer.* Ames portrays Gales Sr. as the embodiment of respectable Jeffersonianism—moderate, pious, and eagerly complicit in the racial, gender, and class exclusions that so marked nineteenth-century Jeffersonian ideology.[4] How had Gales's life project so shifted? When had he ceased making the English working class and begun making the American middle class? What was the process through which his Painite radicalism became Jeffersonian (and eventually Whig) moderation? Historians such as Isaac Kramnick and Michael Durey would argue that Gales did not change at all; rather, they would interpret his moderate Jeffersonianism of the early 1800s as a logical extension of his early 1790s bourgeois radicalism.[5] This essay, by contrast, argues that Gales (as well as many of his formerly radical compatriots) did indeed go through a profound transformation in the 1790s. Although Gales chose to see continuity in his political principles, a close reading of his Sheffield, Philadelphia (1796–97), and Raleigh (1799–1832) newspapers indicates that his political principles changed significantly as he worked himself into the mainstream of the national Jeffersonian party.

The material Gales chose to insert in his newspaper in the run-up to the election of 1800 is particularly revealing. Week after week Gales triangulated his political project against not just aristocratic Federalists but also those supposedly dangerous Jacobins and infidels below him on the social scale. A set of "others" suddenly appeared in Gales's late 1790s newspapers, figures such as the overly talkative woman, the potentially rebellious slave, the amoral infidel, the turbulent journeyman, and the ungrateful apprentice, who seemed to threaten the Jeffersonian ascendancy from below. The conspicuous absence of these figures from his Sheffield paper (and even from his early Philadelphia newspapers) indicates a fundamental shift in his political subjectivity and, more importantly, in the political subjectivity he sought to nurture in his readers. As he increasingly positioned himself and his readers in the middle of a tripartite political division rather than at the bottom of a binary division, his use of key political concepts like equality, rights, and democracy became more moderate. The Joseph Gales of the nineteenth century—the man whose "household" had become "the centre of culture, hospitality, and refined gayety" in Raleigh—had moved quite a way from the man who in 1794 could purportedly "lead 10,000 [working] men by the crook of his finger" in order to stir up a potentially revolutionary "spirit of Clamour & invective against Government." [6] Although he remained a self-professed champion of "democracy" his entire life, the nature of his democratic vision became more explicitly exclusive at precisely the moment he became an established figure in America's Republican Party.

Such a story of a backsliding radical runs the risk of fading into a teleological account of an authentic radical tradition that failed because too many people like Gales chose crass personal prosperity over authentic political principle. I want to avoid such an account, for Gales did not simply suffer from false consciousness or a failure of nerve. There is no reason why we should not believe his claim that his nineteenth-century American moderation flowed logically and unproblematically from his eighteenth-century British radicalism. But we need not take Gales's experience as representative or see the noticeable shifts in his political vision as the only possible responses to his changing context. Hundreds of Joseph's compatriots in the SSCI stayed behind in Sheffield and eventually formed an underground revolutionary cell of the United Englishmen. The participants in this radical underworld that Iain McCalman has so richly described proudly identified themselves as Jacobins and *sans culottes,* and by the late 1790s they were openly espousing the redistribution of wealth and a far more participatory and populist political system than the one that emerged in Joseph Gales's America.[7] Even many American Painites (émigrés and non-émigrés) did not follow Gales's path into the Jeffersonian middle class but instead became key members of the emergent labor and/or deist movements in New York City and elsewhere.

When set in the context of the range of political possibilities generated by the popular political movements of the 1790s, we can see how Gales's political trajectory is representative of only one strand of a Painite tradition that became increasingly fractured and contested over the course of that tumultuous decade.[8] Just because Gales's variety of democratic thought became the dominant one in the early Republic, this does not mean that the transformation he went through was a logical, inevitable working out of a set of ideas that were in place by the late 1780s. Gales, like many of his fellow members of the respectable, self-improving middle classes throughout the Atlantic world, consciously chose to dissociate himself from those self-proclaimed Painites who took the language of the rights of man in more radical directions—toward the anti-authoritarian producer ideology of New York City's freethinking labor radicals, the redistributive egalitarianism of backcountry agrarians and followers of people like Thomas Spence or Thomas Skidmore, or the millennial utopianism of a William Blake or the religious seekers of the Second Great Awakening.[9] When he moved to Raleigh to start his newspaper, Gales chose the path of middling respectability, a path that required him to renounce the other varieties of Painite democratic thought that were proliferating around the Atlantic basin in the early 1800s. Judging from his activities in Sheffield, however, it was by no means a foregone conclusion that he would one day be remembered for producing a moderate American newspaper that "was always on the side of law, order, and good morals."[10]

As this class-coded, nineteenth-century remembering of Gales and his newspaper suggests, his political activities in Raleigh were bound up with another ongoing and interrelated project—the construction and legitimation of an American middle class. While many historians have focused on the long-term material and cultural transformations that accompanied the emergence of the American middle class, this essay examines how the political struggles of the 1790s contributed to this development.[11] It was precisely people like Gales— men who had spent their lives structurally placed between the rich and the poor, the illiterate and the formally educated, the landed and the destitute—who did the most important ideological work of constructing both a recognizably middle-class identity and a public discourse that helped to define and legitimate that identity. As we shall see, the last years of the 1790s were perhaps the most important years in this process, as Jeffersonians sought to distinguish themselves from the aristocratic Federalists to their right and the plebeian Jacobins to their left. In contrast to historical accounts that interpret the ascendancy of America's middling democrats as a logical development fairly free of conflict, this essay argues that this new social and discursive formation emerged quite tenuously and slowly out of an eighteenth-century world where "the people" were regarded as a unified rather than a variegated body. To understand how American democrats became able unapologetically to exclude large portions of the populace from the category of the empowered "people," we must examine how people like Joseph Gales lived the transition from the Painite utopianism of the 1790s to the more circumscribed political aspirations of the nineteenth century's democrats. Recapturing the uncertainty and anxiety of Gales's personal transformation can perhaps help us recover some of the same contingency that marked the transformation of American society more generally.

JOSEPH GALES, SHEFFIELD RADICAL

Until the late 1780s, nothing set Joseph Gales's life story dramatically apart from that of the multitude of other artisanal laborers throughout the Anglo-American world.[12] Gales's father, a village artisan in Eckington, sent Joseph to school until the age of thirteen, at which point he bound him out to a leather maker. Joseph quickly ended that apprenticeship and bound himself to a Manchester printing firm. Pleading unjust treatment and his new master's refusal to teach him the skills of the trade, Gales found another printer, this time in Newark, to take him for the remainder of his indenture. In Newark Gales courted Winifred Marshall, the daughter of a gentry family fallen on hard times. In 1787, at the age of twenty-six, Gales had accumulated enough money, credit, connections, and skill to establish his own printing shop in nearby Sheffield. Gales's early career reveals an ambitious, upwardly mobile artisan, someone who would aggressively seek out better employment conditions and who understood the value of marrying up. Nothing in the scanty archive of his life before 1787, however, reveals a man fired by political principle, unless his as-sertiveness in breaking indentures can be taken as a sign of a generalized arti-sanal resistance to authority.

It was in Sheffield, a working-class city of twenty-five thousand renowned for its political radicalism, that Gales slowly received his political education. Gales's newspapers from the years before 1790 evince a concern for the plight of Sheffield's impoverished laborers, but there is little evidence that Gales was part of any sustained artisanal political culture. If anything his interests seemed to lie with his fellow masters against the journeymen and apprentices who com-prised the majority of the city's inhabitants. Indeed, the first voluntary organi-zation he joined as a young master was one established to track down runaway workers. That said, Gales eagerly supported the two most prominent reformist causes of the late 1780s: the abolition of the slave trade and the repeal of the Test and Corporation Acts. These positions allied him more with nationally oriented gentlemen reformers—dissenters like Granville Sharp, Joseph Priestley, Rich-ard Price, and John Cartwright—than with the artisans of Sheffield.[13] Because the only other newspaper in Sheffield was an avowedly Tory paper, however, the *Register* quickly became the paper of choice for Sheffield's artisan community. Fifty years later Winifred would proudly remember that the *Register* "was to be found in every house of respectability . . . and one at least was taken in every manufacturing shop, so that it was read by at least 10,000 persons of that class, as they clubbed to pay the subscription."[14] In the late 1780s and early 1790s one newspaper could simultaneously serve the communities of "respectable" re-formers and artisans with little sense of contradiction.

With the publication of Paine's *Rights of Man* in 1791 and the popular po-litical action it inspired, Gales's paper became a more vocal advocate for Shef-field's growing democratic movement. From 1791 on, virtually every *Sheffield Register* contained sympathetic accounts of the French Revolution, attacks on Burke's *Reflections,* or excerpts from the democratic pamphlets that espoused the French cause. In July 1791 thousands of Sheffield residents rioted to protest the enclosure of the local commons. While there is no evidence that Gales joined this crowd action, he printed several pieces sympathetic to the rioters' cause. In late autumn of 1791 Gales was one of the "assembly of 5 or 6 me-chanicks"[15] who founded the Sheffield Society for Constitutional Information (SSCI). By January 1792 the organization, composed of "the inferior sort of manufacturers and workers,"[16] had over two hundred members and by May of that year the membership was estimated at twenty-four hundred, thus surpassing the contemporary membership of its metropolitan equivalent, the London Corresponding Society. According to one history of Sheffield, the SSCI became "the hub of a radical propaganda system that centered on the press of Joseph Gales."[17] The *Sheffield Register* quickly became the mouthpiece of the nation's parliamentary reform organizations, printing resolutions, toasts, and pro-reform essays from the scores of societies like the SSCI that emerged throughout Britain in 1792–93. When the government sent troops to Sheffield to keep the peace and marshaled local elites and hired spies to monitor the activities of the SSCI in late 1791, the stakes of Gales's political activism went up. He responded by intensifying the pace of his activities, explicitly choosing not to join any of the other organizations that were formed by the more "respectable" inhabitants "to put a stop to these levellers."[18]

Thanks in part to Gales's organizing efforts, Sheffield became the most important site of political radicalism outside of London.[19] In the summer of 1792 Gales started the previously mentioned *Patriot,* which for a short time had a national distribution and furthered Sheffield's reputation among Britain's democrats.[20] In the fall of 1792 thousands of Sheffield residents took to the streets to celebrate the French victory at Valmy—quite a statement considering that the town also housed a garrison of government troops. Meanwhile the SSCI grew so rapidly that it had "to divide into small Bodies of Ten Persons each, and . . . hold a General Meeting once a Month."[21] The thirty meeting places its members had established could not accommodate all these small gatherings on the same night, so they had to stagger the days on which these cells met. At these small weekly meetings, members discussed a wide range of topics: universal manhood suffrage, annual elections, the injustice of enclosure, the inadequate reward for labor, and the disproportionate suffering that war caused the nation's laborers. According to one hostile observer, Paine's works comprised "the great part of their weekly debates."[22] The organization that Gales had established did more than just lend the power of unreflective numbers to a political persuasion articulated by a few elite leaders. In each of these small meetings new political leaders arose, and established working-class leaders (perhaps people similar to Boston's Ebenezer Mackintosh) established connections to a broader national movement. Only the emergence of such a movement can explain why eight thousand Sheffield residents took the time to walk into Gales's print shop and sign the petition for parliamentary reform that he had helped draft. One can only imagine the thousands of individual conversations that took place in this increasingly politicized space.

Gales embodied a new form of political leadership that the particular cross-class character of early 1790s Painite radicalism necessitated.[23] Unlike upper-class reformers like Joseph Priestley or John Horne Tooke, Gales came into daily contact with the rank and file of the growing democratic movement on the streets and in his workplace. Yet unlike his fellow artisans, Gales corresponded with internationally known figures like Priestley and a few members of parliament. But Gales did not have the luxury of leading the gentleman scientist's or philosopher's life; he was a businessman and artisan who needed to accomplish the daily, grinding work of editing a newspaper and running a small print shop. In Sheffield Gales had earned some extra money by working as an auctioneer, an occupation that brought him into frequent contact with the growing number of northern England's poor farmers and artisans, who faced a future of either wage labor or migration in search of a new start. He saw firsthand the deprivation that the rationalization of the land and the workplace brought to England's poor, and his newspaper never once blamed the poor themselves for their plight. Because he understood the daily struggles of Sheffield's laborers, he did not share the gentleman reformers' utopian and uncritical faith in the beneficence of the free market. Nor did he share their assumption that the "people," if given a chance, would instantly assent to the "self-evident truths" of their reformist platform; rather, Gales understood the necessity of building a popular political organization dedicated to translating Enlightenment theory into democratic practice. Having cultivated connections with both national reformers and Sheffield's workers, Gales provided a crucial link between two very different components of the pro-French reformist coalition.

If we could recapture the texture of Gales's daily interaction with his plebeian compatriots we could more effectively settle the questions about the bourgeois nature of his radicalism. To what extent did he identify with those below him on the socioeconomic scale, and to what extent did he seek to differentiate himself as a member of the particularly virtuous middling sort? Unfortunately the archive is fairly silent on this aspect of Gales's life, offering up only a few examples of his attitude toward Sheffield's laborers. In his newspaper and *The Patriot,* Gales set himself up as the tutor of the working classes, a position that could be read as a gesture of differentiation. Yet by joining a democratically run organization made up of such people, Gales engaged in debate and discussion with them and undoubtedly learned much in the process. Gales's paper was always open to the letters and resolutions of Sheffield's journeymen cutlers, many of whom put forward a sophisticated critique of the free-market labor principles that many larger manufacturers espoused. This gained him the support and admiration of the laborers who made up Sheffield's politicized crowd. When a Church and King mob threatened to destroy his shop in 1793, Gales proudly informed a correspondent in Manchester that "This circumstance . . . had the effect of calling together a wall of defense, for, about an hour afterwards, upwards of a hundred stout democrats stood before us, singing 'God Save Great Thomas Paine!' to the royal tune."[24] Here was a moment of proud defiance through solidarity, and Gales made no apologies for the actions of the crowd. Likewise, in 1794 when a mob had formed and was threatening to pull down the Cutler's Hall where an antireform group was meeting, Gales rushed to the scene, was immediately "carried baldheaded" to the chair, and with a few well-chosen words convinced the crowd to express their political discontent through the SSCI rather than through violence. While this sems to indicate a desire to distinguish himself from "the mob," other evidence suggests that we should look skeptically on his frequent declamations against violence. After all, Gales and one of his journeymen were implicated in a nationwide plot to stockpile pikes in 1794. If the distinction between middle-class and plebeian reformers lay in their attitude toward physical violence, Gales is difficult to locate easily in one camp or the other. It appears that the politics of popular resistance had drawn Gales along the path from reform toward revolution. The only difference between him and the scores of printers and political leaders who were imprisoned or banished to Botany Bay was that Gales was lucky enough to slip out of the country before he was apprehended. And perhaps his flight was the only factor that set his life's course apart from the diehard Jacobins who continued to operate and organize around Sheffield into the early nineteenth century.

Just as the Democratic Republican Societies disappeared in America during the late 1790s, the SSCI and its equivalents throughout Britain also vanished as the reformist community factionalized, largely along class lines. For a short time in the early 1790s the political aspirations of elite, enlightened reformers and their plebeian compatriots had seemed largely compatible. Gales's straddling of these two communities had suited him perfectly for the leadership of an organization like the SSCI, but as the reformist coalition, under the pressure of fierce governmental repression, began to splinter around the issue of peaceful reform vs. violent revolution, Gales was faced with a difficult choice.

His flight to the continent in 1794 saved him from having to make that choice, and upon his arrival in America the emergence of a moderate Jeffersonian coalition offered him an option that had ceased to exist in Britain—he could simultaneously define himself as a friend of the rights of ordinary citizens and as a respectable member of the enlightened elite.

JOSEPH GALES AND THE RADICAL ÉMIGRÉS OF PHILADELPHIA

In July 1795 the Gales family arrived in Philadelphia, a city with a well-established community of native and émigré democrats.[25] Benjamin Franklin Bache's *Aurora* was filled with essays written by radical émigrés like James Callender, and in 1796 Callender would be joined by the man who would become the most notorious foreign incendiary of the 1790s, William Duane. William Young Birch, a printer who had been forced to flee Manchester for printing Paine's works, was beginning to establish himself as one of the leading engravers in the town. Joseph Priestley had recently settled on the Susquehanna and the Galeses immediately joined the Unitarian Church that he had established in Philadelphia. The United Irishmen James Napper Tandy and Archibald Hamilton Rowan would also settle for a brief while in Philadelphia, awaiting the opportunity to return to Ireland in support of an anticipated, French-supported revolution against the English. Philadelphia was also the newly adopted home of "Citizen" Richard Lee, who had printed scores of tracts for the London Corresponding Society at his shop "at the tree of Liberty" in Soho. Morgan John Rhees, a Welsh Baptist who had traveled to Paris with a trunk of Bibles upon hearing the news about the Bastille and had published Welsh translations of Voltaire's works, lived only a few blocks from the Galeses. When Gales started his own newspaper in Philadelphia he printed many accounts of Rhees's utopian community in western Pennsylvania, where, "freed from the oppressor's yoke, and the bustle of your great cities," Rhees and his compatriots hoped to "attend to the voice of nature whistling among the trees the delightful tunes of independence."[26] Gales could not have chosen a more hospitable place to settle, and according to Winifred they received much assistance from this community of "persons who, like ourselves, had sought refuge from the political storm which threatened destruction to all those English friends of Reform who were hardy enough to brave it."[27]

While the Galeses found many politically sympathetic people in Philadelphia, finding work for Joseph was another matter. Gales arrived with neither the capital nor the connections to establish his own shop, so he took temporary work for $10 a week as a journeyman compositor in the shop of Claypool and Dunlop, the editors of the *American Daily Advertiser*. When they discovered that Gales knew how to take shorthand, they employed him to record the debates in Congress for their paper. In a matter of weeks he gained recognition in the city for the remarkable accuracy of his transcriptions. In the fall of 1796 Gales purchased the *Independent Gazetteer* from the widow of its former editor, the locally illustrious anti-Federalist Eleazar Oswald.[28] Trying to carve out a market for another democratic paper in a media-saturated Philadelphia was difficult, so Gales tried to capitalize on Oswald's popularity with those who lived in the rural areas surrounding Philadelphia. He also sought to set himself apart by emphasizing his "many correspondents in England, Germany, Holland, and France who supply him with authentic information," as well as his ability to translate "German and French papers."[29]

Compared to his Sheffield newspaper, Gales's *Independent Gazetteer* was remarkably moderate. While he proudly identified himself as "a firm and determined supporter of the principles of Liberty, Independence and Republican Government," he also declared his opposition "to all violence and licentiousness." In a departure from his previous support for Sheffield's journeymen cutlers, the only time he commented on labor struggles in Philadelphia he criticized the "disorderly manner" in which "a number of Seamen belonging to this port paraded the streets" asking for an "unjust . . . increase in wages."[30] Gales positioned his paper primarily as an aid to commerce, as a vehicle that could "point out where necessary wants may be supplied, and superfluities disposed of." Whereas in Sheffield he had used his newspaper as a means of disseminating political news and opinions, the *Gazetteer* was more interested in promoting the "useful knowledge" and "beneficial information" that could further economic modernization.[31]

This shift in focus could be explained in many ways. As a newcomer with a radical past, Gales probably recognized that this could work against him in his efforts to attract the advertising business of merchants that was so essential to the success of a newspaper. Likewise, there is no evidence that Gales became involved in the popular politics of Philadelphia the way émigrés like William Duane and James Reynolds had. Where Gales's Sheffield paper had served a politicized audience with which he was familiar, he developed few connections with Philadelphia's less organized community of politically minded laborers. In addition, since he had inherited Oswald's largely rural constituency, Gales had to appeal to a readership about which he knew very little. Where Oswald spoke the language of backcountry anti-Federalism fluently, Gales did not have authentic recourse to this particular idiom of late-eighteenth-century radicalism. Recognizing that the style of urban radicalism with which he was familiar would not play particularly well with the modest farmers in Philadelphia's hinterlands, Gales probably decided to play it safe. Finally and perhaps most importantly, Gales arrived in America with an attitude common to many émigrés throughout American history, that America was essentially "a Land of Comfort, where, blessed with health, and being industrious, no one need despair of a comfortable livelihood." [32] Compared to England, where he had experienced governmental repression and witnessed widespread poverty, Gales wishfully viewed his adopted country as a land where collective political struggle was no longer necessary.

Two aspects of Gales's earlier political activism, however, were evident in his Philadelphia newspaper. First, it appears that he sought to introduce his American readers to the pantheon of political activists and thinkers who had emerged in 1790s Britain. As the most recent émigré in Philadelphia, he was well positioned to play such a role. In his first three months as editor of the *Independent Gazetteer,* Gales either recounted the stories of or printed excerpts from the work of many of Europe's leading radicals: John Thelwall, William Godwin, Volney, John Cartwright, Samuel Neilson, William Sampson, Thomas Muir, Joseph Gerrald, Maurice Margarot, and T. F. Palmer. While many American printers had been using stories about Britain's persecuted democrats as a means to reflect on the potentially tyrannical proclivities of the Federalists, Gales avoided extrapolating American meanings from these European stories. [33] All the same, he did important work for American democrats in demonstrating the extent to which they were part of a much broader international movement dedicated to putting Painite principles into practice. In Sheffield Gales had learned how to use a newspaper to create an imagined community of like-minded reformers, and during his time in Philadelphia this goal continued to shape his editorial decisions.

Gales also continued to use his newspaper as a vehicle for disseminating arguments against slavery. In November 1796 he printed a glowing report about the "African Free School at New York" that demonstrated that "the powers of the mind do not depend upon the complexion." The students of the school, according to this report, had been "rendered capable of discharging the duties of Citizens, and of being useful to themselves and to society." [34] Soon after settling in Raleigh Gales would purchase slaves of his own and become a vocal advocate for colonization, but in 1796 he was still hopeful that slavery would soon be eradicated and, most importantly, that former slaves would one day become citizens. Like many other radical émigrés, it took Gales several years to shed an assumption that had been central to the Painite tradition of the early 1790s, that the rights of man should be "extended to the whole human race black or white, high or low, rich or poor."[35]

Gales sold the *Independent Gazetteer* to Samuel Harrison Smith in November 1797, and in 1798 Nathaniel Macon and other Republican members of the North Carolina delegation in Philadelphia encouraged Gales to settle in Raleigh and establish the state's first Republican paper. Gales left no record of this period of his life, so we do not know why he sold his Philadelphia paper or why he decided to move. In any case, by September 1799 the Gales family was settled in Raleigh and on 22 October he published the first issue of the *Raleigh Register*.

FROM SHEFFIELD DEMOCRAT TO RALEIGH REPUBLICAN

Having failed to establish himself in Philadelphia, Gales arrived in Raleigh deeply dependent on his new Republican patrons. They supported him well, garnering the state's printing contract and hundreds of subscribers for him. Raleigh differed greatly from Sheffield and this profoundly shaped the texture of Gales's new publication. The population of Raleigh was less than 750, more than a third of whom were slaves. Gales now served a readership of slaveholders, small farmers, and land speculators, not urban mechanics. Thrust into this new social terrain, he renewed the reformist commitments he had adopted as a young artisan in Sheffield and established social connections with Raleigh's growing community of civic-minded reformers. Indeed, within ten years of moving to North Carolina Gales helped administer or raise money for virtually every "enlightened" and "benevolent" reform effort in the state—the new university in Chapel Hill, the local library, the agricultural reform society, penal reform, colonization, and internal improvements.[36] Where his participation in Sheffield's world of voluntary societies had brought him into contact with the city's reform-minded laborers, in Raleigh his associational life became a means by which he aligned himself with the "respectable" members of North Carolina society—professionals and politicians who sought to distinguish themselves from the "less civilized" portions of the state's population. His cosmopolitanism was undoubtedly one of the most valuable commodities this stranger brought with him to his new home, and he quickly used it to establish a secure place in Raleigh society. In the process, however, his reformism began to function less as a means of joining together with fellow citizens from a fairly wide range of backgrounds, and more as a means of solidifying his connections to a more class-constricted group of upwardly mobile "improvers."

Like most nineteenth-century advocates of economic "improvement," Gales regarded "free commerce" as the best means of achieving national and personal prosperity. As a Sheffield radical he had also espoused free commerce, but as with his associational activities, this position had profoundly different class implications in Raleigh. During the seven years he edited the *Sheffield Register,* Gales and his readers developed an egalitarian structural analysis of commercial society that differed significantly from that of the more optimistic proponents of Smithian economics. Where most members of the mercantile elite saw poverty not as an inevitable facet of commercial society but as an unnatural product of government corruption and monopoly, Gales's Sheffield paper rarely represented the market as an unproblematically benevolent force. There is no evidence that Gales or his readers ever desired to return to a precommercial age, yet they rejected the claim that the market was the only steering mechanism to which society should pay any heed. Instead, Gales and his laboring readers looked to politics (both local and national) as a means to shape commercial society so as to benefit the many without capital as well as the few with it.

In this way the economic context of late-eighteenth-century Sheffield profoundly shaped the reception of Paine's ideas about commerce, natural rights, and equality. Where most American historians have tended to assume that the Painite language of economic improvement and free commerce implied a modern, laissez-faire conception of economics, this was not the case in Britain in the 1790s. The presence of workingmen's political and trade organizations and the heightened degree of industrial development created a situation in which the more economically radical and egalitarian aspects of Paine's thought came to the fore. When the March 1792 general meeting of the SSCI, with Gales in the chair, passed a resolution thanking Paine for his writings, for example, they singled out only one section of his work for particular mention—his "plan for the Support of the Young & the infirm."[37] This was a reference to the section of *The Rights of Man* in which Paine advocated a progressive system of taxation in order to encourage a more equitable distribution of wealth, public pensions for the education of youth and the support of the elderly and infirm, public jobs and material relief for "the casual poor," and publicly funded burials for laborers forced to work "at a distance from their friends."[38] When Gales inserted this SSCI resolution in his *Sheffield Register* it was juxtaposed with an essay from a correspondent who argued against the use of such "general laws" to relieve the plight of the poor, calling instead for the "exercise of private charities."[39] Judging from the other pieces in Gales's paper, we cannot assume that he endorsed such criticisms of Paine's argument; he apparently believed that the poor should demand economic assistance not as a matter "of charity, but of right."[40] Throughout the Atlantic world, such claims for an inclusive (rather than an exclusive) right to property frequently functioned as a critique of commercial society.[41] They rendered wage labor suspect by framing it as a means by which laborers were stripped of the rights to the fruits of their labor. These arguments could also support landless farmers in claims that they had been deprived of their natural right to property. Such statements were not uncommon in Gales's Sheffield and they eventually became central to the British radical movement that grew out of the Painite agitation of the early 1790s. Even though Gales never proposed outright redistribution in his Sheffield newspaper, he frequently commented critically on the social impact of market forces.

Whereas in Sheffield Gales had become a democrat who viewed the free market with a complicated mixture of admiration and reservation, in North Carolina those Painite reservations disappeared.[42] After his move to Raleigh, Gales's newspapers paid scant attention to the plight of those left out by the development of commercial civilization. Gales's increasingly sanguine, Jeffersonian view of commercial society was thus a relatively new feature of his political vision. If one of the key elements of the bourgeois worldview was the notion of the level playing field, or the race of life in which each economic actor starts out even, then Gales's Sheffield newspaper was decidedly not bourgeois.[43] Ironically, it may have been the slave-based economy of his new home that drove him to embrace a more bourgeois conception of economic life. In his newly adopted state the majority of those who were left out by the ideology of "progress" were slaves, and for Gales to support African American economic or political equality was simply beyond the bounds of the publicly utterable.

Another crucial difference between Sheffield and Raleigh was the class structure in which Gales was embedded and his perceived place within that structure. In Sheffield Gales saw himself as a combatant in a battle between an undifferentiated "people" and the entrenched aristocrats and monarchists who ran the government. In America, where "the people" theoretically controlled the government, Gales confronted a society that most Jeffersonians differentiated into three amorphous groupings and one clear-cut category—the mercantile and speculating elite who comprised the Federalist enemy; the virtuous middle composed of established artisans and farmers; the laboring poor; and finally the black slaves who provided the majority of the labor in the South. Dror Wahrman has demonstrated how the notion of a "middling" class emerged in response to the French Revolution and eventually came to shape British political discourse in the late 1790s.[44] If Joseph Gales's newspaper is a reliable indicator of Jeffersonian ideology, we might hypothesize that a similar transformation occurred in American political discourse, as an imagined Jeffersonian middle emerged out of an earlier, undifferentiated discourse of "the people" versus "the aristocrats" or "the many" versus "the few."

Gales described this middling group as uniquely suited to replace an older, outmoded set of social values and practices with a more enlightened, forward-looking approach. While this quarrel with the irrational past expressed itself most frequently as an attack on vestigial aristocratic privileges, it also articulated itself as an attack on equally outdated traditions of popular political action. In Sheffield Gales had played a central role in translating premodern patterns of crowd activity into modern, explicitly political practices of collective action. In America, however, he quickly joined in the Jeffersonian leadership's attempt to delegitimate traditionally plebeian, as well as aristocratic, forms of political activity.

Gales's emerging vision of the middle class's unique political role is exemplified in his shifting attitude toward the role of reason in politics. The Painites of the early 1790s had rested their radical claims for inclusion and political equality on the assumption that all humans possessed the capacity to reason. By the late 1790s this proposition had come under severe attack, and not only from Burkean elitists. The reaction against Enlightenment conceptions of reason also shaped a transatlantic political discourse that stressed the unique rationality of the "middling sort," distinguishing it from the "enthusiasm" and "passion" of the lower classes. Gales's newspapers in late 1799 and early 1800 can be read as an extended meditation on this theme. While he still was capable of waxing rhapsodic, in language that rang with the distant echo of the French Jacobins, about how "the phalanx of Reason is invulnerable," he always made it a point to define reason in a particularly class-coded way, as "sober thought, clear discernment, and intrepid discussion." Gales's newspaper systematically defined the plebian style of angry rhetoric that tapped into the seething resentments of the dispossessed as outside the bounds of legitimate political discourse. Where his Sheffield paper spoke in utopian terms of creating a political system that would bring the reason of every citizen to bear upon the political problems of the nation, his Raleigh newspaper generally focused on the need to keep the less rational portions of the populace out of the political process. Institutions like the SSCI were intended to construct a rational style of mass politics. By 1800 mass rationality (let alone any substantive attempt to create institutions that could foster it) came to be seen as a visionary vestige of the past.

Indeed, one genre that particularly appealed to Gales in the run-up to the election of 1800 was the bemused reflection on the limits of popular rationality. In his first paper issued at Raleigh, Gales included a piece on the irrational "local and hereditary" origins of opinions. While visionaries like Paine might argue that people were capable of judging political matters with rational detachment, this piece argued that "before men are capable of judging for themselves, they adopt the opinions of those whom they reverence or love." Because "the minds of men" as well as their "outward situation[s]" differ dramatically, there would forever be an "infinite diversity of opinion," little of it founded on right reason. While he regarded such opinions, accepted without rational reflection, as "prejudice," nothing in Gales's paper held out much hope that the mass of Americans would ever be able to overcome these barriers to true reason. Gales used an excerpt from the German Romantic philosopher Johann Zimmerman to reinforce this position. Zimmerman noted that the ordinary people of every nation begin their political reasoning from an unreflective position of "vanity and self-conceit," not abstract reason. Indeed, even "negroes . . . though the most stupid among the inhabitants of the earth, are excessively vain." Critical self-reflection, the essence of a Painite vision of inclusive citizenship, became a chimera in such reflections about reason. Likewise, the political unity that Painites had fantasized would arise when collective reason was allowed to function in an unrestrained environment disappeared before a Madisonian fatalism about the inevitability of competing and irreconcilable visions of the good.

This skepticism about reason notwithstanding, Gales never wavered in his commitment to "the natural right of every man to enquire after truth."[45] What had changed by 1800 was his newfound interest in defining a wide range of public utterances as insufficiently rational. At a time when Federalists were denouncing the leading Jeffersonian newspaper editors and pamphleteers as demagogues who inflamed the passions of the people, Gales chose to endorse this interpretation. Framing himself as a friend to moderation and rational public debate, he lumped arch-conservatives like William Cobbett and radical Jeffersonians like William Duane into one category of irresponsible printers who failed to "distinguish between informing the people, and inflaming them."[46] With such arguments Gales banished from the realm of legitimate political discourse the political style of angry, satirical rhetoric that many of Philadelphia's radical émigrés had mastered.

Gales's newspaper also went to great lengths to exclude women from the ranks of those capable of publicly exercising their rational faculties. During the seven-year run of his Sheffield newspaper, Gales published only one piece that could be considered misogynist, while printing scores of essays touting women's intellectual capacities. In 1789, for example, Gales published an essay by "A. Z." that argued that women were kept out of the ranks of philosophers and businessmen only because they had not been educated to fulfill those roles. This correspondent lamented that "in every age and in every country . . . men . . . have either left [women's] minds altogether without culture, or biased them by a culture of a spurious and improper nature; suspicious perhaps that a more rational one would have opened their eyes, shewn them their real condition, and prompted them to have asserted the rights of Nature."[47] Such affirmations of women's rational faculties were replaced in Gales's Raleigh newspaper by a series of anecdotes, poems, and essays emphasizing the "natural" differences between men and women. In his first *Raleigh Register,* for example, Gales printed an excerpt from Rousseau that asserted that "Men say what they think, women what they please. Knowledge is necessary to the one, and taste to the other . . . their discourses ought to have no forms in common, except the forms of truth."[48] Gales followed this up with a February 1800 essay on "the charming prattle of the fair sex," a March poem by Simon Henpeckt that complained of the "perpetual clatter" of his wife's mouth, and a violently misogynist April snippet entitled "Description of a Slut."[49] Gales's decision to include these pieces, which characterize women as incapable of entry into the world of rational discourse, marks a significant retreat from his earlier position as a moderate advocate of women's rights.

As he came to doubt the rational faculties of his fellow citizens, Gales placed greater emphasis on religious faith as the key sinew of American society. In February 1800 Gales chose to excerpt a particularly revealing passage from Washington's Farewell Address in which the president warned that Americans should not "indulge the supposition that morality can be maintained without religion." In several other pieces in his newspaper, Gales endorsed Washington's contention that without popular religious belief there would be no "security for property, for reputation, for life."[50] In another excerpt that same month Gales suggested that the leading men of every town set an example for their less exalted neighbors by going to church regularly.[51] Coming from a man who had once viciously attacked the ways in which the British government used religious doctrine to extract passive obedience from the people, such endorsements of religion's capacity to generate well-behaved citizens were quite remarkable. It was almost as if organized religion had come to fill the space in Gales's political vision once occupied by secular education and explicitly political organizations like the SSCI.

It should come as no surprise that a Jeffersonian newspaper in 1799 or 1800 would distance itself from such "visionary" ideas as women's rights, the equal rationality of all people, and a thoroughly secular (or deist) conception of ethics. What matters is that Joseph Gales had publicly endorsed all of these "Jacobinical" ideas less than a decade earlier. As Gales learned to speak in the idiom of Jeffersonian democracy he systematically shed many of the key elements of his earlier Painite vision of a more democratic future. It is important to note that Gales himself never narrated his transformation from Sheffield's artisan radical into Raleigh's middling democrat. All of his autobiographical writings portray his political career as one animated by an unchanging and consistent set of principles. Making this Whiggish narrative work, however, required a strategic reconfiguration of Gales's Sheffield past.

In the 1830s, when Winifred and Joseph, now prominent citizens of North Carolina and the nation, sat down to write their *Reminiscences* for their descendants, they painted an implausibly tame and respectable picture of Joseph's political activities in Sheffield. While the *Reminiscences* proudly tell of Joseph's popularity "amongst the working class of the community," Joseph appears more as the kind and pacifying patron than as the compatriot. Winifred, for example, noted that Joseph's paper provided "a medium" for the journeymen and apprentices "to lay their grievances before the public," but she also observed that Joseph often wrote these pieces himself. The workers were "gratified at the opportunity of pleading their own cause, and their Employers were glad to find their grievances so moderately stated."[52] Similar accounts of Joseph's ability to curb or refine the passions of the crowd fill the sections on Sheffield. The story about the narrowly averted riot at Cutler's Hall in 1794, for example, became an opportunity to differentiate Joseph's politics from that of the "exasperated mob," that "dreadful Monster." At the time Joseph probably sought to avert a riot for pragmatic political reasons—violence would have brought the full force of the government and army down on his fledgling political organization. The family memory of the episode, however, became an object lesson in the virtues of Joseph's moderation and his differentiation from the crowd. Likewise, when Joseph fled the country and Winifred took over his printing business, "a deputation of six . . . well-intentioned men waited upon me with a paper signed by the Head Workmen of almost every shop, stating that they had 'sworn to protect me and mine, in the absence of my Husband.'" Winifred used this story about "these poor . . . Mistaken men" to wax rhapsodic about the "virtue, benevolence, and affection" of the "lower classes of Society," but she made no mention of Joseph's political action in cooperation with these seemingly naive workers.[53] Their gesture read as a statement of childlike gratitude, not solidarity. Indeed, the *Reminiscences* give no sense of Joseph's daily hard work of building and sustaining a political movement. We see Joseph pacifying the crowd and we hear of his popularity, but the hours of debates in Sheffield's taverns, the innumerable resolution and petition-writing sessions, and the reams of correspondence sent to and received from other democratic societies around Britain go without mention.

Considering the Galeses' position as Whigs in the midst of the resurgence of labor radicalism in the late 1820s and early 1830s, their selective memory about Joseph's role in popular politics makes sense. But this process of taming Joseph's Sheffield past began much earlier. In 1804 his Federalist competitor for the state printing job in North Carolina tried to use Gales's radical past against him. Joseph's response was as measured as Winifred's would be in her *Reminiscences:* "Let not the public misunderstand me, I handled no pike, I urged no violence, I was concerned in no riot. It was by means of a free and independent Press that I became obnoxious to the government."[54] Figuring himself as an innocent printer simply defending himself against an oppressive government, Joseph studiously avoided mentioning his activities in a mass political movement. Indeed, I have yet to find a single instance where Gales, after emigrating to America, publicly discussed his participation in the SSCI. Both the *Raleigh Register* and the *Reminiscences* evince a degree of anxiety about Joseph's past and the plausible paths he had not taken. By the early nineteenth century, the popular political activism that had been a source of pride and identity for Joseph in the 1790s had become a source of potential embarrassment.

"WE ARE ALL REPUBLICANS, WE ARE ALL FEDERALISTS"

In July 1800 Joseph Gales inserted a revelatory snippet in the midst of a series of articles supporting Jefferson's presidential aspirations. Under the heading

"MEMORY," Gales noted that when someone offered to teach Themosticles "the art of memory, he answered that he would rather wish for the art of forgetfulness," because banishing the past enabled one "to look forward to prospects that may brighten."[55] One could not find a clearer statement of that Jeffersonian "principle of hope" that has received so much attention from historians.[56] Yet forgetting, the initial step that made this hope possible, has received less attention as a central component of the principles of 1800. Several recent social histories, however, have reminded us that telling the story of the early Republic as one of opportunity and greater degrees of freedom has always required a measure of forgetting—a selective oversight of those whose lives contradicted that story.[57] To tell the story of the successful Jeffersonian farmers on the nineteenth-century Maine frontier, Alan Taylor reminds us, requires that we also take into account those families who were forced to drift westward and out of the historian's view. Such people were not unfortunate exceptions; they were the necessary sacrifices made on the altar of Maine's development into a liberal, capitalist society.[58] Likewise, Jeanne Boydston's study of the women whose labor continued unabated yet slowly faded from the ranks of what counted as labor in the nineteenth century also fits into this pattern of forgetting in the pursuit of a more comforting and unproblematical narrative of progress.[59]

To accurately assess the relationship between the Painite radicalism of the early 1790s and the principles of 1800, we must also pull away the veil of forgetting that people like Gales constructed. Most of his biographers have followed Gales's lead in distinguishing his political activities in Sheffield from those of the "irresponsible, guillotine-hungry monsters"[60] who experimented with the more radical implications of ideas like liberty and equality. In his Raleigh newspaper Gales frequently went out of his way to denounce Haitians for their "misinterpretation of the principles of Liberty and Equality" or English Jacobins for their "frantic zealot[ry]."[61] Such pronouncements were unexceptional in the Jeffersonian press of 1800, yet Gales's earlier experimentations with revolutionary and emancipationist ideas cast these Jeffersonian truisms in a different light.

Gales's anxiety about his radical past is evident in the way he deployed the contested concept of "Jacobinism" during his first years in Raleigh. In June 1800 he excerpted a section of Thomas Cooper's *Political Essays* in which he ridiculed the Federalists for branding with the term "Jacobin . . . all persons who prefer the principles of American government, and rejoice in the extension of those principles."[62] According to Cooper, Jacobinism was merely a "bugbear" used by Federalists to scare voters into rejecting the true friends of the people. In

August, however, Gales printed a story about an "incorrigible" English "Jacobin" who had apparently plotted to kill the king in order to enable "the poorer classes to obtain a comfortable subsistence." [63] The account was indistinguishable from the scores of similar stories in Federalist newspapers about the supposed Jacobins of America. Gales included such tales about the foolishness of European Jacobinism in order to demonstrate that American democrats were not Jacobins, but at the same time he validated the Federalists' xenophobic claim that such dangerous people did exist elsewhere and posed a potential threat to governments everywhere. In a similar vein Gales printed in late August a report from Cork decrying "the avidity with which every occasion is sought for and seized on by the designing and ill-affected to disturb the peace of the country. Scarce a night passes that meetings of the peasantry . . . do not take place, on the pretended score of swearing the farmers to sell their potatoes, &c. at a certain low rate." [64] Whereas in Sheffield Gales had eagerly sought out stories about popular political unrest and organization throughout the world and framed the participants as compatriots engaged in the same cause, in the run-up to the election of 1800 he reported on such behavior with increasing trepidation.

While he sought to defend Jeffersonian principles as authentically democratic, he went to great lengths to distinguish these ideals and practices from the phantom Jacobinism that the Federalists had so effectively conjured up in the preceding years. In doing so, he ceded important ground to his political opponents. Dangerous Jacobins masquerading as democrats did exist, Gales's newspaper seemed to concede, but they did not inhabit the Jeffersonian coalition. This formulation explains why his newspaper was suddenly so full of characters straight out of the Federalists' worst nightmares—frightening king killers, angry Irish peasants, and immoral atheists. Almost every time Gales's Raleigh newspaper acknowledged those to its political left or down the socioeconomic ladder, it saw tumult, irrationality, and demagoguery. Not coincidentally, it was precisely this image of the lower class that provided some of the crucial ideological glue for the emerging middle class.

The process of constructing a middling, moderate, and "anti-Jacobin" conception of democracy that we see at work in Gales's newspaper occurred across the nation, beginning tentatively when news of the Jacobin Terror reached America, picking up speed with the Bavarian Illuminati scare of 1798 and continuing through the election of 1800. After winning the election, many of the nation's leading Jeffersonians, Joseph Gales included, sought to soothe the partisan passions that had emerged during the previous four years by granting even more approval to their former Federalist enemies' campaign against "Jacobin-ism" and the radical émigrés who supposedly espoused it. Indeed, Jefferson's pronouncement in his inaugural address that "we are all republicans, we are all federalists" left unspoken a third proposition that would soon become obvious to the more radical members of America's Painite community. While the new American leaders were now all Republicans and Federalists, they were ada-mantly not Jacobins.

The leading Jeffersonians' desire to distance themselves from the supposed Jacobins in their ranks was clear from the first day of Jefferson's administration. On inauguration day, 6 March 1801, Philadelphia's democrats celebrated with a grand procession through the city and an evening of festivities. Not surpris-ingly, the city's Federalist newspapers described the day's events with derision: "A strange concourse of men and boys of various colours, and different nations, were seen passing through certain streets in this city . . . some of this throng car-ried guns, others sticks, and others nothing—On enquiry, we find that their object was to *honour* the president—yea to *honor* him!!!" Such dismissive ac-counts of the democratic rabble were predictable from a Federalist editor like John Fenno, but Fenno also noted that many of the Republican leaders seemed to share his distaste for the motley group of celebrants. Indeed, after the grand procession the most prominent and wealthy Jeffersonian leaders adjourned to the elegant Union Hotel for what the *Gazette of the United States* described as an evening of "innocent hilarity," where they "drank to toasts dictated by benevolence and a spirit of conciliation." [65] While the conduct of this respect-able group did "much honor to the gentlemen present," the Jacobins formed their own gatherings where they issued toasts that "breathed nought but the foul breath of sedition and insurrection." Editor John Fenno noted that these Jacobins sang "Ca Ira, The Rights of Man, Marseilles hymn, etc." and proposed toasts that "might be relished by any United Irishmen, French Jacobins, and fugitive members of the English Corresponding Society," but were hardly the type that "might be drunk by Americans." [66] Fenno accurately perceived the ex-tent to which the fragile Jeffersonian coalition was already beginning to fracture along lines of class, ethnicity, and political ideology. As the respectable Repub-licans drank Maeira and toasted George Washington at the Union Hotel, hun-dreds of Irish émigrés and other laboring democrats gathered on the banks of the Delaware to drink whiskey and sing French revolutionary songs.

From the outset of Jefferson's administration, nationally oriented Repub-licans like Joseph Gales, Albert Gallatin, and Alexander James Dallas joined forces with leading Federalists to downplay the divisions between the parties by emphasizing the differences between the nation's new Republican leaders and the "Jacobinical" rabble who had once been a crucial part of their coalition. On the Republican side, leaders like Jefferson systematically distanced themselves from the radical newspaper editors who had most forcefully trumpeted Jefferson's praises during the campaign. Editors like William Duane in Philadelphia, Charles Holt in New London, Phineas Allen in Pittsfield, and Aaron Pennington in Newark were all passed over for government printing contracts in favor of more moderate, even Federalist printers.[67] While Republican leaders indicated their desires for reconciliation through their distribution of patronage, the Federalist press offered the olive branch by legitimating the distinction that respectable Republicans were seeking to establish between themselves and the dangerous Jacobins to their political left. Four days after Jefferson's conciliatory inauguration speech appeared in the *Gazette of the United States,* a regular correspondent to the paper commented favorably on it—quite a gesture for a paper that had not uttered a positive word about Jefferson for years. The *Gazette's* correspondent noted that Jefferson's election coalition had been comprised of two very different "classes of men . . . Democrats and Jacobins." While Democrats were "all the well informed, well disposed citizens" who opposed the Federalists for legitimate reasons, the Jacobins were "the rubbish of our community, consisting chiefly of United Irish fugitives, anglo-democratic outlaws, and . . . the refuse of our native vulgar."[68] Moderate Jeffersonians like Gallatin and Dallas could not have been more pleased. The Federalists, who still held a significant nuber of state and appointed offices and controlled a large proportion of the nation's wealth, agreed to ratify the moderate Republicans' claim that they differed from the radical democrats who had supported them in the election. To an extent, the ongoing crusade to save the country from Jacobinism functioned as the rhetorical glue that prevented the two parties from viciously turning on each other after the election.

After the election of 1800 the category of "Jacobinism" quickly became the repository for a range of political ideas that had once comfortably existed under the banner of "democracy." Cosmopolitan conceptions of citizenship, ideas about women's rights, visions of a government that would ensure a rough measure of economic equality, and plans to create a more inclusive, participatory, and politically efficacious public sphere became increasingly marginal in American public political discourse and were figured as foreign principles, manifestations of an un-American ideology that could prove the undoing of the nation. Prone to seeing American political thought in precisely this manner, as uniquely anti-theoretical and nonideological, American historians have tended to replicate this post-1800 account of the internationalist democratic radicalism of the 1790s. These Painite ideas about economics and politics, however, did not become "Jacobinical" and un-American until the leaders of the Jeffersonians and Federalists sought a rapprochement and found common ground in their banishment of 1790s radicals from the mainstream of American political life. To frame the election as the realization of the democratic strivings of the previous years, Jeffersonians had to position their critics on the left as part of an alien political tradition. And no term better encapsulated dangerous outsider status in the early 1800s than "Jacobin." Perhaps this explains why that term continued to carry significant rhetorical weight for years after Jefferson won the presidency, and why moderate and conservative Jeffersonians like Gales used it almost as frequently as had the Federalists they defeated. So while the election of 1800 made "democracy" a word that respectable leaders could use without apology, this transformation came at a cost. Together, leading Jeffersonians and Federalists sheared the word "democracy" of its previously revolutionary and levelling implications. Such ideas were transformed into perversions of democracy; they became Jacobinical.

Those people who had identified themselves as Painite friends of the rights of man in the 1790s responded in a variety of ways to the new political climate of the 1800s. Some of the more prosperous, pious, or respectable democrats— men like Joseph Gales, Matthew Carey, Thomas Cooper, George Logan, and many others—chose to downplay their earlier radicalism and joined in the fight against Jacobinism. Not surprisingly, many of these men became Whigs in the 1830s. Other 1790s radicals—mostly more obscure men such as William Duane, Joseph Fellows, and David Dennison—tried to keep the spirit of Paine alive, but with little large-scale success. As Alfred Young has argued, one of the major problems in the history of American radicalism has been the difficulty that democratic radicals have had in sustaining their movements over time and across generations.[69] These discontinuities in America's radical democratic tradition have unduly shaped historians' accounts of the 1790s. In singling out the bourgeois and respectable aspects of Paine's thought and framing them as the essence of his project, historians have duplicated Gales's and other moderate democrats' willful forgetting of their radical pasts. The ideology of 1800 successfully figured other incarnations of Painite democratic thought as alien and tangential, and this should be reason enough to treat such propositions with suspicion.

NOTES

1. For representative studies that emphasize the non-bourgeois nature of Painite radicalism, see Gregory Claeys, "The Origins of the Rights of Labor: Republicanism, Commerce, and the Constitution of Modern Social Theory in Britain, 1796–1805," *Journal of Modern History* 66 (1994): 249–90; Gregory Claeys, *Thomas Paine: Social and Political Thought* (Boston, 1989); Jim Smyth, *The Men of No Property: Irish Radicals and Popular Politics in the Late Eighteenth Century* (Basingstoke, UK, 1992); Kevin Whelan, *The Tree of Liberty: Radicalism, Catholicism and the Construction of Irish Identity, 1760–1830* (Notre Dame, Ind., 1996); Jean-Pierre Gross, *Fair Shares for All: Jacobin Egalitarianism in Practice* (Cambridge, Mass., 1997); and Peter Linebaugh and Marcus Rediker, *The Many-Headed Hydra: Sailors, Slaves, Commoners, and the Hidden History of the Revolutionary Atlantic* (Boston, 2000).

2. E. P. Thompson, *The Making of the English Working Class* (New York, 1963), 132, 151–52. See also Albert Goodwin, *The Friends of Liberty: The English Democratic Movement in the Age of the French Revolution* (Cambridge, Mass., 1979), 222, 378–79.

3. *Sheffield Register*, 25 Aug. 1787. This quote appeared in a story about a Quaker school for free blacks in Philadelphia. For Gales's support for the complete abolition of slavery, not just of the slave trade, see *Proceedings of the Public Meeting, Held at Sheffield, in the Open Air, On the Seventh of April, 1794* (Sheffield, England, 1794), 3, 23–25. Henry "Redhead" Yorke delivered this speech, but there is evidence that Gales co-wrote it, and Gales was the chair of the meeting and the secretary of the Sheffield Constitutional Society that sponsored the gathering.

4. William E. Ames, *A History of the National Intelligencer* (Chapel Hill, N.C., 1972).

5. The three most important studies of transatlantic radicalism all follow this interpretive line. See Michael Durey, *Transatlantic Radicals in the Early American Republic* (Lawrence, Kans., 1997); David Wilson, *United Irishmen, United States: Immigrant Radicals in the Early American Republic* (Ithaca, N.Y., 1998); and Richard Twomey, *Jacobins and Jeffersonians: Anglo-American Radicalism in the United States, 1790–1820* (New York, 1989). See also Isaac Kramnick, *Republicanism and Bourgeois Radicalism: Political Ideology in Late Eighteenth-Century England and America* (Ithaca, N.Y., 1990).

6. For the description of Gales's position in Raleigh society see the account written by his son-in-law, William Winston Seaton, *William Winston Seaton of the "National Intelligencer": A Biographical Sketch with Passing Notices of His Associates and Friends* (Boston, 1871), 17. The claim about Gales's popularity with the working men of Sheffield was supposedly made by one of his opponents in Sheffield and was recounted by Winifred Gales in her Reminiscences, Southern Historical Collection, University of North Carolina. Several government spies also testified to the political influence of Gales. The quoted passage comes from a letter from William Dawson to Chamberlayne & White [the solicitors who were heading the investigations into the political activities of English reformers], 15 April 1793, London Public Record Office, TS 11/954.

7. Iain McCalman, *Radical Underworld: Prophets, Revolutionaries, and Pornographers in London, 1795–1840* (Cambridge, Mass., 1988). While McCalman discusses only London in this book, similar communities of radicals emerged in Sheffield and other manufacturing cities throughout England. There are several reports from government spies in Sheffield from the late 1790s that comment on the intricate network of local and itinerant "Jacobins."

8. I discuss the transformation of Painite ideology in 1790s America in my dissertation, "In Paine's Absence: The Trans-Atlantic Dynamics of American Popular Political Thought, 1789–1804" (Ph.D. diss., Northwestern University, 2000).

9. This same process occurred in England, where many former members of the London Corresponding Society, Francis Place most notably, became prominent in the moderate reformist movement, a movement that framed itself against both a corrupt aristocracy and an irresponsible plebeian democracy.

10. William W. Holden, *An Address on the History of Journalism in North Carolina*, 1881, quoted in Santford Martin, "Joseph Gales, Sr., and the *Raleigh Register*," (masters thesis, Wake Forest College, 1948), 2.

11. On the question of middle-class formation in the late eighteenth and early nineteenth centuries, see Carroll Smith-Rosenberg, "Dis-covering the Subject of the 'Great Constitutional Discussion,' 1786–1789," *JAH* 79 (1992): 841–73; C. Dallett Hemphill, *Bowing to Necessities: A History of Manners in America, 1620–1860* (New York, 1999); and Stuart Blumin, *The Emergence of the Middle Class: Social Experience in the American City, 1760–1900* (Cambridge, Mass., 1989).

12. For fuller biographies of Gales, see Robert Neal Elliott Jr., *The Raleigh Register, 1799–1863* (Chapel Hill, N.C., 1955); Willis G. Briggs, "Joseph Gales, Editor of Raleigh's First Newspaper," *The North Carolina Booklet* 19 (1907): 105–30; Clement Eaton, "Winifred and Joseph Gales, Liberals in the Old South," *JSH* 10 (1947): 461–74; W. H. G. Armytage, "The Editorial Experience of Joseph Gales, 1786–1794," *North Carolina Historical Review* 28 (1951): 332–61; Margaret Boeringer, "Joseph Gales, North Carolina Printer," (masters thesis, University of North Carolina at Chapel Hill, 1989); and Martin, "Joseph Gales, Sr."

13. It was crucial for newspaper editors to build patronage connections with prominent men because all newspapers had to be franked by a member of Parliament. At first the prominent anti-slavery activist Wilberforce agreed to support the *Sheffield Register*, but according to Winifred Gales, "when the subject of [parliamentary] reform began to be agitated, he withdrew it" and Lord Grey became the Gales's patron. Gales, Reminiscences, 29.

14. Gales, Reminiscences, 32.

15. Sheffield Society for Constitutional Information to the *English Chronicle*, 15 Jan. 1792, London Public Record Office, TS 11/952/3496(ii).

16. Rev. J. Wildinson to the Rev. H. Zouch, 6 Jan. 1792, Sheffield Archives, Wentworth Woodhouse Muniments. F.44 (a).

17. F. K. Donnelly and J. L. Baxter, "Sheffield and the English Revolutionary Tradition, 1791–1820," *International Review of Social History* 20 (1975): 401.

18. For evidence of these other organizations, see Thomas Ward to John More, 4 Dec. 1792, British Museum, Add. Mss 16920.

19. For accounts of Sheffield politics in the 1790s, see Donnelly and Baxter, "Sheffield and the English Revolutionary Tradition"; Allan W. L. Seaman, "Reform Politics at Sheffield," *Hunter Archaeological Society Transactions* 7 (1957): 215–28; and Goodwin, *Friends of Liberty*, 158–69, 378–84.

20. The Stockport Society for Constitutional Information, for example, issued a series of resolutions in which it praised *The Patriot* for its contribution to the cause: "the work is cheap, and we think we cannot do our country better service, than to recommend it to every Friend of Freedom." Gales immodestly included these resolutions in his *Sheffield Register*, 21 Sept. 1792.

21. *House of Commons, Select Committees: Reports Misc. 1794*, vol. 14, no. 113.

22. [Unnamed correspondent] to the 4th Earl Fitzwilliam, 28 Dec. 1791, Sheffield Archives, Wentworth Woodhouse Muniments. F.44 (a). This letter went on to note that "the pamphlet of Mr. Payne was read with avidity in many of the workshops in Sheffield to the manufacturers who soon manifested a violent zeal for these new opinions so flattering to the lower Classes (especially as understood by them) and these opinions, spreading abroad by the Industry of those new enlightened converts . . . "

23. This analysis of Gales's position as a non-elite political leader has been influenced by David Waldstreicher and Stephen Grossbart, "Abraham Bishop's Vocation: Or, the Mediation of Jeffersonian Politics," *JER* 18 (1998): 617–57.

24. J. Holland and J. Everett, eds., *Memoirs of the Life and Writings of James Montgomery* (London, 1854), vol. 1, 168.

25. For a longer description of the Philadelphia émigré community, see Durey, *Transatlantic Radicals*, 234–35, 187.

26. *Independent Gazetteer,* 14 Oct. 1796.

27. Gales, Reminiscences, 131.

28. Oswald had been a transatlantic radical of another sort, having traveled east across the Atlantic in 1793 to assist the French in their mission to revolutionize the continent. Arriving back in America in 1795 after failing in his endeavor, Oswald died of yellow fever within a few weeks of his return.

29. *Independent Gazetteer,* 10 Sept. 1796.

30. Ibid., 11 Nov. 1796.

31. Ibid.

32. Ibid.

33. For a discussion of how American opposition editors used news about European radicalism to both craft a cosmopolitan critique of the Washington administration and construct an imagined transatlantic community of democratic activists, see Cotlar, "In Paine's Absence," chap. 1.

34. *Independent Gazetteer,* 15 Nov. 1796.

35. Thomas Hardy (Secretary of the London Corresponding Society) to [unnamed corresponding society], 18 April 1792, British Library, Add. Ms. 27811.

36. According to one biographer, Gales eventually served as "the secretary of nearly every benevolent society formed in Raleigh." Martin, "Joseph Gales," 27.

37. Abstract of the Proceedings of the Society for Constitutional Information at a general meeting held at the Freemasons Lodge in Paradise Square, Sheffield, 26 March 1792. Wentworth Woodhouse Muniments, Sheffield City Archives, F44 (a).

38. As a side note to the way Americans have excised this side of Paine from their historical memory, Bruce Kuklick, the editor of the Cambridge University Press's edition of Paine's political writings (*Political Writings* [1989]), chose to exclude the portions of Paine cited here. While these rudimentary plans, which some have seen as the first articulation of a welfare state ideal, were the portion of Paine's work most frequently cited by plebeian democrats in the 1790s, they have come to seem so irrelevant to Paine's message that they could be deleted from his work without comment. For the sections Kuklick edited out, see Philip S. Foner, ed., *The Life and Major Writings of Thomas Paine,* 2d ed., (Secaucus, N.J., 1974), 424–32.

39. *Sheffield Register,* 30 March 1792.

40. Foner, *Writings of Thomas Paine,* 427.

41. I develop this argument further in "In Paine's Absence," chap. 3.

42. I have yet to find a way to demonstrate this absence. Having read all of Gales's North Carolina newspapers from 1799 to 1804, I have not found a single case where he inserted a criticism of the free market similar to the statements he made in his Sheffield paper.

43. Kramnick, *Republicanism and Bourgeois Radicalism,* 53–64.

44. Dror Wahrman, *Imaging the Middle Class: The Political Representation of Class in Britain, c. 1780–1840* (Cambridge, Mass., 1995).

45. *Raleigh Register,* 22 Oct. 1799.

46. Ibid., 29 Oct. 1799.

47. Ibid., 6 Nov. 1789.

48. Ibid., 22 Oct. 1799.

49. Ibid., 18 Feb., 4 March, 22 April 1800. "Description of a Slut. She is all grease; and I know not what use to put her to, but to make a lamp of her, and run from her by her own light."

50. Ibid., 18 Feb. 1800.

51. Ibid., 11 Feb. 1800.

52. Gales, Reminiscences, 27.

53. Ibid., 77.

54. *Raleigh Register,* 10 Dec. 1804.

55. Ibid., 22 July 1800.

56. Joyce Appleby, *Capitalism and a New Social Order* (New York, 1984), chap 4.

57. For a compelling analysis of how historians of the early Republic have tended to overlook the inequalities and intensified forms of unfreedom which accompanied the economic development of the nineteenth century, see Seth Rockman, "The Unfree Origins of American Capitalism" (paper presented at the Library Company of Philadelphia Program in Early American Economy and Society Inaugural Conference, April 2001).

58. Alan Taylor, *Liberty Men and Great Proprietors* (Chapel Hill, N.C., 1990).

59. Jeanne Boydston, "The Woman Who Wasn't There: Women's Market Labor and the Transition to Capitalism in the United States," *JER* 16 (1996): 183–206.

60. Martin, "Joseph Gales," 10.

61. *Raleigh Register,* 29 Oct. 1799 and 5 Aug. 1800.

62. Ibid., 24 June 1800.

63. Ibid., 5 Aug. 1800.

64. Ibid., 26 Aug. 1800.

65. *Gazette of the United States,* 11 March 1801.

66. Ibid., 9 March 1801.

67. For a full account of the relations between Jeffersonian newspaper editors and the Jeffersonian administration, see Jeffrey L. Pasley, *"The Tyranny of Printers": Newspaper Politics in the Early American Republic* (Charlottesville, Va., 2001).

68. *Gazette of the United States,* 11 March 1801.

69. Alfred F. Young, afterword to *The American Revolution: Explorations in the History of American Radicalism,* ed. Alfred F. Young (Dekalb, Ill., 1976), 458.

CHAPTER 15

An Empire for Liberty, a State for Empire
The U.S. National State before and after the Revolution of 1800

Bethel Saler

Near the end of his first year as president, Thomas Jefferson was looking ahead confidently, and not just to the next three years. In a letter to his friend and Virginia governor James Monroe, Jefferson confided his firm faith in Americans' eventual expansion across the North American continent. With characteristic optimism, Jefferson swept aside the seemingly insurmountable obstacles of European imperial claims and the native titles and settlements that currently kept Anglo-Americans "within our own [national] limits." Rather, he held fast to his expectation of "distant times, when our rapid multiplication will expand itself beyond those limits, and cover the whole northern if not the southern continent, with a people speaking the same language, governed in similar forms, and by similar laws."[1] The fact that Jefferson's future vision of a vast American republic was also a plan of breathtaking imperial ambition—an "empire for liberty" in his own famous phrasing—would not have raised many eyebrows among his contemporaries.

This essay explores the importance of empire for American "founders" like Thomas Jefferson, and particularly the way that a national state formed in large part around the administration of that American empire. With their victory over the British in 1783, Americans became sovereigns over a continental empire, or, as George Washington expressed it, "lords and proprietors of a vast continent." [2] Their meditations on just colonial rule, however, had long preceded their formal acquisition of territory. The premise of this essay is that empire was an inescapable fact in the lives of early Americans. Revolutionaries' objections to their own treatment under Britain's imperial rule led them to devise a new model of empire, a distinctly American plan that promised eventual inclusion of colonial territories in the federal union and stressed uniform political structures and principles.

Moreover, in the process of organizing that new model of empire, Americans endowed their national state with considerable central power. The western land cessions granted by individual states to Congress in the early 1780s, for instance, both created a public domain and explicitly invested the national government with exclusive authority to govern it. Congress then enlarged its responsibilities and reinforced its need for central fiscal and military powers through its policies for western state formation as outlined in the Northwest Ordinances of 1784, 1785, and 1787. Additionally, the increasingly more complex colonial relationships forged between the central government and Indian peoples also expanded federal responsibilities. Throughout the 1780s American political thinkers found common cause in their innovative national schemes for developing the colonial West, and they also agreed that the management of that empire should fall under the exclusive control of their federal government.

Historians have traditionally overlooked these points of consensus in their accounts of the political opposition that arose in the 1790s between Republican and Federalist Parties over the structure of republican government. The conventional narrative of this ideological clash ends with the electoral victory of the Republicans in 1800 and the dominance of a decentralized federal system where political power flowed centrifugally outward, residing largely in the semi-autonomous political communities of individual states. [3] But federal responsibilities associated with the American empire—including those of Indian affairs, western state formation, and regulation of trade and foreign diplomacy—continued to occupy the American national state and to warrant centralized fiscal and military powers well after the "revolution of 1800."

When Jefferson became president, he did pare down the national government, but his contribution lay not in dismantling the central state but in reconceptualizing its sphere of operation. Jefferson distinguished between a domestic republic governed by the voluntary will and subordinate jurisdictions of the American people and a central state that managed the peripheries and

protected the nation from foreign dangers. In so doing, he championed a decentralized federal system even while the central government continued to exercise power and authority over its extended domain.

Long before the establishment of American independence or a national state,
the North American colonies were steeped in the ideas and practices of empire. Up until the American Revolution the common history and identity
shared by thirteen otherwise heterogeneous Anglo-American colonies were as
members of the British Empire. In the process of those conjoint experiences,
Anglo-American colonists contributed vitally to the empire's commercial and
ideological development, a development that simultaneously gave rise to a British national identity and an expansive central state.

The distinctive pan-Atlantic identity and structure of the eighteenth-century British Empire, as David Armitage has recently demonstrated, evolved
out of extended public debates over the political and commercial premises of
the British national state as it began to govern an expanding empire. Anglo-
American provincials on the periphery of empire first conceptualized "empire"
in pan-Atlantic terms, celebrating the peace, prosperity, and personal liberties
enjoyed by Britons everywhere. For patriotic Anglo-Americans, empire fostered a sense of identity with the metropolitan center.[4] Thus, when Parliament
replaced its earlier colonial policy of political liberality with greater centralized
control following the British takeover of Canada in 1763, colonists staunchly
objected on the grounds of their rights as "free-born Britons," pointing especially to their legislative autonomy.[5] The ideological nature of the conception of
the British Empire proved useful to American revolutionaries, who drew on
prior arguments about British imperial governance to justify both their grievances and their eventual declaration of independence. In formulating such
arguments, American political thinkers conceived their own ideas about colonial rule. American notions of a republican empire and nation-state, however,
proved no less ideological. Fundamental political differences emerged in the
early national period over the conception of republican governance that, despite consensus on the particulars of federal administration over the colonial
West, still produced two divergent visions of the American Republic and its
empire.

In the immediate aftermath of the Revolution, American revolutionaries
first had to confront their newly acquired status as lords of a "vast continent"

and participants in the accompanying struggles for empire in their western hinterlands. Radical essayist Thomas Paine expressed a familiar sentiment in Europe when he declared land to be "the real riches of the habitable world and the natural funds of America."[6] Certainly the new Republic could now claim a sizeable portion of those natural funds according to their peace treaty with Britain. The Treaty of Paris in 1783 granted the Americans land cessions that more than doubled the territory of the original thirteen colonies. Extending from the coast of Maine west to the Mississippi River, northwest to the Great Lakes, and south to Spanish Florida, more than half of this land mass was Indian country and now, in effect, an American colonial territory.[7]

Americans looked on their western hinterlands as an immediate means of paying their soldiers as well as the site of future demographic and commercial expansion. However, the West also signified instability and danger. The Spanish-American empire threatened just beyond the Mississippi River, offering both another option to Anglo-Americans for colonial settlement and another potential ally for native peoples. Just as importantly, the Spanish controlled New Orleans, the major western entrepot. Meanwhile, in the upper northwest bordering on Canada, the British refused to relinquish their military posts, their traders, and, seemingly, the loyalties of the native peoples. Thus, with their acquisition of colonial territories from Britain in 1783, Americans were thrown into the position of a competing empire within the broader context of ongoing geopolitical conflicts in their western territories.

Just as the expansive West of the Republic rendered the fledgling nation-state an empire fully immersed in broader imperial struggles, so interstate struggles over these same western lands forged a national government and gave substance to a national public. Historians have shown how the western land controversies extending from the late 1770s through the mid-1780s raised the contentious question of state sovereignty within a confederated union.[8] But this early American political controversy also represented an important episode in the mutual construction of the republican empire and national government. On one side of this controversy stood representatives from seven "landed" states (Massachusetts, Connecticut, New York, Virginia, North Carolina, South Carolina, and Georgia) who maintained that their original colonial charters granted them vast territory stretching westward across the continent, or at least as far as the Mississippi River and the Great Lakes. On the other side, representatives from the six "landless" states of Maryland, New Jersey, Pennsylvania, New Hampshire, Delaware, and Rhode Island refused to join a union on such unequal and unjust terms. As the Maryland delegation forcefully put it, the western lands had been "wrested from the common enemy by the blood and treasure of [all] of the thirteen states, [so they] should be considered as a common property."[9]

Eventually the Continental Congress persuaded the "landed" state legislatures to voluntarily cede their western lands for the broader purpose of securing the federal union. Congress pitched its appeals for voluntary cessions on the grounds that cessions would be good for the national political community (as yet only tenuously realized), encouraging the landed states to favor "general security over local attachment."[10] In this way the western hinterlands became a vehicle for cementing the ties of union among the states. Further, by asking for voluntary cessions, Congress did not violate states' sovereignty but instead allowed them to dictate the terms of their cessions. Toward this shared goal of giving form to a confederated nation-state, the "landed" states specifically entrusted their western cessions to the national government as a public domain for the American people. As the Virginia legislature phrased it, the ceded lands "shall be considered as a common fund for the use and benefit" of all current and future members of the United States.[11]

The creation of a public domain endowed both the national "public" and the general government with substance. With few claims to power under the Articles of Confederation, Congress derived authority from its position as conservator of this newly created public domain of western lands—essentially a public empire. And while the Articles of Confederation had given early shape to a national citizenry by stipulating free travel, trade, and general intercourse between citizens of different states, the Continental Congress and the "landed" state legislatures invested this abstract notion of the public with the reality of landed property. In so doing, they made more concrete Congress's position as the national head of an imperially vested American public.

Congress lost no time in acting on its charge as trustee of the public domain by appointing successive committees to plan the transformation of the western territories from Indian "wilderness" into new republican states. In the resulting Ordinances of 1784, 1785, and 1787, congressional committees defined the particular outline of their new republican empire. In doing so, these American policymakers substantially revised defining features of the British Empire to produce a distinctively new model of colonial governance and state formation. In contrast to the permanent colonialism and deference expected of British colonial subjects, republican planners conceived of a temporary colonialism that guaranteed both eventual statehood and equal membership in the Union for settlers in the western territories.[12] In addition, Americans rejected the multiplicity of the English composite monarchy that allowed for diverse internal polities—native and creole—as part of the empire. Rather, they insisted on a uniform model of statehood and a federation premised on basic shared cultural beliefs in "enlightened rationalism,"[13] Anglo-American social and legal customs, and republican ideals.[14]

This peculiarly American blueprint for colonial governance and state formation outlined in the three ordinances also extended, at least on paper, the powers of the central government well beyond those outlined in the Articles of Confederation. In overseeing the radical transformation of property, custom, and ideology that constituted the process of state formation, the national government assumed the authority to define dominant custom and political principles while also enlarging its administration to prepare western territories for statehood.

In the fall of 1783, while still in the midst of negotiations with the Virginia Assembly over its immense cession of northwestern lands, Congress charged a committee to write a general policy for the establishment of a temporary government in the western territories. Chaired by Thomas Jefferson, the committee's "Plan for the Temporary Government of the Western Territory" was approved by Congress in late April 1784 and introduced two of the defining features of the new republican empire. First, exceeding the discrete mandate for a policy of temporary government, the 1784 ordinance mapped out the entire political evolution from federal territory to statehood, even guaranteeing statehood in a charter to Euro-American settlers of the western territories.[15] In so doing, the ordinance ensured the impermanence of the territorial stage by promising equal membership for new western states in the federal union. Second, the Ordinance of 1784 evoked the ideal of homogeneity both by determining the stages of political development for all new territories and by advocating a uniformity in the shape and mathematical plotting of new states. The Ordinance of 1784, for instance, sketched out, in Jefferson's words, "the full contours of nation,"[16] by which he meant the outlines of all current *and* future states, according to uniform, decimal-based latitudinal measurements rather than the irregular lines of topographical features. While the ordinance's proposed outline of new states was speculative at best, it gave American cartographers and surveyors a mathematically based scheme to follow that would produce uniform, ordered states.

In its ambitious plans for the development of the West and the nation, the Ordinance of 1784 also extended the powers of the national government beyond those stipulated by the Articles of Confederation. For instance, the ordinance's blueprint for the determination of all currently disputed state borders and all future state boundaries violated the explicit prohibitions in the Articles of Confederation against Congress's altering the boundaries of any individual state. Thus, by guaranteeing statehood and outlining the entire evolution of political development in the western territories, the ordinance rendered unambiguous the central authority of the national government over that process of state formation, including state boundary definition and the power to confirm statehood.

The subsequent Ordinances of 1785 and 1787 revised and made more concrete both the stages of development of the western territories and the powers of the central government over that process. These later ordinances thus continued to spell out the main characteristics distinguishing the American empire from its British predecessor: its temporariness and the promise of equal standing for settlers in the Union and its insistence on uniformity in the political structure and contours of future states. For instance, in the same spirit of "enlightened rationalism" conveyed by the 1784 ordinance, the Land Ordinance of 1785 codified a mathematically based grid system that would reorganize "wildernesses" into uniform geometric squares—squares that provided the building blocks for future states and for the future state-defined geography of the nation.

The 1785 ordinance not only imposed uniformity on the land but also fostered a commonality between the people in the western territories and the rest of the nation. The ordinance's encouragement of shared customs and principles only reinforced the larger point that the American empire was a place of similarity in contrast to the heterogeneity of the British Empire. For example, the land ordinance committee opted to divide the national domain into townships in the fashion of New England settlement rather than use the southern system of indiscriminate location in which settlers randomly chose their own plots.[17] By accepting a version of the New England system, Congress endorsed the New England emphasis on social harmony through group migrations organized around "friendships religion and relative connections" as William Grayson, a member of the ordinance committee, explained.[18] Such community connections equally tied western migrants to each other and to their eastern homes. Another vehicle for fostering commonality was the high price of $640 for each of the six lots in one township and the provision that they be purchased in advance of settlement. This reflected Congress's desire for particular types of settlers: financially solvent investors and communities of people organized into small land associations. Through all these various stipulations, Congress articulated broad republican principles such as rationality, commercial enterprise, and social harmony that were meant to unite the new territories with the older states and to give definition to the Republic as a whole.

The federal government also gained more administrative bulk from the Land Ordinance of 1785. The Treasury Department expanded its duties in overseeing the land surveys and sales of new territories, the War Department continued its expansive supervision of Indian affairs while also dealing with illegal settlement on the frontiers, and a National Land Office came into existence.

With the Land Ordinance of 1785 in place, the deficiencies of the earlier Ordinance of 1784 for the establishment of a temporary government quickly became apparent to congressional planners. The 1784 ordinance had left it up to settlers to form their own government. By 1786, however, both interested purchasers and congressional policymakers favored greater central authority and guidance from the national government in overseeing the political development of the western territories.[19] Consequently, in that year Congress appointed a committee chaired by James Monroe to produce a new report for "government of the territory of the United States." Monroe's committee stayed true to the idea of a temporary territorial stage peculiar to the American empire, but it provided one critical revision: it replaced the temporary self-government stipulated in the 1784 ordinance with a temporary colonialism in the new Ordinance of 1787 (familiarly known as the Northwest Ordinance). Indeed, the Ordinance of 1787 imposed the colonial rule of the national government over a new territory until it had matured in both population size and political infrastructure such that it could begin to organize its own government and eventually apply for membership in the Union as a new state.

The change to a temporary colonialism reflected the attempt to address the actual conditions of the place where the Northwest Ordinance would first be applied. In other words, the 1787 ordinance committee took a hard look at the "wilderness" that was the Northwest Territory—its diverse population of native peoples, French-Canadian trading families and defiant squatters, its immense geography, and its apparent lack of any kind of civic society or institutions. With this largely alien and "uncivilized" landscape in mind, the committee proposed an initial stage of colonial rule administered by national government officials in the territory, with the promise of progressive stages of internal governance as the number of settlers increased. The stress of the Northwest Ordinance, however, remained on the temporary character of colonial rule over western territories. As James Monroe explained, in comparison to Britain their colonial rule had "this remarkable & important difference that when such districts shall contain the number of the least numerous of the 13 original States for the time being they shall be admitted into the confederacy."[20]

The Northwest Ordinance also revised the principle of homogeneity so that it better addressed the actual conditions in the western lands. The perceived "uncivil" nature of the Northwest Territory, for instance, probably induced the ordinance committee to include some fairly straightforward legal instructions, such as the description of federal rules of descent and conveyance of property. The fact that the committee felt it necessary to lay out so basic a tenet of English common law suggests a presumption that current inhabitants of the Northwest either did not know or chose not to follow such rules of property.[21] Inheritance laws were only one of a whole set of legal and political principles articulated in the Northwest Ordinance that could easily stand as salient national characteristics of the new American Republic, principles that would unite western territories with established states. These included trial by jury, proportional representation, common law, and security of private property and public education. In addition to these, the ordinance encouraged more idealistic commitments from northwestern residents. Some portions of the text sounded like blanket moral injunctions such as that "religion, Morality and knowledge" were necessary for good government or that settlers should act in good faith toward Indian peoples. The inclusion of a prohibition against slavery and "involuntary servitude," on the other hand, suggested that the colonial West functioned not simply as a reflection of the national principles but also as a social experiment from which the republican nation-state itself could learn. All the while, Congress stood at the center of this mutually defining process of empire and state formation, articulating what it deemed the most salient characteristics of the Republic while simultaneously guiding the renewal of the nation through the process of state formation.

Inseparably from its colonial responsibilities over western state formation, the national government also derived central powers from its management of Indian affairs. Government officials interacted with Indian peoples in the course of their dealings in foreign diplomacy and over the administration of the public domain. In the elision of these two primary aspects of federal authority, the central government and Indian nations constructed increasingly more complex colonial relationships that, in turn, demanded an expanded federal administration.

Consistent with its view of Indian polities as foreign or external to the American Republic, Congress claimed the authority to deal with Indian nations as part of its broader responsibility over foreign affairs. Indeed, the government's attempt to maintain peaceful relations with native peoples and to stave off Indian alliances with neighboring British and Spanish colonials constituted perhaps the most immediate and continuous part of its foreign diplomacy. American authorities were all too aware of their country's vulnerability throughout the 1780s and 1790s, while the British still retained their posts in the upper Northwest, the Spanish governed colonies in Florida and Louisiana, and both empires kept up regular trading and diplomatic relations with native peoples living in U.S. territory.[22] Unable to afford a war either with Indian nations or with its imperial neighbors, the government's exchanges with native peoples came to be a mainstay of American foreign diplomacy and helped to justify the expansive powers of the federal state.

At the same time, Indian affairs were a fundamental part of the government's administration of the public domain. This seemed obvious to George Washington, who noted in 1783, "the Settlmnt. of the Western Country and making a Peace with the Indians are so analogous that there can be no definition of the one without involving considerations of the other."[23] The ties between Indian affairs and state formation were also inescapable to a Congress whose administration of the public domain rested on the fiction that these lands were free and available for settlement. In fact, much of federal officials' energies in managing the public domain were taken up with trying to turn that fiction into a reality. American officers sought to acquire title to Indian lands while at the same time protecting Indian country from a number of dangers, including foreign influences, unlicensed traders, private speculation, individual state interference, and illegal settlement.

The national government's exclusive responsibility over Indian affairs gave rise to multifaceted colonial relationships with native peoples that extended the government's involvement into nearly all levels of Indian life, from formal negotiations concerning political alliances, peace, and land boundaries to everyday affairs of trade and social custom. Federal intervention in the daily lives of Indian communities increased especially after Congress assumed the responsibility of "civilizing" native peoples with the vaguely conceived purpose of someday absorbing them into the citizenry—in effect, a promise of temporary colonialism for Indian peoples.

It took nearly a decade of Indian hostilities in the Northwest and South for Congress to adopt a more conciliatory approach to Indian affairs. The inefficacy of demands in 1783 and 1784 for land cessions from "conquered" Indian peoples was soon apparent, as Indian nations repudiated nearly all of the federal treaties based on this principle of conquest. In June 1786 General Clark reported to Congress that several of the western tribes had declared war "in a formal manner against the United States."[24] Three years later, with war between the Americans and the western confederation of Indians raging in the Ohio Valley, Secretary of War Henry Knox advised Congress to replace the policy of cessions based on conquest with that practiced by the British colonial office of purchasing the right of soil from Indian nations. As he observed in his report, the "confederation of a large number of tribes of Indians" holds the "principle of conquest" in "the highest disgust." Paying for Indian cessions, Knox explained, was "the only mode of alienating their lands, to which they will peaceably accede."[25] After 1789, therefore, federal management of the public domain expanded to include extensive treaty negotiations for Indian land cessions that involved the nation in long-term financial relations with tribal groups.

Knox's advice to return to the British precedent of recognizing Indian "right of soil" and paying for Indian land cessions signaled a broader move by the Washington administration toward an Indian policy that articulated the vague promise of a temporary colonialism for native peoples. By the early 1790s federal administrators were speaking of saving Indian populations from being eliminated in the inevitable course of American expansion westward by training them in "civilized" customs and beliefs and so eventually incorporating them into the Republic.[26] Political opponents such as Thomas Jefferson and Timothy Pickering shared this vision—premised on an Enlightenment faith in human improvement—of "civilizing" Indian people so that they could be remade into "native" Americans, citizens of the domestic nation-state, or, in other words, non-Indians and non-colonials.[27] The policy shift that tied the "civilizing" of Indian people with their dispossession further enlarged the scope of the federal government's duties. "Civilizing" measures such as teaching agriculture and domestic arts to Indian men and women became a regular part of the Indian Trade and Intercourse Acts, enacted first in 1790 and at regular intervals thereafter.[28] In addition, U.S. treaty commissioners regularly began to include as part of their treaty settlements programs for the scholastic and mechanical training of native peoples.

Expanded authority over native populations was only possible after the national state had first gained necessary powers under the new Constitution. Prior to this restructuring of the federal union, the Articles of Confederation had strictly circumscribed the government's power to carry out any of its plans for the West. In devising the Articles, representatives from the states had vigilantly guarded against the threat of a centralized state by denying the national government basic fiscal and military powers—to levy taxes, regulate commerce, or raise an army. Further, the Articles' designers qualified even those federal powers they did grant, so that they did not trespass on the sovereignty of the separate states. The consequence was an insolvent and ineffectual Continental Congress whose officers were continually frustrated by individual states' disregard of national authority.

Congressional frustration with state interference was particularly acute in the area of Indian affairs, where the Articles of Confederation both stipulated Congress's authority and muddied the waters with a proviso stating that "the legislative right of any State within its own limits be not infringed or violated." [29] States negotiated treaties with native people, often under very dubious conditions and on occasion in direct competition with the national government. Georgia and North Carolina did nothing to stop white encroachment onto Creek and Cherokee lands, fomenting war with those nations. George Washington complained to Henry Knox that this self-interested conduct on the part of states resulted in "a kind of fatality attending all our public measures." Washington observed that state assemblies which were "supinely negligent & inattentive to every thing which is not local & self inter[e]st[ed]" seemed to characterize the American federal system. Indeed, Washington concluded grimly, "our fœderal Government is a name without substance." [30]

Such sentiment drove nationalists like Washington to the Constitutional Convention in 1787. State representatives gathered in Philadelphia in the early summer, intending to revise the Articles of Confederation and ultimately produce a new framework for the national government. As historian Max Edling has argued, the Constitutional Convention was about state formation.[31] Few delegates disputed that the federal government had suffered under the Articles of Confederation and needed the right to raise money, build an army and navy, and have the powers to regulate commerce and enforce treaties.[32] Many of these reforms, as Alexander Hamilton pointed out, "consisted 'much less in an addition of NEW POWERS to the UNION, than in the invigoration of its ORIGINAL POWERS,' through 'a more effectual mode of administering them.'"[33]

This clarification of original powers certainly was necessary in the case of the national government's authority over matters of empire such as Indian affairs. Gone was the proviso that any congressional action not infringe or violate "the legislative right of any State within its own limits."[34] In place of this ambiguous and contradictory stipulation stood the simply worded recognition of the exclusive authority of the federal government "to regulate commerce . . . with Indian tribes."[35] The total lack of debate over any issue of Indian affairs suggests consensus among the representatives that such colonial concerns should remain under the control of the national government.[36]

Still, while consensus may have existed concerning the government's duty to carry out "the mutual and external" affairs of the nation, a diverse opposition raised a wide range of objections about the new Constitution, focusing particularly on concerns about the preservation of popular liberty.[37] Federalists insisted that individual liberty could flourish only under just laws enacted and enforced by a more energetic, popularly authorized national government. As one Federalist explained succinctly, "our very being depends on social government."[38] Anti-Federalists, on the other hand, expressed a fear about the threat to popular liberty from what they perceived as a "consolidating" national government under the Constitution. Registering a common distrust of centralized power that stretched back to "country" critiques of the British state, anti-Federalists measured liberty by the degree of freedom and direct rule enjoyed by the people; such popular liberty could easily be subverted by an overly centralized government, as the example of the European states made all too clear.[39] This basic conflict amounted in the simplest terms to contrasting views of the relationship between the state and the "people" or the "public." Federalists emphasized the interdependence of the state and the public, the latter authorizing the former to preserve civil society. The anti-Federalists, on the other hand, insisted on a marked distinction between the public and the state. In their view liberty rested in the people and had to be protected from the inherent potential of government to become independent and tyrannical.

These two different orientations were articulated in new ways over the next twenty years within the competing Federalist and Republican visions of the American national state and empire.[40] Though antagonists in these debates agreed on the necessity of avoiding the pitfalls of British imperialism in the government of the American West, their contrasting views of the relationship between the "public" and the national government resulted in two very different-looking republican nation-states and empires.

The Federalists wanted the Republic to resemble the increasingly centralized British national state. Like the British, the Federalists favored energetic central administration over both colonial and domestic realms. Hamilton and his partisan colleagues pressed for military strikes against seditious citizenry and foreign foes alike. In fact, Federalists often saw domestic and foreign threats as inseparable, whether in the form of imported Jacobin convictions among the lower classes or European backing of native hostilities. These "men of enlightened views" justified a fiscally and militarily strong central state on the grounds that it would protect the interests of the national public against the dual dangers of political disorder and social collapse.[41] Government officers drawn from elite society would serve as stewards of the public's interests, with all the paternalist assumptions implied in that role. Indeed, as Jeanne Boydston has argued, Federalists favored limiting political authority to property holders and members of the political and social elite, perceiving "political agency as an act of stewardship, rather than electoral self-representation."[42] Thus, as the putative stewards of the nation over the course of the 1790s, Federalist administrations protected the American public from manifold domestic and foreign dangers to social order, including the Whiskey Rebellion, the seditious speech of "Jacobin" demagoguery and faction, and the specter of French invasion. A consolidated national state was the necessary vehicle for exercising this elite political stewardship.

The transition of power from the Federalists to the Republicans in 1800 has commonly been characterized as a move away from a centralizing state and toward popular and individual state sovereignty. If a principal feature of the early national state, however, was its imperial responsibilities, then Jefferson, who urged American expansion far more avidly than did his Federalist predecessors and opponents, was by far the greater centralizer. Moreover, during his presidency Jefferson sustained Federalist policies on issues of empire, agreeing that Indian affairs, republican state formation, and regulation of trade and intercourse on the western frontiers belonged exclusively to the national government and not the states. Regardless of these continuities, however, Jefferson's ascension to the presidency in 1800 did usher in a sea change in the conception of the national "public," the federal government, and the relationship between the domestic state and its empire. Indeed, the ideological change that marked the transition to power from the Federalists to the Republicans resulted in an altogether different American empire, one that projected a relatively invisible national state concealed in the shadows of an ascendant popular will.

Perhaps the central element of this ideological change was Jefferson's conception of the American public. Despite a bitterly contested election, Jefferson remained unshaken in his romantic view that the American people were united in common sentiments and universal principles. The last decade of Federalist rule represented a "delirium,"[43] a temporary "derangement,"[44] and (in his most high-pitched rhetoric) a reign of witches that had cast a spell that temporarily robbed the American people of their senses.[45] More than merely a conviction that "the large body of Americans" had republican sympathies, Jefferson invoked a core "sameness" that he believed united the American public; they shared basic republican principles—what he called the "spirit of 1776"—as well as national ties as Americans.[46] Jefferson's characterization of the national public in terms of a basic sameness marked an important departure from the Federalists' conception of American society as naturally and unequally divided into the privileged "few" and the disadvantaged "many."[47] The Federalists' belief in the naturalness of social inequality allowed them to advocate a stronger national government in which the "few" carried out their responsibility as stewards for the "many." Jefferson's vision of a republican sameness, on the other hand, projected a general political equality and strict constitutional curbs on centralized power that might interfere with or compromise individual rights and the people's collective will.[48] His conception of the American public implied the dominance of popular sovereignty and localism.

With shared principles and a sense of popular sovereignty at the core of Jefferson's vision of American society, the focus of the national government became the monitoring of the periphery, the western frontiers of the nation-state. In effect, the central state faced outward in this conception; its powers shielded but did not encroach on the domestic public. Indeed, Jefferson described the general government as wrapping its strength around the whole nation and functioning "as a barrier against foreign foes, to watch the borders of every State, that no external hand may intrude, or disturb the exercise of self-government reserved to itself."[49] It was precisely in the need to oversee these peripheries of the Republic that the government justified its centralized fiscal and military powers. Moreover, through its administration of the nation's contiguous colonial territories, the government not only protected popular sovereignty against foreign encroachment but also readied the path for the expansion of popular will.

On many levels Jefferson's republican and freethinking populace was inextricably tied to its empire and so also to the federal government that administered that empire. At the most obvious level, the growth of the American population, in Jefferson's view, would proceed rapidly and require an expansive empire to meet the escalating need for space. He reiterated this vision of a demographically impelled expansion in a letter to James Monroe, who had asked him about a proposal for colonizing "bond 'criminals'" in the wake of Gabriel Prosser's rebellion.[50] Reasoning that white Americans would not want such a colony of black conspirators close to them, Jefferson could not endorse its settlement anywhere in the entire continental United States. This outright refusal rested, of course, on his certainty that the perpetually growing American population would eventually cover the northern and possibly southern American continent with a "people speaking the same language, governed in similar forms and by similar laws."[51] Further, expansion through space was all the more important given Jefferson's conviction that farmers were "the true representatives of the great American interest, and are alone to be relied on for expressing the proper American sentiments." In other words, the life of the farmer embodied the shared principles and national "sameness" that Jefferson invoked, and farmers needed lands to till.[52]

Jefferson also perceived expansion as the sine qua non for the continuing health and viability of the Republic. The duties of the national government in administering western expansion went to the heart of the perpetuation and regeneration of the federal union. The process for creating new states, for instance, as outlined in the 1784, 1785 and 1787 ordinances, engendered in western territorial residents the common national history, principles, and sentiments that Jefferson identified as the unifying ties binding the American people. Thus, by the time a politically mature territory chose to join the Union, it would have experienced a similar if abbreviated colonial history, and it would have adopted the laws and dominant political principles of the older, established states. In these fundamental ways, each "adult" territory would become intrinsically linked to the other states by a uniform political evolution, shared republican principles, and the familial ties existing between young generations of western pioneers and their families to the east.

Given that inhabitants of new territories would be inculcated with a common genealogy and popular republican principles, Jefferson remained sanguine when faced with the specter of a separate confederacy developing out of the newly acquired empire of Louisiana. Political and sentimental ties would be formed in the process of white settlement and state formation so that, as Jefferson explained, "whether we remain in one confederacy, or form into Atlantic and Mississippi confederacies, I believe not very important to the happiness of either part. Those of the western confederacy will be as much *our children and descendants* as those of the eastern, and I feel myself as much identified with that country, in future time, as with this."[53] Working on the peripheries of empire, the national government cultivated this connection of sentiment and kinship between established states and new colonial territories. At the same time, the temporary nature of its colonial rule over western territories meant that the government did not appear to interfere with the collective will of Jefferson's public.

Thus Jefferson's administration carried out policies established in the 1780s but put greater stress on expansion than the Federalists had, and employed a rhetoric of popular sovereignty that underplayed the presence of the national state. In its administration of Indian affairs, however, it was harder to minimize the central powers of government. Still, given Jefferson's conception of a multi-level federal system, the centralized authority of the government over Indian affairs in no sense endangered the ethos of localism and popular sovereignty. On the contrary, each level had its separate and mutually defining place—the national state in foreign policy and popular sovereignty in the domestic realm. Jefferson compared his vision of this carefully weighted federal union to that of a balanced planetary system in which the federal government and the states, "revolving round their common sun, acting and acted upon according to their respective weights and distances, will produce that beautiful equilibrium on which our Constitution is founded."[54]

By maintaining peace and trying to obtain lands from Indian people, the national government protected the American public from "external threats" and "foreign foes" in the West and secured an empire for future generations of Americans. At the same time Jefferson's administration, like its Federalist predecessors, often had to protect native inhabitants from the "external threats" of settlers. In this way, federal responsibility over Indian affairs could at times undercut the republican vision of a perfectly balanced system. Both as secretary of state and as president, Jefferson pledged the government's powers to protect the rights of Indian people, particularly their right of occupancy against the false dealings and incursions of state officials, land companies, and squatters.[55]

In other aspects of Indian affairs as well, Jefferson continued to follow Federalist Indian policies, such as the promise of temporary colonialism for Indian people contingent on their "civilization." But he imbued these policies with his conception of an expansive empire and a nation governed by common principles and popular sovereignty.

The government's project to civilize Indian peoples, for instance, took on a new urgency given Jefferson's stress on American expansion and his consequent blurring of the desire to "civilize" native peoples and the desire to acquire Indian land.[56] His 1803 suggestion to Governor William Henry Harrison that the United States might acquire land by encouraging Indians to go into debt at government trading houses offers one example of Jefferson's mixed motives in this regard.[57] A more common strategy, however, as Jefferson explained to his friend and federal Indian agent Benjamin Hawkins, was "the promotion of agriculture, and . . . household manufacture" in order to wean native people from hunting and "promote among the Indians a sense of the superior value of a little land, well cultivated, over a great deal, unimproved."[58] A perfect balance then could take place where Indian people would be learning to use less land, while "our increasing numbers will be calling for more land, and thus a coincidence of interests will be produced between those who have lands to spare, and want other necessaries, and those who have such necessaries to spare and want lands."[59]

Land acquisition was not the only motive behind the "civilizing" impulse, however. The pragmatic desire for land went hand in hand with a desire to rid native people of their "savagery" so that they could join as one people with the rest of the citizens of the United States. Here again, Jefferson's policy sounded no different from the temporary colonialism promoted by the Federalists. In the context of Jefferson's vision of shared principles and popular sovereignty, though, his administration's "civilizing" measures took on new meaning. By adopting "civilized" customs and beliefs, native people could internalize the values that unified the American public. Once "civilized," Indian tribes would move out from under centralized government control and into the realm of American popular sovereignty.

It is worth noting, however, that the government's abstract promise of eventual inclusion in the Union was contradicted by the political exclusion on the basis of race and gender that crept into state constitutions from the 1790s on. While individual states, urged on particularly by Republicans, broadened their suffrage during this period by dropping property requirements for voting and

office holding, many also became more explicit about gender and racial restrictions on political participation. The introduction of explicit racial and gender
conditions for full political membership in the Union meant that native women
and men, no matter the degree of their "civilization," would still face a barrier
to equal political rights with white males of the republic.

The rise of these racial and gender exclusions qualifies the view that "the
revolution of 1800" represented a victory for the forces of social equality and
popular sovereignty. Similarly, as this essay has argued, the ascendancy of the
Republicans in 1800 did not also signify the end of a strong central state, but far
from it. Historians' claim that no national state existed before the Civil War has
rested on domestic politics rather than on the inextricable ties between the
American nation and its empire during this period. The national state, like the
British central state before it, acquired much of its authority from the administration of its (contiguous) colonial territories. While both Federalists and Republicans could agree on the exclusive authority of the federal government over
the development of American empire, the two parties parted ways on basic republican principles about the relationship of the national state to its domestic
"public." Believing in the naturalness of social inequality and rank, Federalist
administrations supported a strong central state administered by social elites
who acted as putative stewards over the interests of the people in both foreign
and domestic affairs. Jefferson, in contrast, promoted a bifurcated vision of
power that emphasized a "sameness" of shared republican principles and national ties that generated rule by local and popular sovereignty, on the one
hand, and a centralized colonial administration governing an expansive empire, on the other. This shift in the conception of the federal government and
the national "public" ushered in by the election of 1800 produced both a qual-
itatively different empire from that of the Federalists, and a domestic republic
that appeared to operate very successfully within a decentralized federal system.

NOTES

1. TJ to James Monroe, 24 Nov. 1801, L&B, 10:296.

2. Quote taken from Carroll Smith-Rosenberg, "Dis-Covering the Subject of the 'Great Constitutional Discussion,' 1786–1789," *JAH* 79 (1992): 841.

3. For a superb explanation of the early American federal system and the position of territories
within that system, see Peter S. Onuf, "Territories and Statehood," in *Encyclopedia of American Political History*, 3 vols., ed. Jack P. Greene (New York, 1984), 3:1283–1304; see also Richard R. Johns's
historiographical essay for common characterizations among historians of a decentralized federal
system during the early Republic and antebellum periods, "Governmental Institutions as Agents of

Change: Rethinking American Political Development in the Early Republic, 1787–1835" *Studies in American Political Development* 11 (1997): 347–80.

4. Numerous historians have discussed the strong embrace of British national identity by the North American colonies. David Armitage makes the point that a pan-Atlantic conception of the British Empire sprang initially from "a cadre of provincials and imperial officials beyond the metropolis in the second quarter of the eighteenth century" that then was taken up by metropolitan interests. See David Armitage, *The Ideological Origins of the British Empire* (Cambridge, England, 2000), 9. For other discussions of Americans' strong sense of attachment and identity as members of the British Empire, see also Jack P. Greene, "Empire and Identity from the Glorious Revolution to the American Revolution," in *The Oxford History of the British Empire: The Eighteenth Century,* ed. P. J. Marshall (New York, 1998), 208–30, esp. 211–22; and T. H. Breene, "Ideology and Nationalism on the Eve of the American Revolution: Revisions Once More in Need of Revising," *JAH* 84 (1997): 13–39.

5. Greene, "Empire and Identity," 212.

6. Thomas Paine, "Thomas Paine on Government of Western Territory," in *Ohio in the Time of the Confederation,* ed. Archer Butler Hulbert (Marietta, Ohio, 1918), 8.

7. Richard B. Morris, *The Forging of the Union, 1781–1789* (New York, 1987), 10. The definitive Treaty of Paris, signed 19 April 1783, contained the same boundary lines as those stipulated in the Preliminary Articles of Peace in Paris on 30 Nov. 1782. Neither the Definitive Treaty nor the Preliminary Articles mention the Indian peoples inhabiting the lands, nor were native representatives included in the treaty negotiations.

8. For my understanding of the western lands controversy, I have relied particularly on two excellent discussions of this subject from quite different approaches. For a fine treatment of the extended debate prior to the Constitution about the relative powers of the states and the national government and the role of the western lands controversies in that longer debate, see Peter S. Onuf, *The Origins of the Federal Republic: Jurisdictional Controversies in the United States, 1775–1787* (Philadelphia, 1983); and for an interpretation of the controversy that emphasizes the individual interests of state elites, particularly in regard to their investments in land companies, see Merrill Jensen, "The Cession of the Old Northwest," *Mississippi Valley Historical Review* 24 (1936): 27–48.

9. Jerry A. O'Callaghan, "The Western Lands, 1776–84: Catalyst for Nationhood," *Journal of Forest History* 31 (1987): 135.

10. "Pledge of Congress, Oct. 10, 1780," *American History Leaflets: Colonial and Constitutional* (New York, 1892–1910), 22:9–10.

11. Payson Jackson Treat, *The National Land System: 1785–1820* (1910; rept., New York, 1967), 9.

12. For discussions that contrast the politics of deference and permanent colonialism in British Canada with the new expectations of equality in the United States, see Alan Taylor's essay, "A Northern Revolution of 1800? Upper Canada and Thomas Jefferson," in this volume; and Elizabeth Mancke, "Another British America: A Canadian Model for the Early Modern British Empire," *Journal of Imperial and Commonwealth History* 25 (1997): 1–36; and Elizabeth Mancke, "Early Modern Imperial Governance and the Origins of Canadian Political Culture," *Canadian Journal of Political Science* 32 (1999): 3–20.

13. Phrase used by Anthony Pagden, *Lords of All the World: Ideologies of Empire in Spain, Britain and France, 1500–1800* (New Haven, Conn., 1995).

14. Edward Countryman has importantly suggested the devastating shift in Indian peoples' political standing from relatively autonomous subjects of a composite English monarchy to outsiders and wards within the uniform and exclusive model of statehood established by the Americans. See Edward Countryman, "Indians, the Colonial Order, and the Social Significance of the American Revolution," *WMQ* 3d ser., 53 (1996): 342–62. See also Pagden, *Lords of All the World* for an extensive discussion of the different models of imperial rule among the Spanish, French, and English

monarchies, including the perceived strengths of the English composite model. David Armitage explains that a composite monarchy is formed when "a diversity of territories, peoples, institutions and legal jurisdictions is cemented under a single, recognized sovereign authority," Armitage, *Ideological Origins*, 22.

15. Julian Boyd, "Editorial Notes," *TJP* 6:587.

16. TJ to James Madison, 25 April 1784, *TJP* 7:118–19. For Jefferson's vision of a republican empire, see Peter S. Onuf, *Jefferson's Empire: The Language of American Nationhood* (Charlottesville, Va., 2000), and Drew McCoy, *The Elusive Republic: Political Economy in Jeffersonian America* (Chapel Hill, N.C., 1980).

17. William D. Pattison notes that despite the assumption of Payson Treat and others that Congress adopted the New England township system over the southern method of indiscriminate location, the 1785 ordinance clearly reflected a compromise between the two systems, containing aspects of the southern as much as the northern system. For the modifications made by Congress in the New England township model and the aspects of the southern system in the 1785 ordinance, see William D. Pattison, *Beginnings of the American Rectangular Land Survey System, 1784–1800* (Chicago, 1957), 39–40.

18. William Grayson to George Washington, 15 April 1785, *The Papers of George Washington*, ed. W. W. Abbot, (Charlottesville, Va., 1992), 2:499 [hereafter *PGW*].

19. Peter S. Onuf, *Statehood and Union: A History of the Northwest Ordinance* (Bloomington, Ind., 1987), 52–54.

20. James Monroe to TJ, 11 May 1786, *Letters of Delegates to Congress*, ed. Paul H. Smith (Washington, D.C., 1995), 23:278–79 [hereafter *LDC*].

21. Jack Ericson Eblen, *The First and Second United States Empires: Governors and Territorial Government, 1784–1912* (Pittsburgh, 1968), 45–46.

22. Indian groups sometimes played on American anxieties about their alliances with European powers. For instance, in the midst of the Creeks' continued warfare with the state of Georgia over the state's specious claims to their lands, Creek leader Andrew McGillivray pointed to the tribe's signed treaties of alliance and friendship with Spain to try to force federal intervention in the dispute. See Alexander McGillivray to Hon. Andrew Pickens, esq., 5 Sept. 1785, *American State Papers: Indian Affairs* (Washington, D.C., 1832), 1:17–18 [hereafter *ASPIA*].

23. George Washington to James Duane, 7 Sept. 1783, *The Writings of George Washington*, ed. Worthington Chauncey Ford (New York, 1889), 10:311.

24. James Manning to Jabez Bowen, *LDC* 23:344.

25. "Report of the Secretary at War: Indian Affairs" in Clarence Edwin Carter, ed., *Territorial Papers of the United States* (Washington, D.C., 1934), 2:103–5.

26. Bernard W. Sheehan, "The Indian Problem in the Northwest: From Conquest to Philanthropy," in *Launching the "Extended Republic": The Federalist Era*, ed. Ronald Hoffman and Peter J. Albert (Charlottesville, Va., 1996), 212–17; Reginald Horsman, *Expansion and American Indian Policy, 1783–1812* (Norman, Okla., 1967), 54–65.

27. Bernard Sheehan, *Seeds of Extinction: Jeffersonian Philanthropy and the American Indian* (New York, 1973), 3–7. Sheehan identifies the idea of "civilizing" Indian people particularly with Jefferson, or, as he argues, "this basic Jeffersonian commitment bound all these people together in their attitudes toward the Indians. Jefferson led the age, not because his ideas were original, but because they represented a consensus. His prominence as a political leader enhanced the importance of his activities in favor of the Indians. Also his position of influence in scientific affairs gave his opinions on the Indians' future a special stature. In his *Notes* on Virginia, his presidency of the American Philosophical Society, his extensive correspondence with the important minds of the period, and finally his determination, while he held political power, to change the character of tribal society, Jefferson held a central position in the late eighteenth and early nineteenth centuries.

Judged in the light of a widely held body of opinion on the nature of Indian-white relations, the age can be called Jeffersonian" (7). The overall Indian policy promoted by the Washington administration and particularly its willingness to recognize Indian tribal groups as independent nations and therefore as under the aegis of the national government rather than state governments, however, provoked resounding objections from Republicans. See, for instance, Peter S. Onuf's discussion of the objections of John Taylor of Caroline and the general thrust of Republican opposition to Federalist Indian policy in the 1790s in *Jefferson's Empire,* 41–46.

28. Francis Paul Prucha, *American Indian Policy in the Formative Years: The Indian Trade and Intercourse Acts, 1790–1834* (Cambridge, Mass., 1962) is still the most thorough discussion of the Indian Trade and Intercourse Acts.

29. Prucha, *American Indian Policy,* 29–30.

30. George Washington to Henry Knox, 5 Dec. 1784, *PGW* 2:170–72.

31. My understanding of this point and of the constitutional debates more generally comes from Max M. Edling, *A Revolution in Favour of Government: The American Constitution and Ideas about State Formation, 1787–1788* (London, forthcoming); and Saul Cornell, *The Other Founders: Anti-Federalism and the Dissenting Tradition in America, 1788–1828* (Chapel Hill, N.C., 1999).

32. Edling, *A Revolution,* 117–18.

33. Alexander Hamilton, Federalist No. 23, as quoted in Edling, *A Revolution,* 157.

34. Prucha, *American Indian Policy,* 29–30.

35. Ibid., 42.

36. Francis Paul Prucha, *The Great Father: The United States Government and the American Indians,* 2 vols. (Lincoln, Neb., 1984), 50.

37. Saul Cornell's *The Other Founders* provides perhaps the most nuanced reading to date of the diverse and at times internally conflicting arguments made by anti-Federalists, whose different class positions shaped the nature of their objections to the Constitution.

38. Edling, *A Revolution,* 195, 196.

39. Ibid., 31–34, 43, 92; Cornell, *The Other Founders,* 29–31.

40. For the continuing strains of anti-Federalism from the 1790s through the antebellum period, see Richard R. Ellis, "The Persistence of Antifederalism after 1789," in *Beyond Confederation: Origins of the Constitution and American National Identity,* ed. Richard Beeman, Stephen Botein, and Edward C. Carter II (Chapel Hill, N.C., 1987), 295–314; and for its influence on Jefferson and other Republicans, see Cornell, *The Other Founders,* 147–71.

41. Stanley Elkins and Eric McKitrick, *The Age of Federalism: The Early American Republic, 1788–1800* (New York, 1993), 703.

42. See Jeanne Boydston, "Making Gender in the Early Republic: Judith Sargent Murray and the Revolution of 1800," in this volume.

43. TJ to Joel Barlow, 14 March 1801, L&B, 10:222.

44. TJ to Chancellor Robert R. Livingston, 28 Feb. 1799, L&B, 10:118.

45. TJ to John Taylor, 1 June 1798, L&B, 10:46.

46. In contrast, Jefferson characterized the Federalists as a foreign (English) presence. For Jefferson's description of the "Spirit of 1776," see TJ to Samuel Smith, 22 Aug. 1798, and TJ to Thomas Lomax, 12 March 1799, L&B, 10:55–59 and 10:123–25, respectively. For an excellent analysis of Jefferson's perception of the Federalists as foreigners, see Peter S. Onuf, *Jefferson's Empire,* chap. 3. Jefferson trusted that, eventually, hardcore Federalists who were English "in all their relations and sentiments," would be exposed as English subjects, "the mask taken from their faces"; see TJ to General Gates, 30 May 1797, L&B, 9:392.

47. For an extended discussion of the Federalist model of government as a matter of republican stewardship, see Drew McCoy, *The Elusive Republic;* for a discussion of John Adams's changing beliefs, including his intellectual shift toward a defense of rank and permanent privilege based on a

growing conviction that social equality was not possible in human society, see Joyce Appleby, *Liberalism and Republicanism in the Historical Imagination* (Cambridge, Mass., 1992), 188–209.

48. TJ to Benjamin Waring, 23 March 1801, L&B, 10:235–36.

49. TJ to Amos Marsh, 20 Nov. 1801, L&B, 10:293.

50. For this distinction of a demographically impelled expansion rather than one initiated by force, see Alan Taylor, "A Northern Revolution."

51. TJ to James Monroe, 24 Nov. 1801, L&B, 10:296; for the full story of this proposal issued by the Virginia assembly, see Douglas R. Egerton, *Gabriel's Rebellion: The Virginia Slave Conspiracies of 1800 and 1802* (Chapel Hill, N.C., 1993), 150–62.

52. TJ to Colonel Arthur Campbell, 1 Sept. 1797, L&B, 10:420–21; for another plea that the American nation needed to encourage men to live by their hands rather than their heads in order to avoid the social decay of European countries, see TJ to David Williams, 14 Nov. 1803, L&B, 10:428–31. For the elaboration of Jefferson's vision of an expansion through space as a means of staving off the United States' progression toward a corruptive, industrial economy see Drew McCoy, *The Elusive Republic*.

53. Emphasis is mine; TJ to Dr. Joseph Priestley, 29 Jan. 1804, L&B, 10:447. For another declaration of this same sentiment, see TJ to John Breckinridge, 12 Aug. 1803, L&B, 10:407–11.

54. TJ to Peregrine Fitzhugh, 23 Feb. 1798, L&B, 10:3.

55. See, for example, Thomas Jefferson to General Knox, 10 Aug. 1791 L&B, 8:226–27.

56. Horsman, *Expansion,* 109–10.

57. TJ to Governor William Henry Harrison, 27 Feb. 1803, L&B, 10:369–70.

58. TJ to Colonel Benjamin Hawkins, 18 Feb. 1803, L&B, 10:362.

59. Ibid.

CHAPTER 16

A Northern Revolution of 1800?
Upper Canada and Thomas Jefferson

Alan Taylor

In January 1801 Asa Danforth Jr. departed York, the capitol of the British colony of Upper Canada. Created in 1791 along the northern shores of the Great Lakes, Upper Canada was the largest but least populated—and most remote—province in British North America. Designed by imperialists appalled by the American Revolution, the new colony was governed by a Crown-appointed lieutenant governor and executive council that dominated a weak elective assembly and a life-term legislative council. Sensitive to Upper Canada's exposure to American influence (and possible invasion), the colony's official elite were haunted by the American and French Revolutions as catastrophes that must be averted in their province. Ever fearful of subversion, they readily prosecuted as sedition any criticism of their government or any praise of republicanism.

Once across the American border in New York, Danforth wrote to Timothy Green, who was both his ally in republican politics and, unfortunately, his impatient creditor. Lacking enough money to satisfy Green, Danforth instead offered appealing political information about Upper Canada: "You will recollect old Mr. [Peter] Russell, our late administrator, took his seat at the head of affairs about the time you was in the Province. He observed to me on the 2nd day of Jany. last, that if Mr. Jefferson & Mr. Burr should come in at the Head of affairs in the states, the Provinces must give up to the States—or French—the French to him the most awfull." Danforth estimated "that three fourths of the common people would be happy of a Change," if secured in their land titles and if their liberators were American rather than French.[1]

Recently alienated from the government of Upper Canada, Danforth was hardly an impartial observer—but he was also not alone in regarding the province as ready for a republican revolution and in concluding that Jefferson and Burr would help with an invasion. In May 1801 Israel Chapin Jr. reported from western New York, "The subjects of the British talk as if war would take place between Britain and America. . . . The reason they conjecture a war will commence is on account of Jefferson being President. They conceive him friendly to the French & inimical to the English."

In July Col. John A. Graham, a Vermont lawyer turned British spy, reported that ironworkers at Ganonoque in Upper Canada were making pikes to arm for rebellion and corresponding with their political friends in Vermont. In June at York Joseph Willcocks, an Anglo-Irish immigrant and government supporter, noted ruefully, "the people of Ireland are not more discontented than the Lower Class of the People are here." Having fled from the violence of the 1798 republican uprising in Ireland, Willcocks made an informed and sobering comparison. So did William W. Baldwin, an Anglo-Irish immigrant and lawyer who advised his relatives against joining him in Upper Canada because it seemed doomed to an impending rebellion: "Can you believe it, that in these retired regions of the world . . . the greatest discontent reigns among the people," who would, "had they the least prospect of success, tomorrow overturn the order of things in this country." The American election of Jefferson and Burr seemed to provide that prospect.[2]

Upper Canada seemed especially ripe for rebellion because most of the inhabitants were recent (post-1791) immigrants from the United States. Unlike the original, smaller migration of the early 1780s, the newcomers were not true loyalists compelled to leave the states and attracted into Canada by British rule. Instead they were drawn by the especially cheap farmland and low taxes in the underdeveloped province. By 1800 their growing numbers belatedly alarmed the official elite. One jaundiced officer, Col. Thomas Talbot, denounced the American immigrants as "1st. Those who were early enticed by a gratuitous offer of land, without any predilection on their part, to the British Constitution. 2nd. Those who have fled from the United States for crimes, or to escape their Creditors. 3rd. Republicans, whose principal motive for settling in that Country, is an anticipation of its shaking off its allegiance to Great Britain." With such ingredients, rebellion apparently needed only a little encouragement and armed assistance from the newly elected American administration of Thomas Jefferson. Celebrating the recent American election, Asa Danforth Jr. predicted, "Time appears very unfavourable for G. Brittain in the present State of affairs. I should not be surprised if her Jurisdiction should be done away in North America."[3]

In fact, surprisingly little came of the widespread grumbling and alarm manifest in Upper Canada immediately before and after Jefferson's election. The new president refused to fulfill his reputation as an exporter of democratic subversion but instead—in the short term—pursued improved relations with Great Britain. This essay explores both the sources of northern discontent and the limited response to it by Jefferson's administration. That double exploration requires returning to Asa Danforth Jr. and his grievances.

THE DANFORTH ROAD

Thirty years old in 1801, Danforth had been born in Massachusetts. As an adolescent he moved with his parents to Onondaga County, on the New York frontier. As a young man during the early 1790s he incurred heavy debts speculating in New York lands; hoping to reverse his fortunes Danforth played double or nothing by investing in the especially risky land titles of nearby Upper Canada. In 1792 and 1793 an array of speculators, most from New York state, had received grants to entire townships of unsettled land from the generous lieutenant governor, John Graves Simcoe. Known as "nominees," the recipients were supposed to recruit groups of settlers to accelerate the development of the underpopulated colony (which had only fourteen thousand inhabitants in 1791). Simcoe naively assumed that the United States still contained a large, closeted population of loyalists who would flock into Upper Canada if promised cheap land and if guided and assisted by the nominees. With equal naivete Simcoe assumed that the nominees were spokesmen for egalitarian groups of farmers who wished to settle together to sustain a common church.[4]

In fact, most nominees were American land speculators looking for a bargain. They saw nothing to lose because Simcoe demanded no down payments and only modest fees—about five cents per acre—for lands once patented (the final stage in securing a complete land title). By comparison, the United States was then selling townships in more distant Ohio for a dollar per acre, with payment due immediately in full. Simcoe merely stipulated that no patents could issue until the nominees established at least forty settler families per township.

Each family would receive two hundred acres—a generous-size farm—for a mere ten dollars in patent fees. In reward for their exertions in recruiting, provisioning, and equipping the first settlers, the nominees expected at least a bonus of one thousand acres per family, which they could patent at the same minimal rate. By acquiring forty thousand acres (at one thousand acres per family) for about two thousand dollars in later fees, the nominees meant to make a killing by retailing lots at higher prices to subsequent settlers. For their authority the speculators relied on their optimistic interpretation of Simcoe's rather Delphic pronouncements and on the generous land-granting precedent set in the adjoining British province of Lower Canada in 1791.[5]

But making money in frontier land speculation required several years of patience—and the lieutenant governor was by no means a patient man. By 1795 Simcoe became disillusioned with his township program. He was shocked—shocked—to discover that the nominees were land speculators rather than selfless promoters of colonial development and British loyalism. Treating their grants as property rather than as a provisional trust, the nominees bought and sold shares, drawing in new investors who had never been vetted by Simcoe and his executive council. Those new investors included Asa Danforth Jr., Timothy Green (a New York City merchant), and his close business and political associate, Aaron Burr. All three men were active in the Republican Party politics of New York state, with Burr a prominent officeholder, Green his political manager, and Danforth a useful gofer. As Republican operatives the three were the very inversion of the deferential loyalists whom Simcoe had sought to settle his townships. Upon discovering Burr's investment, the British minister to the United States, Robert Liston, warned that such men "of high-flying democratick sentiments . . . would rejoice to see an independent Republick, established in Canada."[6]

Nor was Simcoe impressed with the nominees' exertions to settle their townships. Most minimized their costs by waiting for settlers to move at their own expense into the colony. When nominees did sponsor settlers, many proved to be poor transients who made scant improvements before moving on. The colony's elitist chief justice, John Elmsley, denounced the township settlers as "a few, wretched Vagrants hastily collected from among the Dregs of the Neighbouring States." Or the nominees played a sort of shell game, recruiting resident colonists eager to obtain additional lands—which practice violated the goal of drawing immigrants to the colony. In 1797 a comprehensive investigation by the colony's surveyor general found that only six of the thirty-two townships had obtained the forty-settler minimum; and only one of the six consisted of fully qualified settlers.[7]

In cutting corners and costs, the township nominees simply behaved like other American land speculators, who routinely ignored with impunity any settlement requirements imposed by the indulgent state and federal governments in the United States. Why, the nominees wondered, should the rules be enforced in Upper Canada? And they had their own complaints. Simcoe's vague and inconsistent directives and his slow and inefficient land surveying office often frustrated sincere efforts to locate settlers on particular lots in the proper townships.[8]

An indignant Simcoe vowed to rescue his colony from the American land speculators whom he had unwittingly invited into Upper Canada. He lectured one nominee, "You must perceive that the King's Government is infinitely more desirous of settling a few well-affected Subjects, moral, sober, and religious men, than of a Multitude of Inhabitants & above all that . . . it is careful to prevent this Colony from becoming the Prey of Land Jobbers." For Simcoe regarded land jobbing as the school for "Insurgents, turbulent or seditious People."[9]

In 1795–96 the lieutenant governor arbitrarily revoked fourteen townships and notified the nominees of the other eighteen to complete their settler quota within one year on pain of forfeiture. A year later Simcoe had returned to England, leaving the land mess and the government in the hands of his administrator, Peter Russell. In July 1797 Russell and the executive council abolished the remaining township grants. As a sop to the speculators the council allowed four leading nominees per township personally to receive 1,200 acres each—hardly a fair return for those few who had made a significant effort at considerable cost to recruit bona fide settlers. Denouncing the nominees as "rascals without principle or capital," Chief Justice Elmsley boasted that the council had "prove[d] that the strong arm of Monarchy is not to be pushed aside by those unprincipled & unattached republicans."[10]

Adding insult to injury, the executive council regranted much of the revoked land to themselves or their friends and relatives. Elmsley demanded, "Can lands be in any hands better than in those of the officers of Government, in a country in which the influence of extensive property is so much wanted to give effect to the Laws, & keep the turbulent in good order? & in whose hands can they be more safely placed than ours, who depend so entirely upon the King & the Mother Country." By enriching himself in revoked lands, Elmsley insisted that he also fended off creeping republicanism and built a colonial aristocracy wedded to British rule. Of course the nominees saw it differently, concluding that the councilors were corrupt hypocrites.[11]

In the spring of 1797 Danforth went to Upper Canada in a last-ditch effort to save four townships from revocation. In addition to protecting his own land claims, Danforth represented other investors, including Timothy Green. Obliged to make do with a 1,200-acre award, Danforth resourcefully sought and got another two hundred acres on the dubious grounds that his wife, Olive Langdon, had been a loyalist during the Revolution. Then, however, Danforth imperiled his gains by violating the code expected of true loyalism—which officials regarded as an ongoing character as much as a wartime record. As a newcomer Danforth was initially oblivious to the different rules that distinguished a British colony from an American state. Once deference had yielded 1,400 acres, Danforth quickly shifted to a more aggressive strategy, employing a lawyer to file caveats meant to block the executive council from regranting any lands in the four townships that he represented. A standard legal maneuver in the states, the caveats struck the executive councilors as a rank insult from an impertinent upstart. On 15 December 1798 the council "judged proper to mark its sense of the Indecency as well as the Impropriety of Asa Danforth's Conduct" by rescinding all his land grants and declaring him "unworthy of any future favor from this Government." In March 1799 Danforth apologized, explaining that he had sought the caveats to avoid prosecution in the United States by those he represented, who demanded an aggressive defense.[12]

Although quick to take offense, the executive council could also be forgiving when treated with deference. Apology accepted, Danforth recovered his 1,400 acres. That spring he also entered a potentially lucrative contract for a critical trust: to construct a badly needed road from the provincial capitol, York (now Toronto), eastward 106 miles to the Bay of Quinte, then the main center of the colony's settlement. Run through a dense forest cut by many streams and swamps, the road was an arduous and complex project—but vital to breaking the capitol's winter isolation and integrating the dispersed settlements of the sprawling colony. Such a road also served Danforth's private interest, for he had located his land grants in the country east of York. The executive council agreed to pay Danforth ninety dollars per mile. To help recruit laborers, who could only be had in numbers from New York state, the council authorized Danforth to recommend as many as forty men for grants of two hundred acres, paying the usual small fees. Danforth boasted, "It is not vain in me to say that the Government reposed more trust and confidence in me than they have in an

American in my knowledge." Recognizing his special merit, the councilors had "taken me by the hand & placed me in a Situation to do well." Although frustrated as a nominee, he hoped to recover and prosper as a road-builder.[13]

But there was a catch. Danforth would collect his money in installments only as he completed—and officials inspected—sections of the road. Given his heavy debts and the high costs of importing, provisioning, and paying forty laborers, Danforth needed to make rapid progress and receive steady payments to keep his creditors at bay. By December 1799, when cold and snow compelled a halt, Danforth had completed sixty-three miles of road: it got a mixed review from the official inspector, who noted the "great exertions" but found a few flawed bridges and slopes. The government newspaper applauded: "The report . . . is highly favorable to Mr. Danfor[th], the undertaker, and less imperfections could not be pointed out in so extensive a work." Chief Justice Elmsley, however, read the report in the harshest light, for he despised Americans in general and Danforth in particular as cunning cheats. Following Elmsley's lead, the executive council delivered only half of what they owed for sixty-three miles, reserving the other half pending repairs in the spring.[14]

That left Danforth with too little cash to pay his creditors, principally Timothy Green. In March 1800 Danforth returned to New York state to recruit laborers for renewed road building in the spring. Green's lawyer promptly had Danforth arrested and jailed for debt. In prison Danforth faced perpetual ruin, for unless released he could not complete the road and would forfeit all further payments from the government of Upper Canada. Trapped, Danforth had to accept Green's harsh terms, signing a confession of judgment and a bond for six thousand dollars—about twice what he thought he owed to Green.[15]

By a heroic effort Danforth completed the road, all 106 miles, by mid-December. The official surveyor found the work generally sound but identified a few problems that would need correction in the spring at a probable cost of only $125. Again taking a hard line, the executive council withheld $1,935 from Danforth's payment, pending the spring repairs. They also refused to grant the eight thousand acres due to the workers—who had all sold their rights to Danforth, who would pay the patent fees. The treatment seems especially unfair given that three weeks later Danforth's chief critic, Chief Justice Elmsley, traveled the road and privately praised its "safety and convenience." Certain that Americans were tricksters, the colonial officials protected themselves by defrauding Danforth.[16]

The treatment exposed Asa Danforth to another stint in an American debtor's prison for want of sufficient funds to satisfy Timothy Green. Having once taken pride in his patronage from the executive council, Danforth now felt a special humiliation that turned into fury. He concluded that British officials would never let an American get ahead and become anything more than a common farmer. He complained bitterly that after American entrepreneurs had "built up the Settlements of that Province, & that when the Executive Council saw that our Americans had made Choice of the best lands in the Province, they laid a plan to rescind & take away the Lands theretofore Granted and placed their own locations on the same." He headed for New York to persuade Green to show patience, in return for Danforth's efforts to stir up a rebellion that, by overthrowing the government of Upper Canada, would restore their lost townships.[17]

Danforth took heart, first, from the widespread grumbling he had heard in Upper Canada and, second, from the triumph of Jeffersonian republicanism in the American national election of 1800. In New York Danforth sought out an old acquaintance, who was the new vice president (and almost president), Aaron Burr. Again basking in elite attention, this time Republican, Danforth assured Green, "I have had a long Conversation with Colo. Burr at several times. I am much pleased with him in Many Ideas advanced. I am fully of oppinion that the Great Change of Politics in the United States will afford something very handsome to those who were drag[g]ed from home by fair promises of Genl. Simco[e] & the like." After working with Burr for the spring election of George Clinton as governor of New York, Danforth returned in June 1801 to York in Upper Canada. By letter and visit, Danforth sounded out local leaders known to hold grievances against the government. A political evangelist, Danforth privately announced the republican millennium coming to Upper Canada in a letter to Richard Cockrell: "Many pleasing things have made their appearance since I parted with you at the H[ead] of the Lake. The present aspect is Glorious. I say Glorious, times when Justice and Equity shall take place without partiality and when the Lion shall be Made to lye down with the Lamb, and when a man [who] has exerted himself in a good Work or Noble cause, let him be rewarded accordingly." Of course, the "lion" referred to the symbol of British power as well as to scripture. For Danforth, like the American revolutionaries, only a republic could properly bestow rewards upon the meritorious, however humble their origins, rather than upon the sycophants of official and aristocratic power. As if to confirm that point, in late 1801 the province's new lieutenant governor, the imperious General Peter Hunter, summarily dismissed Danforth's claims to the remaining $1,935 and eight thousand acres owed for the road—perhaps from new suspicions about his loyalty. In January 1802 Danforth again left York to return to New York. Danforth urged his Canadian friends and correspondents to meet him in Albany in February to consult with their New York partners and plan their revolution.[18]

Like Danforth, most of the other suspects were ambitious Americans of middling means, men drawn into Upper Canada during the early 1790s by Simcoe's promises but then frustrated at the end of the decade by the official reaction against the township program. From the official perspective, Danforth and his ilk were classic Yankees: unscrupulous speculators grasping for a wealth properly beyond their lowly station and shifty morals. Of course they saw themselves differently: as able and enterprising men frustrated by a corrupt and oppressive elite of British-born officials. Although the plotters certainly hoped to enhance their fortunes, greed only begins to explain their motivation. As ambitious men of modest origins, they sought property and influence to prove their worth and to defy the sneers of inherited or official privilege. Danforth nicely expressed their eagerness for attention and applause in seeking to extend republican America into Upper Canada: "A Scene will open and many become Actors in the Play. The United States is like a Stage Play. Every Man's Mind is taken up with his part." By contrast, British Canada limited the conspicuous and lucrative roles to the approved clients of the imperial bureaucracy—which found Americans dangerous and untrustworthy. Their disapproval became a self-fulfilling prophecy, as the offended immigrants sought revenge in republican revolution.[19]

The suspects identified by government informants included Ebenezer Allan. In 1794 Allan had sold his mills and land in western New York to accept Simcoe's offer of two thousand acres in the Thames valley, where Allan built a gristmill, sawmill, and distillery. A prominent merchant insisted that Allan was "as active & enterprizing a man as any in the Province." But Allan shocked the official elite by practicing polygamy with Indian women and by grasping for more land by procuring suspect Indian claims and settler rights. In February 1799 a government surveyor accused Allan of attempted bribery and forging settler certificates—charges that led to his indictment in January 1801. In April Chief Justice John Elmsley eagerly issued the arrest warrant. The court proceedings dragged into October, when the magistrates dropped the case, apparently for lack of evidence. Embittered by the prosecution, Allan had the motive to cooperate with Danforth.[20]

According to government informants, the conspirators also included four entrepreneurial and versatile emigrants from New Hampshire: Aaron Greeley, Silvester and Gideon Tiffany, and Davenport Phelps. A land surveyor and mill-wright, Greeley had ventured to settle Haldimand Township until the executive council revoked his grant in 1797—which undercut his considerable invest-ment in a sawmill and gristmill there. In the abortive struggle to save the town-ships, Greeley had worked closely with Danforth.[21]

The Tiffany brothers had taken on an especially tough task: to conduct a newspaper in security-obsessed Upper Canada. During the early 1790s Silvester Tiffany had published a Lansingburgh, New York, newspaper called the *American Spy*—hardly a name to reassure the British. In 1796 he moved to Upper Canada and into a partnership with his younger brother Gideon to print the colony's then lone (and government-sponsored) newspaper, the *Upper Canada Gazette*. The brothers repeatedly offended the official censors, principally Chief Justice Elmsley. In 1797 the Crown prosecuted Gideon for public blasphemy; convicted, he paid a £20 fine and spent a month in jail. Anticipating govern-ment dismissal, Gideon resigned as printer, leaving the press to his brother's management. But Silvester soon reaped his own measure of official disgust. In February 1798 Elmsley fumed that a speech by King George III, "the finest thing in Modern History, & which ought to be circulated in all his Dominions, & got by heart by all his Subjects, has never made its appearance, while every trifle re-lated to the damned States is printed in large characters." In April 1798 the gov-ernment sacked Silvester Tiffany as official printer.[22]

A year later the brothers founded the province's first independent news-paper, *The Canada Constellation* (soon renamed *The Niagara Herald*). The Tif-fanys painfully discovered that, given the limited readership in Upper Canada, no newspaper could thrive without a subsidy from the government. After one losing year, Gideon Tiffany gave up and moved to Delaware Township, in the Thames Valley, where he speculated in land and bought a gristmill and sawmill from Ebenezer Allan. Before retiring, Gideon Tiffany again offended the offi-cial elite by singing "God Save the King" but adding his own verse: "God Save America and keep us from dispotic Powers or Sways till Time shall Cease." Sil-vester Tiffany soldiered on as the sole editor and publisher. In January 1801 he unwisely ridiculed the government newspaper for publishing "An Ode for Her Majesty's Birthday," casting that loyal piece as so wretched that it must have been written by a dog. That comment confirmed the government's resolution to award no printing business to the upstart press, which tottered toward its financial demise at the end of the year.[23]

The Tiffanys' brother-in-law, Davenport Phelps, also emigrated to Upper Canada. A former merchant and occasional lawyer, Phelps speculated in Glanford Township, which the executive council repossessed in 1797. Frustrated by the official elite, Phelps found an unorthodox new patron in Joseph Brant, the Mohawk chief who served as the principal spokesman for the Iroquois Six Nations settled in the Grand River valley of Upper Canada. Resourceful, charismatic, and educated at an Anglo-American school, Brant had mastered the ways of European gentility as well as Native American protocol. With Brant's support Phelps sought Anglican ordination to become a missionary at Grand River, in hopes of procuring a salary from the Society for the Propagation of the Gospel. But once again the government blocked his ambition. In 1798 administrator Peter Russell declared Phelps disloyal because three years earlier he had rallied "a concourse of Farmers" to march on a district courthouse to protest the government's prosecution of a "Person for Seditious Practices." The bishop of Quebec agreed that the Grand River Six Nations were too critical to the security of Upper Canada to risk upon a "Spiritual Instructor who would be disposed to unsettle their notions of loyalty & obedience & weaken their attachment to the Government under which it is their happiness to live." [24]

The rebuff offended Brant, who refused to accept defeat. Instead, in early 1801, he wrote to an American leader whom he had met and impressed during a 1797 visit to Philadelphia: Aaron Burr. Writing to his daughter, Theodosia Burr Alston, Burr extolled Brant's virtues: "He is a man of education—speaks and writes the English perfectly—and has seen much of Europe and America. Receive him with respect and hospitality. He is not one of those Indians who drink rum, but is quite a gentleman; not one who will make you fine bows, but one who understands and practices what belongs to propriety and good breeding." In 1801 Brant sought Burr's help in persuading the Episcopal bishop of New York to ordain Phelps for employment at Grand River. Brant explained, "we should not only be well satisfied to receive a Missionary from a Bishop in the United States, but for various other reasons would prefer one from thence." To justify the request Brant insisted that "religion and morality respect mankind at large, without any reference to the boundaries of civil governments." Of course British officials disagreed radically, insisting that they had to control any Christian mission to the Indians within their boundaries. Because they particularly did not want Brant cooperating with Aaron Burr, the Upper Canadian officials suspected the worst when Theodosia and husband Joseph Alston paid an ostensibly social visit to Grand River in August 1801. What sinister message, wondered the officials, had the Alstons brought from the arch-republican of New York?[25]

Although a staunch loyalist during the American Revolution, Brant had soured on British rule by 1801. In addition to his frustration in the Phelps controversy, he deeply resented British meddling in the land affairs of Grand River. He was determined to manage those lands to secure an endowment and an annual income for the Six Nations, but the government meant to keep the Indians dependent by blocking their land leases and sales. That obstruction drove Brant into an alliance with New York land speculators eager to buy Grand River land. Those speculators included many of the nominees who had invested in the townships of Upper Canada—and wanted them back.[26]

In late 1800 and early 1801 Brant wrote "Secret and Confidential" letters to Thomas Morris, an American congressman, and New York governor George Clinton, seeking their help in securing a large grant of federal land around Sandusky in Ohio. Ostensibly the tract would sustain a mission to encourage Christianity and agricultural progress among any of the Six Nations who chose to live there. But such an American tract could also provide a safety net should the Grand River Six Nations rebel but suffer defeat and need a haven within American lines.[27]

In the spring of 1801 Brant also sent a secret message to the native peoples living to the west around the Great Lakes: the Ottawa, Ojibwa, Pottawattomie, and Huron. If the Grand River Six Nations planned to make a move against Upper Canada, they first had to secure their rear to the west. Brant's message denounced Great Britain as "an ungrateful nation" that "had constantly deceived the Indians." Unfortunately for Brant, the Ojibwa rejected the message and revealed its substance to British officials during the summer, compounding their alarm over the visit of Theodosia and Joseph Alston to Grand River.[28]

In January 1802 Danforth urged Ebenezer Allan to bring Joseph Brant with him to the plotting session at Albany in February. Danforth astutely regarded Brant as critical to wooing the Grand River Six Nations, whose alliance was essential to the security of Upper Canada. No rebellion could prosper without at least their tacit neutrality, while the government probably could not stand if the Six Nations joined the rebels. Closely watched, Brant did not attend Danforth's meeting in Albany in February 1802. Instead he sent his closest confidante and protégé, John Norton.[29]

Unlike the other plotters, Richard Cockrell had been born and educated in England. He had, however, emigrated to and lived in the United States before moving on to Upper Canada. And he possessed a rather American sensibility as a versatile and ambitious gadfly with a dozen schemes for self- and social betterment. Cockrell dabbled in poetry, painting, drawing, and elocution. For an income he surveyed lands and conducted a private school, initially at Newark, later at the Head of the Lake (Ancaster). In 1795 Gideon Tiffany published Cockrell's *Thoughts on the Education of Youth*, a pioneering work of educational theory and the first private (nonofficial) publication in the colony. Befriended by Joseph Brant, Cockrell educated his son, John Brant, and surveyed Grand River lands for illegal sales to speculators, antagonizing the government. In 1800 the quixotic Cockrell further dismayed the administration by running for the assembly, challenging the incumbent and government stalwart David W. Smith, the surveyor general. Equally bold and futile, the race confirmed Cockrell's marginalization from official patronage.[30]

The suspects also shared a bond as Freemasons—members of a secret society with a meritocratic philosophy that especially appealed to ambitious freethinkers. By promoting bonds of mutual trust, freemasonry encouraged the brethren to help one another and keep their shared secrets. On 16 May 1801—as the plot became serious—Sylvester Tiffany published an unusual essay on the front page of his newspaper, asserting that secrecy was an essential social virtue: "A revealer of secrets is the fomenter of mischief and promoter of sedition." Was he sending a reminder to fellow plotters?[31]

In 1801–2 a schism developed in Upper Canadian freemasonry, a rift that closely paralleled the Danforth plot in implication as well as timing. Sylvester Tiffany served as the secretary of the lodge at Niagara when it threw off the negligent leadership of grand master William Jarvis, who had been appointed by the Grand Lodge of England to a life term. The Niagara lodge asserted its right to govern Upper Canadian freemasonry without Jarvis (who was also a high official in the provincial government). In rejecting Jarvis's monarchy in favor of their own republic, the Niagara lodge acted with advice and encouragement from correspondents in the United States. In June 1802 one Canadian brother, Abner Everitt, returned from visiting the United States to report that the American Freemasons "were deeply interested in the action of the Canadian brethren" and "unanimously approve of our proceedings, excepting that we have delayed the forming of an independent Grand Lodge longer than we should have done." The coup had the support of the lodges in the Niagara peninsula, where American settlement was heaviest, and in the Grand River valley, where Brant presided. But Jarvis was championed by the lodges in the eastern and central townships. At the very least, the Freemason uprising parallels the Danforth plot; perhaps it was also an integral part of that scheme. If so, its failure beyond the Niagara peninsula contributed to the collapse of Danforth's plot.[32]

PLOT

By the time the conspirators met in Albany in February and March 1802, their plot was no longer their secret. In January the government of Upper Canada had learned their names and intentions from an anonymous informant. He reported that the conspirators meant to overthrow the government and create a republican state that could join the northern United States in a confederacy that would separate from the southern states. Victory would reward the plotters with their lost townships—and perhaps a bonus of another 1 or 2 million acres. "The American Government," he insisted, "is at the bottom of the plan but will not be seen. Col. Burr and Mr. [George] Clinton are ostensibly the principal leaders." In reporting the information to Lieutenant Governor Hunter, then away at Quebec, Chief Justice Elmsley elaborated

> That the plan is to assemble a considerable force on the frontiers, & at a given signal to enter the Province: that both the men & the Arms necessary for the purpose are ready & can be brought forward at a Moment's warning & that the Invaders will be immediately joined by between One & two thousand of the Inhabitants of this Country. That immediately on their Entry, they are to issue a proclamation declaring that their intention is merely to recover possession of the Townships which were escheated in the Year 1797: that in so doing, no blood is to be shed, unless resistance should make it necessary & that plunder will not be attempted. That on getting possession of York, which will be a primary object, the Members of the Executive Government are to be constrained to grant to the Invaders between 1 & 2 Millions of Acres, which are to be divided among them & for which Col. Burr had pledged himself to use all his influence to obtain a confirmation from Congress whenever the Conquest is completed.

Perhaps the conspirators had talked wishfully of such numbers of men and acres—but they were never as close to their goals as Elmsley breathlessly implied. By speaking of armed American volunteers as real rather than wished for, the conspirators evidently meant to fabricate a rebellion in Upper Canada. Instead they provoked an overreaction by easily spooked officials.[33]

A second government informant attended the winter meetings in Albany, providing additional information that led Elmsley to assure Hunter in April, "We learn that the project is not abandoned, but is to be carried into Execution some time in the Month of Sept., that the places of rendezvous are Oswego & Buffalo Creek & that the manifesto which is to be published on the Entry of the Invaders, is now printing at the office of one Barber in Albany." The new informant was probably Richard Cockrell, who had begun to forward his secret letters from Danforth to the executive council. Once the initial anonymous informant had fingered Cockrell, the government apparently applied sufficient pressure and incentives to get him to change his stripes.[34]

By June Danforth knew that the plot had been revealed but not that his friend Cockrell had turned informant. Writing from New York Danforth informed Cockrell, "I am out of the Jaws of Lions, &c., but the Situation of my friends is different. Therefore I am and must be cautious. I am informed that the great Council fire is prepared to consume me—that is if they could have the privilege of taking me. I feel Easy and unconcerned. I am, thank God, out of their power." Despite the loss of secrecy, Danforth persisted. By late June his pamphlet promoting rebellion had been published in Albany for dissemination in Upper Canada. At least one package of pamphlets did reach the province, sent to Henry Finkle, who had lodged Danforth during his sojourns in Upper Canada. "However," Finkle's son recalled, "the pamphlets were not distributed, and the fact never became generally known." Evidently the elder Finkle could recognize a lost cause and a deadly risk. The arrival of that package of pamphlets proved to be the peak of a rebellion that fizzled. The September date for the invasion and uprising passed uneventfully. By then the plot had become, in the words of Peter Russell, "a tissue of Absurdity & Improbability."[35]

After the fizzle Danforth remained in New York, shifting in and out of debtor's prison depending on Timothy Green's whims. For a time Danforth established a profitable salt-making business, but he had to consign it to Green in 1810. Danforth moved to New York City, where he was last documented in 1821, on the lam from another arrest for debt. In the end it was American creditors rather than British officials who hounded and ruined Asa Danforth Jr. Ultimately the American Republic provided no more reward for his merits than had the British province. Ironically, he remains unwittingly honored in the province that he tried to subvert, for the British never renamed "the Danforth Road," now a major street in Toronto and beyond. In another legacy, Danforth probably inspired the law adopted by the Upper Canadian legislature in early

1804 empowering the government to banish any immigrant alien suspected of sedition.[36]

Most of the other suspects also felt uncomfortable in Upper Canada and began to leave. In 1803 Davenport Phelps and Silvester Tiffany moved to western New York. Based in Geneva, Phelps served as an Episcopal missionary, while Tiffany published a Republican newspaper, the *Ontario Freeman,* at nearby Canandaigua. By 1806 Aaron Greeley also departed Upper Canada, shifting to the Michigan Territory, where he worked as a surveyor and land agent. In 1811 Greeley welcomed the prospect of an American war with Great Britain: "Poor deluded nation. Their corrupt Government, by their insolence and injustice, has led them to the very brink of Destruction." Gideon Tiffany remained in Upper Canada but went into a sort of internal exile from provincial politics. A nineteenth-century local historian remembered Tiffany as "liberal in his sentiments" and said of his politics that "his sympathies were with the weaker party." Joseph Brant also stuck it out in Upper Canada, loudly protesting his loyalty and denouncing the officials who suspected it. In 1806—a year before his death—he promoted the emergence of a legislative opposition party led by Judge Robert Thorpe. Ebenezer Allan also persisted in the province, living long enough to help the Americans in 1812, when they did, at last, invade. The British arrested and jailed Allan, which ruined his health. He died shortly after his release in April 1813.[37]

Richard Cockrell made a profitable peace with the establishment, securing a coveted post as a government surveyor in October 1802—a timing that suggests a reward for his revelations. The oath of office committed Cockrell to "most carefully attend to the Interests of the Crown." He also became a deputy sheriff and in 1810 won promotion to a district judgeship. In 1811 the government awarded him an additional four hundred acres of land. Cockrell's loyalist cycle persisted through the War of 1812, when he served as a militia officer in defense of the province. After the war, however, Cockrell revived his oppositional ways, publishing scathing criticisms of the official elite and endorsing the reform agitation led by the controversial Robert Gourlay.[38]

JEFFERSONIANS

Why did the rebellion plot falter? It depended on a combination of internal uprising and external invasion—both of which failed. Despite the widespread reports of Canadian discontent, most colonists were unprepared to press beyond grumbling to risk their lives and properties on overt rebellion. Beyond the relatively small circle of frustrated speculators, most Upper Canadians were small farmers who had received substantial farms for minimal fees. They would have welcomed a more responsive government, but not at the risk of a revolution that might cast all land titles into legal uncertainty. As late as February 1801 even Danforth hesitated. While reporting Upper Canada as ripe for rebellion, Danforth assured Green: "Do not think by my stating to you in this way, that I shall be a party man in the Hazzard of having my Neck Stretched." If Danforth dithered, we can be sure that the great majority of Upper Canadians preferred to wait and see. The colony's thin population (only thirty-five thousand in 1800), dispersed over bad roads through an immense forest, also discouraged revolutionary coordination and promoted political ignorance and apathy. With the press tightly regulated and Danforth's pamphlet suppressed, few farmers ever heard of the proposed rebellion.[39]

The Upper Canadian farmers would not rebel on their own, without a major American incursion likely to win without them. The conspirators persuaded themselves, and needed to persuade others, that a militant republicanism had triumphed in the United States in 1800–1801 and would promptly sweep into the province. The plotters insisted on their support from Jefferson, Burr, and Clinton to persuade Canadians to regard the proposed rebellion as certain of victory. The wishful thinking of would-be rebels, the paranoia of nervous officials, and the predictions of American intervention inflated a speculative bubble of prospective rebellion—a bubble that popped all too easily when American intervention proved fictional. In the final analysis, the plotters were better speculators than rebels.[40]

Why did the Americans fail to export their "revolution of 1800" to Canada? Of the American leaders, only Aaron Burr seems to have been familiar with, and vaguely encouraging of, the plot against Upper Canada. Opportunistic and irresponsible, Burr was always willing to fish in troubled waters to see what he might catch. Burr also had a flair for inspiring ambitious but frustrated men— especially young men—to take reckless risks on implausible adventures. Danforth gushed, "It is well known that Mr. Burr has bestowed much for the encouragement of certain young Gentlemen who found themselves curtailed by the Incidence of fortune. He has kept them in the Ambitious pursuit of their education. It has been a pain to him to see genius trampled." Essential for boosting the plotters' hopes, Burr's charming encouragement and validation did not suffice to deliver the arms, money, and men for a real rebellion.[41]

Throughout his controversial career, Burr demonstrated a special fascination with grandiose filibustering expeditions meant to reshape the political geography of North America. Certainly the plotters' wild talk of combining Canadian rebellion with an American division into two confederations, north and south, sounds like a Burr touch. A few years later (in 1810), Burr visited Paris to pitch Napoleon on a scheme to invade Francophone Lower Canada and raise a rebellion in Upper Canada among the American born. Burr's French handlers reported his reliance on "friends and agents in Upper Canada, especially near Lakes Erie and Ontario, where a great number of Americans have settled. . . . Mr. Burr has made several trips in this part of America and he enjoys a great deal of influence there." In fact, frustration of the Danforth plot had discredited and scattered Burr's "friends and agents in Upper Canada," rendering revolt more implausible by 1810.[42]

In 1801–2 Danforth had grossly overestimated Burr's power within the national government. Far from certifying ascent, Burr's election to the vice presidency trapped him in conspicuous irrelevance. Governor Clinton and President Jefferson had far more executive power to assist (or retard) a rebellion across the border. But far from working in a revolutionary *troika* with Clinton and Jefferson, Burr had fallen from their grace. They deeply distrusted the vice president, especially after his disingenuous performance in the electoral confusion of early 1801, when the House of Representatives considered making him president at Jefferson's expense. By the end of that year, just when the Upper Canada plot became serious, Clinton and Jefferson were working together to destroy Burr's political standing in New York. They purged his political clients from government posts and used press hacks to savage Burr as a Republican apostate. Consequently, Burr's involvement in the Upper Canada intrigue alone would have sufficed to kill any support by Clinton and Jefferson—who were cooperating to undermine Burr's base, not to expand it into Canada.[43]

And even if Burr had not been involved, Jefferson had abundant pragmatic reasons to discountenance a northern plot—if he ever even knew about it. Jefferson's revolutionary republicanism was largely rhetorical, and in 1801–2 it was dormant. During the early years of the French Revolution, Jefferson had waxed enthusiastic for revolutionary bloodshed on a global scale, making indiscrete statements that clung to his reputation long after he had narrowed his focus to the sufficiently grand enterprise of peacefully securing republican government in the United States. In 1801, as the new president of a large but weak and politically divided nation, Jefferson could ill afford expensive and provocative military interventions across the northern border. First and foremost he needed to consolidate his administration by reassuring the American people—and British officials—that he was no bloodthirsty Jacobin. Between the election and his inauguration, Jefferson took pains to meet with Edward Thornton, the British *chargé d'affaires,* to pledge improved relations. At the same time John Richardson, a British spy sent from Montreal to Albany, reported that a surprising moderation would characterize the new administration.[44]

Even Jefferson's ideological commitment to republicanism worked against risking a northern intervention that would provoke an expensive war with Great Britain. Jefferson considered war barbaric, anachronistic, and antithetical to popular government. And as president he wanted to minimize federal expenditures, the better to pay down the national debt and cut the federal establishment to a minimum. A war with Britain would have doubly devastated his plans, by adding an enormous and prolonged expense while curtailing the overseas trade that funded import duties—the primary source of federal revenue.[45]

In principle Jefferson and his party were committed to the eventual expansion of the United States to embrace all of North America. But it should be emphasized that (prior to 1812) they imagined expansion as gradual rather than immediate; as peaceful rather than military; and as fundamentally driven by demography rather than by state action. In 1791 Jefferson welcomed the invitation extended by Florida's Spanish governor to American settlers: "Our citizens have a right to go where they please. . . . I wish a hundred thousand of our inhabitants would accept the invitation. It will be the means of delivering us peaceably, what may otherwise cost us a war." In 1801 Jefferson assured James Monroe, "However, our present interests may restrain us within our own limits, it is impossible not to look forward to distant times, when our rapid multiplication will expand itself beyond those limits, & cover the whole northern, if not the southern continent, with a people speaking the same language, governed in similar forms, & by similar laws." Here, at the peak of Danforth's plot, Jefferson emphasized the present interest of remaining within current boundaries, postponed expansion to distant times, and assigned agency to reproduction and migration. In 1801 Aaron Burr satirized Jefferson's rhetoric as insisting that the "energies of the men ought to be principally employed in the multiplication of the human race." Although Burr certainly did his part for procreation, he preferred a more muscular government ready to change boundaries by force.[46]

For Jefferson demography was destiny—which absolved policymakers from having to act in the short term. Why provoke trouble on the borders prematurely, when a providential population growth would peacefully secure the continent in the fullness of time? This Jeffersonian cast of mind about expansion resembled his equally vague and distant hope that expansion would somehow combine peacefully with demography to diminish slavery—without requiring risky political action by the living.

Jefferson also had precious little interest in Canada prior to the *Chesapeake* crisis of 1807. Instead there was a southern tilt to Jefferson's expansionist imagination. He showed far more desire for Louisiana, Florida, Texas, and even Cuba. Thoroughly Virginian in his climatology, Jefferson regarded Canada as a frozen tundra hardly suited to civilized life and not worth the expense and danger of a war with the formidable British Empire. By comparison the warmer southern territories were both more appealing and possessed by the relatively weak and vulnerable Spanish. Like most other Americans, Jefferson believed that the Spain was a decadent empire that could be rolled easily and cheaply whenever necessity dictated. And, in contrast to Canada, the Spanish colonies offered a climate attractive to plantation slavery—which in practice Jefferson was especially solicitous to expand. It was not that Jefferson was overtly proslavery. On the contrary, in the consummate paradox of his political career, Jefferson expressed his dread of slavery by urging its expansion. Concerned primarily for slavery's dangers to whites, Jefferson believed that geographic dispersion would avert the concentration of black numbers that would, he feared, lead ultimately to genocidal race war. Louisiana and West Florida were promising places for southern emigrants and their slaves; Canada was not.[47]

Finally, contrary to Danforth's misguided assumption, 1801–2 was an especially inopportune moment for the Americans to challenge the British Empire. In late 1801 the British and French made a preliminary peace, formalized in March 1802 at Amiens. This treaty ended nine years of war, which had been the chief irritant in American relations with Great Britain. With peace restored, the British no longer challenged American neutrality by impressing sailors for the navy or by confiscating ships for their alleged contraband. And without the French to pin most of the British military in Europe, the British could readily send reinforcements to suppress any rebellion in Canada. In Upper Canada in July 1802 Peter Russell astutely assessed the Danforth plot: "if it ever had any foundation, all hopes of its success must have been defeated by the Peace."[48]

On the other hand, the peace of Amiens enabled the French emperor Napoleon to meddle in North America, free from interference by the British fleet. To expand his empire in the Americas, Napoleon had pressured Spain into conceding to France all of Louisiana—the vast domain on the west bank of the

Mississippi, plus the port of New Orleans at the river's mouth. In late 1801 news of the secret cession angered and alarmed American leaders, who considered the French a far more powerful and dangerous neighbor than the Spanish. In particular, Americans longed to possess New Orleans, which controlled access to the sea for the produce raised by settlers in the Mississippi watershed.[49]

Because of the Louisiana crisis, in 1802 Jefferson could not afford to alienate Great Britain with an expedition against Upper Canada. Louisiana was vastly more important to American interests. While most American leaders urged a preemptive military strike to seize New Orleans, Jefferson hoped to avoid war by purchasing the city from Napoleon. If rebuffed, he anticipated what had previously been anathema: an American military alliance with Great Britain against France. In April 1802 Jefferson assured his ambassador in Paris that if Napoleon took possession of New Orleans, "From that moment we must marry ourselves to the British fleet and nation." By no means did Jefferson relish that prospect, devoutly preferring a purchase and continued neutrality, but he had to prepare for the worst.[50]

In sum, Danforth was dead wrong in calculating that conditions in the United States were especially promising to promote rebellion in Upper Canada in 1801–2. In fact, Jefferson's election, Burr's marginalization, the Treaty of Amiens, and the Louisiana crisis combined to compound American inhibitions against a northern intervention. None of this was apparent when Danforth launched his scheme in 1801, but it all became painfully evident in 1802, when he counted on raising money and men in the United States to invade Upper Canada.

Too late for the plotters, American circumstances began to shift in 1803 with the purchase of Louisiana and the renewal of war between France and Great Britain. In possession of New Orleans, the Americans could remain neutral—which led to renewed friction with the British fleet. Anglo-American goodwill slowly deteriorated, leading Jefferson, in 1807–9, to experiment with a commercial embargo meant to pressure the British. As a contingency, Jefferson also began to plan for an American invasion of Canada, but not until 1812 did his successor, James Madison, attempt it. By then it was too late, for most of the local leaders apt to lead a rebellion had been identified, discredited, and scattered by their abortive and frustrating effort a decade earlier.[51]

The invasion failed dismally, which was for the best because the American leaders were not sure what to do with a conquered Canada. Many, including Jefferson, hoped for a permanent conquest, for incorporation into the United

States. But Madison and most of his administration waffled, usually thinking of conquest as a bargaining chip: Canada would be restored to Britain in return for maritime concessions. Two field commanders did issue proclamations inviting an uprising in Upper Canada, but they acted without authority from the national government. Indeed, a revolutionary republic in Canada would have complicated an American attempt to cash in their conquest at a peace settlement. Because the Americans gave such mixed and muted signals, however, it is hardly surprising that so few Upper Canadians were moved to assist the invaders. They had to wonder what would become of them as rebels if the Americans gave the province back. Even in war the Jeffersonians remained ambivalent about acquiring Canada—defying the common generalization that they favored expansion at all times and in all places.[52]

In sum, the abortive Danforth plot illuminates the geographic limits to Jefferson's "revolution of 1800." The president could live within the northern—if not the southwestern—boundaries of the American Republic. Enduring until the 1860s, that tilt in American expansionism combined with the bungling execution of the War of 1812 to preserve Canada as a distinctive polity in North America. Deepened by that war, the Canadian tie to Great Britain and aversion to American ways compounded the distinctions in political culture already manifest in Danforth's day. The commercialism, free press, and democratic electioneering that characterized the United States appalled the rulers of Canada. Contrary to initial expectations, the American electoral revolution of 1800 helped to prolong the partition of North America into distinct Canadian and American regimes and ways of life.

NOTES

1. Asa Danforth Jr. to Timothy Green, 17 Feb. 1801, Danforth file, Misc. Coll., New-York Historical Society (hereafter NYHS).

2. Jane Errington, *The Lion, the Eagle, and Upper Canada: A Developing Colonial Ideology* (Montreal, 1987), 63; Israel Chapin Jr. to Joseph Lyman, 28 May 1801, Crary College, Butler Library, Columbia University; Colonel John A. Graham quoted in E. A. Cruikshank, "The Activity of Abel Stevens as a Pioneer," Ontario Historical Society, *Papers and Records* 31 (1936): 78; Willcocks and Baldwin quoted in Graeme H. Patterson, "Whiggery, Nationality, and the Upper Canadian Reform Tradition," *Canadian Historical Review* 56 (1975): 25. Before the decade ended, Willcocks and Baldwin would turn against the government to become opposition leaders.

3. E. A. Cruikshank, "Immigration from the United States into Upper Canada, 1784–1812: Its Character and Results," Ontario Educational Association, *Proceedings of the Thirty-Ninth Annual Convention* (1900): 263–83; David Mills, *The Idea of Loyalty in Upper Canada, 1784–1850* (Kingston, 1988), 21; Fred Landon, *Western Ontario and the American Frontier* (Toronto, 1941), 69; Robert Grey to Peter Hunter, 16 July 1800, National Archives of Canada (Ottawa) (hereafter NAC), MG 11 CO

42, reel B-285, vol. 325:211; Thomas Talbot to John Sullivan, 27 Oct. 1802, in E. A. Cruikshank, "The Early History of the London District," Ontario Historical Society, *Papers and Records* 24 (1927): 207; Asa Danforth Jr. to Timothy Green, 17 Feb. 1801, Danforth file, Misc. Coll., NYHS.

4. Lillian F. Gates, "Roads, Rivals, and Rebellion: The Unknown Story of Asa Danforth, Jr.," *Ontario History* 76 (1984): 235–37; Lillian F. Gates, *Land Policies of Upper Canada* (Toronto, 1968), 30–31.

5. Gates, *Land Policies of Upper Canada*, 30–31; Jacob Watson to John Graves Simcoe, n.d. Feb. 1794, *The Correspondence of Lieut. Governor John Graves Simcoe, with Allied Documents Relating to His Administration of the Government of Upper Canada*, 5 vols., ed. E. A. Cruikshank (Toronto, 1923–1931), 5:81–82; Silvester Tiffany to Jedediah Morse, 20 Nov. 1796, Misc. Coll., NYHS; John Graves Simcoe, Proclamation, 7 Feb. 1792, Ontario Bureau of Archives, *Fourth Report (1906)* (Toronto, 1907), 171–72.

6. Silvester Tiffany to Samuel Allen, 1 May 1796, Misc. Coll., NYHS; Gates, "Roads, Rivals, and Rebellion," 236; Mary-Jo Kline, ed., *Political Correspondence and Public Papers of Aaron Burr*, 2 vols. (Princeton, N.J., 1983), 1:222 n. 1; Robert Liston quoted in Herbert S. Parmet and Marie B. Hecht, *Aaron Burr: Portrait of an Ambitious Man* (New York, 1967), 113.

7. Augustus Jones, report to the Executive Council, 1 July 1799, NAC, MG 11 (Colonial Office 42), 332, 61–67 (microfilm reel B-287); Chief Justice John Elmsley, report to the Executive Council, NAC MG 11 (Colonial Office 42), 328, 278 (microfilm reel B-288); Gates, *Land Policies of Upper Canada*, 32, 39–41.

8. Davenport Phelps to the Executive Council, 5 Feb. 1796, Public Archives of Ontario (Toronto) (hereafter PAO), Record Group (hereafter RG) 1 (Crown Lands), A-I-1 (Letters Received by the Surveyor General), LII, 1195 (microfilm reel Ms-626/1).

9. For the quotation, see John Graves Simcoe to Mr. Pearce, 26 Oct. 1793 in NAC, MG 23, H I 1, Ser. 4 (Simcoe Transcripts), 7, 43. See also E. B. Littlehales (for Simcoe) to Jacob Watson, 20 Jan. 1795, PAO, RG 1 (Crown Lands), A-I-1 (Letters Received by the Surveyor General), 52, 1044 (microfilm reel Ms-626/1).

10. John Graves Simcoe, proclamation, 26 May 1796, Public Archives of Ontario, *Fourth Report (1906)*, 185–86; Gates, *Land Policies of Upper Canada*, 41; Executive Council minutes, 3 July 1797, and Peter Russell to General Robert Prescott, 4 Feb. 1799, *The Correspondence of the Honourable Peter Russell*, 3 vols., ed. E. A. Cruikshank (Toronto, 1932–36), 1:25, 67; John Elmsley to David W. Smith, 25 Feb. 1798, Smith Papers, Folder B8, 29, Metropolitan Toronto Library (hereafter MTL), Baldwin Room. For the costs and losses by some nominees, see Jacob Watson to John Graves Simcoe, n.d. Feb. 1794, in Cruikshank, *Correspondence of . . . John Graves Simcoe* 5:81; Peter Russell to David W. Smith, 11 Aug. 1796, and William Berckzy to Russell, 1 May 1797, in Cruikshank, *Correspondence of . . . Peter Russell*, 1:205–6 and 3:95.

11. John Elmsley to David W. Smith, 18 Feb. 1798, in Cruikshank, *Correspondence of . . . Peter Russell* 2:84.

12. Asa Danforth Jr. to Timothy Green, 5 March 1797, Green Family Papers, Box 1, Arents Research Library, Syracuse University; Gates, "Roads, Rivals, and Rebellion," 236; Lillian F. Gates, "Asa Danforth," *Dictionary of Canadian Biography* 6 (1821–35): 177; E. A. Cruikshank, ed., "Petitions for Grants of Land: Second Series, 1796–1799," Ontario Historical Society, *Papers and Records* 26 (1930): 153–54. Danforth represented the nominees of Haldimand, Hamilton, Percy, and Cramahe—all located on the north shore of Lake Ontario.

13. Gates, "Roads, Rivals, and Rebellion," 237–39; Cruikshank, "Petitions for Grants of Land, Second Series," 155; Asa Danforth Jr. to Timothy Green, 19 March 1800, Green Family Papers, Box 1, Arents Research Library, Syracuse University.

14. Gates, "Roads, Rivals, and Rebellion," 238–39; Asa Danforth Jr. to David W. Smith, 13 and 16 June 1799, and Danforth to William Chewitt and Thomas Ridout, 9 Sept. 1799, both in PAO, RG 1 (Crown Lands), A-I-6, 2333, 2339, 2410 (microfilm reel Ms-563/3); William Chewett to the

Executive Council, 6 Dec. 1799, PAO, RG 1 (Crown Lands), A-II-1 (Surveyor General Reports), I, 523 (microfilm reel Ms-3696/1); "York," *Upper Canada Gazette* (York), 14 Dec. 1799.

15. Asa Danforth Jr. to Timothy Green, 18 and 19 March 1800, Green to Danforth, 29 March 1800, George Hall to Green, 29 March 1800, Danforth to Green, 22 April and 29 May 1800, all in Green Family Papers, Arents Research Library, Syracuse University.

16. Gates, "Roads, Rivals, and Rebellion," 240–42; Cruikshank, "Petitions for Grants of Land, Second Series," 157; John Elmsley to Peter Hunter, 15 Jan. 1801, Elmsley Letterbook (1800–1802), MTL, Baldwin Room.

17. Asa Danforth Jr. to Richard Cockrell, 4 Jan. 1801, NAC, RG 5, A 1 (Civil Secretary, Upper Canada Sundries), 2:557 (microfilm reel C-4502); the quotation is from Danforth to Timothy Green, 17 Feb. 1801, Danforth File, Misc. Coll., NYHS.

18. Asa Danforth Jr. to Timothy Green, 17 Feb. 1801, Danforth File, Misc. Coll., NYHS; Danforth to Richard Cockrell, 20 July 1801, NAC, RG 5, A 1 (Civil Secretary's Correspondence, Upper Canada Sundries), 2:660 (microfilm reel C-4502); Gates, "Roads, Rivals, and Rebellion," 244. Gates argues that in 1800 Danforth remained a reluctant rebel and that his optimism derived from his hopes that the British home government was about to vindicate the claims of the township nominees. For evidence, Gates cites the 29 June 1801 Privy Council ruling on behalf of one nominee, William Berckzy—but there is no way that London news of 29 June could have reached York by 20 July, when Danforth wrote to Cockrell—given that two months was the shortest possible time for information to cross that divide in 1801. Moreover, Danforth's rhetoric makes more sense if he refers to the dissemination of republicanism. For Aaron Burr's political ties to the Danforth family see Burr to Oliver Phelps, 10 Feb. 1801, Phelps and Gorham Papers, Box 59, New York State Library. For the meritocratic claims of the American revolutionaries, see Gordon S. Wood, *The Creation of the American Republic, 1786–1787* (Chapel Hill, N.C., 1969).

19. Asa Danforth Jr. to Elisha Beaman, 2 March 1802, PAC, RG 5 A 1 (Civil Secretary's Correspondence, Upper Canada Sundries), 2, 708 (microfilm reel C-4502).

20. Asa Danforth Jr. to Ebenezer Allan, 6 Jan. 1802, NAC RG 5 A 1 (Civil Secretary's Correspondence, Upper Canada Sundries), 2:687 (microfilm reel C-4502); Daniel J. Brock, "Ebenezer Allan," *Dictionary of Canadian Biography*, 5 (1983):13; John Askin to Alexander Henry, *The John Askin Papers*, 2 vols., ed. Milo M. Quaife (Detroit, 1928–31), 2:196 ("as active"); Peter Russell to David W. Smith, 10 March 1798, in Cruikshank, *Correspondence of . . . Peter Russell* 2:116; Fred Coyne Hamil, *The Valley of the Lower Thames, 1640 to 1850* (Toronto, 1951), 28; Fred Coyne Hamil, "Ebenezer Allan in Canada," Ontario Historical Society, *Papers and Records* 36 (1944): 84–89; Minutes of the London District Court of General Quarter Sessions of the Peace, Public Archives of Ontario, *Twenty-second Report* (1933) (Toronto, 1934), 14, 19, 25; John Elmsley to Peter Hunter, 6 April 1801, Elmsley Letterbook (1800–1802), MTL, Baldwin Room.

21. Susan Burnham Greeley, "Sketches of the Past," Ontario Historical Society, *Papers and Records* 23 (1926): 248–50.

22. W. S. Wallace, "The First Journalists in Upper Canada," *Canadian Historical Review* 26 (1945): 372–81; PAO, RG 22, Ser. 126 (Court of King's Bench, Rough Termbooks), 2, 24 April and 19 July 1797; John Elmsley to David W. Smith, 25 Feb. 1798, and Executive Council Minutes, 25 April 1798, in Cruikshank, *Correspondence of . . . Peter Russell* 2:104, 144; John White to Peter Russell, 23 April 1798, and Silvester Tiffany to Russell, 30 April 1798, Box 2, Russell Papers, Baldwin Room, MTL.

23. Douglas G. Lochhead, "Silvester Tiffany," *Dictionary of Canadian Biography* 5 (1983): 814–15; "To the Public," *Niagara Herald*, 1 Aug. 1801. For Gideon Tiffany's singing, see Henry Weishuhn to Russell, 13 March 1799, Box 3, Russell Papers, MTL, Baldwin Room.

24. Peter Judd, *The Hatch and Brood of Time* (Boston, 1999), 121–32; Cruikshank, "Petitions for Grants of Land, Second Series," 270; Peter Russell to Bishop Jacob Mountain, 22 Feb. 1798, and Mountain to Russell, 12 June 1798, both in Cruikshank, *Correspondence of . . . Peter Russell*, 2:98, 180.

25. William Leete Stone, *Life of Joseph Brant, Thayendanegea, Including the Border Wars of the American Revolution* (New York, 1838), 2:433–35, 455–56—which includes Burr to Theodosia Burr Alston, 28 Feb. 1797; Isabel T. Kelsay, *Joseph Brant, 1743–1807: Man of Two Worlds* (Syracuse, N.Y., 1984), 547; Aaron Burr to Theodosia Burr Alston, 20 Aug. and 3 Nov. 1801, Brant to Captain Isaac Chapin Jr., 7 May 1801 (quotations), and Davenport Phelps to Aaron Burr, 15 Dec. 1801, *Memoirs of Aaron Burr with Miscellaneous Selections from His Correspondence*, ed. Matthew L. Davis (New York, 1837), 2:152, 155, 163–64.

26. Asa Danforth Jr. to Ebenezer Allan, 6 Jan. 1802, NAC, RG 5 A 1 (Civil Secretary's Correspondence, Upper Canada Sundries), 2:687 (microfilm reel C-4502). For the land controversy at Grand River, see Charles M. Johnston, *The Valley of the Six Nations: A Collection of Documents on the Indian Lands of the Grand River* (Toronto, 1964); Sidney L. Harring, *White Man's Law: Native People in Nineteenth-Century Canadian Jurisprudence* (Toronto, 1998), 36–41. For Brant's alienation, see Major David Shank to Captain James Green, 27 May 1797, Thomas Welch to David W. Smith, 3 Feb. 1798, Peter Russell to John Graves Simcoe, 15 Oct. 1798, and Russell to General Robert Prescott, 22 June 1799, in Cruikshank, *Correspondence of . . . Peter Russell* 1:178, 2:75, 282, and 3:248.

27. Robert Liston to General Prescott, 8 April 1797, in Johnston, *Valley of the Six Nations,* 85; Kelsay, *Joseph Brant,* 621. Kelsay dismisses the charge that Brant was disloyal, insisting that in his letters Brant "said all these things with his tongue very much in his cheek. Joseph had not the remotest idea of leaving Upper Canada, but buying land to make a settlement had a better sound to it than buying land to sell and make a profit." Kelsay's reasoning is suspect. Brant was not seeking to buy land; he wanted a free grant. And in the context of the other evidence, including the approach to Burr and the bishop of New York on behalf of Davenport Phelps, Brant's bid for Ohio land in 1800 – 1801 makes the most sense as a contingency plan in the event that circumstances worsened in Upper Canada. This is not to say that Brant *wanted* to move to Ohio, for he evidently hoped to have his way within Upper Canada.

28. Thomas McKee to William Claus, 14 Sept. 1801, and Chippewa (i.e., Ojibwa) Council, NAC, RG 10 (Indian Affairs), 26, 15378, 15382, (microfilm reel C-11007); Executive Council Minutes, 30 Sept. 1801, NAC, MG 11 (Colonial Office 42), 332, 16–18 (microfilm reel B-287).

29. For Norton's presence in Albany, see Joseph Brant to James Caldwell, 17 Feb. 1802, Thomas Addison Emmett Coll., No. 4623, New York Public Library.

30. J. Donald Wilson, "Richard Cockrell," *Dictionary of Canadian Biography* 6:158–60.

31. Asa Danforth Jr. to Richard Cockrell, 27 Dec. 1801, and Danforth to Ebenezer Allan, 6 Jan. 1802, NAC RG 5 A 1 (Civil Secretary's Correspondence, Upper Canada Sundries), 2:687 (microfilm reel C-4502). At the very least, Richard Cockrell, Ebenezer Allan, Silvester Tiffany, and Joseph Brant were Freemasons. For the nature of freemasonry, see Steven C. Bullock, "The Revolutionary Transformation of American Freemasonry, 1752–1792," *WMQ* 3d ser., 47 (1990): 347–69; Steven C. Bullock, "A Pure and Sublime System: The Appeal of Post-Revolutionary Freemasonry," *JER* 9 (1989): 359–74; *Niagara Herald,* 16 May 1801.

32. John Ross Robertson, *The History of Freemasonry in Canada from its Introduction in 1749 . . .* , 2 vols. (Toronto, 1900), 1:391, 408–10. Robertson noted the American influence and republican implications of the Niagara-led schism. A link to the Danforth plot is my overlay on his interpretation.

33. Informant quoted in Gates, "Roads, Rivals, and Rebellion," 245; John Elmsley to Peter Hunter, 1 Feb. 1802, and Elmsley to Hunter, 14 April 1802, Elmsley Letterbook (1800–1802), MTL, Baldwin Room.

34. Elmsley to Hunter, 14 April 1802, Elmsley Letterbook (1800–1802), MTL, Baldwin Room; Richard Cockrell to David W. Smith, 10 July 1802, NAC, RG 5 A 1 (Civil Secretary's Correspondence, Upper Canada Sundries), 2:758 (microfilm reel C-4502).

35. Asa Danforth Jr. to Richard Cockrell, 26 June 1802, NAC, RG 5 A 1 (Civil Secretary's Correspondence, Upper Canada Sundries), 2:759 (microfilm reel C-4502); Finkle's son quoted in William

Caniff, *History of the Settlement of Upper Canada with Special Reference to the Bay of Quinte* (Toronto, 1869), 226; Peter Russell to William Osgoode, 22 July 1802, PAO, F46 (Peter Russell Papers), reel Ms-75/5. According to the Shaw-Shoemaker bibliography, no copy of Danforth's pamphlet is known to have survived.

36. Gates, "Roads, Rivals, and Rebellion," 250–51. For the new alien and sedition law, see William Renwick Riddell, *The Life of William Dummer Powell: First Judge at Detroit and Fifth Chief Justice of Upper Canada* (Lansing, Mich., 1924), 115–17.

37. Judd, *Hatch and Brood,* 135; Lochhead, "Silvester Tiffany," 815; local historian quoted in Wallace, "First Journalists in Upper Canada," 380; Aaron Greeley to George McDougall, 30 Nov. 1811, Michigan Pioneer and Historical Society, *Pioneer Collections* 8 (1886): 602; Joseph Brant to David W. Smith, 17 July 1802, Smith Papers, Folder B7, 321, MTL, Baldwin Room; Brant speech, 20 Nov. 1802, NAC, RG 10 (Indian Affairs), 26, 15468 (microfilm reel C-11007); Bruce G. Wilson, *The Enterprises of Robert Hamilton: A Study of Wealth and Influence in Early Upper Canada, 1776–1812* (Ottawa, 1983), 157; Carl F. Klinck and J. J. Talman, eds., *The Journal of Major John Norton, 1816* (Toronto, 1970), civ; Brock, "Ebenezer Allan," 14.

38. Richard Cockrell, oath, 8 Oct. 1802, PAO RG 1 (Crown Lands) A-I-1 (Letters Received by the Surveyor General), MF Reel Ms 626/4 p. 1418; Wilson, "Richard Cockrell," 159–60.

39. Asa Danforth Jr. to Timothy Green, 17 Feb. 1801, Danforth File, Misc. Coll., NYHS; Douglas McCalla, *Planting the Province: The Economic History of Upper Canada, 1784–1870* (Toronto, 1993), 13–29, 250.

40. F. Murray Greenwood, *Legacies of Fear: Law and Politics in Quebec in the Era of the French Revolution* (Toronto, 1993), 102–3; Jean-Pierre Wallot, *Intrigues Francaises et Americaines au Canada, 1800–1802* (Montreal, 1965).

41. Asa Danforth Jr. to Timothy Green, 13 March 1804, Document #15411, New York State Library, Albany.

42. Samuel Engle Burr Jr. *Napoleon's Dossier on Aaron Burr: Proposals of Col. Aaron Burr to the Emperor Napoleon* (San Antonio, Tex., 1969), 36, 40; Greenwood, *Legacies of Fear,* 195.

43. Parmet and Hecht, *Aaron Burr,* 171–93; Milton Lomask, *Aaron Burr: The Years from Princeton to Vice President, 1756–1805* (New York, 1979), 296–330.

44. Bradford Perkins, *The First Rapprochement: England and the United States, 1795–1805* (Berkeley, Calif., 1967), 129–32. For Richardson's report, see Wallot, *Intrigues,* 43. For Jefferson at the extreme see his letter to William Short, 3 Jan. 1795, *TJW,* 1004. For Jefferson's cooling attitude toward the French Revolution, see Peter S. Onuf, "'To Declare Them a Free and Independent People': Race, Slavery, and National Identity in Jefferson's Thought," *JER* 18 (1998): 31. Jefferson may not have known much about the Danforth plot. The clearest hint at some knowledge appears in a brief note that he wrote to James Madison on 18 Sept. 1801: "I think it shall be better to postpone an answer to Govr. Clinton on Brandt's proposition till we can be together at Washington. In fact it belongs to the War department" (TJ to Madison, 18 Sept. 1801, Smith, 2:1199).

45. Robert W. Tucker and David C. Hendrickson, *Empire of Liberty: The Statecraft of Thomas Jefferson* (New York, 1990), 16–21, 161.

46. TJ to George Washington, 2 April 1791, *TJP* 20:97; TJ to James Monroe, 24 Nov. 1801, *TJW,* 1097; Burr quoted in Parmet and Hecht, *Aaron Burr,* 170.

47. TJ, newspaper essay, c. Nov. 1784, *TJP* 7:540; John M. Murrin, "The Jeffersonian Triumph and American Exceptionalism," *JER* 20 (2000), 1–25.

48. Perkins, *The First Rapprochement,* 171; Peter Russell to William Osgoode, 22 July 1802, PAO, F46 (Russell Papers), microfilm reel Ms-75/5.

49. Perkins, *The First Rapprochement,* 159–64; Peter S. Onuf, "The Expanding Union," in *Devising Liberty: Preserving and Creating Freedom in the New American Republic,* ed. David Thomas Konig (Stanford, Calif., 1995), 52–56.

50. Perkins, *The First Rapprochement,* 159–64, TJ quoted on 160; Onuf, "The Expanding Union."

51. Gallatin to TJ, 25 July 1807, *Writings of Albert Gallatin,* 3 vols., ed. Henry Adams (Philadelphia, 1879), 1:345.

52. Alfred Leroy Burt, *The United States, Great Britain, and British North America from the Revolution to the Establishment of Peace After the War of 1812* (New Haven, Conn., 1940), 347–48; Reginald C. Stuart, *United States Expansionism and British North America, 1775–1871* (Chapel Hill, N.C., 1988), 59–65.

Notes on Contributors

JOYCE APPLEBY, of the University of California, Los Angeles, is the author of numerous works, including most recently *Inheriting the Revolution: The First Generation of Americans* (2000).

MICHAEL A. BELLESILES, of Emory University, is the author of *Arming America: The Origins of a National Gun Culture* (2000), which won the Bancroft Prize.

JEANNE BOYDSTON, of the University of Wisconsin, is the author of *Home and Work: Housework, Wages, and the Ideology of Labor in the Early Republic* (1990).

SETH COTLAR, of Willamette University, is working on a forthcoming book entitled, "In Paine's Absence: The Trans-Atlantic Dynamics of American Popular Political Thought, 1789–1804."

GREGORY EVANS DOWD, of the University of Michigan, is the author of *A Spirited Resistance: The North American Indian Struggle for Unity, 1745–1815* (1992).

LAURENT DUBOIS, of Michigan State University, is the author of *Les Esclaves de la République: l'histoire oubliée de la première émancipation, 1789–1794* (1998).

DOUGLAS R. EGERTON, of Le Moyne College, Syracuse, is the author of *Rebels, Reformers, and Revolutionaries: Collected Essays and Second Thoughts* (2002).

JOANNE B. FREEMAN, of Yale University, is the editor of *Alexander Hamilton: Writing* (2001), and author of *Affairs of Honor: National Politics in the New Republic* (2001).

JAMES HORN is the Director of the John D. Rockefeller Library at the Colonial Williamsburg Foundation and former Saunders Director of the International Center for Jefferson Studies at Monticello.

JAMES E. LEWIS JR. is the author of *The American Union and the Problem of Neighborhood: The United States and the Collapse of the Spanish Empire, 1783–1829* (1998) and *John Quincy Adams: Policymaker for the Union* (2001).

JAN ELLEN LEWIS, of Rutgers University, Newark, is the author of *The Pursuit of Happiness: Family Values in Jefferson's Virginia* (1983), and co-editor of *Sally Hemings and Thomas Jefferson: History, Memory, and Civic Culture* (1999).

ROBERT M. S. MCDONALD, of the United States Military Academy at West Point, is working on a forthcoming book entitled "Confounding Father: Thomas Jefferson and the Politics of Personality."

JAMES OAKES, of the Department of History at the CUNY Graduate Center, is the author of *Slavery and Freedom: An Interpretation of the Old South* (1990).

PETER S. ONUF, of the University of Virginia, is the author of *Jefferson's Empire: The Language of American Nationhood* (2000), and co-author (with Leonard J. Sadosky) of *Jeffersonian America* (2001).

JEFFREY L. PASLEY, of the University of Missouri-Columbia, is the author of *"The Tyranny of Printers": Newspaper Politics in the Early American Republic* (2001).

JACK N. RAKOVE, of Stanford University, is the author of *Original Meanings: Politics and Ideas in the Making of the Constitution,* which received the 1997 Pulitzer Prize in American history.

BETHEL SALER, of Haverford College, is working on a forthcoming book entitled *The Frontiers of State Formation: Indians, Euro-Americans, and the Making of Wisconsin, 1776–1854.*

JAMES SIDBURY, of the University of Texas, is the author of *Ploughshares into Swords: Race, Rebellion, and Identity in Gabriel's Virginia, 1730–1810* (1997).

ALAN TAYLOR, of the University of California, Davis, is the author of *William Cooper's Town* (1996), which received the 1996 Pulitzer Prize in American history, the Bancroft Prize, and other awards. His most recent book is *American Colonies* (2001).

Index

Place, Francis, 356 n. 9

Plains Indian people, 268

"Plan for the Temporary Government of the Western Territory," 365

Plumer, William, on TJ's banishment of protocol, 158

Pole, J. R., election statistics and, 127–28, 131, 147–49

political culture: of Canada, and relationship with Americans, 403; circular letters and, 96; comfort for ordinary men, philosophy of, 163–64, 342; and households, status of, 245; and Native American women, role of, 271–72; and newspaper publications, role of, 133–47; and political opportunists, fear of, xiv; political parties, and effects on development of, 247; post-1800 changes in, 125, 259; psychology of democracy vs. political philosophy, 168–69; "spirit of 1776" and, 374; and TJ's administration, effects of, 123–24; and traditions, politicization of, 132–34; western territories and, 364–68

political elitism. *See* elitism, political

Political Essays (Cooper), 351

Political Observatory, 140

political parties: business sector, and effects of, 8; cliques vs., 89, 114 n. 2; and democratization, history of, xvi, 131, 355; division between, 353–54, 378; and electoral system, role of, 5–13, 38–39, 54–55; friends vs. loyalties to, 112; and legitimacy of party system, beliefs in, 22; and political culture, development of, 247; radicalism, and common ground between, 355; reform, and role of, 165; social relationships, and effects of, 8; social status of, 114 n. 2. *See also* Democratic-Republicans; Federalists; Republicans; Whigs

polity: and character, role of personal, 89; constitutional policy vs. principle controversy and, 48; corruption and, 87–88, 114 n. 2; democratization, and world, 124; elite perspective of, 89, 93, 115 n. 8, 168; and elitism, role of, 89, 93, 115 n. 8, 168; federal government and, 48, 49, 90–91; and happiness, concepts of, 222, 223, 224; hierarchy in American culture, xiv–xv, xviii; individuals, and role in, 241, 263 n. 5; international instability, and

impacts on, xiii; and partisan ideals, role of, 89, 93–94, 112, 113; presidential candidates and, 45–46; religious beliefs in America, and role in, 194; and reputation, role of personal, 89, 112; and violence and political change, role of, 60; western territories, and geopolitcal conflicts, 363

popular electoral politics: Adams, John on, 90; democratization vs., 124, 264 n. 11; and editors of periodicals, role of, xvi, 358 n. 33, 392; election of 1800, and effects on, 127, 129; federal government and, 373–74, 378; Federalists, and fear of, 128, 129–30, 378; gender issues and, 377; Hamilton on, 57 n. 24; individuals, and role in, 241, 262, 263 n. 5; Native Americans and, 377; presidency and, 124–25; racism and, 377; Republicans and, 126; and states, American, 377; TJ on, 125, 378; Upper Canada and, 390, 406 n. 18; western territories and, 364. *See also* suffrage issues

Pottawattomie people, 394

Preliminary Articles of Peace, 379 n. 7

president: and elections, Constitutional process for, 4–5, 21–24, 35–39, 93–94; foreign policy, and role of, 33–34, 42–44, 46–47; and politics, role in, 40–41, 79; popular electoral politics and, 124–25; powers of, 39–47; presidential veto, bank bill and, 41; Senate, and links to, 39; state linkages with national elections and, 55

Preston, John, 59

Preston, William B., 228

Price, Richard, 336

Priestley, Joseph, 180, 185, 189, 336, 338, 340

Prosser, Thomas Henry, 208

psychology of democracy, xvi, 155–56, 158, 162, 166–71, 168–69. *See also* democratization

"public," national. *See* popular electoral politics

Quasi-War between France and U.S. (1789–1800), xiii, 70, 93, 183, 310, 312–13, 319

racism: American culture and, 200, 377, 378; French Caribbean military policies and, 297; gender, and concepts of, 271; Louverture and, 325; popular electoral politics and, 377; racial hierarchy in American culture, xiv,

Jeffersonian America